Jasmina Grković-Major, Björn Hansen, Barbara Sonnenhauser
Diachronic Slavonic Syntax

Trends in Linguistics
Studies and Monographs

Editor
Volker Gast

Editorial Board
Walter Bisang
Hans Henrich Hock
Natalia Levshina
Heiko Narrog
Matthias Schlesewsky
Amir Zeldes
Niina Ning Zhang

Editor responsible for this volume
Volker Gast

Volume 315

Diachronic Slavonic Syntax

The Interplay between Internal Development,
Language Contact and Metalinguistic Factors

Edited by
Jasmina Grković-Major
Björn Hansen
Barbara Sonnenhauser

DE GRUYTER
MOUTON

ISBN: 978-3-11-068614-2
e-ISBN (PDF): 978-3-11-053143-5
e-ISBN (EPUB): 978-3-11-052939-5
ISSN 1861-4078

Library of Congress Control Number: 2018934491

Bibliographic information published by the Deutsche Nationalbibliothek
The Deutsche Nationalbibliothek lists this publication in the Deutsche Nationalbibliografie; detailed bibliographic data are available on the Internet at http://dnb.dnb.de.

© 2019 Walter de Gruyter, Inc., Berlin/Boston
This volume is text- and page-identical with the hardback published in 2018.
Typesetting: Compuscript Ltd., Shannon, Ireland
Printing and binding: CPI books GmbH, Leck

♾ Printed on acid-free paper
Printed in Germany

Contents

Jasmina Grković-Major, Björn Hansen, and Barbara Sonnenhauser
Introduction —— 1

Part I: The noun phrase

Jürgen Fuchsbauer
Some observations on the usage of adnominal genitives and datives in Middle Bulgarian Church Slavonic —— 13

Hanne Martine Eckhoff
Quantifying syntactic influence: Word order, possession and definiteness in Old Church Slavonic and Greek —— 29

Silvia Luraghi and Milena Krstić
The decay of cases in *Molise Slavonic* —— 63

Part II: The verbal phrase and related topics

Hakyung Jung
Null subjects and person in Old North Russian —— 95

Björn Hansen
On the permeability of grammars: Syntactic pattern replications in heritage Croatian and heritage Serbian spoken in Germany —— 125

Imke Mendoza
Possessive resultative constructions in Old and Middle Polish —— 161

Slobodan Pavlović
Mechanisms of word order change in 12th and 13th century Serbian —— 187

Sandra Birzer
Historical development and contemporary usage of discourse structuring elements based on *verba dicendi* in Croatian —— 209

Part III: The complex sentence

Marina Kurešević
The status and origin of the *accusativus cum infinitivo* construction in Old Church Slavonic —— 261

Björn Wiemer
On triangulation in the domain of clause linkage and propositional marking —— 285

Jasmina Grković-Major
The development of perception verb complements in the Serbian language —— 339

Andrii Danylenko
A tale of two pathways: On the development of relative clause chaining in East Slavonic —— 361

Barbara Sonnenhauser
Relativisation strategies in Slovene: Diachrony between language use and language description —— 387

Index —— 407

Jasmina Grković-Major, Björn Hansen, and Barbara Sonnenhauser
Introduction

This volume is dedicated to the study of the causes and mechanisms of syntactic change in Slavonic languages, including internally motivated syntactic change, syntactic change under contact conditions (structural convergence, pattern replication, shift-induced interference etc.), and the influence of metalinguistic factors such as grammar writing and language ideology. Specific reference is made to the interplay of these factors in the process of syntactic change. Following up the volume 'Diachronic Slavonic Syntax. Gradual changes in focus' (Hansen and Grković-Major 2010), which was dedicated to the (apparent) gradualness of syntactic changes, the intermediary steps involved and the question of how these micro-changes can be detected empirically, the present volume promotes a dialogue between different approaches to the study of diachronic syntax. These approaches include, amongst others, diachronic typology, Construction Grammar, grammaticalization theory, diachronic generative syntax as well as philologically driven textual criticism. Irrespective of the particular approach, all papers strive for a solid empirical grounding of their argumentation. They thereby bring to the fore also questions concerning the limits of corpus-based analyses which arise from the – still – rather restricted historical and diachronic data bases available for most of the Slavonic languages. In this way, the present volume also contributes to discussing data-related questions.

1 Interplay of factors

In the shaping of linguistic patterns over time, factors located on different tiers interact in intricate ways. Thus, adequately approaching diachronic Slavonic syntax, as concerns both the individual languages and overarching patterns, requires considering causes, mechanisms and processes of change that manifest themselves on the linguistic and the metalinguistic level as well as on the level of the data basis itself:

Linguistic factors: The internal driving forces of syntactic change and preconditions for contact-induced syntactic changes need to be identified; these internal and external factors may counteract but also concur, possibly even reinforcing each other.

Metalinguistic factors: The propagation or suppression of particular structural variants as a consequence of their usage in literary documents and their handling by descriptive and prescriptive work may influence the direction of syntactic development; this impact may be non-uniform for the different varieties of a language.

Data related factors: Any account of structural change is subject to limits imposed by the quantitative and qualitative availability of data on the one hand, and the implicit assumptions underlying the way they are described on the other hand; these factors may influence the explanatory power of the analysis provided.

As a prerequisite of describing the interplay of the above mentioned factors, each of them has to be studied carefully in its own right, having in mind the historical and sociolinguistic circumstances in which they were embedded. With their manifold contact languages and contact scenarios, dialectal complexity and their highly diverging standardisation histories, the Slavonic languages provide an interesting test case for the investigation of the interplay between internal development, language contact and metalinguistic factors and may serve the understanding of this intricate interaction also in a more general perspective.

1.1 Linguistic factors: Internal and external causes

It is well-known that language change results from two main driving forces: internal motivations leading to the (partial) restructuring of the respective systems, and external, contact-related factors triggering processes of convergence, replication, transfers etc. Among the main internal preconditions of syntactic change are instability, competition and reanalysis. Language contact as an impetus for language (re-)structuring occurs predominantly in the periods of system instability, when a foreign influence may induce a choice among several internal competing syntactic strategies. With contact persisting not only among structurally, genetically or typologically different languages, but also among closely related languages or among diatopic and diaphasic varieties of one and the same language, external and internal motivations and their consequences are, for the most part, hard to tear apart. The more so, as they may follow the same regularities, as proposed in Kuteva and Heine's (2012) 'integrative model' of grammaticalization.

When it comes to the analysis of external influences, different types of contact scenarios have to be considered, which may trigger different types of structural change in qualitative and quantitative terms, proceeding within different time spans and with different speed. The consequences of oral contact, written contact and contact in translation may be quite different from both a quantitative and qualitative point of view. For the latter scenarios the conditions for and consequences of contact are – at least partially – accessible from the documents themselves, i.e. the linguistic structures and possible metainformation available from, e.g., glosses added by the scribes or commentaries provided by the authors. This is quite different for oral contact, for which, as a rule, only indirect evidence can be found. Moreover, oral contact differs in type and intensity, i.e. contacts in bilingual communities where both languages are preserved (with changes in one of them or both) and contacts which lead to language assimilation and shift leaving substrate patterns in the replacing language. Thomason (2001: 66–67), thus, identifies the presence or absence of imperfect learning as one of the major social predictors of the type of contact-induced change.

1.2 Metalinguistic factors: Selection and propagation

In addition to linguistic factors, metalinguistic aspects need to be considered when it comes to accounting for syntactic change – in particular syntactic change that is primarily traced on the basis of written sources instead of being reconstructed. Such metalinguistic factors are easily overlooked if the focus is on the purely linguistic mechanisms described in Section 1.1. They include the selection and propagation of syntactic structures by the adherence to prestigious original languages and model texts or the selection of specific structures instead of others in the course of the bottom-up emergence of overarching norms or by way of top-down prescription, and – related to the latter – the handling of variation by descriptive and prescriptive work. Pullum (2006) classifies prescriptive claims concerning the correctness of linguistic structures on their justificatory basis, distinguishing nine principles determining ideological prescriptivism: nostalgia, classicism, authoritarianism, aestheticism, coherentism, logicism, commonsensims, functionalism and asceticism (see also Friedman 1997, 2017). Ideologically (wittingly or unwittingly) driven selection as well as prescriptive intervention and description might accelerate the propagation of minor usage patterns which exist as less frequent or stylistically restricted variants. These might in turn become prominent in the linguistic awareness of language users and may thereby, in times of restricted access to literacy, serve as role models for contemporary writers on the one hand, and disproportionally shape the linguistic perception of diachronic data in linguistic analyses on the other hand. It is thus also important to consider variation along the diatopic and diaphasic dimensions.

1.3 Data related factors: Data basis and analysis

Since the factors mentioned above can be identified only based on the data at hand, i.e. on the basis of corpora of different breadth and depth, reflection concerning the data basis needs to be included in any description of syntactic change. This brings to the fore questions concerning the explanatory power of data gained from more or less restricted corpora, i.e. questions of linguistic evidence and the data quality. Possible effects of factors such as corpus planning, adherence to tradition in language usage and linguistic description on the syntactic structures visible in the data at hand may influence the explanatory power of the analyses provided. Data-related aspects thus emerge as an important aspect in observing, describing and explaining structural development.

2 Relevance of Slavonic

The overall purpose of the volume is to give new insights into the development of Slavonic syntactic structures. By investigating the causes, mechanisms and processes of syntactic change prevailing in this group of languages, it addresses more general problems which have been debated in historical linguistics. The Slavonic languages possess a long documented history, their speakers have been in contact with a large number of related and non-related languages. The contact profile, thus, includes other Slavonic varieties, Greek, Latin, Baltic, Romance, Germanic, Albanian as well as Turkish and Finno-Ugric. Contact-induced phenomena have been pointed out and studied by Slavicists since the early 19th century, when Kopitar (1945 [1826]: 139) noted that "Der serbische Dialekt ist ein ganz slawischer, der Form und der Materie nach; der bulgarische ist eine slawische langue romane, die das Material von den Slaven, die Form aber von den – Albanesen, oder Walachen – entlehnt hat" ['The Serbian dialect is completely Slavonic in form and material; the Bulgarian dialect is a Slavonic langue romane which has borrowed the material from the Slavs, but the forms from the Albanians or Vlachs']. This paved the way for Balkan linguistics which was the first to study aspects of syntactic change from an areal perspective. The starting point of areal linguistics is generally considered to be Kristian Sandfeld's seminal book *Balkanfilologien* from 1926 which, besides the analysis of loanwords, which was in focus in the previous works, summarized and systematized the results of the considerable research on the similarities in morphosyntax, found in the Balkan languages. In the years to come many studies were dedicated to the contact-induced syntactic phenomena in the Balkans, including the ones presenting their typology and causes (e.g. Civ'jan 1979). Other parts of the Slavonic language area have also been analysed from an areal and typological perspective, especially the ones belonging to the Circum-Baltic area. These investigations raise important questions about the relation of inherited and areal phenomena (cf. Seržant 2015). The comparative-historical syntax of Slavonic, as a prerequisite for discerning genetic and contact-induced phenomena, has been a fruitful field of research since the 19th century (Miklosich 1865; Potebnja 1941 [1874]). The study of internal developments of Slavonic languages in a comparative Slavonic perspective in the following century offered not only the description but also laid theoretical and methodological foundations for the research (Havránek 1958; Bauer 1972). Relevant for this field of research are also the studies on inner-Slavonic syntactic typology (e.g. Mrazek 1990).

Although many relevant theoretical and methodological issues concerning internal and contact-induced syntactic development have been covered by the previous investigations, some specific aspects of syntactic change have not received much attention. First, whereas most studies on contact-induced change hitherto have focused on pairs of genetically distinct languages, this book also deals with language contact between genetically closely related languages (see also the recent books Rabus 2013 and Besters-Dilger et al. 2014). Second, it discusses the problem of language susceptibility to foreign influences under different circumstances. Third, it includes contributions that address the question of how translations can trigger syntactic change. The data range from the canonical Old Church Slavonic texts and Church Slavonic national recensions (Bulgarian, Serbian), pre-standardized Slavonic vernaculars, to transcribed oral speech of bilingual heritage (minority) speakers in Germany and Italy. In addition, it brings together diachronic studies with recent work on bilingual language use as the latter allow to zoom in on ongoing syntactic changes under the condition of intensive language contact.

3 Contributions

The papers in Part I deal with changes in the noun phrase. Jürgen Fuchsbauer's contribution *Some observations on the usage of adnominal genitives and datives in Middle Bulgarian Church Slavonic* investigates the usage of the two cases in Middle Bulgarian Church Slavonic literary language, taking into account semantic factors which determine it. The comparison of the original and translated works shows that, although one might expect a stronger Greek syntactic influence in the translation, the Graecizing genitive was more frequent in the original text. This indicates the impact of metalinguistic factors on the syntactic system, i.e. the role of an implicit literary language norm of the epoch.

In her article *Quantifying syntactic influence: Word order, possession and definiteness in Old Church Slavonic and Greek* Hanne Martine Eckhoff discusses how to distinguish native from borrowed syntax if a language, such as Old Church Slavonic (OCS), is attested only in translated texts. She demonstrates that in case of OCS adnominal possessive constructions, which exhibit relative syntactic independence, an analysis of the complex interaction of different factors reveals native syntax. However, in cases of replication (OCS word order) which could be attributed to the similarity of the two systems, additional comparative data are needed.

The decay of cases in Molise Slavonic by Silvia Luraghi and Milena Krstić explores changes in a complex, high contact situation between a South Slavonic dialect spoken in Italy and Romance. It is shown that the expansion of prepositions in Molise Slavonic limited the usage of bare cases to the ones encoding the core syntactic arguments: the nominative, the accusative and the dative. The authors explain the causes and mechanisms of this drift toward analytism from the comparative, typological and language contact perspective. The impact of sociolinguistic conditions on linguistic variation between generations is investigated as well.

The papers in Part II focus on the verbal phrase and related topics. In her contribution *Null subjects and person in Old North Russian* Hakyung Jung examines the null subject patterns in Old North Russian within a generative framework. Basing her research on statistical data, she argues that this was a person-based system, and gives an explanation for its reduction from the 10th century to the modern period. As argued by the author, the similarities between Old and Modern Russian, Finnish and Lithuanian in this domain raise the possibility that the development of the Russian system was influenced by the Balto-Finnic substratum.

Replication patterns found in heritage languages are studied in the article *On the permeability of grammars: Syntactic pattern replications in heritage Croatian and heritage Serbian spoken in Germany* by Björn Hansen. In analysing different syntactic phenomena (valence and linking, non-canonical subject constructions, prepositional phrases, word order and agreement), the author distinguishes contact-induced grammaticalization, polysemy copying, and restructuring. This paper exhibits how heritage linguistics, revealing the mechanisms, causes and types of contact induced changes in progress can contribute to historical syntax.

Imke Mendoza's contribution *Possessive resultative constructions in Old and Middle Polish* investigates the development of possessive resultative constructions in Polish. Attested in the earliest written documents in the 14th century, they underwent comparatively few changes up to the modern times, the main one being the increase of adjacency of auxiliary and lexical elements. The author suggests two possible model languages for this construction: German, which had an impact on the spoken language, and Latin, with which Polish was in contact through the written language.

In his paper *Mechanisms of word order change in 12th and 13th century Serbian*, Slobodan Pavlović addresses the question of word order changes in the earliest vernacular written sources, discussing the distribution of enclitics, subject, predicate and object positions and the linearization of the noun phrase. He explains that the changes toward homogeneous and continuous phrasal structures and a centralized sentence are a manifestation of the drift from the non-configurational to configurational language and that this internal process in Old Serbian was intensified by the Balkan Romance influence.

The rise of discourse structuring elements based on *verba dicendi* in Croatian is presented in Sandra Birzer's contribution *Historical development and contemporary usage of discourse structuring elements based on* verba dicendi *in Croatian*. She establishes three periods in their diachronic path and compares Croatian with Russian and Polish, pointing out the differences between the languages. It is argued that German syntactic structures influenced the development of discourse structuring elements based on the past participle, with a possible Czech impact which reinforced the consolidation of the pattern in Croatian.

Part III is focused on complex sentence structures. In her paper *The status and origin of the* accusativus cum infinitivo *construction in Old Church Slavonic* Marina Kurešević examines the origin of the accusative with infinitive in the first Slavonic literary language in a typological and comparative perspective. It is argued that two basic semantic types of this complement structure, one with subjunctive and the other with indicative meaning, evolved independently. The first one is seen as a genuine Slavonic pattern, the other one as a bookish neologism, based on internal language motivation and supported by Greek sentence patterns.

Björn Wiemer's contribution *On triangulation in the domain of clause linkage and propositional marking* introduces the concept of triangulation as an approach to the study of structural features shared between areally and/or genealogically related languages. This holistic concept covers various procedures applied in the research of such phenomena from an areal, genealogical and universal perspective. Its application is illustrated by the case studies of complementizers marking the suspension of assertiveness in clausal complementation: South Slavonic *da* and its North (East and West) Slavonic counterpart *jakoby*.

The paper *The development of perception verb complements in the Serbian language* by Jasmina Grković-Major presents the changes in complementation strategies in a typological, comparative and areal perspective. It is argued that the development of complement clauses was induced by the drift toward a transitive, configurational system. In this gradual process, going through the phase of instability with several competing clausal patterns, Old Serbian was susceptible to foreign influences, which directed further development, as shown by the expansion of *da*-clauses into the indicative domain under Romance influence.

In his contribution *A tale of two pathways: On the development of relative clause chaining in East Slavonic* Andrii Danylenko studies the genesis of relative clauses in East Slavonic, taking into account areal, diachronic, and sociotypological criteria. Distinguishing two developmental pathways, one leading to paratactic subordination, the other to hypotactic subordination, he claims that the former is in correlation with the analytic tendency in the morphosyntax of a language, while the latter is in correlation with the synthetic one, not only in East Slavonic but in other Indo-European languages as well.

Barbara Sonnenhauser analyses the development of relative clauses with the indeclinable *ki* and adjectival *kateri* in her paper *Relativisation strategies in Slovene: Diachrony between language use and language description*. She presents the complex history of the relativisation markers from the earliest written documents to contemporary Slovene, discussing several factors which had been at work in this process: (i) language internal development, i.e. general Slavonic tendencies, (ii) language contacts with German, both as regards the language users and those describing the language, and (iii) metalinguistic factors.

The individual contributions add to the aim of promoting recent developments in the field, both theoretical and methodological, especially as concerns corpus based studies. Accordingly, the case studies gathered in this volume are data-driven, and the analyses are based on sound empirical research conducted on the corpora available for the particular research questions. Dealing with a wide range of phenomena, the contributions reveal an effort to holistically capture and explain the complex interaction of different linguistic and social factors causing and directing syntactic change. We hope that they will contribute to a better understanding of the manifold forces shaping syntactic patterns and stimulate further research in this domain.

References

Bauer, Jaroslav. 1972. *Syntactica slavica. Vybrané práce ze slovanské skladby* [Syntactica slavica. Selected works on Slavonic syntax]. Brno: Universita J. E. Purkyně.

Besters-Dilger, Juliane, Cynthia Dermarkar, Stefan Pfänder & Achim Rabus (eds.). 2014. *Congruence in contact-induced language change. Language families, typological resemblance, and perceived similarity.* Berlin & New York: De Gruyter.

Civ'jan, Tat'jana V. 1979. *Sintaksičeskaja struktura balkanskogo jazykovogo sojuza* [The syntactic structure of the Balkan Sprachbund]. Moskva: Nauka. http://www.inslav.ru/images/stories/pdf/1979_Civjan.pdf (accessed 20 September 2016).

Friedman, Victor A. 1997. One grammar, three lexicons: Ideological overtones and underpinnings in the Balkan Sprachbund. In Kora Singer, Randall Eggert & Gregory Anderson (eds.), *CLS 33: Papers from the panels on linguistic ideologies in contact;*

Universal grammar; Parameters and typology; The perception of speech and other acoustic signals, 23–44. Chicago: Chicago Linguistic Society.

Friedman, Victor A. 2017. Language ideology and language change in the Balkans. A view from the early twenty-first century. *Die Welt der Slaven*. 62 (1). 1–21.

Hansen, Björn & Jasmina Grković-Major (eds.). 2010. *Diachronic Slavonic syntax: Gradual changes in focus* (Wiener Slawistischer Almanach – Sonderband 74). München, Berlin & Wien: Verlag Otto Sagner.

Havránek, Bohuslav. 1958. Metodologická problematika historickosrovávacího studia syntaxe slovanských jazyku [Methodological problems of the historical-comparative analysis of the syntax of the Slavonic languages]. In *K historickosrovnávacímu studiu slovanských jazyku* [Historical-comparative studies on Slavonic languages], 77–88. Praha: Statní pedagogické nakladatelství.

Kopitar, Jernej. 1945 [1826]. Albanesen, Walachen und Bulgaren. *Jerneja Kopitarja spisov*. II. del, 132–164. Ljubljana [originally published 1826 in: *Jahrbücher der Literatur* 34. Wien].

Kuteva, Tania & Bernd Heine 2012. An integrative model of grammaticalization. In Björn Wiemer, Bernhard Wälchli & Björn Hansen (eds.), *Grammatical replication and borrowability in language contact*, 159–190. Berlin: Mouton de Gruyter.

Miklosich, Franz. 1865. Die Verba impersonalia in Slavischen. *Denkschriften der Kaiserlichen Akademie der Wissenschaften*. Philosophisch-historische Classe XIV. 199–244.

Mrazek, Roman. 1990. *Sravnitel'nyj sintaksis slavjanskix literaturnyx jazykov. Isxodnye struktury prostogo predloženija* [Comparative syntax of the Slavonic standard languages. Basic structures of the simple sentence]. Brno: Univerzita J. E. Purkyně.

Potebnja, Aleksandr A. 1941 [1874]. *Iz zapisok po russkoj grammatike* IV [From the notes on Russian grammar IV]. Moskva & Leningrad: Izdatel'stvo Akademii nauk SSSR.

Pullum, Geoffrey K. 2006. Ideology, power, and linguistic theory. https://people.ucsc.edu/~pullum/MLA2004.pdf (accessed 6 August 2016).

Rabus, Achim. 2013. Die Rolle des Sprachkontakts für die slavischen (Standard-)Sprachen (unter besonderer Berücksichtigung des innerslavischen Kontakts). Freiburg: University of Freiburg habilitation thesis. https://app.box.com/s/9ck4rh5d7fyjci4yyyx8 (accessed 11 September 2016).

Sandfeld, Kristian. 1926. *Balkanfilologien. En oversigt over dens resultater og problemer*. [French version: Linguistique balkanique: problèmes et resultants 1930]. København: Bianco Lunos.

Seržant, Ilja A. 2015. Dative experiencer constructions as a Circum-Baltic isogloss. In Peter Arkadiev, Axel Holvoet & Björn Wiemer (eds.), *Contemporary approaches to Baltic linguistics*, 325–348. Berlin & Boston: De Gruyter.

Thomason, Sarah G. 2001. *Language contact. An introduction*. Edinburgh: Edinburgh University Press.

Part I: **The noun phrase**

Jürgen Fuchsbauer
Some observations on the usage of adnominal genitives and datives in Middle Bulgarian Church Slavonic

Abstract: The present study is dedicated to the influence of Greek on Middle Bulgarian Church Slavonic. Its focus lies on the competition of adnominal genitives and datives, which was already typical of Old Church Slavonic. In spite of the decline of the case system in the Middle Bulgarian vernacular, with only the dative surviving up to the 14th century and beyond, in the *Dioptra*, which was transferred from Greek into Church Slavonic around 1350, the genitive prevails in adnominal position. Yet, Greek objective genitives are considerably more frequently rendered by datives, while subjective genitives are almost exclusively translated by genitives. Hence, a semantic criterion exerted a marked impact on the choice of the respective case in the translation. In the *Life of Paraskeva* written by the Bulgarian patriarch Euthymius around 1380 adnominal datives were avoided with even greater consequence. Astonishingly, in this respect at least the Graecizing bias of original works like this even surpasses that of translations from Greek such as the Slavonic *Dioptra*. The preference given to the genitive provides insight into the reasoning of the Middle Bulgarian reformers of Church Slavonic, who expectably favoured archaic forms corresponding to Greek ones, even though they were already obsolete in the contemporaneous vernacular. Most of the adnominal datives in the *Life of Paraskeva* are again objective datives. Obviously, while in the adnominal position the both archaising and Graecizing genitive was generally preferred to the dative, there applied a certain restriction on the use of the genitive as objective adnominal case.

1 Language and translation technique in 14th century Bulgaria

Slavonic literacy was founded in the years of 862 and 863 in Constantinople by an erudite Byzantine cleric with considerable diplomatic experience and an obviously good command of the Slavonic language spoken in his home town

Thessaloniki, namely by Constantine the Philosopher, who is commonly known under his monastic name – Cyril. He was assisted by his brother Methodius and a number of collaborators. The literary idiom which thus came into being has its dialectal basis in Eastern South Slavonic. Initially created for the propagation of the Christian faith in the Great Moravian Empire, it was from 886 onwards resumed in the Bulgarian state. Here it reached its classic status, which is nowadays termed Old Church Slavonic (OCS). Spreading out over Eastern and South Eastern Europe this language adopted certain phonetic features of the local vernaculars, which gave rise to the so called redactions of Church Slavonic. In Bulgaria itself, after a period of decay under Byzantine rule lasting for almost two centuries, the ancient literary language was revived in the renewed empire, which persisted from 1185 until the Ottoman conquest in 1393/96. Since the spoken language had considerably moved away from it, the written idiom, the Middle Bulgarian redaction of Church Slavonic, is characterized by a pronounced artificiality. In addition, especially in the 14th century, the imitation of Greek was taken to extremes, presumably in order to converge the dignity of the Byzantine Hochsprache, which was apparently the aim of the Bulgarian reformers of writing culture of that time. This reformation reached its peak in the acting of patriarch Euthymius of Tărnovo (1375–1393).

Thus, the Church Slavonic literary language had been under a formative influence of Greek from its very beginning. First and foremost, this concerns the literature as such, 80–90% of which represent according to an estimation of Lora Taseva (2013: 129) translations from Greek. The extremely high percentage of translated texts almost naturally resulted in a deep impact of Greek on the linguistic structure of Church Slavonic.

In the course of time, translators into Church Slavonic adopted different approaches to the rendering of their originals.[1] The translations of the Cyrillo-Methodian period are comparatively exact, while, later on, in the School of Preslav a rather free style of transferring texts from Greek was preferred. By contrast, the translations (and revisions) created in the heyday of Middle Bulgarian Church Slavonic literature in the 14th century tended to be extremely literal. Every unit of the Greek original was intended to have its counterpart in Church Slavonic, and the ordering of the single Slavonic units

---

[1] For a periodisation cf., for instance, Ivanova-Mirčeva (1977: 37–48).

should correspond to their counterparts in the Greek text.² The aim of literalistic approaches like this is, in the words of Francis Thomson (1988: 675), "to take the reader to the message and not vice versa". In other words, through the emulation of their Greek exemplars the translators attempted to lead the audience to the sublimeness of the original instead of vulgarizing the latter by rendering the text on a language level which was, in spite of being generally understandable, perceived as ignoble.

The Bulgarian literary language of the 14th century had, as was stated above, considerably moved away from the vernacular, in which the main characteristic feature of the two eastern languages of the Southern branch of Slavonic, Bulgarian and Macedonian, was far advanced, namely the loss of the case system. Its decay, which presumably had already begun to loom in Old Bulgarian³ times,⁴ was, as is generally acknowledged, widely completed in Middle Bulgarian, with only the dative surviving up to the 14th century and beyond (see below). It is commonly assumed that first of all the locative and the instrumental cases were lost (cf., for instance, Ivanova-Mirčeva and Charalampiev 1999: 183), the genitive followed, and finally also the dative, remains of which survive until today (namely the clitic forms of the personal and anaphoric pronouns); nominative and accusative merged. A number of possible causes for the loss of the cases in the Balkan Slavonic languages have been named, such as, the Balkanic environment (i.e. the contact with the other Balkan languages), the phonetic merger of case endings, or the fact that the function of cases could also be fulfilled by alternative

---

2 Trost termed these principles "numerische Entsprechungsidentität" [numeric equivalence] and "Positionsidentität" [positional equivalence] (Trost 1973: 506–507, 1978: 41–42.; cf. also Fuchsbauer 2010: 170–174). The units (Trost speaks of "funktionale und semantische Einheiten" [functional and semantic units]) can be represented by single words as well as by complexes formed by more than one word (e.g., article and noun).
3 I use the term Old Bulgarian for referring to the Slavonic language *spoken* in the Lower Moesian heartland of the First Bulgarian Empire as opposed to the literary idiom OCS. A similar distinction is made between Middle Bulgarian as a spoken and Middle Bulgarian Church Slavonic as a written language.
4 Given the general conservativeness of written languages, and in view of the low literary production of the 12th century and its fragmentary transmission, we can safely assume that linguistic innovations documented at the very beginning of the Middle Bulgarian period – such as the incipient loss of the case system – considerably predate their first attestation. Mirčev (1978: 160) correctly states: "Sledovatelno napălno jasno e, če zagubvaneto na padežnite formi v bălgarskija ezik e stanalo bavno ot X. v. nasam" [It is therefore completely clear that the loss of case forms in the Bulgarian language was slowly proceeding from the 10th century onwards].

means (above all, by prepositional phrases⁵). Nevertheless, in most high quality translations and original works created by Bulgarians in the 14ᵗʰ century cases are used widely correctly. Obviously perceiving the contemporary vernacular as severely solecistic, Bulgarian men of letters of that time strove, and managed, to maintain a language level generally preserving the standard of OCS.⁶

---

5 For instance, already in OCS the agent in passive constructions could be expressed by either the instrumental case or by the preposition *otъ* ('of') + genitive. We encounter an instance in the OCS Gospels, namely in Mark 16:11.

a. Greek:
   e-theá-th-ē   *hyp'*   *aut-ês*
   PST-see-PASS-3SG   by   he/she/it-GEN.SG.F
   'he was seen by her'

b. OCS (codices Zographensis et Marianus)
   viděn-ъ   *by-stъ*   *ejǫ*
   see-PTCP.PASS.PST-NOM.SG.M   be-PST.3SG   he/she/it.INS.SG.F
   'he was seen by her'

c. OCS (codex Assemanianus)
   viděn-ъ   *by-stъ*   *otъ*   *neję*
   Sicut supra, sed   by   he/she/it.GEN.SG.F
   'he was seen by her'

In the codices Zographensis and Marianus Greek *hyp' autês* ('by her') is rendered by the mere case form *ejǫ* (instrumental), while in the codex Assemanianus a prepositional phrase *otъ neję* appears instead (in this case, however, the use of the preposition might also result from the formal imitation of the Greek original). The example demonstrates that in absolutely identical contexts both a mere case form and a prepositional phrase are fully acceptable. It was thus assumed that the availability of alternative constructions rendered cases to a certain decree superfluous.

6 The attitudes of the Middle Bulgarian reformers towards language, texts, etc. unfortunately remained implicit. On the whole, they can only be deduced from extant documents and texts. For example, there seems to be a group of reformers who prefer calques instead of established loanwords (e.g. *posětitelь* instead of *episkopъ* 'bishop'). There are, however, opposite instances, namely that such calques, some of which must have been perceived as overly artificial, were again replaced by loanwords (cf. Fuchsbauer 2015). Neither the "puristic" nor the "anti-puristic" stance is made explicit anywhere. In order to detect such tendencies and to understand eventually the underlying reasoning, the history of the relevant texts has to be studied thoroughly.

2 Case usage in the two Slavonic translations of the *Dioptra*

The Church Slavonic version of the *Dioptra* is a case in point. Its original was written in 1095 by a monk named Philippos, who in the Western tradition usually bears the epithet Monotropos. This work represents a comprehensive didactic poem, consisting of over 7,200 verses. The greater part of it is composed as a dialogue between *psychḗ* and *sárx*, the soul and the flesh, with the latter responding to the former's questions. The whole text was transferred from Greek into Middle Bulgarian Church Slavonic presumably around the middle of the 14th century. The Slavonic version is of high quality both with regard to the rendering of the Greek original and to the language level of the Slavonic text. The translation as such is decidedly literal – the translational principles mentioned above are strictly obeyed.

The loss of cases is hardly noticeable in Middle Bulgarian translations like the one of the complete poem. There exists, however, also a separate Slavonic version of two appendical chapters of the *Dioptra*, the original of which is contained in the codex GIM, Chludov 237. These short extracts were transferred into Middle Bulgarian Church Slavonic by a certain Grubadin in the Hesychast centre of Parorie (cf. Miklas 1994; Fuchsbauer 2010: 261–271; Miklas and Fuchsbauer 2013: 39, 68–69.). They differ noticeably from the Slavonic version of the whole text not only in regard to translation technique[7] – the rendering of the original is not nearly as exact, which is partly due to the fact that the original was apparently read out aloud to the interpreter (cf. Fuchsbauer 2012a). Moreover, even though the cases are on the whole used correctly, certain indications of insecurity in their usage are observable. Above all, prepositional phrases are sometimes utilized instead of bare case forms. For instance, in one of these chapters (A.j.[8]) a

---

[7] This refers to the extremely literalistic approach typical of the Bulgarian translators of the 14th century (cf. above), which differs markedly from moderately literalistic translations of the Cyrillo-Methodian period and the downright free rendering of the originals, as practiced by John the Exarch, a representative of the School of Preslav. Such a free rendering of the original would have been totally uncommon for the Athonite-Tărnovo type of translations. Grubadin's translation is not a deliberately free, but simply a faulty one.

[8] The abbreviation A.j. refers to the appendix "j" of the *Dioptra*; inc. *Pénte eisìn hai ergasíai ...* [There are five activities ...] (cf. Miklas and Fuchsbauer 2013: 16–17, 55).

Greek adnominal genitive is rendered by an adnominal dative in the full translation, but by the preposition *o* ('about') and locatives in the extract translation:

(1) a. Greek *Dioptra*[9]
 mném-ē   *tõn*   *hamartēmát-ōn*   *kaì*
 remembrance-NOM.SG   the.GEN.PL   sin-GEN.PL   and
 toũ   *thanát-ou*   *kaì*   *tẽs*   *mell-oúsēs*
 the.GEN.SG.M   death-GEN.SG   and   the.GEN.SG.F   come-PTCP.GEN.SG.F
 kolás-eōs
 chastisement-GEN.SG
 'the remembrance of the sins, of death, and of the coming chastisement'
 b. Church Slavonic *Dioptra*, full translation:
 pámętь   *sьgrěšeni-omъ*   *i*   *sъmr(ь)t-i*   *i*
 remembrance-NOM.SG   sin-DAT.PL   and   death-DAT.SG   and
 mǫk-ámъ[10]
 pain-DAT.PL
 'the remembrance of the sins, of death, and of the pains'
 c. Church Slavonic *Dioptra*, extract translation:
 pamętь   *o*   *sьgrěšenï-ichь·*   *i*   *o*
 remembrance-NOM.SG   about   sin-LOC.PL   and   about
 sъmr(ь)t-i,   *i*   *o*   *bǫ/d/-(ǫ)št-oi*   *mǫc-ě*
 death-LOC.SG   and   about   be-PTCP.PRS.ACT-LOC.SG.F   pain-LOC.SG
 'the remembrance of the sins, of death, and of the coming pain'

We encounter an instance of downright incorrect case usage in the other appendical chapter contained in Grubadin's extract translation (A.i[11]). Here a derivate of the verb *učiti* ('to teach') governs two objects, the first, *smĕrenomǫdriou*, stands in

---

[9] The complete Slavonic version is quoted according to the best witness, the codex Leopolitanus (L'viv, NB NANU im. Stefanyka MV-418), the Greek text according to the manuscript closest to the translation, i.e. codex Vaticanus gr. 1893 (for the appendical chapters, which are lost here, the codd. Athoniensis Pantokratoros 94 and Vindobonensis theol. gr. 167 are used). The Greek orthography is tacitly normalized.

[10] The participle *melloúsēs* has no equivalent in the Church Slavonic version; it was presumable missing in the interpreter's exemplar.

[11] This abbreviation refers to the appendix "i" of the *Dioptra*, which in the Greek original bears the title *Diákrisis tõn pragmátōn* ('Discrimination of Things'); cf. Miklas amd Fuchsbauer 2013: 16–17, 55).

the dative case, as is usual in OCS,[12] but the second, *naslědïe*, in the accusative. In the Slavonic version of the complete poem in both instances the dative is used. Cf. A.i.4:

(2) a. Greek *Dioptra*

hótan	*tapeinophrosýn-ēn*	*hēm-âs*	*didásk-ēi·*
when	humility-ACC.SG	we-ACC.PL	teach-COND.3SG
kaì	*tês*	*mell-oúsēs*	*dóx-ēs*
and	the.GEN.SG.F	come-PTCP.GEN.SG.F	glory-GEN.SG

éphes-in
pursuit-ACC.SG

'when it teaches us humility and the pursuit of the future glory'

b. Church Slavonic *Dioptra*, full translation:

egda	*smĕrenomǫdri-ju*	*na/s/*	*ouči-tъ*
when	humility-DAT.SG	us.ACC.PL	teach-PRS.3SG
i	*bǫd-ǫšt-ǫę* (for OCS -*ęję*)	*sláv-y*	*želáni-ju.*
and	be-PTCP.PRS.ACT-GEN.SG.F	glory-GEN.SG	wish-DAT.SG

c. Church Slavonic *Dioptra*, extract translation:

egda	*smĕrenomǫdri-ou*	*na/s/*	*naouča-etъ·*
when	humility-DAT.SG	us.ACC.PL	teach-PRS.3SG
i	*bǫd-ǫšt-oi*	*slav-ĕ*	*naslědï-e*
and	be-PTCP.PRS.ACT-DAT.SG.F	glory-DAT.SG	pursuit-ACC.SG

(As was mentioned above, Grubadin translated from recitation; this renders an erroneous adoption of the case of the Greek exemplar not unlikely.)

What is typical is that in the complete translation the adnominal genitive in the phrase *tês mellúses dóxēs éphesin* is rendered by the genitive *bǫdǫštǫę slávy*, but in the partial translation by the dative *bǫdǫštoi slavĕ*. Already in OCS both the genitive and the dative could be used in adnominal position. This competition of two cases in equal function – Večerka (1993: 196) presumes a far reaching, but not unlimited synonymy of genitive and dative in adnominal position – is considered to be one of the "functional doublings" which caused the loss of cases in Bulgarian.

---

[12] As, for instance, in chapter 3 of the *Life of Constantine* (cf. Angelov and Kodov 1973: 90; Lavrov 1966: 41):

dobr-ĕ	*naouči-ti*	*i*	*choudǫžьstv-ou*	*gramatičьsk-omou*
good-ADV	teach-INF	he/she/it.ACC.SG.M	art-DAT.SG	grammatical-DAT.SG

'to teach him the grammatical art well.'

3 The competition of genitive and dative in adnominal position

Generally, Slavonic translators had four possibilities for the rendering of Greek adnominal genitives, namely a genitive, a dative, a prepositional phrase (typically with otъ 'of'), and a relational or possessive adjective. The choice between these was, however, not unrestrictedly free. Rather it may have been influenced or even determined by certain syntactic and semantic criteria (e.g. adjectives are preferred in OCS, if affiliation to a person is expressed and the person's name is not augmented by another word; cf. Večerka 1963: 194; see also Eckhoff, this volume).

Let us consider sentence 9 of the fifth prose chapter of book IV (IV.e.9):

(3) a. Greek *Dioptra*
    allà   nēpí-ōn   taũta   kaì   atel-õn
    but   child-GEN.PL   this.NOM.PL.N and   unfinished-GEN.PL
    andr-õn   kaì   noũ-n   hygi-ẽ   mḕ
    man-GEN.PL and   mind-ACC.SG sane-ACC.SG not
    ech-óntōn   anaplásmat-a
    have-PTCP.PRS.ACT.GEN.PL   imagination-NOM.PL
    'but [these are] the imaginations of children and unfinished men and of ones that do not have a sane mind'
  b. Slavonic *Dioptra*
    nǫ   mladenéčьsk-aa   s-ia   i   nesъvrъšen-ychъ
    but   childish-NOM.PL.N this-NOM.PL.N and   unfinished-GEN.PL
    mǫž-ïi   i   oum-ъ   zdráv-ъ   ne
    man-GEN.PL and   mind-ACC.SG sane-ACC.SG.M not
    im-ęšt-ichъ   nazidáni-a
    have-PTCP.PRS.ACT-GEN.PL   imagination-NOM.PL

Firstly, *nēpíōn* is translated by the adjective *mladenéčьskaa*. If however the adnominal genitive is augmented by other words it cannot be rendered by an adjective. This is the case with the following *atelõn andrõn*, to which in Slavonic corresponds the genitive *nesъvrъšenychъ mǫžïi*. If *ándrōn* were, like *nēpíōn*, rendered by an adjective, i.e. *mǫžьskaja*, the already present adjective *nesъvrъšenaja* for *atelõn* would naturally be related not to *mǫžьskaja*, but to the superordinate noun *nazidanija*. Thus, this sentence would erroneously be understood as "incomplete male imaginations". The same would hold for other words congruent with *andrõn*.

In the first sentence of the same chapter a Greek adnominal genitive is rendered by a dative. Cf. IV.e.1:

(4) a. Greek *Dioptra*
    Hoi   [...] *tõn*   *ke-krym-mén-õn*   *mystērí-ōn*
    the.NOM.PL.M   the.GEN.PL   PFV-hide-PTCP.PASS-GEN.PL secret-GEN.PL
    exetast-aí
    examiner-NOM.PL
    'the examiners of hidden secrets'

  b. Slavonic *Dioptra*
    sъkrъv-én-yimъ   *tainstv-omъ*   *istęzátel-e*
    hide-PTCP.PST.PASS-DAT.PL   secret-DAT.PL   examiner-NOM.PL

We encounter a prepositional phrase in the place of a Greek adnominal genitive for example in verse 825 of the fourth book of the *Dioptra*:

(5) a. Greek *Dioptra*
    kaì   *eíper*   *pro-e-phéteu-s-e*   *toũtó*
    and   if   fore-PST-tell-FUT/AOR-3.SG this.NOM.SG.N
    ti-s   *tõn*   *archaí-ōn*
    anybody-NOM.SG   the.GEN.PL   old-GEN.PL
    'if anybody of the old prophesied that'

  b. Slavonic *Dioptra*
    i   *ašte*   *pr/o/r(o)čъstvova*   *s-e*   *kto*   *w/t/*
    and   if   prophesy[PST.3.SG]   this-NOM.SG.N   who.NOM.SG   of
    drévn-ichъ
    old-GEN.PL

Taking into account the development of the vernacular, one would assume that in Bulgarian translations and original works of the 14th century adnominal datives and prepositional phrases supersede adnominal genitives. Steinke (1968: 84) assumed that in the 13th century the "Genitivverfall bereits das Endstadium erreicht hat" [the loss of the genitive had reached its final stage], whereas the adnominal dative had remained "eine produktive Kategorie" [a productive category]. As the adverbial and prepositional usage of this case was already subjected to considerable restrictions, the adnominal one formed the "Funktionsschwerpunkt" [functional focus] of the dative case (Steinke 1968: 93). According to Steinke, in the 13th century documents he examined the replacement of adnominal genitives by datives is the "am häufigsten zu beobachtende Neuerung der Kasus überhaupt" [on the whole, the innovation in the case system which can be observed most frequently] (Steinke 1968: 62). One would, therefore, expect the usage of genitives for the rendering of Greek adnominal genitives in a 14th century translation like the one of the *Dioptra* to be decidedly restricted. An analysis of the equivalents of Greek adnominal genitives in the fourth book of the poem proved that this is not the case. As a matter of fact, to 39% of the Greek adnominal genitives (at a total of 204 instances) corresponds a genitive in Slavonic. In adnominal position the genitive is thus twice as frequent as the dative with 19%. Relational adjectives account for 22%, possessive adjectives for 15%, prepositional phrases for 5% (cf. Tab. 1). The frequency of the appearance of relational and possessive adjectives is of no immediate relevance for a study of case usage in Middle Bulgarian Church Slavonic. For reasons of completeness, they must be included in the tables (for their usage in OCS cf. Večerka 1963: 193–199).

Tab. 1: Correspondents of Greek adnominal genitives in the Slavonic *Dioptra*

Slavonic correspondents to Greek adnominal genitives	Occurrences	Percentage
Genitive	80	39
Dative	39	19
Relational adjective	44	22
Possessive adjective	30	15
Prepositional phrase	11	5
Total	204	100

In order to determine whether the choice between genitive and dative depends on semantic criteria, I discerned several subtypes of Greek adnominal genitives, namely the *genitivi possessivus, subiectivus, obiectivus, partitivus,* and *definitivus*.[13]

---

[13] This classification is intended to include all semantic fields of the Greek adnominal genitive occurring in the *Dioptra*. The *gen. possessivus* indicates a belonging (e.g. *hē dóxa tōn téknōn toū Theoū* 'the glory of the children of God'). If the dependent noun is the "subject" of an action expressed by the superordinate noun we deal with a *gen. subiectivus* (*éleusis toū Christoū* 'the coming of Christ'), if it is its "object", with a *gen. obiectivus* (*ho ktístēs tōn hapántōn* 'the creator of all'). The *gen. partitivus* characterises something or somebody as being part of a bigger whole (*tis tōn archaíōn* 'anybody of the old'). The *gen. definitivus* explains the content of the superordinate noun (*bathmoì tēs eusebeías* 'steps of piety'; for reasons of simplicity I subsume also semantically related genitives, which like the *genitivus pertinentiae* cannot always be separated clearly from the *gen. definitivus*, under this subtype).

The *genitivus hebraicus*, which shall not be passed over here, does not occur in the fourth book of the *Dioptra*, but in the others, namely in the common phrase *eis aiōnas aiōnōn* (*in saecula saeculorum*). It is translated exclusively by the dative: *vъ věky věkwmъ* (cf. verses 251, 262, 284, 357 of book I; verse 1584 of book II; verse 1275 of book IV; verses 2170 and 2174 of book V).

Table 2 gives the absolute and, in brackets, the relative frequency (in percent) of the Slavonic translation equivalents of these semantic groups. The most frequent correspondents are marked in bold.

Tab. 2: Rendering of Greek adnominal genitives in the Slavonic *Dioptra* according to semantic fields

	Gen.		Dat.		Rel. adjective		Poss. adjective		Prep. phrase		Total
Poss.	30	**(42)**	10	(14)	11	(15)	20	(28)	-	-	71
Def.	27	**(43)**	11	(17)	22	(35)	1	(2)	2	(3)	63
Subj.	13	**(54)**	1	(4)	4	(17)	5	(21)	1	(4)	24
Obj.	9	(24)	16	**(43)**	7	(19)	4	(11)	1	(3)	37
Part.	1	(11)	1	(11)	-	-	-	-	7	**(78)**	9
Total	80		39		44		30		11		204

The table reveals that in the Slavonic version of the *Dioptra* Greek *genitivi possessivi* and *definitivi* are translated nearly three times as often by a genitive than by a dative. As the equivalent of a *genitivus subiectivus* the dative is almost excluded. Remarkably, *genitivi obiectivi* are rendered more frequently by datives than by genitives. With only a few exceptions, prepositional phrases with *otъ* ('of') correspond to *genitivi partitvi*.

The dominance of genitives as equivalents of Greek adnominal genitives in the Slavonic *Dioptra* can be supposed to result from the influence of the original. Additionally, the interpreter may have perceived the dative as being more vernacular than the genitive, which was already obsolete in spoken language. The remarkable preference for the dative as correspondent to the Greek *genitivus obiectivus*[14] demonstrates that the translator was to a certain degree able to distinguish functionally between the two cases. The reason behind this differentiation lies presumably in the basic functions of the two cases, among which is the expression of *partitivity* or *possession* in the case of the genitive and of *affectedness* in the case of the dative. A verbal action expressed by the noun superordinate to a subjective genitive is perceived as being part of or in the possession of the person the genitive refers to (*amor matris* 'the love of the mother'). By contrast, a subordinate noun standing in an objective genitive is seen as being affected by

---

[14] Already Toporov (quoted in Češko 1970: 239) observed for OCS that in adnominal objective constructions datives prevail. To my knowledge, so far no sufficient reason for this has been given.

the verbal action (*amor matris* 'the love to the mother'). By the way, a similar distinction has to be made in English and other languages as well. If *amor matris* is understood as subjective genitive it is translated as 'the love of the mother', if it represents an objective genitive, it will be rendered as 'the love to the mother'. Typically, the preposition *of* has genitive function, while *to* has dative function.

This distinction demonstrates that the translator of the *Dioptra* had a rather subtle feeling for case usage, which he must have acquired in the course of his education. However, his choice was apparently not strictly determined by context, since in identical surroundings both alternatives may appear. An example is offered by the verses 242 and 996 of the fourth book of the poem. Similar Greek phrases are translated with the help of a dative in the first instance, but with the help of a genitive in the second:

(6) Verse IV,242
    a. Greek *Dioptra*

ho	ktíst-ēs	tỗn	hapá-nt-ỗn
the.NOM.SG.M	creator-NOM.SG	the.GEN.PL	all-M/N-GEN.PL

'the Creator of all'

    b. Slavonic *Dioptra*

ʒiž/d/itel-ь	vъsěčьsk-ymъ
creator-NOM.SG	all-DAT.PL

(7) Verse IV,996
    a. Greek *Dioptra*

apò	toũ	ktíst-ou	tỗn	hapá-nt-ỗn
of	the.GEN.SG.M	creator-GEN.SG	the.GEN.PL	all-M/N-GEN.PL

'of the Creator of all'

    b. Slavonic *Dioptra*

ω/t/	ʒižditel-ě (for OCS *-ja*))	vъs-ěchъ
of	creator-GEN.SG	all-GEN.PL

It is not at all astonishing that in a highly imitative 14th century translation like the one of the *Dioptra* syntactical structures were strongly influenced by the Greek model. In view of the archaising bias of the Middle Bulgarian reformers of Church Slavonic literature, one may ask whether at that time any attempts to regulate case usage were undertaken. As is well known, from that period no theoretical works on grammar are extant (except for the treatise of Euthymius' indirect disciple, Constantine of Kostenec, who does not concern himself with morphology or syntax) – and it seems highly doubtful whether any further existed. In order to determine the theoretical basis of the reformation, if such existed at all, we have to examine original texts of its protagonists instead.

The panegyric life of Paraskeva of Epibatai (Petka Tărnovska) written by patriarch Euthymius of Tărnovo between 1376 and 1382 at the behest of Tsar John Šišman (Demina 1980: 183) may serve as an example.[15] In this text the preference for the genitive in adnominal position is even more obvious than in the Slavonic *Dioptra*: 96 adnominal genitives are opposed to 23 adnominal datives. The latter are predominantly represented by *genitivi obiectivi*, e.g.:

(8) nedoug-ωtъ   ωtgnanï-e
    illness-DAT.PL expulsion-NOM.SG
    'expulsion of illnesses' (Kałużniacki 1901: 73)

Some remind of a *dativus commodi*, e.g.:

(9) archïere-ωtъ   sladk-oje   veselï-e
    arch-priest-DAT.PL sweet-NOM.SG.N   delight-NOM.SG
    'sweet delight of the arch-priests' (Kałużniacki 1901: 74)

Thirteen of the 23 instances are found in a comparatively short, but markedly encomiastic section at the end of the *Life of Paraskeva* (pp. 73 and 74 of Kałużniacki's edition). It seems therefore plausible that, since adnominal datives usually denote the affected person, they could also, as opposed to genitives, express a certain *emotional* affectation.

4 Conclusion

Thus, in Euthymius' *Life of Paraskeva* the genitive is used almost exclusively as adnominal case. Astonishingly, in this respect at least this original work appears to be even more Graecizing than a translation from Greek like the one of the *Dioptra*. The preference of the obsolete genitive over the dative demonstrates that the Middle Bulgarian reformers of Church Slavonic deliberately disregarded the development of the vernacular. Instead, they employed a highly artificial literary language, which was formed according to the example of Greek. They did,

---

15 For my investigation I used the edition of Kałużniacki (1901: 59–77), which relies on a Serbian manuscript. A comparison of Kałużniacki's version with the text of the life contained in cod. Zographensis 107, one of the oldest Middle Bulgarian witnesses, did not reveal any significant differences as the usage of genitives and datives in adnominal position is concerned.

however, apparently not manage to formulate compelling rules for the usage of controversial phenomena.[16] This is presumably due to insufficient understanding of the language, which resulted from a lack of grammatical reasoning. The reformers had to rely on Greek grammars and on the deficient Slavonic compilation *On the Eight Parts of Speech*. Only in late 16th and early 17th century Ukraine did grammatical thinking reach a level that made it possible to describe Church Slavonic adequately.

References

Angelov, Bonju & Christo Kodov. 1973. *Kliment Ochridski. Săbrani săčinenija. Tom treti. Prostranni žitija na Kiril i Metodij* [Clement of Ochrid. Collected works. Vol. 3. The long lives of Cyril and Methodius]. Sofija: Izdatelstvo na Bălgarska Akademija na Naukite.

Češko, Elena V. 1970. *Istorija bolgarskogo sklonenija* [History of the Bulgarian declension]. Moskva: Nauka.

Demina, Evgenija I. 1980. ‹Žitie Petki› Evfimija Tyrnovskogo v novobolgarskoj pis'mennosti [Euthymius of Tărnovo's Life of Petka in the modern Bulgarian literature]. In Pen'o Rusev (ed.), *Učenici i posledovateli na Evtimij Tărnovski* [Disciples and followers of Euthymius of Tărnovo]. *Vtori meždunaroden simpozium. Veliko Tărnovo, 20–23 maj 1976*, 183–192. Sofija: Izdatelstvo na Bălgarska Akademija na Naukite.

Fuchsbauer, Jürgen. 2010. *Die Übertragung der Dioptra ins Slavische. Ein Beispiel mittelkirchenslavischer Übersetzungstechnik*. University of Vienna dissertation. http://othes.univie.ac.at/9921/ (accessed October 2016).

Fuchsbauer, Jürgen. 2012a. Identifying listening errors in Slavonic translations? [On some peculiar mistakes in the partial translation of the Dioptra]. In Konstantinos G. Nichoritis (ed.), *Kyrillos kai Methodios. Parakatathikes politismou. Praktika diethnous synedriou „I politismiki klironomia tou ergou ton agion Kyrillou kai Methodiou os paragontas enotitas me tous laous tis N.A. Europis"* (Amyntaio 21–22 Maiou 2010) [Cyril and Methodius. Stocks of culture. Proceedings of the international conference "The cultural heritage of the acts of Sts. Cyril and Methodius as creators of the unity of the peoples of South East Europe" (Amyntaio, May 21–22, 2010)], 155–164. Thessaloniki: Epikentro.

Fuchsbauer, Jürgen. 2012b. Remarks on the grammar of the Slavonic *Dioptra*. Part I: Orthography and phonetics. *Scripta & e-Scripta* 10–11. 105–129.

Fuchsbauer, Jürgen. 2015. Gräzisierung versus Sprachpurismus. Zum Fremdgut im Wortschatz des bulgarischen Kirchenslawisch des 14. Jahrhunderts. In Emmerich Kelih, Jürgen Fuchsbauer & Stefan Michael Newerkla (eds.), *Lehnwörter im Slawischen: Empirische und crosslinguistische Perspektiven* (Sprach- und Kulturkontakte in Europas Mitte. Bd. 6), 140–149. Frankfurt am Main: Peter Lang.

---

[16] The same holds true for spelling, and especially for the usage of the jers and the nasals (cf. Fuchsbauer 2012b).

Ivanova-Mirčeva, Dora. 1977. K voprosu o xarakteristike bolgarskix perevodčeskix škol ot IX–X do XIV veka [On the question of a characteristic of Bulgarian translation schools from the 9th–10th to the 14th century]. *Palaeobulgarica* 1 (1). 37–48.

Ivanova-Mirčeva, Dora & Ivan Charalampiev. 1999. *Istorija na bălgarskija ezik* [History of the Bulgarian language]. Veliko Tărnovo: Faber.

Kałužniacki, Emil. 1901. *Werke des Patriarchen von Bulgarien Euthymius (1375–1393). Nach den besten Handschriften herausgegeben von Emil Kałužniacki.* Wien: Gerold.

Lavrov, Petr A. 1966 [1930]. *Materialy po istorii vozniknovenija drevnejšej slavjanskoj pis'mennosti* [Materials on the history of the rise of the oldest Slavonic literature]. The Hague & Paris: de Gruyter Mouton.

Miklas, Heinz. 1994. Kăde să otišli Parorijskite răkopisi? [Where did the Parorie manuscripts come from?]. In Georgi Dančev (ed.), *Pametnici. Poetika. Istoriografija* (The Tărnovo literary school. Vol. 5. Monuments. Poetry. Historiography). *Peti meždunaroden simpozium, Veliko Tărnovo, 6.–8. septemvri 1989 g. (Tărnovska knižovna škola 5)*, 29–43. Veliko Tărnovo: Univ. Izdat. Sv. Sv. Kiril i Metodij.

Miklas, Heinz & Jürgen Fuchsbauer. 2013. *Die kirchenslavische Übersetzung der Dioptra des Philippos Monotropos. Band 1. Überlieferung. Text der Programmata und des ersten Buches.* Wien: Holzhausen.

Mirčev, Kiril. 1978. *Istoričeska gramatika na bălgarskija ezik* [Historical grammar of the Bulgarian language], 3rd edn. Sofija: Nauka i izkustvo.

Steinke, Klaus. 1968. *Studien über den Verfall der bulgarischen Deklination. Das bulgarische Kasussystem zu Beginn des 13. Jahrhunderts.* München: Sagner.

Taseva, Lora. 2013. Datenbank griechisch-slavischer lexikalischer Parallelen auf der Grundlage von Übersetzungen des 9.–14. Jahrhunderts: philologische Probleme. *Byzantinoslavica* 71. 129–144.

Thomson, Francis J. 1988. Sensus or Proprietas verborum. Medieval theories of translation as exemplified by translations from Greek into Latin and Slavonic. In Klaus Trost, Ekkehard Völkl & Erwin Wedel (eds.), *Symposium Methodianum. Beiträge der Internationalen Tagung in Regensburg (17.–24. April 1985) zum Gedenken an den 1100. Todestag des Hl. Method* (Selecta Slavica 13), 675–691. Neuried: Hieronymus Verlag.

Trost, Klaus. 1973. Die übersetzungstheoretischen Konzeptionen des cyrillisch-mazedonischen Blattes und des Prologs zum Bogoslovie des Exarchen Joann. Zugleich ein Beitrag zur Frage der Autorschaft Konstantin-Kyrills. In *Slavistische Studien zum VII. internationalen Slavistenkongress in Warschau 1973*, 497–525. München: Trofenik.

Trost, Klaus. 1978. *Untersuchungen zur Übersetzungstheorie und -praxis des späteren Kirchenslavischen. Die Abstrakta in der Hexaemeronübersetzung des Zagreber Zbornik von 1469* (Forum Slavicum 43). München: Fink.

Večerka, Radoslav. 1963. Sintaksis bespredložnogo roditel'nogo padeža v staroslavjanskom jazyke [The syntax of the prepositionless genitive in the Old Church Slavonic language]. In Josef Kurz (ed.), *Issledovanija po sintaksisu staroslavjanskogo jazyka* [Studies on the syntax of the Old Church Slavonic language], 183–225. Praha: Izdatel'stvo čechoslovackoj Akademii Nauk.

Večerka, Radoslav. 1993. *Altkirchenslavische (altbulgarische) Syntax II. Die innere Satzstruktur.* Freiburg i. Br.: Weiher.

Hanne Martine Eckhoff
Quantifying syntactic influence: Word order, possession and definiteness in Old Church Slavonic and Greek

Abstract: Canonical Old Church Slavonic (OCS) is the earliest attestation of Slavonic and our only evidence for many Common Slavonic features. Since virtually all of the texts are translations from Greek, separating Greek syntactic features from native Slavonic ones is not straightforward. This article sets out to examine how we can distinguish between native syntax and syntactic influence using statistical modelling (classification trees) and parallel data in two case studies, both extreme cases. The first case study deals with OCS word order, which is known to follow the Greek to a very great extent. The second one concerns adnominal possessive constructions, where OCS displays great independence and translates Greek adnominal genitives into at least five different constructions. In the first case study, we see that Greek word order outranks all other predictors in the statistical model. In the second case study we see that Greek morphosyntactic predictors are outranked by a number of semantic and pragmatic factors. The final classification model also provides a better understanding of the relative weight of these factors than the literature has previously provided. The differences between the results in the two case studies are encouraging: Similar models can be used to weigh language-external against language-internal factors in the less straightforward cases in between those two poles, if we have sufficiently large and sophisticated data sets.

1 Introduction

The Old Church Slavonic (OCS) canon is a cornerstone in Slavonic historical linguistics. The texts are the very first attestations of Slavonic, and they are the sole documentation of a number of Common Slavonic features. However, the texts are virtually all translations from Greek. There is a certain pessimism in the literature about separating Greek features from native Slavonic ones, especially when it comes to syntax. This is obviously a more general question: In languages only attested in translated form, how can we distinguish between native syntax and syntactic influence?

https://doi.org/10.1515/9783110531435-003

This article approaches this question by fitting statistical classification models (classification trees) to detailed parallel corpus data in two OCS case studies. The first case study concerns OCS word order in two syntactic environments: the order of transitive verbs and their direct objects, and the order of an adnominal possessor and its nominal head. In this case study we expect that the OCS distribution is very strongly influenced by the Greek, and this is indeed what we find. OCS replicates the Greek word order almost completely, and other factors do not even surface in the statistical analyses. Thus, we have no evidence to indicate that the two systems are different.

The second and main case study concerns OCS adnominal possessive constructions.[1] Since OCS has a wide range of such constructions, largely rendering Greek adnominal genitives, we expect the syntactic influence from Greek to be small. And indeed, this is what we find: While it *is* to some extent possible to predict the distribution of OCS constructions on the basis of Greek morphosyntactic features, a model using a wider range of language-internal factors produces much better predictions, and shows us that the Greek predictors are just symptoms of the real conditioning factors: animacy, givenness status, possessor discourse prominence, number and adnominal relation type. These factors outrank the Greek predictors and give a much more successful classification. The classification models also provide a better understanding of the relative weight of these factors than the literature has previously provided.

2 Data and method

The two case studies use data from the PROIEL/TOROT treebanks.[2]

The data sets are limited to the Codex Marianus, since this is currently the OCS source available with the richest annotation. The Marianus has been given such priority for several reasons: The OCS Gospel translations are the only texts that are currently available electronically with token-level alignments with the

---

[1] For an examination of Greek influence on the choice of possessive constructions in Middle Bulgarian Church Slavonic, see Fuchsbauer (this volume).
[2] TOROT (The Tromsø OCS and Old Russian Treebank, https://nestor.uit.no, https://torottreebank.github.io/) is an expansion of the Slavonic part of the PROIEL corpus (Pragmatic Resources in Old Indo-European Languages, https://proiel.github.io/). The Codex Marianus (edition: Jagić 1883) was fully annotated in PROIEL, but is also included in TOROT along with the Greek Gospels. The data were all drawn from TOROT in September 2014. Full data sets and R scripts are openly available from the TROLLing data repository at http://hdl.handle.net/10037.1/1028901.

Greek source text. This is so for a reason: The Greek New Testament text used in the PROIEL/TOROT treebanks[3] is certainly not the true source text for the OCS translations, but it is nonetheless considerably closer to what the source text must have been than what we find e.g. for the vitae and homilies in the Codex Suprasliensis.[4] Also, the Codex Marianus must be considered one of the very oldest and linguistically most archaic texts in the OCS canon (cf. e.g. Lunt 2001: 7–9), and was chosen instead of the equally archaic Codex Zographensis because it is some 5000 words longer. The Marianus, and the Gospel manuscripts in general, are, as translations, also much more polished and accomplished than the Suprasliensis translations, with few distorted passages and less Greek interference.

The PROIEL/TOROT treebanks have annotation organised in layers: lemmatisation, morphological and syntactic annotation (dependency grammar) are all in different layers, and word order information is stored independently of the syntactic analyses. In addition, there are various types of customised tagging at sentence, lemma and token level. The custom tagging relevant for this article is lemma-level annotation for animacy, relationality and adjective suffixes.[5] In addition, the token-level alignment with the Greek source text provides access to the layer of givenness status and anaphoricity annotation present in the PROIEL version of the Greek New Testament. This annotation scheme is described in more detail in Section 2.2.

It is to be hoped that the complex, multilayered data provided in the PROIEL and TOROT treebanks can to some extent compensate for the lack of native-speaker intuitions[6] when handling a dead language such as OCS. The complexity of the data calls for statistical methods that can weigh various OCS-internal and -external factors against each other.

2.1 Statistical classification: CART trees and Random Forests

Both word order and choice of possessive construction are phenomena that are expected to be conditioned by a wide range of mutually related factors that all

---

[3] Constantin von Tischendorf (1889): *Novum Testamentum Graece*, Editio octava critica maior, Leipzig: Giesecke & Devrient.
[4] The Codex Suprasliensis is available with full morphosyntactic annotation in TOROT.
[5] For a fuller description of the PROIEL annotation schemes, see Haug et al. (2009).
[6] For OCS, even the notion of native-speaker intuitions is problematic since the language is to some extent a construct for literary purposes. Nonetheless, it clearly does reflect rules and regularities that must stem from the vernacular(s) on which the literary language was based, i.e. the South Slavonic dialect spoken in Thessaloniki, and later Old Bulgarian (see e.g. Birnbaum 1996).

add up to something we might call "discourse prominence", such as animacy, topichood, givenness status, specificity, number and part of speech (nominal realisation type), but also by factors such as phonological length/weight and syntactic complexity. Statistical classification trees are a good way of dealing with such phenomena, since they are well suited for data sets with a large number of predictors and better suited than most models to deal with factors that are internally correlated (multicollinearity), see Tagliamonte and Baayen (2012). They also enable us to provide intuitive visualisations of complex factor interactions. Therefore, classification trees are used to visualise the relative contribution of various predictors in this article, using the ctree() function in the R package "party" (Hothorn, Hornik, and Zeileis 2006).[7]

The classification trees are fitted by recursive partitioning (Strobl, Malley, and Tutz 2009). In such classification trees, an algorithm recursively subdivides the data into ever smaller sets and subsets. At every split, the model selects the best predictor for the split, and so even in the case of correlated factors, it will pick the one that performs best. Splits are visualised as circles representing those factors that can subdivide the data in a statistically significant way. The terminal nodes have representations of the actual distribution in that particular subset, making the evaluation of the splits easier. The terminal nodes will be as homogeneous as possible, but in most cases there will be residual variation unaccounted for by the tree, which gives us an immediate way of assessing the success of the classification. The classification trees are supplemented by Random Forest analyses that provide graphs representing the relative importance of the predictors, using the cforest() and varimp() functions in the "party" package (Hothorn et al. 2006; Strobl et al. 2007; Strobl et al. 2008).

2.2 A note on the information structure annotation in the PROIEL corpus

A great advantage of the PROIEL/TOROT treebanks is that they provide detailed annotation of precisely the kind of information that is expected to be important in the case studies. The PROIEL annotation assigns givenness tags to discourse referents (in the sense of Karttunen 1969). In addition, anaphoric links (from anaphors to antecedents) are assigned, in order to provide data on the properties of immediate antecedents and also on the length and density of anaphoric chains. An

---

[7] See also package documentation in cran.r-project.org/web/packages/party/party.pdf.

addressee-based notion of givenness is employed, based on the idea of *contexts* (cf. Riester, Lorenz, and Seemann 2010) that the addressee may consult in order to establish the reference.

Tab. 1: Contexts and tags in the PROIEL corpus, adapted from Haug, Eckhoff, and Welo 2014.

Context	Specific tag	Non-specific tag	
Discourse	OLD	NONSPEC-OLD	previously mentioned
Scenario	ACC-INF	NONSPEC-INF	accessible by inference
Encyclopaedic	ACC-GEN		accessible from world knowledge
Situation	ACC-SIT		accessible by deixis
—	NEW	NONSPEC	not previously mentioned
	KIND		kind-referring
		QUANT	quantified

The annotation scheme is built on a basic three-way distinction OLD–ACCESSIBLE–NEW in the tradition after Prince (1981). If something has been explicitly mentioned in the previous discourse, it is OLD.[8] The "accessible" category is divided into three by knowledge context: a discourse referent may be accessible by inference, world knowledge or deixis. Finally, if a discourse referent is not available from any knowledge context, it is tagged NEW. In addition, there are parallel tags for non-specific contexts,[9] where direct and indirect anaphora are also relevant. Finally, there are separate tags for kind-referring and quantified nominals.[10]

In both case studies in this article it is reasonable to appeal to the notion "aboutness topic"[11] or (for possessives) a more general notion of topicworthiness. The PROIEL corpus does not offer annotation of complex IS categories, such as topic and focus or contrast. This is primarily due to the difficulty in operationalising criteria for such annotation and achieving high inter-annotator agreement,

---

[8] The tag was only used if the antecedent occurred within a 13-sentence window. If the antecedent was outside that window, the tag OLD-INACT (old inactive) was used. The two tags are collapsed in all statistics in this article.
[9] In the sense that the discourse referent in question only exists inside certain embeddings, such as negation, modality etc., short-term referents in Karttunen's (1969) terms.
[10] For a fuller description and problematisation of the annotation scheme and its theoretical background, see Haug, Eckhoff, and Welo (2014).
[11] As defined by Lambrecht (1996: 131): "A referent is interpreted as the topic of a proposition if in a given situation the proposition is construed as being about this referent, i.e. as expressing information which is relevant to and increases the addressee's knowledge of this referent."

which is always a problem for such annotation, but even more so for the annotation of a dead language scantily attested by written sources. Several annotation experiments gave unsatisfactory results. In comparison, agreeing on givenness status and identification of antecedents is relatively easy.[12] However, it is possible to combine the givenness annotation with other annotated linguistic features in order to identify aboutness topics.

The solution chosen here is identify topics by deconstructing the properties of aboutness topics. An algorithm selects potential topic candidates and scores them for a number of properties known to correlate with topichood cross-linguistically, and which could be annotated for with a reasonable degree of objectivity. The most highly ranked candidate is then selected as the topic for each main verb.[13] The same measure can be used on any nominal as an independent score of topicworthiness.

- Position on the givenness hierarchy (old ranks highest, new is excluded)[14]
- Position on the hierarchy of syntactic relations (subjects rank highest)[15]
- Position on the animacy hierarchy (humans rank highest)[16]
- Word order (first ranks highest)[17]
- Realisation (prodrops, personal pronouns, personal names rank higher)[18]
- Relative saliency: is the topic candidate a member of a longer and tighter anaphoric chain than the competition?[19]
- Properties of the immediate antecedent: does it outrank the intervening referents on the relation, animacy and givenness hierarchies?[20]

---

[12] For interannotator agreement statistics, see Haug, Eckhoff, and Welo (2014).
[13] The algorithm was written by Dag Haug and myself. The scores were adjusted during various experimental runs on a different dataset.
[14] OLD: 15, ACC_SIT: 13, ACC_INF: 10, ACC_GEN: 5, NEW: 0. In addition OLD_INACT is scored 4 and anchored referents (NEW, but with an OLD dependent) are scored 8.
[15] Subject: 10, direct transitive object: 5, oblique argument: 2, complement clause: 1, adverbial: 1, other syntactic relations are scored 0.
[16] The OCS nouns in the PROIEL corpus are annotated for animacy at lemma level, following Zaenen et al. (2004), for more details on the tagging, see Haug et al. (2009). The scores are HUMAN: 10; ORG (human collective): 5; ANIMAL: 3; CONCRETE: 3; TIME, PLACE, NONCONC, VEH(icle): 0.
[17] The linearly first of the topic candidates is scored 15. Note that the word order is mostly taken from the Greek original, but as will be demonstrated in this article, the OCS word order is highly consistent with the original.
[18] +5 for personal pronouns, +5 for human proper nouns, +30 for prodrops unless they are NON-SPEC, KIND, or NEW.
[19] +10 for the candidate with highest relative saliency (number of mentions in the 30 preceding sentences).
[20] +2 each if the antecedent outranks the intervening candidates on these hierarchies.

Experiments with the topic guesser showed that its guesses were about as reliable as a human annotator's judgements. Since there is such a wide range of conceivable prominence features, the guesser may be adapted to the research topic. In a word order study, for instance, word order data can be excluded in order to avoid circularity, but the guesses were not significantly worse.

3 Case study 1: Word order

It is a well-known fact that OCS word order follows the original Greek word order closely. In this case study we look at the word order in two syntactic environments: the order of verbs and direct objects, and the order of adnominal possessors and their heads.

3.1 The order of verbs and direct objects

Table 2 shows us that OCS VO order follows the Greek in 95.5% of the cases. The data set is limited to OCS direct objects which are aligned with a Greek direct object (3747 occurrences).

Tab. 2: Direct object position in OCS and Greek, per cent, n = 3747.

	OCS postverbal object	OCS preverbal object
Greek postverbal object	67.49%	1.97%
Greek preverbal object	2.51%	28.02%

Figure 1 is a classification tree which predicts OCS VO order using the following predictors:
- Greek VO order (is the Greek object preverbal?)
- Greek definiteness (does the Greek object have a definite article?)
- animacy (human, concrete, non-concrete, place, time)
- OCS part of speech
- number
- givenness status (as described in Section 2.2, collapsed to OLD, ACCESSIBLE, NEW, KIND, NON-SPECIFIC)
- topicworthiness (measured as described in Section 2.2)

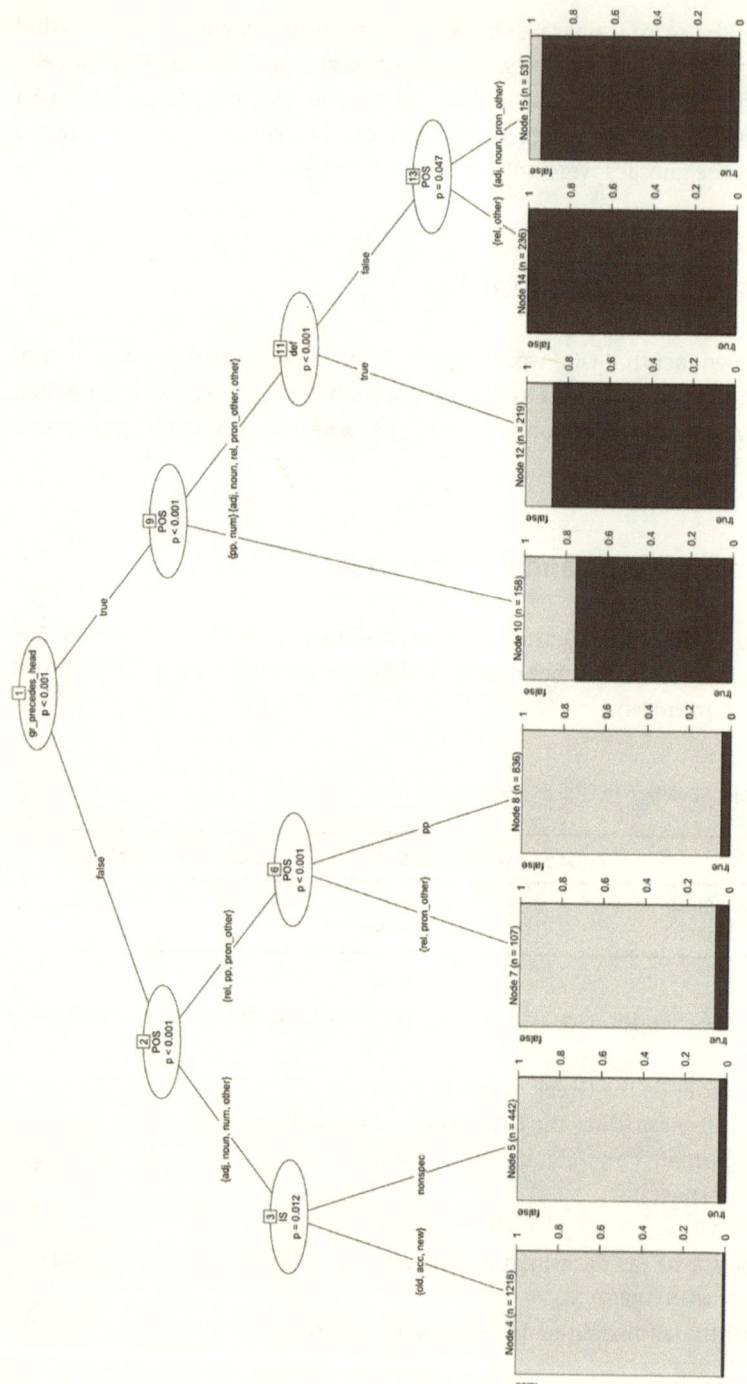

Fig. 1: Classification tree, does the OCS object precede its verbal head?

The tree (Figure 1) has a correct classification rate of 95.5% (baseline = 69.9%, i.e. the result you get if you guess that all OCS objects are postverbal) – if we guess the majority category for all members in each terminal node, the classification will be 95.5% correct. This is exactly the same result you get if you predict OCS VO order from Greek word order alone. Unsurprisingly, then, the single best predictor in Fig. 1 is Greek word order, as the Random Forest variable importance statistics in Fig. 2 show, and on this the first split in the tree is based. However, it is also possible to read a few observations concerning OCS–Greek discrepancies from the tree. First of all, we see that OCS is more likely to follow the Greek if the object is postverbal. Among the branches under the left-hand side of the main split, all terminal nodes have an overwhelming preference for postverbal objects. To the extent that there are deviations at all, they have to do with part of speech: in this group, pronouns are more likely to be prenominal than other objects. Most notably, there is a group of preverbal personal pronoun objects that are translated from postverbal Greek personal pronoun objects (41 occurrences), indicating a real difference (see node 8, example 1).

(1) kъ   tomu   že   ne   sъměaxo[sic!] **ego**   vъprašati ničьsože
    to   that   PRT   not   dared   him   ask   nothing
    ouketi gar   etolmōn   eperōtan   **auton** ouden
    no-longer PRT   dared   ask   him   nothing
    'they did not dare to ask him anything more' (Lk. 20:40)

The deviating examples occur in a few preferred contexts: after *da* in purpose clauses (10 occurrences), directly after a wh-word or a relative pronoun (17 occurrences) between a finite verb and an infinitive or between auxiliary *byti* and an *l*-participle (six occurrences). The deviations must be at least partly due to the complex clitic ordering rules in OCS, since they mostly involve pronominal clitics, cf. Willis (2000), Večerka (1998: 59–63).

On the right-hand side of the split, where the Greek original has a preverbal object, there are slightly more discrepancies. The first split on this side is also conditioned by part of speech: terminal node 10 shows us that if the object is a personal pronoun or a numeral, 24.7% (39) of the Greek preverbal objects are rendered by postverbal ones in OCS. The deviant group consists of personal pronouns with one numeral exception. Thus, it seems that personal pronoun objects are particularly prone to deviate from the Greek word order, but in both directions, and again this is likely to be due to pronominal clitics. The next split is based on Greek definiteness marking.[21] Terminal node 12 forms a subclass of

---

[21] Note that both information status and topic rank are shown by the Random Forest analysis (Fig. 2) to have more impact than Greek definiteness, both of which categories the definite article may be said to express.

objects that are neither personal pronouns nor numerals, and which translate Greek definite objects. This subclass has 12.3% (27) deviant objects, which mostly turn out to be nouns (2).

(2) kto   ti   dastъ   **oblastь**   sijǫ   da   si
    who.NOM   you.DAT   gave   power.ACC   this.ACC that   these.ACC
    tvoriši
    do

    tis   soi   **tēn**   **exousian** tautēn   edōken   hina
    who.NOM   you.DAT   the   power.ACC   this.ACC gave   that
    tauta
    these.ACC poiēis
               do

    'who gave you this authority to do these things?' (Mk. 11:28)

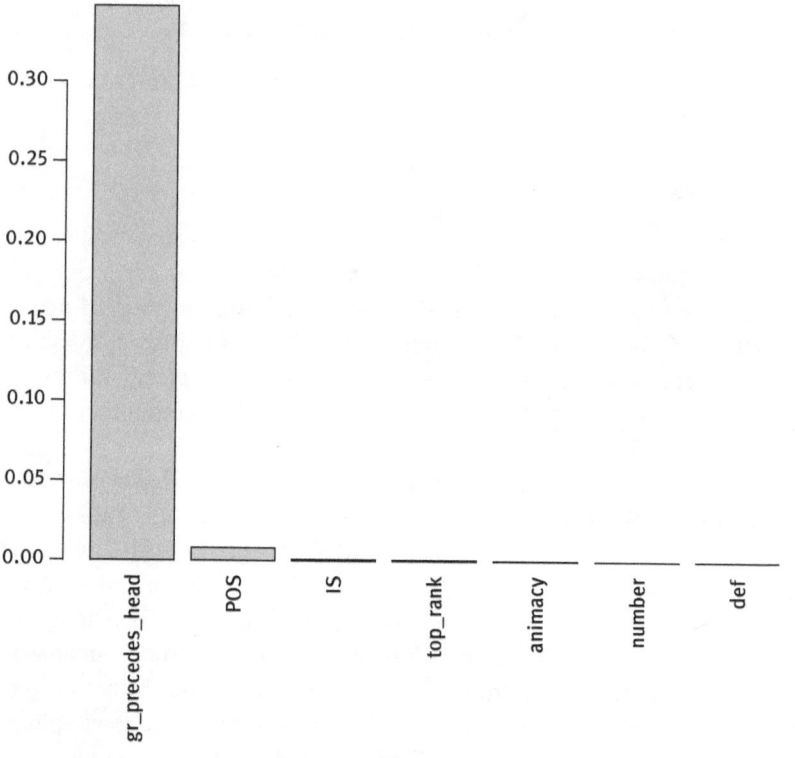

Fig. 2: Relative importance of predictors in Fig. 1.

Thus, Fig. 1 basically tells us what we have already observed: that OCS VO order in most cases faithfully replicates the Greek word order. To the extent that it does not, the deviations mostly have to do with part of speech.

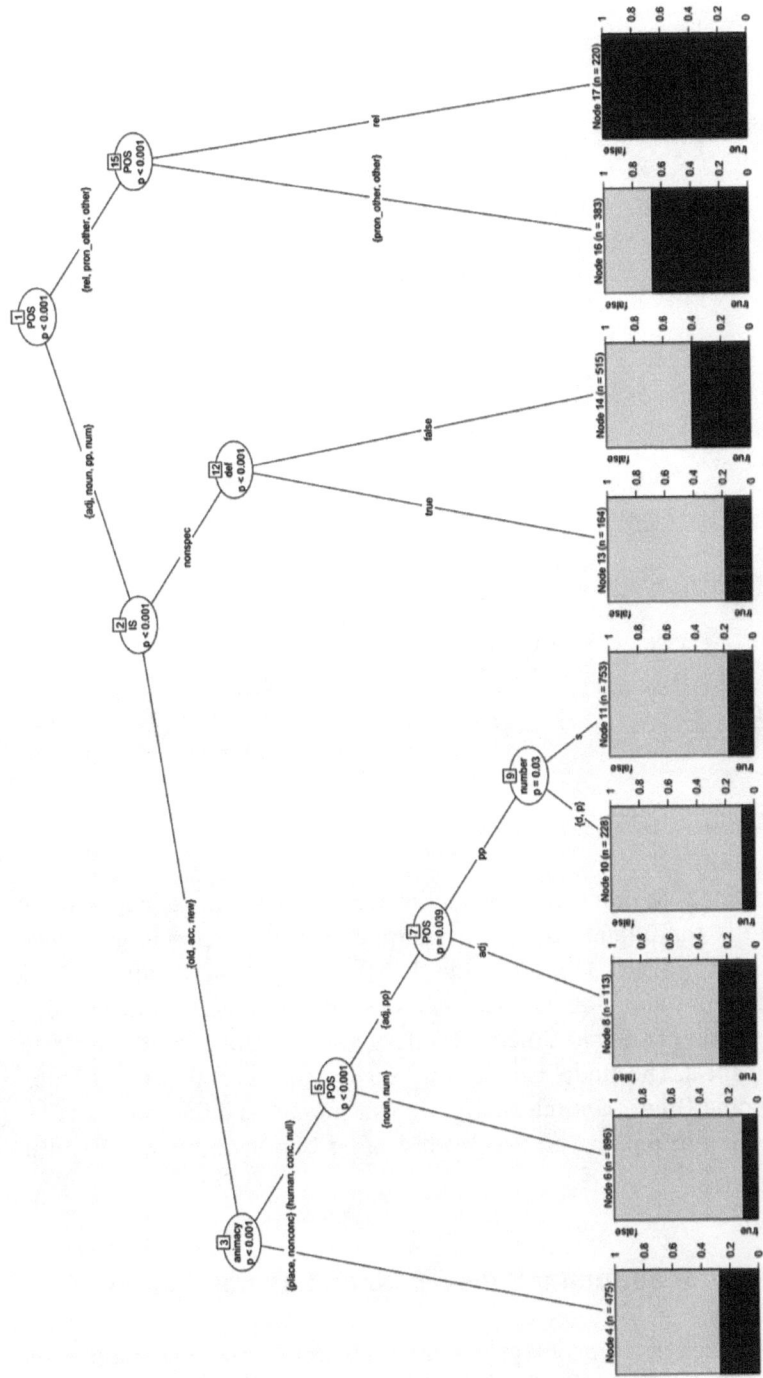

Fig. 3: Classification tree, does the OCS object precede its verbal head? Greek word order is not included among the predictors.

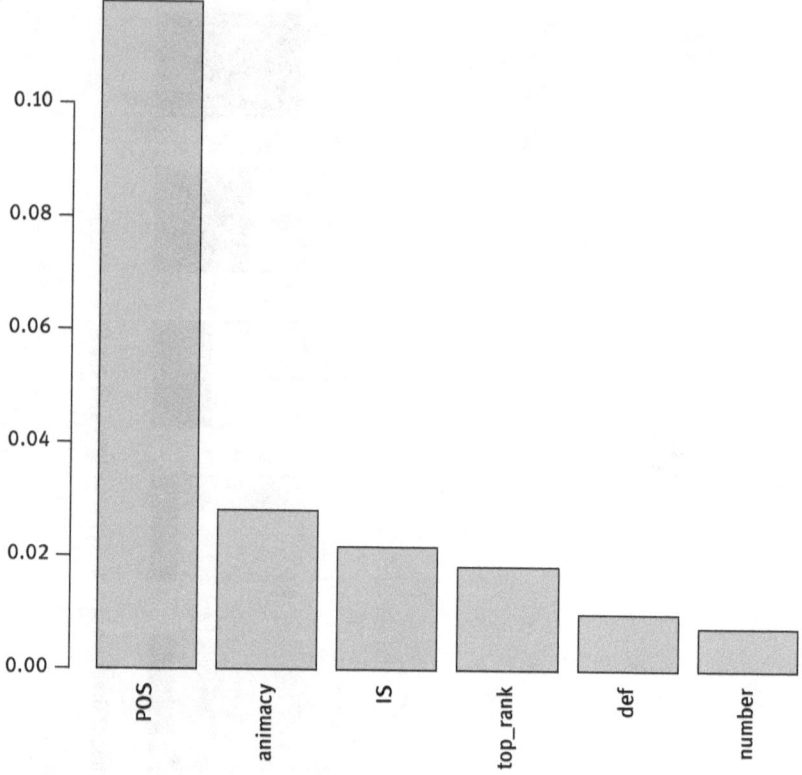

Fig. 4: Relative importance of predictors in Fig. 3.

If we remove Greek VO order from the model, we get a result that suggests that OCS VO order is conditioned by a rich interplay of part of speech, givenness status and animacy (Figs. 3 and 4). Note that the correct classification rate is 79.3%, which is not much above baseline. Most importantly, we have no evidence as to whether OCS and Greek VO order have different conditioning patterns in this respect. The model may simply be a description of the conditioning patterns in Koiné Greek. Optimistically, we can hope that OCS had a similar system and was not replicating Greek word order blindly, but we have little proof of this.

3.2 The order of adnominal possessor and its nominal head

The second environment we look at is that of adnominal possessors and their heads. Instead of classifying noun phrases by semantic criteria, we simply select those OCS NPs that translate an adnominal genitive, dative or denominal adjective with one of the same set of options. This makes for a very wide category of "possessives", including for instance adnominal partitives and objective genitives.[22]

As seen in Tab. 3, possessors are overwhelmingly postnominal both in the Greek and OCS text, and if the OCS has a prenominal possessor, it usually translates a Greek prenominal possessor. The low number of prenominal possessors makes word order unlikely to be a good predictor of the choice of construction type, and overall Greek and OCS possessor–possessee order is 99% identical.

Tab. 3: Order of possessor and possessee in Greek and OCS, n = 1157.

	OCS postnominal	OCS prenominal
Greek postnominal	1110	3
Greek prenominal	8	36

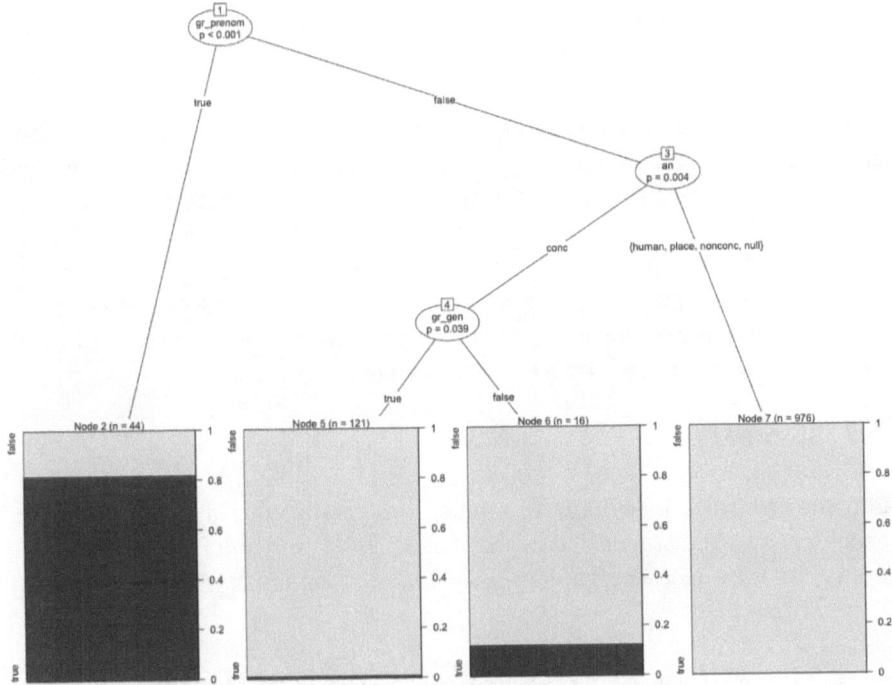

Fig. 5: Order of possessor and possessee in Greek and OCS, n = 1157.

---

22 This choice is further justified in Section 4.

The classification tree shown in Fig. 5 was fitted to the data using the following predictors:
- Greek construction type
- OCS construction type
- possessor animacy (human, concrete, place or non-concrete?)
- possessor modification: is the possessor complex or does it consist of a single word?
- Greek word order (is the Greek possessor prenominal?)
- Greek number
- Greek possessor definiteness
- Greek head definiteness
- Greek part of speech
- relationality: is the head noun relational?
- possessor givenness status (as described in Section 2.2)
- head givenness status
- syntactic relation of the possessor: ATR (attribute), APOS (apposition), PART (adnominal partitive) or NARG (object-like argument of relational noun)?
- topicworthiness (calculated as described in Section 2.2)

It nonetheless shows that the Greek word order provides the main split. The model makes two additional splits using animacy and Greek construction type, but is only able to isolate a class of concrete possessors which do not occur as genitives in the Greek, where a very small minority of the OCS occurrences have a prenominal possessor. We may therefore conclude that there is little evidence in the data to suggest that OCS and Greek differed much in possessor–head order. Whether this is due to the similarity of the two systems or to imitation of Greek word order, we cannot tell from these data alone.

3.3 Summary

Both the two syntactic environments under consideration display a very strong tendency for OCS word order to follow the Greek original word order closely. The Greek word order is by far the best predictor if we want to classify the OCS occurrences.

4 Case study 2: Possessive constructions

4.1 Introduction

Adnominal possession is a field where Greek and OCS differ notably. OCS expresses adnominal possession by way of at least five main construction types with a complex and rather subtle distribution.[23] The constructions involve various types of denominal adjectives, the adnominal genitive and the adnominal dative. In Greek, on the other hand, the adnominal genitive (with different definiteness patterns) dominates completely, and is only marginally supplemented by denominal adjectives and adnominal datives. As we see in Tab. 4, 95.1% of the OCS adnominal possessors correspond to Greek adnominal genitives.[24]

Tab. 4: OCS possessive type by Greek type, n = 1157.

OCS	Agreeing adjective/ participle	Dat	Gen	Other
adj1	0	0	323	2
adj2	36	0	357	1
dat	0	4	102	1
modified gen	0	0	167	4
unmodified gen	2	0	151	7

For the purposes of this article, I will identify four main patterns in OCS.
- **Type 1 adjectives**, derived from nouns denoting humans with the suffixes -*ov*-, -*in*-, -*j*-, -*n'*-, also the adjective *božijь* 'God's': *učenici ioanovi* 'John's disciples' (abbreviated '1' in Figures)
- **Type 2 adjectives**, derived from nouns with the suffixes -*ьsk*-, -*ьn*-,-*ij*-: *učenija fariseiska* 'the teaching of the Pharisees', also the rare adjectives derived from non-human nouns with the Type 1 suffixes (abbreviated '2' in Figures)
- **Adnominal genitive**: *domy vьdovicь* 'the houses of widows' (abbreviated 'g' in Figures)
- **Adnominal dative**: *srьdьca otьcemъ* 'the hearts of the fathers' (abbreviated 'd' in Figures)

As can be seen from the examples, all of these constructions *may* have meanings that most scholars would call possessive (see Eckhoff 2011 for a deeper discussion

---

23 For more details about the distribution of OCS possessive constructions than can be given here, see Eckhoff (2011) and the references therein.
24 Greek adnominal non-inflecting nouns were counted as genitives, typically foreign proper nouns.

of the notion of possession). In fact, as Eckhoff (2011) shows, three main semantic relation types seem to be involved here:
- Anchoring/identification (John's head)
- Classification/labelling (camel's hair, Adam's apple, the Skull Place)
- Elaboration (a piece of bread, the forgiveness of sins, the virtue of abstinence)

The first type is the one that would typically be called possessive by most scholars – the possessor is used to identify the possessee by way of a possessor referent which is already known from context, inference or encyclopaedic knowledge. The relation between possessor and possessee is often one of legal possession or of kinship or other inalienable relations. The two other semantic types are less obviously possessive. The classification type subsumes all "possessive" constructions where the whole construction serves to name a type or a referent. The final type includes object-like arguments of deverbal nouns, adnominal partitives and semantic appositions. The two last semantic types are also regularly expressed with "possessive" constructions cross-linguistically, and we see that the Greek adnominal genitive is common for all three types. Thus, although Type 2 adjectives have their centre of gravity in the field of classification and the adnominal genitive and dative in the field of elaboration, all four construction types interact in the identification field. All four construction types and all three semantic fields are therefore included here, and the terms "possession", "possessor" and "possessee" will be used to refer to all of them.

Most of the literature before Eckhoff (2011) focussed primarily on the semantic, pragmatic and referential properties of the possessor, and little on the properties of the possessee, see for instance Huntley (1984). The present study is therefore also interesting as a test of the relative influence of possessor properties and the valency properties of the possessee.

It should be immediately noted that, as all serious work on OCS possessives acknowledges, the adnominal genitive is in near-complementary distribution with the adjective constructions, an expected adjective construction will regularly be replaced with a genitive if possessor consists of more than one word (3).

(3) glavǫ **ioana krьstitelja**
head.ACC John.GEN baptist.GEN
tēn kefalēn **Iōannou tou baptizontos**
the head.ACC John.GEN the baptising.GEN
'the head of John the Baptist' (Mk. 6:24)

The genitive also occurs instead of expected adjective constructions if the possessor itself is an adjective or a participle. Since this use of the genitive seems fairly mechanical, at least in some semantic fields (Eckhoff 2011: 152–153), all complex adnominal genitives and all adnominal genitives that are themselves adjectives or participles are excluded from the data set in this case study. Only bare noun adnominal genitives are included. Pronouns are not included either in the adnominal genitive or dative class. Furthermore, only constructions with a Greek token alignment are included. This leaves us with a data set of 937 occurrences.

4.2 Greek predictors

Let us first examine to what extent the distribution of OCS possessive constructions is dependent on syntactic factors in the Greek text. The first question to ask is what should count as syntactic factors.

If the Greek original really influenced the OCS choice of possessive construction, we would expect the Greek predictors to be part of speech and case: Greek adnominal genitives would be expected to trigger adnominal genitives, Greek adnominal datives would be expected to trigger adnominal datives, and Greek (denominal) adjectives would be expected to trigger denominal adjectives. The first classification tree (Fig. 6) therefore uses only Greek part of speech[25] and case as predictors. Note that this is a somewhat unorthodox approach: I am deliberately omitting a number of predictors that I expect to be significant merely to look at the success of a model using only predictors that could indicate syntactic influence from Greek. For the full set of predictors, see Section 4.3.

We see that this classification tree is not entirely a failure, as it has a correct classification rate of 50.6% (against a baseline of 41.6%, the outcome if the largest category, type 2 adjectives, is picked every time).

However, we see that the model largely does not tell us what we would expect if the Greek syntax really influenced the choice of OCS possessive construction. The first split sets Greek proper noun and personal pronoun possessors apart from other possessors. This tells us something we already know: that Type 1 adjectives are very frequently derived from (human) proper nouns (4), but we see that this split leads to considerable misclassification as well, since around 30% of the possessors in this group are actually Type 2 adjectives (5).

(4) sěmę **avramle** esmъ
    seed Abraham-j.N.SG are
    sperma **Abraam** esmen
    seed Abraham.INDECL are
    'we are Abraham's seed' (Jn. 8:33)

---

[25] Part of speech labels: Pp (personal pronoun), V- (verb), Ne (proper noun), Nb (common noun), A- (adjective).

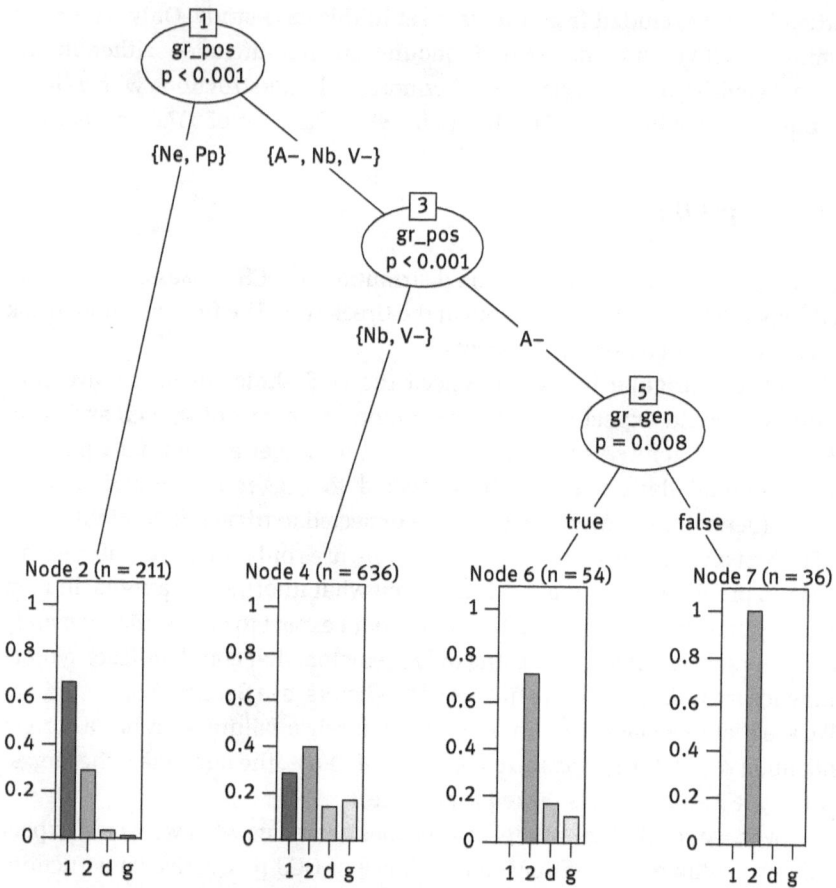

Fig. 6: Classification tree, Greek part of speech and case as predictors.

(5) pride išъ otъ nazareta **galileiskaago**
came Jesus from Nazareth.GEN Galilee-ьsk.GEN.SG
ēlthen Iēsous apo Nazaret tēs **Galilaias**
came Jesus from Nazareth.GEN the Galilee.GEN
'Jesus came from Nazareth in Galilee' (Mk. 1:9)

The second split actually gives us a small indication of possible Greek influence: it tells us that if the Greek possessor is an agreeing adjective (not a nominalisation in the genitive), the OCS will always render it with a Type 2 adjective (6). However, this is a very small group, and since OCS uses denominal adjectives much more than Greek does in any case, this is quite likely to be a case where the two systems overlap.

(6) otecъ   vašъ   **ñbsky**
    father.NOM.SG your   heaven-ьsk.M.NOM.SG
    ho   patēr   humōn **ho** **ouranios**
    the father.NOM.SG   your   the   heavenly.M.NOM.SG
    'your heavenly Father' (Mt. 6:32)

The third split tells us that if the Greek has a dative (or something that is neither a genitive nor an agreeing adjective), it is equally likely to be translated by an adnominal dative (7) or genitive (but the dative is picked in the classification model). This is, again, a tiny class with only 11 members.

(7) vъ   sъvědětelьstvo   **vъsěmъ**   **językomъ**
    in   witness.ACC   all.DAT.PL   nation.DAT.PL
    eis marturion   **pasin**   tois **ethnesin**
    in   witness.ACC   all.DAT.PL   the   nation.DAT.PL
    '(And this gospel of the kingdom will be preached in the whole world) as a testimony to all nations' (Mt. 24:14)

The final split tells us that Greek non-agreeing genitive adjective and participle possessors are preferably translated as Type 2 adjectives. Most of these are occurrences with the adjective ijudeiskъ 'Jewish' (8).

(8) čsrь   **ijudeiskъ**
    king.NOM.SG.   Jew-ьsk.NOM.SG
    ho   basileus   tōn   **Ioudaiōn**
    the   king.NOM.SG.   the   Jew.GEN.PL
    'the king of the Jews' (Mt. 27:37)

Finally, we are left with all the Greek genitive common nouns (621 occurrences), where Type 2 adjectives (9) are only marginally preferred, but where all construction types are really well-represented.

(9) vъ   čemъ   gybělь   **xrizmъnaě**   bystъ
    in   what   waste.NOM.SG   perfume-ьn.NOM.F.SG was
    eis ti   hē   apōleia   autē   tou
    in   what   the   waste.NOM.SG this.NOM.F.SG   the
    murou   gegonen
    perfume.GEN.SG   happened
    'Why this waste of perfume?' (Mk. 14:4)

A Random Forest analysis was run to gauge the relative importance of the predictors (Fig. 7), which shows that Greek part of speech is hugely more important than case as a predictor.

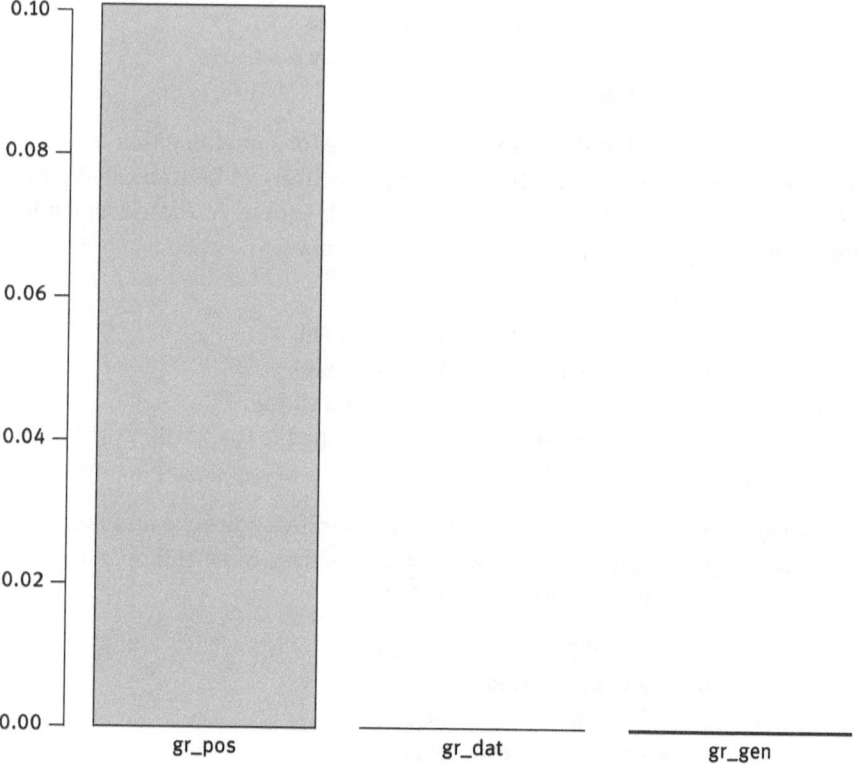

Fig. 7: Relative importance of predictors in Fig. 6.

Let us now try to predict the choice of OCS construction using a larger range of Greek predictors, which cannot necessarily be considered direct influences on the choice of OCS construction. The set of predictors in Fig. 8 include all the predictors in 6, and also the four following Greek predictors: possessor–possessee order, possessor number, definiteness (does the possessor have a definite article?) and head definiteness (does the possessee have a definite article?).

This tree (Fig. 8) is a bit more successful than the one in Fig. 6, with a prediction rate of 54%. This model is a little better at correctly predicting Type 1 adjectives, much better at predicting adnominal datives, and slightly worse at predicting Type 2 adjectives. Neither model ever predicts the genitive.

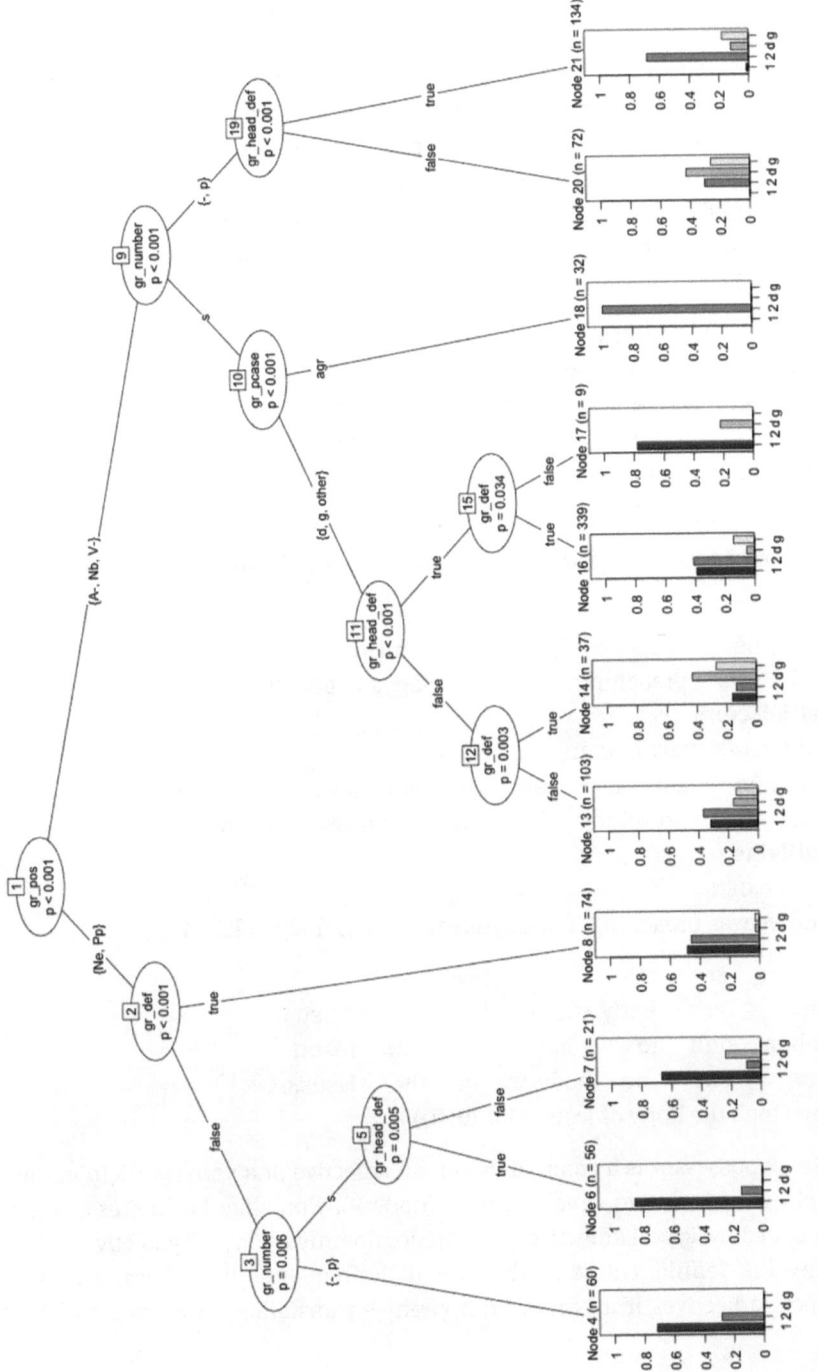

Fig. 8: Classification tree, full set of Greek predictors.

The first split is the same as in Fig. 6. However, there are now two further splits based on number and head definiteness to refine the class of occurrences translated from Greek proper nouns and personal pronouns. Type 1 adjectives are by far the most likely choice if the Greek possessor is indefinite, which follows from the fact that Greek personal proper nouns frequently do not have a definite article when they occur as adnominal genitives (10). The class under node 3 is further refined by taking number and head definiteness into consideration, but Type 1 is the obvious choice in all three subclasses (nodes 4, 6, 7).

(10) vъnide   vъ   domъ   **simonovъ**
     entered   in   house.ACC.SG   Simon-ov.M.ACC.SG
     eisēlthen eis   tēn   oikian   **Simōnos**
     entered   in   the   house.ACC.SG   Simon.GEN
     'he went into Simon's house' (Lk. 4:38)

If the Greek proper noun possessor does have a definite article, on the other hand, a Type 2 adjective translation (11) is almost equally likely as a Type 1 translation (12).

(11) i   bě   propovědaję   na   sъnьmištixъ
     and   was   preaching   on   synagogue.LOC.PL
     galilěiscěxъ
     Galilee-ьsk.NEUT.LOC.PL
     kai   ēn   kērussōn   eis   tas   sunagōgas   **tēs**
     and   was   preaching in   the   synagogue.ACC.PL   the
     Galilaias
     Galilee.GEN
     'and he was preaching in the synagogues of Galilee' (Lk. 4:44)

(12) Prijęste   že   tělo   **išvo**
     took   PRT   body.ACC.SG   Jesus-ov.N.ACC.SG
     elabon   oun   to   sōma   **tou   Iēsou**
     took   PRT   the   body.ACC.SG   the   Jesus.GEN
     'they took the body of Jesus' (Jn. 19:40)

If the Greek possessor is a common noun, an adjective or a verb (participle), the main split is now due to Greek number (node 9). Non-singular possessors are not translated by Type 1 adjectives, but predominantly by Type 2 adjectives if the Greek head is definite (13), and almost equally frequently by datives, genitives and Type 2 adjectives if it is not. With genitive translations, we often see that these indefinite heads are measure expressions, which obligatorily take partitive genitives (14).

(13) bljděte sę otъ kvasa **fariseiska**
watch REFL from leaven.GEN.SG Pharisee-ьsk.M.GEN.SG
blepete apo tēs zumes **tōn pharisaiōn**
watch from the leaven.GEN.SG the Pharisee.GEN.PL
'beware of the leaven of the Pharisees' (Mk. 8:15)

(14) stado **svinii** mъnogo
herd pig.GEN.PL big
agelē **khoirōn** pollōn
herd pig.GEN.PL big
'a great herd of pigs' (Mt. 8:30)

Node 18 again shows that Greek agreeing adjective possessors are consistently translated as OCS Type 2 adjectives. When it comes to Greek genitive and dative singular possessors (node 11), they may be translated into any of the four construction types, but we see in nodes 13, 14, 16 and 17 that the distribution is sensitive to Greek possessor and possessee definiteness. For instance, node 17 again reflects the fact that Greek human unique referents often do not have a definite article, which explains the predominance of Type 1 adjectives in this class. Almost all of the examples are occurrences of *gospodьnь* 'the Lord's' and *božijь* 'God's'.

The Random Forest analysis in Fig. 9 shows us that Greek part of speech is still the most important predictor by far, but that Greek number is also a relatively powerful predictor.

To sum up, although we can make predictions for the OCS outcome that are well above the baseline, Greek morphosyntactic features are not good predictors for the complexities of the distribution of OCS possessive constructions. There is also good reason to believe that the main predictor, Greek part of speech, is really just a symptom of something else: most proper nouns in the New Testament are animate, and virtually all proper nouns are singular. Animate proper nouns are also usually inherently definite[26] and generally have high discourse prominence. All of these are factors known to influence the selection of possessive constructions in OCS, cf. Huntley (1984) and Eckhoff (2011).

---

[26] But they rarely have a definite article in possessive constructions in NT Greek.

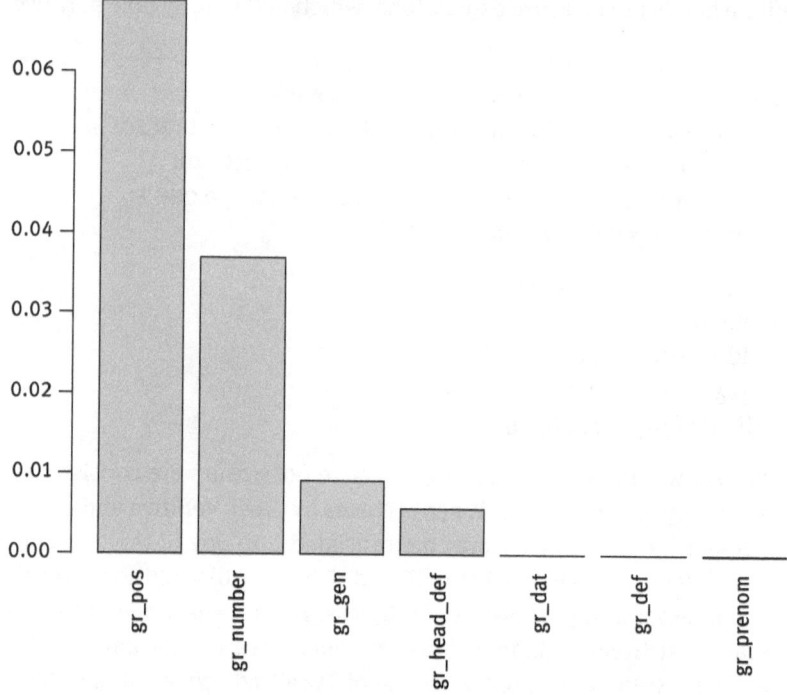

Fig. 9: Relative importance of predictors in Fig. 8.

4.3 Full set of predictors

The second part of the experiment consists of adding a number of predictors expected to affect the choice of OCS possessive construction in building the tree, while still retaining all the Greek predictors we have used so far. The added predictors are the following:
- animacy (human, concrete, place or non-concrete?)
- possessor modification: is the possessor complex or does it consist of a single word?
- relationality: is the head noun relational?
- possessor givenness status (as described in Section 2, simplified to old, accessible, new, non-specific)
- head givenness status (same simplification)
- syntactic relation: ATR (attribute), APOS (apposition), PART (adnominal partitive) or NARG (object-like argument of relational noun)?
- topicworthiness (calculated as described in Section 2.2)

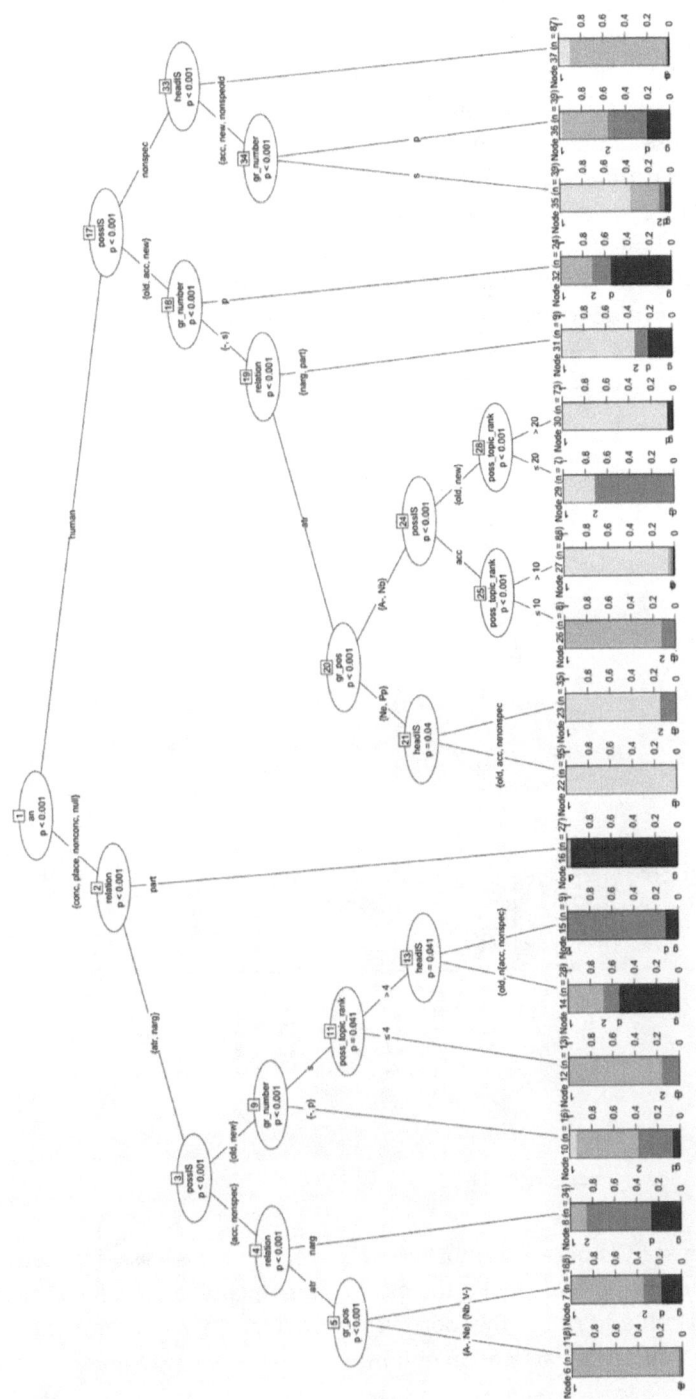

Fig. 10: Classification tree, all predictors.

Adding these predictors produces a much more successful classification tree (Fig. 10): the correct classification rate rises to 80.1%. The tree, like the previous trees, does best with the adjective constructions, but this tree is the first that also has some success in predicting dative and genitive constructions (33 of 107 datives and 54 of 118 genitives are correctly classified). A Random Forest analysis (Fig. 11) of the relative weight of the predictors shows that while Greek part of speech still has some prediction power, it is outranked by a number of semantic and pragmatic predictors. The most powerful predictor is now animacy, followed by topicworthiness, syntactic relation, possessor givenness status, number and head givenness status.

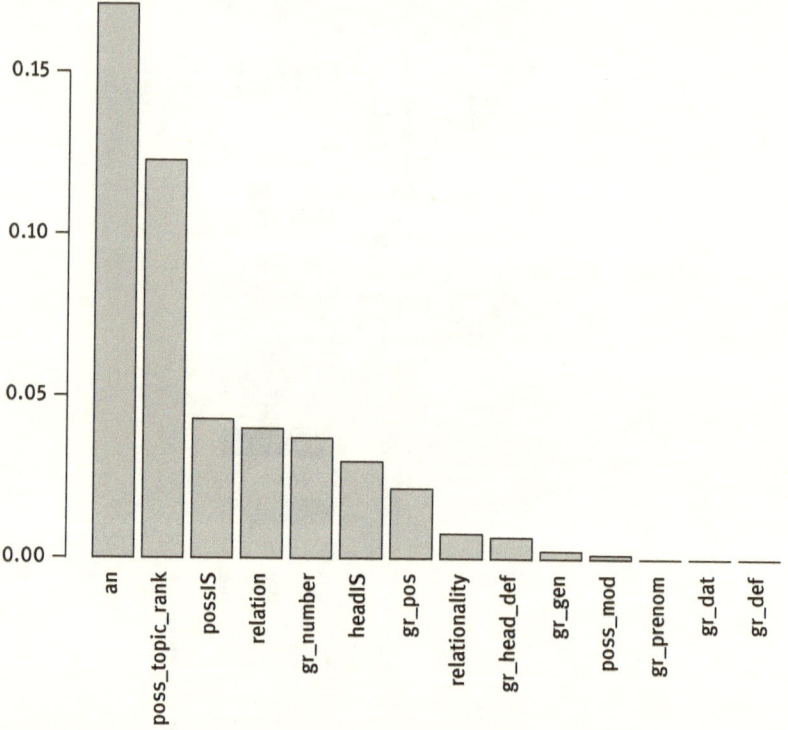

Fig. 11: Relative importance of predictors in Fig. 10.

In Fig. 10, the main split is between human and non-human possessors. When the possessor is human, Type 1 is by far the most common choice. However, the classification tree is able to refine this observation by identifying several subclasses where Type 1 adjectives are not an option.

The first split in this class is based on givenness status. If the possessor has non-specific or generic reference,[27] Type 1 adjectives are a much less likely option. The only subclass where they occur fairly frequently is that seen in node 35, where the possessee is not OLD and the possessor is singular. This class turns out to include a number of fixed collocations (*synъ božijь* 'the son of God'), more or less fixed toponyms (*selo skǫdьlьnikovo* 'the Potter's Field') and patronymics. As pointed out by Eckhoff (2011: 139–140), these constructions are on the borderline between anchoring/identification semantics (the whole NP refers to a uniquely identifiable referent and has a uniquely identifiable possessor) and classification/labelling semantics (the whole collocation is conventionalised as a fixed name of something). There are also occurrences where a non-specific possessor serves as an anchor, but this is the minority of cases (15).

(15) Priemlęi   prka   vъ   imę   **proroče**
     receiving prophet   in   name.ACC.SG   prophet-j.N.ACC.SG
     mьzdǫ   **proročǫ**   priemletъ
     reward.ACC.SG   prophet-j.F.ACC.SG   receives

     ho   dekhomenos   prophētēn   eis   onoma   **prophētou**
     the   receiving   prophet   in   name.ACC.SG   prophet.GEN.SG
     misthon   **prophētou**   lēmpsetai
     reward.ACC.SG   prophet.GEN.SG   will-receive
     'Whoever welcomes a prophet as a prophet will receive a prophet's reward'
     (Mt. 10:41)

Thus, node 35 finds the group of examples where it is enough for the possessor to be human and singular to be realised as a Type 1 adjective. The usual requirement that it also be definite (discourse-old or accessible) or at least specific is overridden.

Apart from the occurrences in node 39, Type 2 adjectives are a much better choice for non-specific or generic human possessors, as seen in node 36 and 37 – the former holds plural non-specific human possessors (16), and the latter almost solely consists of a large number of occurrences of the collocation *synъ člověčьsky* 'the Son of Man' (both exemplified in (17)).

---

[27] The NONSPEC label collapses possessors with no information status with KIND, NON_SPEC and QUANT possessors, see Section 2.2.

(16) se   sь   člvkъ   ědъca   i   vinopiica.   **mytaremъ**
     behold this   man   glutton and wine-drinker tax-collector.DAT.PL
     drugъ   i   **grěšьnikomъ**
     friend and   sinner.DAT.PL
     idou   anthrōpos phagos kai oinopotēs,   **telōnōn**
     behold   man   glutton and wine-drinker tax-collector.GEN.PL
     philos kai **hamartōlōn**
     friend and sinner.GEN.PL
     'behold, a gluttonous man and a drunkard, a friend of tax collectors and sinners!'(Mt. 11:19)

(17) sn̄   bo   **člvčsky**   imatъ prědati sę   vъ
     son.NOM.SG for   man-ьsk.M.NOM.SG   has   betray   REFL in
     rǫcě   **člvčsce**
     hand.ACC.DU man-ьsk.F.ACC.DU
     ho   gar huios   **tou   anthrōpou** mellei paradidosthai eis
     the   for son.NOM.SG the   man.GEN.SG   will   be-betrayed   in
     kheiras   **anthrōpōn**
     hand.ACC.PL   man.GEN.PL
     'for the Son of Man shall be delivered into the hands of men' (Lk. 9:44)

Returning to node 17, the second branch of the split encompasses specific human possessors (i.e. old, new or accessible). In this group, Type 1 adjectives are the prevalent choice (18).

(18) vъnide   vъ   domъ   **zaxariinъ**
     entered into house.ACC.SG   Zechariah-in.M.ACC.SG
     eisēlthen eis ton oikon   **Zakhariou**
     entered   into the house.ACC.SG Zechariah.GEN.SG
     'she entered the house of Zechariah' (Lk. 1:40)

The major exception (node 32) is again plural human possessors, they are prevalently realised as genitives (19).

(19) po   čъto   učenici   tvoi   prěstǫpajǫtъ prědaniě   **starecъ**
     by   what   disciples   your   transgress   traditions elder.GEN.PL
     dia ti   hoi   mathētai sou   parabainousin tēn
     by   what   the   disciples you.GEN   transgress   the
     paradosin   **tōn   presbuterōn**
     traditions   the   elder.GEN.PL
     'Why do your disciples break the tradition of the elders?' (Mt. 15:2)

Note that while Greek human proper nouns are consistently translated as Type 1 adjectives (nodes 22, 23, example 18), the translation of Greek human common nouns appears to depend on topicworthiness (nodes 26, 27, 29, 30): if the topicworthiness score is high enough, a Type 1 adjective is a better choice. In example (20), the possessor has a topicworthiness score of 27, since it is human and discourse-old.

(20) i   vъšedъ   vъ   domь   **farisěovъ**   vъzleže
     and   entered   in   house.ACC.SG   Pharisee-ov.M.ACC.SG   reclined
     kai   eiselthōn eis   ton   oikon   **tou** **Pharisaiou**
     and   entered   in   the   house.ACC.SG the Pharisee.GEN.PL
     kateklithē
     reclined
     '(One of the Pharisees asked him to eat with him.) And he went to the Pharisee's house and reclined at the table' (Lk. 7:36)

According to our classification tree, then, the main predictors of construction type for human possessors are possessor givenness status, head givenness status and number. Type 1 adjectives do not render human plurals, and have competition when it comes to express non-specific human possessors or ones with low topicworthiness scores. The tree does not pick up on relationality or argument status, except in the very small class isolated in node 35.

Non-human possessors are a different story. In this group, the first split in the tree (node 2) is based on adnominal relation type: adnominal partitives are almost exclusively genitives (21).

(21) ěko   i   kaplę   **krъve**   kapljǫštę   na   zemljǫ
     like   even   drops   blood.GEN.SG   dripping   on   ground
     hōsei   thromboi   **haimatos**   katabainontos   epi   tēn   gēn
     like   drops   blood.GEN.SG   dripping   on   the   ground
     '(and his sweat became) like drops of blood falling on the ground' (Lk. 22:44)

The next split (node 3) is based on possessor givenness status, but oddly, the split has accessibles and non-specifics/generics on the one side, and old and new referents on the other side, which makes one suspect that the classification may really depend on a combination of other factors.

If the possessor is accessible or non-specific/generic, Type 2 adjectives are generally the best choice, but we see that this also depends on the argument structure of the head noun. In node 8, we see that nominal arguments in this class are preferably datives (22). Thus, the non-human side of the classification tree appears to confirm Eckhoff's (2011) claim that nominal argument structure is a factor in the distribution of OCS possessive constructions.

(22) otъstǫpite   otъ   mene   vьsi   dělatele   **nepravьdě**
     step-away   from   me   all   doers   evil.DAT.SG
     apostēte   ap'   emou   pantes ergatai   **adikias**
     step-away   from   me   all   doers   evil.GEN.SG
     'Depart from me, all you workers of evil!' (Lk. 13:27)

The other branch in the split in node 3 concerns old and new inanimate possessors. Here the tree resorts to number to make the classifications: again, Type 2 adjectives is the best choice if the possessor is non-singular (as the plural, but previously mentioned nails in example 23). However, datives and genitives are well-represented in all subnodes here, and preferred with singulars, and many of them have relational head nouns (24).

(23) vь   ězvǫ   **gvozdiinǫjǫ**
     in   wound.ACC.SG   nail-in.F.ACC.SG
     eis ton   topon   **tōn   hēlōn**
     in   the   place.ACC.SG the   nail.GEN.PL
     '(Unless I see in His hands the imprint of the nails, and put my finger) into the nail wounds (and put my hand into his side, I will not believe)' (Jn. 20:25)

(24) i   rečeta   g̃nu   **domu**
     and   tell   master   house.GEN.SG
     kai   ereite   tēi   oikodespotēi   **tēs   oikias**
     and   tell   the   master   the   house.GEN.SG
     '(Follow him to the house that he enters,) and say to the owner of the house' (Lk. 22:11)

4.4 Summary

The classification tree in Fig. 10 comes much closer to accounting for the complex interactions of factors in the distribution of OCS adnominal possessive constructions than the two trees with Greek predictors only. It is able to predict all construction types to some extent, and it has a much higher correct classification rate. Moreover, it confirms the impression that the Greek high-ranking predictors are really symptoms of something else: The importance of part of speech as a predictor in Figs. 6 and 8 mostly reflects the importance of animacy, uniqueness and specificity in the choice of OCS possessive construction. The importance of Greek definiteness as a predictor reflects the importance of givenness status. Number is important in both Figs. 8 and 10, but it is important as a referential feature, not as a Greek syntactic influence.

We also see that Fig. 10 supports many of the conclusions in Eckhoff (2011) without using the semantic classifications in that material as input. As in Eckhoff (2011), both the referential properties of the possessor and the valency properties of the possessee turn out to be important, although the former are perhaps given more weight in the classification tree. Both analyses strongly suggest that the distribution of OCS possessive constructions was independent of the Greek source text.

Finally, it seems clear that the classification tree is not able to capture *all* the intricacies of the OCS possessive system, in particular the generalisations in the lower splits of the tree (expectedly) seem much more arbitrary than the ones in the higher splits. Also, the lack of generalisations cross-cutting human and non-human possessors seems implausible.

5 Conclusions

The central question of this article is "In languages only attested in translated form, how can we distinguish between native syntax and syntactic influence?" I approached this question by using Greek and OCS parallel data with detailed annotation for morphology (mostly inflectional, but also derivational), syntax, givenness status and various semantic features, and subjecting these data to statistical analysis in order to evaluate the relative weight of various predictors in two case studies.

The two case studies were extremes when it comes to syntactic influence: In the first case study, which deals with the order of transitive verbs and their objects, and with the order of adnominal possessors and their heads, we found a case that suggested nearly complete replication. In the statistical analysis, the Greek word order was the supremely best predictor, and only marginally allowed other predictors to surface in the classification tree. It is of course possible that the strong association is (partly) due to the fact that the two systems were very similar, but we cannot substantiate this claim quantitatively. Only studies of non-translated early Slavonic texts can resolve this question.

The second case study, on the other hand, of OCS adnominal possessive constructions, proved to be a case of nearly complete independence. A number of semantic, pragmatic and referential features turned out to outrank Greek morphosyntactic predictors. As a bonus, the weighting of these factors elaborates and supports earlier research based on manual semantic classification.

The differences between the results in the two case studies are encouraging: Similar models can be used to weigh language-external against language-internal factors in the less straightforward cases in between those two poles, if we have sufficiently large and sophisticated data sets.

References

Birnbaum, Henrik. 1996. Language contact and language interference: The case of Greek and Old Church Slavonic. *Suvremena lingvistika* 41–42 (1–2). 39–44.
Eckhoff, Hanne Martine. 2011. *Old Russian possessive constructions: A Construction Grammar approach*. Berlin: De Gruyter Mouton.
Fuchsbauer, Jürgen (this volume). Some observations on the usage of adnominal genitives and datives in Middle Bulgarian Church Slavonic.
Haug, Dag Trygve Truslew, Marius Jøhndal, Hanne Martine Eckhoff, Eirik Welo, Mari Johanne Bordal Hertzenberg & Angelika Müth. 2009. Computational and linguistic issues in designing a syntactically annotated parallel corpus of Indo-European languages. *Traitement Automatique des Langues* 50 (2). 17–45.
Haug, Dag Trygve Truslew, Hanne Martine Eckhoff & Eirik Welo. 2014. The theoretical foundations of givenness annotation. In Kristin Bech & Kristine Gunn Eide (eds.), *Information structure and syntax in Germanic and Romance languages*, 17–52. Amsterdam: John Benjamins.
Hothorn, Torsten, Kurt Hornik & Achim Zeileis. 2006. Unbiased recursive partitioning: A conditional inference framework. *Journal of Computational and Graphical Statistics* 15 (3). 651–674.
Hothorn, Torsten, Peter Buehlmann, Sandrine Dudoit, Annette Molinaro & Mark Van Der Laan. 2006. Survival Ensembles. *Biostatistics* 7 (3). 355–373.
Huntley, David. 1984. The distribution of the denominative adjective and the adnominal genitive in Old Church Slavonic. In Jacek Fisiak (ed.), *Historical syntax*, 217–236. Berlin: Mouton.
Jagić, Vatroslav. 1883. *Quattuor evangeliorum versionis palaeoslovenicae Codex Marianus glagoliticus*. Berlin: Weidmann.
Karttunen, Lauri. 1969. Discourse referents. In *Proceedings of the 1969 Conference on Computational Linguistics, COLING '69*, 1–38. Stroudsburg, PA: Association for Computational Linguistics.
Lambrecht, Knud. 1996. *Information structure and sentence form: Topic, focus, and the mental representations of discourse referents*. Cambridge: Cambridge University Press.
Lunt, Horace G. 2001. *Old Church Slavonic grammar*, 7th edn. Berlin: De Gruyter Mouton.
Prince, Ellen F. 1981. Toward a taxonomy of given-new information: The two genitives of English. In Peter Cole (ed.), *Radical pragmatics*, 223–256. New York: Academic Press.
Riester, Arndt, David Lorenz & Nina Seemann. 2010. A recursive annotation scheme for referential information status. In *Proceedings of the Seventh International Conference*

on *Language Resources and Evaluation (LREC '10)*, 717–722. Valletta, Malta: European language resources distribution agency.

Tagliamonte, Sali A. & R. Harald Baayen. 2012. Models, forests and trees of York English. Was/were variation as a case study for statistical practice. *Language Variation and Change* 24 (2). 135–178.

Strobl, Carolin, Anne-Laure Boulesteix, Achim Zeileis & Torsten Hothorn. 2007. Bias in Random Forest Variable Importance Measures: Illustrations, Sources and a Solution. *BMC Bioinformatics* 8(25). http://www.biomedcentral.com/1471-2105/8/25.

Strobl, Carolin, Anne-Laure Boulesteix, Thomas Kneib, Thomas Augustin & Achim Zeileis. 2008. Conditional Variable Importance for Random Forests. *BMC Bioinformatics* 9(307). http://www.biomedcentral.com/1471-2105/9/307.

Strobl, Carolin, James Malley & Gerhard Tutz. 2009. An introduction to recursive partitioning: Rationale, application and characteristics of classification and regression trees, bagging and Random Forests. *Psychological Methods* 14 (4). 323–348.

Večerka, Radoslav. 1989. *Altkirchenslavische (altbulgarische) Syntax I. Die lineare Satzorganisation*. Freiburg: U.W. Weiher.

Willis, David. 2000. Verb movement in Slavonic conditionals. In Susan Pintzuk, George Tsoulas & Anthony Warner (eds.), *Diachronic syntax: Models and mechanisms*, 322–48. Oxford: Oxford University Press.

Zaenen, Annie, Joan Bresnan, M. Catherine O'Connor, Jean Carletta, Andrew Koontz-Garboden, Tom Wasow, Gregory Garretson & Tatiana Nikitina. 2004. Animacy encoding in English: Why and how. In *Proceedings of the 2004 ACL Workshop on Discourse Annotation*, 118–125.

Silvia Luraghi and Milena Krstić
The decay of cases in *Molise Slavonic*[1]

Abstract: This paper discusses the use of cases in Molise Slavonic, a high contact South Slavonic variety spoken in Southern Italy by about 1,000 speakers. Based on available texts and on data from informants, we show that cases are still realized by older, fluent speakers, even though the extent to which they actually contribute to distinguishing meanings is limited. As a consequence, case morphology is no longer mastered by younger semi-speakers. The absence of fluent speakers among young generations is thus leading to the decay of the case system. Patterns of reduction of case meanings in Molise Slavonic are similar to those found in other high contact Slavonic varieties.

1 Introduction

Molise Slavonic is a highly endangered, or moribund according to Ethnologue (http://www.ethnologue.com/language/svm), minority language spoken by a few hundred speakers in Molise, Southern Italy. In spite of the high contact situation in which speakers live today, relative isolation in the past has helped preserve nominal morphology.[2] In the past century, and especially over the last few decades, sociolinguistic conditions have changed dramatically as a consequence of enhanced means of communication. In this paper, we try to assess the bearing of such changes on the use of cases and on their morphological realization.

The paper is organized as follows. In Section 1 we provide information about the language and its speakers. We then proceed to discussing attested uses of bare cases and cases with prepositions over a century's time span (Section 2). In Section 3 we discuss tendencies detected in Molise Slavonic in the framework of developments known from other Slavonic languages, and illustrate current trends in case usage and morphological realization. We show that nowadays there are major differences between the conservative variety of older, fluent speakers, and the varieties of semi-speakers, which are bringing about a complete decay of case

---
1 We would like to thank the editors of the volume for helpful comments on an earlier version of this paper. The usual disclaimers apply.
2 As is well known, isolated areas are particularly conservative, see Anttila (1989: 297) and Luraghi (2010a: 254), while language contact favours the spread of innovation.

morphology. Crucially, only semi-speakers remain among young generations. Section 4 contains the conclusions.

1.1 Molise Slavonic

Molise Slavonic (originally called *na-našu* or *na-našo* 'in our way', Italian *slavo molisano* or *slavisano*, henceforth MS) is a Southern Slavonic variety which belongs to the Serbo-Croatian (henceforth SC) dialectal subgroup, and has been in close contact with Romance varieties for more than five centuries. Croatian speakers from Dalmatia settled in the area between the 15th and 16th century CE. MS is now spoken in three villages of Molise in the province of Campobasso: Acquaviva, Montemitro and San Felice. Only in the first two villages is MS still spoken by a significant part of the population, which, however, does not include younger generations. In San Felice MS is mastered only by a small number of older speakers. The number of active speakers has decreased dramatically after the Second World War: while the 1961 census gives a figure of 4,038 speakers, the corresponding figure at the 2001 census was 2,064, and Breu and Piccoli (2012) give an estimate of 1,000 extant speakers. Among our informants, active speakers who claim to have a native competence in the language were all above age 35 at the time of our research, many of them much older. Settlements are shown in Fig. 1, adapted from Krstić (2014: 115). Figure 1 shows the location of the three villages of Acquaviva, Montemitro and San Felice, along with other settlements in which MS was spoken in the past.

When the Croats settled in Molise in the 15th–16th century, they found an indigenous population speaking a Southern Italian vernacular variety, Moliseans, and this situation remained virtually the same for several centuries. Only in the second half of the 20th century did the Italian population increasingly switch from Moliseans to regional and standard Italian. Thus, the sociolinguistic situation is complex, as contact with MS involves at least three Italo-Romance varieties: Moliseans, regional Italian, and standard Italian.[3]

The dialectal affiliation of MS within the SC group is not easy to gauge, and has been a matter of discussion for over a century (see Krstić 2014 for a survey). SC displays a major dialectal split between Čakavian, Kajkavian and Štokavian varieties. Today, Kajkavian is spoken only in the surroundings of Zagreb and in the northern part of Zagorje; Čakavian dialects are spoken in Istria and Dalmatia, while Štokavian (or Neo-Štokavian) dialects are spoken in the internal part of

---

[3] For a definition of regional, as opposed to standard Italian, see Berruto (1987).

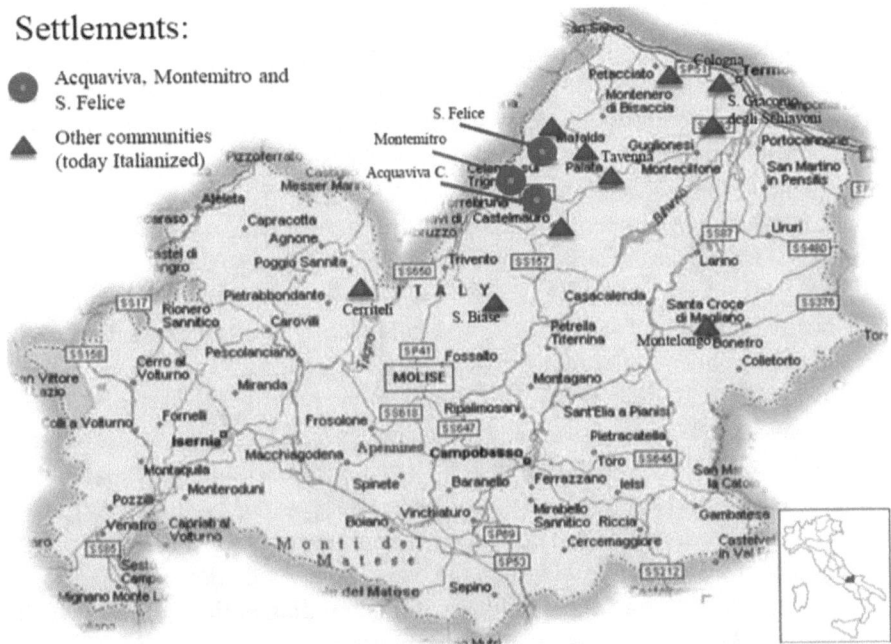

Fig. 1: Croatian settlements in Molise.

Croatia, Serbia, Montenegro, and Bosnia and Herzegovina, and provide the basis for modern Serbo-Croat-Bosnian. Notably, this was not the original situation at the time when settlers left the Croatian coast and moved to Molise, so a Dalmatian origin does not per se imply affiliation to the Čakavian branch of SC. Many elements point to a relation with the Ikavian sub-branch of Štokavian (see Krstić 2014), but Čakavian elements are also present, as shown for example in rules for clitic placement. While in standard SC features P2 (second position) enclitics, in MS clitics cannot be hosted by a finite verb, so in case of verb initial sentences they are proclitic, and precede the verb, similar to Slovenian and to Čakavian dialects (Krstić and Luraghi 2013).

1.2 Noun morphology

The most important innovation of MS with respect to standard SC is the loss of the neuter gender, and the ensuing emergence of a two-gender system, with a distinction between masculine and feminine. However, some neuter forms still persist in classes of pronouns (especially demonstrative), of adjectives and in participles mostly in impersonal constructions. Inflectional classes are also reduced to two, and coincide with genders. Gender distinctions are neutralized in the plural. Animacy distinctions, whereby animate masculine nouns are kept distinct from inanimate in most Slavonic languages, still persist in MS, although not systematically, as we discuss in Section 2.2.

Number features two values, singular and plural, with some dual vestigial forms in older texts (see Rešetar 1997[1911]: 124, 174). Extant cases are the nominative/vocative, the accusative, the genitive, the dative, and the instrumental. The locative case has merged morphologically with the dative, while parts of its functions have been taken over by the prepositional accusative (see the discussion in Section 2.2). As in other SC varieties, adjectives have a long and a short form limited to the nominative; only the former can be used in attributive function. They have a five case inflection; gender distinction is limited to the singular, which also features remnants of neuter. The five-case system is well preserved for personal pronouns, which also have clitic variants for the dative and the accusative and, for the third person singular, the two gender distinction.

In spite of phonological reduction in the articulation of final vowels (which, however, varies among varieties, with Montemitro presenting more conservative forms than Acquaviva), cases are productively realized morphologically, as shown by the fact that Italian loanwords are well integrated and display regular case inflection (Marra 2009: 99). Nominal, adjectival, and pronominal inflection are shown in Tabs. 1, 2 and 3a, b. The tables are adapted from Rešetar (1997) and show the dialect of Montemitro where final vowels are well preserved. In the dialect spoken in Acquaviva, final vowels can be centralized or dropped. This difference is also reported in Rešetar (1997), so it has remained stable over time (see further Barone 1995; Breu and Piccoli 2000: 390–402).

Tab. 1: Noun inflection in MS (Montemitro).

	–o stems *pop* 'priest'		–a stems *žena* 'woman'	
	Singular	Plural	Singular	Plural
Nominative	pop	pope	žena	žene
Genitive	popa	popi/ø	žene	ženi/ø
Accusative	popa-pop	pope	ženu	žene
Dative	popu	popami/i	žen	ženami/i
Instrumental	popom	popami/i	ženom	ženami/i

Tab. 2: Adjective inflection in MS (Montemitro).

	Long form *dobri* 'good'			
	Masculine	**Feminine**	**Neuter**	**Plural**
Nominative	'dobri	'dobra	'dobro	'dobre
Genitive	'dobroga	'dobre	'dobro	'dobrixi
Accusative	'dobri~'dobroga	'dobru	'dobro	'dobre
Dative	'dobromu	'dobru	/	'dobrimi
Instrumental	'dobrim(e)	'dobrom	'dobrom	'dobrimi
	Short form *dobar*			
Nominative	'dobar	do:'bra	do:'bra	do:'bre

Tab. 3a: Pronominal inflection in MS (Montemitro).

	Stressed forms				
	Singular		**Plural**		
	1	2	1	2	3
Nominative	ja	ti	mi	vi	one
Genitive	mena	teba	nasa	vasa	njixi
Accusative	mena	teba	nasa	vasa	njixi
Dative	men	teb	nami	vami	njimi
Instrumental	menom	tebom	nami	vami	njimi
	Unstressed forms				
Genitive	/	/	/	/	/
Dative	mi	ti	nami	vami	njimi
Accusative	ma	ta	nasa	vasa	xi
Instrumental	/	/	/	/	/

Tab. 3b: Pronominal inflection in MS (Montemitro).

	Stressed forms		Unstressed forms	
	3 m.	3 f.	3 m.	3 f.
Nominative	on	ona	/	/
Genitive	njega	nje	/	/
Dative	njemu	njoj	mu, mu	ju, ju
Accusative	njega	nju	ga, ga	ju, ju
Instrumental	njime	njom	/	/

1.3 The data

The data for our work come from different sources and cover a time span of 150 years, which makes possible a number of diachronic considerations. An early description of MS with some texts is Vegezzi-Ruscalla (1864). Some of these texts have been re-edited and included in Cirese's (1957) collection. Rešetar (1997) has been until recently the largest collection of texts in MS. Breu and Piccoli (2011, 2012) collected oral narratives from Acquaviva, Montemitro and San Felice over a time span of about 20 years preceding the years of publication.[4]

Marra (1999) devoted a study to the form and usages of cases in MS, completely based on her own field research, which provides valuable data for our study. As we noted in Section 1.1, among the informants that we contacted directly no speaker is below age 35. Marra, instead, worked with a number of younger speakers, who were children at the time of her research and are presently below age 30. This difference owes to the fact that we only considered speakers who regard themselves as having a native competence of MS, while Marra also elicited her data from speakers who learned MS in their childhood, but rather view themselves as Italian native speakers. Informants in this group can be considered semi-speakers (see Marra 1999: 26–35).[5] As we will see in Section 3.5, this difference has important consequences on the morphological realization of cases by individual speakers. Note further that Marra's data come from the more innovative variety spoken in Acquaviva.

For the purposes of the present chapter, we used the data in the above publications, supplemented with the data collected in Krstić (2014) for her study of the

---

[4] More texts are available online at http://lacito.vjf.cnrs.fr/archivage/index.htm#europe.
[5] We follow Marra's (1999) definition of semi-speakers as imperfect bilingual speakers, who have some competence in a language which enables them to speak it, but feel more at ease in the other language. Semi-speakers varieties are "markedly aberrant in terms of fluent speakers' norm" (Dorian 1981: 107). As a result, semi-speakers tend to switch to the language in which they feel more comfortable, and only when solicited do they use the language in which they do not feel fluent. Following Dorian (1982), semi-speakers have had a limited input in the minority language, and their learning process has been imperfect. This is a frequent situation for vernaculars in Italy: a generation of fluent speakers decides not to pass down the vernacular to their children, and opts for standard Italian. The children are still exposed to the vernacular, because fluent speakers use it among them, however, the children's competence remains mostly passive, as they are not actively solicited to use it. They can in principle decide to use the vernacular, but if they do, they feel uncomfortable especially when addressing fluent speakers still present in the community. As a result, their varieties remain far from the fluent speakers' norm, which they have little chance to acquire. See further Dorian (1977) on the role of semi-speakers in language death, and Berruto (1987) on Italian vernaculars.

MS gender system and in Krstić and Luraghi's (2013) study of clitic placement. The data for Krstić (2014) were gathered during different fieldwork periods in the two villages of Montemitro and Acquaviva in the time span from 2010 to 2014. There were 23 informants selected, divided into two age groups. The youngest bilingual informant was in her late twenties at the time of the first fieldwork visit. Teenagers and students were not included because of their limited proficiency in MS. Since the oldest participant was in his eighties at the time when fieldwork was carried out, informants were further divided depending on whether their bilingualism concerned the Molisean vernacular and MS or regional Italian and MS. We then elicited more data from the informants that Krstić had selected for her earlier research, limited to Montemitro, whose variety is more conservative than the variety spoken in Acquaviva.

2 Use of cases

In this section, we review the morphology and the use of cases in the texts of our corpus. Whenever possible, we also indicate diachronic developments detectable in the data.

2.1 Nominative/vocative

The vocative case has merged with the nominative in MS. The only form that is preserved is *Bože* 'oh God!' which, however, is isolated and disconnected from nominal paradigms, a development that has parallels in some other Slavonic languages, such as Russian.

The main morphological opposition for nominative singular is between zero for masculine and *-a* for feminine, while in the plural the two genders are syncretic (see Tabs. 1 and 2). The nominative is the case of the subject and of the nominal predicate, as shown in (1).[6]

(1) *Marko   je   njevog   ospit   nasbolji.*
     Marko.NOM.SG.M be.PRS.3SG POSS.3SG.M guest.NOM.SG.M best.NOM.SG.M
     'Marko is his best guest.'

---

[6] Examples are from our own field research if not otherwise indicated. The glosses follow the conventions in the *Leipzig Glossing Rules* (http://www.eva.mpg.de/lingua/resources/glossing-rules.php)

The nominative can also occur as complement of the preposition *di* 'at, to', as shown in (2) and (3).

(2) *Grem   di   medik   sutra.*
    go.PRS.1SG to   doctor.NOM.SG.M tomorrow
    'I'm going to the doctor tomorrow.'

(3) *Je   poša   di pišina.*
    AUX.3SG   go.PTCP.PST.SG.M to swimming.pool.NOM.SG.F
    'He went to the swimming pool.'

This preposition derives from grammaticalization of the adverb *gdi* 'where' > *di* (Breu 1996: 36–37), and was originally used in constructions that also contained the verb 'be', as in (4).

(4) *Ova   dica   su   pol   di je
    DEM.NOM.PL   child.NOM.PL   AUX.3PL go.PTCP.PST.PL at be.PRS.3SG
    non[a].*
    grandmother.NOM.SG.F
    'These kids went to (their) grandmother.'
    (Rešetar 1997: 158)

Marra (1999) reports the same construction from one of her oldest informants, as shown in (5).

(5) *dit   da   faštidjə di su   os.*
    child.NOM.SG.M   give.PRS.3SG bother   at be.PRS.3PL bee.NOM.PL
    'The child bothers the bees.'
    (Marra 1999: 135)

As argued in Marra (2012) and (2013), the original construction contained a sentence 'where X is', which explains the occurrence of the nominative. In a later development, the auxiliary was dropped, and *di* was reanalyzed as a preposition in this construction, but the nominative remained. This development is relatively recent, as shown by the fact that only the construction with the copula occurs in the texts collected by Rešetar, and by the persistence of this earlier pattern in some older speakers. The adverb *di* also remains elsewhere with its original meaning.

Marra (2012) points to the occurrence of constructions with the adverb *ndo* 'where' and the verb *stare* 'be located' in Molisean as a possible source for the MS construction. Remarkably, grammaticalization of the adverb 'where' as an allative/locative preposition has other parallels, and is maybe more common. For example, in South American Spanish varieties the adverb *donde* 'where' has undergone the same development, mostly with human landmarks, as shown in (6) and (7).

(6) Yo   almorzaba   todos   los   jueves   donde el
    1SG.NOM   dine.IMPF.1SG   every.PL   the.PL   thursday.PL at   the
    tío   Lucho
    uncle   Lucho
    'On Thursday, I always had lunch at uncle Lucho's.'

(7) vuelve   donde   tus   padres!
    return.IMP.2SG   to   POSS.2SG.PL   parent.PL
    'Go back to your parents!'
    (Examples from M. Vargas Llosa, *La tía Julia y el escribidor*)

Also in this case, the construction was brought about when the auxiliary *estar* 'be' was dropped; the form *donde* also preserves its original function as an adverb. In MS, in which nouns are consistently inflected for case, the development of this new preposition had the effect, among other things, of introducing the nominative case into prepositional phrases, and may have served as a starting point for its extension.

2.2 Accusative

The accusative case is consistently realized by speakers especially in Montemitro, while the ending of the feminine may be dropped in Acquaviva, as noted in Section 1.2. The animacy based distinction for the accusative singular of masculine nouns was already inconsistent at the time when Rešetar prepared his text collection, as shown in his own examples, in which a proper name in (8) and an animate noun in (9) feature nominative-accusative syncretism.

(8) Ko   [z]na   si   ti   vidija
    who.NOM.SG   know.PRS.3SG   AUX.2SG   2SG.NOM   see.PTCP.PST.SG.M
    moj   Lez?
    POSS.ACC=NOM.SG.M   Lez.ACC=NOM.SG.M
    'Who knows if you've seen my Lez?'
    (Rešetar 1997: 154)

(9) Ja   jena   sin   jimam.
    1SG.NOM   one.ACC=NOM.SG.M   son.ACC=NOM.SG.M   have.PRS.1SG
    'I've got (only) one son.'
    (Rešetar 1997: 153)

However, the distinction is still available to speakers. In Acquaviva, it is reported especially in older informants by Marra (1999, 2009), who also found occurrences in which the animacy distinction is extended to nouns that were originally neuter. Let us consider example (10):

(10) *Poznaš   onga   diteta   ka   sa*
     know.PRS.2SG   DEM.ACC=GEN.SG.M   child.ACC=GEN.SG.M   that   REFL
     zova   džuvan?
     call.PRS.3SG   džuvan.NOM.SG.M
     'Do you know that kid called Giovanni?'
     (Marra 2009: 100)

In (10) the masculine noun *diteta* 'child' has the form of the genitive/accusative. Notably, this noun is neuter in SC; consequently, it regularly features the syncretism of the nominative and the accusative. In MS, the noun became masculine as a consequence of the loss of neuter gender.

Our own informants from Montemitro display both accusative/genitive and accusative/nominative syncretism, and the same patterns emerge from the data collected in Breu and Piccoli (2011, 2012) for both villages. Notably, loanwords can also show the animacy based accusative/genitive syncretism, as *vukata* (nom. kursiv) 'lawyer' in (11) and *kolega* (nom. *koleg*) in (12).

(11) *Sa   zva   vukata   za   prosit*
     AUX.1SG   call.PTCP.PST   lawyer.ACC=GEN.SG.M   for   ask.INF
     na   mala   mburmacijuni.
     one   little   information.ACC.PL
     'I called the lawyer to ask him some information.'

(12) *Učer   sa   pozna   njevoga*
     yesterday   AUX.1SG   meet.PTCP.PST.SG.F   POSS.3SG.ACC=GEN.SG.M
     kolega.
     colleague.ACC=GEN.SG.M
     'Yesterday I met his colleague.'

In the variety of Acquaviva, in the *allegro* style feminine endings may be realized as reduced vowels or even dropped (see Rešetar 1997; Breu 2010; Marra 2009), but they are consistently produced in Montemitro. Pronouns preserve the nominative/accusative distinction much more consistently than nouns (there is no possible syncretism for personal pronouns), and adjectives agree with nouns quite consistently inflecting in the accusative (Marra 2009). Non-emphatic forms of accusative pronouns are clitic, as *ga* in (19). Example (13) contains accented accusative forms of second and third person singular pronouns. Notably, these forms are not only different from nominative forms, but also from the corresponding forms of the genitive in vowel length, as in (14)–(15) from Montemitro.

(13) o   ubivaš   ti   njega   o   ubivam   ja
     either   kill.PRS.2SG   2SG.NOM   3SG.ACC   or   kill.PRS.1SG 1SG.NOM
     teba!
     2SG.ACC
     'Either you kill him, or I kill you!'
     (Breu and Piccoli 2011: 278)

(14) Je   vidija   ['mene]
     AUX.3SG   see.PTCP.PST.SG.M   1SG.ACC
     'He saw me.'

(15) Se   straši   do   [me:'ne]
     REFL   be.afraid.PRS.3SG   of   1SG.GEN
     'He is afraid of me.'

The prosodic difference shown above, which is reported by Rešetar (1997) and has been confirmed by our informants from Montemitro, is remarkable, as it introduces a distinction between genitive and accusative in the first and second person pronouns, which is unique in SC. The original pattern in Croatian dialects was genitive/accusative *méne*, dative *mené*. This is still preserved in some Neo-Štokavian dialects in Posavina, but standard Croatian generalized the baritone short falling accent from the genitive/accusative, while in standard Serbian the dative pattern was generalized, but then the accent was retracted (Ranko Matasović p.c.).

Apart from encoding the direct object, the accusative frequently occurs in prepositional phrases. In particular, it occurs with spatial prepositions and, differently from SC, it can encode both motion and location. In particular, the prepositions *u*, *na*, *utra* take the accusative in MS, as shown in examples (16)–(20).

(16) Je   si   kupila   hižu   u
     AUX.3SG   REFL   buy.PTCP.PST.SG.F   house.ACC.SG.F in
     naš   grad.
     POSS.1PL.ACC.SG.M   town.ACC.SG.M
     'She bought a house in our town.'

(17) Je   uliza   u   njevogu   maginu.
     AUX.3SG   enter.PTCP.PST.SG.F   in   POSS.3SG.ACC.SG.F car.ACC.SG.F
     'She got into his car.'

(18) ...ke   je   razbila   pur   gozdja   na
    ...that AUX.3SG   break.PTCP.PST.SG.M   also iron.ACC.PL on
    balkun.
    balcony.ACC.SG.M
    'He broke some iron on the balcony.'
    (Breu and Piccoli 2012:18)

(19) Večer   mat   je   ga   ponila
    Yesterday   mother.NOM.SG.F   AUX.3SG   ACC.3SG.M take.PTCP.PST.SG.F
    na   školu
    to   school.ACC.SG.F
    'Yesterday mother took him to school.'

(20) utra   nu   butilju   je   bot
    inside   one.ACC.SG.F   bottle.ACC.SG.F   be.PRS.3SG frog.NOM.SG.M
    'Inside a bottle, (there) is the frog.'
    (Marra 2012: 274)

The preposition *po* 'by, around' also takes the accusative in MS, even though some morphologically conditioned occurrences with the dative are also reported in the literature (see Section 2.4). Case alternation does not bring about any semantic difference. Examples with the accusative are (21) and (22).

(21) Sma   ga   frundal   po   Berlin.
    AUX.1PL   ACC.3SG.M   meet.PTCP.PST.PL   around   Berlin.ACC.SG.M
    'We met him (somewhere) in Berlin.'
    (Breu and Piccoli 2011: 63)

(22) Po   štale   biše   kano   na   oblak!
    around   barn.ACC.PL   be.IMPF.3SG   like   one   cloud.NOM.SG.M
    '(All) around the barn (there) was (something) like a cloud!'
    (Breu and Piccoli 2012: 86)

In time expressions, with words indicating portions of time, the accusative can also be used without prepositions, as in the expression *učer* 'in the evening', or with names of days, as *nelju* 'on Sunday'.

2.3 Genitive

The genitive is used adnominally or as complement of prepositions. In Montemitro, the genitive singular is consistently realized by fluent speakers both in the masculine and in the feminine, while in the more innovative variety of Acquaviva, according to Marra (1999), the ending of the feminine singular is often zero. Zero realization is more frequent in semi-speakers. In the masculine, zero realization brings about genitive-accusative-nominative syncretism, and this also often happens in the feminine, as the accusative ending is sometimes dropped in Acquaviva. However, things are not only connected with accidental phonological developments as it may seem, as even proper nouns borrowed from Italian that do not have a zero nominative can occur in prepositional phrases with *do* in the place of the genitive. As this also happens in Montemitro, we return to this issue further on in this section. It must further be remarked that according to Marra (2012) the form of the preposition *do* has been influenced by Italian *da* 'from', as the SC cognate has the form *od*. Marra also thinks that the existence in SC varieties of another preposition, *do*, which means 'up to', may have played a role. Notably, this preposition takes the genitive in SC and has left no traces in MS.

Most often, as adnominal modifiers, the genitive is reinforced by the preposition *do* 'of, from'. With proper nouns, denominal possessive adjectives typical of Slavonic languages are also a possibility, especially for speakers from Acquaviva. Speakers from Montemitro prefer prepositional phrases in this context, but notably they can use *do* both with the genitive and with the nominative. Examples are (23)–(31).

(23) *Sa   vaza   pumbu   do   vode*
     AUX.1SG take.PTCP.PST.SG.F   pump.ACC.SG.F   of   water.GEN.SG.F
     za   lakvat   hjura.
     for   hose.INF   flower.ACC.PL
     'I took a water-pump to hose flowers.'

(24) *Se   arkordaš   ke   držahmo   ono*
     REFL   remember.PRS.2SG   that   hold.IMPF.1PL   DEM.ACC.SG.N
     tete   Adaldžize...
     aunt.GEN.SG.F   Adalgisa.GEN.SG.F
     'Do you remember that we kept aunt Adalgisa's thing [= land] ...'
     (Breu and Piccoli 2012: 24)

(25) *Ovi   ljud   je   muž   do*
     DEM.NOM.SG.M   person.NOM.SG.M   be.PRS.3SG   husband.NOM.SG.M   of
     moje   sestre
     POSS.1SG.GEN.SG.F   sister.GEN.SG.F
     'That guy is my sister's husband.'

(26) *Divojka   do   Marko   je   još*
     girl.NOM.SG.F   of   Marko.NOM.SG.M   be.PRS.3SG   still
     na   študendesa.
     one.NOM.SG.F   student.NOM.SG.F
     'Marko's girlfriend is still a student.'

(27) Sinoć   si   vidila   brata   do
    last night AUX.1SG   see.PTCP.PST.SG.F   brother.ACC.SG.M   of
    Marka.
    Marko.GEN.SG.M
    'Last night I saw Marko's brother.'

(28) Župa   Markina   je   čuda   duga.
    jacket.NOM.SG.F   Marko.POSS.ADJ.NOM.SG.F   be.PRS.3SG much   long
    'Marko's jacket is very long.'

(29) nosahu   one   stvare   do rama.
    carry.IMP.1SG   DEM.ACC.PL thing.ACC.PL   of copper.GEN.SG.M
    'I have carried that copper thing.'
    (Breu and Piccoli 2012: 29)

(30) Vam   na   toc   torte!
    take.IMP.2SG   one.ACC.SG.M   slice.ACC.SG.M cake.GEN.SG.M
    'Take a slice of cake!'

(31) se   strašahu   čuda   do štregi.
    REFL   be.afraid.IMPF.1SG much   of witch.GEN.PL
    'I was very much afraid of witches.'
    (Breu and Piccoli 2012: 128)

Crucially, the likelihood for speakers to use the bare genitive or the prepositional phrase is not the same in all types of occurrence. In particular, occurrences such as (23) always feature a prepositional phrase. Animate nouns can occasionally occur in the plain genitive and indicate possessor, as *tete Adaldžize* in (24). Example (25) shows a prepositional phrase with a genitive noun and an agreeing possessive adjective. In (26)–(28) we find three different possibilities for proper nouns: *do* with the nominative, *do* with the genitive, or a possessive adjective. Example (29) shows that the genitive of material is also normally reinforced by *do*, while (30) features a partitive genitive. This is the only type of expression in which all speakers consistently use the bare case, without *do*. The same distribution was also noted by Rešetar (1997: 141), while Marra (1999) does not discuss partitive expressions. The retention of the bare case in partitive expressions is easily explained through the comparatively rigid structure of such expressions, in which the first member is necessarily a word that indicates a quantity. In partitive expressions the noun that indicates the whole can be reinterpreted as appositional to the quantifying noun, and the whole phrase acquires a partitive meaning, rather than depend on an independent meaning of the case.

Prepositional phrases with *do* also indicate source, as in (32) and (33).

(32) *Je   umbrala   do   straha.*
     AUX.3SG   die.PTCP.PST.SG.F   from   fear.GEN.SG.M
     'She died from fear (=because of fear).'
     (Breu and Piccoli 2012: 191)

(33) *Profesor   je   jiskodija   do
     professor.NOM.SG.M   AUX.3SG   go.out.PTCP.PST.SG.M   from
     aule*
     classroom.GEN.SG.F
     'The professor went out of the classroom.'

In addition, the genitive occurs with other prepositions, such as *mbač(a)* 'in front of, near', *ndžera* 'in front of', *zdola* 'below' and *zgora* 'over'.

2.4 Dative

The dative case is very persistent in MS, as it is not only used consistently by speakers but, in its function as indirect object marker, it is never reinforced by a preposition. Examples are numerous, and include pronouns, proper and common nouns, as shown in (34)–(36).

(34) *Ja,   onmu   ditatu   sa   ja
     1SG.NOM   DEM.DAT.SG.M   kid.DAT.SG.M   AUX.1SG   1SG.NOM
     dala   čuda voti   mblika.*
     give.PTCP.PST.SG.F   many times   milk.GEN.SG.F
     'Me, I gave so many times milk to that child.'
     (Breu and Piccoli 2012: 408)

(35) *Nimaše   što   da(t)   dicami.*
     not.have.IMPF.3SG   what   give.INF   kid.DAT.PL
     '(S)he didn't have anything to give her children.'
     (Breu and Piccoli 2012: 210)

(36) *Sa   poj   reć   timi   mbladimi
     now   go.IMP.2SG   say.INF   DEM.DAT.PL   young.DAT.PL
     te   stvare!*
     DEM.ACC.PL   thing.ACC.PL
     'Now go and tell to those young people these things.'
     (Breu and Piccoli 2012: 56)

Apart from encoding the indirect object, the dative has virtually no other productive function. Some traces of an older usage as a locative are attested even today, in the first place in semi-adverbial prepositional phrases such as *na rukami* 'by hand', *na nožami* 'on foot' (Breu 2008: 84). The preposition *po* 'by, around' still takes the dative as shown in (37) and (38), but note that its function has been partly taken over by *niz* 'downwards', a preposition that normally takes the accusative (Breu 2008: 88–89 also indicates occasional usage with the dative and with the genitive). In addition, according to Breu (2008), even *po* can be used with the accusative especially for masculine singular nouns in Montemitro. As a consequence, one can have both *po gradu* as in (37) or *po grad* with the accusative.

(37) *Kada   druge   stojahu   po   gradu,*
     when   other.NOM.PL   stay.IMPF.3PL around   town.DAT.SG.M
     ja   gredahu...
     1SG.NOM   go.IMPF.1SG
     'While the others remained in town, I was going...'
     (Breu and Piccoli 2012: 244)

(38) *E   ga   nosahu   po   spidalu.*
     and   3SG.ACC.SG.M   carry.IMPF.1SG   around   hospital.DAT.SG.M
     'And I was carrying him around in the hospital.'
     (Breu and Piccoli 2011: 19)

Marra (1999: 160, 163) also reports some occasional (and lexically limited to some body parts) bare plural datives indicating location: *rukami* 'in the hands', and *justami* 'in the mouth'. Some other occurrences are collected in Rešetar (1997: 114), which point to an earlier extension of the bare plural dative to nouns with spatial referents, as in (39).

(39) *on   sìdi   škalami*
     3SG.M   sit.PRS.3SG   stairs.DAT.PL
     'He is sitting on the stairs.'
     (Rešetar 1997: 114)

Such expressions have no parallel in SC, in which the dative in locative function does not occur without prepositions. Considering the peculiar distribution in MS (only a limited number of plural nouns, with common lexical features), these forms must be considered adverbs, rather than forms motivated by an independent meaning of the case.

2.5 Instrumental

The instrumental case endings are well preserved; however, the instrumental is regularly reinforced by the comitative preposition *s* even in its instrumental function. Examples are (40)–(42).

(40) *Pa,   mi   bihmo   sèt   person   doma*
      then   1PL.NOM   be.IMPF.1PL   six   person.NOM.PL   home.DAT.SG.M
      di   moja   mat,   se   idaše
      at   POSS.1SG.NOM.SG.F   mother.NOM.SG.F   REFL   eat.IMPF.3SG
      s   teserom.
      with card.INS.SG.F
      'At that time, we were six persons at my mother's home, we had ration cards for food.'
      (Breu and Piccoli 2012:31)

(41) *Si   se   uspeja   zgora   stolice   s*
      AUX.2SG   REFL   climb.PTCP.PST.SG.F   above   chair.GEN.SG.F   with
      jenime   zgabelem.
      one.INS.SG.M   stool.INST.SG.M
      'I climb on a chair with one stool.'

(42) *Si   činija   nu   kuću   za*
      AUX.1SG   make.PTCP.PST.SG.F   one.ACC.SG.F   house.ACC.SG.F   for
      kučka   s   jenom   kasetom   do   driva.
      dog.GEN.SG.M   with   one.INST.SG.F   box.INS.SG.F   of   wood.GEN.PL
      'I made a dog's house from a wooden box.'

The only expression in which the bare instrumental is consistently preserved is the perlative expression *putam*, as in (43).

(43) *Svak   gre   njevogam   putam.*
      everyone.NOM.SG.M   go.PRS.3SG   POSS.3SG.INS.SG.M   way.INS.SG.M
      'Everyone goes his own way.'

The perlative expression *putam* must be considered an adverb, as other perlative expressions normally feature the preposition *po*. Notably, this is the only function of the instrumental case which does not correspond to the meanings of the Italian comitative preposition *con*.

2.6 Locative

In the variety of Montemitro, Breu (2008) points to occurrences of a locative ending *-o*, which can indicate both location and direction. Examples are (44) and (45).

(44) E   ove   bihu   funde   ke   se
     and   DEM.NOM.PL   be.PRS.3PL   fountain.NOM.PL   that   REFL
     idjaše   na   vodo.
     go.IMPF.3PL   in   water.LOC.SG.F
     'And those were fountains where (we) were going to take water.'
     (Breu and Piccoli 2012:63)

(45) oš   se   čini   prčesijuna   po   grado.
     and   REFL   do.PRS.3SG   procession.NOM.SG.F   in   village.LOC.SG.M
     'And the procession was made in the village.'
     (Breu and Piccoli 2012:124)

Notably, the *-o* locative is only attested for a limited number of lexemes, which are likely to occur in spatial expressions, as well as in several spatial adverbs. Breu (2008: 92–97) discusses the emergence of this new locative, and describes two possible scenarios for its development. In the first place, he points to the existence of an *-o* ending for adverbs, as in *dobro* 'good', that derive from old short forms of neuter adjectives. However, he views as unlikely a development whereby this adverbial ending could become a case ending for nouns, although lexically limited, or limited to a non-productive partial class of nouns, as he puts it (Breu 2008: 93), and provides a second possible explanation, by which the *-o* locative should be connected with the old neuter accusative. Following this view, the extension involves the following steps: the accusative replaced the dative in locative expressions (a development that sets MS apart from other SC varieties, see Section 3.1), neuter nouns now have *-o* forms in locative function. Then the neuter disappeared, and some former neuter masculine nouns retained the neuter form, only in locative expressions. Later, the *-o* ending also extended to some feminine nouns that did not originate from ancient neuters. It must be added that feminine nouns in Montemitro partly preserved the use of the dative with prepositions such as *u* and *na* when they occurred with attributive adjectives until recent times. The extension of the *-o* ending to some lexically restricted feminine forms would then be part of the replacement of the dative in locative expressions by other means. Notably, Breu's second scenario implies a chronology by which the loss of the dative/accusative distinction within prepositional phrases precedes the loss of the neuter gender.

Both if one views adverbs as primary origin of -*o* locatives, or considers them reflexes of neuter nouns, forms that feature this ending belong to a small set of lexemes, which, as we noted above, are likely to occur in locative expressions. As dative forms preserved in locative function, -*o* locative forms can be considered adverbial expressions, in which the case ending does not bring any independent meaning. The new MS locative can be compared to so-called sub-cases (see Brown 2007; see further Blake 2001: 22–23) in other languages, the most readily available parallels being the Latin locative and the Russian second locative. As the Latin and the Russian sub-cases, the MS locative is lexically restricted, and alternates with other, more productive expressions (see Luraghi 2010b). Even the origin of the three locatives is partly similar, as they originated from cases or paradigms that had been dropped due to earlier morphological simplification (loss of the locative case in Latin, merger of the -*o* and the -*u* declension in Russian, and, if we follow Breu's second scenario, loss of neuter gender in MS).

3 Discussion

In Section 2 we have shown that cases are morphologically quite persistent in MS, in spite of some over-extension of the nominative. However, their meaning has arguably undergone bleaching, as is shown by reinforcement of the genitive through *do* and of the instrumental through *s*. In addition, the fact that prepositions do not allow for case alternation also points toward a lower contribution of the independent meaning of cases within prepositional phrases. In this section, we discuss the data that we have reviewed in Section 2 in the light of developments in other Slavonic languages, starting from SC (3.1). We show similar developments that concern the extension of prepositions within the Slavonic family (3.2), and then proceed to setting them in the framework of possible influence from Italian (3.3). Then we survey the data of semi-speakers' varieties (3.4), mostly based on Marra (1999). We discuss once again the relation between cases and prepositions in MS (3.5), and conclude showing that current developments reflect a process of on-going language death (3.6).

3.1 Cases and prepositions: MS and other SC varieties

Except for the vocative, which has disappeared in MS, the case inventory remains the same as in other SC varieties. With respect to the standard variety, the usage of prepositions is much more extended. In particular, in standard SC the instrumental does not take any preposition when it indicates instrument or means, the preposition *s* being limited to comitative, and the genitive is not reinforced by any preposition when it functions as adnominal modifier. Remarkably, however, in Čakavian varieties spoken on the Dalmatian coast, the genitive is frequently reinforced by *od*, the SC cognate of MS *do*, at least in the spoken register. Lisac (2009: 309, our translation) remarks that "in Central Čakavian [...] *od* is used with the genitive due to Romance influences, e.g. *otac od moje prijateljice* 'father of my friend' [...] in Grobnik, or *od divojke* 'of the girl' in Senj".

A major difference between MS and standard SC (and in general most Slavonic varieties) is the loss of case variation for indicating locative vs. allative with the prepositions *na* and *u*.[7] In SC varieties, cognates of these prepositions take the accusative for allative function and the dative in locative function (in other Slavonic languages the latter function is normally taken by the prepositional locative, which has merged with the dative in SC). Much to the contrary, in MS the two prepositions no longer allow for case alternation, except for some marginal or semi-adverbial expressions (see Section 2.2). In general, both locative and allative functions are indicated by prepositions with the accusative. To be sure, case alternation with prepositions such as *na* and *u* is not limited to Slavonic: rather, it is typical of virtually all Indo-European languages that have preserved case inflection in nouns. Indeed, such alternation is known for example from German (e.g. *in* plus dative for locative vs. *in* plus accusative for allative), Latin (e.g. *in* plus ablative for locative vs. *in* plus accusative for allative), and other Indo-European languages. We return to the possible reason for this change in 3.3. The productivity of the accusative within prepositional phrases is also shown by its partial extension to prepositional phrases with *po* in the variety of Montemitro.

In the field of spatial relations, MS also shows a limited innovation in the lexically restricted usage of the bare dative plural in locative function, as well as in the creation of a sub-case, the new locative singular, in Montemitro. Arguably, however, rather than reflections of a growing meaningfulness of cases, such occurrences, which are limited to a small set of words, must be considered as adverbial forms disconnected from inflectional paradigms.

---

[7] However, it must be noted that such confusion also occurs in some other SC non-standard varieties, in which *na* and *u* may take both the accusative and the locative, with case variation often disconnected from the locational or directional meaning of specific prepositional phrases. As one reviewer points out, this situation is attested already in the 13th century, spreading in the 14th and 15th, and is usually attributed to Romance influence. See Pavlović (2006).

There is no counterpart of the MS preposition *di* with the nominative, even though the adverb 'where' also has the form *di* in Čakavian varieties, as a consequence of a common development whereby /g/ was elided in front of /d/.

3.2 Cases and prepositions: Other Slavonic languages

Among other South-Slavonic languages, the extension of prepositions has primarily affected languages that have lost case inflection, that is, Bulgarian and Macedonian (see Tomić 2006). In these languages, the prepositions that have replaced the instrumental and the genitive are largely the same as those that are used for reinforcing the same cases in MS. In particular, the instrumental with the function of instrument or means has been replaced by cognates of *s*, while with the genitive the situation is slightly more complex. Indeed, syncretism of the dative with the genitive typical of the Balkan languages partly also affected prepositional phrases, with the result that not only the preposition *ot* (cognate of MS *do*) replaced the genitive, but partly also the preposition *na*, which is one of the prepositions that replaced the dative in other usages (see Feuillet 1996 and below, Section 3.3). Another development of MS that has a parallel in the languages that have lost case morphology is the merger of locative and allative functions with prepositions: Bulgarian and Macedonian cognates of MS *na* and *u* indicate both functions.

The semantic extension of *s* or its cognates from comitative to instrumental meaning, and its consequent generalization to most functions of the instrumental case (except perlative) is an ongoing development in many Slavonic varieties. It reflects the Companion Metaphor, first described in Lakoff and Johnson (1980), which predicts that the semantic role Instrument is encoded in the same way as the semantic role Comitative, and follows the commonly attested path of extension (Luraghi 2001). Recently, the extension of *s* and its cognates in Slavonic languages that have long been spoken in high contact situations has been described in terms of contact induced grammaticalization in the sense of Heine and Kuteva (2005), due to influence of Romance and Germanic languages, in Nomachi and Heine (2011). Danylenko (2015) challenges Nomachi and Heine's assumption of Romance and/or Germanic influence as the triggering factor for such a semantic extension. He thinks that the semantic extension is likely to arise in Slavonic languages in contact situations, irrespective of the contact language, and reflects a tendency toward increasing analyticity.[8] He also points to

---

[8] As one of the reviewers points out, the spread of *s* in SC has been discussed thoroughly by Ivić (1954), as also acknowledged in Danylenko (2015).

the Balkan languages, in which *s* underwent the semantic extension in question without an especially dramatic impact of Romance languages. We return to this issue in Section 3.3.[9]

3.3 Language contact

Alleged Romance influence is pervasive in MS. Concerning cases and prepositions, reinforcement of the genitive through *do* and of the instrumental through *s* are commonly viewed as triggered by Romance (Venetian) influence (see Marra 2012, 2013), as is the reinforcement of the genitive through *od* in some coastal varieties of Croatian (see Section 3.1). However, things may not be as simple as they seem to be. As we noted in Section 3.2, discussing possible Romance or Germanic influence as a trigger for the extension of *s* in Slavonic varieties, Danylenko (2015) argues that it is the contact situation itself, and not the specific pattern in the contact languages, that triggers this extension. Thus, we do not have a replication here: rather, the tendency to extend the meaning of *s* as to include the Instrument role is so to speak inherent in Slavonic languages, and emerges in situations in which such languages display a drift toward analyticity.

Let us now consider the extension of MS *do* and of its SC cognate *od* as a genitive marker. The original meaning of this preposition, which, similar to *s*, has cognates in other Slavonic languages, is 'from'. To be sure, this is not the only preposition that indicates source in SC: two other prepositions also occur, *iz* 'out of', with an elative meaning, and *s* plus genitive 'off', with a sublative meaning. Neither preposition has cognates in MS: at first sight, this could also be considered a consequence of Italian influence, as Italian only has one ablative preposition (see Marra 2013, who also suggests that contact with Italian is responsible for the metathesis *od* > *do*). However, if we turn to the Balkan languages, what strikes us as relevant is that both Bulgarian and Macedonian only feature a single ablative preposition, i.e. *ot*, the cognate of *od* and *do*. As noted in Section 3.2, this preposition partly replaced the genitive in Macedonian. Again, as in the case of *s*, the Balkan languages, which have been for a long time in a high contact situation not (only) involving Romance or Germanic languages, show a development

---

[9] It must be noted that a trend toward analyticity is detectable in most, if not all languages of Europe and not only in connection with (total) language contact, as shown in the collection of papers in Hinrichs and Büttner (2004).

which is similar to the development in MS, and that consists in simplification.[10] Note further that both Standard Italian and Molisean feature two different prepositions, *di* and *da* (Molisean *de* [də] and *da*) with the meaning 'of' and 'from' respectively, contrary to other Romance languages (e.g. French *de* or Spanish *de*, both meaning 'of, from'). This means that Italo-Romance varieties did not offer a direct target for the extension of *do* as genitive marker. As in the case of *s*, one could argue that Slavonic languages in contact situations develop in the direction of higher analyticity, and that this implies replacement of the genitive with a cognate of MS *do*, and possibly also reduction of ablative prepositions.

In this framework, we can also add the loss of the opposition between locative and allative in prepositional phrases (Section 2.2). This change, too, has been ascribed to Italian influence (Breu 2008): indeed, Italian encodes both allative and locative with the same prepositions, and, as it does not feature morphological case, there is no formal distinction between allative and locative expressions, either in Standard Italian or in other vernacular varieties, including Molisean. Note however that case alternation with cognates of *na* and *u* in SC is not especially meaningful. Prepositionless allative and locative expressions are virtually inexistent, and some other prepositions, such as *po*, always take the same case but can indicate both motion and stative location. Such a situation explains how the loss of cases in Bulgarian and Macedonian resulted in polysemy of allative and locative for cognate prepositions of MS *na* and *u*. A similar situation must have arisen in Vulgar Latin preceding the loss of cases, as case variation within prepositional phrases was already redundant in Classical Latin, as argued in Luraghi (1989), and is apparently a common stage in the drift toward analyticity.

It is still interesting to note that similar developments in Bulgarian, Macedonian and MS have another parallel within the Balkan area. Modern Greek displays polysemy of comitative and instrumental with the preposition *me*, does not distinguish between allative and locative expressions, for both of which the preposition *s'* can be used, and the preposition *apo* 'from' also replaced some of the genitive's meanings. This was not the situation in Classical Greek. At that stage, Greek kept the encoding of comitative and instrumental distinct, as the former was encoded by *metá*+gen. and the latter by the plain dative; *apó* did not replace the genitive and there was a second primary preposition, *ek*, that indicated elative, and locative and allative expressions were consistently kept distinct by the occurrence of two different prepositions, *en*, which encoded the locative

---

[10] As remarked in Section 3.2, the genitive has been replaced by *na* in Bulgarian, and partly also in Macedonian, due to syncretism of the genitive with the dative, which is typical of the Balkan area.

and later disappeared, and *eis*, which encoded the allative, and started extending to locative at the time of the New Testament (see Luraghi 2003, 2005).

In conclusion, it is not completely clear whether reinforcement of the genitive through *do*, extension of *s* to instrumental function, and merger of locative and allative expressions through the loss of case variation with prepositional phrases must be regarded as typical developments of Slavonic languages in contact with Romance and Germanic varieties, common developments within the Balkan area, or common developments of the languages of Europe in the drift toward analyticity in generic contact situations.

3.4 Semi-speakers

As we have remarked in Section 1, Marra (1999) collected her data both from fluent, native speakers, and from semi-speakers. The two sets of speakers display major differences in the field of case morphology. While cases are usually well preserved by fluent speakers, including those who reduce final vowels, semi-speakers display over-extension of accusative and nominative forms within prepositional phrases. This is especially visible with the instrumental case, which is very well preserved by fluent speakers, but often replaced by semi-speakers, who also tend to replace the preposition *s* with a loanword from Italian, *ko* or *kon* (cf. Italian *con* 'with').

Considering the evidence over the whole time span in which MS is documented, one observes a quite stable realization of cases even in the more innovative variety of Acquaviva, in which final vowels may sometimes be centralized (see Breu and Piccoli 2000; Breu 2010). Up to the present, fluent speakers do not indicate any ongoing reduction of the case system. The situation changes dramatically with semi-speakers, as we will discuss in Section 3.5 and 3.6.

3.5 Cases and prepositions in MS

As we have shown above, with respect to SC the case inventory of MS remains largely the same, the only notable difference being the loss of the vocative. Case distinctions are preserved, partly also including the animacy based distinction within masculine nouns. In addition, a new distinction has arisen between the genitive and the accusative accented forms of first and second person singular pronouns.

In spite of the substantially well preserved case morphology, the use of bare cases is seriously limited by the expansion of prepositions. Not that prepositions have replaced cases: rather, cases are reinforced by prepositions. This happens virtually always for the instrumental, and most often also for the genitive, whose usage as bare case is very limited. Apart from the nominative and the accusative, only the dative is still consistently used without prepositions, and indicates the third argument of trivalent verbs. Thus, the remaining cases used productively without prepositions are those that encode core arguments required by the verbal valency, that is, the nominative, the accusative, and the dative.

Several inflected forms are used adverbially, or in fixed expressions: this is the case of the perlative instrumental *putam* in example (43), and of the plain or prepositional dative in occurrences such as *na rukami, na nožami, rukami, škalami* described in Section 2.4. The second locative described by Breu (2008) in the variety of Montemitro also occurs in a limited number of adverbial or semi-adverbial expressions. In addition, partitive expressions in which the genitive occurs without prepositions are likely also constructions that are processed as single units by speakers.

Let us now consider the loss of case variation within prepositional phrases with *na* and *u*. In SC, accusative/dative alternation is connected with the allative/locative distinction. However, this distinction is also expressed by the verb, and the extent to which case variation really conveys an independent meaning is very limited (see Luraghi 1989 for a discussion of the same issue in Latin). Thus, the loss of case variation can easily come about as a consequence of case distinction having become redundant in a specific environment. If we turn to the use of the genitive and the instrumental in MS, we can see that the almost obligatory occurrence of a preposition also has the effect of making case endings redundant.

To be sure, case endings are retained and consistently realized by fluent speakers who have learned MS as their mother tongue, but they are no longer learned by semi-speakers, who are in the first place Italian speakers, and have learned MS as an L2. Marra (1999) reports zero realization of the prepositional genitive in younger speakers. Note that dropping of the ending with masculine nouns produces a syncretism of the genitive with the nominative and with the accusative, which is already systematically realized as the nominative by semi-speakers. Even in the case of masculine nouns not ending in zero, replacement of the genitive with the nominative is a possibility available even to fluent speakers, as we have shown in Section 2.3. Feminine forms are somewhat more persistent, even though semi-speakers tend to replace them with nominative or accusative forms, or even with zero (Marra 1999: 148–149). Notably, zero is also a possibility for the nominative and the accusative singular feminine in Acquaviva, the community in which Marra elicited her data. The difference between fluent and semi-speakers is even clearer in the case of the instrumental. As we have shown in Section 2.5, fluent speakers never fail to realize this case ending. Semi-speakers, on the other hand, replace it with the accusative or with zero (Marra 1999: 152–156). According to Marra, replacement is more frequent within prepositional phrases that indicate instrumental, which are also those in which the loanword *ko*, *kon* is more likely to occur instead of *s*.

The remaining three cases, nominative, accusative, and dative, encode grammatical relations. They are not made redundant by prepositions, as the genitive and the instrumental, however, they are highly predictable from the verbal valency. In the variety of semi-speakers in Acquaviva, where even fluent speakers may drop the ending of the accusative feminine (see Section 1.2), all three cases can be dropped in the singular for both genders, thus resulting in syncretism of all three grammatical cases. Distinctions are retained for pronouns (see Marra 1999: 188–190), which constitute a large portion of the total occurrences of accusative and dative arguments. That pronouns have more case distinctions than nouns is frequent cross-linguistically. Limiting our observations to the Slavonic languages, one can note that even the Balkan languages that have lost case inflection for nouns still retain a number of distinction for pronouns (see Tomić 2006: 49–108).

3.6 Language death and the decay of the case system

Marra (1999: 193–200) describes in detail patterns of case loss in the varieties of semi-speakers, and points to frequency and to phonological weight as causes for more consistent retention of certain endings, such as the accusative singular feminine or the instrumental. In any case, as fluent speakers are virtually inexistent among young generations, the impact of semi-speakers is driving the MS case system to its final decay. As we have shown in Section 3.5, the extension of prepositions is not triggered by the loss of case distinctions. Rather, the drift toward analyticity proceeds the other way around: prepositions are introduced to reinforce cases, and this makes cases increasingly meaningless. Thus, even though fluent speakers consistently realize cases, semi-speakers no longer learn them, as their contribution to distinguishing meanings is minimal. The same process has been highlighted for Bulgarian by Mayer (1923). In addition, peripheral cases are the first ones to be dropped, as also noted in the case of Bulgarian by Feuillet (1992). The drift toward analyticity is reflected even in Slavonic languages in which cases are productively used: remarkably, the locative case mostly occurs with prepositions in all Slavonic languages.

Such stages in the reduction of case systems are not only limited to Slavonic languages. Other Indo-European languages present similar patterns, such as Germanic languages or Ancient Greek. Apparently, cases that encode core arguments are more persistent than cases that indicate adverbial constituents, and in general distinctions that concern grammatical relations are more likely to be expressed by cases at least in Indo-European languages, while distinctions that indicate the semantic roles of adverbial constituents are often encoded by prepositional phrases (see Luraghi 1991). Moreover, frequency also plays a role in the tendency for cases to be lost or retained. Luraghi (2004) shows that low token frequency was one of the triggers for the loss of the instrumental case and later of the dative in Ancient Greek. Note, however, that in Greek low frequency was connected with a high degree of allomorphy. In MS, the instrumental case, though virtually always reinforced by the preposition *s*, is quite persistent even in semi-speaker varieties, and, contrary to expectations, this especially concerns the instrumental plural. Notably, the instrumental plural has the same ending in different paradigms; in addition, as Marra (1999: 197) points out, it is syncretic with the dative plural, which is also realized more frequently than the singular.

The 150-year time span covered by MS sources show a remarkably stable case system, with only minor changes. To the contrary, changes reported by Marra in the variety of her younger informants are dramatic, and lead her to conclude that "[...] the speed at which changes are taking place indicate a different process with respect to a normal evolution, and point toward ongoing language death." (Marra 1999: 206, our translation). Limited to the case system, this abrupt change has been made easier by the fact that case distinctions had already become largely redundant when MS underwent the changes that had limited their meaningfulness. This change may well have been the result of total language contact, as described in Breu (2012, 2014).[11]

4 Conclusion

In this paper, we have described the usage of cases and prepositions in MS. Based on text collections, available research on cases, and our own field work we have shown that cases are generally preserved by fluent speakers. However, the meaningfulness of cases is severely reduced by the extension of prepositions, and

---

[11] Hansen (this volume) studied replication of syntactic patterns in heritage Serbian/Croatian spoken in Germany. Notably, the speech community mostly comprises second and third generation speakers. This constitutes a crucial difference between heritage Serbs/Croats in Germany and speakers of Molise Slavonic, who have been in Italy for several centuries, arguably experiencing a situation of total language contact since the time of their settlement.

consequent limitation of bare cases to the encoding of verbal arguments. Such a situation creates the background conditions for the loss of morphological case, which can currently be observed among semi-speakers. Patterns of reduction in the meaningfulness of cases, including the extension of prepositions and the loss of case variation within prepositional phrases are similar in MS and in other Slavonic languages that attest to a drift toward analyticity. Such developments are typical of high contact situations, and apparently they are not necessarily connected with a specific contact language.

References

Anttila, Raimo. 1989. *Historical and comparative linguistics*. Amsterdam: John Benjamins.
Barone, Charles. 1995. *La parlata croata di Acquaviva Collecroce: Studio fonetico e fonologico*, Firenze: Olschki.
Berruto, Gaetano. 1987. *Sociolinguistica dell'italiano contemporaneo*. Roma: La Nuova Italia Scientifica.
Blake, Barry J. 2001. *Case*, 2nd edn. Cambridge: Cambridge University Press.
Breu, Walter. 1996. Überlegungen zu einer Klassifizierung des grammatischen Wandels imSprachkontakt (am Beispiel slavischer Kontaktfälle). *Sprachtypologie und Universalienforschung* (STUF) 49 (1). 21–38.
Breu, Walter. 2008. Der slavische Lokativ im Sprachkontakt. Ein Beitrag zur Binnendifferenzierung des Moliseslavischen. In Peter Kosta & Daniel Weiss (eds.), *Slavistische Linguistik 2006/2007*, 59–101. München: Sagner.
Breu, Walter. 2010. La ristrutturazione della categoria del genere grammaticale nello slavomolisano. In Patriza Del Puente (ed.), *Atti del Secondo Convegno di Dialettologia 'Dialetti: per parlare e parlarne'*, 35–37. Rionero in Vulture (PZ): Calice Editori.
Breu, Walter. 2012. The grammaticalization of an indefinite article in Slavic micro-languages. In Björn Wiemer, Björn Hansen & Bernhard Wälchli (eds.), *Grammatical replication and borrowability in language contact*. Berlin: De Gruyter Mouton, 275–322.
Breu, Walter. 2014. Funkcii nastojaščego i imperfekta soveršennogo vida i perfekta nesoveršennogo vida v molizsko-slavjankom mikrojazyke [The functions of the perfective present/imperfect and the imperfective perfect in the Molise Slavonic micro-language]. *Scando-Slavica* 60 (2). 321–350.
Breu, Walter & Giovanni Piccoli. 2000. *Dizionario croato molisano di Acquaviva Collecroce. Dizionario plurilingue della lingua slava della minoranza di provenienza dalmata di Acquaviva Collecroce in Provincia di Campobasso. Dizionario, registri, grammatica, testi.* (con la collaborazione di Snježana Marčec). Campobasso: Arti grafiche La regione.
Breu, Walter & Giovanni Piccoli. 2011. *Südslavisch unter romanischem Dach. Die Moliseslaven in Geschichte und Gegenwart im Spiegel ihrer Sprache. Teil I. Texte gesprochener Sprache aus Acquaviva Collecroce* (Sagners Slavistische Sammlung 32, 1). München: Otto Sagner.
Breu, Walter & Giovanni Piccoli. 2012. *Südslavisch unter romanischem Dach. Die Moliseslaven in Geschichte und Gegenwart im Spiegel ihrer Sprache. Teil II. Texte gesprochener Sprache aus Montemitro und San Felice del Molise* (Sagners Slavistische Sammlung 32, 2). München: Otto Sagner.

Brown, Dunstan. 2007. Peripheral functions and overdifferentiation: The Russian second locative. *Russian Linguistics* 31 (1). 61–76.

Cirese, Alberto Mario. 1957. *I canti popolari del Molise*. Vol. 2. Rieti: Nobili.

Danylenko, Andrii. 2015. On the mechanisms of the grammaticalization of comitative and instrumental categories in Slavic. *Journal of Historical Linguistics* 5 (2). 267–296.

Dorian, Nancy C. 1977. The problem of the semi-speaker in language death. *International Journal of the Sociology of Language* 12. 23–32.

Dorian, Nancy C. 1981. *Language death: The life cycle of a Scottish Gaelic dialect*. Philadelphia: University of Pennsylvania Press.

Dorian, Nancy C. 1982. Language loss and maintenance in language contact situations. In Richard Lambert & Barbara Freed (eds.), *The loss of language skills*, 44–59. New York: Newbury House Publishers.

Feuillet, Jack. 1992. Réflexions sur la perte des cas en bulgare. *Revue des études slaves* 64 (3). 539–546.

Feuillet, Jack. 1996. *Grammaire synchronique du bulgare*. Paris: Institut d'études slaves.

Hansen, Björn (this volume). On the permeability of grammars: Syntactic pattern replications in heritage Croatian and heritage Serbian spoken in Germany.

Heine, Bernd & Tania Kuteva. 2005. *Language contact and grammatical change*. Cambridge: Cambridge University Press.

Hinrichs, Uwe & Uwe Büttner. 2004. *Die europäischen Sprachen auf dem Weg zum analytischen Sprachtyp*. Wiesbaden: Harrassowitz.

Ivić, Milka. 1954. *Značenja srpskohrvatskog instrumentala i njihov razvoj: Sintaksičko-semantička studija* [Meanings of the Serbo-Croatian instrumental case and their development]. Beograd: Institut za srpski jezik SANU.

Krstić, Milena. 2014. *La categoria del genere grammaticale nel croato molisano (con particolare riferimento all'interferenza linguistica)*. Rome: University of Rome 'La Sapienza' dissertation.

Krstić, Milena & Silvia Luraghi. 2013. Clitic placement in Molisean Croatian. Paper read at the 46th Annual Meeting of the Societas Linguistica Europaea (SLE). Split, 18–21 September.

Lakoff, George & Mark Johnson. 1980. *Metaphors we live by*. Chicago: University of Chicago Press.

Lisac, Josip. 2009. *Hrvatska dijalektologija 2. Čakavsko narječje* [Croatian dialectology 2. The Čakavian dialect]. Zagreb: Golden Marketing – Tehnička knjiga.

Luraghi, Silvia. 1989. The relation between prepositions and cases within Latin prepositional phrases. In Gualtiero Calboli (ed.), *Subordination and other topics in Latin: Proceedings of the Third Colloquium on Latin Linguistics*, 253–271. Amsterdam & Philadelphia: John Benjamins.

Luraghi, Silvia. 1991. Paradigm size, possible syncretism, and the use of cases with adpositions in inflectional languages. In Frans Plank (ed.), *Paradigms: The economy of inflection*, 57–74. Berlin & New York: Mouton de Gruyter.

Luraghi, Silvia. 2001. Some remarks on Instrument, Comitative, and Agent in Indo-European. *Sprachtypologie und Universalienforschung* (STUF) 54 (4). 385–401.

Luraghi, Silvia. 2003. *On the meaning of cases and prepositions: The expression of semantic roles in Ancient Greek*. Amsterdam & Philadelphia: John Benjamins.

Luraghi, Silvia. 2004. The evolution of the Greek nominal paradigms: Economy and case syncretism from Mycenean to Modern Greek. *Classica et Mediaevalia* 55. 361–379.

Luraghi, Silvia. 2005. The history of the Greek preposition *metá*: From polysemy to the creation of homonyms. *Glotta* 81. 130–159.

Luraghi, Silvia. 2010a. *Linguistique historique et indoeuropéenne*. Louvain-la-Neuve: Peeters.

Luraghi, Silvia. 2010b. Adverbial phrases. In Philip Baldi & Pierluigi Cuzzolin (eds.), *New perspectives on historical Latin syntax 2. Constituent syntax: Adverbial phrases, adverbs, mood, tense*, 19–107. Berlin & New York: Mouton de Gruyter.

Marra, Antonietta. 1999. *Il sistema dei casi nel nanaš dei Croati molisani. Processi di mutamento, decadenza e morte di una lingua*. Pavia: University of Pavia dissertation.

Marra, Antonietta. 2009. L'uso del caso accusativo nei parlanti slavo-molisani. In Paola Desideri & Carlo Consani (eds.), *Alloglossie e comunita alloglotte nell'Italia contemporanea. Teorie, applicazioni e descrizioni, prospettive. Atti del XLI Congresso Internazionale di Studi della Societa di Linguistica Italiana*, 95–119. Roma: Bulzoni.

Marra, Antonietta. 2012. Contact phenomena in the Slavic of Molise: Some remarks about nouns and prepositional phrases. In Martine Vanhove, Thomas Stolz, Aina Urdze & Hitomi Otsuka (eds.), *Morphologies in contact*, 265–282. Berlin: Akademie Verlag.

Marra, Antonietta. 2013. Borrowed prepositions: Contact-induced forms, meanings, and structures in Slavic minority languages in Romance environments. Paper presented at the 46th Annual Meeting of the Societas Linguistica Europaea (SLE). Split, 18–21 September.

Mayer, Karl H. 1923. *Der Untergang der Deklination im Bulgarischen*. Heidelberg: Winter.

Nomachi, Motoki & Bernd Heine. 2011. On predicting contact-induced grammatical change. Evidence from Slavic languages. *Journal of Historical Linguistics* 1 (1). 48–76.

Pavlović, Slobodan. 2006. *Determinativni padeži u starosrpskoj poslovnopravnoj pismenosti* [Determinative cases in Old Serbian business and legal documents], Novi Sad: Matica Srpska.

Rešetar, Milan. 1997[1911]. *Le colonie serbocroate nell'Italia Meridionale*. Traduzione italiana, prefazione, note, bibliografia a cura di Walter Breu e Monica Gardenghi (1st edn. *Die Serbokroatischen Kolonien Süditaliens*. [1911]. Wien: Alfred Hölder). Campobasso: Amministrazione Provinciale.

Tomić, Olga Mišeska. 2006. *Balkan Sprachbund: Morpho-syntactic features*. Dordrecht: Springer.

Vegezzi-Ruscalla, Giovenale. 1864. *Le colonie serbo-dalmate del circondario di Larino, Provincia di Molise (Campobasso). Studio Etnografico*. Torino: Tipografia degli Eredi Botta.

Part II: **The verbal phrase and related topics**

Hakyung Jung
Null subjects and person in Old North Russian[1]

Abstract: This paper investigates the licensing mechanism of null subjects in Old North Russian, reflected in the Novgorod birch-bark letters (11th–15th cc.). The null subject system is based on a strict person-split, which indicates that person agreement licenses null subjects. The data shows that in the *l*-past tense, inflected auxiliaries and overt subjects are complementarily distributed in 1st/2nd person. As the D-feature in Tense may be checked either by overt subjects in Spec,TP or by V-to-T movement that results in verbal agreement, the complementary distribution of overt subjects and auxiliaries in 1st/2nd person may be interpreted as a competition between two strategies to check the D-feature. In 3rd person *l*-past sentences, the lack of both overt subjects and auxiliaries is normative, which I attribute to the lack of a person feature in 3rd person. Thus, the contrast of different null subject patterns between 1st/2nd and 3rd persons is reduced to the [+person] and [–person] opposition. This contrast is parallel to the cross-linguistic contrast between canonical null subject languages with rich verbal agreement and radical null subject languages without verbal agreement. The distributional patterns of null subjects suggest that variations in subject pronominalization should be viewed as a result of grammar competition, and not as a purely pragmatically motivated phenomenon. The Old and Modern Russian null subject patterns resemble those of Lithuanian and Finnish, which raises the possibility of Balto-Finnic substratum effects in the developmental process of the Russian null subject system.

1 Introduction

With the goal of capturing the licensing mechanism of null subjects within a generative framework, this paper examines the distributional patterns of null

---

[1] This paper has been developed on the basis of my previous work, published under the title "Null Subjects and Person in the Old Novgorodian Dialect" in *Russian Language and Literature* 49. 193–228, 2015 (written in Korean). I thank three of the reviewers for their valuable comments and suggestions.

subjects in Old North Russian of the 11th–15th centuries (ONR).[2] ONR refers to a regional variety of Old Russian, reflected in birch bark letters (*BBL*) from northern Russian areas including Novgorod, Pskov, and Staraja rusa. Although ONR is distinguished from "Standard Old Russian" based on the southern dialects centred in Kiev, in terms of certain linguistic features (Zaliznjak 1987: 115), the null subject system does not seem to be one of the distinctive dialectal features. Null subjects in Old Russian manuscripts from southern and central Russian areas behave similarly to those from the north, while their patterns are less consistent than ones reflected in *BBL*. This difference can be attributed to the distinct genres and registers of manuscripts rather than to different dialectal systems (see Section 5.1).[3] I follow Zaliznjak (2004, 2008), Meyer (2011), and Kibrik (2013), assuming that as far as the null subject system is concerned, *BBL* best reveals a general picture of colloquial, near-spoken Old Russian.[4]

In this paper, I particularly focus on the role of person features in null subject licensing. I argue that a person-split (1st/2nd vs. 3rd) and the treatment of 3rd person ([-person]) are a core aspect of the null subject system in ONR, showing that the two distinct null subject patterns found in *BBL* are organized based on the presence/absence of person agreement, which is directly related to the typology of null subject languages. Departing from traditional, pragmatically oriented explanations of subject pronominalization, I argue that a competition between two syntactic strategies to satisfy the subject requirement results in variations in subject realization in ONR. I further compare the ONR null subject system with the more restricted null subject patterns in Modern Russian. While modern northern dialects sporadically maintain old dialectal features inherited from ONR (e.g., nominative

---

[2] The paper contains the following abbreviations: ACC (accusative), AUX (present tense auxiliary), *BBL* (birch bark letters), COMP (complementizer), CP (complementizer phrase), DAT (dative), DP (determiner phrase), EPP (Extended Projection Principle), GEN (genitive), INF (infinitive), NOM (nominative), NP (nominal phrase), N-P (non-past), OCR (Old Central Russian), OCS (Old Church Slavonic), ONR (Old North Russian), OSR (Old South Russian), PL (plural), PRST (present), PST (past), PTCPL (participle), REFL (reflexive), SG (singular), Spec (specifier), T (tense), TP (tense phrase), V (verb).

[3] Kwon (2009) takes the position that ONR is distinguished from Old South Russian and Old Central Russian in terms of the compatibility of AUX and overt subjects in a sentence. However, I maintain the view that the difference should rather be attributed to Old Church Slavonic's degree of influence on specific manuscripts (see also Zaliznjak 2004, 2008).

[4] Most existing studies on Old Russian null subjects examine manuscripts of diverse genres and mixed styles. However, in order to obtain coherent results from research, it is more useful to focus on a single type of text spanning over a long period of time. In this respect, a study exclusively focusing on *BBL* can be beneficial as this source rather consistently reflects a spoken variety of Old Russian during five centuries.

objects, *okan'e*), no evidence has been reported to claim they still utilize old null subject system. It is important to note that the person-based system of ONR (and Old Russian in general) is not attested in both standard and dialectal varieties of Modern Russian. I intend to show what changes caused Old Russian to lose the person-based null subject patterns. I further compare Old and Modern Russian with Finnish and Lithuanian to explore the possibility that old and new null subject patterns in Russian may be construed as Balto-Finnic substratal features.

The structure of this paper is as follows: Section 2 briefly illustrates different types of null subject languages and introduces the basic framework, in which I examine the distribution of ONR null subjects. Section 3 provides a critical review of existing studies on Old Russian null subjects. Section 4 presents statistical data collected from *BBL* and analyses the distributional patterns of null subjects, factored by tense and person. Section 5 compares null subject systems in Old and Modern Russian, Finnish, and Lithuanian from a historical and comparative point of view. Section 6 contains the conclusion.

2 The syntax of null subjects

2.1 Null subject languages

Null subjects, or *pro*, refer to non-overt, pronominal, referential subject arguments in finite clauses, which are usually differentiated from non-overt subject arguments in non-finite clauses (traditionally called PRO). As shown in (1), in English, a non-null subject language, a subject pronoun must be overtly realized. Otherwise, the sentence is ungrammatical. In contrast, a subject may be either null or overt in Spanish and Croatian, as illustrated in (2a) and (2b) respectively. Overt pronoun subjects are used for emphasis/contrast or in order to avoid referential ambiguity in these languages.

(1) *(*We*) went to the theater.*

(2) a. (*Nosotros*) hemos encontrado el libro.
    we   have.PL found.PTCP the book
    'We have found the book.'

 b. (*Ti*) možeš   reći   što   god hoćeš.
    you   can.2SG say.INF whatever want.2SG
    'You can say whatever you want.'

Typologically, null subject languages are classified into several types. First, in consistent null subject languages, a pronominal subject can appear in a null form regardless of its grammatical features, such as person and number, and the type of the clause in which it occurs. Romance languages, including Italian and Spanish, are typical consistent null subject languages. Slavonic languages such as Serbian/Croatian also belong to this category. Next, in partial null subject languages, the use of a null subject is constrained by certain grammatical features of the argument (e.g., person) and conditioned by specific syntactic environments (e.g., embedded clauses). Finnish, Hebrew, and Marathi are classified into this category. Finally, radical or discourse null subject languages freely allow null subjects without syntactic constraints as long as the referents of the null subjects are identifiable from the context. East Asian languages such as Japanese, Chinese, and Korean belong to this group. While consistent and partial null subject languages usually feature rich verbal agreement morphology, radical null subject languages generally lack verbal inflection.[5]

2.2 Licensing of null subjects and person features

Null subject licensing conditions have been investigated from various theoretical perspectives, yet the majority of the analyses present similar insights on the function of agreement features, at least in consistent null subject languages. For instance, from a functionalist view, verbal agreement morphology that marks the person feature of a subject functions as a pronoun and replaces the subject (Givón 1976; Bybee 1988; Hopper and Traugott 2003; Siewierska 2004). The grammaticalization phenomenon, in which pronouns shift to verbal agreement morphology, is presented as direct evidence in this line of proposals. This insight is recaptured from a generative perspective: null subjects are licensed by syntactic operations, such as the valuation/checking of agreement features (or *phi*-features) and the D-feature in Tense. The proposals are largely divided into two camps, depending on whether the presence of empty pronouns (*pro*) in the subject position (Rizzi 1986) is assumed. They are further elaborated based on how the subject requirement, i.e., D-feature checking in Tense (the Extended Projection Principle/EPP: Chomsky 1995) is implemented.

In this paper I take a generativist, in particular, non-*pro* approach: there is no 'empty pronoun' in the subject position and agreement can function as a subject (Borer 1986). In order to satisfy the EPP, languages can either fill the subject

---

[5] There is another type of null subject language. Expletive null subject languages such as German allow null subjects, but they cannot be referential. I do not mention this type because it is irrelevant to the discussion in this paper.

position (Spec,TP) with an overt subject, which checks the D-feature in the Tense head via spec-head agreement, or raise a verb to Tense so that the verb can check the D-feature in Tense (*à la* Borer 1989; Platzack 2003). Verb movement to Tense (V-to-T movement) is directly related to the licensing of null subjects, because when a verb moves to Tense, it checks the D-feature, which un-necessitates an overt subject in Spec,TP. This view is deduced from the Rich Agreement Hypothesis, which suggests that V-to-T movement results in rich subject agreement on a finite verb (Taraldsen 1978; Roberts 1985, 1999; Borer 1986; Kosmeijer 1986; Pollock 1989; Holmberg and Platzack 1990, 1995; Alexiadou and Anagnostopoulou 1998; Rohrbacher 1999; Koeneman and Neeleman 2001; Platzack 2003; Holmberg 2005; Biberauer and Roberts 2009; Koeneman and Zeijlstra 2014). Under this line of thinking, agreement has a pronominal nature, as it expresses all the grammatical features and thematic relations that are realized by pronouns. Thus, agreement can allow subject drop.

Among agreement features that are checked by an overt subject or a raised verb, it is a person feature that is relevant to the EPP requirement. Following Ritter (1995), Shlonsky (1997), and Boeckx (2002), who argue that the EPP is essentially reduced to the requirement that person features be in Spec,TP or T, I assume that person features are essentially pronominal, associated with D^0 (see also Postal 1970; Abney 1987) and that person agreement occurring on Tense satisfies the EPP, checking the D-feature in T.[6] A language lacking V-to-T movement requires an overt subject to fill the subject position in order to check the D-feature in Tense, just like English. When a language has V-to-T movement, the language tends to feature null subjects, like Italian.[7]

In ONR, the present tense forms of the auxiliary *byti* ('to be') of *l*-perfect (or *l*-past, as I choose to call it in this paper) move to Tense and check the D-feature as well as the person feature in Tense, just as overt pronouns in Spec,TP would do. The pronominal nature of the auxiliary (AUX) in ONR is empirically confirmed by the complementary distribution of AUX and overt pronominal subjects in this language, as illustrated in (3a)–(3c) (Zaliznjak 2008: 240). As will be discussed in detail in Section 4, this complementary distribution is sensitive to person

---

[6] Number and gender features are not pronominal because they can also occur with nouns and adjectives. In the case of person features, only 3rd person ([–person]) is available for nouns and adjectives. Then, is a person feature equivalent with a D-feature? I reserve a definitive judgment with respect to this question, as some languages lack V-to-T movement caused by a strong D-feature but show person agreement on finite verbs (e.g., Russian: Bailyn 1995).

[7] There are languages occupying an intermediate status, having enough inflectional richness for V-to-T movement but not enough for null subjects. For instance, French features V-to-T movement but no null subjects (Koeneman and Neeleman 2001).

features: only 1st/2nd person AUXs participate in this distribution while 3rd person AUXs do not, which is critical to my analysis.[8]

(3) a. *dalŭ*   *jesmĭ*   (participle – AUX)
       give.PTCP AUX.1SG
    b. *azŭ*   *dalŭ*   (subject – participle)
       I.1SG   give.PTCP
    c. **azŭ*   *jesmĭ*   *dalŭ*   (subject – AUX – participle)

Pattern (3a) consists of a participle and AUX, which is the most unmarked pattern in ONR when the frequency of occurrence is considered (Zaliznjak 2008: 170–172; see also Section 4). Pattern (3b), consisting of an overt pronoun subject and a participle, is also used, but not as frequently as (3a). Pattern (3c), containing both a subject and AUX, is extremely rare in ONR. This complementary distribution of a pronoun subject and AUX supports Borer's (1986) idea that agreement functions as a subject (see also Jung and Migdalski [2015] for related discussions).

3 Existing accounts of null subject patterns in Old Russian

3.1 Borkovskij (1949, 1968, 1978)

Among existing works on Old Russian null subjects, Borkovskij's extensive research (1949, 1968, 1978) provides abundant data and statistics. The major findings of his work are (i) the use of null subjects is prevalent in 1st/2nd person (since verbal agreement morphology sufficiently indicates referents); (ii) in 3rd person, null subjects are predominant; (iii) the use of overt pronouns is motivated by 'logical stress' (*logičeskoe udarenie*) that occurs under special emphasis, highlighting, juxtaposing, etc.

Borkovskij (1968) briefly notes that functionally unmotivated occurrences of overt pronouns may be due to the lack of *l*-perfect auxiliaries that express person and number. In other words, the use of null subjects is not only determined

---

[8] About transliterations in this paper: one reviewer suggests that the Cyrillic sign for the front nasal (Ѧ) should not be transliterated with *ę*, but rather with *ja*, since denasalization took place in East Slavonic. However, in this paper I maintain the transliteration of 'Ѧ' with *ę* because transliteration is not primarily concerned with representing the exact sounds of the original but rather with representing the characters. The same goes with the representations of reduced vowels.

by stylistic rules but also by syntactic, structural conditions. As Meyer (2011: 95) notes, this is completely distinct from Borkovskij's previous theories in favour of the discourse-pragmatic aspects of the phenomenon, and closer to the 'verb impoverishment' hypothesis, stressing the conditional relationship between the loss of verb inflection morphology and the loss of null subjects. However, Borkovskij does not clarify whether agreement features of AUX determine the use of null subjects and how this factor interacts with discourse-pragmatic factors.

Borkovskij (1968) addresses null subjects in 3rd person separately as a case of argument ellipsis in bi-segmental sentences (*dvusostavnye predloženija*), i.e., as a pure stylistic matter. According to him, argument ellipsis typically occurs when the referent is easily inferred from the context (especially in the genre of *gramoty*. He notes that the use of 3rd person pronoun *onŭ* 'he' increased from the 15th century on, while null subjects declined.

3.2 Zaliznjak (2004, 2008)

Zaliznjak (2004) exclusively investigates *BBL* (11th–15th cc.). Zaliznjak observes a strict complementary distribution between overt subjects and AUX in 1st/2nd person *l*-perfect (see Zaliznjak 2004: 170–172, 178–179; see also Xaburgaev 1978: 47; Meyer 2011: 109). He notes that in 3rd person, neither overt subject pronouns nor AUX are used.[9] In Old Russian manuscripts auxiliation patterns in 3rd person vary depending on the genre and local contents. While 3rd person AUX forms are practically non-existent in *BBL*, they are attested in Old Church Slavonic (OCS)-oriented texts. Chronicles and *Žitie protopopa Avvakuma* ('The Life of Avvakum') occupy an intermediate position in this respect.

Zaliznjak shares Borkovskij's view that the use of null subjects was the norm in Old Russian, which eventually shifted to a new rule of using overt subjects everywhere. Overt pronoun subjects have been used since the earliest period (11th–12th cc.) though they were not very prevalent. Zaliznjak argues that overt subjects were only motivated in the context of vocatives, contrast, topic shift, etc. The null subject system became unstable in younger pieces of *BBL*, and overt subjects began to be used in any syntactic context without pragmatic motivation (Zaliznjak 2004: 172).

---

9 Similar distributional patterns of AUX and overt pronouns in each person are observed in the case of the copula *byti* in combination with adjectival and nominal predicates.

Zaliznjak concludes that the AUX system began to visibly change during the second half of the 16th century. With respect to the correlation between the drop of AUX and the rise of overt subjects, Zaliznjak's view is similar to those of Lomtev (1956) and Xaburgaev (1978): he argues that the increase of overt pronouns does not result from the drop of AUX, and the opposite is actually the case.[10] That is, the change in subject pronominalization brought about AUX drop. I revisit this causal direction issue in Section 5.1 and suggest another explanation.

3.3 Meyer (2011)

Meyer, in his extensive work on Old Russian null subjects (2011), also provides analyses of statistical data from *BBL*. His observation on the complementary distribution of AUX and overt subjects in 1st/2nd person generally confirms Zaliznjak's view. However, Meyer's analysis differs from Zaliznjak's as he argues that the complementary distribution may indicate that verb impoverishment is the cause of the loss of null subjects, while, in principle, the opposite situation is also possible (p.109). In other words, both 'AUX drop → subject realization' (Jakobson [1935] 1971a; Kibrik 2011) and 'subject realization → AUX drop' (Lomtev 1956; Xaburgaev 1978; Zaliznjak 2004) are possible. Meyer supports the verb impoverishment hypothesis by comparing the rates of AUX drop and subject pronominalization across all persons and tenses in Old Russian manuscripts. According to Kroch's Constant Rate Effects (1989), if two phenomena are correlated and thus explained by one common factor, the two changes must proceed at an identical speed or rate diachronically. In Meyer's work, the rates of AUX drop and subject pronominalization appear parallel with each other, which indicates both changes are parametrically correlated. This result supports my own conclusion on the correlation between the loss of AUX and the loss of null subjects in 5.1.

Null subjects without verbal agreement morphologies (AUX in ONR) and verbal agreement morphologies along with overt subjects are both in fact problematic for the verb impoverishment hypothesis. Meyer regards the first case, in 1st and 2nd persons, as formulaic omissions or contextual ellipsis. In the case of 3rd person, he argues that the lack of agreement itself marks 3rd person. He also compares ONR with Common Czech (*obecná čeština*), in which in 1st/2nd person overt subject realization accompanies AUX drop. In Standard Czech, both overt subjects

---

[10] Zaliznjak (2004: 172) states that AUX drop began in copular sentences with nominal predicates, such as *a ne sestra je vamo* 'and for you I am not a sister' (*BBL* 644, 12th c.). I do not discuss this issue in this paper. See relevant discussions in Claudi (2014: 62–65).

and AUX are realized in 1st/2nd person. In 3rd person, AUX is not marked in either variety.[11] I argue against Meyer's proposal of the "null" morphology denoting 3rd person in Section 4.2.

3.4 Questions and issues

All three aforementioned studies on Old Russian null subjects observe a general correlation between AUX and null subjects and the absolute prevalence of 3rd person null subjects, although they suggest different motivations behind the phenomena. I believe that there are several general issues that have not yet been satisfactorily addressed or resolved in some or all of these works.

First, it remains highly arbitrary to determine whether discourse-pragmatic factors, such as topicality and contrast, are entirely responsible for the use of null/overt subjects in specific cases. For instance, in 1st/2nd person either null or overt subjects may be used, although the former is favoured. Is this due to the absence/presence of "logical stress" (in Borkovskij's terminology)?

Second, while the person-based split is commonly admitted, it has not been explained at all why 3rd person null subjects do not behave in the same manner as 1st/2nd person null subjects. Why are null subjects more frequent in 3rd person than in 1st/2nd person? What general principle motivates the split between 1st/2nd person and 3rd person in Old Russian? In 3rd person *l*-past (or *l*-perfect) sentences, overt subjects do not appear in a complementary distribution with AUX, unlike in 1st/2nd person. Is this related to the lack of overt pronoun subjects in 3rd person?

---

11 However, Czech has shown auxiliation variation historically. Dickey (2013) attributes auxiliary variation in 3rd person in Old and Middle Czech to a semantic distinction between current relevance expressed by auxiliated *l*-participles and neutral preterit marked by non-auxiliated *l*-participles. The explanation is based on the original function of the Slavonic auxiliary *byti* 'be' as an expression of current relevance (i.e., resultative, stative) due to its profiling of a present-tense state. 3rd person compound past tense was unmarked in terms of the denotation of current relevance and thus had auxiliary variation. As 3rd person is neutral in terms of event participation, it appeared in narrative context more frequently than 1st and 2nd persons. As aorist, which originally assumed a narrative function, was lost, 3rd person compound past tense took this function over and came to pattern with AUX drop. However, as Dickey (2013: 111–112) also admits, this functional account is difficult to apply to the lack of AUX in 3rd person in Old Russian because in earliest Old Russian manuscripts, such as *BBL* of the 11th c., 3rd person AUX drop was already firmly established, regardless of the temporal/aspectual meaning of bare *l*-participles. Moreover, the loss of aorist and imperfect occurred much earlier in Old Russian than in Czech. In Old Russian auxiliaries are already fully grammaticalized as person markers in the 11th century-*BBL* (see Section 4).

Third, the direction of the causal relationship between subject pronominalization and the loss of AUX needs to be further illuminated. Although Zaliznjak believes that overt pronominalization resulted in AUX drop, there is no clear evidence in favour of this possibility.

Finally, it would be worth examining what place ONR occupies in the typology of null subject languages and how the Old (North) Russian null subject system evolved into the Modern Russian system.

In the following sections, I attempt to provide answers to these questions by analysing data from *BBL*.

4 Null subjects in ONR

I performed statistical research on null subject patterns in *BBL*, tracking the use of null and overt pronoun subjects in different persons, tenses, and periods. In this section, I present the results of my research and analyse the ONR situation based on the aforementioned theoretical assumptions. I exclude aorist and imperfect from the discussion, because relevant examples are very few in these tenses and they appear to be strongly influenced by registers.[12] I use the term '*l*-past' to refer to the tense that is traditionally called '*l*-perfect,' because it is hard to specify whether this tense form functions as a perfect or as a simple past, especially in dealing with forms without AUX. I also have to note that I do not count cases that are syntactically ambiguous due to the damage/loss of immediately preceding or following words.[13]

4.1 Data statistics

First of all, not surprisingly, the prevalence of null subjects in non-past and *l*-past is clearly observed. The ratio of null and overt subjects used in *BBL* is 76% (222 cases) vs. 24% (72 cases) in non-past, and 86% (243 cases) vs. 14% (39 cases) in *l*-past. As shown in Tab. 1, the proportion of null subjects in the non-past diachronically decreases constantly: 90% (11th c.) → 86% (12th c.) → 71% (13th c.) → 63% (14th c.) → 73% (15th c.). In the 15th century the ratio rises a bit but this may be attributed to the scarcity of manuscripts from this period. In contrast, in the

---

[12] Aorist and imperfect are rare, typically used in texts that are written in formal styles (see also Zaliznjak 2004: 142).
[13] The differences in flat numbers of the data in my research and Meyer's (2011) are mostly owing to this.

case of *l*-past, the frequency of null subjects does not change much, and a rather high ratio is maintained for null subjects throughout the centuries: 83% (11ᵗʰ c.) → 84% (12ᵗʰ c.) → 89% (13ᵗʰ c.) → 85% (14ᵗʰ c.) → 100% (15ᵗʰ c.). Here again, the 15ᵗʰ century should be treated as an exception given the limited quantity of texts.

Tab. 1: The decrease/increase of null/overt subjects (11ᵗʰ–15ᵗʰ cc.).[14]

Periods	(S) + non-past	S + non-past	(S) + *l*-past	S + *l*-past
11ᵗʰ c.	9 (90%)	1 (10%)	5 (83%)	1 (17%)
12ᵗʰ c.	88 (86%)	14 (14%)	87 (84%)	17 (16%)
13ᵗʰ c.	50 (71%)	20 (29%)	47 (89%)	6 (11%)
14ᵗʰ c.	47 (63%)	27 (37%)	87 (85%)	15 (15%)
15ᵗʰ c.	27 (73%)	10 (27%)	17 (100%)	0 (0%)
Total	222 (76%)	72 (24%)	243 (86%)	39 (14%)
	294 (100%)		282 (100%)	

An increase of overt subjects is also seen in specific expressions. For instance, most of the letters contain fixed forms of greetings and farewells. One of the most frequently used phrases is "I bow to you." While earlier letters contain formulaic Ø *klanęju ti sę* with a null subject, as in (4a), later letters tend to have *jazŭ tobe klanęju sę* with an overt subject, as exemplified in (4b).

(4) a. i   Ø   poklanęju   ti   sę.
       and   bow.NPST.1SG   you.DAT.2SG   REFL.ACC.SG
       'And I bow to you.'
       (*BBL* no. 798, late 12ᵗʰ c., Zaliznjak 2004: 321)
    b. a   ięza   tobe   koloneju-sę.
       and   I.NOM.1SG you.DAT.2SG   bow.NPST.1SG-REFL
       (*BBL* no. 501, late 13ᵗʰ–early 14ᵗʰ cc., Zaliznjak 2004: 558)

The use of null and overt subjects appears in an interesting correlation with person features, given the ratios between 1ˢᵗ/2ⁿᵈ person and 3ʳᵈ person in each tense in Tab. 2. In the non-past, among all overt subjects throughout the *BBL* manuscripts, 1ˢᵗ/2ⁿᵈ person pronouns occupy 99% of the uses, while 3ʳᵈ person pronouns only occupy 1%. All 3ʳᵈ person non-past pronominal subjects are covert, except for one case. The same situation is observed in the *l*-past. Among

---

[14] In these statistics, data dated to two consecutive centuries by Zaliznjak (2004) have been classified as belonging to the later century (e.g., from late 11ᵗʰ c. to early 12ᵗʰ c. > 12ᵗʰ c.).

all overt subjects, there are 37 occurrences of 1st/2nd person pronouns (95%) while only two cases of 3rd person pronouns are observed (5%).

Tab. 2: 1st/2nd person vs. 3rd person by tense and subject.

Person	S + non-past	S + *l*-past	(S) + non-past	(S) + *l*-past
1/2	71 (99%)	37 (95%)	157 (71%)	166 (68%)
3	1 (1%)	2 (5%)	65 (29%)	77 (32%)
Total	72 (100%)	39 (100%)	222 (100%)	243 (100%)

Based on the results in Tab. 2, we can clearly see that in 3rd person, in both tenses, a null subject is normative in *BBL*, while in the other persons both null and overt subjects are available for use. The only instance of an overt 3rd person pronominal subject in the non-past is given in (5), and the two instances of the *l*-past containing an overt 3rd person pronoun are provided in (6a) and (6b). The use of overt 3rd person pronouns seems to be an innovation that became more prominent after the 15th c. (see also Borkovskij [1949] for a similar analysis).

(5) ate [e]no sotesyvaete
 let.COMP he.NOM.3SG cut.NPST.3SG
 'Let him cut...'
 (*Gramota Tver.* 5, 13th–14th cc., Zaliznjak 2004: 569)

(6) a. ože ono poexalo
 that he.NOM.3SG came.PTCP
 'that he came...'
 (*BBL* no. 531, 12th–13th cc., Zaliznjak 2004: 416)
 b. i onŭ prislalŭ kŭ Fedosy
 and he.NOM.3SG sent.PTCP to Fedos'je
 'And he sent (a note) to Fedos'je.'
 (*BBL* no. 3, 14th c., Zaliznjak 2004: 646)

The ratio between overt and null subjects in each person and tense in Tab. 3 also confirms distinct subject patterns in different persons.

Tab. 3: Overt vs. null subjects by person and tense.

Subject	1st/2nd p. non-past	3rd p. non-past	1st/2nd p. *l*-past	3rd p. *l*-past
S	71 (31%)	1 (2%)	37 (18%)	2 (3%)
(S)	157 (69%)	65 (98%)	166 (82%)	77 (97%)
Total	228 (100%)	66 (100%)	203 (100%)	79 (100%)

As shown in Tab. 3, in the 1st/2nd person non-past, the use of overt subjects reaches 31%, while the use of null subjects marks 69%. In the 1st/2nd person *l*-past, overt subjects occupy 18% whereas null subjects amount to 82% of all the subjects. However, in the case of the 3rd person non-past and *l*-past, overt subjects only occupy 2% and 3%, while null subjects reach as high as 98% and 97%, respectively. This shows that in both tenses the percentage of null subjects is much higher in 3rd person than in 1st/2nd person, although null subjects are still preferred in 1st/2nd person.

When overt subjects are used in 1st/2nd person, AUX is almost always absent (91.9%). As noted by Zaliznjak (2004) and Meyer (2011), when null subjects are used in 1st/2nd person, overt AUX is absolutely prevalent. Two cases out of 166 1st/2nd person *l*-past sentences with null subjects lack AUX but even these cases are only superficial because the *l*-participle is conjoined with the preceding *l*-participle, sharing AUX between them. Thus, in 1st/2nd person, overt subjects appear in a strict complementary distribution with AUX. Conversely, in 3rd person *l*-past with null subjects, 76 examples out of 77 (99%) lack AUX. As already shown in (6a) and (6b), there are only two instances of 3rd person *l*-past with overt subjects. Both examples lack AUX. This means that it is normative to omit both subject and AUX in 3rd person.

This clearly differentiates 1st/2nd person and 3rd person in *l*-past. The fact that either overt pronouns or AUX, but not both, must be realized in 1st/2nd person indicates that AUX functions as a subject in 1st/2nd person. In other words, the 1st/2nd person feature must be morphologically expressed either by subjects or by AUX.[15] Alternatively, in 3rd person, the lack of both subject and AUX demonstrates that the person feature need not be (or cannot be) represented at all. I will discuss the syntactic implications of this contrast in the next section. As Meyer (2011: 110) notes, an increase of both AUX-drop and 1st/2nd person subject pronominalization is observed during the 14th–15th centuries.

4.2 Problems and analysis

From the data described thus far, several observations can be made. First, in *BBL* the ratio of null subjects (in all tenses and persons) to whole subject pronouns decreased towards the 15th century, while overt subjects increased and became

---

[15] As a reviewer pointed out, it should be noted that here the AUX that raises to Tense and functions as a subject is not a subject pronoun that occupies the subject position (Spec,TP). The former is a head while the latter is a phrase. It is the person feature as well as the D-feature in AUX that performs the subject function. However, AUX as a real pronoun subject, which occupies the subject position and triggers agreement on finite verbs, is indeed attested in Old Russian. See the discussion and data in 5.1.

more prevalent. This tendency is clear in the case of non-past but not in *l*-past, in which the proportion of null subjects against overt subjects remains rather high (see Tab. 1). The overall decrease of null subjects is not surprising given the fact that Modern Russian lost null subjects, except in very restricted environments. However, it is curious why the decrease of null subjects is more prominent in non-past than in *l*-past. Why is the loss of null subjects so slow in *l*-past? A partial answer to this question may be found in a possible correlation between the loss of null subjects and the loss of AUX in *l*-past, given the solid complementary distribution between AUX and overt subjects. The late loss of AUX (16th c.–) may be responsible for the late loss of null subjects in *l*-past. What then caused the loss of AUX and what causal relationship may be established between the loss of null subjects and AUX drop? I come back to these questions in Section 5.1.

The complementary distribution of AUX and overt subjects in 1st and 2nd persons is shown not only by the lack of overt subjects in the presence of AUX but also by the lack of AUX in the presence of overt subjects. This observation is crucial because it shows that only one of the two morphological means (subject or AUX) to represent a person feature may be chosen. In contrast with 1st/2nd person, in 3rd person it is the norm that neither subject nor AUX is overtly realized. How can we explain this along with the complementary distribution in 1st/2nd person?

The split between 1st/2nd and 3rd persons in terms of subject realization has been examined from pragmatic perspectives in the literature. One of the widely discussed discourse-pragmatic features in this respect is "informativeness," a concept that originates from Greenfield and Smith (1976), which is based on Grice's ([1967] 1975) quantity maxim. According to Greenfield and Smith, informative arguments tend to be omitted. As Serratrice (2007: 185) succinctly summarizes, informative arguments, whose referents are not highly salient and/or accessible, are more likely to be realized overtly than uninformative arguments, which are highly salient and accessible. 1st and 2nd person referents are always highly salient and accessible as they identify discourse participants (the speaker and the addressee). Thus, their referents' informativeness status will be low and they are more likely to be omitted. In contrast, 3rd person referents are more ambiguous than 1st/2nd person referents, and their informativeness status is higher. Therefore, 3rd person referents are more likely to be overtly realized. This type of person-split in terms of subject realization (null subjects in 1st/2nd person vs. overt subjects in 3rd person) has been empirically well supported: this kind of split has been observed in partial null subject languages and has also been noted in child language acquisition (see discussions in Clancy 1993; Allen 2000; Skarabela and Allen 2002, among others). When viewed from this theoretical and empirical background, the ONR situation is very peculiar: while productive null subjects in 1ˢᵗ and 2ⁿᵈ persons are as expected, it is strange that null subjects are absolutely predominant in 3ʳᵈ person.

Given this peculiarity, let us first consider why 3ʳᵈ person *l*-past lacks AUX. Meyer proposes that AUX in 3ʳᵈ person has "null" morphology. The lack itself of overt AUX denotes 3ʳᵈ person, just as *jesmĭ* signals 1ˢᵗ person. If his claim is on the right track, 3ʳᵈ person null or zero morphology should have been replaced by overt subjects more frequently, given that 1ˢᵗ and 2ⁿᵈ AUXs are often replaced by overt subjects, such as *języ̌* 'I' and *ty* 'you.' However, 3ʳᵈ person pronominal subjects (e.g., *onŭ* 'he', *ona* 'she') are very rarely attested in *BBL*.[16] I suggest that instead of morphologically null forms, there is really nothing in the AUX position in 3ʳᵈ person, just like there is nothing in the subject position (Spec,TP), rather than null *pro* in a null subject sentence (see Section 2.2 for the 'no empty pronoun' approach). I argue that the lack of AUX in 3ʳᵈ person can be explicated if 3ʳᵈ person is interpreted as non-person ([–person]). Jakobson ([1957] 1971b) and Benveniste (1966) note the split between 1ˢᵗ/2ⁿᵈ and 3ʳᵈ persons and defined 3ʳᵈ person as "impersonal" and "non-personne," respectively, based on the semantic and morphological defectiveness or unmarkedness of 3ʳᵈ person across languages (see also Greenberg 1966: 44). When it comes to null subject patterns, the person-split may be reduced to a contrast between [+person] and [–person]. When a person feature is active (or present, +), null subjects are syntactically licensed by this feature. In contrast, when the sentence lacks an active person feature, there is no need to represent a person feature, hence no need for AUX or overt subjects. Thus, while either an overt subject or AUX must represent the person feature in 1ˢᵗ/2ⁿᵈ person, in 3ʳᵈ person, there is no such person feature to be represented by an overt element. As a result, null subjects are licensed freely everywhere in 3ʳᵈ person. In this sense, the null subject system in ONR operates based on two different mechanisms.

What then determines the use of overt pronouns in 1ˢᵗ/2ⁿᵈ person? The use of overt subject pronouns has been explained as motivated by discourse-pragmatic

---

[16] In 1ˢᵗ and 2ⁿᵈ persons, only pronouns can be overt subjects, but in 3rd person, nouns and demonstratives as well as pronouns can become overt subjects. Can this explain the extremely few occurrences of 3ʳᵈ person subject pronouns in *BBL*, as suggested by Lindseth (1998: 62)? I believe that the answer is no. Even when noun subjects (demonstrative subjects are very rare in *BBL*) are taken into account, the difference in occurrence between 1ˢᵗ /2ⁿᵈ and 3ʳᵈ person overt subjects is still outstanding. Moreover, while 1ˢᵗ and 2ⁿᵈ person overt subjects often appear in the beginning and the middle of the texts, 3ʳᵈ person noun subjects are usually presented only once, earlier in the texts, and thus cannot syntactically function as the antecedents of null subjects in later parts of the texts. In some texts, 3ʳᵈ person null subjects are used despite the complete absence of their antecedent nouns in the given text (see Zaliznjak 2008: 257).

factors (i.e., logical stress: Borkovskij 1949, 1968, 1978; Zaliznjak 2004). However, when the extremely low frequency of 3rd person overt pronouns is considered, it would be strange to say that overt subjects are pragmatically required much less often in 3rd person than in 1st/2nd person. The contrast in the frequency of overt pronouns in different persons indicates that the relatively frequent use of overt pronouns in 1st/2nd person cannot be attributed to pragmatic factors. Istrina (1923) argues that the use of overt subject pronouns in Old Russian is not functionally motivated. Meyer (2011) also points out the highly arbitrary nature of 'logical stress': whenever an overt subject is found, its pragmatic motivation can be easily justified from the context, but there is no independent way to verify this motivation.

The strict complementary distribution between overt subjects and AUX shows that both overt subjects and AUX play the role of subject, and that their primary function is not expressing emphasis or contrast. In consistent null subject languages, pragmatically motivated overt pronouns do not replace AUX. See (7) for Croatian (see also (2a) for Spanish). In (7), the overt pronoun subject has an emphatic effect stressing that it was "I" who bought the refrigerator. Here, AUX cannot be dropped. Thus, the complementary distribution in ONR is evidence against a functional account for the use of overt subject pronouns in ONR (and in Old Russian in general).[17]

(7) Ja   sam   jučer   kupio   novi, bijeli hladnjak.[18]
    I.1SG   AUX.1SG yesterday bought.PTCPL new   white refrigerator
    'Yesterday I bought a new white refrigerator.'

In this respect, purely pragmatically motivated overt pronouns are found in rare examples containing both overt pronouns and AUX, such as in (8).

(8) a   ty   atče   jesi   ne   vŭzalŭ   kunŭ
    and you.2SG if.COMP   AUX.2SG   NEG taken.PTCP   kuna.GEN.PL
    texŭ
    those.GEN.PL
    'and you, if have not taken that money'
    (*BBL* no. 109, 11th–12th cc., Zaliznjak 2004: 249)

---

17 In *l*-past sentences without AUX, overt pronoun subjects first occupy the subject position (Spec,TP) and then optionally further move to the Topic/Focus position (Spec,CP), depending on pragmatic motivations. Thus, the regular and fundamental function of a pronoun subject is to fill the subject position, while its function as Topic or Focus is secondary and optional.
18 I thank my Croatian native informant Tomica Šćavina for this example.

In (8), the AUX *jesi* functions as a subject whereas the overt pronoun *ty* functions as a Topic, which is supported by its position preceding the complementizer *atče* (thus occupying Spec,CP).[19] The rare cases of 3rd person overt subjects can also be construed as Topic or Focus, located in Spec,CP. 3rd person overt Topic pronouns must have been reanalysed as true subjects in Spec,TP (cf. Gelderen's subject cycle [2011]).

To summarize, in 1st/2nd person overt pronoun subjects may assume certain discourse-functional roles, such as Topic and Focus, but that is secondary and optional, and the foremost reason for their presence is to check the D-feature in Tense. Under this analysis, in 1st/2nd person, two distinct grammars for checking the D-feature competed for dominance in ONR. As a result of this grammar competition, the option of realizing subjects and omitting AUX became more frequent, and eventually the option of null subjects waned.

The contrast between person and non-person in ONR resembles the cross-linguistic split between consistent null subject languages, such as Italian and Spanish, and radical null subject languages, such as Japanese and Korean. As noted earlier, person agreement is a key factor that licenses null subjects in consistent null subject languages. As for radical null subject languages, the lack of person agreement and insufficient inflection has been thought to play a role for liberal null subject patterns (Huang 1984; Rizzi 1986; Tomioka 2003; Neeleman and Szendrői 2007; Saito 2007, among others). For instance, Tomioka (2003) argues that in radical null subject languages nouns are bare NP-arguments lacking a DP layer. Due to the lack of the D-feature, overt pronouns cannot satisfy the EPP requirement (if the EPP can be assumed for these languages), and null subjects are allowed whenever the reference is contextually supported. Overt pronouns are used to mark discourse functions and occupy Spec,CP. As I assume that the D-feature is in the disguise of a person feature in ONR, the situation in radical null subject languages is the same as that of 3rd person in ONR.[20] From a typological point of view, it is interesting that two cross-linguistically distinguished null subject strategies are employed in one language, realizing the contrast of [+person] vs. [−person].

Finally, if the loss of AUX accompanied the loss of null subjects since null subjects were licensed by person agreement on AUX, as I have argued thus far, why were null subjects also lost in non-past sentences, in which verbal agreement

---

[19] The overt pronoun *ty* in sentence (8) could be a vocative phrase.
[20] This analysis is also in line with the argument on radical pro-drop languages: there is no evidence for person feature impoverishment, where there is no person marking in the first place (Müller 2007).

morphologies remain maximally distinctive by person and number (no impoverishment) even in Modern Russian? Two possibilities may be suggested. First, this could be because the presence of one particular impoverishment rule affecting Tense (i.e., in *l*-past) sufficed to block null subject licensing by Tense as a whole (Müller 2007: 7). Alternatively, if the loss of AUX was caused by the loss of inflected past tenses in Old Russian (feature weakening/impoverishment of Tense), which happened before the 12th c. in spoken Russian, as will be discussed in Section 5.1, and if only past tenses are defined as true tenses specified as [+tense] (as preterit tense is a marked member of the tense category [Andersen 2001: 23–24]), the null subject system associated with Tense was lost as the [+tense] feature in Tense was lost.[21] Non-past tense is non-tense ([–tense]) and, therefore, could not retain Tense-associated null subjects after the tense system change in Old Russian.

5 Historical and comparative issues

5.1 From Old Russian to Modern Russian

As noted in the beginning of this paper, ONR is differentiated from Old South Russian (OSR) and Old Central Russian (OCR) in terms of various linguistic features. However, the person-based null subject system of ONR is also operative in OSR/OCR, although the patterns in *BBL* are clearer than in OSR/OCR-based manuscripts. Meyer (2011: 107–122) observes that in most Old Russian manuscripts null subjects absolutely prevail regardless of person (see also Choo 2003 for a similar conclusion). Thus, it is not very problematic to assume an evolutionary process in the Old Russian null subject system, on the basis of the ONR situation by the 15th century. For instance, Zaliznjak (2004, 2008) regards the language of *BBL* as reflecting a spoken vernacular of Old Russian, as far as null subjects and auxiliation are concerned.

However, it should be noted that *BBL* is distinguished from Old Russian chronicles in terms of 3rd person pronoun subjects and AUX (Zaliznjak 2004, 2008). According to Meyer's sample study, the *Laurentian Chronicle* (14th c.) contains a certain number of 3rd person non-past sentences containing overt subjects, which is not the case in *BBL*. It is also observed in Claudi's research (2014: 117) on the *Hypatian Chronicle* (15th c.) that 3rd person *l*-perfect (*l*-past in this paper) sentences

---

21 The *l*-perfect tense consisting of a present tense auxiliary and an adjectival *l*-participle cannot be regarded as containing inflectional morphology devoted to denote [+past]. The same applies to *l*-past that evolved from *l*-perfect.

tend to include AUX, which differs from the ONR system. All these differences may be dialectal, reflecting differences between null subject systems of ONR and OSR/OCR. Alternatively, it can be attributed to distinct genres that employ different languages and styles. For instance, the level of influence of OCS matters because OCS and OCS-influenced texts of "bookish nature" tend to contain AUX in 3rd person (cf. Zaliznjak 2008: 257) and feature some optionality of 3rd person pronouns (Meyer 2011: 107). Most *BBL* texts are private letters written in a spoken vernacular, while chronicles occupy an intermediate position (Zaliznjak 2008: 258), being more influenced by OCS (e.g., frequent uses of aorist) than *BBL*.[22]

In Old Russian, the person-based split begins to visibly change only in the 17th century: in *Žitie protopopa Avvakuma* the null subjects' proportion compared to overt subjects in non-past decreases to 79.55% (1st/2nd person) and 72.92% (3rd person). Meyer believes that still there is no difference from the previous periods, except for the overall frequency. However, in my view, this is already different from the situation in the 11th–15th cc., in which null subjects are more dominant in 3rd person than in 1st/2nd person. Another peculiarity found in Meyer's research is that in his sample from *Domostroj* (16th c.), there are 25 occurrences of 3rd person null subjects in the perfect (p. 118). As Meyer uses the term "the perfect" to refer to 'AUX + *l*-participle' (which I refer to as '*l*-past with AUX' in this paper) in order to distinguish it from "the past," which refers to bare *l*-participle forms, this data indicates that 3rd person AUX is used regularly in this text. This is also different from the earlier situation, in which both subject and AUX are absent in 3rd person.

The emergence of a more restricted null subject system is one of the notable changes that the Russian language underwent from the 10th century to the modern period. While Old Russian is generally thought to be a null subject language, Modern Russian is either considered to be a non-null subject language (Franks 1995; Avrutin and Rohrbacher 1997) or a (partial) null subject language (Růžička 1986; Müller 1988, 2006, 2007; Demjjanow and Strigin 2000; Perlmutter and Moore 2002). What is important for the current discussion is that the use of null subjects has become restricted.

In Modern Russian a null subject can occur in coordinated or consecutive sentences (see McShane 2009), which may rather be viewed as a contextually

---

[22] As a reviewer pointed out, it should be noted that the evaluation of language and style may not be applied to a genre or a specific manuscript as a whole, because, even in the same text, different languages can be used depending on the local contents. However, the null subject patterns in different genres are approximately in accordance of the degree of the OCS influence. If the use of 3rd person AUX is attributed to the OCS influence, it is possible to draw the conclusion that the lack of 3rd person AUX in *BBL*, the corpus least influenced by OCS, reflects the Old Russian colloquial patterns.

licensed ellipsis.[23] However, in Russian null subjects are also used in the case of co-reference with main clause subjects, as illustrated in (9a), and when a subject has a non-specific, general meaning ('they'), as exemplified in (9b).[24]

(9) a. *Ona   skažet,   kogda   Ø   priedet.*
       she   will say.3SG   when   will come.3SG
       'She$_i$ will tell when she$_i$ will come.'

   b. *V   èto   vremja   goda   Ø   sobirajut   griby.*
      in   this   time   year.GEN.SG   collect.PL   mushrooms
      'In this season, they collect mushrooms.'

I have argued above that the ONR null subject system consists of two separate mechanisms based on the presence and absence of a person feature. In 1st/2nd person ([+person]), either an overt subject or AUX must realize the person feature. In 3rd person, there is no person feature, and therefore there is no need for AUX or an overt subject. Modern Russian has lost the old, syntactically constrained null subject system. The loss of null subjects that are licensed by person agreement in association with the D-feature in Tense is particularly interesting since V-to-T movement, which is also triggered by the D-feature in Tense (see Section 2.2), has been lost in Russian as well. The high position of the auxiliary verb preceding the negation in the Old Russian sentence in (8), repeated in (10), and the low position of the verb following the temporal adverb in the Modern Russian sentence in (11) show that V-to-T movement was possible in Old Russian while it was lost in Modern Russian (see the related arguments in Bailyn 1995; Slioussar 2007; Dyakonova 2009; Jung 2011 on the lack of V-to-T movement in Modern Russian).

(10) *a   ty   atče   jesi   ne   vŭzalŭ*
     and   you.2SG   if.COMP   AUX.2SG   NEG   taken.PTCP
     kunŭ   texŭ
     kuna.GEN.PL   those.GEN.PL
     'and you, if have not taken that money'
     (*BBL* no. 109, 11th–12th cc., Zaliznjak 2004: 249)

(11) *Ja   dumaju,   čto   Ivan   často   celuet   (*často)*
     I   think   that.COMP   Ivan.NOM   often   kisses
     Mašu
     Maša.ACC
     'I think that Ivan often kisses Masha.'
     (Bailyn 1995: 58)

---

[23] For a discussion concluding that a null subject is a case of ellipsis, see Duguine (2013).
[24] I thank my Russian informant Vadim Slepchenko for the examples in (9a)–(9b).

Both the loss of V-to-T movement and the loss of null subjects in Old Russian are motivated by the change in the way the D-feature in Tense is checked in Old Russian, and are thus parametric. As a morphological aspect system developed, Old Russian lost inflected aspectual past tenses, such as aorist and imperfect, and came to denote past tense by means of the participial forms in -*l*. In spoken Old Russian, imperfect and aorist were, at the latest, out of use in the 12th century (Xaburgaev 1978; Issatschenko 1983: 355–356; Uspenskij 1987: 144–151).[25] This change in the tense system arguably caused feature weakening/impoverishment of Tense (cf. Jung and Migdalski 2015; *contra* Müller 2006, 2007), which resulted in the loss of V-to-T movement. Due to the loss of V-to-T movement, AUX could not raise and check the D-feature in Tense and overt pronouns came to fill the subject position obligatorily (loss of null subjects). AUX, which used to perform the subject function, became unmotivated (see Jung 2014). The functional redundancy of AUX was resolved in two different ways: AUX either simply dropped or was reanalysed as a real subject pronoun occupying Spec,TP and triggering verb agreement.[26] The latter change is reflected in the Old Russian example in (12):

(12) *povestuju,* *što* **jesmĭ** *nynĕ* *na* *dorogu* *jexati.*
 tell1SG COMP AUX.1SG now on road go.INF
 xoščŭ
 want.1SG
 'I tell you that I will leave now.'
 (*The Third Pskov Chronicle*, 1473, Zaliznjak 2004: 179)

In (12), the AUX *jesmĭ* functions as the overt pronominal subject of the finite verb *xoščŭ*. It triggers person agreement in the same way that the pronoun *azŭ* 'I' does (Zaliznjak 2004: 179; Kwon 2009). AUX-as-subject (*jesmĭ, jesi*, etc.) and original pronouns (*azŭ, ty*, etc.) must have been in competition, but the latter won over the former and was generalized (Zaliznjak 2004; Kwon 2009; Jung 2013).[27]

---

25 For an opposite view, see Matthews (1960).
26 The change of AUX into a subject pronoun is the reverse of Gelderen's (2011) Subject Agreement Cycle and can be analyzed as a case of degrammaticalization (Kwon 2009; Jung 2013).
27 Kwon (2009) contends that AUX-as-subject occupying Spec,TP was generalized in ONR, based on the instances of AUX preceding the negation, as in (10) (*jesi*$_{AUX}$ *ne*$_{NEG}$ *vŭzalŭ*$_{PTCPL}$). However, while the AUX-negation-participle order is a general phenomenon across Old Slavonic languages and has been found in the earliest manuscripts, clear examples of AUX-as-subject, i.e., AUX triggering agreement on finite verbs, are very rare in Old Russian manuscripts (including *BBL*). Thus, I believe that it is more adequate to assume that the widely attested AUX that is higher than the negation is located on Tense, which is naturally predicted when V-to-T movement is active in a language.

Thus, AUX was lost, regardless of whether it was dropped or it was reanalysed as a pronoun subject. Under this analysis, both the loss of AUX and the loss of null subjects are consequences of the tense system change in Russian. This argument differs from the views held by Zaliznjak, Kibrik, and others concerning the causal direction between subject pronominalization and AUX drop, in that the two phenomena resulted from another change in Old Russian.

5.2 Finnish/Lithuanian vs. Old and Modern Russian

Balto-Finnic substratum effects have often been discussed in relation to various phonological, morphological, and syntactic traits of ONR, and sometimes are also brought up in relation to Old Russian in general. For instance, the neutralization of *c* and *č*, the *u* 'at' + genitive possessive construction (Veenker 1967; Décsy 1967),[28] and nominative objects (Timberlake 1974) are thought to be Balto-Finnic substratal features. It is argued that some substratal features of northern dialects, such as the *u* + genitive, expanded to other regions and eventually became primary features of Modern Russian (McAnallen 2011). I speculate that null subject patterns could also be such an instance. Null subject patterns in Modern Lithuanian, Modern Finnish, and Old Russian (including ONR) have an important common feature, while Modern Lithuanian and Finnish also share other null subject patterns with Modern Russian.

Finnish is one of the most representative partial null subject languages, allowing null subjects in 1st/2nd person and banning them in 3rd person (13a)–(13f). Finnish also allows null subjects in embedded clauses when they are co-referential with main clause subjects, as exemplified in (14a). Finally, non-specific, generic subjects appear null, as shown in (14b).

(13) a. *(Minä) puhun   englantia*
        I   speak.1SG   English
       'I speak English.'
     b. *(Sinä) puhut   englania*
        you   speak.2SG   English
       'You speak English.'

---

28 However, see Xodova (1966), Mirčev (1971), and Vasilev (1973) for different views. See also McAnallen (2011) for a comprehensive discussion of this possibility.

c. *(Hän)   puhuu   englantia
   he/she   speak.3SG   English
   'He/She speaks English.'
d. (Me)   puhumme   englantia
   we   speak.1PL   English
   'We speak English.'
e. (Te)   puhutte   englantia
   you   speak.2PL   English
   'You speak English.'
f. *(He)   puhuvat   englantia
   they   speak.3PL   English
   'They speak English.'
   (Holmberg 2005: 539)

(14) a. Juhani$_i$ kertoi   että   (hän$_i$)   oli   ostanut   talon.
        Juhani   said   that   he   have.PST.3SG   bought   house
        'Juhani said that he had bought a house.'
        (Holmberg, Nayudu and Sheehan 2009: 65)
     b. Kesällä   herää   aikaisin.
        in-summer wake.PRS.3SG   early
        'In the summer one wakes up early.'
        (Holmberg, Nayudu, and Sheehan 2009: 63)

The same patterns are observed in Lithuanian. As illustrated by Šereikaitė (2013: 51–52), Lithuanian also exhibits a person-split: 1st and 2nd person pronouns are optionally null in the declarative main and embedded clauses and interrogatives, while 3rd person definite overt subjects cannot be dropped in the matrix clause or in the interrogative. Additionally, 'indefinite-personal' sentences lack an overt subject and have an indefinite generalized implicit logical subject (Ambrazas 1997: 600). A 3rd person definite subject is optionally null in the embedded clause when bound by the matrix subject.

Overall, the Finnish and Lithuanian null subject systems are similar to the Old Russian (and ONR) system, as they show a person-based split. However, Finnish and Lithuanian, on the one hand, and Old Russian on the other, display very opposite patterns in dealing with 3rd person. The Finnish/Lithuanian system is restricted in 3rd person, while the Old Russian system is quite liberal in 3rd person. This demonstrates how languages assign distinct featural values to the same grammatical category (3rd person), or how the same featural value ([−person]) may be realized across languages.

It is worth noting that the null subject patterns in (14a)–(14b) are very similar to those in (9a)–(9b) in Modern Russian.[29] While Russian lost the old person-based system completely, it developed the patterns in (9a)–(9b) in the same way that Finnish/Lithuanian did. Given the similarities in null subject patterns between Old and Modern Russian and Finnish/Lithuanian, I conjecture that the Russian and Finnic/Baltic null subject systems have shared many traits historically. Of course, it would be illuminating if the Old Finnic/Baltic system were directly compared to the Old Russian system, but unfortunately, relevant data and literature on the Old Finnic/Baltic system are not available for this paper. However, the resemblance between the null subject systems of Finnish/Lithuanian and Old and Modern Russian may offer a possibility of historical substratum effects, which is worthy of in-depth exploration in the future.

6 Conclusion

In this paper I have investigated the null subject system of ONR, based on subject realization patterns and conditions reflected in *BBL*. The ONR null subject system, based on a person feature split, is a prime case that realizes Borer's (1986) proposal of agreement performing the subject function. The data shows that *l*-past AUX and overt subjects are complementarily distributed in 1st/2nd person, while the use of null subjects is prevalent in 3rd person. In non-past, the situation is similar. In 1st/2nd person, null subjects are more favoured than overt ones. In 3rd person, a null subject is almost always the only possible option.

As the D-feature in Tense may be checked and agreement can be realized in two ways (either by overt subjects in Spec,TP or by V-to-T movement), the complementary distribution of overt subjects and AUX in 1st/2nd person *l*-past sentences may be interpreted as a competition between two strategies to check the D-feature. In 3rd person, the lack of both null subjects and AUX is normative, which I attribute to the lack of a person feature in 3rd person. The contrast of null subject patterns between 1st/2nd person and 3rd person can be reduced to the [+person] and [−person] opposition, which is parallel to the cross-linguistic contrast between canonical null subject languages with rich agreement and radical

---

[29] The indefinite null subjects in Russian example (9b) and Finnish example (14b) are semantically not identical. While the Russian null subject in 3rd person plural has a non-specific and arbitrary meaning, as in Eng. ***They*** *speak many different languages in Russia*, the Finnish 3rd person singular null subject has a generic and general interpretation, as in Eng. ***One*** *should work hard to make money*. See Holmberg, Nayudu, and Sheehan (2009: 63–64).

subject languages with no agreement. Variations in subject pronominalization and auxiliation should be viewed as grammar competition, and not as a purely pragmatically motivated phenomenon.

Modern Russian has a null subject system that is much more restricted than the Old Russian system. The Old and Modern Russian null subject patterns resemble those of Lithuanian and Finnish in different ways, which raises the possibility of Balto-Finnic substratum effects in the developmental process of the Russian null subject system.

References

Abney, Steven P. 1987. *The English noun phrase in its sentential aspect*. Cambridge, Mass.: MIT dissertation.
Alexiadou, Artemis & Elena Anagnostopoulou. 1998. Parametrizing AGR: Word order, V-movement and EPP-checking. *Natural Language and Linguistic Theory* 16. 491–539.
Allen, Shanley E.M. 2000. A discourse-pragmatic explanation for argument representation in child Inuktitut. *Linguistics* 38 (3). 483–521.
Ambrazas, Vytautas (ed.). 1997. *Lithuanian grammar*. Vilnius: Baltos Lankos.
Andersen, Henning. 2001. Markedness and the theory of linguistic change. In Henning Andersen (ed.), *Actualization: Linguistic change in progress*, 21–57. Amsterdam: John Benjamins.
Avrutin, Sergej & Bernhard Rohrbacher. 1997. Null subjects in Russian inverted constructions. In *Proceedings of the Fourth Annual Workshop on Formal Approaches to Slavic Linguistics*, 32–53. Ann Arbor: Michigan Slavic Publications.
Bailyn, John Frederick. 1995. *A configurational approach to Russian 'free' word order*. Ithaca, New York: Cornell University dissertation.
Benveniste, Émile. 1966. *Problèmes de linguistique générale*, 1. Paris: Gallimard.
Biberauer, Theresa & Ian Roberts. 2009. Subjects, tense and verb-movement. In Theresa Biberauer, Anders Holmberg, Ian Roberts & Michelle Sheehan (eds.), *Parametric variation: Null subjects in minimalist theory*, 263–302. Cambridge: Cambridge University Press.
Boeckx, Cedric. 2002. Quirky agreement revisited. Ms., University of Illinois.
Borer, Hagit. 1986. I-subjects. *Linguistic Inquiry* 17. 375–416.
Borer, Hagit. 1989. Anaphoric AGR. In Osvaldo Jaeggli & Kenneth Safir (eds.), *The Null Subject Parameter*, 69–109. Dordrecht: Kluwer Academic Publishers.
Borkovskij, Viktor I. 1949. *Sintaksis drevnerusskix gramot. Prostoe predloženie* [Syntax of Old Russian charters. The simple sentence]. L'vov: Izd.-vo L'vovskogo gosudarstvennogo universiteta.
Borkovskij, Viktor I. (ed.). 1968. *Sravnitel'no-istoričeskij sintaksis vostočnoslavjanskix jazykov: Tipy prostogo predloženija*. [Comparative-historical syntax of the East Slavonic languages. Types of simple sentence]. Vol. 2. Moskva: Nauka.
Borkovskij, Viktor I. 1978. *Istoričeskaja grammatika russkogo jazyka: Sintaksis. Prostoe predloženie* [Historical grammar of Russian: Syntax. The simple sentence]. Moskva: Nauka.
Bybee, Joan.1988. The diachronic dimension in explanation. In John Hawkins (ed.), *Explaining language universals*, 350–379. Oxford: Blackwell.
Chomsky, Noam. 1995. *The minimalist program*. Cambridge, Mass.: The MIT Press.

Choo, Sukhoon. 2003. *The decline of null pronominal subjects in Old Russian*. Bloomington: Indiana University dissertation.

Clancy, Patricia. 1993. Preferred argument structure in Korean acquisition. In Eve Clark (ed.), *The Proceedings of the Twenty-fifth Annual Child Language Research Forum*, 307–314. Stanford, CA: CSLI.

Claudi, Tommaso. 2014. *The status of subject pronouns in Old Russian: A diachronic analysis*. Pavia: University of Pavia MA thesis.

Décsy, Gyula. 1967. Is there a Finnic substratum in Russian? *Orbis* 16 (1). 150–160.

Demjjanow, Assinja & Anatoli Strigin. 2000. Case assignment to conceptual structures: The Russian instrumental. In Marcus Kracht & Anatoli Strigin (eds.), *Papers on the interpretation of case* (Linguistics in Potsdam 10), 75–107. Potsdam: Institut für Linguistik.

Dickey, Stephen M. 2013. See, now they vanish: Third-person perfect auxiliaries in Old and Middle Czech. *Journal of Slavic Linguistics* 21 (1). 77–121.

Duguine, Maia. 2013. *Null arguments and linguistic variation: A minimalist analysis of pro-drop*. UPV/EHU & Université de Nantes dissertation.

Dyakonova, Marina. 2009. *A phase-based approach to Russian free word order*. Amsterdam: University of Amsterdam dissertation.

Franks, Steven. 1995. *Parameters of Slavic morphosyntax*. Oxford: Oxford University Press.

Gelderen, Elly van. 2011. *The linguistic cycle: Language change and the language faculty*. New York: Oxford University Press.

Givón, Talmy. 1976. Topic, pronoun, and grammatical agreement. In Charles N. Li (ed.), *Subject and topic*, 81–114. New York: Academic Press.

Greenberg, Joseph H. 1966. Some universals of grammar with particular reference to the order of meaningful elements. In Joseph. H. Greenberg (ed.), *Universals of language*, 2nd edn., 73–113. Cambridge, Mass.: MIT Press.

Greenfield, Patricia Marks & Joshua H. Smith. 1976. *The structure of communication in early language development*. New York: Academic Press.

Grice, H. Paul. 1975 [1967]. Logic and conversation. In Donald Davidson & Gilbert Harman (eds.), *The logic of grammar*, 64–75. Encino, CA: Dickenson.

Holmberg, Anders. 2005. Is there a little *pro*? Evidence from Finnish. *Linguistic Inquiry* 36 (4). 533–564.

Holmberg, Anders, Aarti Nayudu & Michelle Sheehan. 2009. Three partial null-subject languages: A comparison of Brazilian Portuguese, Finnish and Marathi. *Studia Linguistica* 63 (1). 59–97.

Holmberg, Anders & Christer Platzack. 1990. On the role of inflection in Scandinavian syntax. In Werner Abraham, Wim Kosmeijer & Eric Reuland (eds.), *Issues in Germanic syntax*, 93–118. Berlin & New York: Mouton de Gruyter.

Holmberg, Anders & Christer Platzack. 1995. *The role of inflection in Scandinavian syntax*. New York and Oxford: Oxford University Press.

Hopper, Paul J. & Elizabeth Closs Traugott. 2003. *Grammaticalization*, 2nd edn. Cambridge: Cambridge University Press.

Huang. James C.-T. 1984. On the distribution and reference of empty pronouns. *Linguistic Inquiry* 15 (4). 531–574.

Issatschenko, Alexander V. 1983. *Geschichte der russischen Sprache. Das 17. und 18. Jahrhundert*. Vol. 2. Heidelberg: Carl Winter.

Istrina, Evgenija S. 1923. *Sintaksičeskie javlenija Sinodal'nogo spiska I Novgorodskoj letopisi* [Syntactic features of the Synodal copy of the First Novgorod Chronicle]. Petrograd.

Jakobson, Roman. 1971a [1935]. Les enclitiques slaves. In *Selected writings: Volume II*, 16–22. The Hague: Mouton de Gruyter.
Jakobson, Roman. 1971b [1957]. Shifters, verbal categories, and the Russian verb. In *Selected writings: Volume II*, 130–147. The Hague: Mouton de Gruyter.
Jung, Hakyung. 2011. *The syntax of the be-possessive: Parametric variation and surface diversities*. Amsterdam: John Benjamins.
Jung, Hakyung. 2013. On the syntax of the so-called auxiliary clitic in Old North Russian. Paper presented at Formal Description of Slavic Languages 10, University of Leipzig, 6 December.
Jung, Hakyung. 2014. The syntax of the *be*-auxiliary and D-feature lowering in Old North Russian. Paper presented at Formal Approaches to Slavic Linguistics 23, University of California at Berkeley, 2 May.
Jung, Hakyung & Krzysztof Migdalski. 2015. On the degrammaticalization of pronominal clitics in Slavic. In *Proceedings of Formal Approaches to Slavic Linguistics* 23, 143–162. Ann Arbor: Michigan Slavic Publications.
Kibrik, Andrej A. 2011. *Reference in discourse*. Oxford: Oxford University Press.
Kibrik, Andrej A. 2013. Peculiarities and origins of the Russian referential system. In Dik Bakker & Martin Haspelmath (eds.), *Languages across boundaries: Studies in memory of Anna Siewierska*, 239–274. Berlin: De Gruyter Mouton.
Koeneman, Olaf & Ad Neeleman. 2001. Predication, verb movement and the distribution of expletives. *Lingua* 111 (3). 189–233.
Koeneman, Olaf & Hedde Zeijlstra. 2014. The rich agreement hypothesis rehabilitated. *Linguistic Inquiry* 45. 571–615.
Kosmeijer, Wim. 1986. The status of the finite inflection in Icelandic and Swedish. *Working Papers in Scandinavian Syntax* 26. 1–41.
Kroch, Anthony. 1989. Reflexes of grammar in patterns of language change. *Language Variation and Change* 1 (3). 199–244.
Kwon, Kyongjoon. 2009. The Subject Cycle of pronominal auxiliaries in Old North Russian. In Elly van Gelderen (ed.), *Cyclical change*, 157–184. Amsterdam & Philadelphia: John Benjamins.
Lindseth, Martina. 1998. *Null-subject Properties of Slavic languages: With special reference to Russian, Czech, and Sorbian*. München: Sagner.
Lomtev, Timofej P. 1956. *Očerki po istoričeskomu sintaksisu russkogo jazyka* [Essays on the historical syntax of Russian]. Moskva: Izdatel'stvo Moskovskogo universiteta.
Matthews, William Kleesmann. 1960. *Russian historical grammar*. London: Athlone Press.
McAnallen, Julia. 2011. *The history of predicative possession in Slavic: Internal development vs. language contact*. Berkeley: University of California dissertation.
McShane, Marjorie. 2009. Subject ellipsis in Russian and Polish. *Studia Linguistica* 63 (1). 98–132.
Meyer, Roland. 2011. *The history of null subjects in North Slavonic: A corpus-based diachronic investigation*. Regensburg: University of Regensburg Habilitation thesis.
Mirčev, Kiril. 1971. Predlog 'u' v posessivnoj funkcii v istorii bolgarskogo jazyka [The preposition 'u' in the possessive function in the history of Bulgarian]. In *Issledovanija po slavjanskomu jazykoznaniju: Sbornik v čest' šestidesatiletija prof. S. B. Bernštejna* [Studies in Slavonic linguistics: Festschrift on the occasion of the 60th birthday of prof. S. B. Bernštejn], 79–84. Moskva: Nauka.
Müller, Gereon. 1988. *Zur Analyse subjektloser Konstruktionen in der Rektions-Bindungs-Theorie. That-trace-Effekte und pro-Lizensierung im Russischen*. Ms., Universität Frankfurt/Main.

Müller, Gereon. 2006. Pro-drop and impoverishment. In Patrick Brandt & Eric Fuss (eds.), *Form, structure, and grammar. A Festschrift presented to Günther Grewendorf on occasion of his 60th birthday*, 93–115. Berlin: Akademie Verlag.
Müller, Gereon. 2007. *Some consequences of an impoverishment-based approach to morphological richness and pro-drop*. Ms., University of Leipzig.
Neeleman, Ad & Krista Szendrői. 2007. Radical pro drop and the morphology of pronouns. *Linguistic Inquiry* 38 (4). 671–714.
Perlmutter, David M. & John Moore. 2002. Language-internal explanation: The distribution of Russian impersonals. *Language* 78 (4). 619–650.
Platzack, Christer. 2003. Agreement and null subjects. In Anne Dahl, Kristine Bentzen & Peter Svenonius (eds.), *Nordlyd: Proceedings of the 19th Scandinvian Conference of Linguistics* 31 (2). 326–355. University of Tromsø Working Papers. Septentrio Academic Publishing.
Pollock, Jean-Yves. 1989. Verb movement, Universal Grammar, and the structure of IP. *Linguistic Inquiry* 20 (3). 365–424.
Postal, Paul M. 1970. On so-called pronouns in English. In Roderick A. Jacobs & Peter S. Rosenbaum (eds.), *Readings in English Transformational Grammar*, 56–82. Waltham, Mass.: Ginn.
Ritter, Elizabeth. 1995. On the syntactic category of pronouns and agreement. *Natural Language and Linguistic Theory* 13. 405–443.
Rizzi, Luigi. 1986. Null objects in Italian and the theory of pro. *Linguistic Inquiry* 17 (3). 501–557.
Roberts, Ian G. 1985. Agreement parameters and the development of English modal auxiliaries. *Natural Language and Linguistic Theory* 3 (1). 21–58.
Roberts, Ian G. 1999. Verb movement and markedness. In Michel DeGraff (ed.), *Language creation and change: Creolization, diachrony, and development*, 287–328. Cambridge, Mass.: MIT Press.
Rohrbacher, Bernhard Wolfgang. 1999. *Morphology-driven syntax: A theory of V to I raising and pro-drop*. Amsterdam: John Benjamins.
Růžička, Rudolf. 1986. Funkcionirovanie i klassifikacija pustyx kategorij v russkom literaturnom jazyke [Functioning and classification of empty categories in standard Russian]. *Zeitschrift für Slawistik* 31 (3). 388–392.
Saito, Mamoru. 2007. *Notes on East Asian argument ellipsis*. Ms., Nanzan University & University of Connecticut.
Serratrice, Ludovica. 2007. Null and overt subjects at the syntax-discourse interface. Evidence from monolingual and bilingual acquisition. http://dspace.library.uu.nl/bitstream/handle/1874/296781/bookpart.pdf?sequence=2 (accessed 5 May 2016).
Shlonsky, U. 1997. *Clause structure and word order in Hebrew and Arabic. An essay in comparative Semitic syntax*. New York: Oxford University Press.
Siewierska, Anna. 2004. *Person*. Cambridge: Cambridge University Press.
Skarabela, Barbora & Shanley Allen. 2002. The role of joint attention in argument realization in child Inuktitut. In Barbora Skarabela, Sarah Fish & Anna H.-J. Do (eds.), *Proceedings of the Twenty-sixth Annual Boston University Conference on Language Development*, 620–630. Somerville, Mass.: Cascadilla Press.
Slioussar, Natalia. 2007. *Grammar and information structure: A study with reference to Russian*. Utrecht: Utrecht University dissertation.
Šereikaitė, Milena. 2013. *Lithuanian passives and passive-like constructions (with comparison to English)*. Trondheim: Norwegian University of Science and Technology MA thesis.

Taraldsen, Knut Tarald. 1978. On the NIC, vacuous application and the that-trace filter. Indiana University Linguistics Club.

Timberlake, Alan. 1974. *The nominative object in Slavic, Baltic, and West Finnic*. München: Sagner.

Tomioka, Satoshi. 2003. The semantics of Japanese null pronouns and its cross-linguistic implications. In Kerstin Schwabe & Susanne Winkler (eds.), *The interfaces: Deriving and interpreting omitted structures*, 321–340. Amsterdam: John Benjamins.

Uspenskij, Boris A. 1987. *Istorija russkogo literaturnogo jazyka (XI–XII vv.)* [History of the Russian literary language (11th–17th c.)]. München: Verlag Otto Sagner.

Vasilev, Christo. 1973. Ist die Konstruktion *U Menja Est'* russisch oder urslavisch? *Die Welt der Slaven* 18. 361–367.

Veenker, Wolfgang. 1967. *Die Frage des finnougrischen Substrats in der russischen Sprache*. Bloomington, Ind.: Indiana University.

Xaburgaev, Georgij A. 1978. Sud'ba vspomogatel'nogo glagola drevnix slavjanskix analitičeskix form v russkom jazyke [Development of the auxiliary verb of the Old Slavonic analytical forms in Russian]. *Vestnik MGU. Ser. 9, Filologija* 4. 42–53.

Xodova, Kapitolina I. 1966. Sintaksis predloga 'u' s roditel'nym padežom v staroslavjanskom jazyke [Syntax of the preposition 'u' with genitive in Old Church Slavonic]. *Scando-Slavica* 12. 96–114.

Zaliznjak, Andrej A. 1987. O jazykovoj situacii v drevnem Novgorode [On the language situation in Old Novgorod]. *Russian Linguistics* 11 (2–3). 115–132.

Zaliznjak, Andrej A. 2004. *Drevnenovgorodskij dialekt* [The Old Novgorod dialect]. Moskva: Jazyki slavjanskoj kul'tury.

Zaliznjak, Andrej A. 2008. *Drevnerusskie ènklitiki* [Old Russian enclitics]. Moskva: Jazyki slavjanskoj kul'tury.

Björn Hansen
On the permeability of grammars: Syntactic pattern replications in heritage Croatian and heritage Serbian spoken in Germany

A svako mi kaže kad me čuje (.)
da sam ko... da ne lijepo pričam. (T 9)

Abstract: This paper addresses the syntax of second generation speakers of Serbian and Croatian in Germany. It is based on an empirical analysis of interviews and written essays. The author presents a first typology of syntactic changes which have occurred in comparison to L1 speakers of standard Štokavian whose language is taken as the monolingual baseline of comparison. The paper addresses the following research questions: i) What types of syntactic pattern replication are found in the speech of Croatian/Serbian-German bilinguals? ii) Are all types of syntactic pattern replication known from other contact settings attested and are there specific types? iii) Are the replications of patterns mediated by or even directly linked to lexical elements? The data clearly show that syntactic features are easily replicated if they are linked to lexical elements. In all cases of syntactic pattern replication, we see a clear link with lexical entries. Schematic syntactic rules are only indirectly affected by language contact in the sense that contact can trigger the loss of categorical distinctions.

1 Introduction[1]

This paper aims to contribute to our understanding of the permeability of grammatical systems in situations of intensive language contact with special focus on syntactic features. The point of departure of our considerations is Weinreich's statement from 1953 that the locus of language contact is not the language system, but the mind of the bilingual individual. As is well known, in contrast to the replication of lexical elements it is much more difficult to detect syntactic structures which have developed due to language contact, i.e. due to the fact

---

[1] I would like to thank Daniel Romić (KU Eichstätt) not only for his invaluable comments, but mainly for his pioneering field work. All errors and inadequacies remain mine.

that the speaker uses two languages on a regular basis. We would like to explore the extent and limits of the replication of syntactic structures found in heritage languages. As pointed out by Silva-Corvalán (1993: 19), since the early studies by Weinreich (1953) and others, there is a widespread belief that in situations of language maintenance, the grammatical system is rather impermeable to the direct transfer of foreign elements. The replication of grammatical patterns is claimed to be confined to features that either fit with the structure of the receiving language or that correspond to its own internal tendencies. Thomason (2001: 63), however, challenges this view. On the basis of evidence provided by a large number of contact linguistic studies from different areas, she argues that any structural feature can be transferred from one language to another. A further question addressed by many scholars concerns the interrelation between lexical and syntactic change. For example, Winford (2003: 61), who admits the possibility of far reaching syntactic restructuring, argues that "such structural change is practically always mediated by lexical transfer". Silva-Corvalán (1998: 225–226), who works on heritage Spanish in California, even claims that "what is borrowed across languages is not syntax but lexicon and pragmatics". We would like to contribute to the controversy on the permeability of syntactic systems by studying the language use of Croatian and Serbian bilinguals living in Germany. These data will be analysed for the types of syntactic pattern replication from German to Croatian and Serbian. We do not aim at a full account of the specific structures found in these heritage languages. Instead, we present a first qualitative inventory of types of contact induced changes of syntactic patterns. More specifically, in our paper we will address the following research questions:
1. What types of syntactic pattern replication are found in the speech of Croatian/Serbian-German bilinguals?
2. Are all types of syntactic pattern replication known from other contact settings attested and are there specific types?
3. Are the replications of patterns mediated by or even directly linked to lexical elements?

In accordance with Dorleijn and Backus (2013), we would like to point out the relevance of heritage linguistic studies. Heritage linguistics can considerably contribute to historical syntax because heritage languages allow us to study change in on-going contact settings in the sense that they provide snapshots of change in progress. In contrast to changes which took place in the past, the linguist has direct access to speakers and can elicit specific data.

Our paper is structured in the following way. First, we will give a short overview of the state of the art in heritage linguistic studies on Croatian and Serbian in Germany including the number of speakers in relation to the distribution of the first and the second generation. In the second section, we will present a typology of syntactic pattern replications. The empirical Part three containing the data gives an overview of the specific phenomena found in a research corpus. In the final Chapter, we will sum up our findings and come back to the three research questions. Our paper draws on the data and findings from Hansen, Romić, and Kolaković (2013), which being published in Croatian might not be accessible to the English readership. Some of the data have been discussed in Romić (2016).

2 Croatian and Serbian as heritage languages

According to the available statistical data, in Germany there are roughly one million people with a so-called *Migrationshintergrund* 'migration background' (a term used in German statistics) from the former Yugoslavia, the vast majority of whom can be assumed to have at least some knowledge of Croatian and Serbian (or Bosnian/Croatian/Serbian BCS as it is officially called in German universities).[2] In the year 2008, 692,944 migrants living in Germany hold Bosnian (158,158), Croatian (225,308) or Serbian and Montenegrin citizenship (236,451).[3] Among them, 148,428 persons are born in Germany (48,995 declared Croats, 27,387 Bosnians, 34,517 Serbs und 37,529 Montenegrins). The group of second and third generation migrants born in Germany encompasses 292,000 persons (66,000 with Bosnian, 122,000 with Croatian and 104,000 with Serbian background); for more statistical data, see Hansen, Romić, and Kolaković (2013) and Romić (2016). The latter offers a holistic account of the current BCS-German bilingualism by correlating the migrants' language use with sociolinguistic factors like identity construction and linguistic attitudes.

Since the foundation of the discipline, language contact has been a fundamental issue in Slavonic philology. Whereas previously the focus has been mainly on the outcome of the contact between standard languages, in the eighties of the 20th century Slavists in the traditional immigration countries developed an increasing interest in the language use of Slavonic migrant communities and in the structural changes triggered by bilingualism (cf. Sussex 1993). The first studies dealt with the language use in the US, Australia and Sweden and contributed to the rise of the new linguistic subdiscipline called 'Heritage linguistics', a term coined and popularized by Maria Polinsky, Silvina Montrul and others.

---

[2] In the following I will use the terms Serbian/Croatian and BCS as synonyms.
[3] Cf.: Bundesamt für Migration und Flüchtlinge, Grunddaten der Zuwandererbevölkerung in Deutschland, Working Paper 27, S. 32.

In the nineties, Slavists started to be interested in Russian and Polish as spoken in Germany (for overviews see Anstatt 2008, 2011 on Russian and Warchoł-Schlottmann 1996; Błaszczyk 2015 on Polish).

In comparison to e.g. Russian, Serbian and Croatian heritage languages have received less attention. Due to the lack of space we will not give a full account of the current state of the art and will instead refer the reader to the overview of heritage linguistic studies on Croatian and Serbian in Romić (2016), Hansen, Romić, and Kolaković (2013), S. Savić (1989), Zubčić (2010) and Vuletić (2013). There are a few studies on the language of the Croatian and Serbian diaspora in the US (e.g. Albin and Alexander 1972; Jutronić-Tihomirović 1985; J. M. Savić 1995), in Australia (e.g. Dimitrijević-Savić 2004, 2008; Hlavac 2003), in New Zealand (e.g. Stoffel 2002/2003), and in Sweden (Ďurovič 1983). Although BCS belongs to the 'old' immigrant languages of Germany in the sense that speakers came to Germany in the context of labour migration in the sixties and seventies of the twentieth century (so-called *Gastarbeiter*), it has been the subject of very few studies. Therefore, the research on heritage BCS spoken in Germany considerably lags behind in comparison to the English speaking world. The research on Serbian/Croatian has a mainly sociolinguistic orientation as e.g. Stölting (1980) and Schlund (2006). Raecke (2007a, 2007b) and Mrazović (1989) were the first to offer some preliminary observations regarding the structural properties of Croatian and Serbian in Germany. Their hypothesis is that heritage BCS is in a process of structural convergence with German as the dominating language (also J. M. Savić 1995; Dimitrijević-Savić 2004, 2008 on heritage Serbian in English speaking countries). Raecke even goes so far as to call this language 'German with Croatian words' – 'Hrvatski u Njemačkoj: njemački s hrvatskim riječima' (Raecke 2007a: 151). It is not difficult, however, to show that this is an incorrect generalization. It suffices to compare one of his examples with the glossed underlying German sentence:

(1) Ja   sam   je   pitala   što   ona
    I   **aux.1SG** she.ACC   **ask.PTCP.F.SG** what   she
    Ich   habe   sie   gefragt   was   sie
    I   **have.1SG** she.ACC   **PTCP.ask.PTCP** what   she
    poslije predavanja radi.
    after   lesson.GEN.SG do.3.SG
    nach   **dem** Unterricht   macht.
    after   **ART.DAT.SG** lesson do.3SG
    'I asked her what she would do after the class.'
    (Raecke 2007a: 152)

The glossing reveals syntactic differences in the structures of the two sentences: the form of the predicate, different types of auxiliaries, subject-predicate agreement, articles, case marking etc. The Croatian sentence is well formed according to all syntactic rules of standard Croatian; it only shows two pragmatic deviations: first, the use of the personal pronoun *ja* would require emphasis or contrast focus which is not the case here. Second, the predicate *radi* is in the clause final position which in standard or native varieties is perceived as somewhat odd, but not as ungrammatical.

3 Theoretical basis: A typology of syntactic pattern replications

Before analysing the data, we need to discuss some theoretical aspects of the replication of grammatical patterns. Being aware of the fact that any typology of syntactic pattern replications depends on the syntactic theory applied, we elaborate a largely descriptively oriented typology which is compatible with basic assumptions of Construction Grammar in the version presented in Fried and Östmann (2004), but can also be spelled out in other frameworks. Our point of departure are the mainly functionally oriented volumes Harris and Campbell (1995), Heine and Kuteva (2005), Winford (2003) and Wiemer, Wälchli, and Hansen (2012) which contain in-depth discussions of the scope and boundaries of contact-induced grammatical changes.

To start with, following Heine and Kuteva (2005: 2) we can distinguish the following general kinds of linguistic transfer:
a) Form, that is, sounds or combinations of sounds,
b) Meanings (incl. grammatical and lexical),
c) Form-meaning units,
d) Syntactic relations, that is the order of meaningful elements,
e) Any combination of a) through d).

In our contribution we are going to focus on the replication of grammatical meanings mentioned under b) and the replication of syntactic structures d).

There is a plethora of terms used in the contact linguistic literature for denoting processes of transfer. Just to name a few: 'interference' (Weinreich 1953), 'replication' (Matras and Sakel 2007), 'imitation' (Wasserscheidt, in print), 'structural borrowing' (Winford 2003), 'grammatical calquing' (Turk 2013), 'convergence' (can relate to reciprocal influences, Matras 1998; Myers-Scotton 2002), 'code copying' (Johanson 2002) and some more. The term 'interference' is problematic as it is associated with a negative evaluation of 'errors'. As shown in our discussion of example (1) above, the terms 'congruence' and 'convergence' are highly imprecise as it is not clear which structural features they actually refer to. The term tends to trade on a relatively low degree of explicitness and on intuitive understandings of the categories involved. In example (1) we saw 'convergence' mainly in the domain of the ordering of the elements but neither in the make-up of the predicate nor in subject-predicate agreement. As pointed out by many scholars (e.g., Heine and Kuteva 2005), the structures of the replica language are rarely completely identical with the ones in the model language. Recent research has provided clear evidence that transfer is a highly creative process involving some sort of participation of the bilingual individual. Therefore, we should refrain from terms with a static connotation like 'transfer', 'convergence' or 'code-copying'. Instead we opt for Matras' and Sakel's term 'replication' because it reflects the active involvement of the bilingual speakers and their creativity. Accordingly, a fundamental distinction is drawn between MAT(erial) and PAT(tern) replication. MAT replication occurs "when morphological material and its phonological shape from one language is replicated in another language", while PAT replication is at issue "where only the patterns of the other language are replicated, i.e. the organization, distribution and mapping of grammatical or semantic meaning, while the form itself is not borrowed" (Sakel 2007: 15). The basis for PAT is a creative process of "interlingual identification of linguistic subsystems", i.e. a category in the replica language R is identified with a category in the model language M.

As a basis for our study, we will use a general typology of morpho-syntactic PAT which we would like to illustrate on the basis of native varieties of Croatian and Serbian. We will present data from the standard languages, non-standard varieties spoken in Croatia and Serbia, and finally from Molise Slavonic, a seriously endangered minority language spoken in the Molise Region of southern Italy with fewer than 1,000 active speakers the ancestors of whom migrated from Dalmatia in the 16th century. These instances of PAT are the result of historical language contacts and have given rise to syntactic structures firmly entrenched in these varieties. Inspired by Heine and Kuteva (2005) and Kuteva and Heine (2012), we propose a cross-linguistic typology of PAT consisting of three types:
1. contact induced grammaticalization
2. polysemy copying
3. restructuring (also encompassing loss)

These types differ along two dimensions: a) involvement of form-function units vs. syntactic relations, b) degree of grammaticality of the input and the output category. In a next step, we will confront this typology with the data found in our corpus of heritage Croatian and Serbian (see Section 3).

3.1 Contact induced grammaticalization

Grammaticalization is usually understood as a process leading from lexical to grammatical and from grammatical to more grammatical forms. In the case of contact induced grammaticalization, the contact triggers the rise of a grammatical construction in the R language which did not exist in R before. This implies that language contact can be a "stimulus of grammaticalization, but once such a process has been triggered its path is more or less predictable and essentially in accordance with principles of grammaticalization, and [...] these principles are the same irrespective of whether or not language contact is involved" (Heine and Kuteva 2005: 1). Therefore, the grammaticalization process as such is triggered by M, but the output of the process in R need not be the same as in M. This is the case in the development of the preposition *za* 'for' in colloquial Croatian and in the Serbian dialects e.g. of the Banat region (Vojvodina) which replicate the *zu*-infinitive of German.[4] Wiemer and Hansen (2012: 129–131) argue that whereas Slavonic syntax originally prohibits the usage of prepositions with the infinitive, here the preposition *za* came to govern an infinitive which takes over some functions of the German *zu*-infinitive. We are dealing with the grammaticalization path preposition > infinitive marker (further data in Vukojević 2008):

Colloquial Croatian
(2a) *To   je   za   umrijet   od   smijeha.*
     this be.PRS.3SG   for   die.INF   from   laughter.GEN.SG

German
(2b) *Das   ist   zum   Totlachen.*
     this be.PRS.3SG   to.DEF.ART   dead.laugh.INF
     'It is so that you could die laughing.'

The new *za*-construction has a much more restricted usage as compared to the model *zu*-infinitive in German. It is, for example, not used in constructions with complement taking predicates like e.g. *versprechen* + *zu*-infinitive 'to promise to'.

---

4 Popović (1960: 567) argues that in the Dalmatian dialects this structure might have been influenced by the Italian model *Ovo je najboļi način za izgubiti$_{Inf}$ sve – Questo é il migliore modo per perdereInf tutto.*

The crucial moment is that the output of this process is a structure which is more grammaticalized than the input.

A further example of contact induced grammaticalization is from Molise Slavonic spoken in southeastern Italy: Here, the numeral 'one' is grammaticalized into an indefinite article and is used e.g. in generic contexts like in Italian (Breu 2012: 287):

Molise Slavonic
(3) *Na   džokatol   dobri   uči   dita.*
    INDEF.ART   toy   good.NOM.SG   teach.3SG   child

Italian
(3a) *Un   buon   giocattolo   educa   il   bambino.*
     INDEF.ART   good.NOM.SG   toy   teach.3SG   DEF.ART   child
     'A good toy educates the child.'

The concept of contact induced grammaticalization has been developed on the basis of situations of 'usual' language contact involving a long time period of bilingualism across generations. To our knowledge, Błaszczyk (2015) is the first to introduce this concept to a heritage linguistic study. Analysing data from heritage Polish spoken in Germany, she detected minor steps in the grammaticalization of pre-articles which can be explained by the influence of German. In our study, we will try to corroborate the hypothesis that contact induced grammaticalization can take place within two generations.

3.2 Polysemy copying of a grammatical function

As with contact induced grammaticalization, here an existing element develops a new function. The differences, however, are that a) the functions in M and R are identical, b) we are dealing with an abrupt process, and c) the input and output category have the same degree of grammaticality. One of the most basic processes in language contact, traditionally regarded as a type of interference (cf. Weinreich 1953), is a change in the distribution or meaning of a linguistic sign which results from the interlingual identification of that sign with an element from some contact language. A polysemous construction or form F in M is replicated in R by first identifying it with a form G in R in one function and then extending the use of G to one or several other functions b (Wiemer and Wälchli 2012: 27).

An example would be from Molise Slavonic where the imperfect, originally a purely tense-aspect form, developed the function of a conditional. This is a

Model language M: Form F has the functions a+b
Replica language R: Form G has the function a

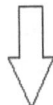

Model language M: Form F has the functions a+b
Replica language R: Form G has the functions a+b

Fig. 1: Polysemy copying

replication of the polysemy pattern of the conditional of colloquial Italian which functioned as the model language. Here is an example from Breu (1999: 247):

Molise Slavonic
(4) Si znadahu ne kjikjarijahu s njime.
    if know.IMPF.1SG not talk.IMPF.1SG with him

Colloquial Italian
(4a) Se lo sapevo non parlavo con lui.
     if it know.IMPF.1SG not talk.IMPF.1SG with him
     'If I had known I wouldn't have talked to him.'

We treat this change as polysemy copying and not as grammaticalization because function a 'past imperfect' and b 'conditional' do not differ as to the degree of grammaticalization.

3.3 Restructuring

Restructuring of a structural pattern involves neither grammaticalization nor polysemy copying; here, no new categories arise. We use the term in the following sense:

> Restructuring involves those kinds of contact-induced change where there are no new grammatical categories created; what happens is simply that, as a result of language contact, an existing structure is rearranged or replaced with some other structure. One type of restructuring involves a loss of grammatical category, that is, a change whereby a language, as a result of contact, loses in categorial distinctions. (Kuteva and Heine 2012: 179)

A well-studied example is the restructuring of complement clauses which took place in the Balkan languages. A semi-finite construction with the complementizer *da* took over the functions of the old infinitive which was gradually being lost. In Bulgarian and Macedonian this process is nearly complete nowadays, whereas in Serbian the old infinitive and the new construction still compete with each other. The new South Slavonic construction consists of the complementizer *da* and a verbal form inflecting for person and number (for more details see Hansen, Wald, and Kolaković in print). It can be called semi-finite as it inflects for person and number but not for tense and mood. Since Sandfeld (1926) it is commonly held that the loss and replacement of the infinitive was triggered by Middle Greek which is known to be the first Balkan language to show this innovation (for details see Joseph 1983). This change is reflected in the variation in Modern Serbian, e.g. in example (5) we have the 'old' construction modal verb plus infinitive and in example (6) the 'new' analytical construction consisting of the complementizer plus a finite verb.

(5) Svi   zajedno   i   zaposleni   i
    all   together   and   employee.NOM.PL   and
    roditelji   i   deca   **moramo**   **raditi**
    parent.NOM.PL   and   child.NOM.PL   must.1PL   work.INF
    na   tome.   (osjosifpancic.rs)
    on   this.LOC.SG
    'Together, meaning the employees, the parents and the children, we have to work on that.'

(6) **Moramo**   **da**   **radimo**   prave   stvari
    must.1PL   COMP   work.1PL   real.ACC.PL   thing.ACC.PL
    na   pravi   način.   (sport26.rs)
    on   real.ACC.SG   way
    'We have to do real things.'

Whereas in Standard Serbian both constructions co-exist, in the Torlak dialects spoken in the Eastern Serbian-Macedonian border region, the *da*-construction has completely replaced the infinitive (s. Sobolev 1998: 60) which would be a case of restructuring leading to the loss of a morpho-syntactic category.

4 Pilot studies Hansen, Romić, and Kolaković (2013) and Romić (2016)

As there is a deplorable lack of data, we conducted pilot studies in order to get a first overall impression of the processes of change which have affected the language system of Croatian and Serbian as spoken in Germany. We used a qualitative corpus containing maximally natural production data of the speech of second generation speakers born in Germany. The corpus was compiled by Daniel Romić. These natural data from qualitative semi-structured hidden interviews were complemented by a minor set of written production data consisting of three essays written in a language class for heritage speakers at U Regensburg. We are aware of the fact that the latter does not fulfil the requirements of a reliable data source. Therefore these data are exclusively used for additional independent evidence.

The primary criterion for choosing an interviewee apart from having been born in Germany or having emigrated before the age of five was active bilingualism, understood functionally as the ability to produce texts in both languages and switching from one language to the other, when it is necessary. The interviewees had not lived in one of the countries of former Yugoslavia for a longer time and had attended school exclusively in Germany. Both parents immigrated to Germany and a variety of Štokavian was used as the family languages. The interviewees had no formal training in BCS at university or adult education centres ('Volkshochschule') with the exception of the so-called 'additional classes' ('dopunska nastava'). We deliberately refrained from control of the education background factor and interviewed people both with higher education and without. We recruited the interviewees by snowball sampling as used in qualitative sociological research. The interviews were conducted by Daniel Romić who, being a heritage speaker of Croatian himself, contacted his acquaintances which helped to create an informal atmosphere and reduced the risk of the known problem of yeah-saying or social desirability bias. Social desirability bias refers to the fact that in interviews people will often try to present themselves in the best possible light which can lead to a language use they assume to be in accordance with expected standard norms. All interviews were carried out in maximally natural settings like private houses, bars or restaurants. For a more detailed description of the corpus and a sociolinguistic analysis of the data we refer to Romić (2016).

Tab. 1: Socio-linguistic profiles of interviewees

Transcript á 35–100 minutes (tokens)	Age	Sex	Citizenship/ Country of birth	Educational Background
T 1 (3.354)	33	male	HR/DE	Basic secondary (Hauptschule)
T 2 (2.451)	32	male	SRB/DE	General secondary (Realschule) plus Vocational training (Geselle)
T 3 (3.561)	27	male	HR/DE	Graduate degree

Tab. 1 (continued)

Transcript á 35–100 minutes (tokens)	Age	Sex	Citizenship/ Country of birth	Educational Background
T 4 (1.038)	30	male	SRB/DE	General secondary (Realschule) plus Vocational training (Geselle)
T 5 (2.821)	26	female	HR/DE	Graduate degree
T 6 (4.662)	24	female	HR/DE	General secondary (Realschule)
T 7	30	female	BH/BH (emigrated as toddler)	Basic secondary (Realschule) plus Vocational training (Geselle)
T 8 (3.298)	32	male	SRB/DE	Basic secondary (Realschule) plus Vocational training (Geselle)
T 9 (2.945)	31	female	DE/DE	Graduate degree
T 10 (2.139)	25	female	SRB/DE	Graduate degree
T 11 (2.161)	31	female	HR/DE	Graduate degree

Tab. 2: Socio-linguistic profiles of the authors of the essays

Essay	Age	Sex	Citizenship/ Country of birth	Educational Background
E 1	20	female	SRB/DE	University student
E 2	20	female	SRB/Canadian (emigrated as toddler)	University student
E 3	26	male	DE/DE	University student

Before we present the data, we have to address the question of the so-called baseline of comparison (henceforth BL). In other words, if we want to detect contact induced changes in the syntactic system of heritage Serbian and Croatian we have to make clear which variety or varieties of BCS we are going to compare our data with. As heritage speakers are not exposed to the standard languages through schooling, heritage languages should generally be compared with spoken language (Polinsky 1995: 373). In contrast to Russian which shows relatively weak regional variation, BCS is divided into three national standards. Apart from that, there are major differences between regional dialects especially within Croatia. A major problem for the identification of the baseline of comparison specifically for Croatian and Serbian, however, is the considerable lack of available data and empirical descriptions of spoken standard variants. Therefore, we will rely on different sources of linguistic descriptions in order to determine the baseline. Apart from the grammar handbooks which reflect the codified standard norms, we also draw from dialectological studies and especially from stylistic handbooks and interactive on-line resources dedicated to language cultivation (Croatian *jezični savjetnici*, Serbian *jezički savetnici*).[5] These contain discussions of 'good' and 'bad' language use and provide us with information about variation in actual language use. We are especially interested in the language structures which are evaluated negatively and therefore banned from the standard norms.

5 Syntactic structures affected by PAT in heritage Croatian and Serbian

The corpus data described in the previous section were analysed to determine which syntactic categories are affected by PAT and which types of PAT are attested. Due to the small size of the corpus we will restrict ourselves to a purely qualitative analysis and, therefore, will refrain from any frequency data. In the first step, we identify syntactic structures affected by PAT which helps us to find out which constructions are more susceptible to pattern replication and which are rather impermeable to replication. As replication is based on an act of interlingual identification we try to identify structures in the model language, i.e. we are looking for possible equivalents in German which can be assumed to have functioned as the source model. In the second step, we determine the type of PAT and discuss the validity of the typology presented in Section 2.

5.1 Valence and linking

In describing the combinatorial properties of verbs we must address the association between the semantic event participants or frame elements required by the meaning of the predicate and the morpho-syntactic realization of these frame elements (Fried and Östman 2004: 40). As the frame elements are directly linked to the lexical meaning of the verb they are too specific for drawing generalizations about their morpho-syntactic encoding. Therefore, the lexico-syntactic

---

5 e.g. bujicarijeci.com, hrvatskiplus.org, maturski.net, hrvatskijezik.eu, kakosepise.com.

representation of verbs consists of "two layers of information: a frame and a valence. The frame captures all the idiosyncratic information needed for our understanding of the meaning of a given predicate. The valence in contrast represents the corresponding event pattern in a highly schematized form, and though it represents a subset of frame elements, it is not necessarily fully predictable from the frame" (Fried and Östman 2004: 42–43). Whereas the valence determines the set of morpho-syntactically relevant frame-level participants, the associations between these participants and their morphosyntactic expression is represented in so-called linking constructions. In the following we will discuss some cases of changes in the syntactic properties of verbs which are triggered by the identification with German model verbs. We will try to determine whether we are dealing with changes in the frame semantics which would be a syntactic change mediated by lexical change or with the replication of an abstract linking construction.

At least, four test persons from our corpus used selected predicates taking complements in the Accusative case in a way that deviates from BL usage (Romić 2016). These are:

(7) […] **napravila sam Croaticum** […] to je
 make.PST.SG.F AUX.1SG Croaticum it be.3SG
 kao Sprachkurs. (T 5)
 like language-class
 'I attended the Croaticum, it is a sort of language class.'

(8) […] sad **pravi majstorsku školu**
 now make.3SG vocational.ACC.SG school.ACC.SG
 subotom. (T 2)
 saturdays
 'Now he attends the vocational school on Saturdays.'

(9) ima nekih koji
 have.3SG some.GEN.PL which.NOM.PL
 naravno posle hauptschule mogu ići
 of.course after Hauptschule can.3PL go.INF
 kao **mittlere Reife** da **prave.** (T 5)
 like mittlere Reife COMP do.3PL
 'There are people who after having finished 'Hauptschule' can continue school to get 'Mittlere Reife' (General Certificate of Secondary Education)'.

The sentences (7)–(9) contain the abstract verb *praviti* and its perfective counterpart *napraviti* which can best be translated as 'to make'. In contrast to English *to make* and, for us more relevant, the German verb *machen*, native Croatian and Serbian *(na-)praviti* shows more semantic restrictions on the level of frame elements. The Serbian Valency Dictionary Djordjević and Engel (2013: 448–449) describes the first frame element as *Agent*, and the second as *AFF* (*ected entity*) with the specifications *eff* and *mut*. The former represents the role that the entity comes into existence or disappears, and the latter denotes that the entity changes. The semantic role *effected entity* is illustrated by the uses of the verb *napraviti* with the noun *kolač* 'cake' or *galama* 'noise' occupying the slot of the second argument:

Standard Serbian
(10) Moram   još   brzo   **napraviti**   kolač.
     must.1SG still quickly make.INF   cake
     'I still have to bake a cake quickly.'

Similarly, the Croatian Valence dictionary CROVALLEX assigns the semantic role or how the authors call it *functor* PAT(ient) to the second frame element.

napraviti (nàpraviti) fin 83

[1] napraviti (nàpraviti)$_1$ ≈ **izraditi, stvoriti, sastaviti**
-frame: **AGT$_{0\_or\_1}^{obl}$ PAT$_4^{obl}$ ORIG$_{od+2}^{typ}$**
-example: Vreću sam napravio od starog šatorskog krila
-class: **build/create/prepare**

[2] napraviti (nàpraviti)$_2$ ≈ **počiniti, uzrokovati**
-frame: **AGT$_{0\_or\_1}^{obl}$ PAT$_4^{obl}$**
-example: Račanova vlada je napravila veliki gaf
-class: **accomplish**

Crovallex (accessed 16 May 2015)

Fig. 2: *napraviti* in Crovallex

As *praviti* obligatorily invokes the frame element *effected* or *affected entity* it comes as no surprise that in the collocation with the lexeme *kurs* 'course' which corresponds to the context in the heritage examples (7–9) it renders the meaning 'to create' and not 'to attend' as can be seen in this example taken from the Serbian web corpus srWaC:

(11) U   prethodnom   projektu   radili   smo
     in   previous.LOC.SG project.LOC.SG   work.PST.PL.M   AUX.1PL
     za   Srbiju,   kreirali   digitalnu
     for   Serbia.ACC.SG   create.PST.PL.M   digital.ACC.SG
     biblioteku, **pravili**   on-line   kurseve
     library.ACC.SG makePST.PL.M   course.ACC.PL

za digitalizaciju. (yc.rs)
for ditigitalization.ACC.SG

'In the previous project, we worked for the Serbia, we created a digital library and worked out on-line courses for digitilization.'

This indicates that in baseline varieties *(na-)praviti*[6] has a second frame element with the representation *effected* or *affected entity*. In examples (7), (8) and (9), however, the slot for the second argument is filled with nouns denoting educational processes or institutions in the sense that the agent attended a school or course. Predicates denoting processes of visiting an institution also have two frame elements, but they differ in their semantic roles. The first frame element encoded as the subject in the Nominative has the role of a 'learner' which is much less agent-like and comes closer to an experiencer, because the participant does not create or effect the element occupying the slot of second frame element. The entity of the second frame element does not undergo any changes depending on the activity of the first frame element. If we want to explain the change in the syntactic behaviour of the verb *(na-)praviti* in heritage language, we need to look for a corresponding structure in the source language which functions as the model. We would argue that this new structure developed because the bilingual speakers identified the verb *(na-)praviti* with its German counterpart *machen*. If we analyse the entry of *machen* in the German Valence dictionary E-Valbu we see that the first meaning *machen* 1 'etwas herstellen' semantically coincides with the meaning of *(na-)praviti*. Cf. the example in the screenshot of the dictionary entry:

machen 1 (lesartspezifische Angaben) [Artikelkopf]

Strukturbeispiel:	jemand/etwas macht etwas
Im Sinne von:	jemand/etwas lässt etwas durch Handlungen entstehen; herstellen, anfertigen
Satzbauplan:	K_{sub} . K_{akk}
Beispiele:	(1) Soll ich uns eine Tasse Kaffee machen?
	(2) Jeden Frühling machen die Vögel ihre Nester in unserer Hecke.
	(3) Ich habe nach einem Rezept meiner Großmutter Glühwein gemacht.
	(4) Muss jede Generation von Wissenschaftlern eine neue Theorie machen?

E-Valbu (accessed 16 May 2015)

Fig. 3: *machen* 1 in E-Valbu

---

[6] There are some differences in the use of *(na-)praviti* in Croatian and Serbian which, however, are not relevant for our discussion.

The entry contains the meaning definition 'someone / something brings something to existence; produce, create' and illustrative examples with the following arguments occupying the position of the second valence slot: *Kaffee* 'coffee', *Nester* 'nests', *Glühwein* 'mulled wine', and *neue Theorie* 'new theory'. We explain the rise of the new usage of *(na-)praviti* in the sense 'to attend, to complete' as in example (7)–(9) by the replication of a further meaning of *machen* labelled in E-Valbu as *machen 9*:

machen 9 (lesartspezifische Angaben) [Artikelkopf]

Strukturbeispiel:	jemand macht etwas
Im Sinne von:	jemand absolviert etwas
Satzbauplan:	K$_{sub}$, K$_{akk}$
Beispiele:	(1) Wann machst du deine Fahrprüfung? (2) Im nächsten Semester mache ich mein Examen in Germanistik und Anglistik.
Belegungsregeln:	• K$_{sub}$: NP im Nom/ProP im Nom/GWS • K$_{akk}$: NP im Akk/ProP im Akk/GWS
Passivkonstruktionen:	Werden-Passiv werden: (3) Das Saarland führt als erstes westliches Bundesland das achtjährige Gymnasium ein, an dem nach zwölf statt 13 Schuljahren Abitur gemacht werden kann. (die tageszeitung, 23.11.2000, S. 6)

E-Valbu (accessed 16 May 2015)

Fig. 4: *machen 9* in E-Valbu

This meaning described as 'to complete' allows for a different set of frame elements in the second valence slot. Here, we find nouns denoting educational processes like *Fahrprüfung* 'driving test' or *Examen in Germanistik und Anglistik* 'exam in German and English studies'.

Using the terms proposed by Fried and Östman (2004) we could argue that this pattern replication triggered by the cross-linguistic identification of the verbs *(na-)praviti* and *machen* exclusively affects the lexical level of the frame elements. There are no changes in the minimal valence; i.e. as in the baseline varieties, *(na-)praviti* has two valence slots associated with the frame elements labelled in the same way for the status +distinguished argument and -distinguished argument. Neither are there any changes in the linking with the morphological level. Both in baseline BCS and in heritage usage *(na-)praviti* merges with the same linking constructions; i.e. the first valence is encoded as the subject in the Nominative and the second as the direct object in Accusative case. The change which has taken place is best to be explained as the copying of a polysemy pattern on the level of the frame elements which complies with our definition polysemy copying as defined in Section 2:

Model language German: Verb *machen* has the meanings 1 and 9
Replica language Croatian/Serbian: Verb *(na-)praviti* has the meaning 1

⇩

Model language German: Verb *machen* has the meaning 1 and 9
Replica language Croatian/Serbian: Verb *(na-)praviti* has the meaning 1 and 9

Fig. 5: *(na-)praviti* and polysemy copying

Although they look similar, we would argue that the case of the specific use of the verb *početi* in example (12) slightly differs from *(na-)praviti*.

(12) Deca   imaju   mogućnost   da   **počnu**   još
     child.NOM.PL have.3PL   possibility COMP   start.3PL   yet
     jedan   **jezik**   u   školi. (E 1)
     one.ACC.SG.M language.ACC.SG.M   in   school.LOC.SG
     'The Children have the possibility to start learning another language in school.'

Serbian and Croatian *početi* and their German counterparts *anfangen/beginnen* are labile verbs which means that they participate in both transitive and intransitive argument structure without any change in its formal marking as can be illustrated by the following German sentences (own example):

(13a) Er   begann   die   Arbeit.
      he   begin.PST.3SG   the   work
      'He started the job.'

(13b) Die   Arbeit   begann.
      the   work   begin.PST.3SG
      'The job started.'

Mainly due to this specific property, all three verbs are highly polysemious: Djordjević and Engel (2013: 391–393) list seven meanings for *početi* and E-Valbu ten for *anfangen* and eleven for *beginnen*. *Početi* and *anfangen/beginnen* show a largely identical polysemy pattern and a very similar frame and valence structure. One of the very few differences between *početi* in baseline varieties and German *anfangen* and *beginnen* can be seen in the following contexts involving non-processual entities as second arguments (*početi* 3 in Djordjević and Engel 2013: 391, *anfangen* and *beginnen* are interchangeable).

(14)   Mario   begann   mit   dem
       Mario   begin.PST.3SG   with   DEF.ART.DAT.SG
       großen   Schrank.
       big.DAT.SG   wardrobe

(14a) Mario   begann   den   großen
       Mario   begin.PST.3SG   DEF.ART.ACC.SG   big.ACC.SG
       Schrank.
       Wardrobe

(14b) Mario   je   počeo   s
       Mario   AUX.3SG   begin.PST.SG.M   with
       velikim   ormarom.
       big.INS.SG   wardrobe.INS.SG

(14c) *Mario   je   počeo
       Mario   AUX.3SG   begin.PST.SG.M
       veliki   ormar.
       big.ACC.SG   wardrobe

In contrast to the verb pair *(na-)praviti – machen*, there is no difference in the set of frame elements: both *početi* and *anfangen/beginnen* have a semantic structure where the first frame element is an agent and the second a non-processual or even concrete entity as in the case of *Schrank/ormar* 'wardrobe'. The difference, however, is the linking with the morpho-syntactic level: whereas *anfangen/ beginnen* allows for the Accusative or the prepositional phrase with *mit* 'with', baseline *početi* 3 is restricted to the Accusative. In the sentence example (12) the bilinguals replicated the morpho-syntactic linking of the German model. In BL varieties one would expect either an encoding with an explicit verb of learning in the infinitive like *počnu učiti jezik* or the linking with a prepositional phrase as in *počnu s još jednim jezikom*. We would like to emphasize that no new meaning is added to the inventory of the replica language, neither a new linking construction. Instead, the bilinguals replace the linking construction by another one which matches the morpho-syntactic structure of the model verb in German. Therefore, we are dealing with an instance of restructuring. Further examples of this type of PAT are found with the verb *igrati* 'to play' and the existential verb *imati*:

(15)   *Ima*   *ima*   *igraju*   **igraju**   **hrvatsku**
       have.3SG have.3SG   play.3PL   play.3PL   Croatian.ACC.SG
       ligu. (T 3)
       league.ACC.SG
       'Yes, there is one, yes, they play, they play in the Croatian league.'

In contexts of German sporting reports, especially in headlines, one can find the following equivalent:

(15a) *Sie* **spielen erste Liga**.
 they play.3PL first.ACC.SG league

Here, the verb *igrati* is identified with German *spielen* which in this meaning allows the encoding of the frame element 'a group of sports teams competing against each other' either in a prepositional phrase as in *Sie spielen in der kroatischen Liga* or in a direct object in the Accusative as in example (15a).[7] A similar shift in case marking is found in the use of the existential verb *ima* which is identified with German *es gibt*:

(16) *tamo u... ima njemačku poštu*
 there at have.3SG German.ACC.SG post-office.ACC.SG
 ili Telekom u Zagrebu. (T 5)
 or Telekom in Zagreb.LOC.SG
 'There at... in Zagreb there is a German post office or Telekom.'

Whereas in baseline use, *ima* as an existential verb requires Nominative if the noun denotes a countable object in singular (*ima [njemačka pošta]*$_{Nom}$) and in all other cases genitive (Ivić, M. 1981: 23), the speaker in example (16) replicates the linking pattern of the German translational equivalent *es gibt* which takes the Accusative (*es gibt [eine deutsche Post]*$_{Acc}$).

To sum up, the instances of PAT found in the area of valence and linking constructions presented in this section can be analysed either as polysemy copying or restructuring. We could not find any case of contact induced grammaticalization. We have shown that all of these contact induced changes are directly linked to lexical entries and do not affect the inventory of schematic syntactic mechanisms. The changes coincide with what Silva-Corvalán (1998: 231–233) calls 'lexico-syntactic calques'.

5.2 Non-canonical subject constructions

In this section, we look into the instantiation of the arguments on the level of the subject phrase. Some scholars claim that heritage varieties of Serbian and Croatian are characterised by an overuse of personal pronouns in subject

---

[7] The BL use can be illustrated by the dictionary entry in Djordjević and Engel (2013: 143) where *igrati* 4 in the position of the second valence only allows for arguments like *fudbal* 'football'.

position which they explain with a resetting of the pro-drop parameter (Dimitrijević-Savić 2008: 65–66; Raecke 2007b: 387). We will neither corroborate nor refute this claim because we simply lack empirically valid studies on the use of pronouns in spoken baseline varieties. A first superficial glance at the spoken data in Hinrichs and Hinrichs (1995) and the corpora located at the University of Tübingen[8] shows that subject pronouns are more frequently used than in written standards. Therefore, we are not in a position to evaluate our heritage data.

In our corpus, we did not find any specific cases of the encoding of canonical subjects understood as subject phrases instantiating the first valence which are marked for Nominative and which control agreement with the predicate. However, what we did find were interesting cases of the instantiation of non-canonical, i.e. non-nominative subjects. The first pattern we would like to discuss involves experiencer constructions where the first valence is instantiated in an oblique case. In our data we found an example of the following type which deviates from the baseline equivalent given here in ex. (17):

(17) **Njemu**   je   još   više   sram. (T 3)
     he.DAT   be.3SG   more   more   shame

Base line usage:
(17a) **Njega** je   još   više   sram.
      he.ACC   be.3SG   more   more   shame
      'He is even more embarrassed.'

Here, the experiencer is not encoded in the Accusative as is the rule with this type of predicate in native BCS. If the bilingual speaker uses the Dative case instead, we can certainly assume that he or she is replicating the German pattern which also uses the Dative.

German translation:
(17b) **Ihm**   ist   das   noch   peinlicher.
      he.DAT   be.3SG   that   still   more.embarrassing

The bilingual speaker, however, does not create a new experiencer construction, but extends the use of the existing dative experiencer which is used with the majority of evaluative predicates (e.g. *ugodno mi je* 'it is pleasant to me'). As a matter of fact, only a small number of these predicates requires the Accusative. These include predicates of nominal origin like *sram* 'shame' used in example (17).

---

[8] Corpora of the Tübinger SFB 441 (http://u-002-ssfbv001.uni-tuebingen.de/sfb441/corpora/index-de.html): 'Bosnian Interviews' (59.138 tokens) and 'Novosadski korpus of Spoken Language 1980/2000' (30.145 tokens).

The next case we would like to discuss concerns the instantiation of the non-overt subject (big PRO) in sentences involving control constructions. One of our Croatian interviewees said:

(18) On   me   ***forsira*** PRO   ***govoriti***   hrvatski. (T 5)
      he   I.ACC force.3SG   speak.INF   Croatian.ACC.SG
      'He insists on me speaking Croatian.'

The peculiarity is the use of the infinitive instead of a *da*-clause which would not only in native Serbian, but also in Croatian be the expected form (ex. 18a). As there are no entries in the valence dictionaries, we queried the verb in Croatian Web Corpus hrWaC 2.0. Without going into detail, we found that the use of *forsirati* plus infinitive is extremely rare.[9] Obviously, the speaker has replicated the corresponding structure of German which in this context uses the infinitive (according to E-Valbu, *zwingen* allows a complement clause with *dass* only with the correlative element *dazu*).

Base line usage:
(18a) On   me   ***forsira***   da   ***govorim***
      he   I.ACC force.3SG   COMP   speak.1SG
      hrvatski.
      Croatian.ACC.SG

German translation:
(18b) Er   zwingt   mich   Kroatisch   ***zu sprechen.***
      he   force.3SG I.ACC   Croatian   to speak.INF

As to our findings in the area of subject encoding, we treat the contact induced changes in examples (17) and (18) as instances of restructuring. As we have only single examples, we cannot say whether this specific feature is linked to the lexical entries *sram* and *forsirati* or whether we are dealing with the replication of an abstract linking construction independent of these lexical entries.

5.3 Prepositional phrases

We also find instances of PAT in the area of prepositional phrases. These are extensions into new functions, i.e. polysemy copying, on the one hand, and

---

9 hrWaC 2.0 The query [lemma="forsirati" & !tag="Vmn*"] [] {0,2}[tag="Vmn"] within <s/> gave 171 hits, (0.1 WpM), nearly none of them, however, displayed the model *forsirati* + Inf.

shift in the use of cases, on the other. The first can be illustrated on the basis of example (19) where the bilingual extends the use of the preposition *kroz* which is restricted to inanimate entities to a human referent. Whereas in BL Croatian *kroz* is restricted to a spatial (*kroz šumu* 'through the forest') and a temporal meaning (*kroz 3 meseca* 'in three months')[10] here it is used in an instrumental sense. The basis is the identification with the German equivalent *durch*.

(19) [...] *samo mama je* **kroz Nas**
only mum AUX.3SG through we.ACC
naučila Njemački. (T 6)
learn.PST.SG.F German.ACC.SG

Baseline usage:[11]
(19a) *mama je* **od nas** *naučila Njemački.* (T 6)
mum AUX.3SG from we.ACC learn.PST.SG.F German.ACC.SG

German translation:
(19b) *mama hat* **durch uns** *Deutsch gelernt.* (T6)
mum AUX.3SG through we.ACC German PTCP.learn.PTCP

(20) (...) **kroz** *taj* **studium** *uđem*
through this.ACC.SG study enter.1SG
u gehobene Dienst. (T5)
in intermediate service
German: *durch [dieses Studium]*$_{Acc}$
'By this training I will be promoted to the intermediate service.'

(21) [...] *al sam još bolje*
but AUX.1SG still better
naučila **kroz to**
learn.PST.SG.F through this
jer (*sam od malena uvijek bila kod babe i kod djede*). (T 5)
because
German translation: *dadurch, dass*
'I learnt even more, as from childhood, I have been visiting Grandpa and Grandma.'

Example (21) is interesting because the German model is structurally different from the replica which shows the creativity of the bilingual speaker: *kroz to jer* is

---

10 see Hrvatski jezični portal, http://hjp.novi-liber.hr/.
11 see the dictionary entry in Djordjević and Engel (2013: 143)

made up of a preposition, a deictic adjectival pronoun and a conjunction whereas *dadurch dass* contains a deictic adverbial pronoun.

The second type of PAT concerns instances where the preposition has the same function, but comes to govern a new case. There are several such instances attested in the transcript of the Croatian speaker T3. Whereas in BL Croatian, the preposition *protiv* 'against' exclusively governs the genitive, he uses it with the Accusative. He must have replicated the government pattern of the German equivalent *gegen* + Accusative.

(22) i   dobili   jednu   jednu   utakmicu
     and   get.PST.PL.M   one.ACC.SG   one.ACC.SG   match.ACC.SG
     i [...] **protiv**   Mađare   dva-dva   odigrali. (T 3)
     and   against   Hungarian.ACC.PL   2:2   play.PST.PL.M
     'We had one match against the Hungarians, we played 2:2.'
     Baseline usage: *protiv Mađarā*$_{Gen}$
     German translation: *gegen [die Ungarn]*$_{Acc}$

The same holds for the use of *preko* which in BL varieties governs the Genitive being replaced by *preko* + Accusative modelled on German *über* + Accusative.

(23) ehm   gledaju   prvi   hrvatski.
     erm   watch.3PL   first.ACC.SG   Croatian.ACC.SG
     HRT-jedan.   To   dobije   **preko**
     HRT.ACC.SG   this   get.3SG   via
     taj   **kabel.** (T 3)
     this.ACC/NOM.SG   cable.ACC/NOM.SG
     'erm, they watch First Croatian Television, HRT1. One gets it via cable.'
     Base line usage: *preko [toga kabla]*$_{Gen}$
     German translation: *über [Kabel]*$_{Acc}$

A slightly different case is represented by the use of the preposition *na* with nouns denoting languages. In this context, even four test persons (T 3, T 6, T 11, T 12) used an adjectival form in the Nominative (or Accusative) as *na njemački*. In BL varieties, the preposition *na* in non-directional contexts requires the Locative case *na njemačkom*.

(24) ja   ne   moram   prevest   nešto   da
     I   not   must.1SG   translate.INF   something   COMP
     si   prvo   **na**   **njemački**   mislim. (T 3)
     REFL.DAT   first   on   German.NOM.SG.M   think.1SG
     'I don't have to translate, that ... I first think in German.'

(25) ja   psujem   uvijek   **na**   **hrvatski.** (T3)
    I   curse.1SG always   on   Croatian.NOM.SG.M
    'I always curse in Croatian.'

(26) oni   su   dosta   dugo   u   Njemačkoj
    they   be.3PL   enough   long   in   Germany.LOC.SG.F
    pa   im   brže   ponekad   ili   lakše
    and   they.DAT quicker   sometimes or   easier
    nešto   objasniti **na**   **njemački.** (T 11)
    something   explain.INF on   German.NOM.SG.M
    'They've been in Germany for a pretty long time, so it's sometimes faster or easier to explain something to them in German'.

This structure is somehow modelled on the German phrase which consists of the preposition *auf* plus a non-inflecting adjective (*auf Deutsch, auf Kroatisch*), but the morpho-syntactic structures in both languages are different. The German language names differ from the heritage structure because the former has a zero ending, and the latter the default ending of the Nominative Singular Masculine: *Kroatisch-Ø* vs. *hrvatsk-i$_{Nom/Acc.Sg.M}$*. This case nicely illustrates the limits of PAT: the heritage speakers do not create a new morphological form which would be something like *hrvatsk-Ø*, but match the German adjective containing a zero-ending with the default ending of the Croatian adjective declensions which happens to be the form of the Nominative Singular Masculine.

Summarizing our data concerning prepositional phrases, we are dealing with either polysemy copying or with restructuring. In all cases, we see a clear link with lexical entries.

5.4 Word order

A major number of instances of PAT concerns word order rules. The authors who claim that heritage varieties of Serbian and Croatian show convergence with the dominating language (i.e. English or German) usually refer to changes in word order patterns (e.g. Raecke 2007a, 2007b). In the following we will show some word order patterns which deviate from base line usage and will discuss if they can be assumed to have developed under German influence. We will argue, however, that even in these cases we see considerable differences in the serialization between the heritage clause and the assumed German model. First, we will discuss specific cases affecting the word order of clitics and, second, we will then present some peculiarities in word order of the verbal phrase.

5.4.1 The syntax of Clitics

Clitics in Serbian and Croatian are special. They have morphonological properties of both word forms and affixes. Syntactically they are characterized by specific word order rules setting them apart from other phrases with the same argument function. Clitics underlie the second position effect (2P principle) which means that they usually attach to the first element in the clause, either to the first constituent or the first accentuated phonological word. The 2P principle is further complicated by the fact that certain elements cannot host a clitic; e.g. many conjunctions and so-called heavy constituents function as barriers in the sense that they trigger a shift of the clitic to the third position. A second syntactic mechanism is the template principle according to which clitics have to appear in a cluster with a fixed serialization. Although there exists a large body of literature on the syntax of BCS clitics, we know very little about variation in spoken BL varieties.[12]

Violations of the 2P principle are relatively rare which means that the second generation speakers of our test corpus still have a general command of it. We found some cases of a clitic third position where the first element in the clause does not function as a barrier, i.e. we are not dealing with heavy constituents or elements which in BL varieties trigger clitic third position. This is especially found in essay E2 and in the speech of test person T6:

(27) *Ljudi često **se** plaše stvari*
people.NOM.PL often REFL fear.3PL thing.GEN.PL
koje ne poznavaju i koje
which.ACC.PL not know.3PL and which.ACC.PL
su njima strane. (E 2)
be.3PL they.DAT foreign.NOM.PL
'Often people are afraid of things they do not know and which are foreign to them.'

(28) *[A: Mentalitet je drugačiji.]*
A: The mentality is different.
B: Je [...] sto posto i to
be.3SG hundred percent and this
*drži **te**.* (T 6)
hold.3SG you.ACC.SG
'A: The mentality is different. B: Yes, for sure it is and this holds you.'

---

[12] To fill this gap, we have started a special research project dedicated to the "Microvariation in pronominal and verbal enclitics in Bosnian, Croatian and Serbian. Empirical studies on spoken language, including dialects and heritage languages" (HA 2659/6-1, funded by DFG 2015–2018).

(29) tako   da   su   pjevači   [...] i
     so   COMP   be.3PL   singer.NOM.PL   and
     koncerti   i   ima   je/jedan   kao [...]
     concert.NOM.PL and   have.3SG   one   like
     loša   osoba   koja   hoće
     bad.NOM.SG   person.NOM.SG   which.NOM.SG   want.3SG
     ih   srediti. (T 6)
     they.ACC   fix.INF

'So that there are singers and concerts and there is one bad person who wants to kill them.'

(30) [znaš li zašto su tvoji roditelji u njemačku došli? Recimo tvoj tata.]
     Da   bude   **mu**   bolje   u   životu. (T 6)
     COMP   AUX.3SG   he.DAT   better   in   life.LOC.SG

[Do you know why your parents came to Germany? For example, your father?] 'He wanted to have a better life.'

In example (27) the first element in the clause is a bare accentuated noun which fulfils the function of the subject of the clause. In base line varieties, subjects of this type are obligatory hosts for clitics. The following examples (29) and (30) are even clearer because the complementizer *da* or the relativizer *koji* always trigger 2P (cf. Radanović-Kocić 1988: 99–101). These violations of 2P do not lead to a word order similar to German and, thus, cannot be explained by a straightforward replication of a corresponding category.

Some of the test persons show violations of the template principle; in example (31) the clitics do not cluster but occur in different positions of the clause (should be *su se*):

(31) Družile   se   dobro   ali   one   **su**
     be.friends.PST.PL.F   REFL   well   but   they   AUX.3PL
     neke   **se**   vratile   pa   ona   ostala.[...](T 9)
     some   REFL   return.PST.PL.F   but   she   stay.PST.SG.F

'They were friends, but some went back while she stayed.'

The following examples are interesting as the speaker T 9 does not only violate the cluster principle but also the morphological haplology rule of the standard language which requires the deletion of the tense auxiliary third person singular *je* if co-occurring with the reflexive *se* (*je* + *se* > *se*).

(32) Ahm,   kad   **je**   završio   **se**   rat
     erm   when   AUX.3SG   finish.PST   REFL   war

> *prestali   su   ić   tamo.* (T 9)
> stop.PST.PL   AUX.3PL   go.INF   there
> 'Erm, when the war was finished they no longer went there.'
> Base line usage: *Ahm, kad **se** završio rat prestali su (.) ić tamo [...]*

(33) *nije   niko   ozdravio   od*
    NEG.AUX.3SG   nobody   get.well.PST   from
    *njiha [...]   al   smirijo   **je**   **se***
    they.GEN   but   reconcile.PST.SG.M   AUX.3SG   REFL
    sa   ocom. (T 9)
    with   father.INST
    'None of them got well, but he made it up with his father.'
    Base line usage: *al smirijo **se** sa ocom.*

Further peculiarities concern the use of the full form of the personal pronoun instead of the clitic. In BL, full pronouns are used in the context of contrastive focus which is not the case with the pronoun *njima* in example (27) above repeated here for convenience:

(27) *Ljudi   često   **se**   plaše   stvari*
    people.NOM.PL   often   REFL   fear.3PL   thing.GEN.PL
    koje   ne   poznavaju   i   koje
    which.ACC.PL   not   know.3PL   and   which.ACC.PL
    *su   **njima**   strane.* (E 2)
    be.3PL   they.DAT   foreign.NOM.PL
    'Often people are afraid of things they do not know and which are foreign to them.'
    Base line usage: *[...] koje su im strane.*

All these uses of clitics illustrated in the examples (27) to (33) deviate from BL varieties, but the question is whether we are dealing with a type of PAT. As a matter of fact, it is difficult to find a corresponding element of cross-linguistic identification in the model language, as German has no 2P clitics comparable to the ones of BCS. It also does not have the distinction between full and clitic forms of pronouns and auxiliaries. Therefore, we would argue that we are dealing with the beginning of the loss of a syntactic category.

5.5 Agreement

In several transcripts of oral speech we find deviations in the area of agreement marking. These can either be explained as slips of the tongue triggered by spontaneous language use, or as first signs of the erosion of the category. All types of phrases carrying agreement marking can be affected, and we find mismatches in all three agreement categories, i.e. in gender, case and number.

The most salient one is probably the mismatch within nominal phrases. In example (34), the controlling noun is in the neuter gender (*vreme*) and the target demonstrative pronoun in the masculine gender (*taj*).

(34) i   na   **taj**   vreme   šta   da
     and   on   this.ACC.SG.M   time.ACC.SG.N   what   COMP
     uspijem?   weißt   schon. (T 4)
     manage.1SG   know$_{German}$ already$_{German}$
     'What can I do in this time, *you know what I mean* (German).'

Or mismatches in case: in BL varieties the preposition *na* governs either the Accusative or Locative case whereas in example (35) both cases are mixed (*jednoj*$_{prep}$ and *ruku*$_{acc}$). This usage seems to be based on a conflation of the text structuring phrase *u jednu ruku* 'on the one hand' with the local phrase *na jednoj strani* 'on the one side'.

(35) onda   kaže   na   **jednoj**   **ruku**   isto
     then   say.3SG   on   one.LOC.SG.F   one.ACC.SG.F   same
     što   nisam   bio   uvek. (T 4)
     what   NEG.AUX.1.SG   be.PST   always
     'then she says the same on the one hand that I was never there.'

A further instance of a mismatch in case (Nominative vs. Accusative) is found in the nominal phrase *one turski krovove* in example (36). The demonstrative *one* and the head *krovove* are in the Accusative plural whereas the modifying adjective *turski* is in the Nominative Plural.

(36) čekaj   po ...   po   Bausubstanz   nije
     wait.IMP   on   on   basic.structure   NEG.AUX.3SG
     naše   kuće   ne   prave   se   s
     our.NOM.PL   house.NOM.PL   NEG   make.3PL   REFL   with
     ovakvim   sa   ćoškovima   ne   i   kod   nas
     such.INS.PL   with   corner.INS.PL   NEG   and   at   we.GEN
     su   **one**   **turski**   **krovove**. (T 4)
     be.3PL   this.ACC.PL   Turkish.NOM.PL.M   roof.ACC.PL
     'hang on, as to the basic structure it is not. Our houses are not built with these corners, no. There are those Turkish roofs.'

Apart from agreement in nominal phrases, there are mismatches also in the agreement between subject and predicate. In example (37), the fronted predicate is marked for the singular (*je*) whereas the subject for plural (*satelitske antene*).

(37) i na toj ruševini **je**
 and on this.LOC.SG hulk.LOC.SG be.3SG
 satelitske ovaj ahm *antene.* (T11)
 satellite.ADJ.NOM.PL.F this uhm antenna.NOM.PL.F
 satellite.ADJ.ACC.PL.F antenna.ACC.PL.F
 'and in this hulk there are /is ‚how do you call it, er, satellite dishe(s).'

One possible explanation for this structure might be the identification with the German existential construction *es gibt* governing the Accusative (see the discussion of ex 16 above). In contrast to that, example (38) has a predicate with a feminine singular marker which does not fit with the subject in the neuter singular. One possible explanation for this agreement pattern might be that the speaker identifies the Croatian word *prvenstvo* 'championship' with German *die Meisterschaft* which happens to have feminine gender.

(38) *bila* *je* *svetsko*
 be.PST.SG.F AUX.3SG world.ADJ.NOM.SG.N
 prvenstvo u *Zagrebu.* (T 3)
 championship.NOM.SG.N in Zagreb.LOC.SG
 'The World championship took place in Zagreb.'

The question arises if the cases of agreement mismatches in examples (34)–(38) discussed above can be treated as instances of PAT or as the incomplete acquisition of the agreement rules. As a matter of fact, German like Croatian and Serbian has an elaborated agreement system involving the same three grammatical categories gender, number and case. The difference is only in the number of cases (German 4 vs. Croatian/Serbian 6), the high number of homophonous forms in German and the marking of gender with verbs in the past tense.

6 Conclusions

In our paper we have addressed the question of the permeability of grammatical systems in situations of intensive language contact by analysing a data corpus of the language use of Croatian and Serbian heritage speakers living in Germany. Whereas Silva-Corvalán (1998: 225–226) claims that 'what is borrowed across languages is not syntax but lexicon and pragmatics', Thomason

(2001: 63) argues that in situations of intensive language contact anything can be replicated. We have distinguished three possible types of the replication of syntactic structures (PAT): a) contact induced grammaticalization, b) polysemy copying, and c) restructuring. We presented an overview of the syntactic features affected by contact induced changes found in the data corpus. We showed that especially valence and linking constructions are susceptible to PAT. In these cases, we were dealing with either polysemy copying or with restructuring. Neither in valence and linking constructions, nor in any other area, did we find clear examples of contact induced grammaticalization. This finding might indicate that the latter takes place only over a longer time period involving more than two generations of speakers (contra Błaszczyk 2015). For a better understanding of contact induced grammaticalization we need more heritage linguistic studies.

Apart from that, we discussed specific cases of the use of clitics and of agreement marking which deviate from base line usage. It turned out, that some speakers showed violations of rules of the clitic system. This might be treated as a case of restructuring involving the loss of a category on the basis that the model language German does not have these types of clitics. A different case is presented by inconsistent agreement marking. These changes which developed during the transmission of the language from the first to the second generation do not directly fit the definition of PAT because they are not based on an act of interlingual identification. As a matter of fact, German has an agreement system which even if it is based on a smaller case system shows similarities with Serbian and Croatian.

Addressing the final research question if the replications of patterns are mediated by or even directly linked to lexical elements we come to the conclusion that our data clearly show that syntactic features indeed are easily replicated if they are linked to lexical elements. In all cases of PAT, we see a clear link with lexical entries. Schematic syntactic rules are only indirectly affected by language contact in the sense that contact can trigger the loss of categorical distinctions. The data from heritage Serbian and Croatian thus corroborate Silva-Corvalán's findings from Spanish in the US.

References

Albin, Aleksandar & Ronelle Alexander. 1972. *The speech of Yugoslav immigrants in San Pedro, California*. The Hague: Martinus Nijhoff.
Anstatt, Tanja. 2008. Russisch in Deutschland: Entwicklungsperspektiven. *Bulletin der deutschen Slavistik* 14. 67–74.
Anstatt, Tanja. 2011. Sprachattrition. Abbau der Erstsprache bei russisch-deutschen Jugendlichen. *Wiener Slawistischer Almanach* 67. 7–31.

Błaszczyk, Izabela. 2015. *Ausdruck von (In)definitheit bei polnisch-deutschen Bilingualen. Eine Analyse am Beispiel des Demonstrativums „ten" und des Zahlworts „jeden"*. Saarbrücken: AkademikerVerlag.

Breu, Walter. 1999. Der Konditional im Moliseslavischen. Ein Beitrag zur Kontaktlinguistik. In Karsten Grünberg & Wilfried Potthoff (eds.), *Ars Philologica. Festschrift für Baldur Panzer zum 65. Geburtstag*, 243–253. Frankfurt a.M: Lang.

Breu, Walter. 2012. The grammaticalization of an indefinite article in Slavic micro-languages. In Björn Wiemer, Bernhard Wälchli & Björn Hansen (eds.), *Grammatical replication and borrowability in language contact*, 275–322. Berlin & Boston: De Gruyter Mouton.

Crovallex 2.0008: Croatian Valency Lexicon of Verbs, Version 2.0008. http://theta.ffzg.hr/crovallex (accessed 16 May 2015).

Dimitrijević-Savić, Jovana. 2004. Contact-induced change in a case of language shift: The Serbian language in Australia. *Zbornik Matice srpske za filologiju i lingvistiku* XLVII (1–2). 75–92.

Dimitrijević-Savić, Jovana. 2008. Convergence and attrition: Serbian in contact with English in Australia. *Journal of Slavic Linguistics* 16 (1). 57–90.

Djordjević, Miloje & Ulrich Engel. 2013. *Srpsko-nemački rečnik valentnosti glagola. / Wörterbuch zur Verbvalenz. Serbisch-Deutsch*. München: Sagner.

Dorleijn, Margreet & Ad Backus. 2013. Loan translations as the missing link between lexical and structural effects of contact. Paper given at SLE 2013 University of Split, 18–21 September.

Ďurovič, L'ubomír. 1983. Lingua in Diaspora: Studies in the language of the second generation of Yugoslav immigrant children in Sweden. *Slavica Lundensia* 9. 21–94.

E-Valbu: Das elektronische Valenzwörterbuch deutscher Verben. http://hypermedia.ids-mannheim.de/evalbu/index.html) (accessed 16 May 2015).

Fried, Mirjam & Jan-Ola Östman. 2004. Construction Grammar: A thumbnail sketch. In Mirjam Fried & Jan-Ola Östman (eds.), *Construction Grammar in a cross-language perspective*, 11–87. Amsterdam & Philadelphia: Benjamins.

Hansen, Björn, Daniel Romić & Zrinka Kolaković. 2013. Okviri za istraživanje sintaktičkih struktura govornika druge generacije bosanskoga, hrvatskoga i srpskoga jezika u Njemačkoj [A framework for the research on syntactic structures of heritage Croatian, Bosnian and Serbian as spoken by the second generation in Germany]. *Lahor* 15. 9–45.

Hansen, Björn, Veronika Wald & Zrinka Kolaković (in print). Subjektkasus und Finitheit: Eine korpusbasierte Studie zur Mikrovariation und zur Entwicklung kroatischer Modalkonstruktionen. *Zeitschrift für slavische Philologie*.

Harris, Alice C. & Lyle Campbell. 1995. *Historical syntax in cross-linguistic perspective*. Cambridge: Cambridge University Press.

Heine, Bernd & Tania Kuteva. 2005. *Language contact and grammatical change*. Cambridge: Cambridge University Press.

Hinrichs, Uwe & Ljiljana Hinrichs. 1995. *Serbische Umgangssprache*. Wiesbaden: Otto Harrassowitz.

Hlavac, Jim. 2003. *Second-generation speech. Lexicon, code-switching and morpho-syntax of Croatian-English bilinguals*. Bern: Lang.

Hrvatski jezični portal. http://hjp.novi-liber.hr/ (accessed 16 May 2015).

hrWaC 2.0.: Croatian Web Corpus 2.0. http://nl.ijs.si/noske/wacs.cgi/corp_info?corpname=hrwac (accessed 20 June 2015).

Ivić, Milka. 1981. Srpskohrvatski glagolski oblici za iskazivanje pojava koje postoje u sadašnjosti. [Serbocroatian verbal forms used for the expression of existence in the present]. *Južnoslovenski filolog* XXXVII. 13–24.

Johanson, Lars. 2002. Contact-induced change in a code-copying framework. In Mari C. Jones & Edith Esch (eds.), *Language change: The interplay of internal, external and extra-linguistic factors*, 285–313. Berlin: Mouton de Gruyter.

Joseph, Brian D. 1983. *The synchrony and diachrony of the Balkan infinitive: A study in areal, general, and historical linguistics*. Cambridge: Cambridge University Press.

Jutronić-Tihomirović, Dunja. 1985. *Hrvatski jezik u SAD* [The Croatian language in the US]. Split: Logos.

Kuteva, Tania & Bernd Heine. 2012. An integrative model of grammaticalization. In Björn Wiemer, Bernhard Wälchli & Björn Hansen (eds.), *Grammatical replication and borrowability in language contact*, 159–190. Berlin: De Gruyter Mouton.

Matras, Yaron. 1998. Convergent development, grammaticalization, and the problem of 'mutual isomorphism'. In Winfried Boeder, Christoph Schroeder, Karl Heinz Wagner & Wolfgang Wildgen (eds.), *Sprache in Raum und Zeit: In memoriam Johannes Bechert*, 89–103. Tübingen: Narr.

Matras, Yaron & Jeanette Sakel (eds.). 2007. *Grammatical borrowing in cross-linguistic perspective*. Berlin: Mouton de Gruyter.

Mrazović, Pavica. 1989. Neke karakteristike govornog i pisanog nemačkog i srpskohrvatskog jezika dece migranata u SR Nemačkoj. [Some features of spoken and written German and Serbocroatian of children of immigrants in the Federal Republic of Germany]. In Svenka Savić (ed.), *Interkulturalizam kao oblik obrazovanja dece migranata van domovine* [Interculturalism as a form of education of the children of migrants outside their homeland], 70–77. Novi Sad: Filozofski fakultet.

Myers-Scotton, Carol. 2002. *Contact linguistics: Bilingual encounters and grammatical outcomes*. Oxford: Oxford University Press.

Polinsky, Maria. 1995. American Russian: Language loss meets language acquisition. In *Formal approaches to Slavic linguistics. Cornell meeting*, 370–406. Ann Arbor: Michigan Slavic Publications.

Popović, Ivan. 1960. *Geschichte der serbokroatischen Sprache*. Wiesbaden: Otto Harrassowitz.

Radanović-Kocić, Vesna. 1988. *The grammar of Serbo-Croatian clitics: A synchronic and diachronic perspective*. Urbana-Champaign: University of Illinois dissertation.

Raecke, Jochen. 2007a. Hrvatski u Njemačkoj: njemački s hrvatskim riječima? [Croatian in Germany: German with Croatian words?]. *Lahor* 2 (2). 151–159.

Raecke, Jochen. 2007b. Wenn Migrantenkinder als Studierende die Sprache ihrer Eltern sprechen – was können sie dann? *Zeitschrift für Slawistik* 52 (4). 375–398.

Romić, Daniel. 2016. „Ja sam ti ono pola-pola, wie das Gericht beim Kroaten": Sprachidentität und -struktur der zweiten Generation ex-jugoslawischer Migrantennachkommen in Deutschland. In Kerstin Kazzazi, Angela Treiber & Tim Wätzold (eds.), *Migration – Religion – Identität. Aspekte transkultureller Prozesse*, 185–218. Wiesbaden: Springer.

Sakel, Jeanette. 2007. Types of loan: Matter and pattern. In Yaron Matras & Jeanette Sakel (eds.), *Grammatical borrowing in cross-linguistic perspective*, 15–29. Berlin: Mouton de Gruyter.

Sandfeld, Kristian. 1926. *Balkanfilologien. En oversigt over dens resultater og problemer* [1968 Linguistique balkanique. Problèmes et résultats.]. København: Bianco Lunos.

Savić, Jelena M. 1995. Structural convergence and language change: Evidence from Serbian/English code-switching. *Language in Society* 24 (4). 475–492.
Savić, Svenka. 1989. Dokle smo došli? [What have we achieved?]. In Svenka Savić (ed.), *Interkulturalizam kao oblik obrazovanja dece migranata van domovine* [Interculturalism as a form of education of the children of migrants outside their homeland], 8–42. Novi Sad: Filozofski fakultet.
Schlund, Katrin. 2006. Sprachliche Determinanten bilingualer Identitätskonstruktion am Beispiel von Deutsch-Jugoslawen der zweiten Generation. *Zeitschrift für Slawistik* 51 (1). 74–93.
Silva-Corvalán, Carmen. 1993. On the permeability of grammars: Evidence from Spanish and English contact. In William J. Ashby, Marianne Mithun & Giorgio Perissinotto (eds.), *Linguistic perspectives on Romance languages: Selected papers from the XXI linguistic symposium on Romance languages, Santa Barbara, February 21–24, 1991*, 19–44. Amsterdam & Philadelphia: Benjamins.
Silva-Corvalán, Carmen. 1998. On borrowing as a mechanism of syntactic change. In Armin Schwegler, Bernard Tranel & Myriam Uribe-Etxebarria (eds.), *Romance linguistics: Theoretical perspectives. Selected papers from the 27th linguistic symposium on Romance languages*, 225–246. Amsterdam & Philadelphia: Benjamins.
Sobolev, A. N. 1998. Dialekty vostočnoj Serbii i zapadnoj Bolgarii [The dialects of eastern Serbia and western Bulgaria]. In *Malyj dialektologičeskij atlas balkanskix jazykov. Materialy vtorogo rabočego soveščanija* [Small dialectological atlas of the Balkan languages. Materials of the second working meeting], 59–77. Sankt-Peterburg: Institut lingvističeskix issledovanij RAN.
srWaC: Serbian Web Corpus. http://nl.ijs.si/noske/wacs.cgi/corp_info?corpname=srwac (accessed 20 June 2015)
Stoffel, Hans-Peter. 2002/2003. Dialect and standard language in a migrant situation: The case of New Zealand Croatian. *Croatian Studies Review* 2. 1–23.
Stölting, Wilfried. 1980. *Die Zweisprachigkeit jugoslawischer Schüler in der Bundesrepublik Deutschland*. Wiesbaden: Otto Harrassowitz.
Sussex, Roland. 1993. Slavonic languages in emigration. In Bernard Comrie & Greville G. Corbett (eds.), *The Slavonic languages*, 999–1036. London & New York: Routledge.
Thomason, Sarah G. 2001. *Language contact. An introduction*. Edinburgh: University Press.
Turk, Marija. 2013. *Jezično kalkiranje u teoriji i praksi. Prilog lingvistici jezičnih dodira* [Linguistic calquing in theory and in use. A contribution to language contact]. Zagreb: Hrvatska Sveučilišna Naklada.
Vukojević, Luka. 2008. Infinitivne posljedične konstrukcije [Infinitival consequential constructions]. *Rasprave Instituta za hrvatski jezik i jezikoslovlje* 34 (1). 449–462.
Vuletić, Julijana. 2013. Srpsko-nemački jezički kontakti sa osvrtom na istraženost jezika Srba u Nemačkoj danas [Serbian-German language contact with special reference to current studies on the language of Serbs in Germany]. *Nasleđe* 10 (24). 87–106.
Warchoł-Schlottmann, Małgorzata. 1996. Język Polski w Niemczech – Perspektywy zachowania języka etnicznego u najnowszej emigracji [Polish in Germany – Perspectives of language maintenance in recent emigration]. *Przegląd Polinijny* 22. 31–50.
Wasserscheidt, Philipp (in print). Construction Grammar and code-mixing. In Justyna Robinson & Monika Reif (eds.), *Cognition, culture and codes: Current perspectives on multilingualism*, 26p, Berlin.

Weinreich, Uriel. 1953. *Languages in contact. Findings and problems*. New York & Den Haag: Mouton.
Wiemer, Björn & Björn Hansen. 2012. Assessing the range of contact-induced grammaticalization in Slavonic. In Björn Wiemer, Bernhard Wälchli & Björn Hansen (eds.), *Grammatical replication and borrowability in language Contact*, 67–155. Berlin: De Gruyter Mouton.
Wiemer, Björn & Bernhard Wälchli. 2012. Contact-induced grammatical change: Diverse phenomena, diverse perspectives. In Björn Wiemer, Bernhard Wälchli & Björn Hansen (eds.), *Grammatical replication and borrowability in language contact*, 3–64. Berlin: De Gruyter Mouton.
Wiemer, Björn, Bernhard Wälchli & Björn Hansen (eds.). 2012. *Grammatical replication and borrowability in language contact*. Berlin: De Gruyter Mouton.
Winford, Donald. 2003. *An introduction to Contact Linguistics*. Malden: Blackwell.
Zubčić, Sanja. 2010. Speech of Croatian emigrants in the overseas countries and countries of Western Europe: The level of research attained. *Croatian Studies Review* 6 (1). 141–162.

Imke Mendoza
Possessive resultative constructions in Old and Middle Polish

Abstract: The possessive resultative construction (PRC) of Modern Polish has been a topic of interest in Polish linguistics for quite some time. One of the main issues is its relationship to a grammaticalized perfect and the question of whether there is an ongoing process of grammaticalization to a new perfect in contemporary Polish. However, the discussions do not take the earlier stages of Polish into account. This paper analyses the syntactic and semantic features of possessive resultatives in Old and Middle Polish with regard to their diachronic dimension and their areal setting. Particular emphasis is placed on the delineation of possessive constructions proper and possessive resultatives. The analysis shows that there have been almost no changes to this category since the first written documents. The construction has thus basically stayed the same for 600 years. It is further suggested that the Polish PRCs are the outcome of a language contact induced process. There are two possible source languages: Latin and German. However, the question of which one of the two was in fact responsible for the possessive resultative cannot be answered definitively, due to the scarcity of relevant data from the earliest period.

1 Introduction

Polish possessive resultative constructions (PRCs) have received some attention, particularly over the past two decades. The discussion focuses on Modern Polish only and revolves around the question whether PRCs are being grammaticalized to a new perfect.[1] There is almost no research on older stages of Polish, nor is there a debate on the diachronic and systematic relations of PRCs to possessive constructions proper.

---

1 The first one to suggest a "new perfect" was probably Nitsch (1954 [1913]). See also Kątny (1999); Kątny (2005); Łaziński (2001); Piskorz (2012); Piskorz, Abraham, and Leiss (2013); Sawicki (2011); Topolińska (1968); Weydt and Kaźmierczak (1999).

https://doi.org/10.1515/9783110531435-007

In my paper, I first analyse the semantic and syntactic features of Old and Middle Polish and the relation of PRCs to possessive constructions proper. Then I compare Old and Middle Polish PRCs with their modern counterparts, and discuss possible origins of Polish PRCs. In the last section, I draw conclusions.

My corpus consists of Old and Middle Polish texts from the 14th–18th centuries. I used the "Polish Diachronic Online Corpus" (PolDi) at the University of Regensburg, the database of Polish 17th c. documents compiled by Andrzej de Vincenz and Gerd Hentschel (Database),[2] and a number of Old Polish texts I downloaded from the site http://www.ijppan.krakow.pl/index2.php?strona=korpus_tekst_star.[3] The corpus comprises different genres, such as religious texts (bible, Apocrypha, hymns, sermons), official and legal documents, religious and mundane poetry and prose, wills, letters, and texts from *Merkuriusz Polski*, the first Polish newspaper.[4]

2 Definition of resultative constructions

A resultative construction (RC) is a morpho-syntactic structure that refers to the state after an event and thereby implies the change of state that caused the state referred to by the RC.[5] This is illustrated by the following graph:

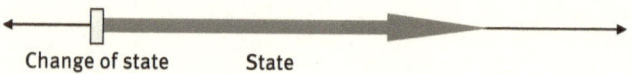

Change of state   State

Fig. 1: Resultative construction.

There are three different types of resultative constructions: subject-oriented RCs, object-oriented RCs and possessive RCs.[6] Subject-oriented RCs have grammatical

---

2 This database is not accessible online.
3 This site has been turned off some time ago, the texts are now available under https://www.ijp-pan.krakow.pl/publikacje-elektroniczne/korpus-tekstow-staropolskich.
4 The appendix lists all the documents I analysed.
5 Other terms are "statal perfect" (Maslov 1988: 64–65) or "resultative perfect" (Resultativperfekt, Breu 1988: 54–55). For definitions see also Nedjalkov and Jaxontov (1988); Giger (2003: 12–26); Wiemer and Giger (2005: 1–3); Mel'čuk (1998: 76).
6 See Wiemer and Giger (2005: 1–10) and Nedjalkov and Jaxontov (1988: 8–11) for a detailed description of the different types of RC.

subjects identical to the grammatical subject of a construction that describes the event immediately preceding the state. Compare the actional construction in (1) with the corresponding subject-oriented RC (2):

(1) (Polish)
Jan   przejął   się   losem   brata.[7]
Jan.NOM.SG.M   worry.3SG.PST.M   REFL   fate.INS.SG.M   brother.GEN.SG.M
'Jan worried about his brother's fate'

(2) Jan   był   przejęty   losem
    Jan.NOM.SG.M   be.3SG.PST.M   worry.PP.NOM.SG.M   fate.INS.SG.M
    brata.
    brother.GEN.SG.M
    'Jan was troubled by the fate of his brother'

In object-oriented RCs, the direct object of the corresponding actional construction is identical with the grammatical subject of the respective RC, cf. (3) and (4):

(3) (Russian)
Lesopil'ščiki   srubili   derevo.
lumberjack.NOM.PL   chop.PST.PL   tree.ACC.SG.N
'The lumberjacks chopped down a tree.'

(4) Derevo   srubleno.
    tree.NOM.SG.N   chop.PP.NOM.SG.N
    'The tree has been felled.'

Possessive resultative constructions are characterized by a possessive or quasi-possessive relation between the grammatical subject and the second argument of the verb the participle is derived from. Cf. (5) with a possessive relation between the speaker and a car:

(5) (Polish, Kątny 1999: 104)
    Od   tygodnia   mam   samochód   zepsuty.
    from   week.GEN.SG.M   have.1SG.PRS   car.ACC.SG.M   broken.PP.NOM.SG.M
    'My car has not been working for a week.'

From a semantic point of view, PRCs are somewhere between stative constructions on the one hand, and perfects on the other hand. Stative constructions

---

[7] Ex. (1)–(4) are taken from Wiemer and Giger (2005: 6).

designate states without implying a change of state, while perfects denote a change of state, and only imply the state after the event. Cf. Figs. 2 and 3:

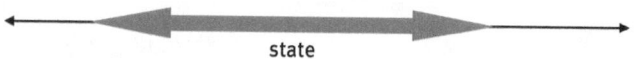

state

Fig. 2: Stative construction.

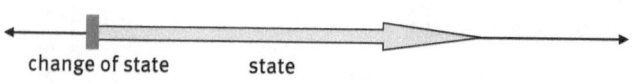

change of state   state

Fig. 3: Perfect.

Stative constructions, PRCs and perfects are different stages on a grammaticalization path that can lead all the way to a narrative past tense. The grammaticalization processes from PRCs to a perfect and from a perfect to a narrative past tense have been thoroughly researched and well documented, particularly in the Germanic and Romance languages.[8] The relationship between statives and PRCs has received less attention.

3 Characteristics of possessive resultative constructions in Old and Middle Polish[9]

3.1 Syntax

The constitutive elements of Polish PRCs are a) a form of the verb *mieć* 'to have', b) a direct object, and c) a passive participle (PP). Following Giger (2003: 269–270), I take the syntagm "*mieć* + participle" in a PRC to be a complex predicate with *mieć* being the copula and the participle the copular complement. This is illustrated by example (6), where the participle *wyćwiczonego* is part of the complex predicate *mieć wyćwiczonego*:

---

[8] There is an abundance of literature on this subject, the following list names only a few titles: Dentler (1997); Detges (2000); Grønvik (1986); Jacob (1995); Kuroda (1999); Pinkster (1987).
[9] For the purposes of this paper, there is no need to differentiate between Old and Middle Polish, since PRCs have not changed much since the first attestations in the 14th c. (cf. Mendoza 2013).

(6) (Mid 18th c., Chmielowski; Database)
Xiążę   ieden   Francuski   tak
prince.NOM.SG.M one.NOM.SG.M   french.NOM.SG.M   so
miał   wyćwiczonego   psa,   że   stół
have.3SG.PST.M train.PP.ACC.SG.M dog.ACC.SG.M that table.ACC.SG.M
nakrywał   dla gościa,
cover.3SG.PST.M for guest.GEN.SG.M
'A French prince had trained his dog to set the table for the guest.'

3.1.1 Object and agreement

In Old and Middle Polish (OMP), the object is an obligatory element of PRCs. In the overwhelming majority of cases, it is a noun phrase (including pronouns). Propositional objects, as in (7) and (8), are rather rare. In (7), the object is the relative adverb *jako* 'how' which refers to a proposition in the preceding text. The object in (8)[10] is a verbal complement, preceded by the complementizer *że*:

(7) (Mid 15th c., Biblia królewej Zofii; PolDi)
jiż   czynią   po   żydowsku   a   po   jerusalemsku
REL.NOM.PL.M   do.3SG.PRS   by   Jewish   and   by   Jerusalem_like
pełniąc,   jako   masz   w   zakonie   bożem
fulfill.CVB   how   have.2SG.PRS in   law.LOC.SG.M god.INS.SG.M
popisano
write.PP.ACC.SG.N
'who do [it] the Jewish and the Jerusalem way, complying with the way it has been written for you in the law by God'

(8) (19th c., Jewlaszewski; PolDi)
miał   sobie   przepowiedziane   od   jakiegoś
have.3SG.PST.M REFL.DAT   predict.PP.ACC.SG.N   from   some.GEN.SG.M
przejeżdżającego   cygana,   że   zginie   od   [...]
travelling.GEN.SG.M   gypsy.GEN.SG.M that   die.3SG.PRS   from
'He was predicted by a travelling gypsy, that he would die from [...]'

---

10 Example (8) is taken from a 19th c. translation of a 16th c. Belorussian text. Strictly speaking, it does not belong to OMP, but since it is the only example of this kind in my corpus, I decided to include it in the analysis.

Example (9) presents another unusual object, namely a metalinguistic expression (*"milczenie"* 'silence'):

(9) (1618, P. Kochanowski; Database)
Że po wszytkich komorach mają napisane
that on all.LOC.PL.F cell.LOC.PL.F have.3PL.PRS write.PP.ACC.SG.N
„Milczenie"
silence
'that they have "silence" written in all cells'

The participle agrees with the object in case, number and gender. In affirmative sentences object and participle show the accusative, in negative sentences the genitive case, cf. (10):

(10) (1627, Birkowski; Database)
rąk nie miał nigdy związanych
arm.GEN.PL.F NEG have.3SG.PST.M never tie.PP.GEN.PL.F
'His never had his arms tied up'

With objects that do not have morphological marking, like propositional objects, the participle takes the form of NOM.SG.N, cf. (7) and (8) above. If a complex object consists of non-agreeing word forms, the participle agrees with the morphologically dependent element. In (11), the adjective *większego* (GEN.SG.N) depends on the pronoun *coś* and the participle agrees with the adjective (*zgotowanego*, GEN.SG.N):

(11) (Mid 17th c.., L. Opaliński; Database)
ale coś większego mamy od
but something.ACC.SG bigger.GEN.SG.N have.1PL.PRS from
Boga nam zgotowanego
god.GEN.SG.M we.DAT prepare.PP.GEN.SG.N
'but that we have something greater prepared for us by God'

3.1.2 Expression of beneficiary

The grammatical subject of a PRC is the beneficiary of the situation, i.e. it is affected by the situation in a positive or in a negative way. Sometimes, the beneficiary is referred to by a second phrase, cf. the dative of the personal pronoun (*nam*) in (11) above, the dative pronoun *sobie* in (12), and the prepositional phrase *na się* in (13):

(12) (2nd half of 17th c., J.A. Morsztyn; Database)
    że   Kraków   mają   sobie   powierzony
    that   Cracow.ACC.SG.M have.3PL.PRS   REFL.DAT   entrust.PP.ACC.SG.M
    'that they were entrusted with [the city of] Cracow'

(13) (Early 15th c., Naborowski; Database)
    Niechaj   mam   rozgniewane   na   się   wszytkie
    PAR   have.1SG.PRS   upset.PP.ACC.PL.M   on   REFL.ACC   all.ACC.PL.M
    bogi
    god.ACC.PL.M
    'may I have all gods be upset with me'

It is mostly three-place predicates like *zlecać, obiecać, przepowiedzieć, przysłać* that have a second expression of beneficiary.

The additional beneficiary phrase is usually coreferent with the subject. Very seldom do we find constructions like (14) with a non-coreferent beneficiary. The second beneficiary, referred to by *dla niej* 'for her', is different from the subject:

(14) (1618, P. Kochanowski; Database)
    iż   ma   zbudowany   klasztor   dla
    that   have.3SG.PRS   build.PP.ACC.SG.M   monastery.ACC.SG.M for
    niej
    she.GEN.SG
    'that he had a monastery built for her'

3.1.3 Word order

There is no fixed word order for the constituents of a PRC. All six possible combinations of *m[ieć]*, O[bject] and P[articiple] are attested in the documents, as the following examples demonstrate:

Type A: *m* O P
(15) (1496–1501, Pamiętnik Janczara; PolDi)
    mają   osobny   namiot   rozbity
    have.3PL.PRS   special.ACC.SG.M   tent.ACC.SG.M   put_up.PP.ACC.SG.M
    'they have their own tent put up'

Type B: O *m* P
(16) (Mid 17th c., Listy do Marysi; PolDi)
    i   żegnania   mam   ponotowane
    and   farewells.ACC.PL.N have.1SG.PRS note.PP.ACC.PL.N
    'and I have noted the farewells'

Type C: O P *m*
(17) (Early 17th c., P. Kochanowski; Database)
    I   żołądek   tak   dawno   wypróżniony   mając
    and   stomach.ACC.SG.M so   long_ago empty.PP.ACC.SG.M have.CVB
    'And having had the stomach emptied long ago'

Type D: P *m* O
(18) (Mid 18th c., Chmielowski; Database)
    na   który   wlepione   ma   oczy
    on   REL.ACC.SG.M glue.PP.ACC.PL.N have.3SG.PRS eye.ACC.PL.N
    'at which he was staring'

Type E: *m* P O
(19) (Early 17th c., P. Kochanowski; Database)
    chcąc   mieć   ugaszony   wielki   ogień
    want.CVB have.INF extinguish.PP.ACC.SG.M big.ACC.SG.M fire.ACC.SG.M
    'wanting to have the fire extinguished'

Type F: P O *m*
(20) (Late 18th c., Krasicki; PolDi)
    iż   wzwyż   wyrażoną   klauzulę   mam
    that   above   express.PP.ACC.SG.F clause.ACC.SG.F have.1SG.PRS
    'that above I have expressed the clause'

The patterns occur with varying frequency, cf. the following Table:

Tab. 1: Frequency of word order patterns in Old and Middle Polish.

Type A [*m* O P]	Type B [O *m* P]	Type C [O P *m*]	Type D [P *m* O]	Type E [*m* PO]	Type F [P O *m*]
36%(148)[11]	31%(129)	9%(37)	4%(18)	18%(74)	2%(8)

The most frequent pattern is type A [*mieć* O P], with type B [O *mieć* P] following close behind. These two patterns make up two-thirds of all examples.

---

[11] The numbers in brackets indicate the absolute number of attestations.

Obviously, the preferred position for the participle is the final position. The least favoured position is its initial position: The patterns D and F amount to only 6%.

Let us take a look at the adjacency of *mieć* and participle, since it is a function of the grammaticalization of the finite verb. Interestingly enough, the most frequent type A does not enable adjacency of *mieć* and the participle. The types B, C, D, and E, which allow contact between the constituents, occur both with and without adjacency. In examples (16)–(19) above, *mieć* and participle are adjacent (*mam ponotowane, wypróżniony mając, wlepione ma, mieć ugaszony*). In the following examples the two verb forms are separated by different elements: prepositional phrases (21), (22), pronouns (23) or even two phrases (numeral and prepositional phrase in (24)):

Type B:
(21) (Early 17th c., Birkowski; Database)
począł krucyfix on głową ktorą
begin.3SG.PST.M crucifix.ACC.SG.M he head.INS.SG.F REL.ACC.SG.F
miał / na prawą stronę
have.3SG.PST.M on right.ACC.SG.F side.ACC.SG.F
skłonioną / na lewicę obracać
incline.PP.ACC.SG.F on left_side.ACC.SG.F turn.INF
'he started to turn the crucifix to his left with the help of his head, which he had inclined to the right side'

Type C:
(22) (Late 15th c., Pamiętnik Janczara; PolDi)
a koźdy swą chorągiew
and everyone.NOM.SG.M self.ACC.SG.F banner.ACC.SG.F
ma od Cesarza daną
have.3SG.PRS from emperor.GEN.SG.M give.PP.ACC.SG.F
'and everyone had been given their banner by the Emperor'

Type D
(23) (Late 18th/ early 19th c., Kopeć; PolDi)
który tem okrętem miał sobie
REL.NOM.SG.M this.INS.SG.M ship.INS.SG.M have.3SG.PST.M REFL.DAT
przysłane pismo od Katarzyny
send.PP.ACC.SG.N letter.ACC.SG.N from Katarzyna.GEN.SG.F
Imperatorowej
Imperatowa.GEN.SG.F
'who had himself a letter from the Empress Catherine sent with this ship'

Type E:
(24) (1480, Ortyle Oss.)
Kiedy mają   dwa   miedzy   sobą   murowaną
when   have.3PL.PRS two   between REFL.INS   lay_bricks.PP.ACC.SG.F
ścianę
border.ACC.SG.F
'when two have a bordermade of brick between them'

Type C
(25) (1618, P Kochanowski; Database)
Twarz   upłakaną,   włosy   roztargane
face.ACC.SG.F   cry.PP.ACC.SG.F   hair.ACC.PL.M   tousle.PP.ACC.PL.M
miała
have.3SG.PST.F
'She had her face tear-stained, her hair tousled'

Type D
(26) (1614, Szymonowic; Database)
a   ci   zmówione   już   mieli   Za
and   this.NOM.PL.M   agree.PP.ACC.PL   already   have.3PL.PST.M for
się   dwie   siestrze
REFL.ACC   two   sister.ACC.DU.F
'and these had had marriage promised to two sisters for themselves'

However, even though there seem to be no restrictions as to the syntactic or semantic nature of the insertions, the majority of the patterns B, C, D, and E show adjacency. In groups B and E the adjacent constructions amount to almost 60%, in C and D there are only three non-adjacent attestations out of 31 (C) and two out of 18 (D).

3.2 Semantics

3.2.1 Verb

The participle in a resultative construction is always formed from a terminative verb (Wiemer and Giger 2005: 4–5). Non-terminative or durative verbs, i.e. verbs that denote an action with no inherent limitation, do not occur in resultative constructions by definition. If there is no inherent boundary and no intrinsic goal to the action, there is no change of state the construction can imply. Therefore, examples like (27) are always designations of states:[12]

(27) (Early 17th c., P. Kochanowski, Database)
że	masz	swą	kochaną	Izabellę
that	have.2SG.PRS	self.ACC.SG.F	love.PP.ACC.SG.F	Izabella.ACC.SG.F

'that you have your beloved Izabella'

The participles are typically based on transitive and perfective verbs. Intransitive or imperfective participles, however, are also possible. The participle in (28) is derived from the intransitive *zepsuć się* 'break' and the participle *ćwiczone* 'practiced' in (29) is imperfective:

(28) (Mid 18. Jh., Chmielowski)
Jeźliby	tedy	kto		przez	czary	miał
if	then	someone.NOM		by	spell.ACC.PL.M	have.3SG.PST.M
wzrok		zepsuty				
vision.ACC.SG.M		damage.PP.ACC.SG.M				

'if someone then has had their vision damaged by spells'

(29) (1496–1501, Kronika turecka; PolDi)
które	miedzy	sobą	ćwiczone	mają
REL.ACC.PL.N	among	REFL.INS	practice.PP.ACC.PL.N	have.3SG.PRS

'what they have practiced amongst each other'

3.2.2 Object

From a semantic point of view, the objects of a PRC are manifold. In fact, there are virtually no restrictions as to their semantic characteristics. Objects of a PRC can be alienable or inalienable (30), affected (31) or effected (32), they cover the whole

---

[12] One could play devil's advocate and argue that examples like (27) demonstrate quite the opposite, namely the expansion of the PRC to constructions with durative verbs, and that they show a very advanced stage of grammaticalization. However, there is no evidence for such a far-reaching grammaticalization process, be it OMP or Modern Polish. If there were such a process, we would expect to find examples without agreement of participle and object or without an object altogether on a regular basis. Examples of this kind, however, are virtually non-existing in OMP (see 3.1.1 above) and rare in Modern Polish (cf. Mendoza 2013 and the literature cited therein).

animacy scale (cf. the collective noun in (33), which refers to human beings), they can be count nouns or uncountable nouns (34), and they mostly refer to things (or persons), but sometimes also to events (35):

(30) (2nd half of 17. c., Listy do Marysi; PolDi)
i   już   głowę   napełnioną   mając   ideą
and   already   head.ACC.SG.F   fill.PP.ACC.SG.F   have.CVB   idea.INS.SG.F
piękności   Bukieta   swego
beauty.GEN.SG.F   bouquet.GEN.SG.M   self.GEN.SG.M
'and having his head filled with ideas of the beauty of his bouquet'

(31) (17th/18th c., Kopeć; PolDi)
mając   tedy   zapłacone   konie   i   inne
have.CVB   then   pay.PP.ACC.PL.M   horse.ACC.PL.M   and   other.ACC.PL.M
zapasy
supply.ACC.PL.M
'having then paid the horses and other supplies'

(32) (Mid 17th c., Odymalski; Database)
A   brama,   która   czoło   wydawała   te
and   gate   REL.NOM.SG.F   front.ACC.SG.N   give.3SG.PST.F   this.ACC.PL.N
w   sobie   słowa   napisane   miała:
in   self.DAT   word.ACC.PL.N   write.PP.ACC.PL.N   have.3SG.PST.F
'and the gate that formed the front, had these words written on it:'

(33) (Mid 17th c., W. Odymalski; Database)
że   już   miał   wojska
that   already   have.3SG.PST.M   armed_forces.ACC.PL.N
zebrane   w   Opolu
gather.PP.ACC.PL.N   in   Opole.LOC.SG.N
'that he had already gathered the armed forces in Opole'

(34) (1627, Birkowski; Database)
znowu   wesołość   y   całość   miał
again   mirth.ACC.SG.F   and   wholeness.ACC.SG.F   have.3SG.PST.M
przywróconą
restore.PP.ACC.SG.F
'he had restored mirth and wholeness again'

(35) (2nd half of 18th c., Krasicki; PolDi)
i   tę   sarnę   stratę   inszymi
and   this.ACC.SG.F   deer.ACC.SG.F   loss.ACC.SG.F   other.INS.PL.F

korzyściami	*dawno*	*już*	*mam*		*nagrodzoną*
profit.INS.PL.F	long_ago	already	have.1SG.PRS		reward.PP.ACC.SG.F

'and I already have compensated for the loss of the deer by other profits a long time ago'

3.2.3 Subject and agent

The subject of a PRC is usually human. However, one can find the occasional non-animated subject as in (32) above (*brama* 'gate') or (36) below (*Tunis* '[the city of] Tunis'):

(36) (Mid 17th c., P. Kochanowski; Database)
Widzi   y   Tunis,   co   ma
see.3SG.PRS PRT Tunis.ACC.SG.M REL have.3SG.PRS
otoczony   Brzeg   swego   morza
surround.PP.ACC.SG coast.ACC.SG.M   self.GEN.SG.N sea.GEN.SG.N
górami   wielkiemi
mountain.INS.PL.F big.INS.PL.F
'[he] sees [the city of] Tunis, which had its sea coast surrounded by big mountains'

As noted before, the grammatical subject is the beneficiary of the situation and is not necessarily identical with the agent. The agent's identity is irrelevant and often unknown. Certain three-place verbs like *dać* 'give', *obiecać* 'promise', *wyznaczyć* 'assign', *zlecić* 'order' even prevent subject-agent-identity, cf. (8) and (22). If the agent is explicitly named, it is usually done so by a prepositional phrase *od* + GEN (cf. ex. (8), (11), (22), and (23)), very rarely by a noun phrase in the instrumental case (cf. *bożem* in ex. (7)). Example (28), here repeated as (37), presents an interesting case, insofar as the "agent" *czary* 'spells' is not human. Moreover, it is expressed not by *od* + GEN, but by *przez* + ACC.:[13]

(37) (Mid 18th c., Chmielowski; Database)
Jeźliby tedy kto   przez   czary   miał
if   then someone.NOM   through spell.ACC.PL.M have.3SG.PST.M
wzrok   zepsuty
vision.ACC.SG.M   damage.PP.ACC.SG.M
'If someone then has had their vision damaged by spells'

---

[13] Incidentally, *przez* + ACC. is used to express the agent in passive sentences in Modern Polish.

3.3 Possessive constructions proper vs. possessive resultative constructions

Possessive constructions with *mieć* and a passive participle are the source constructions for PRCs. In possessive constructions proper, the participle has an attributive function. They describe a relation of possession that holds between the grammatical subject and the object, which, in turn, is being modified by a participle. Possessive constructions do not relate to an event or change of state. The following example illustrates the possessive construction "*mieć* + participle". The subject (*jeden matacz, albo szarletan* 'a swindler, or charlatan') is the possessor of the object (*pies morski* 'seal'). The participle *ćwiczony* 'trained' modifies the object and does not imply a change of state:

(38) (Mid 18th c., Chmielowski; Database)
Jeden   Matacz,   albo   Szarletan,
one.NOM.SG.M   swindler.NOM.SG.M or   charlatan.NOM.SG.M
miał   psa   morskiego   ćwiczonego,
have.3SG.PST.M dog.ACC.SG.M   maritime.ACC.SG.M train.PP.ACC.SG.M
którego [...]
REL.ACC.SG.M
'a swindler, or charlatan had a seal, which [...]'

The notion of possession is not easy to define. Some authors trace possession back to other dimensions such as location or existence.[14] Others, like Seiler (2001: 38), take it to be a cognitive and linguistic domain of its own. Most researchers agree, however, that possession is not a categorial concept, but is organized in terms of prototype(s) and periphery (cf. Heine 1997; Seiler 2001; Taylor 1995, and references therein). Prototypical relations between possessor and possessum are inalienability, control of possessor over possessum and permanence of possessive relation (Heine 1997: 33–41; Taylor 1995: 202–203; Langacker 1995). Each feature is relative rather than categorial, even inalienability (Seiler 2001).

The fuzziness of the domain of possession is one of the reasons why it is at times difficult to decide whether we are dealing with a PRC or a possessive construction proper. This is particularly true with objects that relate to the subject

---

14 Heine finds possession "a relatively abstract domain of human conceptualization" (1997: 45) and derives possessive expressions from certain event schemata, such as Action, Location, Accompaniment, and Existence.

in a way that is prototypical for possessive relations, like inalienability or total control of the subject over the object. Most of the constructions "*mieć* + "typical possessum" + participle" are possessive constructions proper but, as examples (10), (17) and others demonstrate, not necessarily so.

The same holds for constructions with imperfective participles. The majority of "*mieć* + impf. participle"-structures are possessive constructions, but there are also attestations for PRCs with imperfective participles, cf. example (29).[15]

Sometimes the syntactic environment gives a hint. If a "*mieć* + participle"-construction occurs in conjunction with another, unambiguous element, it will be interpreted according to this unambiguous element.[16] This mechanism is illustrated by the following examples. In (39), the second conjunct is a noun phrase modified by an adjective (*święta suknia* 'sacred garment'). Hence, the participle *rozdarty* 'torn' will most probably be interpreted as attributive and the construction "*mieć* + participle" as a possessive construction proper:

(39) (Mid 15th c., Biblia królowej Zofii; PolDi)
    mając   rucho   rozdarte   i   świętą
    have.CVB   train.ACC.SG.N rip.PP.ACC.SG.N   and   holy.ACC.SG.F
    suknią
    garment.ACC.SG.F
    'having a torn train and a sacred garment'

In (40), the parallelizing effect works the opposite way. The construction "*mieć* + participle" is conjoined with an object-oriented resultative construction formed by *być* + participle (*ani nogi spętane były* 'nor were his legs shackled'). Therefore, it is safe to assume that *rąk nie miał nigdy związanych* ('he never had his hands tied up') is to be interpreted as a resultative construction also:

(40) (1627, Birkowski; Database)
    rąk   nie   miał   nigdy   związanych/   ani
    arm.GEN.PL.F   NEG   have.3SG.PST.M never   tie.PP.GEN.PL.F   NEG
    nogi   iego   spętane   kiedy   były
    leg.NOM.PL.F   his   shackle.PP.NOM.PL.F   ever   be.3PL.PST.F
    'He never had his arms tied up, nor were his legs ever shackled'

---

15 Labocha (1988: 236) interprets "*mieć* + imperf. participle" as possessive by definition. In my opinion, this is premature, at least when dealing with older documents.
16 This phenomenon is an instantiation of the so-called parallelizing effect (*Parallelisierungseffekt*, Lang 1977: 47–58). It means that the reading of the conjuncts in a coordination will be aligned with regard to certain features, e.g. literal or metaphorical interpretation.

In some cases, the construction "*mieć* + participle" is accompanied by a spatial adverbial, thereby strengthening the stative meaning, and thus rendering a possessive interpretation preferable. Consider (41) with the local expression *w swej ręce* 'in one's hand':

(41) (Mid 17th c., Biblia królowej Zofii; PolDi)
a   list   miał   w   swej
and   letter.ACC.SG.M   have.3SG.PST.M   in   self.LOC.SG.F
ręce   pisany   tymi   słowy
hand.LOC.SG.F   write.PP.ACC.SG.M   this.INS.PL.N   word.INS.PL.N
'and he had a letter in his hand, written with these words'

On the other hand, there are some features that clearly set off PRCs from possessive constructions. Constructions with a propositional object are always PRCs, since there is no real possessive relation between subject and object. Further unequivocal indications for PRCs are agentive phrases and additional beneficiary phrases. Both an explicitly expressed agent and an explicitly expressed beneficiary direct the attention on the event that caused the change of state. Once the change of state comes into play, the construction in question cannot be a stative and possessive one.

4 Possessive resultative constructions in OMP and in Modern Polish

The analysis has shown that PRCs constitute a clearly defined group of constructions in OMP, albeit a very small one.[17] PRCs in OMP possess the following features:

- a) The object is obligatory, but not obligatorily a noun phrase,
- b) the participle agrees with the object or with the (morphologically) dependent element of a complex object,
- c) all possible word order constellations are attested, adjacency of the participle and *mieć* is not obligatory,
- d) the subject is the beneficiary, not (necessarily) the agent; sometimes there is an additional beneficiary phrase,
- e) the participle is derived from a terminative, usually perfective and usually transitive verb,
- f) there are no semantic restrictions concerning the object.

---

17 Cf. the numbers in the appendix.

When comparing PRCs in OMP with those in Modern Polish, one soon comes to realize that they have not changed much. One difference is that in Modern Polish it seems to be possible to have a PRC with a non-agreeing participle or even without an object at all.[18] A more noticeable development, however, concerns the word order patterns. Like in OMP, all patterns are possible, the most frequent types being A, B and E. Hence, Modern Polish also disfavours combinations with the participle in initial position or *mieć* as the final element. According to Piskorz's database of contemporary Polish, the ranking of the different patterns is nearly identical, with one striking difference. The patterns A and E have changed places. The most frequent type in Modern Polish is E [*m* P O], whereas in Old and Middle Polish it is A [*m* O P]:

Tab. 2: Comparison of relative frequency of word order patterns in OMP and contemporary Polish

Type	A [*m* O P]	B [O *m* P]	C [O P *m*]	D [P *m* O]	E [*m* PO]	F [P O *m*]
OMP	36%	31%	9%	4%	18%	2%
CP[19]	17,9%	28,9%	5,3%	5,8%	38,9%	3,2%

In modern Polish, the patterns that allow adjacency of the participle and *mieć* are the most frequent, patterns that do not allow contact (i.e. patterns A and F), make up only 21% of all cases. According to Piskorz (2012: 232–234), adjacency is almost obligatory in patterns E and B. The separation of *mieć* and the participle by other elements results in loss of acceptability or in a possessive, i.e. attributive reading. The difference between Modern Polish and OMP in the frequencies of patterns A and E is hence a corollary of the greater demand for adjacency in Modern Polish.

Adjacency of a finite verb and a non-finite form within a complex predicate is an indicator for the auxiliarization of the finite verb. At first glance, the increasing dominance of adjacent word order patterns in PRCs seems to be evidence of a more advanced grammaticalization stage of *mieć* in Modern Polish compared to OMP. But if we analyse the word order changes against the background of the

---

[18] Weydt and Kaźmierczak (1999) and Piskorz (2012), but cf. Łaziński (2001) for a more critical approach.
[19] CP = Contemporary Polish. The numbers are taken from Piskorz (2012: 231).

overall word order patterns in OMP, another interpretation becomes feasible. Unlike Modern Polish, OMP does not require adjacency of auxiliary and lexical elements. Consider examples (42) and (43) where the forms that constitute future tense forms are separated by the pronoun *nas* 'us', (42), and the noun phrase *ognistymi kulami* 'with glowing balls', (43):

(42) (Early 17th c., Listy staropolskie; Database)
będzie	nas	chciał		wszystkimi	sposobami
be.3SG.FUT	we.ACC	want.L-PTCP.SG.M		all.INS.PL	kind.INS.PL
awokować	od	przedsięwzięcia		naszego	
withdraw.INF	from	untertaking.GEN.SG.N		our.GEN.SG.N	

'he wants to withdraw us from our undertaking by all means'

(43) (Early 17th c., Listy staropolskie; Database)
bo	was	będę	ognistymi	kulami
for	you.ACC.PL	be.1SG.FUT	glowing.INS.PL	ball.INS.PL

palił!
burn.L-PTCP.SG.M
'for I will burn you with glowing balls'

In Modern Polish, insertions between auxiliary and lexical element are restricted to very short word forms like pronouns and particles (cf. *będzie to śpiewał* '[he] will sing this', *zostało już zrobione* '[this] has been done'). Considering this, the increase of adjacent patterns could be interpreted as a process relating to the relative position of auxiliaries in general and not as a function of a grammaticalization process within PRCs.

Given the fact that PRCs underwent comparatively few changes since their first occurrence in the 14th century, I opt for the second interpretation.

5 Possible origins of possessive resultative constructions

PRCs exist in all West Slavonic languages. At the same time, German possesses a *haben*-perfect, which developed from a PRC consisting of *haben* 'to have' and a past passive participle. This suggests that German played a part in the emergence of PRCs in Polish (and other West Slavonic languages). A look at the linguistic facts and the sociolinguistic situation in medieval Poland seems to support this hypothesis. PRCs must have developed before the 14th century, since they occur in the earliest written documents. At that time, there was a large German speaking population living in Poland, so that we can assume intense language contact, intense enough to warrant structural borrowing.[20] However, as I have argued in Mendoza (2013: 95–96), there is another possible model language for PRCs, namely Latin. Latin was the written language in medieval Poland and was gradually replaced by Polish from the 14th century onwards. Latin possesses PRCs with *habere* 'to have' + perfect passive participle (PPP), which originated in Classical Latin. In Late Antiquity and the Middle Ages, the construction *habere* + PPP was also used with a perfect meaning. This usage, however, was considered poor style (cf. Stotz 1998: 331: "nicht sonderlich gepflegt") and the use of *habere* + PPP was gradually brought back to its resultative meaning, which soon prevailed (Thomas Lindner, p.c.).

The emergence of a new grammatical category as a result of language contact can be aptly described using Heine and Kuteva's (2003, 2005) concept of grammatical replication, which they characterize as follows:

> "a. Speakers notice that in language **M** there is a grammatical category **Mx**.
> b. They create an equivalent category **Rx** in language R on the basis of use patterns available in **R**.
> c. To this end, they draw on universal strategies of grammaticalization, using Ry in order to develop **Rx**.[21]
> d. They grammaticalize category **Ry** to **Rx**." (Heine and Kuteva 2005: 81)

The outcome of a grammatical replication (Rx) is not always identical to the model category in language M (Mx). In particular, replica categories tend to be less grammaticalized than the original category (Heine and Kuteva 2005:119).

Using Heine and Kuteva's model, we would have to presume that speakers of Polish (= R) noticed the category "*haben*-perfect" (= Mx) in German or *habere*-PCRs in Latin (= M) and created PRC (= Rx) by drawing on possessive constructions proper with *mieć* (= Ry).

If we compare Latin and German as candidates for a possible model language, we find that Latin is the more likely candidate, because the Latin construction matches the Polish PRC more closely than the German one does. In German, the process of grammaticalization of a full-fledged perfect was

---

20 Cf. Thomason and Kaufman's well known borrowing scale (1988: 74–76).
21 Another type of grammatical replication is the so-called replica grammaticalization, i.e. the recreation of the (assumed) chain of grammaticalization itself: "To this end, they [the speakers, *I.M.*] replicate a grammaticalization process they assume to have taken place in language M, using an analogical formula of the kind [My > Mx] : [Ry > Rx]." (Heine and Kuteva 2005: 92). Heine and Kuteva (2005: 92–93) concede, however, that "it is not always possible on the basis of the evidence available to distinguish neatly between ordinary and replica grammaticalization".

completed in the 12th century (Fleischer and Schallert 2011: 125–129; Grønvik 1986). Hence, we would have to assume that the grammaticalization process in Polish started out using a language with a full perfect as a model only to be cut short at a very early stage, where it remained more or less until today. This renders a somewhat unusual scenario, even if we factor in possible differences between Mx and Rx.

However, it is impossible to decide definitively, which language was used as a model language. Even when we try to take register and text genre into account, we find ourselves at a dead end. Contact between Polish and Latin happened through writing, whereas German-Polish contact took place largely via the spoken word. One can argue that Latin-Polish interference manifests itself rather in written registers, while German influence would be found predominantly in spoken language. To be sure, in Modern Polish PRCs are usually used in spoken and not in written language. But due to the lack of evidence of spoken OMP, it is not easy to answer this question for the earliest periods. As my studies have shown, PRCs are not confined to a certain text genre or register. Moreover, in the *roty przysiąg sądowych*, which reflect spoken Polish of that time to a certain extent, I have found only one attestation of PRCs so far (1401; Roty kościańskie Nr. 168, cf. Mendoza 2013).

6 Conclusion

The possessive resultative is an infrequent, yet distinctive construction in OMP and has resisted major changes when compared to its Modern Polish equivalent. Only when it comes to word order patterns do we notice a clear difference. OMP prefers patterns that place the participle at the end ([*mieć* Object Participle] and [Object *mieć* Participle]), the adjacency of *mieć* and the participle is not relevant. In Modern Polish, on the other hand, the adjacency of *mieć* and the participle has become more important. Modern Polish strongly favours patterns that enable adjacency, the final position of the participle plays only a secondary role. This development seems, at first glance, to indicate the further auxiliarization and grammaticalization of *mieć*, but is probably just an instance of a more general process, namely the clustering of (any) auxiliary and lexical element (participle or infinitive).

The emergence of PRCs in Polish is, in all likelihood, a result of contact-induced grammaticalization. The starting point could have been the German *haben*-perfect or the *habere*-based PRC of Renaissance Latin. At this point, it is not possible to decide which it was. It is even conceivable that the two languages were reinforcing each other's influence.

Appendix: List of documents analysed

Document name or author's name	Number of wordforms	Number of PRC	Date of origin
Psałterz floriański	37.424	1	late 14th c.
Kazania świętokrzyskie	2.629	0	14th c.
Psałterz puławski	40.191	1	late 15th/early 16th c.
Ewangeliarz zamojskich	5.818	0	2nd half of 15th c.
Biblia królowej Zofii	167033	8	1453–1455
Kazania gnieźnieńskie	9.814	0	early 15th c. Jh.
Kazania na dzień wszech świętych	4.194	0	mid 15th c.
Modlitwy Wacława	13.113	0	ca. 1470
Modelitewnik najwojki	7.563	1	late 15th c.
Kodeks działyńskich	14.962	4	ca. 1450
Kodeks świętosławów	38.041	8	1449–1450
Ortyle z rękopisu Biblioteki Ossolińskich	40.937	1	ca. 1480
Polskie zabytki wierszowane do końca XV wieku[22]	19.195	0	14th and 15th c.
Kronika Turecka (Pamiętniki Janczara)	48347	6	1496–1501
Rozmyślanie przemyskie	123.441	10	early 16th c.
Ortyle Maciejowskiego	36.999	1	early 16th c.
List chana perekopskiego z roku 1500 do króla Jana Olbrachta	344	0	1500
Łukasz Górnicki, Droga do zupełnej wolności	14773	0	late 16th c.
Naborowski, Daniel	30.695	5	1593–1640
Testamenty	36.747	8	1595–1774
Szarzyński, Mikołaj	9340	1	1601
Listy staropolskie z epoki Wazów	44.000	9	1601–1665
Jurkowski, Jan	35.642	5	1604–1607
Skarga, Piotr	4.483	0	1610

---

22 Collection of religious and mundane poetry from the 14th and 15th c. (Bogurodzica, Legenda o św. Dorocie, Legenda o św. Aleksym, Dialog mistrza Polikarpa ze Śmiercią, Wiersz Słoty o chlebowym stole and others).

Document name or author's name	Number of wordforms	Number of PRC	Date of origin
Żółkiewski, Stanisław	24.310	3	1612
Szymonowic, Szymon	26.205	4	1614
Kochanowski, Piotr	367.363	97	1618
Birkowski, Fabian	106.050	10	1627
Sarbiewski, Maciej Kazimierz	4630	0	1635
Twardowski, Samuel 1	15.119	1	1638
Morsztyn, Jan Andrzej	109.189	30	1638–1693
Poczobut Odlanicki, Jan Władysław	48.017	6	1640–1684
Miaskowski, Wojciech	34.271	0	1640–1641
Opaliński, Łukasz	29.852	5	1641–1661
Gawiński, Jan	4.722	2	1650
Opaliński Krzysztof	52.747	6	1650
Morsztyn, Zbigniew	39.750	6	1653–1689
Zimorowic, Szymon	13.719	1	1654
Twardowski, Samuel 2	28.214	11	1655
Odymalski, Walerian	82.144	15	1655–1673
Merkuriusz Polski	70.124	11	1661
Zimorowic, Józef Bartłomiej	14.546	3	1663
Lubomirski, Stanislaw Herakliusz	104.809	14	1664
Szemiot, Stanisław Samuel	56.296	7	1674–1684
Kochowski, Wespazjan	5.637	2	1684
Potocki, Wacław	233.554	12	1690–1691
Komunija duchowna swiętych Borysa i Gleba	18.091	2	before 1693
Niemirycz, Krzysztof	10.354	0	1699
Listy do Marysieńki	115959	6	2nd half of 17th c.
Chmielowski, Benedykt	125.783	15	1745–1756
Konstytucja	5189	0	1791
Kopeć, Józef	31474	16	late 18th/early 19th c.
Krasicki, Ignacy	41334	8	2nd half of 18th c.
Pamiętnik Jewłaszewski[23]	14162	2	1860

---

[23] Polish translation of a 16th c. Belorussian original.

List of abbreviations

1	first person
2	second person
3	third person
ACC	accusative
CVB	converb
F	feminine
FUT	future
GEN	genitive
INF	infinitive
INS	instrumental
L-PTCP	*l*-participle
M	masculine
N	neuter
NOM	nominative
PRT	particle
PL	plural
PRP	present participle
PRS	present
PST	past
PP	passive participle
SG	singular

References

Breu, Walter. 1988. Resultativität, Perfekt und die Gliederung der Aspektdimension. In Jochen Raecke (ed.), *Slavistische Linguistik 1987: Referate des XIII. Konstanzer Slavistischen Arbeitstreffens Tübingen 22.–25.9.1987*, 42–74. München: Sagner.

Database: Andrzej de Vincenz & Gerd Hentschel. Datenbank polnischer Texte des 17. Jahrhundert.

Dentler, Sigrid. 1997. *Zur Perfekterneuerung im Mittelhochdeutschen: Die Erweiterung des zeitreferentiellen Funktionsbereichs von Perfektfügungen*. Göteborg: Acta Univ. Gothoburgensis.

Detges, Ulrich. 2000. Time and truth: The grammaticalization of resultatives and perfects within a theory of subjectification. *Studies in Language* 24 (2). 345–377.

Fleischer, Jürg & Oliver Schallert. 2011. *Historische Syntax des Deutschen. Eine Einführung*. Tübingen: Narr.

Giger, Markus. 2003. *Resultativa im modernen Tschechischen. Unter Berücksichtigung der Sprachgeschichte und der übrigen slavischen Sprachen*. Bern, Berlin, Bruxelles, Frankfurt a.M., New York, Oxford & Wien: Peter Lang.

Grønvik, Ottar. 1986. *Über den Ursprung und die Entwicklung der aktiven Perfekt- und Plusquamperfektkonstruktionen des Hochdeutschen und ihre Eigenart innerhalb des germanischen Sprachraumes.* Oslo: Solum Forlag.

Heine, Bernd. 1997. *Possession. Cognitive sources, forces, and grammaticalization.* Cambridge: University Press.

Heine, Bernd & Tania Kuteva. 2003. On contact-induced grammaticalization. *Studies in Language* 27 (3). 529–572.

Heine, Bernd & Tania Kuteva. 2005. *Language contact and grammatical change.* Cambridge: Cambridge University Press.

Jacob, Daniel. 1995. Von der *Subjekt*-Relevanz zur Gegenwartsrelevanz: Gebrauch und Entwicklung der Perfektperipharase *aver* + Partizip Perfekt Passiv im Altspanischen. *Romanistisches Jahrbuch* 46. 251–286.

Kątny, Andrzej. 1999. Zu Zustandskonstruktionen mit *mieć* 'haben' im Polnischen und ihren Entsprechungen im Deutschen. In Andrzej Kątny & Christoph Schatte (eds.), *Das Deutsche von innen und von außen: Ulrich Engel zum 70. Geburtstag*, 97–106. Poznań: Wydawnictwo naukowe UAM.

Kątny, Andrzej. 2005. Zu Zustandskonstruktionen mit *mieć* 'haben' im Polnischen und ihren Entsprechungen im Deutschen (Revisited). In Danuta Stanulewicz (ed.), *De lingua et litteris: Studia in honorem Casimiri Andreae Sroka*, 335–341. Gdańsk: Wydawnictwo Uniwersytetu Gdańskiego.

Kuroda, Susumu. 1999. *Die historische Entwicklung der Perfektkonstruktionen im Deutschen.* Hamburg: Buske.

Labocha, Janina. 1988. Czasownik *mieć* z imiesłowem biernym w polszczyźnie mówionej [The verb *mieć* 'have' with passive participle in spoken Polish]. *Język Polski* 68 (4–5). 233–242.

Lang, Ewald. 1977. *Semantik der koordinativen Verknüpfung.* Berlin: Akademie-Verlag.

Łaziński, Marek. 2001. Was für ein Perfekt gibt es im modernen Polnisch? Bemerkungen zum Artikel „Gibt es ein Pefekt im modernen Polnisch?" von H. Weydt und A. Kaźmierczak (Linguistik online 4, 3/99). *Linguistik online* 8 (1/01). http://www.linguistik-online.de/1_01/Lazinski.pdf (accessed 17 July 2015).

Langacker, Ronald W. 1995. Possession and possessive constructions. In John R. Taylor & Robert E. MacLaury (eds.), *Language and the cognitive construal of the world*, 51–79. Berlin & New York: Mouton de Gruyter.

Maslov, Jurij S. 1988. Resultative, perfect, and aspect. In Vladimir P. Nedjalkov (ed.), *Typology of resultative constructions*, 63–85. Amsterdam & Philadelphia: Benjamins.

Mel'čuk, Igor' A. 1998. *Kurs obščej morfologii. Tom II* [Course on general morphology. Vol. II]. Moskva & Vena: Jazyki Russkoj Kul'tury.

Mendoza, Imke. 2013. Verhinderte Grammatikalisierung? Zur Diachronie von Resultativkonstruktionen mit *mieć* 'haben' im Polnischen. *Wiener Slawistischer Almanach* 72. 77–102.

Nedjalkov, Vladimir P. & Sergej J. Jaxontov. 1988. The typology of resultative constructions. In Vladimir P. Nedjalkov (ed.), *Typology of resultative constructions*, 3–62. Amsterdam & Philadelphia: Benjamins.

Nitsch, Kazimierz. 1954 [1913]. Nowy czas przeszły złożony [A new compound past tense]. In *Wybór pism polonistycznych* [Selected Polonistic writings], 272–275. Wrocław: Zakład im. Ossolińskich.

Pinkster, Harm. 1987. The strategy and chronology of the development of future and perfect tense auxiliaries in Latin. In Martin Harris & Paolo Ramat (eds.), *Historical development of auxiliaries*, 193–223. Berlin & New York: Mouton de Gruyter.

Piskorz, Jadwiga. 2012. *Die Grammatikalisierung eines neuen Perfekts im Polnischen: Ein Beitrag zur Entwicklungslogik des Perfekts.* München: Sagner.

Piskorz, Jadwiga, Werner Abraham & Elisabeth Leiss. 2013. Doppelter Grammatikalisierungszyklus und funktionale Universalgrammatik. Am Beispiel des analytischen Perfekts und des Präteritums in der Sprachgeschichte des Polnischen. *Die Welt der Slaven* 58. 276–307.

PolDi: Polish Diachronic Online Corpus. http://rhssl1.uni-regensburg.de/SlavKo/korpus/poldi (accessed 21 July 2015).

Roty kościańskie: Henryk Kowalewicz & Władysław Kuraszkiewicz (eds.). 1967. *Wielkopolskie roty sądowe XIV–XV wieku. T. III: Roty kościańskie* [Greater Polish juridical oaths of the 14th–15th c. Vol. III: The *Kościan oaths*]. Warszawa: Państwowe Wydawnictwo Naukowe.

Sawicki, Lea. 2011. The perfect-like construction in colloquial Polish. *Zeitschrift für Slawistik* 56 (1). 66–83.

Seiler, Hansjakob. 2001. The operational basis of possession: A dimensional approach revisited. In Irène Baron, Michael Herslund & Finn Sørensen (eds.), *Dimensions of possession*, 27–40. Amsterdam & Philadelphia: Benjamins.

Stotz, Peter. 1998. *Handbuch zur Lateinischen Sprache des Mittelalters. Band 4: Formenlehre, Syntax und Stilistik.* München: Beck.

Taylor, John R. 1995. *Linguistic categorization. Prototypes in linguistic theory*, 2nd edn. Oxford: Clarendon Press.

Thomason, Sarah G. & Terrence Kaufman. 1988. *Language contact, creolization, and genetic linguistics.* Berkeley: University of California Press.

Topolińska, Zusanna. 1968. Miejsce konstrukcji z czasownikiem *mieć* w polskim systemie werbalnym [The place of the construction with the verb *mieć* 'have' in the Polish verbal system]. *Slavia Orientalis* 17. 427–431.

Weydt, Harald & Alicja Kaźmierczak. 1999. Gibt es ein Perfekt im modernen Polnisch? *Linguistik online* 4 (3/99). www.linguistik-online.ch/3_99/weydt.pdf (accessed 15 July 2015).

Wiemer, Björn & Markus Giger. 2005. *Resultativa in den nordslavischen und baltischen Sprachen: Bestandsaufnahme unter arealen und grammatikalisierungstheoretischen Gesichtspunkten.* München: LINCOM.

Slobodan Pavlović
Mechanisms of word order change in 12th and 13th century Serbian[1]

Abstract: This paper reviews the origin and the mechanism that led to word order change in the oldest Serbian mercantile and legal manuscripts, originating from the late 12th to the late 13th century. The Old Serbian language exhibits a dual nature with respect to sentence linearization. As the first word order rule, the linearization of stressed words is quite variable, while the second rule dictates that the ordering of enclitics and enclitic clusters, mostly attached to Wackernagel's position, remains fixed. While the dominant word order established in the Serbian language in the 12th and 13th centuries was SVO, it still allowed for alternatives (VSO, OVS, SOV, VOS, OSV). More importantly, the frequency of SVO rule increased with time, corresponding to 43.2% during the first half of the 13th century to 57.7% during the second half of the 13th century. During this period, the position of enclitics was defined by their specific functions. The sentential enclitic *li* takes the second place in the sentence. The noun-phrase enclitics, as a rule, now occupy the second place in the noun-phrase. The normal position for the predicate-phrase enclitics is immediately after the clause-front position and was observed with an 88% frequency. Outside of this position, predicate enclitics tend to occur closer to the verb, with nearly eight times lower frequency. These linearization tendencies can be explained by the development of configurational syntax, defined by syntactic phrase structures and centralized sentences.

1 Introduction

The linear ordering of sentence elements is one of the crucial syntactic parameters used for defining the typological profile of a particular language, but also for defining its diachronic development. Ever since B. Delbrück's work (1878: 13, 17–24), the SOV sentence model was considered to be the basic Proto-Indo-European word order of sentence elements. This claim was confirmed in

---

[1] This paper is a synthetic view of the Serbian sentence linearization in the 12th and 13th centuries, which has been the topic of the author's study in the past two years. This study was conducted within the project *The history of the Serbian language* (№ 178001), financed by the Ministry of Education, Science, and Technological Development of the Republic of Serbia.

https://doi.org/10.1515/9783110531435-008

subsequent works by several researchers in the next century (cf. Lehman 1974; Gamkrelidze and Ivanov 1984: 320–325). The change of this pattern is related to a typological change from the active-stative into the nominative-accusative language type (Gamkrelidze and Ivanov 1984: 267–319), i.e. to the development of verbal transitivity (Grković-Major 2013: 8–54). Thus, the diachronic typological research overlaps with the synchronic typological research of J. Greenberg (1963).[2] As Serbian has a dual nature in terms of sentence linear ordering – orthotonic sentence elements have a more or less free distribution, while the distribution of enclitics is regularly fixed (cf. Browne 1974; Radanović-Kocić 1988; Schütze 1994; Popović 1997; Dimitrova-Vulchanova 1999; Franks and Holloway King 2000; Diesing, Filipović Đurđević, and Zec 2009; Spencer and Luís 2012) – it seems useful to look into this aspect of linguistic phrasing in the oldest Serbian texts from the 12th and 13th centuries, in order to detect potential changes and identify the mechanism of those changes. The research focuses on 1) the distribution of enclitics; 2) the position of the subject, predicate and object as the key sentential elements and 3) the ordering of noun phrase elements.

The corpus of this study consists of Old Serbian administrative manuscripts, originating from the late 12th to the late 13th century (a total of 44 charters and letters). The examples are labelled according to the list of the manuscripts in the book *The Old Serbian dependent clause from the 12th to the 15th century* (Pavlović 2009). The structure of the research corpus is defined by Old Serbian functional diglossia, in which Serbian Church Slavonic (as the language of sacral literacy) and Serbian vernacular language are used for complementary communicative functions (cf. Grković-Major, this volume). The written use of vernacular Serbian was limited to the administrative texts of mercantile and legal type until the end of the 15th century. It is important to note that the Serbian medieval vernacular texts may reflect an oral tradition, promoted especially by public reading legal and mercantile agreements.

---

[2] The earlier history of typological sentence linearization research can be traced back to G. Girard, who, in the mid-18th century classified languages according to the order of subject (S), predicate (V) and object (O) into analogous (in which sentence linearization follows the natural course of thinking) and transpositive ones (in which sentence linearization does not follow the natural course of thinking) (Ramat 2011: 17). Nevertheless, the real philological predecessor of Greenberg's typological studies can be traced, according to G. Graffi (2011: 26), only in Gabelenz's research into word order in the late 19th century.

2 Distribution of enclitics

The position of enclitics in Old Serbian is governed by two confronted distributional concepts: 1) the old Wackernagel, post-frontal sentential concept, according to which the second, tonally depressed, sentence position attracts clitics as non-tonic grammatical components (Delbrück 1878: 48; Wackernagel 1892: 406; Comrie 1980: 86),[3] and 2) the new post-frontal phrasal concept, according to which enclitics link to their corresponding phrases according to their syntactic function (Franks and Holloway King 2000: 234–240; Pancheva 2005: 150–157; Zaliznjak 2008: 68; Spencer and Luís 2012: 171–177; Pavlović 2013: 35–67; Zimmerling and Kosta 2013: 194–196). Based on their function, Old Serbian enclitics can be divided into a) the sentential (S) enclitic *li*, which is related to a clause as a whole; b) the predicate phrase (VP) enclitics, which are morphologically or syntactically related to the predicate phrase and c) noun phrase (NP) enclitics, which are the constituents of the noun phrase.

2.1 The sentential enclitic *li*

The sentential enclitic *li*, which is a syntactic indicator of the illocution of the utterance, is always related to the post-frontal, Wackernagel sentence position (1):

(1) ako   li   sie   prestuplu   da   me   °bъ
    if   S.ENCL   this   break-1SG.PRS   OP.PRT   me   God
    sudi.
    condemn-3SG.PRS
    'Should I break this promise, may God condemn me.' (№ 4.11)

2.2 Noun phrase enclitics

Dative enclitics of personal pronouns with the meaning of possessive determiners of the corresponding noun, can be found in any position in the clause as a post-frontal constituent of a noun phrase, where they function as dependent elements. Hence the position of noun phrase enclitics in the Serbian language of the

---

[3] B. Comrie (1980: 86) discusses a possible explanation of Wackernagel's law in the light of the attraction of enclitics "into the position between the topic (theme) and the comment (rheme) of the sentence, i.e. into the main intonation break within the sentence".

12th and 13th centuries depends on the position of the head noun, which is usually the orthotonic catalyst of the noun phrase (2):

(2) izlezohъ   prě/d/   bratomь   mi   vla/d/slavomъ.
    escape-1SG.AOR   in front of   brother   me-DAT.ENCL   Vladislav
    'I escaped in front of my brother Vladislav.' (№ 5.3)

Noun phrase enclitics can be attached to the post-initial (Wackernagel's) sentence position only if their noun phrase takes a sentence initial position (3):

(3) °sto   ti   °crstvo   da   ne   stvoritъ
    holy   you-DAT.ENCL   Imperial Majesty   OP.PRT   not   make-3SG.PRS
    mirъ   bezъ   nasъ   sъ   urošemъ.
    peace   without   us-GEN.PL   with   Uroš
    'May Your Holy Imperial Majesty not make peace with Uroš without us.' (№ 23.13)

2.3 Predicate phrase enclitics

The enclitics featuring in the predicate phrase (VP) are the enclitic (primarily aorist) forms of the verb *byti* as the constituent of the conditional form, the present enclitics of the verbs *jesъmь* and *htěti*, the dative and accusative enclitic forms of personal pronouns, including the enclitic forms of the reflexive pronoun. Verbal enclitics are involved in the predicate phrase as the morphological indicators of the person and number of analytical verbal forms (conditional, perfect and future), and the copulative predicate. Pronominal enclitics, on the other hand, usually establish a syntactic relationship, with the finite verbal form which is the head of the predicate phrase, thus filling up the argument positions required by the argument structure of the given verb.

Old Serbian predicate phrase enclitics take Wackernagel's position (i.e. the post-initial position in the clause) in 88% of the cases (of the total of 483 examples), (4):

(4) ako   mi   °bъ   da   i   budu
    if   me-DAT.ENCL   God   give-3SG.PRS   and   be-1SG.PRS
    gospodarъ ‖ kako   sъmь   bylъ   da
    lord   as   be-AUX.ENCL.1SG.PRS   be-PTCP.PFV   OP.PRT
    si   hode...
    REFL.DAT.ENCL   go-3PL.PRS
    'Should God allow me to be the ruler as I have been, your people may go [trade].' (№ 5.9)

In 12% of the cases these enclitics are separated from the frontal sentential catalyst (as the orthotonic host), which means that the statistical ratio between the predicate phrase enclitics in Wackernagel's position and those in other positions is 7.3 : 1 in favour of the post-frontal sentence position.

This ratio varies with the types of enclitics, reaching the highest value 20.7 : 1 in verbal enclitics, and the lowest 4.5 : 1 in the enclitic forms of the reflexive pronoun, which means that the reflexive pronoun is the most susceptible to movement from the post-initial sentence position.

The violation of Wackernagel's principle of the distribution of these enclitics is motivated by the need for homogeneity inside the predicate phrase: a) in 74% of the cases these enclitics are incorporated in the non-initial optative periphrasis *da + present* with the particle *da* as the catalyst, (5), b) in 15% of the cases it is the accusative enclitic *se*, which is in the verb-postposed position as the marker of reflexivity, (6), c) in 6% of the cases it is the dative enclitic of personal pronoun postposed to the head verb, (7), and d) in 5% of the cases it is the predicate phrase enclitic which is positioned before the head verb, with a clearly marked tendency of direct concatenation with it, (8):

(5) od °/d/nъšnega °dne: ‖da ti
    since today day OP.PRT you-DAT.ENCL
    smo prъěteli.
    be-AUX.ENCL.1SG.PRS friends
    'May we be your friends as of today.' (№ 8.6)

(6) banъ bosnъski: veliki ‖kle se knezu
    prince Bosnian great pledge-3SG.AOR REFL.ACC.ENCL prince
    doubrovčkomou.
    Dubrovnik-POSS.ADJ
    'The great prince of Bosnia pledged to the prince of Dubrovnik.' (№ 7.1)

(7) sije ‖oučinivъ imъ i outvrъdihъ.
    this make-ACT.PTCP.PST them-DAT.ENCL and establish-1SG.AOR
    'This was made and established by me.' (№ 5.8)

(8) mi i naša opъkina pravo ‖i verъno
    we and our municipality righteously and faithfully
    sъmo derъžali.
    be-AUX.ENCL.1SG.PRS keep-PTCP.PFV
    'We and our municipality have kept it righteously and faithfully.' (№ 12.4)

It should be noted that in almost half of the examples of Wackernagel's predicate phrase enclitic, a verbal form has the function of the orthotonic host, i.e. catalyst. In 13% of the cases the lexical component of the analytical verbal form has the function of the catalyst and in 35% of the cases the particle *da*, as the constituent part of the optative periphrasis *da + present* has the function of the orthotonic host. Those are the structures in which the post-frontal sentential and post-frontal phrasal concepts of distribution of enclitics overlap.

3 Subject, predicate and object positions

Identifying the rule of the ordering of subject, predicate and object implies, as M. Dryer remarked (2007: 79), defining the positional relationship of 1) the predicate and the subject, 2) the predicate and the object, and 3) the subject and the object, where the third relation is contained in the first two, since subject-object relationship is always realized through the predicate.

3.1 Models of subject-predicate ordering

The statistical analysis of sentences which contain an explicitly stated subject alongside the predicate indicates that in the Serbian language of the 12th and 13th centuries the subject predominantly preceded the predicate. The frequency ratio between the SV and VS models of subject-predicate ordering is approximately 1.9 : 1 (65% : 35%) in favour of the SV model, which could therefore be regarded as the default model. This frequency ratio can vary with the type of predicate with which the subject occurs.

The ratio between the SV (see the a-examples) and VS (see the b-examples) models remains at a more or less average value (65% : 35%) in the cases when the predicate is a transitive verb with an explicitly stated object (65.1% : 34.9%) (9):[4]

(9) a. SVO ě radoe diěkъ banъ pisahъ
I Radoje scribe prince-POSS.ADJ write-1SG.AOR
ovu knjigu
this book
'I, Radoje, the scribe of ban, have written this book.' (№ 1.16)

(9) a. SOV my samoga krivca da daemo.
we himself culprit OP.PRT give-1PL.PRS
'We should give away the culprit himself.' (№ 28.30)

---

[4] Sentences with an indirect object do not show significant deviation (cf. Pavlović 2013: 81–84).

(9) a. OSV globe   nitъkore da   ne   vъzyma.
            tax   nobody   OP.PRT not take-3SG.PRS
            'Taxes shall not be taken by anyone.' (№ 29.126)

(9) b. VSO vidě   kralevъstvo   mi   tolikou o/d/
            see-3SG.AOR Royal Majesty   me-DAT.ENCL   such   from
            nihъ   počъstь.
            them-PL.GEN   honour
            'My Royal Majesty has witnessed such an honour from them.' (№ 5.7)

(9) b. VOS stvori   sie   ja stefan   vladislavъ.
            create-3SG.AOR this   I   Stefan   Vladislav
            'This has been created by me, Stefan Vladislav.' (№ 15.1)

(9) b. OVS sie   vse pisa   kra/le/vъstvo   mi
            this all write-3SG.AOR   Royal Majesty   me-DAT.ENCL
            'This has all been written by My Royal Majesty.' (№ 35.9)

A more significant deviation from the average relationship is found in the cases where the preposing of the subject would cause the separation of the direct object from the transitive verb, as the head of the predicate phrase. Namely, despite a limited number of cases, it is evident that the OVS model with the subject postposed after the predicate is more frequent than the opposite OSV model with the preposed subject (2.6 OVS : 1 OSV). This is most probably caused by the homogenizing of the predicate phrase with the transitive verb as the head and object as the subordinate constituent.

Compared to the average frequency ratio of the SV and VS models of sentence linearization, the frequency of the SV model, on the one hand, increases with positional verb predicates, i.e. verbs of speaking and, on the other, decreases with verbs of motion. With existential verbs, the subject is more commonly preposed than postposed. The ratio of preposing (see the a-examples) and postposing (see the b-examples) of the subject to the verbs of speaking is approximately 8.6 : 1 (10), to the positional verbs the ratio is approximately 5 : 1, (11), to the motion verbs it is approximately 1.5 : 1, (12), and to the existential verbs it is approximately 1 : 2.7, (13):

(10) a. ě banъ: bosъnъski kulinъ: prisezaju   /te/bě
         I prince   Bosnian   Kulin   pledge-1SG.PRS   you-DAT
         kneže   krъvašu.
         prince-VOC   Gervase
         'I, the prince of Bosnia Kulin, pledge allegiance to you, prince Gervase.'
         (№ 1.5)

(10) b. *piše   kralev'stvo   mi   knezu*
       write-3SG.PRS Royal Majesty   me-DAT.ENCL   prince-DAT
       dubrov'čьskomu.
       Dubrovnik-POSS.ADJ
       'My Royal Majesty is writing to the prince of Dubrovnik.' (№ 37.1)

(11) a. *carinikъ   tvoj   da   stoji   u   nasь.*
       customs officer   your   OP.PRT   stay-3SG.PRS   at   us-GEN
       'Let your customs officer stay with us.' (№ 8.32)

(11) b. *da   si   sěde   tvoě   sela   svobodьno.*
       OP.PRT   REFL.DAT.ENCL   stay-3PL.PRS   your   villages   freely
       'May your villages remain free.' (№ 11.4)

(12) a. *Koupьci   ih   da   si   hode   po*
       customers   they-GEN OP.PRT   REFL.DAT.ENCL   go-3PL.PRS   over
       zemlji   kra/l/vstva   mi.
       land   Royal Majesty   me-DAT.ENCL
       'Let their customers go around the land of My Royal Majesty.' (№ 39.4)

(12) b. *pride   kra/l/v/s/tvou   mi   igoumenь*
       approach-1SG.AOR   Royal Majesty   me-DAT.ENCL   prior
       jevstaθije.
       Jevstatije
       'Prior Jevstatije approached My Royal Majesty.' (№ 33.1)

(13) a. *pravina   da   estь.*
       justice   OP.PRT   be-3SG.PRS
       'May there be justice.' (№ 6.9)

(13) b. *tu   běše   sudija   boleslavь.*
       there   be-3SG.IMP   judge   Boleslav
       'Judge Boleslav was there.' (№ 44.6)

A significant deviation from the default model of subject-predicate positioning is found in existential sentences, which have VS as the primary linearization model, and not SV as in other sentence types. Existential verbs confirm the existence of a denotatum, which carries the communicative focus, and is therefore placed after the verb (as a rule, the rheme is related to the sentence ending).[5] This sentence type confirms that the communicative sentence perspective was

---

[5] A similar tendency was recorded in Old Russian texts, although the dominance of the VS model in existential sentences was much more striking (6.3 VS : 1 SV) (McAnallen 2009: 221).

relevant already in the 12th and 13th centuries, and so was the communicative focus of the sentence ending.

3.2 Models of predicate-object ordering

The statistical analysis of sentences which contain an explicit object with the predicate shows that the default position of the direct object in the Serbian language of the 12th and 13th centuries was dominantly after the predicate. The frequency ratio between the VO (i.e. predicate – direct object) and OV (i.e. direct object – predicate) order is approximately 2.1 : 1 in favour of the VO order, which gives it the status of the basic model. This frequency ratio insignificantly varies with the occurrence of an explicit subject in sentences with a transitive verb.

In relation to the average frequency relation of the VO and OV models of sentence element ordering, the frequency of the VO model is comparatively lower in sentences without an explicit subject, and higher in sentences with an explicit subject. The ratio of the preposed (see the a-examples) and postposed (see the b-examples) direct object in relation to the predicate in sentences without an explicit subject is approximately 1.8 : 1, (14), and in sentences with an explicit subject it is 2.7 : 1, (15):[6]

(14) a. *dahъ   sela   ou   hlъmscy   zemly.*
       give-1SG.AOR villages in   Hum-POSS.ADJ   land
       'I have given the villages in the land of Hum.' (№ 29.83)

(14) b. *sizi   dvě   tisuki   da   daju   na*
        these   two   thousands   OP.PRT   give-3PL.PRS   on
        dmitrovъ   °dnъ.
        Dmitar-POSS.ADJ day
        'Let them give these two thousand on Dmitar's day.' (№ 37.10)

(15) a. SVO *vladimirъ   ne   plenoval   tvoju   zm/l/u.*
             Vladimir   be-NEG.3SG.PRS ravage- PTCP.PFV your   country
             'Vladimir did not ravage your country.' (№ 12.11)

(15) a. VSO *prizva   kralevъstvo   mi   arhije[]pa*
             summon-3SG.AOR Royal Majesty   me-DAT.ENCL   archbishop
             arsjanija.
             Arsenije
             'My Royal Majesty has summoned the archbishop Arsenije.'
             (№ 29.25)

---

[6] Sentences with an indirect object do not show statistical significance (cf. Pavlović 2013: 81–84).

(15) a. VOS I   ne   ostavi   mene   vla/d/ka   moi.
            and   not   leave-3SG.AOR   me-ACC   God   my
            'And my God did not desert me.' (№ 2.44)

(15) b. SOV ěa   vašega   čověka   da   puštu.
            I   your   man   OP.PRT   release-1SG.PRS
            'I shall release your man.' (№ 24.14)

(15) b. OSV siju   crkvu   da   niktore   ne   razlouči.
            this   church   OP.PRT   nobody   not   divide-3SG.PRS
            'May no one divide this church.' (№ 33.2)

(15) b. OVS drugu   polovinu   da   ima   opьkina.
            other   half   OP.PRT   have-3SG.PRS   municipality
            'Let the municipality of Dubrovnik come into possession of the other half.' (№ 23.47)

The stabilization of the VO sentence pattern is one of the crucial indicators of the typological change from an active-stative (i.e. non-configurational) into a nominative-accusative (i.e. configurational) language type (Gamkrelidze and Ivanov 1984: 267–319), where an inactive actant, through the development of syntactic transitivity, acquires the status of an object conceptualized as the goal onto which an activity is "physically or metaphorically conveyed" (Grković-Major 2013: 9). The new syntactic concept meant the change of the old phrasal *A (active actant) – In (inactive actant) – V* order into the new SVO phrasal linear order where the object, analogous to its purpose, follows the predicate represented by a transitive verb. It is obvious that at the earliest stage of the development of Old Serbian literacy the frequency of the new VO model grew at the expense of the old OV model. The frequency ratio between the VO and OV models in the first half of the analysed period (up to the mid-13th century) is approximately 1.5 : 1, while in the second half of the period (after the mid-13th century) it increased to 2.9 : 1.

Together with the postposing of the object in relation to the predicate, there is an evident strengthening of the homogeneity of the predicate phrase. In sentences where the transitive verb is accompanied with an explicit subject, the direct object can be remote from the verb, which is its head constituent (as in the VSO and OSV models), but such structures were only found in every fifth case. The relation of homogeneous predicate phrases made up of a transitive verb and a direct object (without an interposed subject) and the non-homogeneous ones (with an interposed subject) in the first half of the period analysed (up to 1250) is approximately 3.1 : 1, and in the second half of the period (after 1250) it gets as high as 7.3 : 1. Such a relation clearly indicates the strengthening of the predicate phrase as the core of the new centralized sentence.

The process of postposing the object in relation to the predicate could be viewed as the process of preposing the predicate in relation to the object. Namely, there are two distinct distributional mechanisms that could have simultaneously led to the movement of the old Serbian predicate to the post-initial sentence position, which automatically left the orthotonic object in the post-predicative position.[7] These are the tendency towards homogenizing the predicate phrase on the one hand, and the influence of Wackernagel's rule of post-frontal sentence distribution of verbal enclitics on the other.

3.3 Development tendency

If we analyse the frequency relations of sentence models with an overt subject and direct object (which is the primary focus of the typological and diachronic research of sentence linearization), it is apparent that as early as in the Serbian-language mercantile and legal manuscripts of the 12th and 13th centuries the SVO model is more frequent than all other models in total: SVO 51.1%, VSO 14.6%, OVS 13.5%, SOV 8.3%, VOS 7.3%, OSV 5.2%. In addition, this model obviously showed an increasing tendency: before the mid-13th century this model is found in 43.3% of the cases, and after 1250 until the late 13th century in 57.7% of the cases.

4 Linearization of the noun phrase

The homogenization of the Serbian noun phrase was finalized even before the emergence of the first written texts, so that the examples of its discontinuity in the Old Serbian texts occur only in traces, (16)–(17):

(16) vsakou globou da ouzima °crkvъ malou
every-ACC tax-ACC OP.PRT take-3SG.PRS church small [tax]-ACC
i velikou.
and big [tax]-ACC
'The Church shall take every tax, both low and high.' (№ 45.41)

(17) kletvu da ima °stgo simeona.
curse-ACC OP.PRT have-3SG.PRS holy-POSS.GEN Simeon-POSS.GEN
'May the curse of St. Simeon come upon him.' (№ 188.36)

---

[7] A similar phenomenon was attested in medieval Romance texts (cf. Wanner 1996: 554).

The frequency ratio of remote and adjacent modifiers of the head noun is approximately 1 : 250 in favour of the adjacent position, which means that the distance of the modifier and the head noun was reduced to only 4% as early as in the oldest Serbian texts. In the Serbian language of the 12th and 13th centuries the noun phrase was a stable category with the noun as the centripetal core, which does not allow the modifiers to be remote.

The distribution of the modifying constituents of the noun phrase is still not uniform, either in variable types of modifiers or within the same modifier type. Modifiers exhibiting agreement (concordant modifiers) are dominantly preposed, while the non-concordant ones are dominantly postposed. The frequency ratio between the preposed and postposed concordant modifier is approximately 3 : 1 in favour of preposing, while the ratio between the preposed and postposed non-concordant modifier in the genitive or dative case is approximately 1 : 9.1 in favour of postposition.

4.1 Noun phrase with a concordant modifier

However, the dominant preposed location of a concordant modifier in the Serbian language of the 12th and 13th centuries is remarkably uneven and closely related to the modifier type. Thus, the ratio of preposed location of pronominal modifiers decreases from the relational (general, negative, indefinite and demonstrative) adjectival pronouns to possessive pronouns. The frequency ratio of preposed (see the a-examples) to postposed (see the b-examples) relational pronouns is approximately 12.3 : 1, (18)–(19), while with the possessive pronoun this relation is approximately 2.9 : 1 in favour of the preposed location, (20).

(18) a. *da   imъ   ně   nikere   sile.*
    OP.PRT   them-DAT   be-NEG.3SG.PRS   no-GEN   pressure-GEN
    'May they not be forced to anything.' (№ 4.8)

(18) b. *da   vi   ně   desetka   nikogare.*
    OP.PRT   you-DAT.PL.ENCL   be-NEG.3SG.PRS   tax-GEN   no-GEN
    'May you pay no tax.' (№ 10.6)

(19) a. *pisah   siju: knigu.*
    write-1SG.IMPF this-ACC   book-ACC
    'I wrote this book.' (№ 1.16)

(19) b. *da   e   na   nas   kletva   siě.*
    OP.PRT   be-AUX.ENCL.3SG.PRS   on   us-ACC   curse-NOM   this-NOM
    'May this curse come onto us.' (№ 8.11)

(20) a. da   si   sěde   tvoě   sela
       OP.PRT   REFL.DAT.ENCL   stay-3PL.PRS your-NOM   villages-NOM
       svobodьno.
       freely
       'May your villages remain free.' (№ 11.4)

(20) b. trьžnici   vaši   da   gredu   na   brьskovo.
       merchants-NOM your-NOM   OP.PRT   go-3PL.PRS   on   Brskovo
       'Your merchants may go to Brskovo.' (№ 27.23)

With adjectival attributes, the uneven distribution is yet more apparent. The ratio of preposed (see the a-examples) to postposed (see the b-examples) qualifying adjectives is 13.5 : 1, (21). With possessive adjectives the ratio is approximately 1.2 : 1 in favour of preposed distribution, (22), and with categorizing adjectives the ratio is reversed, being 1 : 2.6 in favour of the postposed location, (23):

(21) a. da   mu   se   ne   uzme   ni
       OP.PRT   him-DAT.ENCL   REFL.ACC.ENCL   not   take-3SG.PRS   neither
       Tьnkь   konьcь.
       thin-NOM thread-NOM
       'May not even a thin thread be taken from him.' (№ 6.13)

(21) b. tko   e   priětelь   věrьnь   vьzdě
       who   be-AUX.ENCL.3SG.PRS   friend-NOM   faithful-NOM   always
       e   priětelь.
       be-AUX.ENCL.3SG.PRS   friend-NOM
       'A faithful friend is always a friend.' (№ 24.17)

(22) a. kako   grede   cjasta   ou   radova   kjučyšta.
       as   go-3SG.PRS   path-NOM   in   Rade-POSS.ADJ.ACC   hamlet- ACC
       'As the path goes in Rade's hamlet.' (№ 29.76)

(22) b. ě   radoe   diěkь   banь   pisahь   ovu
       I   Radoje   scribe-NOM   prince-POSS.ADJ.NOM   write-1SG.AOR this
       knjigu.
       book
       'I, Radoje, the scribe of ban, have written this book.' (№ 1.16)

(23) a. htitor   bystь   mnogim   manastyremь   vь
       benefactor   be-3SG.AOR   many-DAT.PL   monastery-DAT.PL   in
       srьp/s/koi   oblasti
       Serbian-LOC   land-LOC
       'I have been the benefactor of many monasteries in Serbian lands.' (№ 16.2)

(23) b. *stefan   vladislavь   pomokiju   ⁰bžiovь*
     Stefan   Vladislav   help-INS.SG   God-POSS.ADJ.INS.SG
     kralь   srьp/s/ki.
     king-NOM.SG   Serbian-NOM.SG
     'Stefan Vladislav, the king of Serbs, with God's help.' (№ 14.7)

The majority of postposed concordant determiners are adverbial and pronominal indicators of categorical and individual possession. The frequency ratio of the postposed possessive pronouns and all other postposed adjectival pronouns is approximately 3 : 1 in favour of the possessive pronouns. The frequency ratio of the postposed category and possessive adjectives on the one hand, and all other postposed adjectives on the other, is approximately 7.1 : 1 in favour of the categorical possessive adjectives. If, on the one hand, these data of the Serbian language are compared to the Old Church Slavonic texts, where the possessive pronouns are preposed in 0.2% in *Psalterium Sinaiticum* to 42.8% in *Rila folia* (Večerka 1989: 78), and on the other to the Old Russian texts from the 11th to the 14th century, where possessive pronouns, for example, are preposed only in 21.7% (Sannikov 1968: 61–69), it is obvious that the concordant modifier in the Slavonic languages moved from the post-position to the pre-position in relation to the head noun.[8] The shifting of the concordant modifiers from post-position to pre-position is most persistently rejected by adjectival and pronominal indicators of individual and categorical possession, i.e. by category and possessive adjectives and possessive pronouns.

4.2 Noun phrase with a non-concordant modifier

Non-concordant, i.e. genitive and dative attributes are dominantly postposed since the oldest extant Old Serbian texts. The frequency ratio of the postposed (see the a-examples) to the preposed (see the b-examples) genitive noun

---

[8] Although such statistical tendencies suggest that the primary position of the Slavonic concordant modifier is postposition after the head word (cf. Lapteva 1959), a number of authors are of a different opinion (for example, Kozlovskij 1901; Vondrák 1908). A high frequency of postposed modifiers in old Slavonic texts is sometimes uncritically interpreted from the viewpoints of foreign influences, primarily Greek, even when Old Russian examples were in question (cf. Lapteva 1959: 99–102).

modifier is approximately 8.4 : 1, (24), and of the dative nominal modifiers it is 16.9 : 1, (25):

(24) a. *da   si   ju   prodaju   po*
       OP.PRT   REFL.DAT.ENCL   her- ACC.ENCL   sell-3PL.PRS   round
       zemli   kralevъ/s/tva   mi.
       country-LOC   Royal Majesty-POSS.GEN   me-DAT.ENCL
       'Let them sell it in my kingdom.' (№ 27.26)

(24) b. *°gna   i   oca   svojego   °stgo   kr/l/a*
        master-GEN   and   father-GEN   his-GEN   holy-GEN   king-GEN
        stefana   povelěnije   razouměvъ.
        Stefan-GEN   command-ACC   understand-ACT.PTCP.PST
        'Having understood the command of his master and father, holy king Stefan.' (№ 22.11)

(25) a. *koga   °bъ   izvoli   byti   g/d/na*
        whom-ACC   God   appoint-3SG.PRS   be-INF   lord-ACC
        srъb'skoi   zemli.
        Serbian-POSS.DAT   land-POSS.DAT
        'Whom God has appointed the lord of the Serbian land.' (№ 38.36)

(25) b. *tomu   selou   mega*
        that-POSS.DAT   village-POSS.DAT   border
        'The border of that village.' (№ 16.12)

4.3 Development tendency

Taking into consideration that the genitive and dative non-concordant attributes, as a rule, also surface as the indicators of individual or categorical possession, it can be concluded that possessive pronouns and adjectives have been kept in the post-position after the head noun by their semantics, i.e. possessiveness in the broadest sense of the word,[9] while the other force, pushing them to the pre-position, was morphological (case-number-gender) agreement, whose "distributional pressure" will eventually prevail.

---

[9] It should be noted here that the majority of personal pronouns emerged as a combination of the original genitive and the corresponding possessive suffix. Cf. *naš* (**nas + jь*) etc.

5 Change in linearization as a result of typological change

The changes in the sentence linear order of the Serbian language of the 12th and 13th centuries were motivated by the need to establish homogeneous and continuous phrasal structures, as well as a centralized sentence (cf. Grković-Major 2010). This tendency is obvious in the case of the orthotonic sentence elements, but it is also observed in the distribution of atonal, enclitic components.

5.1 Wackernagel's law and establishing homogeneous phrasal structures

While the sentential enclitic *li* is always related to the post-frontal sentence position in accordance with Wackernagel's law, the noun phrase enclitics are linked to the post-frontal phrasal position – regardless of the place taken by the noun phrase as the "host". Predicate phrase enclitics prefer post-frontal sentence position (88%), but in almost every eighth example these enclitics are displaced from this position by attaching to the post-frontal position of a non-initial predicate phrase.

The fact that noun phrase enclitics are consistently attached to their noun phrase, while the predicate enclitics are dominantly attached to the post-frontal sentence position, is probably determined by the different syntactic status of their phrasal hosts in sentences.

In other words, if the noun phase enclitic does not attach to its "mobile" phrase, it cannot manifest its noun phrase character (as the possessive determiner). A predicate phrase enclitic, on the other hand, even when remaining in Wackernagel's position, does not lose its predicate phrase quality, because the predicate phrase is the core of the centralized sentence, and "sentence space" is the effective domain of the predicate phrase.

5.2 SVO ordering and development of syntactic transitivity

Since it is obvious that at the earliest stage of the development of Old Serbian literacy the frequency of the VO model grows at the expense of the OV model, it can be assumed, in accordance with the principle of growth, that the object in the late Proto-Slavonic language could have been dominantly preposed in relation to the predicate. This is in line with the contemporary theory of change from an active-stative into a nominative-accusative language type in the

Indo-European languages (cf. Gamkrelidze and Ivanov 1984: 267–319). The old active-stative *A – In – V* (i.e. SOV) model of sentence linearization is replaced by the new nominative-accusative SVO model of sentence element ordering through the development of syntactic transitivity (Grković-Major 2013).

The change of the language pattern types is a long-lasting, phase process (cf. Radovanović 2009), during which the new model, whose frequency increases, acquires the dominant status of the natural, unmarked order, while the other models, being far less frequent, acquire the status of marked models in terms of their distribution or pragmatic meanings (cf. Dryer 2007: 73–78).

The stabilization of the SVO model of sentence linearization in the Serbian language of the 12th and 13th centuries obviously corresponded to the stabilization of the noun phrase with the preposed concordant attribute and postposed non-concordant attribute. Although "there is no evidence for any universal relationship between the order of adjective and noun and the order of object and verb" (Dryer 1988: 208), Dryer identifies the SVO order and AdjN model as the Indo-European dominant model (1988: 189). What is typologically significant is the stabilization of the homogeneous, continuous noun phrase, whose constituents are in a contact relationship with the head noun.

5.3 From non-configurational to configurational syntax

The changes in word order motivated by the homogenization of phrase structures and the centralized sentence are a manifestation of the typological transition of the Serbian language from the non-configurational to configurational syntax as an expression of highly developed verbal transitivity. The term non-configurational syntax emerged in the theoretical framework of generative grammar, i.e. of the Government and Binding Theory in the 1980's as a label of specific syntactic systems without an integrated sentence hierarchy.[10] Syntactic non-configuration is characterized by an increased autonomy of particular words in the sentence structure, which significantly strengthens the importance of morphological forms, i.e. paradigmatic relations. At the sentence linearization level, syntactic non-configuration is manifested, among

---

[10] Analysing the Warlpiri language of Central Australian Aborigines, K. Hale (1983: 5) remarks that the grammatical system of this language "exhibits a number of properties which have come to be associated with the typological label 'non-configurational'". K. Hale introduced the terms configurational and non-configurational in the late 1970's, so that N. Chomsky (1981: 128), referring to Hale's findings, takes Japanese as a typical example of a non-configurational language.

other things, through a free word order and discontinuity of phrase structures (cf. Webelhuth 1984–1985: 203; Rögnvaldsson 1995: 3; Pavlović 2013: 11–34).[11]

Configurational syntax is characterized by the opposite features, i.e. a) more or less fixed word order and b) phrase structure constituency characterized by a homogeneous predicate and noun phrase, even at the cost of moving the enclitics outside the Wackernagel position.[12]

Non-configuration and configuration are two poles of a developmental continuum (cf. Radovanović 2009), and Serbian of the 12th and 13th centuries emerges as a language that intensively approaches a configurational typological pole in terms of sentence linearization.[13]

Such a typological shift of the Serbian language may have been triggered by substrate and adstrate "pressures". The development of configurational syntax is intensified by the development of literacy, and Old Serbian syntax of written texts was under the influence of Romance literacy with a highly developed syntactic configuration. Medieval Romance languages' influence on the Serbian written language syntax is primarily manifested through the so called diplomatic forms, which defined the discourse structure of the Old Serbian charters.

It is therefore not surprising that the violation of the Wackernagel principles of distribution of predicate phrase enclitics is twice more frequent in the Old Serbian charters written in the south-western Serbian offices, which were exposed to more intensive Romance influence than in the texts of the offices

---

[11] The spread of linguistic interest in syntactic configuration in the domain of diachronic Indo-European studies was on the one hand motivated by attested elements of non-configurational syntax in certain, particularly older Indo-European languages, and on the other, by realizing that syntactic configuration is a developmental continuum which ranges from the striking non-configurational structure, typical of older syntactic systems (such as Homeric Greek), to marked configurations, typical of most contemporary Indo-European languages (for example, Modern Greek). After a period of generativist research into syntactic configuration, mainly of non-Indo-European languages in the 1980's (e.g. Jelinek 1984; Kiss 1987; Marácz and Muysken 1989), there has been an increased interest of this phenomenon in Indo-European languages, such as German (Haider 1982; Webelhuth 1984–1985), Homeric Greek (Taylor 1988), Old Icelandic (Faarlund 1990; Rögnvaldsson 1995), Latin (Luraghi 2010) and in Indo-European languages in general (with a focus on prepositional expressions) (Hewson and Bubeník 2006).

[12] Dunn's findings (1989: 16) can be understood in this context. According to him, in the period from 750 BC to 100 AD, Old Greek pronominal enclitics increasingly moved away from the post-frontal sentence position, attaching to the contact postposition in relation to the head verb. On the other hand, the fact that Wackernagel's distribution principle of enclitics is related to languages with non-configurational syntax is proved by non-Indo-European languages, such as Warlpiri of Central Australian Aborigines (cf. Nash 1986: 55–64, 185–187), or the North American Indian Salish language (cf. Jelinek 1996).

[13] On the phase nature of syntactic configuration see Golumbia (2004: 15).

in the east.[14] This is the context in which H. Hock's view can be understood (2010: 66), according to which the emergence of a linguistic type is the manifestation of geographic (horizontal), rather than historical (vertical) transition.

List of abbreviations

ACC	accusative
ACT	active
ADJ	adjective
AOR	aorist
AUX	auxiliary
DAT	dative
ENCL	enclitic
IMP	imperfect
OP	optative
PL	plural
POSS	possessive
PFV	perfective
PRS	present
PRT	particle
PST	preterite
PTCP	participle
REFL	reflexive
S	sentence
SG	singular

---

14 Considering the position of pronominal (en)clitics in Old Italian, Old Spanish and Old Portuguese written texts, D. Wanner (1996: 554) notices the tendency of these enclitics to attach either to the initial sentence element (according to the Wackernagel principle), or, alternatively, to the corresponding finite verb. This tendency, attested in old Romance languages – which could have spread by means of diplomatic forms to the Serbian diplomatic texts – was probably typical of Balkan Romance influence (i.e. the Balkan Romance substrate such as coastal Dalmatian or continental Proto-Vlachian), since the close contact position of predicate phrase enclitics in relation to the finite verb is typical of contemporary Romanian and Albanian, but also in Bulgarian (Dimitrova-Vulchanova 1999: 90–101).

References

Browne, Wayles. 1974. On the problem of enclitic placement in Serbo-Croatian. In Richard D. Brecht & Catherine Chvany (eds.), *Slavic transformational syntax*, 36–52. Ann Arbor: University of Michigan.
Comrie, Bernard. 1980. Morphology and word order reconstruction: Problems and prospects. In Jacek Fisiak (ed.), *Historical morphology*, 83–96. The Hague, Paris & New York: Mouton de Gruyter.
Chomsky, Noam. 1981. *Lectures on government and binding: The Pisa lectures*. Dordrecht & Cinnaminson: Foris Publications.
Delbrück, Berthold. 1878. *Die altindische Wortfolge aus dem Çatapathabrāhmaṇa*. Halle: Verlag der Buchhandlung des Waisenhauses.
Diesing, Molly, Dušica Filipović Đurđević & Draga Zec. 2009. Clitic placement in Serbian: Corpus and experimental evidence. In Sam Featherston & Susanne Winkler (eds.), *The fruits of empirical linguistics. Volume 2: Products*, 59–73. Berlin & New York: Mouton de Gruyter.
Dimitrova-Vulchanova, Mila. 1999. Clitics in the Slavic languages. In Henk van Riemsdijk (ed.), *Clitics in the languages of Europe*, 83–122. Berlin & New York: Mouton de Gruyter.
Dryer, Matthew S. 1988. Object-verb order and adjective-noun order: Dispelling a myth. *Lingua* 74 (2–3). 185–217.
Dryer, Matthew S. 2007. Word order. In Timothy Shopen (ed.), *Language typology and syntactic description. Volume I: Clause structure*, 61–131. Cambridge: Cambridge University Press.
Dunn, Graham. 1989. Enclitic pronoun movement and the ancient Greek sentence accent. *Glotta* 67. 1–19.
Faarlund, Jan Terje. 1990. *Syntactic change. Toward a theory of historical syntax*. Berlin & New York: Mouton de Gruyter.
Franks, Steven & Tracy Holloway King. 2000. *A handbook of Slavic clitics*. Oxford: Oxford University Press.
Gamkrelidze, Tamaz V. & Vjačeslav V. Ivanov. 1984. *Indoevropejskij jazyk i indoevropejcy. Rekonstrukcija i istoriko-tipologičeskij analiz prajazyka i protokul'tury* I. [Indo-European and the Indo-Europeans. A reconstruction and historical typological analysis of a proto-language and a proto-culture I]. Tbilisi: Izdatel'stvo Tbilisskogo universiteta.
Golumbia, David. 2004. The interpretation of nonconfigurationality. *Language & Communication* 24 (1). 1–22.
Graffi, Giorgio. 2011. The pioneers of linguistic typology: From Gabelentz to Greenberg. In Jae Jung Song (ed.), *The Oxford handbook of linguistic typology*, 25–42. Oxford: Oxford University Press.
Greenberg, Joseph H. 1963. Some universals of grammar with particular reference to the order of meaningful elements. In Joseph H. Greenberg (ed.), *Universals of language*, 58–90. Cambridge, MA: MIT Press.
Grković-Major, Jasmina. 2010. The role of syntactic transitivity in the develoment of Slavonic syntactic structures. In Björn Hansen & Jasmina Grković-Major (eds.), *Diachronic Slavonic syntax. Gradual changes in focus* (Wiener Slawistischer Almanach – Sonderband 74), 63–74. München, Berlin & Wien: Otto Sagner.
Grković-Major [Grković-Mejdžor] Jasmina. 2013. *Istorijska lingvistika: Kognitivno-tipološke studije* [Historical linguistics: Cognitive-typological studies]. Sremski Karlovci & Novi Sad: Izdavačka knjižarnica Zorana Stojanovića.

Grković-Major, Jasmina (this volume). The development of perception verb complements in the Serbian language.
Haider, Hubert. 1982. *Dependenzen und Konfigurationen. Zur deutschen V-Projektion.* Wien: Universität Wien, Institut für Sprachwissenschaft.
Hale, Ken. 1983. Warlpiri and the grammar of non-configurational languages. *Natural Language & Linguistic Theory* 1 (1). 5–47.
Hewson, John & Vít Bubeník. 2006. *From case to adposition: The development of configurational syntax in Indo-European languages.* Amsterdam & Philadelphia: John Benjamins.
Hock, Hans H. 2010. Typology and universals. In Silvia Luraghi & Vit Bubenik (eds.), *The Continuum companion to historical linguistics*, 59–69. London & New York: Continuum International Publishing Group.
Jelinek, Eloise. 1984. Empty categories, case, and configurationality. *Natural Language & Linguistic Theory* 2 (1). 39–76.
Jelinek, Eloise. 1996. Definiteness and second position clitics in Straits Salish. In Aaron L. Halpern & Arnold M. Zwicky (eds.), *Approaching second: Second position clitics and related phenomena*, 271–297. Stanford, CA: Center for the Study of Languages and Information.
Kiss, Katalin É. 1987. *Configurationality in Hungarian.* Dordrecht, Boston, Lancaster & Tokyo: Reidel.
Kozlovskij, Ignaz. 1901. Zwei syntaktische Eigenthümlichkeiten der russischen Sprache. *Archiv für slavische Philologie* 23. 95–106.
Lapteva, Olga A. 1959. Raspoloženie drevnerusskogo odinočnogo atributivnogo prilagatelnogo [Distribution of the Old Russian single attributive adjective]. In Viktor V. Vinogradov (ed.), *Slavjanskoe jazykoznanie. Sbornik statej*, 98–112. Moskva: Akademija nauk SSSR.
Lehman, Winfred P. 1974. *Proto-Indo-European syntax.* Austin: University of Texas Press.
Luraghi, Silvia. 2010. The rise (and possible downfall) of configurationality. In Silvia Luraghi & Vit Bubenik (eds.), *Continuum companion to historical linguistics*, 212–229. London & New York: Continuum International Publishing Group.
Marácz, László & Piter Muysken (eds.). 1989. *Configurationality: The typology of asymmetries.* Dordrecht: Foris Publications.
McAnallen, Julia. 2009. The competing roles of SV(O) and VS(O) word orders in Xoždenie igumena Daniila. *Russian Linguistics* 33 (2). 211–228.
Nash, David G. 1986. *Topics in Warlpiri grammar.* New York & London: Garland Publishing.
Pancheva, Roumyana. 2005. The rise and fall of second-position clitics. *Natural Language & Linguistic Theory* 23 (1). 103–167.
Pavlović, Slobodan. 2009. *Starosrpska zavisna rečenica od XII do XV veka* [The Old Serbian dependent clause from the 12th to the 15th century]. Sremski Karlovci & Novi Sad: Izdavačka knjižarnica Zorana Stojanovića.
Pavlović, Slobodan. 2013. *Uzroci i mehanizmi sintaksičkih promena u srpskom jeziku* [Causes and mechanisms of syntactic changes in the Serbian language]. Sremski Karlovci & Novi Sad: Izdavačka knjižarnica Zorana Stojanovića.
Popović, Ljubomir. 1997. *Red reči u rečenici* [Word order in the sentence]. Beograd: Društvo za srpski jezik i književnost Srbije.
Radanović-Kocić, Vesna. 1988. *The grammar of Serbo-Croatian clitics: A synchronic and diachronic perspective.* Urbana-Champaign: University of Illinois dissertation.
Radovanović, Milorad. 2009. *Uvod u fazi lingvistiku* [Introduction to fuzzy linguistics]. Sremski Karlovci & Novi Sad: Izdavačka knjižarnica Zorana Stojanovića.

Ramat, Paolo. 2011. The (early) history of linguistic typology. In Jae Jung Song (ed.), *The Oxford handbook of linguistic typology*, 9–24. Oxford: Oxford University Press.

Rögnvaldsson, Eiríkur. 1995. Old Icelandic: A non-configurational language? *North-Western European Language Evolution* 26. 3–29.

Sannikov, Vladimir Z. 1968. Soglasovannoe opredelenie [Congruent determination]. Viktor I. Borkovskij (ed.), *Sravnitel'no-istoričeskij sintaksis vostočnoslavjanskix jazykov. Členy predloženija* [Comparative-historical syntax of the East Slavonic languages: Sentence constituents], 47–95. Moskva: Nauka.

Schütze, Carson T. 1994. Serbo-Croatian second position clitic placement and the phonology-syntax interface. *MIT Working Papers in Linguistics* 21. 373–473.

Spencer, Andrew & Ana R. Luís. 2012. *Clitics. An introduction*. Cambridge: Cambridge University Press.

Taylor, Ann. 1988. From non-configurational to configurational: A study of syntactic change in Greek. *The Penn Review of Linguistics* 12. 1–15.

Večerka, Radoslav. 1989. *Altkirchenslavische (altbulgarische) Syntax I. Die lineare Satzorganisation*. Freiburg. i. Br.: Weiher.

Vondrák, Václav. 1908. O místě attributivního adjektiva a substantivního genitivu ve větě [On the position of attributive adjectives and adnominal genitives in the sentence]. In *Zbornik u slavu Vatroslava Jagića* [Festschrift for Vatroslav Jagić], 151–158. Berlin: Weidmannsche Buchhandlung.

Wackernagel, Jacob. 1892. Über ein Gesetz der indogermanischen Wortstellung. *Indogermanische Forschungen* I. 333–436.

Wanner, Dieter. 1996. Second position clitics in medieval Romance. In Aaron L. Halpern & Arnold M. Zwicky (eds.), *Approaching second: Second position clitics and related phenomena*, 537–578. Stanford, CA: Center for the Study of Languages and Information.

Webelhuth, Gert. 1984–1985. German is configurational. *The Linguistic Review* 4 (3). 203–246.

Zaliznjak, Andrej A. 2008. *Drevnerusskie ėnklitiki* [Old Russian enclitics]. Moskva: Jazyki slavjanskix kul'tur.

Zimmerling, Anton & Peter Kosta. 2013. Slavic clitics: A typology. *STUF – Language Typology and Universals* 66 (2). 178–214.

Sandra Birzer
Historical development and contemporary usage of discourse structuring elements based on *verba dicendi* in Croatian

Abstract: Modern Croatian features four functional domains which are marked by constructions based on two non-finite forms of verba dicendi, namely the adverbial participle *govoreći* 'speaking' and the past participle *rečeno* 'said':
a) stance-marking with the prototypical construction ADV + non-finite *verbum dicendi* (e.g. *iskreno govoreći / rečeno* 'frankly speaking');
b) contextualization with the prototypical construction *govoreći / rečeno* + ADJ.INS + NOUN.INS (e.g. *nogometnim žargonom rečeno* 'speaking (lit. said) in soccer jargon');
c) quotative indexing with the prototypical construction *govoreći / rečeno* + NOUN.INS+ NOUN.GEN (e.g. *govoreći rječnikom sv. Pavla* 'lit. speaking in the language of St. Paul')
d) direct speech marking with the help of "plain" *govoreći*.

Only with the formant *rečeno* 'said' is the construction semi-productive, which implies a crystallization of functions: "plain" *govoreći* seems to be developing towards an exclusive marker of direct speech, whereas *rečeno* 'said' is turning into the preferable formant for all the modified constructions that are associated with discourse functions.

The diachronic part of the paper is concerned with the development of the four constructions mentioned above and proposes an explanation for the current crystallization of functions: firstly, the semantic structure of *reći* 'say' predisposes this verb for discourse functions. Secondly, historical language contact with German may have enhanced the rooting of discourse structuring constructions with *rečeno* 'said' in Croatian, as German also features a semi-productive construction based on the past participle *gesagt* 'said' that serves discourse functions.

1 Introduction

Many languages – not only Slavonic ones – feature discourse structuring elements (henceforth DSEs) based on *verba dicendi*, e.g. B/C/S *iskreno rečeno* 'frankly speaking', POL *dokładnie mówiąc* 'precisely speaking', RUS *mjagko govorja* 'mildly speaking' or GER *kurz gesagt* 'in short (lit. shortly said)'. As the number of DSEs formed this way is rather high for each language (e.g. 109 types formed with *mówiąc* in POL and 39 formed with *govorja* in RUS (cf. Birzer (accepted)), this may be considered a semi-productive way of forming DSEs. Furthermore, the Slavonic languages display the specificity that many of them employ two different morphological forms of *verba dicendi* for the formation of these DSEs. The simultaneous adverbial participle may be labelled the "fixed participant" in this process, as all Slavonic languages mentioned above feature it, (1)–(4).[1] Additionally, Russian employs the infinitive of *skazat'* 'say' (5), Polish the anterior adverbial participle *powiedziawszy* 'having said' (6), B/C/S (7) and Czech (8) the passive past participle neuter *rečeno* and *řečeno* 'said' respectively.

(1) RUS
Irina-NOM *imela status ljubovnicy, a v Azerbajdžane étot*-ADJ.NOM *status*-NOM *ne prestižen,* **mjagko**-ADV ***govorja***-AP.
'Irina had the status of a lover, and in Azerbaidjan this status is not prestigious, mildly speaking.'
(Tokareva, V. *Svoja pravda*, 2002)

(2) POL
Halina ma płaszcz. Taki-ADJ.NOM *płaszcz*-NOM *to skarb, choć na pozór nic specjalnego – znoszony, trochę za długi i zbyt szeroki,* **krótko**-ADV ***mówiąc***-AP, *niemodny*.
'Halina has got a coat. Such a coat is a treasure, although to all appearances it is nothing special – worn out, a bit too long and a bit too wide, in short, unmodern.'
(*Granica wytrzymałości.* // Dziennik Polski. 2006-06-03)

(3) B/C/S
Ambicija nam je bila osvojiti bar bod, ali **iskreno**-ADV ***govoreći***-AP *nismo*-1PL *ga zaslužili*.
'It was our ambition to win at least this point, but honestly speaking we did not deserve it.'
(HNK_v25 subcorpus, gs20030325sp18906)[2]

---

[1] All examples are taken from the respective national corpora if not marked otherwise. For the B/C/S examples the Croatian National Corpus was employed for reasons explained below. Morphosyntactic characteristics of the DSEs, such as the missing coreference between the adverbial participle (AP) and the first argument of the matrix sentence (probably illustrated best by the feminine or neuter AP and the male first argument in (4)), as well as interpunction issues will be discussed in Section 2.
[2] Unfortunately, the HNK_v25 subcorpus of the Croatian National Corpus does not allow one to identify the text title behind the ID number of the text.

(4) CZ
... *muž*-NOM.SG.M [...] *byl*- NOM.SG.M *starý a těžce nemocný*, **tak**-ADV **říkajíc**-AP.F/N *jednou nohou v hrobě*.
'The man was old and very ill, so to say (lit. so saying) with one leg in the grave.'
(Goldberg, L. *Virus*, 2005)

(5) RUS
Tut, vidite li, est' dva puti – **tak**-ADV **skazat'**-INF, *put'*-NOM *Cholmsa i put'*-NOM *Puaro*.
'There exist, you see, two ways – so to say, Holmes's way and Poirot's way.'
(Belousova, V. *Vtoroj vystrel*, 2000)

(6) POL
Tego już, **szczerze**-ADV **powiedziawszy**-AP, *dokładnie nie pamiętam*.
'This, frankly speaking, I do not remember in detail.'

(7) B/C/S
O Slovačkoj, **iskreno**-ADV **rečeno**-PTCP.PASS, *nisam mnogo znao*.
'About Slovakia, frankly speaking, I did not know much.'
(HNK_v25 subcorpus, fo2005br162cl4078)

(8) CZ
Hospoda, tedy **lépe**-ADV **řečeno**-PTCP.PASS *firma, je psaná na jméno Sartanová*.
'The pub, so better said the company, was registered under the name Sartanová.'
(Jonquet, T. *Tarantule Uvězněná paměť*. 2005)

The two forms compete with each other in the sense that they form doublets in combination with some select elements, mainly adverbs (e.g. RUS *čestno govorja / skazat'*, POL *szczerze mówiąc / powiedziawszy*, B/C/S *iskreno govoreći / rečeno* 'frankly speaking'), but only one of the patterns is semi-productive, whereas the other one has only a few highly lexicalized representatives. What makes B/C/S and Czech special is the fact that one of the "competitors", namely the passive past participle neuter displays structural similarities with the corresponding German construction (henceforth Cxn) ADV + *gesagt* 'said' that also employs the passive participle. As Birzer (2012a) showed that language contact with French and its pattern *á / pour* ADV *parler*-INF seems to have given rise to the two competing constructions ADV + *govorja* and ADV + *skazat'* in Russian, there is reason to examine the question whether the constructions with the passive past participle neuter in B/C/S and Czech are the result of language contact with

German; the more so, as especially Croatian (cf., among others, Rammelmeyer 1975; Golubović 2007; Štebih 2003) and Czech have been in long-term contact – both oral and written – with German, and German calques in Czech served as a model for replication in other Slavonic languages, among them Croatian (cf. Turk and Sesar 2003). In both languages the construction with the past participle is also a semi-productive one. Another peculiarity of B/C/S not paralleled by Czech, namely the fact that *govoreći* functions also as marker of direct speech, led us to make Croatian the subject of our study. The choice of Croatian over Bosnian and Serbian is motivated by two reasons. Firstly, Croatian is considered the variety on which German has exerted the most influence (cf., among others, Rammelmeyer 1975) and, secondly, Croatian offers the most comprehensive online-accessible text corpus, the Croatian National Corpus, comprising even a subcorpus of classics ranging from the 16th to the 20th century.[3]

This paper is organized as follows. In the following section a short definition of the term DSE is given. The third section discusses the corpus data that serves as the basis for our investigation. The functions of *govoreći* and *rečeno* in Contemporary Croatian are described in the fourth section, whereas the fifth section traces how *govoreći* acquired the functions of a direct speech marker and DSE, and *rečeno* that of a DSE. Conclusions will be presented in the sixth section.

2 Defining DSEs

Most literature on DSEs in B/C/S uses the terms *diskursivna* or *pragmatska partikula* 'discourse / pragmatic particle' (cf. Ivić 2005: 46; Dedaić and Mišković-Luković 2010) and *diskursivan marker* (cf. Popović 2009: 186–187), inspired by the terminology proposed for DSEs in English.

The term *discourse marker* bears some advantages, but also shortcomings. In contrast to *discourse* or *pragmatic particle*, the term *marker* does not provide implications on the item's size or affiliation with a certain word class (cf. Fischer 2006: 5). Mosegaard-Hansen (2006: 28) illustrates this attitude rather to the point:

> the term *discourse marker* is not a cohyponym of, for instance, *interjection, conjunction, modal particle, focus particle,* or *sentence adverbial*. I consider these latter terms to be names for specifiable syntactic categories which may or may not exist in a given language, whereas *discourse marker* names a function which may be fulfilled by items from several of these categories.

---

[3] For a list of sources included in the subcorpus "Klasici" cf. http://www.hnk.ffzg.hr/Izvori_Klasici.html

At first glance, it seems there is nothing to be added to this definition. However, an issue that remains unclear is the exact working principle of a *marker*. This will become clearer if we draw on the function of grammatical markers in morphology, where the term *marker* has probably been borrowed from. Each grammatical category forms a paradigm of values. The grammatical marker is member of the paradigm and expresses one value of the category. In other words, the marker not only signals that the given grammatical category is at work, but at the same time also bears one of its values. DSEs, however, behave in various ways concerning the representation of values. We will demonstrate this with the help of examples (9)–(10).

(9) *Na pitanje o tome koji bi mu redatelj najviše odgovarao za ekranizaciju "Ken Parkera", Milazzo je odgovorio "John Ford, ali on*-NOM *je,* **nažalost**-ADV, *mrtav".*
'On the question which director would suit him most for the film adaptation of "Ken Parker", Milazzo answered "John Ford, but, unfortunately, he is already dead".'
(HNK_v25 subcorpus, CW040199811051407hr)

(10) *... nacionalizacija*-NOM, *konfiskacija*-NOM, *eksproprijacija*-NOM ... **ukratko**-ADV **rečeno**-PTCP.PASS – *ozakonjena*-ADJ.NOM *otimačina*-NOM, *[se] rastegnula na mnoge hektare najbolje zemlje ...*
'... nationalization, confiscation, expropriation ... in short – legalized seizure, has extended itself over many hectars of the best land.'
(HNK_v25 subcorpus, gs20021023sb14745)

Nažalost 'unfortunately' in (9) is a stance marker and – just like a grammatical marker – signals not only that stance marking is at work, but also embodies one "value" of stance – a negative one in this case. *Ukratko rečeno* 'in short (lit. shortly spoken)' is a reformulation marker (on reformulation markers in general cf. Saz Rubio and Fraser 2003). It signals that a reformulation follows, but does not constitute the reformulation. Furthermore, the discourse markers may bear two functions at the same time, e.g. stance marking and reformulation (cf. examples (29)–(32) in Section 4.1). Thus, the so-called discourse markers differ concerning the realization of the discourse function(s) they mark. If we adhere to Mosegaard-Hansen's definition that a "*discourse marker* names a function which may be fulfilled by items from several of these categories" (2006: 28), we would need to exclude reformulation markers (such as examples (4), (8), (10)) and possibly other subgroups as well) from *discourse markers*, as they do not themselves fulfil the function they signal. However, our items under investigation fulfil all of these functions depending on the context they occur in.

Moreover, there are items called *veznički prilozi* ('connecting adverbs'). They are distinguished by the fact that svojim leksičkim sadržajem izriču odnos rečenice u kojoj stoje prema drugim rečeničnim sadržajima, izrečenim ili samo pomišljenim. Takvim prilozima i priložnim izrazima nije obično mjesto kraj predikata, kao drugim priložnim oznakama što jest, nego na početku rečenice. (Katičić 2002: 169)

[by their lexical content they express the relationship of the clause in which they stand to other clausal contents, overtly expressed or only imaginary ones. The usual place for such adverbs and adverbial expressions is not the verge of the predicate, as for the other existing adverbial features, but the beginning of the clause. Translation – S. B.]

This coincides with the features of Slavonic connectives offered by Mendoza (2009: 983) following Pasch et al. (2003: 331). Thus, a connective is

a) *nicht flektierbar*, vergibt b) *keine Kasusmerkmale* an seine syntaktische Umgebung, seine Bedeutung ist c) eine *zweistellige Relation*, deren Argumente d) *propositionale Strukturen* sind, die e) als *Satzstrukturen* ausdrückbar sein müssen.

[a) non-inflective, does not assign b) case to its syntactic surrounding, its meaning is c) a binary relation, whose arguments are d) propositional structures which e) need to be realizable as syntactic structures. (Translation – S. B.)]

Furthermore, Mendoza (2009: 984) mentions that the meaning of some conjunctions (CONJ), which may be considered to be prototypical connectives, can be specified by the help of so-called concretizators (*Konkretisatoren*), which in their turn also function as connectives in their own right. This also holds for the Croatian items under investigation, as (11) shows.

(11) ... *Europska*-ADJ.NOM *bi unija*-NOM *u optimalnom obliku mogla postati "federacijom nacionalnih država" ili*-CONJ, ***drukčije***-ADV ***rečeno***-PTCP.PASS, *konfederacija u kojoj bi nacionalni parlamenti dobili važniju ulogu stvaranjem zajedničkog tijela, "kongresa"* ...
'... the European Union in an ideal configuration could become a "federation of national states" or, in other words (lit. otherwise said), a confederation in which the national parliaments would acquire a more important role by the formation of a collective authority, a "congress"... '
(HNK_v25 subcorpus, vj20010601gl03)

However, our items occur not only in the sentence-initial position, as is expected of *veznički prilozi*. This is explained by the fact that apart from the connective function, our items fulfil some more functions from the realms of topic management and expressing the speaker's stance, for example hedging (12). Here, *blago rečeno* 'mildly speaking' does not connect two propositional structures, but scopes over just one structure, namely *gangsterski* 'gangster-like'.

(12) *Takav*-DEM.NOM *pristup*-NOM *politici je,* **blago-ADV rečeno-PTCP.PASS**, *gangsterski*.
'Such an approach to politics is, mildly speaking, gangster-like.'
(HNK_v25 subcorpus, fo2003br63cl1560)

Thus the term *veznički prilog* is also too narrow for the items under investigation.

Therefore, we propose the term *discourse structuring element*, as it does not entail any formal restrictions, but the constituent *structuring* implies scope over certain structures independently from the DSE's syntactic position.

We recur to Rathmayr (1985) for defining the properties of DSEs. Rathmayr offers an enumeration of defining properties of particles serving as so-called pragmalexemes, which we adapt for DSEs. In addition to these general properties some specific properties exist that are derived from formal aspects of the subgroup under investigation, i.e. DSEs that are based on the adverbial participle *govoreći* 'speaking' and the participle *rečeno* 'spoken'.

Rathmayr's properties are the following:

a) syntactic eliminability due to irrelevance for the content, i.e., the proposition (1985: 42). As example (13a) shows, the elimination of the DSE *iskreno rečeno* 'frankly speaking' does not change the proposition of the sentence. This coincides with Fraser (2006: 189), who establishes integration into a discourse segment without contribution to its proposition as a defining criterion. However, this criterion is a semantic rather than a syntactic one.

(13) *O Slovačkoj,* **iskreno-ADV rečeno-PTCP.PASS**, *nisam*-1SG *mnogo znao*.
'About Slovakia, frankly speaking, I did not know much.'
(HNK_v25 subcorpus, fo2005br162cl4078)
a. *O Slovačkoj nisam*-1SG *mnogo znao*.
'About Slovakia I did not know much.'

b) DSEs cannot be subject to questions, i.e. just like particles (cf. Rathmayr 1985: 72) DSEs do not serve as answers to (probe) questions.

b. *Šta nisam znao*-1SG *o Slovačkoj?* – **Iskreno*-ADV *rečeno*-PTCP.PASS.
'What did I not know about Slovakia? – Frankly speaking.'

c) as a third criterion Rathmayr (1985: 72) lists the non-negatability of particles, which also holds for DSEs (14).

(14) a. **Ne   iskreno   govoreći / *iskreno   ne   govoreći   ne*
       NEG   frankly   speak-AP / frankly   NEG   speak-AP   NEG
       očekujem   ništa   posebno.
       expect-1SG.PRS   nothing-ACC   special
       'Not frankly speaking / frankly not speaking, I do not expect anything special.'

b. *Ne   iskreno rečeno /   *iskreno   ne   rečeno
   NEG   frankly speak-PTCP.PASS.N   frankly   NEG   speak-PTCP.PASS.N
   ne   očekujem   ništa   posebno.
   NEG   expect-1SG.PRS nothing-ACC special
   'Not frankly speaking / frankly not speaking, I do not expect anything special.'

d) Rathmayr (1985: 72) gives two more defining criteria typical for particles, namely that they are unstressed and cumulative with other particles. However, these fit only partially for DSEs. Firstly, DSEs may bear secondary stress if they consist of several words. Secondly, not all DSEs may be used cumulatively. Probably this is due to the length of some DSEs based on semiproductive constructions, but restrictions also seem to exist due to functional reasons. Concretisation constitutes an occasion for cumulation. Mendoza (2009: 983) states that

> [d]ie Bedeutung bzw. Funktion von multifunktionalen koordinierenden Konjunktionen kann durch die Kombination mit sog. Konkretisatoren spezifiziert werden [...], wobei die Konkretisatoren alleine wiederum meistens ebenfalls Konnektorenfunktion übernehmen können.

> [the meaning respectively function of multifunctional coordination conjunctions may be specified by combination with so-called concretisators [...], whereupon the concretisators in turn may in most cases also take over the function of connectives on their own. (Translation – S. B.)]

In contrast to Russian and Polish, where this kind of cumulation seems to concern only DSEs with a primarily connective function, usually reformulation markers, Croatian allows for it independent of the DSE's function, as examples (15)–(17) show. (15) contains the stance marker *iskreno govoreći* 'frankly speaking', (16) features *usput rečeno* 'by the way (lit. spoken)', a marker for the introduction of further, digression-like information, and (17) contains the reformulation marker *točnije rečeno* 'more precisely (lit. spoken)'.

(15) *Ovakav*-ADJ.NOM *odgovor*-NOM *sasvim je nedovoljan*-ADJ.NOM, *a*-CONJ ***iskreno***-ADV ***rečeno***-PTCP.PASS *i netočan*-ADJ.NOM.
'Such an answer is completely unsatisfactory, and frankly speaking inaccurate.'
(HNK_v25 subcorpus, vj20030827ko03)

(16) ... *svoj rođendan nisam*-1SG *nikad javno i na javnim mjestima slavio*, *a*-CONJ ***usput***-ADV ***rečeno***-PTCP.PASS *ne slavim*-1SG *ga od 1991*.
'I never celebrated my birthday openly and in public places, and by the way, I have not celebrated it at all since 1991.'
(HNK_v25 subcorpus, na249_r03)

(17) ... *novi*-ADJ.NOM **ili**-CONJ, ***točnije***-ADV ***rečeno***-PTCP.PASS, *novi-stari*-ADJ.NOM *izvršni*-ADJ.NOM *producent*-NOM *te manifestacije* ...
'... the new or, more precisely, the new-old executive organizer of this event ...'
(HNK_v25 subcorpus, v230fil01)

Furthermore, Russian and Polish allow cumulation in cases where the DSEs in question serve different discursive needs (cf. Birzer accepted), whereas no such instances were found in our Croatian corpus data.[4]

All DSEs consisting of multi-word units display other characteristic traits that are at least partially derivable from their semantics and syntax.

The semantic criterion defines possible constituents of multi-word DSEs. As this definition is elaborated best in Russian grammar AG-80,[5] we will apply it to Croatian as well. According to it, multi-word DSEs contain verbs, nouns, adverbs and phraseological units with the meaning of "mysli, reči, vosprijatija, ocenki, ėmocional'nych, intellektual'nych, volevych, uzual'nych sostojanij, raznoobraznych otnošenij, svjazej i zavisimostej, mery, stepeni, kačestvennosti ili količestvennosti [thought, speech, perception, evaluation, of emotional, cognitive, volitional, habitual states, of various relationships, connections and dependencies, of measure, degree, quality or quantity – translation S. B.]" (AG-80: § 2220). The importance of semantics might imply that morphological and (morpho)syntactic features play a minor role. However, only the specific interplay of semantics and morphosyntax allows us to distinguish DSEs from other (syntactic) constructions.

Since the objects of our investigation are formed with the patterns ADV + AP or ADV + PTCP respectively, we will restrict our description of morphosyntactic criteria to the features of these two formation types.

For the ADV + AP type, undoubtedly the most important syntactic issue is the loss of obligatory coreference[6] between the covert subject of the adverbial participle and the first argument of the matrix verb. Instead the speaker (SP) is the covert subject of the adverbial participle (18). The aforementioned coreference is the characteristic trait of prototypical adverbial participles (19).

---

4 Tagged corpora are suited best for this kind of search. Unfortunately, the Croatian National Corpus offers only one small subcorpus of tagged texts, the cw2000 corpus, in which no corresponding matches have been found. The non-tagged HNK_25 was searched for all instances of *govoreći* and *rečeno*, followed by manual post-processing, also with no corresponding matches.
5 Compare the following enumeration with e.g. Katičić (2002: 169) cited above, who deems it sufficient to mention that the items in question have special lexical content, but fails to describe it more precisely.
6 Coincidental coreference may still occur if the first argument of the matrix clause is in the first person.

(18) ... Ø_sp iskreno   govoreći,   to   nije   moj   problem ...
         frankly   speak-AP   this-NOM   not-is   my-NOM   problem-NOM
'Frankly speaking, this is not my problem.'
(HNK_v25 subcorpus, vj20000211un19)

(19) Ø_j Govoreći   o   birokraciji,   ministar_j   Petrović_j
     speak-AP   about   bureaucracy-LOC   minister-NOM   Petrović-NOM
     je   istaknuo
     AUX.3SG   stress-PTCP.SG.M
     da se protiv toga problema mora boriti svaki hrvatski građanin.
     that every Croatian citizen must fight this problem
     'Speaking about bureaucracy, Minister Petrović stressed that every Croatian citizen must fight this problem.'
     (HNK_v25 subcorpus, CW008199803051004hr.S17)

The loss of obligatory coreference, together with the speaker as the covert subject of the AP and the irrelevance of the AP for the proposition of the matrix clause, indicates that the adverbial participle ceases to function as a secondary predication, a trait all adverbial participles share – even those that may not be considered prototypical due to the coreference of their covert subject with a matrix verb argument other than the first one (cf. Katičić 2002: 491–492; ex. 22).[7]

(20) Odlazeći_j   od   njih,   zanesen_j,   /   Mene_j   muče
     go_away-AP   from   them   excited-NOM.SG.M   me   torment-PRS.3PL
     vrele   žudnje.
     torrid-NOM.PL   desire-NOM.PL
     'On leaving them, excited, / torrid desires torment me.'
     (Tadijanović cited in Katičić 2002: 492)

The situation is somewhat different with the past participle passive *rečeno*. The passive diathesis rests upon the demotion of the agent,[8] and in the majority of cases the demoted agent is not realized syntactically (cf. Katičić 2002: 156–158; Kunzmann-Müller 1994: 65–68). Thus, we may only state that, in the

---

[7] In fact, the loss of secondary predication status implies that the affected item be no longer labelled as an adverbial participle. Yet for reasons of convenience we will retain this denomination. Concerning the new status of the items under investigation, the assignment poses some problems. As has been described above, the items behave like particles, but, on the other hand, they also show resemblance to items like *na žalost* 'unfortunately' that are traditionally labeled as sentence adverbials.

[8] The promotion of the patient is not addressed here, as it is irrelevant for the point we want to make.

case of DSEs based on *rečeno*, the speaker is the only possible semantic argument to fill the role of demoted agent out of a whole range of potentially eligible ones (21).

(21) *Iskreno   rečeno,   to   nije   moj   problem.*
     frankly   speak-PTCP.PASS.N this-NOM   not-is   my-NOM   problem-NOM
     'Frankly speaking, this is not my problem.'
   = *Iskreno   rečem   da   to   nije   moj   problem*
     frankly   speak-1SG   COMP   this-NOM   not-is   my-NOM   problem-NOM
     'I say frankly that this is not my problem.'
   ≠ *Ivan   iskreno   reče   da   to   nije   moj*
     Ivan-NOM   frankly   speak-3SG   COMP   this-NOM   not-is my-NOM
     problem
     problem-NOM
     'Ivan says frankly that this is not my problem.'

Other aspects of valence need to be considered as well. The concerned items are derived from polyvalent verbs. In our case we are dealing with the polysemous verbs *govoriti* 'speak, say' and *reći* 'speak, say' that require an agent producing the message and, in the majority of their meanings (among them the most frequently used ones), the message itself with the semantic role content. The semantic role content is represented syntactically in various ways – as NP (22), PP (23) or complement clause (24).[9]

(22) a. *Ivan   ne   govori   istinu.*
        Ivan-NOM   NEG   say-PRS.3SG   truth-ACC
        'Ivan is not telling the truth.'
     b. *On   je   odbio   reći   ime   osobe*
        he-NOM   AUX.3SG   refuse-PTCP.SG.M   say-INF   name-ACC   person-GEN
        s   kojom   se   pregovara ...
        with   REL.INS.SG   REFL   negotiate-PRS.3SG
        'He refused to say the name of the person with whom was being negotiated.'
        (HNK_v25 subcorpus, cw116200005051304hr)

---

9 For reasons of space we cannot discuss each meaning and each valency pattern separately. Therefore, we restrict ourselves to the analysis of the two semantic arguments that are pivotal for the development of the items under investigation.

(23) a. *Ivan   je   otvoreno   govorio   o   mnogim*
     Ivan-NOM   AUX.3SG   openly   speak-PTCP.SG.M   about   many-LOC.PL
     pitanjima.
     issue-LOC.PL
     'Ivan spoke openly about many issues.'
  b. *Što   je   rekao   o   njezinoj   bolesti*
     what-ACC   AUX.3SG   say-PTCP.SG.M   about   her-POSS.LOC   illness-LOC
     liječnik?
     doctor-NOM
     'What did the doctor say about her illness?'
     (HNK_v25 subcorpus, izv vjnovak_nove)

(24) a. *Ivan   govori   da   će   doći   do   Zagreba.*
     Ivan-NOM   say-PRS.3SG   COMP   AUX.FUT   go-INF   to   Zagreb-GEN
     'Ivan says that he will come to Zagreb.'
  b. *U tom slučaju,   ne   bih   mogao   reći   da*
     In this case,   NEG   AUX.COND.1SG   can-PTCP.SG.M   say-INF   COMP
     će   proces   početi   za tri godine
     AUX.FUT.3SG   process-NOM   begin-INF   within three years
     'In this case, I could not say that the process will start within three hours.'
     (HNK_v25 subcorpus, cw1172000005121003hr)

DSEs based on the adverbial participle inherit this argument structure in an adapted version (on the historical aspects of the adaptation process in Russian and Old Church Slavonic cf. Birzer 2012a, 2012b). The speaker is the only agent to fill the first argument position. Each DSE is integrated into a clause or sentence which may be considered the "heir" of the originally second argument with the semantic role content (12).

Example (21) gives reason to raise the question of whether we are dealing with an instance of clause restructuring in the sense that the formerly superordinate clause becomes a parenthesis in the formerly subordinate clause. This question will be addressed in the section on historical development.

3 Corpus data

As has been mentioned above, our analysis relies on corpus data. The Croatian National Corpus offers several subcorpora. Unfortunately, by the time of our data retrieval in summer 2013 only the subcorpus cw2000 was tagged morphologically. As a corpus of newspaper texts containing just 118 000 tokens is too small for our needs, we resorted to the morphologically untagged HNK_v25 corpus for the synchronic description. We refrained from the usage of web corpora such as hrWaC, as most texts from the web are rather colloquial and close to oral communication and thus hardly comparable to historical texts, which are the main focus of this paper. For the diachronic description we made use of the untagged subcorpus "Klasici", containing 65 classical pieces of Croatian literature with an overall token number of 3.6 million words (for a list of the works included cf. http://www.hnk.ffzg.hr/Izvori_Klasici.html) and the Marulić subcorpus of the Croatian National Corpus with all texts of the 15th century writer (81,000 words). As the two historical corpora are still not comprehensive enough to answer our research question, we supplemented them with texts from the University of Zagreb's *Zbirka književnih djela na hrvatskome jeziku* (http://dzs.ffzg.unizg.hr/popis.htm) and Kašić's translation of the Bible.

Since contemporary Standard Croatian is based on Štokavian, but the material for our historical analysis comprises Čakavian and Kajkavian data as well, some words are in order on this seeming inconsistency. The literature on the history of Croatian stresses the fact that even rather early texts such as the Missals of 1483 and 1494 or the *Korizmenjak* (1508) display a mixture of elements from all three dialect groups (cf. Moguš 1995: 37, 41, 45, Holzer's discussion (2007: 22–23) of the use of isoglosses for delineating Croatian dialects from other South Slavonic dialects takes the same direction). Although the processes in the 16th and 17th centuries are described differently in the literature, all authors nonetheless stress the mutual influence of all three dialects on the respective standard varieties: Poljanec (1931: 114–115) speaks of the "širenje štokavskog dijalekta na severozapad na račun kajkavskog, a s južne strane na zapad na račun čakavskog dijalekt" [expansion of the Štokavian dialect to the Northeast at the expense of Kajkavian, and from South to West at the expense of the Čakavian dialect. – translation S. B.]. At the same time, he stresses the dialects' mutual influence on one another, e.g. Čakavian influence on the Štokavian of the Dubrovnik circle (cf. Poljanec 1931: 116) or Štokavian elements in the Kajkavian of Juraj Zrinjski's press (cf. 1931: 130). Moguš (cf. 1995: 56–76) probably draws a more apposite picture by describing the mutual influence and interdependencies between the dialects as a *koiné* situation: "Two types of common language, or two literary *koinés*, were formed in sixteenth century Croatia. One developed in the west and south, and the other, [sic!] in the north. [...] any dialect spoken in Croatia, i.e., Čakavian, Štokavian, and Kajkavian, could have become the basis of the Croatian literary language. In this respect, the three dialects were equally important, although they were not equally represented in terms of quantity" (Moguš 1995: 75–76). Although Moguš also states an expansion of Štokavian beginning in the 17th century (cf. 1995: 106 for the regression of Čakavian), he also makes it clear that all three dialects continued to influence each other and thus the emerging "All Croatian" standard throughout the 18th century: "This [Kajkavian] standard was interwoven with Čakavian and Štokavian elements, which helped create its distinct character. In addition to that, the Kajkavian areas had been open to Štokavian influences even before, but in the eighteenth century the reverse was also true" (Moguš 1995: 154). Therefore, we decided to consider texts from all three dialect areas for our diachronic analysis. The more so, as phonetics / phonology and inflectional morphology, where the most fundamental differences between the dialects may be expected, are rather irrelevant for our research question.

In HNK_v25 we restricted our search to the two expressions *govoreći* and *rečeno* forming the verbal element in the explored DSEs. As we do not know which historical syntactic structure(s) served as the point of departure for the modern construction, we decided to consider more inflectional forms and *verba dicendi*. Of the 22 *verba dicendi* in Croatian Church Slavonic enumerated by Mihaljević (2011: 64) we picked the semantically unspecified ones *glagolati*, *govoriti*, *kazati*, *reči* and *skazati*, all with the meaning 'speak' or 'say' (with the exception of *kazati*, which then meant 'show' or 'point', but today has the meaning 'speak').

The untagged historical subcorpora and digitized texts were searched for the following expressions:
glagol.*
govor.*
kaza.*
kaž.*
rek.*
reče.*
skaza.*
skaž.*

Needless to say that all (half)automatic searches were followed by manual post-processing.

As Kašić's Bible translation is not available in digitized form, it was searched for the same verbs with the help of the index in the edition from 1999. The index enumerates all attested forms of a lexeme together with selected instances, which means that we could not trace all instances.

4 Constructions with *govoreći* and *rečeno* in Contemporary Croatian

Although DESs in B/C/S have become an issue rather recently (cf. the works cited in Section 2), to the best of our knowledge DSEs based on *govoreći* and *rečeno* have not been analysed so far.

Several works on *verba dicendi* and on language contact that are relevant for our research have been published; however, as these are all – except one – concerned with historical data and contact situations, we will discuss them in Section 5. Pranjković (2007) constitutes the aforementioned exception. He analyses the complements and (at least partially) the modifiers and adjuncts of *verba dicendi* and shows that each meaning of the two polysemous verbs *govoriti* and *reći* displays a specific pattern of complements, modifiers and adjuncts. In the following we will have a closer look at the patterns that show structural parallels with our DSEs. The first relevant pattern concerns *govoriti* and is tied to contexts where the process of conveying a message is focused (this and the following cf. Pranjković 2007: 134). In this case *govoriti* displays no complement but a modifier or adjunct describing the "qualitative circumstances" (*kvalitativna cirkumstancijalnost*, Pranjković 2007: 134), e.g. *govoriti lijepo*-ADV 'speak nicely' or *govoriti s prekidima* 'speak with interruptions'. The parallels to *govoreći* in the DSEs under investigation are twofold. Firstly, the verb is accompanied by a modifier but realizes no complements. Secondly, of the rather infinite multitude of adverbs that are potentially eligible as modifiers of *govoriti*, some describe not the quality or manner of articulation (e.g. *govoriti glasno* 'speak loudly'), but the quality and / or outer form of the content (e.g. *govoriti lijepo* 'speak nicely'), just as DSEs like *iskreno govoreći* 'frankly speaking' convey the speaker's evaluation of the proposition the DSE is integrated in.

Furthermore, Pranjković points out that *govoriti* also occurs with some more or less lexicalized accusative complements whose semantics can be expressed alternatively with an adverb, e.g. *govoriti gluposti* vs. *glupo* 'speak stupid things vs. stupidly' or *govoriti pametne stvari* vs. *pametno* 'speak sensible things vs. sensibly' (2007: 134–135). Quite interestingly, in these cases "u prvi plan izbija predmet nego kvaliteta govorne manifestacije" [to the foreground comes the subject or quality of the utterance – translation S. B.]. In other words, the evaluation of the utterance by the speaker plays a prominent role, just as it does with our DSEs.

Reći seems to prefer complement clauses (25) over NPs for denoting the content of the speech act (cf. Pranjković 2007: 136 as well as the following); PPs are rather unusual. In the cases where *reći* takes an NP as its complement, the noun has to be modified by an adjective (26). This can be interpreted in the way that *reći* has its semantic focus rather on the conveyance of content than its mode of articulation. With the DSEs under investigation this semantic feature is even more distinct, as the mode of articulation is absolutely irrelevant. Amongst others, this can be seen from the fact that the DSEs can be used in written discourse without substituting the respective *verba dicendi* by *pisati* 'write' or other verbs denoting written communication.

(25) Rekli   su   svima   da   ne   moraju   dolaziti.
     speak-PTCP   AUX.3PL   all-DAT.PL   COMP   NEG   must-3PL   come-INF
     'They told everybody that they needn't come.'
     (after Pranjković 2007: 136)

(26) Reći   će   vam   zanimljive   stvari
     tell-INF AUX.FUT.3SG   you-DAT   interesting-ACC.PL   thing-ACC.PL
     o   glagolima   govorenja.
     PREP   verb-LOC.PL   speaking-GEN
     'He will tell you interesting things about *verba dicendi*.'
     (after Pranjković 2007: 136)

As quite a few adjectives (among them the ones Pranjković gives in his examples: *lijep* 'nice' and *zanimljiv* 'interesting') are evaluative, the necessity of (evaluative) modification allows us to draw a parallel with our DSEs. The fact that *reći* prefers complement clauses allows us to formulate the hypothesis that the loss of (matrix) clause status was one step in the development of our DSEs. The combination of these three factors, i.e. the focus on content conveyance (in contrast to polysemous *govoriti*, where content conveyance is just one meaning out of several), the predilection of complement clauses and the necessity of an (evaluative) modifier in all other cases, together with the higher general of usage of *reći* in comparison to *govoriti* is probably an explanation of why DSEs based on *rečeno* predominate numerically over those based on *govoreći*.

We will now have a look at the functions of DSEs based on *govoreći* and *rečeno*. In doing so, we follow the categorization proposed in Birzer (accepted) as far as possible.

4.1 The stance-marking function

ADV + *govoreći* / *rečeno*[10] is not only the most common construction based on *verba dicendi*, but it is also the prototypical construction for stance-marking, although some instantiations of other construction types, such as e.g. *jednostavnijim*-ADJ.INS *rječnikom*-NOUN.INS *rečeno* 'in simpler words (lit. with simpler language said)' may also fulfil this function.

---

[10] ADV + *govoreći* / *rečeno* is used here as representative, i.e. it stands for all instances with the adverb in pre- and postposition to the verb. This also applies for all other constructions that will be discussed below.

The stance-marking function has 38 representatives based on *govoreći* and 94 representatives based on *rečeno*. To get a more precise picture, we will compare the token frequencies for all representatives (Chart 1) as well as the semantics of the most frequent representatives for *govoreći* and *rečeno* respectively (Chart 2). Since all frequencies are drawn from the same corpus, HNK_v25, we can do without conversion into a words per million count.

As Chart 1 shows, the representatives can be divided into occasional formations with very low usage frequency, an intermediate field, and formations with very high usage frequency. The latter ones may be considered lexicalized. Whether lexicalization also applies to the intermediate field, deserves consideration at least for those representatives with a frequency of 11 to 50.[11]

Chart 1: Number of stance-marking DSEs of the type ADV + *verbum dicendi* with indication of their token frequency and their verbal basis.[12]

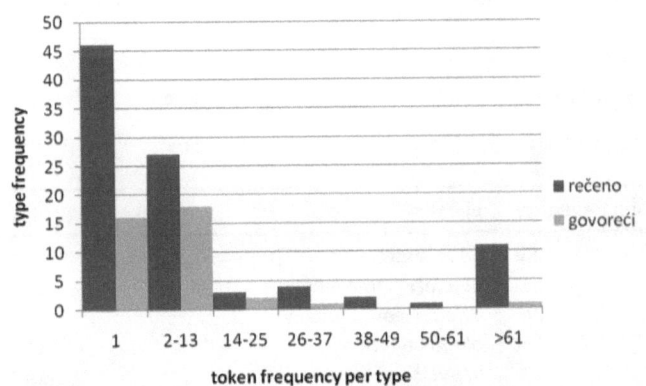

The fact that the mere number of representatives for the *rečeno* constructions outweighs the number of *govoreći* constructions not only in the low, but also by far in the high (token frequency > 51) and intermediate fields (token frequency 10–50) may be interpreted as evidence that the *rečeno* construction is semi-productive. Many of the most frequent *govoreći* constructions have direct (e.g. *iskreno govoreći / rečeno* 'frankly speaking' or *uvjetno govoreći / rečeno* 'conditionally speaking') or synonymous counterparts (e.g. *pošteno govoreći* 'honestly

---

[11] This study is a qualitative one. For a quantitative treatment of similar data cf. Birzer (accepted).
[12] To ensure comparability, the bins of the histogram are of equal size and have been generated on the basis of the data points for *govoreći*.

speaking vs. *iskreno govoreći / rečeno* 'frankly speaking') among the most frequent *rečeno* constructions. Furthermore, if we disregard frequency counts, it turns out that each *govoreći* construction has a direct counterpart among the *rečeno* constructions. This might be indicative for the *govoreći* constructions to be analogical forms of the *rečeno* constructions.

Quite interestingly, synonymous series also exist among representatives of one construction type, e.g. *usput / uzgred rečeno* 'by the way (said)', *najkraće / ukratko / kratko / sažeto / kraće rečeno* 'in short (lit. most shortly / more shortly / shortly said)' or *iskreno / pošteno / otvoreno govoreći* 'frankly / honestly / openly speaking', to mention just a few.

The functions of the construction are (partially) derivable from their semantics. On the pragmatic level, the construction expresses speaker's stance towards the proposition. On the syntactic level, the construction may function as a connective. Both functions are inherent in the construction, but depending on the semantics of the adverb inserted into the construction, their manifestation varies.

Chart 2: Representatives of stance-marking with token frequency > 10 in HNK25.

govoreći		*rečeno*	
element	token frequency	element	token frequency
iskreno 'frankly'	73	*bolje* 'better'	360
općenito 'generally'	33	*najblaže* 'most mildly'	277
objektivno 'objectively'	24	*uvjetno* 'conditionally'	265
uvjetno 'conditionally'	18	*blago* 'mildly'	176
pošteno 'honestly'	13	*usput* 'by the way'	147
realno 'frankly (lit. really)'	12	*jednostavno* 'plainly'	102
otvoreno 'frankly (lit. openly)'	11	*najkraće* 'in shortest term (lit. most shortly said)'	102
pojednostavljeno 'simply'	10	*pojednostavljeno* 'simply'	99
		iskreno 'frankly'	81
		točnije 'more exactly'	75
		uzgred 'by the way'	73
		jednostavnije 'more plainly'	59
		preciznije 'more precisely'	44
		drukčije 'in other words (lit. in another way said)'	39
		ukratko 'in short'	34
		uzgred budi 'by the way'	34
		grubo 'roughly'	32
		usput budi 'by the way'	30

Chart 2 (continued)

\multicolumn{2}{c}{*govoreći*}	\multicolumn{2}{c}{*rečeno*}
element	token frequency	element	token frequency
		kratko 'in short (lit. shortly said)'	24
		najjednostavnije 'most plainly'	24
		sažeto 'in short (lit. shortly said)'	14
		kraće 'in still shorter terms (lit. shorter said)'	10

Thus, connectivity is less pronounced with *iskreno govoreći / rečeno* 'frankly speaking', but speaker's stance figures prominently (compare (27), where speaker's stance is dominant, with (28), where connectivity is also at work); whereas with *najkraće govoreći / rečeno* 'in short' connectivity is dominant (29) and the speaker's stance plays only a minor role (compare (29) with (30), where stance is more in focus).

(27) EXTRA : *Jeste li očekivali takav uspjeh? – Ne,* **iskreno**-ADV **rečeno**-PTCP.PASS *nisam*-1SG *se nadao pobjedi.*
'EXTRA: Have you expected such a success? – No, frankly speaking I did not hope for victory.'
(HNK_v25 subcorpus, na138_08)

(28) *Čini mi se da sam previše introvertirana ili, bolje rečeno, izbirljiva, pa čak i komotna.* **Iskreno**-ADV **rečeno**-PTCP.PASS, *kad se ugase*-3PL *reflektori*-NOM.PL *pozornice, prilično sam*-1SG *dosadna osoba* .
'It seems to me that I am too introverted or, more precisely (better said), fastidious, even also easy-going as well. Frankly speaking, when the theatre lights are turned off, I am a rather boring person.'
(HNK_v25 subcorpus, na146_12)

(29) *Sigurno je, međutim, da je premijer Ehud Barak, koji je preživio glasovanje o povjerenju vladi, doživio snažan udarac izborom Katsava za novoga, osmoga izraelskog šefa države. Otpao je*-3SG, **najkraće**-ADV **rečeno**-PTCP.PASS, *njegov*-POSS.NOM *vrlo blizak*-ADJ.NOM *politički*-ADJ.NOM *istomišljenik*-NOM.
'Meanwhile it is sure that prime minister Ehud Barak, who has survived the cabinet's no-confidence vote, experienced a strong blow by Katsav's election as the new, eighth Israeli head of government. In short (lit. most shortly said) his very close political like-minded friend has been moved aside.'
(HNK_v25 subcorpus, vj20000802gl03)

(30) *Sarajevske vlasti za Herceg Bosnu ne plaćaju ni jednog bosanskog dinara, a Hrvatska za održavanje samo četiri gardijske brigade HVO-a izdvaja – točno i precizno – 105 milijuna američkih dolara godišnje. To*-DEM.NOM *je*-3SG, ***najkraće***-ADV ***rečeno***-PTCP.PASS, *apsurdna*-ADJ.NOM *bilanca*-NOM *povijesnog HDZ-ova projekta na tlu susjedne države.*
'The authorities in Sarajevo do not pay a single Bosnian dinar for Herceg-Bosna, but Croatia spends for the maintenance of just four infantry brigades of the HVO [Croatian Defence Council – S. B.] – exactly and precisely – 105 million US dollars per year. That is, in short (lit. most shortly said) the absurd balance of accounts of the HDZ's historic project on the soil of a neighbouring country.'
(HNK_v25 subcorpus, na135_13)

4.2 The contextualizing function

govoreći / rečeno + ADJ.INS + NOUN.INS is the prototypical construction representing contextualization. A contextualizer relates (part of the) proposition within a certain discourse – be it modern terminology for old and well-known phenomena (cf. especially (31) or different style registers that characterize certain types of discourse, (32)–(33).

(31) *Odmah nakon uvođenja [godine 1910 – S. B.], tramvaj*-NOM *je*-3SG *u Dubrovniku,* ***današnjim***-ADJ.INS ***jezikom***-INS ***rečeno***-PTCP.PASS, *bio pravi hit.*
'Directly after the implementation in 1910, the tramway in Dubrovnik was, using (lit. speaking in) contemporary language, a real hit.'
(HNK_v25 subcorpus, HR510209A)

(32) *Može li vjernik dati glas stranci koja se protivi izgradnji crkve?* ***Sportskim***-ADJ.INS ***rječnikom***-INS ***govoreći***-AP, *to*-DEM.NOM *je*-3SG *isto kao da član Hajduka navija za Partizan!*
'Can a believer give his vote to a party that opposes the building of a church? In terms of sports (lit. speaking in sportive language), this is the same as if a member of Hajduk supported Partizan!'
(HNK_v25 subcorpus, gs20050516hr41161b)

(33) *Dinamov*-ADJ.NOM *trener*-NOM *Ilija*-NOM *Lončarević*-NOM *u maksimirskom klubu još uvijek radi*-3SG *bez ugovora, ili*-CONJ ***kolokvijalno***-ADV ***rečeno***-PTCP.PASS *– radi*-3SG *"na crno".*
'The trainer of Dinamo, Ilija Lončarević, still works in the club of Maksimir without a contract, or, in colloquial language (lit. colloquially said) – he "moonlights".'
(HNK_v25 subcorpus, vj20010424sp03)

Apart from the construction with ADJ.INS + NOUN.INS, contextualizers can also be based on adverbs, (33).

Chart 3: Representatives of contextualizing sorted after token frequency.

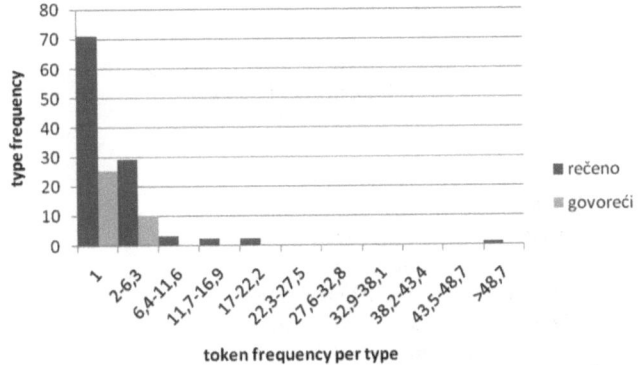

Regarding the distribution of instantiation types and synonymy, Charts 3 and 4 show a picture similar to Charts 1 and 2. However, one difference deserves special mention: judging from the token frequencies of representatives, it looks like the prototypical construction *govoreći / rečeno* + ADJ.INS + NOUN.INS is not as productive as the ADV + *govoreći / rečeno* construction is in general. Yet the fact that along with *nogometnim riječnikom / nogometnim žargonom / nogometnom terminologijom rečeno* 'speaking (lit. said) in soccer language / jargon / terminology' there exists also *nogometno rečeno* 'speaking (lit. said) in a soccer way' gives reason to assume that at least some of the adverbs used in the contextualizing function are derived from the *govoreći / rečeno* + ADJ.INS + NOUN.INS construction.

Chart 4: Representatives of contextualizing with token frequency > 3.

govoreći		*rečeno*	
element	token frequency	element	token frequency
slikovito 'figuratively'	6	*slikovito* 'figuratively'	54
simbolički 'symbolically'	3	*laički* 'in layman's terms (lit. amateurishly)'	19
stručno 'technically'	3	*simbolično* 'symbolically'	19
		figurativno 'figuratively'	13
		metaforički 'metaphorically'	12
		pučki 'in popular language (lit. popularly)'	10

Chart 4 (continued)

govoreći		rečeno	
element	token frequency	element	token frequency
		nogometnim riječnikom 'in football language'	9
		narodski 'in folk language'	7
		hrvatski 'in plain language (lit. Croatian)'	6
		popularno 'in the language of the masses (lit. popularly)'	6
		simbolički 'symbolically'	6
		kolokvijalno 'colloquially'	5
		slikovitije 'more figuratively'	5
		karikirano 'in caricature fashion'	4
		današnjim jezikom 'in today's language'	3
		diplomatski 'in diplomatic language'	3
		među nama 'between us'	3
		naški 'in our language'	3
		pravnički 'in legal terms'	3

4.3 The quotative index

Govoreći / rečeno + NOUN.INS + NOUN.GEN is the prototypical construction for this function. The quotative index can be roughly described as "non-verbal clauses (or copula clauses without a canonical subject topic) with a foregrounding function with scope over a nominal that refers to the source, aka [also known as – S. B.] speaker, of an associated direct quote" (Güldemann 2012: 134; for a more detailed description and discussion of the pros and cons of Güldemann's approach cf. Birzer accepted). Quotative indices combine two functions: Apart from identifying the source of quotation, they also connect two discourses with each other. They link the discourse into which the citation is integrated to the one from which the citation was taken. Weiss (2012) describes the mechanism at work as follows: As basis for the connection [between citation and the text it is integrated into – S. B.] functions the metatextual operation of comparison, i.e. an implicit or explicit parallel between the actual [...] situation [...] and the content of the xeno-text [the quote – S. B.]" [translation – S. B.].

Since referring to quotation sources is a rather individual process in several senses (an individual speaker may use a quotation and give the index or not), most quotative indices are attested just once. They all base on *rečeno*, (34)–(36). It is also possible to use the constructions *rečeno / govoreći* + ADJ.INS + NOUN.INS (34) and ADV + *rečeno* / *govoreći* (35) as a quotative index if the respective adverb or adjective is derived from the (proper) noun that takes the genitive in the prototypical construction.

(34) ... *živimo u zvjerinjaku ali zato smo svoji na svome, ili – **rečeno**-*PTCP.PASS *jezikom*-INS ***pokojnoga***-ADJ.GEN ***Gojka***-GEN ***Šuška***-GEN *– kad nas već okružuju*-3PL *lopovi*-NOM*, bolje da su to naši lopovi nego tuđi.*
'... we live in a menagerie, but consequently we are our people on our ground, or – using the words of the late Gojko Šušak (lit. said in the language of the late Gojko Šušak) – when villains surround us, it is better that they are our villains than foreign ones.'
(HNK_v25 subcorpus, na147_k08)

(35) *Za razliku od svojih tranzicijskih parnjaka u zemljama gdje,* ***Držićevim***-POSS.ADJ.INS ***rječnikom***-INS ***rečeno***-PTCP.PASS "*ruka*-NOM *maha*-3SG", *a često polete i odgojne palice, meci i mine, današnje stanovništvo bivše Istočne Njemačke nema vidljivog razloga svoje javne istupe ...*
'In contrast to its transitional mates in countries where, using Držić's wording (lit. said in Držić's language) "the arms are in a frenzy", and truncheons, bullets and mines often fly, today's population of former East Germany does not have an obvious reason for its public furore ....'
(HNK_v25 subcorpus, na208_r02)

(36) ... *Bleiburg*-NOM *nosio*-3SG *neizbrisiv pečat tragedije i bio*-3SG *smatran*-PTCP.PASS.NOM, ***matoševski***-POSS.ADV ***rečeno***-PTCP.PASS, "*teškim križem jedne nacije*".
'... Bleiburg carried the tragedy's inerasable stamp and was considered, using Matoš's words (lit. said in Matoš's way) "the grave crux of one nation".'
(HNK_v25 subcorpus, vj20030430st01)

4.4 The direct speech marking function

This function is a specificity of Croatian, as it has not been attested for Russian and Polish. Only "plain" *govoreći* can be used in this function, (37)–(39). At first glance, the direct speech marker looks like a prototypical adverbial participle whose covert subject is co-referent with the subject of the matrix clause (cf. Katičić 2002: 489–490). However, this is only half the picture, as *govoreći* may also figure in sentences introducing direct speech where it is the only predicate, although such cases are rather few in number (40). Croatian is less rigid about adverbial participles with an overt, non-co-referent subject (cf. Katičić 2002: 491–492) than other Slavonic languages, but, to the best of our knowledge, the possibility of an adverbial participle forming the only predicate in a sentence has never been allowed for in the grammaticography of contemporary Croatian – even if *govoreći* is co-referent with the subject of the preceding sentence, as in (40). This may be considered an argument for classifying plain *govoreći* as a special marker of direct speech.

Another idiosyncratic feature can also be interpreted as evidence that plain *govoreći* is not a "normal" adverbial participle, but a marker: it occurs directly after a finite *verbum dicendi*, which is semantically more complex and renders the manner of speaking, (37)–(39). From the point of view of semantics and information structure, the finite verb is sufficient to introduce the rendering of speech content, but *govoreći* specifies that the content is rendered in its original form, i.e. as direct speech, and not as reported speech or "digested" in the form of a complement clause or PP, (41).

(37) *Pokraj nje bila su prevrnuta dječja kolica, a djevojčica*-NOM *je*-3SG *plakala* ***govoreći***-AP: *"Što si napravio mojoj mami!?"*
'Next to her the pram was turned over, and the girl cried, saying: "What have you done to my mama!?"'
(HNK_v25 subcorpus, gs20050702ck42973)

(38) *Valpurga*-NOM *se smijala*-3SG *tome* ***govoreći***-AP: *- Eto ....*
'Valpurga laughed about this, saying: "That is, ..."'
(HNK_v25 subcorpus, vjnovak_stip)

(39) *Veselin*-NOM *Šljivančanin*-NOM, *major*-NOM, *postrojio je*-3SG *pred sobom liječnike i ... držao im moralno-političko vaspitanje* ***govoreći***-AP: *"Evo bre doktori, ..."*
'Veselin Šljivančanin, a major, made the doctors deploy in front of him and gave them a moral-political instruction, saying: "Look you doctors ...."'
(HNK_v25 subcorpus, gs20031118hr25841)

(40) *Nisam, međutim, dobro razumjela. – Niste dobro razumjeli? – Ne. Gouldov se otac ponovno stao*-3SG *smijati, odmahujući*-AP *glavom. Ali ne* ***govoreći***-AP: *– Da poludiš.*
'"However, I haven't understood well." – "You haven't understood well?" – "No." Gould's father started to laugh again, shaking his head. But not saying: "You are driving me crazy."'
(HNK_v25 subcorpus, vj20021218ku08)

(41) *... on*-NOM *me nazvao*-3SG *mobitelom* ***govoreći***-AP *mi da je otišao u Gospić ....*
'... he called me by mobile phone, telling me that he had gone to Gospić.'
(HNK_v25 subcorpus, gs20040614os31492)

This allows us to draw an interesting diachronic parallel to Croatian Church Slavonic, where a cumulation of two *verba dicendi* was also used for marking speech report. Mihaljević (2011: 75) states that "[o]nly in examples where the reporting marker is a combination of two verbs of speaking, the second being *reĉi* or *glagolati*, the speech report must always follow the reporting verb." This allows us to propose the hypothesis that the contemporary direct speech marker *govoreći* is the result of a diachronic development, in whose course the rules for the positioning of speech markers slackened and *govoreći* achieved the status of the exclusive marker of direct speech. We will come back on this hypothesis in Section 5.

Taxis embedding is another issue, as plain *govoreći* seems to be on the way to losing it. The adverbial participle (henceforth AP) of imperfective verbs marks the simultaneity of the situations denoted in the AP clause and its matrix clause. Roughly speaking, the tense of the matrix clause predicate serves as a point of reference for the relative tense of the AP (for a more detailed discussion of taxis and its implications cf. Xrakovskij 2003). When the AP is the only predicate in a sentence, as in example (40), the AP is deprived of its point of taxis reference. Example (40) is very enlightening, as it contains two simultaneous APs, *odmahujući glavom* 'shaking his head' and *govoreći* 'speaking'. The point of reference for *odmahujući* is *stao se smijati* 'he began to laugh'. Although, strictly speaking, the head-shaking should coincide only with the beginning of the laughing, it is more likely that head-shaking and laughing coincide in their temporal extension. Now to *govoreći*. As it has no matrix verb of its own, its placement on the time axis remains unclear. It may be conceived as a) a non-implemented alternative to *odmahujući glavom* 'shaking his head', which would imply simultaneity with the (start of) laughing; b) an alternative to the combination of laughing and head-shaking, which would imply posteriority in relation to the preceding dialogue; c) a possible, but non-implemented reaction following the combination of laughing and head-shaking, thus implying posteriority in relation to it. Example (42) provides a similar picture. Here, *govoreći* has a matrix verb, but the temporal extension of the situations denoted by AP and matrix verb differ considerably: the matrix verb *otvoriti vrata* 'open the door' denotes a momentary situation, whereas *govoriti* 'speak' denotes a perdurative action. This reason as well as common knowledge make it rather improbable that the two situations take place simultaneously, and rather plausible that the speaking antecedes the opening of the door, i.e. is anterior.

(42) *Ja te željno očekujem! – To **govoreći**-AP, otvori-3SG vrata svoje sobe i, stojeći na pragu, dobaci mu prstima cjelov.*
 '"I wait for you ardently!" Saying this, she opened the door of the room, and, standing on the threshold, she blew him a kiss with her fingers.'
 (HNK_klasici subcorpus, J. Tomić. *Melita*. 1899)

Finally, some words on semantics and valency are in order. In contrast to *reći*, the exact mode of articulation is much more central for many meanings of *govoriti*, just as well as the syntactic realization of content (cf. Pranjković 2001: 136). Thus it is not too surprising that an inflectional form of *govoriti* becomes a marker of direct speech, and an inflectional form of *reći* is part of a semi-productive pattern for forming DSEs. Another contrast to the three functions described above is the fact that plain *govoreći* as a direct speech marker lacks the semantic component 'the speaker'.

Therefore, considering all facts rendered in this section, we may assume that plain *govoreći* occupies an intermediate position between the prototypical adverbial participle and DSE.

5 Historical development

5.1 State of the art

As our research question is the diachronic development of DSEs based on *verba dicendi* and the role language contact plays in it, we need to cover the state of the art of three issues: the historical development of DSEs, *verba dicendi* in the history of Croatian, and the role of language contact therein.

To the best of our knowledge, the diachronic development of DSEs in the South Slavonic languages is a rather understudied subject, the more so if one is not concerned with elements that are usually subsumed under the label *discourse markers*, i.e. particles or interjections. However, we would like to point out that a study on the historical development of DSEs based on the AP *govorja* 'speaking' has already been conducted for Russian (Birzer 2012a), where eight developmental steps have been established:

1) APs of the *verba dicendi glagolati, rešči* and *govoriti* 'speak' function as markers of direct speech with the semantics 'X is saying Q. X is not the author of P; the speaker is author of P.'[13] At this stage the direct speech forms a sentence of its own. The contextual information gradually integrates into the AP's semantics.

---

13 In this quotation semantic explications in the style of the Moscow Semantic School have been used (cf. Apresjan 2005). The variable X represents semantic arguments of content words; P and Q those of function words. Although *verba dicendi* are without doubt content words, the variables P and Q have been used in order to mark those arguments that are retained on the historical way to DSE.

2) Bleaching out of the semantic components connected with sound production; loss of the corresponding syntactic arguments.
3) Tightening of the paradigm: only AP *govorja* marks speaker's evaluation Q of a situation P.
4) Loss of obligatory co-reference between the covert subject of AP and first argument of the matrix clause.
5) AP loses clause status.
6) Collocation of the former and a restricted number of manner adverbs; collocations convey speaker's stance to Q.
7) Collocation forms sentence with Q.
8) Phonological reduction of the collocation; remaining manner adverb conveys meaning of the whole collocation.

(Birzer 2012a: 246–247)

Quite interestingly, inflectional forms of Old Church Slavonic and Old Russian *verba dicendi*, among them APs, functioned as markers of direct speech, quite often in cumulation with a second *verbum dicendi* (cf. Birzer 2012a: 238, 2012b). In later times, this function was fulfilled exclusively by the AP *glagolja* 'speaking', which finally also went out of use in the 18th century (cf. Birzer 2012a: 240). So Russian, in contrast to Croatian, features no more markers of direct speech based on *verba dicendi*.

Verba dicendi have received much attention in the historical linguistics of B/C/S. Mihaljević (2011) gives an account of the semantic arguments of Croatian Church Slavonic *verba dicendi* and their syntactic realization. In his analysis of the possible syntactic realizations of the semantic role 'content', he elaborates on the problems for analysis that (complement) clauses pose (cf. Mihaljević 2011: 69–75). His analysis of speech report markers is of special interest for us.

Mihaljević states that "a reporting marker can be a combination of any verb of speaking with the verb *reći* or *glagolati*. In that case the speech report is always direct speech" (2011: 74). However, judging from Mihaljević's examples, a single, semantically more complex *verbum dicendi* also seems to be sufficient as a reporting marker. These markers may also form a parenthesis or be postponed (cf. Mihaljević 2011: 74–75), but "[o]nly in examples where the reporting marker is a combination of two verbs of speaking, the second being *reći* or *glagolati*, the speech report must always follow the reporting verb" (Mihaljević 2011: 75). If we consider example (42) from Modern Croatian, where the direct speech marker *govoreći* is postponed, it turns out that *govoreći* occupies a less fixed position than the Croatian Church Slavonic reporting markers based on *reći* or *glagolati*.

Hudeček explores foreign influence on the syntactic structures of *verba dicendi* and *cogitandi* in the Čakavian literary language up to the 17th century

(2001) and in the Croatian literary language from the 17th century up to the first half of the 19th century (2003). Unfortunately – as complement clauses are much more interesting for our research question – in both cases Hudeček analyses only arguments syntactically realized as NPs and PPs. These structures deviate in case assignment and choice of prepositions from Modern Croatian, and Hudeček aims to establish which role structural influence from foreign languages played in these deviations. For the Čakavian literary language up to the 17th century, she identifies Latin and Italian as the main sources for the replication of syntactic structures (cf. Hudeček 2001: 97); for the Kajkavian literary language from the 17th to the first half of the 19th century she postulates a strong influence from German (Hudeček 2003: 117). Unfortunately, Hudeček does not confirm her claims by providing appropriate data from the source languages even in cases where this can be accomplished easily, e.g. the Latin source for Kašić's Bible translation. Finally, we would like to mention that there exists manifold literature on (adverbial) participles in Old Serbian (cf., among others, Grković-Major 2003), but, unfortunately, the (morpho)syntactic issues discussed cannot be exploited for our needs.

The role of language contact in the history of Croatian has been an issue for a long time. As our assumption is that German syntactic structures influenced the rise of DSEs based on *rečeno*, we will discuss only works concerned with German influence. The focus of most studies has been on the borrowing of lexical material (cf. among others Striedter-Temps 1958; Schneeweis 1960; Grotzky 1978; Golubović 2007). Štebih (2003: 305) pays some attention to the replication of morphological patterns (and partially morphosyntactic ones, such as reflexivization) in the verbal sector, but this entails only the replication of Croatian patterns by German loans that share the semantics of the pattern-giving Croatian verb, and not the replication of German syntactic patterns in Croatian. Rammelmeyer (1975) explores German loan translations in B/C/S. In doing so, he finds that many past participles passive in B/C/S are borrowed from German (cf. Rammelmeyer 1975: 107; Turk and Sesar 2003: 329–330). Quite interestingly, several of Rammelmeyer's examples serve discourse functions: (43) has text referential function, and (44) expresses the speaker's doubt about the applicability of a concept to a given entity, i.e. conveys speaker's stance.

(43) B/C/S
　　gore-spomenut　　　　　　　　　*gore-naveden*
　　above-mention-PTCP.PST.PASS　　above-adduce-PTCP.PST.PASS
　　G
　　oben　　　erwähnt　　　　　　　oben　　　angeführt
　　above-ADV　mention-PTCP.PST.PASS　above-ADV　adduce-PTCP.PST.PASS
　　'above mentioned'

(44) B/C/S
 tako-zvan
 so-call-PTCP.PST.PASS
 G
 so-genannt
 so-call-PTCP.PST.PASS
 'so-called'

The evidence that in general German structural patterns played a role in the formation of participles serving discourse functions strengthens our hypothesis that the specific construction with *rečeno* also developed under German influence.[14] Three more factors also support our hypothesis: Firstly, according to Turk and Sesar (2003: 337) German is considered to be the language to which the Slavonic languages resorted for the replication of patterns and to be the mediator for the adaptation of patterns from the classical and other European languages. This statement deserves a critical comment. Without doubt German exerted some influence on all Slavonic languages, but it was by far not the only influential language; the extension of its influence over linguistic domains such as lexicon, morphology and syntax varied considerably depending on the intensity of language contact,[15] and the influence was not equally strong in all historical time periods, so it is quite difficult to determine which patterns were replicated directly and which ones via a mediator language. However, Croatian was in contact with German for a rather long time, which makes the replication of German patterns very probable. The same also applies to Czech, which leads us to the second factor. Czech is considered to be the mediator language via which calques from German were passed on to other (South) Western Slavonic languages (cf. Turk and Sesar 2003: 327). Since Czech also features DSEs based on the past participle passive *řečeno* 'spoken', it might be that Czech influence reinforced the consolidation of the *rečeno* pattern in Croatian. Thirdly, structural calques seem to enhance the existence of doublets with a different (morpho)syntactic structure (cf. Turk and Sesar 2003: 335). This

---

14 Examples of direct translations would be very enlightening, but the identification and accessibility of historical parallel texts poses a major problem. With respect to German-Croatian parallel texts, the *corpora juris* of the Austrian Crownlands probably constitutes the largest resource. Some of them are available online at http://alex.onb.ac.at/cgi-content/alex-iv.pl but only as graphical images without the possibility of automatic search. Therefore, we refrained from searching this database. Furthermore, only DSEs of the type (43–44) and possibly reformulating DSEs can be expected due to the text genre.

15 For example, the German influence on Russian is restricted to loanwords in the lexicon, whereas Czech replicated constructions (cf. e.g. Berger 2009).

might explain the existence of the competing discourse structuring constructions based on *govoreći* and *rečeno* respectively.

5.2 Analysis of diachronic data

Our data allows us to establish three periods in the diachronic development of DSEs based on *govoreći* and *rečeno* respectively. The first one ends with the first half of the 17th century and covers the development of *govoreći* into a marker of speech report. From the second half of the 17th century onwards constructions with *govoreći* and *rečeno* respectively begin to function as DSEs and to develop the morphosyntactic features characteristic for these DSEs. Finally, in the 19th century the DSEs expand their field of usage, which can be seen from increasing type and token frequency.

5.2.1 Development until the first half of the 17th century

As has been mentioned above, in this period *govoreći* acquires its status as a marker of speech report.[16] The comparison of secular and religious writing, namely Kašić's Bible translation, proved to be very helpful, as the two text genres differ in the usage of *verba dicendi* and their morphological forms for marking speech report. As the examples below will show, in the secular texts only the AP *govoreći* is used for marking speech reports. It appears both in a cumulation with another (semantically more complex) *verbum dicendi* and as the sole predicative element; its syntactic position relative to the speech report varies. On the other hand, Kašić uses only cumulations of *verba dicendi* for marking speech reports; the marker always precedes the speech report, i.e. is syntactically fixed, but is formed of various *verba dicendi* in various morphological forms. This may be attributed to archaic style – the more so as Church Slavonic redactions are known to display such variety in the marking of speech reports (cf. among others Daiber 2009; Birzer 2012b) – but is helpful for our analysis, as it allows us to draw some conclusions on earlier language stages.

In example (45) *govoreći*, the prototypical marker of speech report, functions as a "normal" AP with complements and a matrix verb that is not a *verbum*

---

[16] Why *marker of speech report* is preferred to *direct speech marker* will become clear in the course of this section.

dicendi. The aim of this example is showing that the features of speech report markers enumerated above are indeed decisive for setting markers apart from mere inflectional forms of *verba dicendi*. It is also noteworthy that in this context *govoreći* does not introduce any speech report.

(45) *Mojses*-NOM ***govoreći*-AP** *na gori z Bogom, puk*-NOM *se pristraši*-3SG *i odstupi*-3SG *od gore, čuvši trublje i glas strašan Božji.*
'While Moses was speaking on the mountain with God, the people got scared and retreated from the mountain, having heard the blare and God's awesome voice.'
(HNK_Marulić subcorpus)

Let us now have a look at instances of speech report marking. We will set out with cases where the marker is part of a cumulation of *verba dicendi*. In all these cases, the complements go with the first, semantically more complex *verbum dicendi* (46), whereas the second one is bare, irrespective of the chosen verb and its morphological form.[17] The marker always precedes the speech report. It is also noteworthy that in some cases (47) the semantically more complex verb has an non-finite form, whereas the second *verbum dicendi* is finite – and not vice versa. This can be explained by the higher syntactic independency participles and APs enjoyed in earlier times (cf. Grković-Major 2003). Finally, (53)–(54) are two examples that illustrate why the elements under investigation need to be labelled *markers of speech report* and not *markers of direct speech*: it is not clear whether the prophecies introduced by the markers are renderings of direct speech or periphrases, and are thus citations. Furthermore, (54) can also be treated as evidence that *rečeno* has not yet acquired any discourse function. It is part of a regular passive construction where even the facultative PP encoding the agent is realized syntactically. At the same time, this example shows quite nicely that already in the 17th century *reći* obviously had its semantic focus rather on the conveyance of information than the mode of its articulation, as the Lord does not speak Himself but uses the prophet as instrument.

---

17 This holds even for those few cases – 2 of more than 30 analysed ones – where the two *verba dicendi* are placed in reverse order:
(1) kursiv (Kašić, Lk 8,8)
(2) ... kursiv ... (HNK_Klasici subcorpus, Hektorović, Petar: *Ribanje i ribarsko prigovaranje*, 1556.)

(46) *ere Gñ*-NOM *govorio jest*-3SG *Davidu* **rekši**-PTCP.ACT: *U ruci sluge moga Davida sahraniti ću puka moga Izraela od ruke filistejske i od svieh nepriatelja njegovich.*
'So the Lord spoke to David saying: "In the hands of my servant David I will save my folk Israel from the Philistines' hand and from all its foes."'
(Kašić, 2 Sam 3:18)

(47) *Odgavarajući*-AP *tad Job*-NOM, **reče**-3SG:"..."
'Then answering Job said: "...."'
(Kašić, Job 26:1)

(48) ... *kamenovahu*-3SG *Stiepana*-ACC, *zovećega*-PTCP.ACT.ACC *i* **govorećega**-PTCP.ACT.ACC: *Gñe Jesuse, primi duha moga.*
'... they lapidated Stiepan, who was crying and speaking: "Lord Jesus, accept my soul."'
(Kašić, Dj 7:58/Acts 7:59)

(49) *Koja*-NOM *[Sara*-NOM – S. B.] *se nasmija*-3SG *potajno,* **govoreći**-AP: ....
'This one [Sara] laughed in secret, saying: "..."'
(Kašić, Post/Gen. 18:12)

(50) *Zanika*-3SG *Sara*-NOM **govoreći**-AP: *Niesam se nasmijala, strahom pristrašena.*
'Sara denied, saying: "I did not laugh, paralysed by fear."'
(Kašić, Post/Gen. 18:15)

(51) *Panucij*-NOM *poče*-3SG *Bogu zahvaljivati*-INF **govoreći**-AP: *Hvala mi ti budi, o slatki Bože moj ...*
'Panucij began to praise God, saying: "Be this my praise to you, oh my sweet God ...."'
(HNK_Marulić subcorpus)

(52) ... *moj*-POSS.NOM *drug*-NOM *Sladmil*-NOM *opita*-3SG *me* **govoreći**-AP: *– Ako ti nî trudno, reci mi ....*
'... my friend Sladmil asked me, saying: "If it is not difficult for you, tell me ...."'
(HNK_klasici subcorpus, Zoranić P. *Planine*. 1569)

(53) *I ispunjuje*-3SG *se u njih proročanstvo*-NOM *Isaije*-GEN *proroka*-GEN **govorećega**-PTCP.ACT.GEN: *Sluhom ćete slišati i nećete razumieti: i gledajući gledati ćete i nećete vidieti.*
'And in them is fulfilled the prophecy of Esaias, which saith, By hearing ye shall hear, and shall not understand; and seeing ye shall see, and shall not perceive.' (King James Bible translation)
(Kašić, Mt 13:14)

(54) *A ovo sve bi učinjeno neka bi se izpunilo što-*NOM *je-*3SG **rečeno-**PTCP.PASS.N
*od Gospodina po proroku-*DAT *govorećemu-*PTCP.ACT.DAT: *Evo će dievica
u utrobi imati i roditi će sina i zvati će se ime njegovo Emanuel, koje
istomačeno jest S nami Bog.*
'Now all this was done, that it might be fulfilled which was spoken of the
Lord by the prophet, saying, Behold, a virgin shall be with child, and shall
bring forth a son, and they shall call his name Emmanuel, which being
interpreted is, God with us.' (King James Bible translation)
(Kašić, Mt 1:22)

The second type of contexts is characterized by the following features: the marker is incurred without a second *verbum dicendi* and has no complements or adjuncts. It is optionally accompanied by the deictic adverb *tako* 'so'. Quite interestingly, in secular texts only *govoreći* occurs in this context (55), whereas religious texts feature other, even finite verbal forms (56).[18] If one still considers *govoreći* to be the member of a verbal paradigm and not a lexicalized element, it has to be described as a predicate that has been promoted from secondary predication in a complex sentence to primary predication in a sentence consisting only of the predicate. In comparison to the cumulative speech report marker its position is relatively free, as it can be inserted into the speech report as parenthesis.

(55) *On ju tišeći-*AP *tisućkrat i tisuć milo pritiskajući-*AP *celunu-*3SG: *– Nemoj se –*
govoreći-AP *– dušice moja, rascviljevati.*
Consoling and a thousand and thousand times pressing her heartily,
he kissed her: "Don't," saying, "my darling, moan."'
(HNK_klasici subcorpus, Zoranić P. *Planine.* 1569)

(56) *Zanika-*3SG *Sara-*NOM *govoreći-*AP: *Niesam se nasmijala, strahom
pristrašena. A Gñ*ⱼ*-*NOM: *Nie tako,* **reče**ⱼ*-*3SG; *pače si-*2SG *se nasmijala.*
'Then Sarah denied, saying, I laughed not; for she was afraid. And he said,
Nay; but thou didst laugh.' (King James Bible translation)
(Kašić, Post/Gen. 18:15)

Based on the description of prototypical contexts and features of speech report marking, we will now discuss intermediate cases that allow us to reconstruct the marker's development.

---

18 Since the finite verb forms are attested only in contexts where the second *verbum dicendi* is in the 3SG, it is impossible to determine whether they are already fossilized or not.

The first group of intermediate cases consists of instances where the marker still takes the addressee of the speech report as complement. This may happen in the cumulative construction, (57), as well as in cases where the marker is incurred independently of a second *verbum dicendi*, (58).

(57) .... *dvižuć*-AP *dlan u nebo moleći*-AP; *Bogu* **govoreći**-AP: *O Bože*, ...
'.... moving the palm to heaven in prayer (lit. praying), speaking to God: "Oh God, ..."'
(HNK_Marulić subcorpus)

(58) **Govoreći**-AP *njemu: Vid* ...
Speaking to him: "Eyelight..."
(HNK_klasici subcorpus, Hektorović, P. *Ribanje i ribarsko prigovaranje*. 1556.)

In the second group complex sentences are gathered. The *verbum dicendi* is predicate of an AP clause with an overt subject; the subject of the AP clause and matrix clause do not coincide. The AP clause follows immediately after the direct speech; the deictic adverb *tako* 'so' anaphorically relates to the direct speech (59)–(60). Except that *tako* 'so' comes directly after the speech, no fixed order of constituents in the AP clause can be discerned.

(59) *Anica našim hoće reći* .... – **Tako**-ADV **Dubjak**-NOM **govoreći**-AP, *dojdosmo*-1PL *uz goru* ...
'"Anica wants to speak to our people ..." With Dubjak speaking so, we came to the mountain ...'
(HNK_klasici subcorpus, Zoranić, P. *Planine*. 1569)

(60) ... *pripravni ste reći, dali trudi moji nećete podleći*. – **Tako**-ADV **govoreći**-AP *Isus*-NOM *s učenici, ugleda*-3SG *hodeći na njih oružnici* ...
'.... you are ready to say that you will not follow my teachings." Speaking so with his disciples, Jesus saw armed men approaching them ....'
(HNK_Marulić subcorpus)

In both groups of context, the dropping of complements may serve as an explanation for the development of the syntactically independent marker attested in (57)–(58).

Generally, the semantically more complex *verba dicendi* in "cumulative" contexts fall into two groups: verbs with the semantic component 'conveyance of information', such as *odgavarati* 'answer' or *moliti se* 'pray' and verbs with the component 'manner of articulation', such as *smijati se* 'laugh' or *vapiti* 'cry (out)'. The semantics of the former ones implies an addressee for the information and interestingly, markers with the addressee as complement occur only in those intermediate cases, where the semantically more complex *verbum dicendi* belongs to the semantic group of information conveyance. As both *verba dicendi* have the same subject, the addressee can easily be shifted from one verb to the other and the former AP can be detached into a sentence of its own. In cases where the subject of the preceding sentences is different, the point of reference for the marker is made explicit with the help of a "detached" nominative, (56).

In the second group, the relative syntactic independence of the AP clause with an overt subject enhances its syntactical autonomy from the matrix clause. The situations under consideration are also characterized by the conveyance of information, so it can be assumed that the same mechanisms as described above for the first group of contexts takes place in a second step.

Finally, we would like to discuss one curious example (61) that sheds light on how the marker might have acquired the function of citation marking. The example contains two syntactical structures with a *verbum dicendi* each, namely *govoreći tako* 'speaking so' and *kako on reče* 'as he said', which frame the speech report. The speech report or citation itself is introduced with the complementizer *da*. As has been shown above, *govoreći tako* prototypically functions as a marker of direct speech, although the verb *govoriti* of course does take complement clauses encoding indirect speech or citations. To make things more complicated, deictic *tako* 'so' inhibits a complement clause, as *tako* 'so' moves the concrete mode of articulation or the concrete wording (or both) into the focus – information which indirect speech cannot provide. Nearly the same problem arises with *kako on reče* 'as he said'. *On reče* 'he said' is no marker and takes a complement clause without any problems, but *kako* 'how', which works as anaphoric deictic referring to the speech content in this context, drastically reduces the probability of *on reče* doing so. Therefore, we propose that the two syntactical structures containing a *verbum dicendi* be considered as markers of the beginning and end of indirect speech. Such marking was helpful with the inconsistent punctuation in historical times, because the beginning and end of the indirect speech were difficult to detect as all pronouns – except the 2nd person – have to be transformed into 3rd person – the most frequent person in narrations (cf. Večerka 2002: 417–419 for Old Church Slavonic). Given that there are no examples found where the initial marker occurs in a cumulative construction and introduces a citation, it can be assumed that the usage as a citation marker was developed via analogy to the marking of direct speech. Since the combination of *govoreći tako* and *da* constitutes a double marking, *da* is in fact obsolete. The more so, as more prototypical examples of citation marking, (53)–(54), involve contexts that explicitly refer to the source of information and thus make it obvious that a citation will follow.

(61) **Govoreći**-AP **tako**-ADV: *da će svih zgubiti ki ne htiše,* **kako on reče**.
'Saying so: that he will kill [another possible interpretation would be *izgubiti* 'lose'] all who do not want, as he said.'
(HNK_Marulić subcorpus)

5.2.2 The second half of the 17th and the 18th centuries

This time period witnesses the first developmental steps towards DSEs with a stance marking and contextualizing function. Already at this early stage a division line between constructions based on *govoreći* and *rečeno* respectively can be distinguished: although in our corpus *govoreći* with a discourse function is attested four times as often as *rečeno*, we found just one instance where *govoreći* fulfils the contextualizing function, whereas *rečeno* occurs three times in contexts of stance marking or contextualization.

Govoreći is now the only marker of speech report and no intermediate cases are incurred. As in the preceding time period, contexts with two *verba dicendi*, (63)–(64), dominate numerically over those with *govoreći* occurring alone, (65)–(66). In the latter case, the syntactic position of *govoreći* is still less limited, as it can also follow the direct speech. Since the features of this usage have been described extensively in the preceding section, we will not discuss it further.

(62) ... *videći sada mostove široke i tvrde, počeše*-3PL *ga blagosivljati*-INF **govoreći**-AP: *"Ej junače, uvik živio!"*
'... seeing there the broad and solid bridges, they began to praise him saying: "Hey hero, may you live forever!"'
(HNK_klasici subcorpus, Relković, M. A. *Satir iliti divji čovik.* 1762)

(63) *"... Vidiš lađu eto, ... kako srićno brodi", kaže*-3SG **govoreći**-AP, *"igra se po vodi kao ptić leteći ...."*
'"...Do you see this ship, how smoothly it runs," he says speaking, "it floats through the water like a flying bird ...."'
(HNK_klasici subcorpus, Kanižlić, A. *Sveta Rožalija.* 1759)

(64) ... *zavapi*-3SG **govoreći**-AP: *'Bismo, er nijesmo veće: ...*
'.... he cried of fear, saying: "We were, but aren't no more: ...".'
(HNK_klasici subcorpus, Đurđević, I. *Uzdasi Mandalijene pokornice.* 1720)

(65) *Dižem*-1SG *ruke kao poletit*-INF *želeći*-AP: *"Ah, tko bi mi dao krila!"* **govoreći**-AP.
'I move my hands like wishing to fly: "Ah, who would give me wings!" saying.
(HNK_klasici subcorpus, Kanižlić, A. *Sveta Rožalija.* 1759)

(66) *Da ustavi tebe, neće*-3SG *"Tko si?" reći*-INF *ni odbit*-INF *od sebe "Natrag!"* **govoreći**-AP.
'In order to stop you he won't say "Who are you" nor will he repel you from himself by saying "Back!".'
(HNK_klasici subcorpus, Kanižlić, A. *Sveta Rožalija.* 1759)

Furthermore, there is also one instance of *govoreći* marking a citation (67). Once again, the marker precedes the citation and the source of information is made explicit.

(67) *Imala si prid ovim junake, kako kaže pismo i kronike, koji uvik slavno vojevaše, ovo ime Slavonci dobiše s Aleksandrom od Macedonije, koji njima dade*-3SG *dopuštenje baš u pismu* **tako**-ADV **govoreći**-AP*: "Da ne može nitko posli reći neg da ste nam bili pomoćnici, ..."*
'You had heroes, as the charter and the chronics relate, who always fought gloriously and who this name Slavonci received with Alexander of Macedonia, who gave them the permission in the very charter so saying: "So nobody will later be able to say anything but that you have been helpful ....".'
(HNK_klasici subcorpus, Relković, M. A. *Satir iliti divji čovik.* 1762)

The 18th century is also the time when *govoreći* and *rečeno* occur for the first time in progenitors of the contemporary DSEs.

Example (68) is enlightening, as the clause *pravo je rečeno* 'it is rightly said', merges two functions that are of interest for us. The analytical verb form *je rečeno* introduces the quotation of a saying. But in contrast to (61), where an inflectional form of *reći* 'speak' marks the end of an indirect speech, not deictic *kako* 'how / as', but the adverb *pravo* 'rightly / correctly' is used, which expresses the speaker's stance towards applying the cited saying to the situation described in the preceding text segment. This may be considered an evidence that stance-marking DSEs developed out of constructions for speech report marking by substituting deictic elements such as *tako* 'so' or *kako* 'how / as' through adverbs (a similar observation has been made for Russian DSEs of the same pattern, cf. Birzer 2012a: 227). This development is not too surprising, as DSEs – at least in their function as stance markers – are deictic as well. Quite interestingly, in Modern Croatian the construction finds its continuation in *pravo govoreći* 'rightly speaking', which is attested twice in the HNK_v25 corpus.

(68) *Pođe s ovoga svita kralj slovinski isto vrime udari na Ljutovida neizbrojena vojska cesara Ludovika, kojoj ne mogući Ljutovid odoliti, pobiže u srbsku zemlju i bi primljen od vojvode srbskoga u dvor svoj; ali se Ljutovid ukaza nepoznan i žestoko neharan, jer pogubivši svoga dobročasnika učini se gospodar od njegova grada i svega bogatstva.* **Pravo**-ADV *je*-3SG **rečeno**-PTCP.PASS*: "Ne čini dobra nepoznanu, da te zlo ne nađe".*
'The Slavonic king [i.e. Borna – S. B.] had departed from this world and at that time uncountable armed forces of Emperor Ludovik made an attack against Ljutovid, and Ljutovid, unable to resist them, fled to the Serbian lands and was received by the Serbian duke in his court; but Ljutovid turned out unthankful and terribly disrespectful, because having killed his benefactor he made himself sovereign of his city and all riches. Rightly it is said: "Don't do good to an unknown person, so evil will not find you."'
(HNK_klasici subcorpus, Kačić-Miošić, A. *Razgovor ugodni naroda slovinskoga.* 1759)

(69) ... *skoro sasvim durchaus ništa ne valjade. Al **po**-PREP **duši**-DAT **naški**-POSS.DAT **govoreći**-AP, umrit ćemo, ...*
'... nearly in general nothing turns around. But speaking according to our soul, we will die ....'
(HNK_klasici subcorpus, Relković, M. A. *Satir iliti divji čovik*. 1762)

Finally, we would like to mention two expressions that serve textual reference. On the one hand, this is the parenthetical clause *kako je gori rečeno* 'as has been said above', (70)–(71), and the attributive participle *rečeni* 'aforesaid'. Both refer to information that has already been introduced into the discourse at an earlier point in the text. In principle, expressions of the type *kako je gori rečeno* 'as has been said above' have the potential to become DSEs with a non-finite verbal element via deletion of the auxiliary. However, the expression is not attested in any form at later stages. *Rečeni* 'aforesaid', (72), figures also in contemporary texts; as a participle it is a non-finite verb form, but the fact that it has attributive function does not comply with our definition of DSEs. Therefore, we will not describe its further development.

(70) ... *Memed*-NOM .... *u njega [kašteo – S. B.] stavio*-3SG *svoje vojnike,* **kako**-ADV **je**-3SG **gori**-ADV **rečeno**-PTCP.PASS, *Skenderbeg, ne mogući podnositi Turke u svojoj državi, otiđe od grada do grada kupit vojsku za osvojit* **rečeni**-PTCP.PASS.ACC *kašteo*-ACC.
'... Memed placed his soldiers in it [the fort – S. B.], as was said above, Skenderbeg not being able to stand Turks in his state, went from town to town to buy soldiers for the conquest of the aforesaid (lit. said) fort.'
(HNK_klasici subcorpus, Kačić-Miošić, A. *Razgovor ugodni naroda slovinskoga*, 1759.)

(71) kako   je   gori   rečeno
as   AUX.3SG above say-PTCP.PST.N
wie   oben   gesagt   /   erwähnt   (wurde)
as   above   say-PTCP.PST.N mention-PTCP.PST.N AUX.3SG
'as has been said / mentioned above'

(72) *rečeni*
say-PTCP.PST.M
be-sagt
PREFIX-say.PTCP.PST
'aforesaid'

Structurally, Examples (68) and (70)–(72) are rather close to the contemporary constructions ADV + *rečeno* and (ADJ.INS) *jezikem*.INS *rečeno*; (68) may even be considered a predecessor of the former construction. Since the contemporary constructions also display alternation between *rečeno* and *govoreći*, the question arises how this alternation came into being.

We know from the history of other Slavonic languages that the alternation between two inflectional forms of *verba dicendi* in constructions with the same functions and similar structure is a result of language contact (cf. Birzer 2012a for Russian). Therefore, it seems worth checking this hypothesis for Croatian *rečeno* as well.

Popović (1960: 554: 622) gives a comprehensive survey of the source languages for syntactic replications, loan words and loan translations in Croatian; unfortunately, especially his account of syntactic replications cannot be considered exhaustive. Nonetheless, it helps to identify possible source languages. As the Croatian constructions have structurally and functionally similar counterparts in other Indo-European languages (among them other Slavonic ones such as e.g. Russian, Polish and Czech (see the introductory Section) and non-Slavonic ones such as e.g. English *frankly speaking*-AP, French *à dire*-INF *frai* 'frankly speaking' or German *ehrlich gesagt*-PTCP.PASS 'frankly speaking') it can be excluded that the respective Croatian constructions are the result of language contact within the *Balkansprachbund*. To capture as many source languages as possible, we decided to consider literature on language contact concerning all three varieties, i.e. Bosnian, Croatian and Serbian. Three major sources of influence are cited there: the first source are the Romance languages, with French as the source language and Italian as both the source and mediating language (cf. Musić 1972; Popović 2005; Franolic 1976; Šoć 2002). Two authors deserve special mention: Popović (2005: 157–166) gives a good theoretical survey of calque types, but applies his theoretical insights only randomly to data from French-Serbian language contact. Musić (1972: 117–119) offers a fine description of semantic influence and syntactic pattern replication from Italian. However, none of them mention the constructions under investigation as cases of language contact with Romance, and the fact that both French and Italian favour constructions with the infinitive as equivalents for the Croatian constructions described above, makes Romance language contact a rather unlikely explanation. Russian (Ajduković 1997) may also be excluded for structural reasons, as its relevant constructions are formed with the help of either the adverbial participle or the infinitive. Thus only German remains, which has exerted quite some influence on Croatian (for the probably most detailed account, also from a historic perspective, cf. Striedter-Temps (1958); Rammelmeyer (1975) and Turk and Sesar (2003) show that loan translations from German also imply pattern replication) and also displays structural convergence: just like Croatian *rečeno*, the element *gesagt* 'said' of the corresponding German construction is a past participle passive. Apart from the structural parallelism, several facts from our data support the assumption that German influence indeed played a role in the enhancement of DSEs based on *rečeno*. Firstly, from their first attestation stance marking DSEs and their precursors are in their majority formed with the help of *rečeno*, the form that is structurally similar to the German equivalent. Furthermore, as example (70) shows, in the 18th century many more expressions existed with a structural parallelism to German (71) than attested today. This may be interpreted as a hint that many more pattern replications from German circulated in the 18th century, but not all of them got rooted in Croatian.

5.2.3 The 19th and 20th centuries

The 19th century witnessed the consolidation of the structures that had emerged in the 17th and 18th centuries. However, we would like to set out with examples that allow us to reconstruct a possible developmental path. For the DSEs based on *rečeno*, the status as a passive clause containing a finite form of the auxiliary *biti* 'be' is the point of departure. In (73) *rečeno* is part of an analytic VP with the auxiliary *biti* 'be'; in the two paratactic clauses, the first semantic participant of the verbs differs – for *reći* 'say' it is the person whose direct speech is rendered, and for *činiti se* 'seem' it is the narrator. Different first semantic participants and / or first arguments within a sentence are one of the conditions for the development of DSEs (cf. Birzer 2012a). It is also noteworthy that *Ovo je bilo rečeno kao u zanosu* 'this was said seemingly in ardour' also expresses the speaker's stance towards his statement – a function DSEs fulfil as well.

(73)   ... *mi iz starih familija – khm – istom u takovoj staroj plemićkoj kući dišemo pravi zrak. Odmah osjeća čovjek – khm – da se nalazi – khm – u sigurnom domaćem gnijezdu.* - **Ovo**-DET.NOM **je**-3SG **bilo rečeno**-PTCP.PASS **kao**-ADV *u zanosu* ... .
'... we from old families – hmm – only in such an old aristocratic house do we breathe the right air. You feel immediately – hmm – that you are – hmm – in the secure native nest. – This was said seemingly in ardour ....'
(HNK_klasici subcorpus, Gjalski, Ks. *Pod starimi krovovi*. 1886)

Sentence (74) is a fine example for the transition of the adverbial participle *govoreći* from secondary predicate to part of a DSE. Coreference between the first semantic participant of the matrix verb and the adverbial participle is still given. It is the speaker who constitutes this participant – they are also the subject of the DSE developing out of the secondary predication.

(74) – *Ne boj se mene! I ja*-NOM *znam*-1SG – ***među***-PREP ***nama***-PERS.1SG.INS
govoreći-AP – *za novu gospodu*
'Don't be afraid of me! I also know – speaking between us – of the new authorities ...'
(HNK_klasici subcorpus, Šenoa, A. *Prosjak Luka*. 1879)

In (75)–(76) we are dealing with two instances where the construction with *govoreći* marks reformulation. Quite interestingly, the conjunction *ili* 'or' has the same function; thus the question arises whether we are dealing with a cumulation of connectives – namely the conjunction *ili* 'or' and the construction with *govoreći* – or whether the construction with *govoreći* has not yet reached the status of connective. Following Mendoza (2009: 983) we may assume that in the case of *govoreći* the cooccurence with a conjunction is also typical for the transitional phase in which the construction is gaining "connective power". Quite interestingly, the coreference between the first arguments of the matrix clause and adverbial participle is already lost at this stage; the speaker is the covert subject of *govoreći*.

(75) *A neće l' se i vama, djevice Doro, osladiti usne zlatnom kapljicom iz srebrne čaše kad vas pozove bog Hymen u svoj hram ili,* ***jasnije***-ADV ***govoreći***-AP, *kad se udadete*-2PL?
'And won't your lips sweeten you, damsel Dora, with a draught from the silver goblet when the God Hymen calls you to his temple or, more clearly speaking, when do you marry?'
(HNK_klasici subcorpus, Šenoa, A. *Zlatarovo zlato*. 1871)

(76) ... *da ste*-2PL *novovjeki*-ADJ.NOM *filozofi*-NOM *ili,* ***s***-PREP ***dopuštenjem***-INS ***govoreći***-AP, *hrvatski*-ADJ.NOM *literati*-NOM.
'... that you are new-age philosophers or, if you will pardon my saying so (lit. with permission speaking), Croatian men of letters.'
(HNK_klasici subcorpus, Kovačić, A. *U registraturi*. 1888)

If one considers all instances of discourse structuring constructions based on *govoreći* and *rečeno* in the 19th century, it turns out that the number of types increases rapidly (cf. Chart 3). The collocations vary not only in their structure – with adverbs (e.g. *ukratko* 'shortly') and PPs (e.g. *među nama* 'between us') – but also in their functions: for example, *iskreno* 'frankly' and *blago* 'mildly', express speaker's stance, whereas e.g. *jasnije* 'more clearly' and *ukratko* 'shortly' serve reformulation and *matematički prozaično* 'mathematically prosaically' contextualizes the statement in a certain discourse. Thus all functions described in Section 4 for Contemporary Croatian are accounted for the first time at the latest in the 19th century. An explanation for the explosion of forms and functions in the 19th century will be given below after discussing *govoreći* as a direct speech marker, since an interaction between these functions can be assumed.

Chart 3: Types of the constructions with *govoreći* and *rečeno*.

types of the construction with *govoreći*	types of the construction with *rečeno*
jasnije 'more clearly speaking'	*matematički prozaično* 'mathematically prosaically speaking (lit. said)'
hladno 'in cool fashion speaking'	*ukratko* 'in short (lit. shortly said)'
među nama 'between us speaking'	*s dopuštenjem (budi)* 'if you will pardon my saying so (lit. with permission speaking)'
iskreno 'frankly speaking'	*u zanosu* 'in ardour speaking (lit. said)'
s dopuštenjem 'if you will pardon my saying so (lit. with permission speaking)'	*blago* 'mildly speaking (lit. said)'
pravo 'rightly speaking'	*ne za grijeh (budi)* 'not in vain speaking (lit. not for a sin said)'

Let us now consider *govoreći* as a direct speech marker. In the 18th century it was able to take a multitude of syntactic positions and enjoyed a high degree of syntactic independence, as it could occur as the only predicative element in a sentence and thus was not necessarily subject to coreference with the first syntactic argument of a matrix clause. Furthermore, *govoreći* functioned both as a direct speech marker and as quotative index. The latter function is not attested in our data from the 19th century, which is most probably due to corpus size, as we find examples in the centenaries before and after. The syntactic behaviour related to the former function changes in the 19th century. Casually speaking, the development may be described as "back to the roots", (77)–(78): *Govoreći* always co-occurs with another, finite *verbum dicendi* describing the manner of speaking; this *verbum dicendi* syntactically precedes *govoreći* and functions as the matrix verb for the latter. In other words, *govoreći* behaves like a prototypical adverbial participle whose covert subject is coreferent with the first argument of the matrix verb. Furthermore, *govoreći* itself is always in immediate preposition to the direct speech it introduces.

(77) *Irena*-NOM *Ostalinski*-NOM, *ona krasna udovica, uvijek mu je*-3SG *riječ prekidala* **govoreći**-AP: *šuti, ti si još dijete!*
 'Irena Ostalinski, this beautiful widow, interrupted him all the time, saying: "Be silent, you are still a child!"'
 (HNK_Klasici subcorpus, Kumičić, E. *Olga i Lina*. 1881)

(78) *No što im nejasno bijaše ili što nije išlo na njihov račun – na to pristajahu*-3PL *govoreći*-AP: *"ah, to bi bilo dobro."*
'But whatever remained unclear or whatever did not turn out the way they had expected it – they always agreed on the following, saying: "ah, this would have been good."'
(HNK_Klasici subcorpus, Leskovar, J. *Propali dvori.* 1896)

Thus, in comparison to the usage of *govoreći* as a marker of direct speech, we are witnessing a retrogressive development in the sense that the direct speech marker *govoreći* readopts the features of a prototypical adverbial participle.

Croatian is not the only Slavonic language in which the types for discourse structuring constructions based on *verba dicendi* rise dramatically in the 19th century. A highly probable explanation for this phenomenon is a new narrative technique of the so-called *erlebte Rede* (henceforth *experienced speech*) that comes into existence along with the emergence of realism[19] and remains in use thereafter:

> Mit E.R. [erlebter Rede – S. B.] bezeichnen wir jene Stellen in einem schriftlichen oder mündlichen Text, die in einer gegebenen Rede die Frage aufkommen lassen, wer da "eigentlich" spricht (denkt/wahrnimmt). Also: E.R. als Irritation der Redeinstanz und in deren Folge: E.R. als Form der Interferenz von Primär- und Sekundärtext [...]
>
> [As experienced speech we describe those passages in a written or oral text which within a given speech raise the question of who is "actually" speaking (thinking/experiencing). So: experienced speech as irritation of the speech authority and in its result: experienced speech as interference of primary and secondary text [...] [– translation S. B.] (Hodel 2001: 49)

Experienced speech poses the question of the speaker, and DSEs can give an answer to this question: several of the (secondary) characteristics of experienced speech directly correspond to one of the functions the (prototypical) construction types under investigation display:
a) the "wertungsmässige" (evaluative) characteristic (cf. Hodel 2001: 45) of experienced speech implies a differing evaluation of the same situation and complies with the discourse structuring function of speaker's stance with its prototypical construction ADV + *govoreći* / *rečeno*. Within experienced speech "kann einmal die "Sinnposition" (smyslovaja pozicija) des Sprechers, d.h. die „gegenständliche Zusammensetzung" des Gesagten im Vordergrund stehen, ein andermal der "Ausdruck" (vyraženie) selbst [at one time the speaker's "positioning of meaning" (smyslovaja pozicija) may be in the

---

[19] I owe many thanks to Robert Hodel for pointing this out to me.

foreground, and another time the "expression" (vyraženie) itself]" (Hodel 2001: 29). In linguistic terms this means that either the situation and thus the proposition can be evaluated by experienced speech, or its formal side, i.e. the chosen lexeme or construction to describe the situation. This complies with our finding that, among the DSE types expressing speaker's stance, some focus rather on evaluation (e.g. *iskreno rečeno* 'frankly speaking'), i.e. foreground the speaker's evaluation of the situation, and some focus on their reformulating potential (e.g. *ukratko rečeno* 'in short'), i.e. concentrate on the (lexical and / or constructional) means for describing a situation; but all types bear the potential for both foci.

b) the contextualizing function and its prototypical construction *govoreći / rečeno* + ADJ.INS + NOUN.INS may be considered a "remedy" for the irritation evoked by the unmarked interference of primary and secondary text (cf. Hodel 2001: 29–32), as it indicates the source discourse, i.e. the primary text, from which a chunk in the secondary text was taken.

c) another issue that is typical for experienced speech is the so-called "zitierende (citatnaja) Rede [... die] reicht von einzelnen Lexemen bis zu "subjektiven Redemassiven" [quoting (citatnaja) speech which ranges from single lexemes up to "whole subjective passages of speech" – translation S. B.]" (Hodel 2001: 32). In our opinion, the situation that an "Enunziator EN ist eine von der Sprecherinstanz SI zu unterscheidende Äußerungsinstanz, die anhand unterschiedener sprachlicher Manifestationen bestimmbar ist [enunciatior EN is an authority of utterance to be distinguished from the speaker authority SI and can be identified by differing lingual manifestations – translation S. B.]" (Hodel 2001: 39) also applies to quotative speech. The latter relates to the quotative index function with its prototypical construction *govoreći / rečeno* + NOUN.INS + NOUN.GEN that allows one to identify the enunciator, who is encoded as noun in the genitive.

The described parallels between the narrative technique of experienced speech and the constructions under investigation make it highly possible that the emergence of this technique enhanced the rise of type and token frequencies for these constructions.

While the proportion of types for the *govoreći* and *rečeno* constructions was approximately equal in the 19th century, this changes in the 20th century. As our corpus data shows (cf. Chart 4), *govoreći* features not only much fewer collocation types than *rečeno* – which moreover include synonyms of DSEs based on *rečeno*,[20] but their token frequencies are also much lower. Furthermore, "plain"

---

20 Not all of these synonyms are listed in Chart 4, as some of them have a token frequency below ten.

govoreći in the speech marker function (so to say a "void collocation") takes the second place regarding token frequency. This may be interpreted as follows: The constructions with *govoreći* and *rečeno* respectively stand at the beginning of a crystallization of functions.²¹ The *govoreći* construction reduces the number of types with discourse structuring functions, which may finally result in "plain" *govoreći* with speech marking function as only remaining type. In fact, this comes close to a cyclic process, as historically the marking of speech was the point of departure for the development of DSEs based on *verba dicendi*. The reduction of types with discourse structuring functions is facilitated by the fact that all these types of the *govoreći* construction are doubled by synonymous types of the *rečeno* construction. As a consequence of the process described for the *govoreći* construction, the *rečeno* construction becomes the only construction with discourse structuring functions.

Chart 4: Collocations types of *govoreći* and *rečeno* with token frequency > 10 in HNK25.

govoreći		rečeno	
element	token frequency	element	token frequency
iskreno 'frankly'	73	*bolje* 'better'	360
direct speech marker	54	*najblaže* 'most mildly'	277
općenito 'generally'	33	*uvjetno* 'conditionally'	265
objektivno 'objectively'	24	*blago* 'mildly'	176
uvjetno 'conditionally'	18	*usput* 'by the way'	147
pošteno 'honestly'	13	*jednostavno* 'plainly'	102
realno 'frankly (lit. really)'	12	*najkraće* 'in shortest term (lit. most shortly said)'	102
otvoreno 'frankly (lit. openly)'	11	*pojednostavljeno* 'simply'	99
pojednostavljeno 'simply'	10	*iskreno* 'frankly'	81
		točnije 'more exactly'	75
		uzgred 'by the way'	73
		jednostavnije 'more plainly'	59
		preciznije 'more precisely'	44
		drukčije 'in other words (lit. in another way said)'	39
		ukratko 'in short'	34
		uzgred budi 'by the way'	34

---

21 Following Doroszewski (1958), Hansen (2001: 400) defines crystallization as following: "Kristallisation ist ein Prozess, in dem von vielen Einheiten nur eine oder einige übrig bleiben und andere Konkurrenten verschwinden. [Cristallization is a process, in which out of many units only one or a few remain and other competitors vanish. – translation S. B.]"

Chart 4 (continued)

govoreći		rečeno	
element	token frequency	element	token frequency
		grubo 'roughly'	32
		usput budi 'by the way'	30
		kratko 'in short (lit. shortly said)'	24
		najjednostavnije 'most plainly'	24
		sažeto 'in short (lit. shortly said)'	14
		kraće 'in still shorter terms (lit. shorter said)'	10

6 Conclusion

Since DSEs based on *verba dicendi* constitute a phenomenon that can be found in many Slavonic languages, among them Russian (cf. Birzer 2012a) and Polish (cf. Birzer 2013), in this section we would like to tend to those characteristics that contrast the development in Croatian from Russian and Polish.

In all three languages DSEs developed out of the adverbial participle of a *verbum dicendi*, which was originally used as marker of direct speech. Syntactically, the covert first argument of the AP gradually loses coreference with the first argument of the matrix verb; finally, the speaker becomes covert subject of the AP. In all three languages, the construction containing the AP is paralleled by another construction containing another non-infinite form of a *verbum dicendi* (the infinitive *skazat'* 'say' in Russian and the anterior adverbial participle *powiediawszy* 'having said' in Polish) but fulfilling the same functions, i.e. we are dealing with competing constructions. Language contact plays a role in the development of DSEs based on *verba dicendi* in all three languages: Russian replicates the construction with infinitive from French, and Polish uses replicated lexical matter from Latin for forming the adverbs that go into the DSEs. Still, Croatian sets itself apart from the other discussed languages in the following respects:

a) impact of language contact

In Contemporary Russian and Polish, the constructions with the (simultaneous) AP have the highest type and token frequencies and form a semi-productive pattern for forming DSEs based on *verba dicendi*. Thus, language contact plays only a minor role, as in the case of Russian it led to the existence of a second, non-productive pattern for forming DSEs, and in Polish lexical borrowing resulted in a few adverbs out of a large range of adverbs that are potentially eligible in the construction ADV + AP. In Croatian, however, the replicated pattern with *rečeno* has become the semi-productive pattern for forming DSEs based on *verba dicendi*.

b) direct speech marking

Of the three languages discussed, Croatian is the only one that has retained the AP *govoreći* in the function of direct speech marker, i.e. in the function that has to be considered the point of departure for the development of DSEs based on *verba dicendi*. In the 19th century the direct speech marker *govoreći* loses much of the syntactic independency it had gained in the centuries before and is confined to usage in sentences containing a second *verbum dicendi* that is semantically more complex and functions as matrix verb for *govoreći*. Therefore, one may assume a

c) developmental circle of *govoreći*

The aforementioned syntactic and semantic prerequisites for *govoreći* as a speech marker also existed at the initial point of the historical development of DSEs based on *govoreći*.

d) crystallization of functions

Croatian is the only language where the competition of constructions based on different (inflectional forms of) *verba dicendi* is resolved via a beginning crystallization of functions: The construction with *rečeno* is the only semi-productive pattern for forming DSEs based on *verba dicendi* and is at present already able to convey all the functions DSEs based on *verba dicendi* may display. *Govoreći*, on the other hand, seems to develop into an exclusive marker of direct speech, as it is a non-productive pattern for forming DSEs with low type and token frequency and (with one exception) the token frequency of *govoreći* as a direct speech marker is much higher than for the DSE types based on *govoreći*.

References

AG-80: Švedova, Natalija J. (ed.). 1980. *Russkaja grammatika. Tom I–II* [Russian Grammar. Vols. I–II]. Moskva: Nauka.

Ajduković, Jovan. 1997. *Rusizmi u srpskohrvatskim rečnicima. Principi adaptacije. Rečnik* [Russisms in Serbo-Croatian dictionaries. Principles of adaptation. Dictionary]. Beograd: Foto Futura.

Apresjan, Jurij D. 2005. O Moskovskoj semantičeskoj škole [On the Moscow Semantic School]. *Voprosy jazykoznanija* 1. 3–30.

Berger, Tilman. 2009. Einige Bemerkungen zum tschechischen Absentiv. In Tilman Berger, Markus Giger, Sibylle Kurt & Imke Mendoza (eds.), *Von grammatischen Kategorien und sprachlichen Weltbildern – Die Slavia von der Sprachgeschichte bis zur Politsprache. Festschrift für Daniel Weiss zum 60. Geburtstag*, 9–28. München & Wien: Wiener Slavistischer Almanach.

Birzer, Sandra. 2012a. From subject to subjectivity: Russian discourse structuring elements based on the adverbial participle *govorja* 'speaking'. *Russian Linguistics* 36 (3). 221–249.
Birzer, Sandra. 2012b. Von der (in)direkten Rede zum Kommentar. *Verba dicendi* in griechischen und altkirchenslavischen Konstruktionen der Redewiedergabe. In Björn Hansen (ed.), *Diachrone Aspekte slavischer Sprachen* (Slavolinguistica 16), 197–209. München & Berlin: Otto Sagner.
Birzer, Sandra. 2013. Zur historischen Entwicklung der auf *mówiąc* 'sprechend' basierenden *komentarze metatekstowe* (metatextuellen Kommentare). Paper presented in the procedure of appointment for the position of W1 professor at the University of Hamburg. 27 June.
Birzer, Sandra (accepted). Formal unity and functional diversity: a corpus-linguistic approach to Russian and Polish adverbial participles with the meaning 'speaking' between discourse and grammar (working title). In Mirjam Fried & Eva Lehečková (eds.), *Conjunctions vs. contextualizers*. John Benjamins.
Daiber, Thomas. 2009. Direkte Rede im Russisch-Kirchenslavischen. Zum pragmatischen Wert des *jako recitativum*. In Juliane Besters-Dilger & Achim Rabus (eds.), *Text, Sprache, Grammatik. Slavisches Schrifttum der Vormoderne. Festschrift für Eckhard Weiher*, 363–386. München: Otto Sagner.
Dedaić, Mirjana N. & Mirjana Mišković-Luković (eds.). 2010. *South Slavic discourse particles*. Amsterdam: John Benjamins.
Doroszewski, Witold. 1958–1969. *Słownik języka polskiego. 1–10*. [Polish dictionary. 1–10]. Warszawa: Państwowe Wydawnictwo Naukowe.
Fischer, Kerstin. 2006. Introduction. In Kerstin Fischer (ed.), *Approaches to discourse particles*, 1–20. Amsterdam et al.: Elsevier Ltd.
Franolić, Branko. 1976. *Les mots d'emprunt Français en Croate*. Paris: Nouvelles éditions latines.
Fraser, Bruce. 2006. Towards a theory of discourse markers. In Kerstin Fischer (ed.), *Approaches to discourse particles*, 189–204. Amsterdam et al.: Elsevier Ltd.
Golubović, Biljana. 2007. *Germanismen im Serbischen und Kroatischen*. München: Otto Sagner.
Grković-Major, Jasmina. 2003. Predikativni gerund u starosrpskom jeziku [The predicative gerund in Old Serbian]. *Zbornik Matice srpske za filologiju i lingvistiku* XLVI (1). 23–34.
Grotzky, Johannes. 1978. *Morphologische Adaptation deutscher Lehnwörter im Serbokroatischen*. München: Trofenik.
Güldemann, Tom. 2012. Thetic speaker-instantiating quotative indexes as a cross-linguistic type. In Isabelle Buchstaller & Ingrid van Alphen (eds.), *Quotatives: cross-linguistic and cross-disciplinary perspectives*. 117–142. Amsterdam: John Benjamins.
Hansen, Björn. 2001. *Das Modalauxiliar im Slavischen. Semantik und Grammatikalisierung im Russischen, Polnischen, Serbischen/Kroatischen und Altkirchenslavischen*. (Slavolinguistica 2). München: Otto Sagner.
Hodel, Robert. 2001. *Erlebte Rede in der russischen Literatur. Vom Sentimentalismus zum Sozialistischen Realismus*. Band 1. Frankfurt/Main: Peter Lang.
Holzer, Georg. 2007. *Historische Grammatik des Kroatischen: Einleitung und Lautgeschichte der Standardsprache*. Frankfurt/Main et al.: Peter Lang.
Hudeček, Lana. 2001. Glagoli govorenja i mišljenja u hrvatskome čakavskom književnom jeziku do 17. stoljeća – strani sintaktički utjecaji [Verbs of speaking and thinking in the Croatian Čakavian literary language up to the 17th century – foreign syntactic influences]. *Rasprave Instituta za hrvatski jezik i jezikoslovlje* 27. 95–112.
Hudeček, Lana. 2003. Dopune glagolima govorenja i mišljenja i srodnih značenja u hrvatskome književnom jeziku od 17. do polovice 19 stoljeća – strani sintaktički utjecaji [Complements

to verbs of speaking and thinking and of related meanings in the Croatian literary language from the 17th to the first half of the 19th century – foreign syntactic influences]. *Rasprave Instituta za hrvatski jezik i jezikoslovlje* 29. 103–129.

Ivić, Milka. 2005. *O rečima. Kognitivni, gramatički i kulturološki aspekti srpske leksike* [On words. Cognitive, grammatical and cultural aspects of the Serbian lexicon]. Beograd: Biblioteka XX vek.

Kašić, Bartol. 1999. *Biblia Sacra: versio illyrica selecta, seu declaratio vulgatæ editionis latinæ, Bartholomæi Cassij curictensis e Societate Iesu Professi, ac sacerdotis theologi, ex mandato Sacræ Congregationis de propag: fide, Ano 1625*. Ed. Hans Rothe, Christian Hannick. Paderborn et al: Schöningh.

Katičić, Radoslav. 2002. *Sintaksa hrvatskoga književnog jezika*, 3rd edn. [Syntax of the Croatian literary language, 3rd edn.]. Zagreb: Hrvatska akademija znanosti i umjetnosti.

Kunzmann-Müller, Barbara. 1994. *Grammatikhandbuch des Kroatischen und Serbischen*. Frankfurt/Main: Peter Lang.

Mendoza, Imke. 2009. Anaphorische Mittel: Konnexion. In Sebastian Kempgen, Peter Kosta, Tilman Berger & Karl Gutschmidt (eds.), *Die slavischen Sprachen: Ein internationales Handbuch zu ihrer Struktur, ihrer Geschichte und ihrer Erforschung / The Slavic languages: An international handbook of their structure, their history, and their investigation*. Band 1. (HSK Band 32.1), 982–990. Berlin & New York: Mouton de Gruyter.

Mihaljević, Milan. 2011. Verba dicendi in Croatian Church Slavonic. *Zbornik Matice srpske za filologiju i lingvistiku* LIV (1). 63–77.

Moguš, Milan. 1995. *A history of the Croatian language: Toward a common standard*. Zagreb: Globus.

Mosegaard-Hansen, Maj-Britt. 2006. A dynamic polysemy approach to the lexical semantics of discourse markers (with an exemplary analysis of French *toujours*). In Kerstin Fischer (ed.), *Approaches to discourse particles*, 21–41. Amsterdam et al.: Elsevier Ltd.

Musić, Srđan. 1972. *Romanizmi u severo-zapadnoj Boki Kotorskoj* [Romanisms in the northeastern Bay of Kotor]. Beograd: Filološki fakultet Beogradskog univerziteta.

Pasch, Renate, Ursula Brauße, Eva Breindl & Ulrich Hermann Waßner (eds.). 2003. *Handbuch der deutschen Konnektoren: linguistische Grundlagen der Beschreibung und syntaktische Merkmale der deutschen Satzverknüpfer (Konjunktionen, Satzadverbien und Partikeln)*. Berlin: de Gruyter.

Poljanec, Franja (ed.). 1931. *Istorija srpskohrvatskog književnog jezika: s pregledom naših dijalekata i istorijskom čitankom* [History of the Serbo-Croatian literary language: with an overview of our dialects and a historical textbook]. Beograd: Narodna prosveta.

Popović, Ivan. 1960. *Geschichte der serbokroatischen Sprache*. Wiesbaden: Harrassowitz.

Popović, Ljudmila. 2009. Leksičke inovacije u elektronskom diskursu srpskog i hrvatskog jezika [Lexical inovations in the electronic discourse of the Serbian and Croation language]. In Branko Tošović (ed.), *Die Unterschiede zwischen dem Bosnischen / Bosniakischen, Kroatischen und Serbischen. Lexik – Wortbildung – Phraseologie*, 183–203. Wien – Berlin: LIT Verlag.

Popović, Mihailo. 2005. *Reči francuskog porekla u srpskom jeziku* [Words of French origin in the Serbian language]. Beograd: Zavod za udžbenike i nastavna sredstva.

Pranjković, Ivo. 2007. Glagoli govorenja i njihove dopune [Verbs of speaking and their complements]. *Zbornik Matice srpske za slavistiku* 71–72. 133–141.

Rammelmeyer, Matthias. 1975. *Die deutschen Lehnübersetzungen im Serbokroatischen. Beiträge zur Lexikologie und Wortbildung*. Wiesbaden: Franz Steiner Verlag.

Rathmayr, Renate. 1985. *Die russischen Partikeln als Pragmalexeme*. München: Otto Sagner.
Saz Rubio, Mª Milagros del & Bruce Fraser. 2003. *Reformulation in English*. http://people.bu.edu/bfraser/ (accessed 18 October 2016).
Schneeweis, Edmund. 1960. *Die deutschen Lehnwörter im Serbokroatischen in kulturgeschichtlicher Sicht*. Berlin: De Gruyter & Co.
Striedter-Temps, Hildegard. 1958. *Deutsche Lehnwörter im Serbokroatischen*. Wiesbaden: Otto Harrassowitz.
Šoć, Branko. 2002. *Romanizmi i grecizmi u crnogorskom jeziku* [Romanisms and Graecisms in Montenegrin]. Cetinje: Centralna narodna biblioteka Crne Gore "Đurđe Crnojević".
Štebih, Barbara. 2003. Adaptacije germanizama u iločkom govoru [The adaptation of Germanisms in the Ilok dialect]. *Rasprave Instituta za hrvatski jezik i jezikoslovlje* 29. 293–323.
Turk, Marija & Dubravka Sesar. 2003. Kalkovi njemačkoga podrijetla u hrvatskome i u nekim drugim slavenskim jezicima [Calques of German origin in the Croatian and some other Slavonic languages]. *Rasprave Instituta za hrvatski jezik i jezikoslovlje* 29. 325–338.
Večerka, Radoslav. 2002. *Altkirchenslavische (altbulgarische) Syntax IV. Die Satztypen: Der zusammengesetzte Satz*. Freiburg. i. Br.: Weiher.
Xrakovskij, Viktor S. 2003. Kategorija taksisa (obščaja xarakteristika) [The category of taxis (general characterisation)]. *Voprosy jazykoznanija* 2. 32–54.
Weiss, Daniel. 2012. Deputaty ljubjat citaty: ssylki na ksenoteksty v Gosdume [Deputies love citations: references to foreign texts in the Russian parliament]. In Nina N. Rozanova. *Russkij jazyk segodnja. Vypusk 5: Problemy rečevogo obščenija*, 64–75. Moskva: Flinta & Nauka.

Part III: **The complex sentence**

Marina Kurešević
The status and origin of the *accusativus cum infinitivo* construction in Old Church Slavonic[1]

Abstract: The aim of this paper is to determine the status and origin of the *accusativus cum infinitivo* construction (AcInf.) in Old Church Slavonic (OCS), i.e. whether it is a syntactic Graecism or a genuine Slavonic construction. The approach to the problem includes the language internal reconstruction, and also the comparative and typological perspective on the problem.

Depending on the context, two basic semantic types of AcInf. complement can be recognized: a) with subjunctive and b) with indicative meaning. They evolved independently. It is shown that AcInf. expressing subjunctive meaning emerged as the result of the language-internal process, whereby the other type emerged from an interplay between internal tendencies and language contact factors. The former represents a genuine Slavonic pattern in OCS and the latter can be labelled as a bookish neologism, i.e. a feature that has internal language motivation supported by Greek sentence patterns.

The main corpus for the research consists of data collected from OCS Codex Marianus and the Serbian Alexander Romance, a Serbian Church Slavonic text. Additional data are taken from the relevant studies dealing with this topic in Old Serbian and Old Russian.

1 Introduction

Due to the development of new methodological approaches in the research of Old Church Slavonic (OCS) syntax, which include a typological perspective on the problem as well,[2] some OCS syntactic patterns can be reinterpreted. One of them

---
[1] The research was conducted within the project *The history of the Serbian language* (№ 178001) financed by the Ministry of Education, Science, and Technological Development of the Republic of Serbia.
[2] Such methodology is, for example, applied in J. Grković-Major's papers, especially those concerning OCS syntactic patterns (cf. e.g. Grković-Major 2008, 2010a, 2011).

https://doi.org/10.1515/9783110531435-010

is the *accusativus cum infinitivo* (AcInf.) construction, especially the one occurring after communicative and cognitive verbs, e.g.:

(1) kogo   glagoljǫtъ   mę   člověci   byti
    whom-ACC   say-3PL.PRS   I-ACC   people-NOM.PL.M   be-INF
    'Who do people say I am'
    (CM Mt. 16:15)

There is no agreement concerning the status of this structure. Many authors consider it to be a syntactic Graecism (cf. Miklosich 1868–1874: 871–872; Vondrák 1928: 276, 415; Vaillant 1952: 395–396; Gardiner 1984: 138; Pacnerová 1964: 550; Gaderka 1964: 528–530; MacRobert 1986: 158). Others assume that the construction might have been of domestic origin in Slavonic languages since it is found in the texts written in Old Serbian (Grickat 2004: 165). Only rarely is a connection between AcInf. and the construction of double accusative made (Potebnja 1958: 375–378; Georgieva 1968: 89–93). Večerka states that it was located at the periphery of the OCS system expressing meanings that were primarily conveyed by other means, such as *accusativus cum participio* or *dativus cum infinitivo* (Večerka 1996: 196–197; Večerka 2002: 446). According to Večerka (2002: 439), it is a genuine Slavonic pattern, synonymous with optative and imperative clauses, but it was not extensively used as an equivalent of declarative clauses.

Determining the status and origin of a construction in OCS – whether it is a syntactic Graecism or a genuine Slavonic construction – is not easy. The situation becomes more complicated if we know that among syntactic Graecisms in OCS two more layers can de distinguished: syntactic calques ("syntaktische Nachahmungen (Calques)", Večerka 1989: 28) and bookish neologisms ("schriftsprachliche Neologismen", Večerka 1989: 28), which differ mainly in their internal language motivation.[3] The main reason for this is the set of internal and external factors

---

[3] R. Večerka explains these terms in more detail in his later paper (Večerka 1997: 373, 375). He uses the term syntactic calques to denote "literal imitation of Greek constructions by means that are otherwise impossible, unusual or grammatically 'incorrect' in OCS, occur rarely in the earliest translations (their number is then higher in later texts), but still do exist there". By bookish neologisms he means features that "cannot possibly be considered calques in the usual sense of the word, but neither can they be taken as living domestic means: they have no analogies in other Slavonic languages [...] and in a certain form and extent exist only in OCS" (Večerka 1997: 375). Bookish neologisms are features that emerged either by stylization according to the foreign (especially Greek) syntactic patterns or by increasing the frequency of individual means or constructions in OCS in cases where it had several synonymous means, all structurally immanent to the Slavonic language system, some of which may have been on the road to its disappearance. E.g. the emergence of subordinate clauses introduced by the Slavonic language elements as their

which led to the emergence of the syntactic structures known from the oldest OCS texts. So far, it has been noted that the structure of the simple sentence, the use of cases and tenses in OCS were in accordance with the Slavonic system (Grković-Major 2001: 9–11). The Greek influence is seen especially in expressing semantic subordination, particularly in certain infinitive and participial constructions, and in the way compound sentences were formed (Bauer 1972: 77–84; Gramatika 1993: 520). This conclusion is not surprising, especially with regards to two linguistic facts: one of them is that some uses of infinitive and participial constructions are characteristic of literary language, so they could not have been used in colloquial use, and the other is that, at the time of the creation of OCS, Slavonic dialects did not have formalized means for expressing semantic subordination, so the Greek or Latin sentence patterns were replicated for the purpose of translating (Bauer 1972: 212; Večerka 1997: 373–374).

However, the Greek influence on OCS syntax was often exaggerated. Almost every OCS feature which was found in Greek but not in Slavonic vernacular texts was considered to be a bookish one. Lately, it has become clear that on such occasions besides the comparative method, one should take into account two more dimensions of analysis: language internal reconstruction and typological perspective (Grković-Major 2010a: 193–194). Besides this, it was pointed out that tendencies in the evolution of language should also be taken into consideration (Jarceva 1956).

The AcInf. has commonly been defined as the infinitive construction with the accusative subject, which is different from the subject of the matrix verb (Gaderka 1964: 505). Such a definition describes several construction types which differ in semantic relation between the accusative and the matrix verb, as well as in the meaning of the whole clause. Thus, in order to determine the status of the construction in OCS, we will first analyse the syntactic and semantic contexts in which it appears in OCS, as well as the competing constructions and semantics they express (the implementation of language internal reconstruction) (Section 2). Then, we will compare their usage with the situation in Church Slavonic (CS) and Slavonic vernacular texts (implementation of the comparative method) (Section 3). After that, facts from some old Indo-European languages

---

conjunctions is explained in the first way, while the increased frequency of some uses of participial constructions is explained in the second way (Večerka 1997: 373–377).

Moreover, it has to be emphasized that this terminology is just one of many possible options. Using the terminology of recent theories on language contact and the replication of syntactic structures, it seems that the term syntactic calque used in this paper mostly corresponds to the term grammatical replication, and the term bookish neologism to the notion labelled grammatical borrowing (cf. Wiemer and Wälchli 2012).

will be taken into consideration in order to get a wider typological perspective of their usage (Section 4). Finally, we will try to define the causes and mechanisms which led to the emergence of AcInf. in OCS and its further development in CS, taking into account extra-linguistic factors as well (Section 5).

2 *Accusativus cum infinitivo* in OCS

2.1 Typology of AcInf. in OCS

In order to determine whether AcInf. is a genuine or a borrowed construction in OCS, it is important to distinguish two basic types of syntactic contexts in which it appears: it is usually used as a verb complement and very rarely as an independent construction.

When used as a complement, it is governed by different verb classes: transitive verbs of movement (e.g. *poslati* 'to send sb. to do sth.'), jussive (e.g. *moliti* 'to ask sb. to do sth.'), causative (e.g. *tvoriti* or *sъpodobiti*, 'to make sb. do sth.'), cognitive (e.g. *mьněti* or *věděti* 'to consider sth./sb. as sth.'), communicative (e.g. *glagolati* 'to say sth. about sth./sb.'), verbs of doing (e.g. *sъtvoriti* or *postaviti* 'to make sth./sb. be/become sth.') and very rarely desiderative verbs (e.g. *hotěti* 'to want sth./sb. to be/become sth.'). From a diachronic point of view, in all these syntactic contexts the nominal in the accusative can be considered to be an object (taken in a wider sense) of the verb.[4] The lexical semantics of the matrix verb determines the semantic relation between the accusative and the matrix verb,[5] as well as the meaning of the whole clause. Three types of syntactic and semantic contexts in which the AcInf. complement appears in OCS can be distinguished. *Type A*: if used with jussive, causative or transitive verbs of movement, the nominal in the accusative denotes their patient and the verb in the infinitive expresses the purpose of the action given by the matrix verb. Thus, the infinitive exhibits the role of an adverbial modifier of the matrix verb.

---

[4] In early PIE this accusative actually represented a residue of the adverbial protoaccusative, meaning 'in reference with *x*', which was gradually being grammaticalized into object argument due to the typological drift of PIE and its daughter languages (Grković-Major 2010b: 64–65). Residues of such archaic use of the accusative case are also confirmed in New Testament Greek (Blass and Debrunner 1961: 84, 86), in Old Baltic (Schmalstieg 1988: 232, 236), as well as in other old Slavonic languages (Miklosich 1868–1874: 373–376; Potebnja 1958: 295–299; Gortan-Premk 1971: 23–29; Grković-Major 2010b: 65–68).
[5] Our classification of AcInf. constructions is based upon Potebnja's (1958: 375).

(2) molěše   i   vъniti   vъ   domъ   svoi
    ask-3SG.IMPF   he-ACC   enter-INF   in   house-ACC.SG.M   his
    'He asked him to enter his house'
    (CM Lk. 8:41)

(3) tvoritъ   jǫ   prěljuby dějati
    make-3SG.PRS   she-ACC   commit adultery-INF
    'He makes her commit adultery'
    (CM Mt. 5:32)

(4) posъla   raby   svojǫ   kъ   dělatelemъ
    sent-3SG.AOR   servants-ACC.PL.M   his   to-PREP   tenants-DAT.PL.M
    prijęti   plody   jego
    take-INF   fruits-ACC.PL.M   his
    'He sent his servants to the tenants to get his fruits'
    (CM Mt. 21:34)

Type B: if used with cognitive or communicative verbs, the nominal in the accusative denotes a theme and it is followed by another accusative which modifies it. In this type of construction, the infinitive of the verb *byti* 'to be' is used to underline the predicative character of the second accusative (Večerka 2002: 439–440). The whole construction expresses the content of the matrix verb, i.e. it is an indirect statement.

(5) da   ne   kъto   mьnitъ   mę   bezumna   byti
    that   not   who-NOM   consider-3SG.PRS   I-ACC   fool-ACC.SG.M   be-INF
    'That someone doesn't consider me to be a fool'
    (Christ, Slepč, Šiš, according to Večerka 2002: 446)

(6) kogo   glagoljǫtъ   mę   člověci   byti
    whom-ACC   say-3PL.PRS   I-ACC   people-NOM.PL.M   be-INF
    'Who do people say I am'
    (CM Mt. 16:15)

Finally, *type C*: if used with the verb *sъtvoriti* 'to make sb. be/become sth.' or with the verb *hotěti* 'to want sb. to be/become sth.', the first accusative denotes the beneficiary of the matrix verb. It is modified by another (predicative) accusative and the infinitive of the verb *byti* 'to be', used in order to underline its predicative character.

(7) sъtvorjǫ   vy   byti   lovъca   člověkomъ
    make-1SG.PRS   you-ACC   be-INF   fisher-ACC.DU.M   men-DAT.PL.M
    'I will make you become fishers of men'
    (CM Mk. 1:17)

(8) hoštǫ   že   vy   prěmǫdry   byti
    want-1SG.PRS PRT you-ACC wise-ACC.PL.M be-INF
    vъ blagoje, krotky   že   vъ zъloje
    in good   meek-ACC.PL.M   PRT in evil
    'I want you to be wise in good and meek in evil'
    (Rim 16.19 Christ, according to Gaderka 1964: 528)

The common syntactic feature of all these constructions is represented by the first accusative, which exhibits a double role, the object of the main verb and the subject of the action or state given by the infinitive or by the nominal predicate.

Unlike this, the accusative in an independent construction (*type D*) exhibits only the role of a subject of the action or state given by the infinitive. According to Gaderka (1964: 528–530), it appears very rarely as a complement of impersonal verbs or as an adverbial of purpose. The following example reveals that only the subject of the infinitive of the verb *byti* 'to be' can be expressed by the accusative, while the subject of the infinitive of the other verbs is expressed by the dative.

(9) izvěstnъno   ny   jestъ   po
    known-PST.PASS.PTCP.NOM.SG.N   we-DAT   be-3SG.PRS   according to
    božijamъ kъnigamъ   ne   tok'mo   nebesъnymъ sylamъ
    God's books-DAT.PL.F   not   only   heavenly powers-DAT.PL.F
    priti.   nъ   i   samogo Boga   nevidimo
    come-INF   but   even   God himself-ACC.SG.M   invisibly
    sъ   nami   byti   vъ   sъ   časъ
    with-PREP   we-INS   be-INF   in-PREP   this   hour-ACC.SG.M
    'It is known to us accoridng to God's books that not only heavenly powers will come, but God himself will be with us invisibly in this hour.'
    (Treb 95b 4, according to Gaderka 1964: 530)

OCS also used other syntactic strategies to express the same meaning. In types A, B and C contexts those were the supine, finite clause introduced by the conjunctions *jako/da*, *accusativus cum participio* (AcPtc.) and the double accusative.

Semantically equivalent constructions reveal the inherent meaning of AcInf. in different contexts. The supine, which is found only with transitive verbs of movement (10), and the clause introduced by the conjunction *da* with transitive verbs of movement, jussive and the causative ones (11) suggest the subjunctive[6]

---

[6] The term subjunctive is used in contrast to indicative. Subjunctive proposition expresses attitudes such as desires, intentions, indeterminacy, uncertainty etc. (Kristal 1988: 125).

character of the proposition. On the other hand, the clause introduced by the conjunction *jako* with communicative and cognitive verbs marks its indicative character (12). AcPtc. (13) and the construction of double accusative (14) are confirmed in type B and C contexts and their usage suggests the indicative meaning of the proposition.

(10) *posъla   i   na sela svoě   pastъ   svinii*
     sent-3SG.AOR   he-ACC   into his fields feed-SUP   pigs-GEN.PL.F
     'He sent him into his fields to feed pigs'
     (CM Lk. 15:15) (SUP = supine)

(11) *sъtvori   dъva na desęte   da   bǫdǫtъ   sъ*
     make-3SG.AOR   twelve-ACC.PL   to-CONJ   be-3PL.PRS   with-PREP
     nimъ.   i   da   posylaatъ   ję   propovědati
     he-INS   and   to-CONJ   send-3PL.PRS   they-ACC   preach-INF
     'He made the twelve to be with him and to send them out to preach'
     (CM Mk. 3:14)

(12) *estъ   otc͞ъ   moi   slavęi*
     be-3SG.PRS.   father-NOM.SG.M   my   glorify- PRS.ACT.PTCP.NOM.SG.M
     mę.   egože   vy   gl͞ete   ěko
     I-ACC   he-ACC   you-NOM   say-2PL.PRS   that-CONJ
     б͞ъ   našъ   estъ
     God-NOM.SG.M   our   be-3SG.PRS
     'It is my Father who glorifies me and of whom you say that is our God'
     (CM Jn. 8:54)

(13) *mъněvъša   že   i*
     suppose-PST.ACT.PTCP.NOM.DU.M   PRT   he-ACC
     vъ družině   sǫštъ
     in group   be-PRS.ACT.PTCP.ACC.SG.M
     'Supposing him to be in the group'
     (CM Lk. 2:44)

(14) *Irodъ   bo   boěaše sę   ioana.*
     Herod-NOM.SG.M   because   fear-3SG.IMPF   of John-GEN.SG.M
     vědy   i   mǫža
     know-PRS.ACT.PTCP.NOM.SG.M   he-ACC   man-ACC.SG.M
     pravedъna   i   sveta
     righteous-ADJ   and-CONJ   holy-ADJ
     'For Herod feared John knowing that he is a righteous and holy man'
     (CM Mk. 6:20)

2.2 AcInf. in Codex Marianus

In order to determine the distribution of the syntactic strategies described in the Section 2.1. and the quantitative relationship between the competing means, we analyzed the Codex Marianus (CM 1960), one of the oldest OCS manuscripts, whose text is believed to be the closest to the Slavonic archetype of the Gospel translation (EM: 7).

Results of the research are presented in the Tabs. 1 and 2.

Tab. 1: Competing means in CM: subjunctive field of use.

	acc. + inf./sup.	acc. + *da*-clause
Type A		
causative verbs of movement (e.g. *posъlati*)	10x /+7x	10x
causative verbs (e.g. *sъpodobiti*)	21x	3x
jussive verbs (e.g. *moliti*)	3x	9x
Type D	/	/

Tab. 2: Competing means in CM: indicative field of use.

	double acc.	1st acc. + *jako* + 2nd acc.	AcInf. (1st acc. + 2nd acc. + *byti*)	DatInf. (dat. + *byti*)	AcPtc. (1st acc. + 2nd acc. + *sǫšt-*)	1st acc. + *jako*-clause
Type B						
cognitive verbs (e.g. *vĕdĕti*)	5x	7x	2x	/	1x	1x
communicative verbs (e.g. *glagolati*)	24x	/	5x	1x	2x	4x
Type C						
verbs of doing (e.g. *tvoriti* [*sę*])	17x	1x	1x	/	1x	/
desiderative verbs (e.g. *hotĕti*)	/	/				

We can see that in type A contexts non-finite constructions with accusative subjects prevail in comparison to *da*-clauses. In type B contexts, the double accusative and its variant, the double nominative, and the construction of *accusativus* + *jako* + *accusativus* dominate in comparison to their counterparts with the infinitive or participle form of the verb *byti* 'to do'. In this type of syntactic context finite structures introduced by the conjunction *jako* instead of the second accusative are found very rarely. In type C contexts with the verb *tvoriti (sę)* 'to make sb. be/become sth.' constructions with double cases prevail, whereby AcInf., AcPtc. and the *accusativus* + *jako* + *accusativus* constructions are confirmed in one example respectively. The construction is not found with desiderative verbs, nor in independent use.

Comparison with the Greek text[7] reveals that this OCS translation mostly follows the original, although we observe four differences as well. All four OCS examples with AcPtc. correspond to the Greek constructions with the infinitive (15a), (15b). However, in one example we encounter AcInf. as an equivalent to the Greek finite clause introduced by the conjunction *hóti* (16a), (16b).

(15a) OCS
  mьněvъša   *že*   *i*
  suppose-PST.ACT.PTCP.NOM.DU.M   PRT   he-ACC
  vъ družině   *sǫštъ*
  in the group   be-PRS.ACT.PTCP.ACC.SG.M

(15b) GR
  nomísantes dè   *autòn*   *eĩnai*
  suppose-AOR.ACT.PTCP.NOM.PL.M   he-ACC   be-INF
  en tẽ: sinodía
  in the group
  'Supposing him to be in the group'
  (CM Lk. 2:44)

(16a) OCS
  oni   *že*   *viděvъše*   *i*
  they-NOM   PRT   see-PST.ACT.PTCP.NOM.PL.M   he-ACC
  po moru   *hodęštъ.*   *nepъštevašę*
  on the sea   walk-PRS.ACT.PTCP.ACC.SG.M   think-3PL.AOR
  Ø   *prizrakъ*   *byti*
  Ø-ACC   apparition-ACC.SG.M   be-INF

---

[7] The Greek Bible text is quoted according to Novum Testamentum Graece (2012).

(16b) GR

hoi dè   idóntes   autòv   epì tē:s thalásse:s
they-NOM   see-AOR.ACT.PTCP.NOM.PL.M   he-ACC   on the sea
peripatŭnta   édoxan   hóti
walk-PRS.ACT.PTCP.ACC.SG.M   think-3PL.AOR   that-CONJ
fántasmá   estin
apparition-NOM.SG.F   be-3SG.PRS
'When they saw him walking on the sea, they thought of him to be an apparition'
(CM Mk. 6:49)

These differences indicate that the earliest translators of the Gospels did not blindly adhere to the Greek text. They indicate not only that the AcPtc. is of genuine Slavonic nature, but also that AcInf. is not as artificial as it is commonly said. More precisely, it could be seen as a part of the Common Slavonic heritage. In order to evaluate this claim we will try to draw on evidence from the CS and Slavonic vernacular texts. Since in the liturgical CS texts the situation is the same as in OCS, of particular interest are the texts written in the Slavonic vernaculars or in non-liturgical CS,[8] i.e. Orthodox Slavonic (Picchio 1980: 32–33). Orthodox Slavonic represents a system open to syntactic innovations from Slavonic vernaculars, with a very low percentage of calques. It is mainly used in narrative texts of profane character. Thus, it represents an important, though secondary, source for the study of vernacular syntactic features.

3 AcInf. in Slavonic perspective

3.1 AcInf. in Slavonic languages

The representative examples from Slavonic vernaculars are taken from the relevant studies dealing with this topic in Old Serbian and Old Russian.[9]

---

[8] Medieval literacy in Slavia Orthodoxa is characterized by the homogeneous diglossia, a situation in which two genetically closely related languages, in this case the CS and Slavonic vernaculars, were in complementary distribution. The former had the function of the high style and was used in sacral texts (e.g. in liturgical ones), while the latter had the function of the low style and was used in the texts of profane character (e.g. in medieval charters and letters). It was the homogeneous diglossia that enabled the formation of the Church Slavonic of the lower functional style (or Orthodox Slavonic, according to Picchio 1980: 32–33), which combines features inherited both from OCS and those originating from the vernacular (Grković-Major 2007: 443–446).

[9] For the Old Serbian situation see Pavlović (2009: 58, 299–300); Gortan-Premk (1973: 286–287); Zima (1887: 312); Miklosich (1868–1874: 395). For the Old Russian situation see Lomtev (1954: 30–36, 44); Potebnja (1958: 301–307, 377).

Slavonic vernacular texts exhibit the common usage of AcInf. in causative constructions, as in (17a), (17b), and the double accusative with communicative, cognitive and perception verbs, see (18a), (18b) throughout the historical period of Slavonic literacy.

(17a) Old Serbian
ni   da   mogu   nikadare   zabraniti
nor-NEG   that-CONJ   can-1SG.PRS never   forbid-INF
ni   ustaviti   niedne moe ljudi ni vlahe ni srьble
nor-NEG   stop-INF   any of my men, or Vlachs or Serbs-ACC.PL.M
slobodno hoditi   u dubrovnikъ   trъgovati
freely   walk-INF   into Dubrovnik   trade-INF
'nor that I can ever forbid or stop any of my men, nor Vlachs or Serbs freely walk into Dubrovnik to trade'
(Kos. 1451, N° 656.24, according to Pavlović 2009: 298)

Pušti   mene   do   djevojke   doći.
Let-2SG.IMP   I-ACC   to-PREP   girl-GEN.SG.F   come.to-INF
'Let me reach to the girl'
(Petr. 2, 676, according to Zima 1887: 312)

(17b) Old Russian
Pristavi   k   nimъ   muži   svoi
sat-3SG.AOR   to-PREP   they-DAT   men-ACC.PL.M   his
pokazati   imъ   cerkovъnuju krasotu
show-INF   they-DAT   church beauty-ACC.SG.F
'He sat his men to show them the church beauty'
(Ip.$_2$, 23, according to Potebnja 1958: 376)

(18a) Old Serbian
U licu   ga   kažu   plemenita
in the face   he-ACC   say-3.PL.PRS   noble-ACC.SG.M
'They say about him, that he is noble in the face'
(Juk. 256, according to Zima 1887: 312)

(18b) Old Russian
knjazja   svoego   živogo   vědjače
prince-ACC.SG.M   his   alive-ACC.SG.M   consider-PRS.GER
'considering of his prince to be alive'
(Ip., 64 (303), according to Potebnja 1958: 305)

Postavi   *Methodьja*   *episkopa*
make-3.SG.AOR   Methodius-ACC.SG.M   bishop- ACC.SG.M
v Panonii
in Pannonia
'He made Methodius become a bishop in Pannonia'
(Lavr., 11 (27), according to Potebnja 1958: 303)

Rarely, AcInf. with perception verbs is found in Old Serbian texts. The infinitive within the structure has subjunctive meaning.

(19)   Old Serbian
      ne   *vidě*   *ga*
      not-NEG.   see-3.SG.AOR   he-ACC.SG.M
      Men(e)lauš   *c(a)rь*   *ubiti*
      Menelaus-NOM.SG.M   King- NOM.SG.M   kill-INF
      'The king Menelaus did not see him to kill (him).'
      (Rom. o Tr. 247, according to Grickat 2004: 165)

AcInf. with communicative and cognitive verbs is found only in non-liturgical CS texts, probably as a hallmark of the literary language, cf. (20a) and (20b).

(20a)   Serbian Church Slavonic
        mudra   *bo*   *mi*   *ego*
        wise-ACC.SG.M   PRT   I-DAT   he-ACC
        i   *sьmyslьna*   *skazajutь*   *byti*
        and-CONJ   reasonable-ACC.SG.M   tell-3.PL.PRS   be-INF
        'They told me about him that he is a wise and reasonable man.'
        (SAR 127r/5–7)

(20b)   Russian Church Slavonic
        i   *vzjaše*   *ego*   *mnjašte*
        and-CONJ   take-3.PL.AOR.   he-ACC   think-PRS.PTCP.ACT.NOM.PL.M
        ego   *mertva*   *byti*
        he-ACC   dead-ACC.SG.M   be-INF
        'and took him, considering him to be dead'
        (Pat. Peč, according to Georgijeva 1968: 91)

Having these data in mind, we argue that AcInf. in the subjunctive use is a genuine Slavonic construction, whereby its indicative meaning is secondary, derived from the construction of the double accusative. Unlike Miklosich (1868–1874: 388), Potebnja (1958: 301) stated that the construction of the double accusative was probably of common Slavonic character since it is found not only in Slavonic vernaculars, but in other Indo-European languages as well. In the history of Slavonic languages these constructions with subjunctive and indicative meaning developed in different ways depending on the syntactic and semantic context (cf. Section 5).

3.2 AcInf. in the Serbian Alexander Romance

In order to compare the situation in OCS with the situation in CS, we conducted research on the Serbian Alexander Romance (SAR 1985), a text of profane character written in Serbian Church Slavonic of the lower functional style, i.e. Orthodox Slavonic. The critical edition (SAR 1985) used for this research is based on the 16th century Serbian Church Slavonic text, which originated in the Prizren-Timok dialectal area (Jerković 1983: 225–227).[10] Although it is a transcript from the 16th century, it preserves a version very similar to the archetype, which is believed to be written at the end of the 13th century in Dubrovnik and its surroundings or in Duklja (Marinković 2007: 309). The language of the text demonstrates many archaic syntactic and morphological features,[11] which are believed to be due to its folklore base.[12] Such language realization was conditioned by the genre and content of the text. SAR belongs to narrative prose, specifically to the romance of chivalry in which the main content represents historical events interwoven with legends and anecdotes. Thus, its thematic implies the inclusion of certain constructions from oral literature. Therefore, this type of text can preserve certain archaic features that were out of use in literary language or in everyday speech.

The results of our research of SAR are shown in Tables 3 and 4. They illustrate a slightly different situation from CM.[13] In type A contexts, infinitive constructions with accusative subjects are also predominant in comparison with the *da*-clause (structures with supine were not found). But in contrast to the situation in CM, in SAR they are more frequent than the finite clause. In type B contexts, unlike in CM, AcInf. and AcPtc. prevail in comparison with the double accusative, while the finite clause introduced by the conjunction *jako* instead of the second

---

[10] This is mainly inferred from some very rare phonetic and morphological features which deviate from the CS norm, such as the preservation of the semivowel in all its etymological positions.
[11] This fact is confirmed by a lot of linguistic evidence, such as: the usage of particle *da* in its optative and adjunctive function, the absence of anaphoric objects, the usage of the adverbial accusative and double accusative with many verb classes, the usage of predicative participles etc. (Grković-Major 2008: 72; Kurešević 2010a, 2014).
[12] Many linguists pointed out that oral literature or dialects could preserve some archaic features that have been out of use in literary language or in everyday speech (Bauer 1972: 27; Ambrazas 1990: 28; Večerka 2009: 181–182).
[13] 'Different' in the sense that they reflect different quantitative relations between competing means.

accusative is not confirmed. In type C contexts we found only the double accusative. AcInf. is not found with desiderative verbs, nor in independent use (type D context).

Tab. 3: Competing means in SAR: subjunctive field of use.

	acc. + inf. /sup.	acc. + *da*-clause
Type A		
causative verbs of movement (e.g. *posъlati*)	14x	2x
causative verbs (e.g. *sъpodobiti*)	21x	1x
jussive verbs (e.g. *moliti*)	3x	1x
Type D	/	/

Tab. 4: Competing means in SAR: indicative field of use.

	double acc.	1st acc. + *jako* + 2nd acc.	AcInf. (1st acc. + 2nd acc. + *byti*)	DatInf. (dat. + *byti*)	AcPtc. (1st acc. + 2nd acc. + *sǫšt-*)	1st acc. + *jako*-clause
Type B						
cognitive verbs (e.g. *věděti*)	10x	/	13x	5x	4x	/
communicative verbs (e.g. *glagolati*)	2x	/	12x	2x	/	/
Type C						
verbs of doing (e.g. *tvoriti [sę]*)	16x	/	/	/	/	/
desiderative verbs (e.g. *hotěti*)	/	/	/	/	/	/

The situation in SAR can be explained in two ways: a) infinitive constructions are preserved as a characteristic of the literary language or b) they reflect the stage of evolution of the vernacular at the time the text was written.[14]

---

[14] The preservation of language features which existed in the vernacular at the time when the text was written reflects the power of the textual form and language tradition of a particular genre, which played an important role in the preservation of language norms during the medieval period of Slavonic literacy.

In order to give a precise answer to that question, we have to get a wider typological view of the AcInf. use.

4 AcInf. in Indo-European perspective

AcInf. existed in many old Indo-European languages, such as Classical Latin and Greek, Hittite, Sanskrit, Gothic, Old English etc. where it was usually found with jussive, causative, perception, communicative and cognitive verbs (Hahn 1950; Potebnja 1958: 375; Disterheft 1980: 193–194; Wackernagel 2009: 330–332).

The historical syntax of Indo-European languages proves that, although AcInf. was their common feature, the scope of its usage was not the same in all of them.[15] For example, in Greek and Latin (Hahn 1950; Moorhouse 1955) the construction in some contexts had the subjunctive, while in others the indicative meaning. Since it is impossible to connect these two types of its usage genetically as it had been believed earlier, they must have evolved independently. The construction used with communicative and cognitive verbs (expressing the indicative meaning) was brought into connection with the accusative followed by a predicative modifier (in fact with the double accusative). In contrast to Latin, the double accusative, which is considered to be dependent on primitive parataxis (Jacquinod 1995), is found in the New Testament Greek very often (Blass and Debrunner 1961: 86) alongside with its counterpart, the same construction followed by the infinitive *eĩnai*, without any change in their meaning (Culy 2009). The further development of the double accusative and AcInf. in Latin and Greek shows that they were gradually replaced by finite clauses (Pichkhadze 2012: 53).

On the other hand, Old Baltic languages have AcPtc. with communicative, cognitive, and also perception verbs (Ambrazas 1990: 141–145). The genuine character of the construction is proven by its systematic reliance on the use of the double accusative or on the use of the so-called cognate accusative, found in the same contexts as a residue of the time when the accusative case had a wider scope of use.[16]

---

15 For example, in Latin and Greek it has been confirmed in type B, C and D contexts, in Sanskrit in type B and C contexts, while in CS and Russian in type A, B and C contexts (Potebnja 1958: 375).
16 Cf. endnote 4.

5 Emergence of AcInf. in OCS: Explanations of the causes and mechanisms

The history of Proto-Indo-European and its daughter languages can be seen as the evolution from an active towards a nominative language type, with the rise of syntactic transitivity as its manifestation (Gamkrelidze and Ivanov 1995: 267–276).

Grković-Major (2008, 2010b) pointed out some consequences of the rise of transitivity in Slavonic languages: a) syntactic government became a basic principle in sentence organization, b) the nominative and accusative were grammaticalized as subject and object cases respectively, c) gradual disappearance of nominal constructions for expressing semantic subordination and their replacement by the finite structures etc. All these changes gave the central role to the predicate which increased the intra-sentence, as well as inter-sentence, cohesion and consequently led to the formation of compound sentences.

If we look at AcInf. in OCS in the context of the development of syntactic transitivity, we might get a new perspective on its origin and status. Used both as a complement and as an independent construction, it represents a nominal construction which had an important role in the syntactic organization of the sentence in earlier stages of many Indo-European languages (Meillet 1965: 204; Lehmann 1980).[17] The history of IE languages shows that such nominal forms were gradually replaced by their verbal counterparts (Bauer 2000: 349). In this process, structures with a loose syntactic relation to the matrix verb were replaced earlier than those that built a stronger syntactic relation.[18]

Regarding the fact that the independent AcInf. is rarely found in OCS (Gaderka 1964: 528–530) and that it does not exist in our corpus nor have we found it in vernacular texts, we can conclude that it was not a genuine Slavonic construction. Thus its use in OCS can be labelled as a syntactic calque proper of the Greek pattern. This is also confirmed by internal language facts, which show that OCS used another absolute construction in this syntactic position – *dativus cum infinitivo* (Večerka 2002: 340–341) or a finite clause introduced with the *jako da* or *da* conjunction (Gramatika 1993: 506).

---

[17] For instance, the subordination was expressed by nominal assets (such as participles, absolute constructions, double case constructions, verbal nouns, etc.), which were overtly paratactically organized.
[18] A good example of the foregoing is the history of the dative absolute in Slavonic languages (Grković-Major 2008: 77–78, 2010b: 69).

On the other hand, if the AcInf. complement was a calque of the Greek pattern, as it is commonly believed, it would have not been confirmed so often in some CS texts of profane character (that is, in Orthodox Slavonic). Thus we assume that it had support in the Slavonic system. Its origin differs depending on whether it expresses the subjunctive or indicative meaning.

AcInf. in type A contexts (subjunctive meaning) reflects earlier morphology: the direct object represents the grammaticalized patient and the grammaticalized verbal noun in dative denotes the purpose of the action given by the matrix verb. This is a genuine Slavonic syntactic strategy, as proven by its further development: in Old Serbian the infinitive in such constructions was gradually replaced by *da*-clauses, as a manifestation of a typological drift from the nominal to the verbal language type. This process was supported by language contact in the Balkans (Grković-Major 2004; Pavlović 2006). In contrast to the Serbian situation, in Russian the infinitives with accusative subjects with some jussive and causative verbs still represent a productive category (Lomtev 1954: 44).

AcInf. used in type B and C contexts (indicative meaning) had a different history. It cannot be brought into a genetic relationship with type A because neither does the accusative express a prototypical patient, nor does the infinitive express purpose. It should be brought into connection with the double accusative construction, which was of common Slavonic character, as Potebnja (1958: 301) pointed out. If the double accusative construction is a trace of the system in which the subordinate nominal predicate was expressed by apposition, its variant, AcInf. (i.e. the accusative with the infinitive of the verb *byti* 'to be'), can be considered to be the next stage in the process, as it is recorded in Koine Greek (Culy 2009). A comparison with the Baltic situation in this respect indicates that internal language motivation for its emergence did exist.

The history of Slavonic languages shows that double accusative constructions with the communicative, cognitive and verbs of doing, (18a) and (18b), could develop in two ways: 1) the second accusative was either transformed into complement clause or 2) it was replaced by the instrumental case. The development of AcInf. could have gone through the same scenario. Both changes were caused by the rise of syntactic transitivity, i.e. by internal language drift towards the establishment of the sentence with formally differentiated semantic roles and one predicative centre.

The first way of development was characteristic for the double accusative and AcInf. with communicative verbs. The second accusative, as the second predicative centre in the sentence, was first replaced by a complement clause whose subject was coreferential with the object of the matrix verb, (21a) and (21b). In the next stage, the accusative in the matrix clause was lost.

(21a) Old Serbian
Tebe   kažu   da   si
you-ACC say-3.PL.PRS that-CONJ   be-AUX.2.SG.PRS
junak   dobar
hero-NOM.SG.M   good-ADJ
'They say about you, that you are a good hero'
(Petr. 2, 345, according to Zima 1887: 312)

(21b) Old Russian
Mьstislava   povědaša   ože
Mstislav-ACC.SG.M   tell-3.PL.AOR   that-CONJ
pošel   s   Telebugoju   na Lvovъ
go.to-3.SG.PRF   with-PREP   Telebuga-INS   to Lvov
'they told about Mstislav, that he was gone with Telebuga to Lvov'
(PSRL II: 900.2–3, according to Pichkhadze 2012: 57)

The second way of development was characteristic for the double accusative and AcInf. with verbs of doing, naming and cognitive verbs. According to Borkovskij and Kuznecov (1963: 364) it speaks not just in favour of its predicative character, but also of its greater dependence on the matrix verb.

(22a) Old Serbian
Nemojte   činiti   kuću
do not-2.PL.IMP.NEG   make-INF   house-ACC.SG.F
moga oca   kućom   od   prodavac
my father-GEN.SG.M   house-INS.SG.F   of-PREP   seller-GEN.PL.M
'Do not make my father's house become house of sellers'
(D. Ranjina, according to Gortan-Premk 1973: 287)

(22b) Old Russian
postavi   mja   popomь   arhepiskopъ
make-3.SG.AOR   I-ACC   priest-INS.SG.M   Archbishop-NOM.SG.M
svjatyj   Nifontъ
holy-ADJ   Nifont-NOM.SG.M
'Archbishop holy Nifont made me become a priest'
(Novg. I, 9, according to Potebnja 1958: 492)

6 Conclusion

Having in mind AcInf.'s systematic reliance on the use of double accusative, its attestation in ancient Indo-European languages and its further development in Slavonic languages, we argue that the emergence of the AcInf. construction in OCS with communicative, cognitive and verbs of doing can be explained as a result of the interplay of language-internal (the spread of syntactic transitivity) and contact-induced processes (the influence of literary Greek or Latin). The appearance of the copula in this type of construction, used in order to underline the predicative character of the second accusative, could have been caused by a typological drift from the nominal to the verbal language type. The question is why, in the OCS examples, the copula appears more often with the infinitive than with the participle, although only the latter is believed to be more in compliance with the Slavonic system (Večerka 2002: 447–449). One of the possible answers is that the interplay between the internal tendencies and language contact factors could have been a trigger for the adoption of a sentence pattern that was not completely in accordance with the system of the recipient language. The other possible answer can be drawn from the invariant meaning of the infinitive and participle. Since the infinitive of stative verbs (e.g. 'to be') characterizes the whole sentence as a statement, it is more associated with communicative and cognitive verbs, while their participle, expressing procedural meaning, is more associated with perception verbs. We assume that this was the situation in late Common Slavonic. The Greek influence in the case of AcInf. in type B and C contexts, as in the case of some other archaic constructions (cf. Grković-Major 2008: 77–78), could give prominence to the archaic construction among several competing strategies for expressing the same meaning.

AcInf. in type B and C contexts retained its bookish character through the whole period of CS literacy. Like some other nominal (participial and infinitive) constructions which were lost in the early history of Slavonic languages, it became *differentia specifica* of CS literary languages. As such, in the lower registers of CS, i.e. Orthodox Slavonic, it could be used as a syntactic strategy with a specific stylistic value: unlike finite clauses, it could indicate unreliable, reported information (cf. Kurešević 2010b).

(23) *priličnaa   glagoljut   mi   te   byti*
     similar-ACC.SG.M say-3PL.PRS   I-DAT   you-ACC   be-INF
     Aleksandru   o človeče.
     Alexander-DAT.SG.M oh, man-VOC.SG.M
     'They tell me, oh man, that you look like Alexander.'
     (SAR: 122r/7–9)

Finally, if AcInf. with communicative and cognitive verbs in (O)CS is attested in many ancient Indo-European languages, had internal language motivation, as well as a special pragmatic function, we should consider it to be a bookish neologism rather than a syntactic calque. Its emergence in OCS confirms the claim of Jakobson (1962: 241) that syntactic borrowings from one language to another are possible only in case of the same developmental tendencies that lie at their basis.

Sources

CM: Jagić, Vatroslav (ed.). 1960 [1883]. *Quattuor Evangeliorum versionis palaeoslovenicae Codex Marianus glagoliticus*. Graz: Akademische Druck- und Verlagsanstalt.
SAR: Marinković, Radmila & Vera Jerković (eds.). 1985. *Srpska Aleksandrida. Sveska druga* [Serbian Alexander Romance. Volume II]. Beograd: Srpska akademija nauka i umetnosti.

References

Ambrazas, Vytautas. 1990. *Sravnitel'nyj sintaksis pričastij baltijskix jazykov* [Comparative syntax of participles in the Baltic languages]. Vil'njus: Mokslas.
Bauer, Brigitte. 2000. *Archaic syntax in Indo-European: The spread of transitivity in Latin and French*. Berlin & New York: Mouton de Gruyter.
Bauer, Jaroslav. 1972. *Syntactica slavica. Vybrané práce ze slovanské skladby* [Syntactica slavica. Selected works on Slavonic syntax]. Brno: Universita J.E. Purkyně.
Blass, Friedrich & Albert Debrunner. 1961. *A Greek grammar of the New Testament and other early Christian literature* (translated and revised by Robert W. Funk). Cambridge: Cambridge University Press & Chicago: University of Chicago Press.
Borkovskij, Viktor I. & Petr S. Kuznecov. 1963. *Istoričeskaja grammatika russkogo jazyka* [Historical grammar of the Russian language]. Moskva: Akademija nauk SSSR.
Culy, Martin M. 2009. Double case constructions in Koine Greek. *Journal of Greco-Roman Christianity and Judaism* 6. 82–106.
Disterheft, Dorothy. 1980. *The syntactic development of the infinitive in Indo-European*. Columbus, Ohio: Slavica Publishers.
EM: *Evangelie ot Matfeja v slavjanskoj tradicii* [The gospel according to Mark in the Slavonic tradition]. 2005. Sankt-Peterburg: Sankt-Peterburgskij gosudarstvenyj universitet, Filologičeskij fakul'tet, Sinodal'naja biblioteka Moskovskogo Patriarxata & Rosijskoe biblejskoe obščestvo.
Gamkrelidze, Thomas V. & Vjačeslav V. Ivanov. 1995. *Indo-European and the Indo-Europeans. A reconstruction and historical analysis of a proto-language and a proto-culture. Part I: The text*. Berlin & New York: Mouton de Gruyter.
Gardiner, Sunray C. 1984. *Old Church Slavonic. An elementary grammar*. Cambridge, London, New York, New Rochelle, Melbourne & Sydney: Cambridge University Press.
Georgieva, Valentina L. 1968. *Istorija sintaksičeskix javlenij russkogo jazyka* [History of the syntactic phenomena in the Russian language]. Moskva: Prosveščenie.
Gortan-Premk, Darinka. 1971. *Akuzativne sintagme bez predloga u srpskohrvatskom jeziku* [Accusative phrases without a preposition in the Serbo-Croatian language]. Beograd: Institut za srpskohrvatski jezik.

Gortan-Premk, Darinka. 1973. O evolutivnim tendencijama akuzativnih sintagmi bez predloga u srpskohrvatskom jeziku [On evolutionary tendencies of accusative phrases without a preposition in the Serbo-Croatian language]. *Južnoslovenski filolog* XXX (1–2). 281–295.

Gramatika: Ivan V. Duridanov (ed.). 1993. *Gramatika na starobălgarskija ezik. Fonetika. Morfologija. Sintaksis* [Old Church Slavonic Grammar. Phonetics. Morphology. Syntax]. Sofija: Bălgarska Akademija na Naukite.

Grickat, Irena. 2004. *Studije iz istorije srpskohrvatskog jezika* [Studies from the history of the Serbo-Croatian language]. Beograd: Narodna biblioteka Srbije.

Grković-Major [Grković-Mejdžor], Jasmina. 2001. *Pitanja iz staroslovenske sintakse i leksike* [Issues of Old Church Slavonic syntax and lexicon]. Novi Sad: Filozofski fakultet.

Grković-Major [Grković-Mejdžor], Jasmina. 2004. Razvoj hipotaktičkog *da* u starosrpskom jeziku [Development of the hypotactic *da* in Old Serbian]. *Zbornik Matice srpske za filologiju i lingvistiku* XLVII (1–2). 185–203.

Grković-Major [Grković-Mejdžor], Jasmina. 2007. *Spisi iz istorijske lingvistike* [Studies in historical linguistics]. Sremski Karlovci & Novi Sad: Izdavačka knjižarnica Zorana Stojanovića.

Grković-Major [Grković-Mejdžor], Jasmina. 2008. Ka rekonstrukciji praslovenske sintakse [Towards the reconstruction of Proto-Slavonic syntax]. *Zbornik Matice srpske za slavistiku* 73. 71–83.

Grković-Major [Grković-Mejdžor], Jasmina. 2010a. O konstrukciji akuzativa s participom (tipološki i kognitivni aspekti) [On the *accusativus cum participio* construction (typological and cognitive aspects)]. *Južnoslovenski filolog* LXVI. 187–204.

Grković-Major, Jasmina. 2010b. The role of syntactic transitivity in the develoment of Slavonic syntactic structures. In Björn Hansen & Jasmina Grković-Major (eds.), *Diachronic Slavonic syntax. Gradual changes in focus* (Wiener Slawistischer Almanach – Sonderband 74), 63–74. München, Berlin & Wien: Otto Sagner.

Grković-Major [Grković-Mejdžor], Jasmina. 2011. Dativ + infinitiv: praindoevropsko poreklo i slovenski razvoj [Dative + Infinitive: its Proto-Indo-European source and Slavonic development]. *Zbornik Matice srpske za filologiju i lingvistiku* LIV (1). 27–44.

Hahn, Adelaide E. 1950. Genesis of the infinitive with subject-accusative. *Transactions and Proceedings of the American Philological Association* 81. 117–129.

Gaderka, Karel. 1964. Sočetanija sub"ekta, svjazannogo s infinitivom, v staroslavjanskix i cerkovnoslavjanskix pamjatnikax [Combinations of subject with the infinitive in (Old) Church Slavonic manuscripts]. *Slavia* XXXIII (4). 505–533.

Jakobson, Roman. 1962. *Selected writings I. Phonological studies*. The Hague: Mouton & Co.

Jacquinod, Bernard. 1995. Regression and creation in the double accusative in Ancient Greek. In Henning Andersen (ed.), *Historical linguistics 1993: Selected papers from the 11th International Conference on Historical Linguistics, Los Angeles, 16–20 August 1993*. Amsterdam & Philadelphia: John Benjamins.

Jarceva, Viktorija N. 1956. Problema vydelenija zaimstvovannyx èlementov pri rekonstrukcii sravnitel'no-istoričeskogo sintaksisa rodstvennyx jayzkov [The problem of distinguishing borrowed elements in the reconstruction of historical and comparative syntax of related languages]. *Voprosy jazykoznanija* 6. 3–14.

Jerković, Vera. 1983. *Srpska Aleksandrida. Akademijin rukopis (br. 352). Paleografska, ortografska, i jezička istraživanja* [The Serbian Alexander Romance. Academy's manuscript (No. 352). Palaeographic, orthographic and linguistic studies]. Beograd: Srpska akademija nauka i umetnosti.

Kristal, Dejvid. 1988. *Enciklopedijski rečnik moderne lingvistike* [A dictionary of linguistics and phonetics]. Beograd: Nolit.

Kurešević, Marina. 2010a. O upotrebi partikule/veznika *da* u Srpskoj Aleksandridi [On the usage of the particle/conjunction *da* in the Serbian Alexander Romance]. *Godišnjak Filozofskog fakulteta u Novom Sadu* XXXV (2). 243–258.

Kurešević, Marina. 2010b. O konkurentnoj upotrebi akuzativnih konstrukcija (sa participom i infinitivom) i dopunske rečenice u Srpskoj Aleksandridi [On the competitive usage of the accusative constructions (with infinitive and participle) and complement clause in the Serbian Alexander Romance]. *Zbornik Matice srpske za filologiju i lingvistiku* LIII (1): 79–92.

Kurešević, Marina. 2014. *Hipotaktičke strukture u Srpskoj Aleksandridi: funkcionalnostilski aspekti* [Hypotactic structures in the Serbian Alexander Romance: Functional-stylistic aspects]. Novi Sad: Filozofski fakultet.

Lehmann, Winfred. 1980. The reconstruction of non-simple sentences in Proto-Indo-European. In Paolo Ramat (ed.), *Linguistic reconstruction and Indo-European syntax: Proceedings of the Colloquium of the 'Indogermanische Gesellschaft', University of Pavia, 6–7 September 1979*, 113–144. Amsterdam: John Benjamins.

Lomtev, Timofej P. 1954. *Iz istorii sintaksisa russkogo jazyka* [From the history of Russian syntax]. Moskva: Gosudarstvennoe učebno-pedagogičeskoe izdatel'stvo ministerstva prosveščenija RSFSR.

MacRobert, Catherine Mary. 1986. Foreign, naturalized and native syntax in Old Church Slavonic. *Transactions of the Philological Society* 84 (1). 142–166.

Marinković, Radmila. 2007. *Svetorodna gospoda srpska: istraživanja srpske književnosti srednjeg veka* [Holy Serbian lords: Studies of the Serbian literature of the Middle Ages]. Beograd: Društvo za srpski jezik i književnost Srbije.

Meillet, Antoine. 1965. *Uvod u uporedno proučavanje indoevropskih jezika* [Introduction to the comparative study of Indo-European languages]. Beograd: Naučna knjiga.

Miklosich, Franz. 1868–1874. *Vergleichende Syntax der slavischen Sprachen*. Wien: Wilhelm Braumüller.

Moorhouse, Alfred C. 1955. The origin of the infinitive in Greek indirect statement. *American Journal of Philology* 76 (2). 176–183.

Novum Testamentum Graece: Barbara Aland & others (eds.). 2012. *Novum Testamentum Graece*. 28th revised edition. Stuttgart: Deutsche Bibelgesellschaft.

Pacnerová, Ludmila. 1964. Sintaksis infinitiva v staroslavjanskix evangel'skix kodeksax s točki zrenija texniki perevoda [Syntax of infinitive in Old Church Slavonic Gospel codices from the viewpoint of translation techniques]. *Slavia* XXXIII (4). 534–557.

Pavlović, Slobodan. 2006. Sistemski podsticaj za konektivnu unifikaciju asertivnosti i voluntativnosti u starosrpskom jeziku [Systemic stimulus for the conjunction unification of the assertive and voluntative meanings in Old Serbian]. *Zora* 44. 181–190.

Pavlović, Slobodan. 2009. *Starosrpska zavisna rečenica od XII do XV veka* [The Old Serbian dependent clause from the 12th to the 15th century]. Sremski Karlovci & Novi Sad: Izdavačka knjižarnica Zorana Stojanovića.

Picchio, Riccardo [Rikkardo Pikkio]. 1980. Church Slavonic. In Alexander M. Schenker & Edward Stankiewich (eds.), *The Slavic Literary Languages: Formation and Development*, 1–33. New Haven: Yale Cocilium on International and Area Studies.

Pichkhadze, Anna A. 2012. Subject of subordinate clause as object with verbs of perception, thought, and communication in Old Russian. *Slověne* 1 (1). 52–60.

Potebnja, Aleksandr A. 1958. *Iz zapisok po russkoj grammatike. Tom I–II* [From the notes on Russian grammar. Volume I–II]. Moskva: Akademija nauk SSSR.

Schmalstieg, Wiliam R. 1988. *A Lithuanian historical syntax*. Columbus, Ohio: Slavica Publishers.

Vaillant, André [Andre Vajan]. 1952. *Rukovodstvo po staroslavjanskomu jazyku* [Old Church Slavonic grammar]. Moskva: Izdatel'stvo po inostrannoj literatury.

Večerka, Radoslav. 1989. *Altkirchenslavische (altbulgarische) Syntax I. Die lineare Satzorganisation.* Freiburg. i. Br.: Weiher.

Večerka, Radoslav. 1996. *Altkirchenslavische (altbulgarische) Syntax III. Die Satztypen: Der einfache Satz.* Freiburg. i. Br.: Weiher.

Večerka, Radoslav. 1997. The influence of Greek on Old Church Slavonic. *Byzantinoslavica* LVIII (2). 363–386.

Večerka, Radoslav. 2002. *Altkirchenslavische (altbulgarische) Syntax IV. Die Satztypen: Der zusammengesetzte Satz.* Freiburg. i. Br.: Weiher.

Večerka, Radoslav. 2009. Entwicklungsvoraussetzungen und Triebkräfte der Slavischen Syntax. In Björn Hansen & Jasmina Grković-Major (eds.), *Diachronic Slavonic syntax. Gradual changes in focus* (Wiener Slawistischer Almanach – Sonderband 74), 181–194. München, Berlin & Wien: Otto Sagner.

Vondrák, Wenzel. 1928. *Vergleichende slavische Grammatik. Bd. 2: Formenlehre und Syntax.* (Göttinger Sammlung indogermanischer Grammatiken und Wörterbücher). Auflage Göttingen: Vandenhoeck and Ruprecht.

Wackernagel, Jacob. 2009. *Lectures on syntax with special reference to Greek, Latin, and Germanic.* Oxford: Oxford University Press.

Wiemer, Björn & Bernhard Wälchli. 2012. Contact-induced grammatical change: Diverse phenomena, diverse perspectives. In Björn Wiemer, Bernhard Wälchli & Björn Hansen (eds.), *Grammatical replication and borrowability in language contact*, 3–66. Berlin & Boston: De Gruyter Mouton.

Zima, Luka. 1887. *Ńekoje, većinom sintaktične razlike između čakavštine, kajkavštine i štokavštine* [Some, mostly syntactic differences between Čakavian, Kajkavian, and Štokavian dialects]. *Djela JAZU* VII. 1–343.

Björn Wiemer
On triangulation in the domain of clause linkage and propositional marking

Abstract: This article presents mutually connected pilot studies on the development of certain complementizers capable of introducing propositional complements in South and North (= West + East) Slavonic, and it deliberates the concepts and methods necessary for triangulation. By the latter I understand approaches that aim at equilibrating the relative share of three factors in language change and the rise of areal clines and clusters: (i) genealogical affinity (i.e. inherited features), (ii) areal closeness (involving contact-induced change), and (iii) typological tendencies (often considered as universals) driven by general cognitive and communicative preconditions of speech. On this backdrop, three central issues are discussed. First, what are the conditions for the emergence and entrenchment of complementizers that, in one way or other, mark the suspension of assertiveness in clausal complementation? Second, how are these patterns of complementation related, both systematically and diachronically, to particles serving roughly the same functions? And, third, do the patterns we observe in synchronic terms correspond to more interesting areal distributions? The units analysed for South Slavonic are *da* and, to some extent, *kako*, for North Slavonic *jako + by > jakoby* (with variants). Within Slavonic, *da* and *jakoby* have evolved basically in complementary areal distribution, although the range and overall importance of *da* for South Slavonic syntax is much more considerable than of *jakoby* for North Slavonic. Also, the geographic direction for innovative features in the use of *jakoby* is opposite (from west to east) to functional innovations that have occurred with *da* in South Slavonic (from east to west). A preliminary comparison with 'as if'-units in continental West Germanic reveals that the inner-North Slavonic cline for *jakoby* seems to inscribe well into a larger cline running through the middle of the European continent.

1 Introduction

Recently, Robbeets and Cuyckens (2013) wrote a well-considered survey on how to approach "shared grammaticalization from an integrated perspective, including areal as well as genealogical and universal motivations and by searching for ways to distinguish between these factors" (2013: 1). Other authors have inquired into such approaches as well, first of all in the context of contact-induced grammaticalization (cf., for instance, Kuteva and Heine 2012). I want to claim that such integrative attempts do not essentially depend on whether we are dealing with grammaticalization (or with whatever one wants to subsume under 'grammaticalization') or 'only' associated language change phenomena. Instead, one should approach **any** sort of structural features (and the processes leading to their rise like, first of all, reanalysis and analogical expansion) shared between areally and/or genealogically related languages from a triangulation perspective, as was sketched in Wiemer, Seržant, and Erker (2014).

In Section 2, I will introduce the concept of triangulation and discuss theoretical issues relevant for further progress in this direction. The remaining part of this article is meant to be an application of triangulation to the domain of complex sentences; this includes a demonstration of how certain types of clausal complementation are diachronically and systematically related to the marking of suspended assertiveness and of propositions. I will look at the rise of clausal complementation in South Slavonic (*da* and other connectives; Section 3), on the one hand, and in West and East Slavonic (Section 4), on the other, using case studies on Polish *jakoby* and its Russian equivalents as a starting point. Sections 3 and 4 complement each other in inner-Slavonic areal terms. In fact, we will see that the southern and the northern part of Slavonic (after early divisions of a more homogeneous dialect continuum), roughly, show diametrically opposed directions of areal clines (from SE to NW in South Slavonic and from SW to NE in West and East Slavonic) and that both clines are based on different choices of cognate morphemes from Proto- or Common Slavonic. Section 5 summarizes the findings and provides conclusions.

I want to emphasize that what is to follow are case studies in a global sense, as they cannot pretend, in one go, to fill a lot of research gaps which I will indicate in passing. Instead, I will be glad if my contribution helps understand why and where in-depth studies will have to follow.

2 On triangulation, areal patterns and types of language change

The following remarks are meant to point out some critical methodological issues, but they are not intended as a comprehensive discussion. For this reason, I will be rather selective with references. I will first comment on triangulation (2.1) and then provide an argument for the careful treatment of the term 'grammaticalization' against the background of some other, maybe more simple, types of linguistic change (2.2).

2.1 Triangulation in a nutshell

By adapting the quote from Robbeets and Cuyckens (2013: 1) adduced above, an overarching goal of diachronic linguistics can be phrased in the following way: for a dedicated area, one should approach **shared structural features** "from an integrated perspective, including areal as well as genealogical and universal motivations and by searching for ways to distinguish between these factors". Since we are dealing with three dimensions (or viewpoints), this endeavour can also be dubbed 'triangulation'. Triangulation is a blanket term covering procedures with which phenomena of structural convergence in a dedicated area are systematically assessed by cross-verification of complementary approaches that concentrate on at least one of three kinds of backgrounds. These backgrounds are typological, or even universal, tendencies (basically Greenbergian markedness relations; see below), areal and contact linguistics (including dialect geography), and historical-comparative linguistics (with its main goal of establishing the common "heritage" from some ancestor variety); cf. Wiemer, Seržant, and Erker (2014: 25). The weaknesses of one approach are to be counterbalanced by the strong sides of the complementary ones.[1]

We get the triangle we are looking for if we account for the following (deliberately simplified) considerations. Historical-comparative linguistics primarily deals with the etymological sources of linguistic fabric (phonemes, morphemes) and their paradigmatic organization within languages that can be traced back to some sort of common ancestor, and aims to describe how these initial forms and their paradigms diversified over time. The investigation "back in time" to shared sources often ends up in reconstructions, especially (as is so often the case) if there are not enough data with sufficient time-depth. The same endeavour can, in principle, be pursued with respect to the syntactic organization of languages with an assumed "common ancestor", but the comparative reconstruction of syntax has encountered many more obstacles than the reconstruction of phonology and phonetics or of morphological paradigms based on regularities

---

[1] Triangulation was first introduced in the social sciences (Olson 2004) where the primary goal was to ensure an optimal degree of validity ("Are the data/observations adequate for what we want to investigate?") and reliability ("Are the data/observations exact enough?; "Do we have control over all factors of variation?"; "Are the data robust enough, so that they can be gained after repetition?") in the elicitation and interpretation of data. Within the scope of triangulation, we can differentiate (a) methods (field work, experiments, interviews, etc.), (b) access to data types (corpora, field notes, questionnaires, reference grammars, introspection, etc.), and (c) disciplines. Of course, these different "dimensions" of triangulation intersect with (or condition) each other to a certain extent.

of sound change, analogy and an understanding of the structure of paradigms as such. Moreover, aiming to reconstruct proto-stages, historical-comparative linguistics, up to a certain stage, neglected (or even excluded) contact with language varieties from outside the genealogical group. It thus, in a sense, pretended that language-contact (at least from outside the genealogically grown dialect continuum) did not play any significant role in changes and the diffusion of innovations (or, conversely, the retention of more ancient features); cf. Wiemer (2007). In this respect, contact linguistics and areal typology have been natural – and necessary – methodological antipodes to historical-comparative linguistics, as they amend the missing but essential consideration that features may also be shared between genealogically unrelated languages because representatives of speaker groups communicate not only in their dialectal continua, but also with speakers of dialects that are much less related in genealogical terms. Finally, a third basic dimension to be accounted for in research into areal clustering and the spread of innovative (or the retention of archaic) features is found in the consideration of properties of the structural organization of languages that simply occur more frequently in the world, or at least in some considerable part of it. Prior to the appearance of areal linguistics, typology pursued the endeavour of, first and foremost, uncovering unity in diversity, i.e. those structural principles which are common to all languages as well as the range of variation that is possible. Typology also aims to understand what a natural language can look like, and which properties appear to be rather incompatible with one another. This endeavour has not been abandoned but rather has been relativized by the obvious assumption that speaker communities have always communicated with one another and that diffusion across boundaries of previously different (and genealogically unrelated) languages is unavoidable and natural.[2]

Nonetheless, large-scale comparisons of which structural features and which kinds of change can be observed allow for more reliable generalizations concerning 'usualness' vs. 'rarity'. The largest possible scale is, of course, the whole world. Large-scale comparisons, however, may also be conducted on the basis of continent-wide areas. Therefore, if some dialects (languages) L_{1-n} that are unrelated in genealogical terms share a feature based on etyma with (roughly)

---

[2] Here I abstract away from language- or dialect-internal variation (homogeneous speaker communities do not exist) and secondary convergence within an already diversified dialect continuum, which can always occur. In fact, it is an open question as to whether secondary convergence between dialects of the "same" or very closely related languages (e.g., between German and Dutch, or Polish and Slovak) does not correspond to areal clusters on larger scales and between genealogically unrelated languages.

the same meaning, and the relation between this initial meaning and the shared function in L_{1-n} has hardly or not at all been attested in other regions of the world (nor in "relatives" of the languages in question), one can be quite confident that this feature has spread via contact. This is how Stolz and Stolz (2001) argue with respect to Náhuatl (Aztecan), Ch'ol (Penutian) and Zapotec (Oto-Manguic) in Mesoamerica: these languages are not genealogically closely related, but they have been spoken in contiguous areas for a long time, and all of them have developed postpositions with the meaning 'back, behind' deriving from the noun 'shoulder' in each particular language. These expressions are no cognates of each other, and the semantic evolution 'shoulder > behind' is extremely rarely attested worldwide (contrary to, e.g., 'behind' derived from other body parts like 'back'; cf. Heine and Kuteva 2000: 47–48). On this basis, Stolz and Stolz concluded that diffusion by contact is the most plausible explanation for the spread of this particular semantic and structural shift occurring in genealogically unrelated languages. For similar reasons, Koptjevskaja-Tamm and Wälchli (2001) argue for a complex contact-superposition zone in the Circum Baltic Area: there are a large number of convergences that strike the eye because they are rare, affect varieties of not too closely related languages spoken in a coherent area, and do not occur (at least not to the same extent) in closely related languages of immediately neighbouring areas. These features then most probably have spread due to contact between unrelated languages. More often than not, such convergences do not accumulate in "isogloss bundles". We cannot continue these issues in more detail here.

It has recently been debated to what extent the geographic range of an area can be decreased to become very small, like the Balkans, and apply the same quantificational methods as for large-scale comparisons (cf., for instance, Wälchli 2012). However, in any case, a crucial thing to be taken into account here is that not every feature can sensibly be assessed in areal terms if one looks for worldwide (or continent-wide) correspondences. First, some features may be restricted to (or salient in) only some part of the world (say, Europe), and within this already restricted, but still reasonably large area one again finds pockets in which deviations from this (sub)continent-wide standard can be observed. Thus, a feature that stands out against the background of a middle-scale area may seem to be "normal" if compared to a world-wide survey. To state this, though, would hinder us in concluding that, in comparison to its more immediate areal surrounding, this feature has spread among rather unrelated languages in a restricted area (set apart also from "relatives" of languages belonging to that spread zone) and thus deprive us of valuable conclusions concerning the significance of language contact. Second, in order to detect clusters (bundles of convergences) on geographically low scales, very subtle differences often have to be looked at that cannot be studied on larger scales because data are too scant (or unreliable) and the differences at hand may be irrelevant for many languages (cf. Wiemer 2004).

Briefly, in order to say that some feature F stands out, the geographic format and genealogical background against which F becomes salient must be indicated; this background, as a rule, does not comprise the whole world, and it is often more sensible to assess it in the context of considerably smaller areas. This background provides one of the two dimensions that I will refer to as 'marked' (vs. 'unmarked') linkage devices. The other dimension is a functional (semantic) and distributional one: the 'marked' member of an opposition occurs in a more restricted sort of context and/or it can often be replaced by an 'unmarked' (or 'neutral') member. I am aware of the multifaceted usage of the term 'markedness', and that it is probably a term that can eventually be supplanted by more precise and adequate terms (Haspelmath 2006). With this proviso in mind, my exploitation of this term basically follows its usage by Croft (2003), i.e. as a notion that asks for multidimensional correlations which are based on observations made on as large a number of languages (or linguistic situations) as possible. Nothing more is implied here with saying that a feature or unit is 'marked' (vs. 'neutral').

2.2 On types of language change

Most scholars would probably subscribe to the claim that contact-induced change and areal clustering start from minor usage patterns (as explained, for instance, in Heine and Kuteva 2005), or that some kind of variation for given features (on an etic level) is necessary for contact to trigger change which emerges into functionally differentiated patterns of use (as emic distinctions); these, in turn, can eventually become entrenched in a speech community as new grammatical constructions and oppositions (cf., e.g., Joseph 2013 on sound change in West Germanic and the functional re-distribution and syncretism of case in Indo-Iranian). There is no reason to assume that this basic assumption would not be valid for other structural domains, such as clause linkage and connectives, hereby including not only subordinators (conjunctions, complementizers), but also various sorts of 'particles' with scope over states of affairs or propositions. All these are so-called minor parts of speech. Particles differ from subordinators (in the traditional sense) in that they do not take part in the constituent structure of clauses, although they modify various layers of the clause (or sentence). Particles in many respects behave like other distinct words of the given language or like simple clitics (compare, e.g., Russ. *že*, Germ. *ja*, *wohl*), but they are usually not restricted to a particular position in the clause. Of course, the delimitation of particles against conjunctions and complementizers is fluctuant, but for the purposes of this paper, it is not necessary to enter into this intricate discussion.

What is essential is that particles can indicate some linkage to another clause, or utterance, and they can modify the content of an utterance in a way comparable to that of subordinators. But this way of linking pertains to a pragmatic level, not to a level of syntactic analysis. Subordinators often develop out of particles, and changes through which the latter turn into the former can only be captured in larger contexts of syntactic tightening. This process, in turn, not only is still too poorly understood, but also has too hastily been resumed under the rubric of grammaticalization.[3]

Since I do not intend to go into a principled discussion of what makes grammaticalization distinct from other types of language change, I will satisfy this topic here with just one brief remark. In a concisely written article, Lehmann (2002: 1) delimited grammaticalization from lexicalization in the following way: "A sign is lexicalized if it is withdrawn from analytic access and inventorized. On the other hand, for a sign to be grammaticalized means for it to acquire functions in the analytic formation of more comprehensive signs." Thus, lexicalization brings about irregularity and loss of internal structure so that a formerly composite unit can only be accessed holistically. On the contrary, grammaticalization requires that some unit *x* can productively be applied to other units belonging to a relatively open class *A*, and that the combination of both remains transparent. What holds true for the rise of lexical units applies to constructions as well; for, as a rule, constructions are claimed to be schemata or combinations of different units (or unit types) that can be processed only holistically. Thus, regardless of whether we conceive elements like *da, jako(by), kako* or *čto(by)* to be lexical units or units that mark some grammatically relevant function (e.g., suspension of assertiveness) within a clausal construction (or sentence frame) – and which are, for this reason, considered as "analytical mood markers" or the like – we always have to determine their place (as for a slot) in a unit of a larger format. These units would be the "more comprehensive signs" pointed out by Lehmann in the above quote.[4] Here is not the place to demonstrate that we often arrive at quite paradoxical results if we attempt to figure out more comprehensive signs for function words (in particular, for particles); what are these more comprehensive signs if not clauses or utterances to which they refer in a very loose way? The only point I want to make at present is that what I will be dealing with in the following

---

[3] Maybe one reason is that particles, conjunctions and complementizers are included under so-called 'function words', and this labelling suffices for many to regard them as products of grammaticalization.

[4] The extent to which this kind of reasoning may be transferred to different types of Construction Grammar can be left open here. At least, Lehmann himself judges this transfer skeptically (p.c.) because, among other things, there are so many different notions of what counts as a 'construction'.

is the diachronic development in both semantic (functional) and syntactic (structural) terms of a small amount of syncategorematic units, all of which operate on the level of clauses (either simple ones or their combinations). These units will be understood, first and foremost, as lexical items, and I am interested in changes of their syntactic distribution and global directions of areal diffusion. The latter will be considered mainly within Slavonic regardless of whether these units resulted from univerbation of previous simpler units or not.

After all, the question of whether these cases can be considered as instances of grammaticalization is unnecessary for the points to be made. Instead, what is really important is to demonstrate the precondition of minor usage patterns (or seemingly free variation) and the influence of factors that might have supported their evolution into structures with neat functional oppositions on the level of simple clauses and in clause linking (complex sentences).

3 Complex sentences and marking of suspended assertiveness

In the following, I will investigate three issues. First, what are the conditions for the emergence and entrenchment of complementizers that, in one way or other, mark the suspension of assertiveness in clausal complementation? Second, how are these patterns of complementation related, both systematically and diachronically, to particles serving roughly the same functions? And, third, do the patterns we observe in synchronic terms correspond to more interesting areal distributions? I will illustrate these issues with one prominent example each for the South Slavonic (Section 3) and North Slavonic regions (understanding the latter just as the conjunction of West and East Slavonic) in Section 4. Each example has common Slavonic roots, which will be surveyed first. The prominent example of South Slavonic is the general connective *da*, ubiquitous and indispensable in South Slavonic syntax (see 3.1). Its North Slavonic counterpart, though considerably less prominent (in terms of token frequency as well as of significance for discourse syntax and clause combining), is comparison markers consisting of *jako* (< CS. **jako*[5]) 'how' and an agglutinated segment *by*, which diachronically derives from the general Slavonic subjunctive marker but lost its distinct morpheme status by taking part in univerbation: *jako* + *by* > *jakoby* (see 4.2).

---

[5] In examples below, this unit will sometimes be written as *ěko* depending on the source of citation. The different spelling is due to different transliteration principles and does not reflect any difference in etymology (J. Grković-Major and P. Sobotka, p.c.).

As we will see below, both *da* and *jako* are well attested as general devices of marking some kind or other of unreal state of affairs, be it in speech acts with directive (or other non-assertive) illocutions (*da*) or as a marker of imaginative, unreal or approximative comparison (*jako*). There does not seem to be any doubt as to their diachronically primary use as particles, in the sense that neither *da*, nor *jako(by)* originally marked any sort of subordination (in structural terms) but only became integrated into clausal subordination (as conjunctions or complementizers) at later stages. Later (and contemporary) stages in which they occur as heterosemic[6] lexemes (function words) should best be treated as synchronic manifestations of layering: earlier and later usage types (or functions) co-exist because the older types did not vanish after the newer ones established themselves more firmly in the speech community.

Remarkably, regarding the second question formulated above (the correlation between synchronic distribution and diachronic pathways), a preliminary answer emerges from a global observation, namely: *jakoby* occurs (although rather infrequently and unevenly in diastratic terms) in West and East Slavonic whereas *da* is the universal marker of suspended assertiveness (or 'non-factivity') in early South Slavonic and has remained restricted to this general function in its eastern part (= Balkan Slavonic). With regard to each other, the global functional distribution of these two connectives within Slavonic seems to have reached complementary distribution. It will, thus, be of interest to learn how both *da* and *jako* (with or without *by*) were exploited in Old Church Slavonic and in the earlier stages of West and East Slavonic. To these areal considerations we may add the question of inner-Slavonic clines, which I will address at several points below.

3.1 From a demonstrative to the most ubiquitous South Slavonic connective

The history of the connective *da* in the Slavonic-speaking territory should be divided into three parts: first, its etymology (from times prior to written documentation); second, its development in Old Church Slavonic (OCS) and other ancient attested stages of Slavonic; third, its development in South Slavonic (while it practically died out or kept a very marginal status in clause linkage in North Slavonic; see 3.2). This subsection is organized according to these three parts.

---

6 On the notion of 'heterosemy' cf. Lichtenberk (1991). A related notion is 'transcategorization' as proposed in Ježek and Ramat (2009).

3.1.1 Etymological background

The etymology of *da* has been the object of some disputes. The predominant claim seems to be that *da* continues the ablative form of an IE demonstrative (*dōd.ABL), from which it developed into a kind of particle with the meaning 'from then onwards', assumed for Common Slavonic (CS; cf. Grković-Major 2004, among others). Genadieva-Mustafčieva (1970: 15) and Večerka (1993: 81, 1996: 29) considered it most likely that OCS *da* descended from an interjection, a consideration which would have parallels in other IE languages derived from IE demonstrative *t*-roots (e.g., ancient Greek δή, Lat. ***do**-nec, quan-**do***).[7] A third view was expressed by Gołąb (1984: 171). On the basis of authoritative etymological dictionaries, he argued that *da* descended from the imperative singular **dadjь!* of the Proto-Slavonic verb *dati 'give'. This etymology would neatly explain why *da*, irrespective of its syntactic status, first occurred with an optative or hortative[8] function. However, Gołąb (1984: 179) claimed that the verbal origin of *da* applied only to its use as a particle ("mood marker"), while the homonymous complementizer (his "conjunction") derived from the demonstrative pronoun (i.e. in accordance with the first hypothesis). We thus face not only the problem of alternative etymological explanations, but also and even more so reluctance (Gołąb 1984) toward explaining the complementizer-use of *da* as the result of reanalysis and generalisation (as did Grković-Major 2004; see 3.3). After all, although it may not be excluded that the pre-Slavonic history of *da* had two different sources which happened to converge (because of homonymy?) at some Proto- or Common Slavonic stage, we can safely assume that, at the time of OCS, *da* was used as **one** clitic morpheme for which any of its presumable etymological origins had become obliterated anyway. It seems justified to take the stage of OCS as the point of departure and to surmise that this stage was a sufficiently faithful manifestation of how *da* was used in a yet not very heterogeneous Slavonic-speaking dialect continuum of that period.

---

7 Večerka also considered the possibility of "elementare Sprachverwandtschaft" of an echo-lalic origin. Such a remark relates to a variety of typological tendencies as one of the "corners" in triangulation, which would be based on common articulatory preferences. This might be checked against a reasonably reliable basis (e.g., from a world-wide survey) only provided one knows the generalizable (and yet not too vague) meaning of such interjections which would serve as a *tertium comparationis*; furthermore, one would have to obtain reliable enough etymologies of the compared units in languages that undoubtedly did not have any contact among each other.
8 Consider the generally well attested path from 'give' to 'let' (e.g. in analytical causatives).

3.2 OCS: From particle to complementation and "analytic morphology"

With growing inner-Slavonic dialectal differentiation, the development of *da* in the South Slavonic territory became very different from its fate in North Slavonic. In the latter, *da* either faded away entirely (and quite early, as in Polish and Czech), or it survived almost only as a clause-initial particle or conjunction. For example, in standard Russian it has persisted as an adversative conjunction or sort of hortative marker.[9] To my knowledge, nowhere in East Slavonic has *da* acquired complementizer status, let alone become a tightly integrated component of verbal complexes, as it has in South Slavonic (see 3.3). As pointed out by Grković-Major (2004: 186–187), the general areal distribution of *da* supports the idea that West Slavonic is the most conservative (and, in fact, rudimentary) part of a former dialect continuum (since practically only particle use in the original optative meaning has been attested at best),[10] while the East Slavonic territory is intermediary in that it shows *da* at least in coordinative linkage, and only in South Slavonic has *da* evolved into a fully-fledged subordinator (and beyond that).

One cannot but emphasize that it has remained a matter of much debate as to which extent, and against which analytical basis, patterns of subordination can reliably be stated for early stages of languages. A discussion of this matter goes beyond the aims of this article. The most recent and comprehensive account of the usage of *da* in OCS is certainly comprised in Večerka's fundamental compendium of OCS syntax. I will thus rely mainly on his account.

Večerka roughly divided the usage types of *da* into three types: (i) as an optative-hortative particle (in independent clauses), (ii) as a subordinator (conjunction[11] or complementizer), (iii) as a component of periphrastic verb forms (referred to as 'analytic mood'). In the latter function, *da* always combined with the present indicative, these complex forms differed from the usual indicative by their imperative-optative meaning (Večerka 1993: 79, 1996: 65). Thus, whatever its syntactic status was, *da* transmitted its original optative meaning and marked the suspension of assertiveness. With this function as a

---

9 For more details and references cf. Mendoza (1996) and Wiemer (2017: §4.3.1).
10 It is claimed that *da* has survived in some West Slavonic dialects but, even if this is correct, the areas it is found in are scattered and the occurrences haphazard (cf. Sedláček 1970: 59; Grković-Major 2004: 186, also for more references).
11 As such, it occurred in various functions (final, consecutive, conditional, etc.). According to Genadieva-Mustafčieva (1970: 16–17), the final function was the most widespread and probably first one; it often corresponded to a Greek final infinitive construction (see fn. 16).

complementizer, it was in opposition to *jako*,[12] which did not carry a functional load like this and got lost quite early in favour of *kako* (for Old Serbian cf. Grković-Major 2004: 199); see 3.2.

Arguably, the use of *da* as a particle was diachronically primary to the two others (Wiemer 2017: §4.3). Regardless of this, the borderlines between any two of the three aforementioned functional types (i–iii) were, more often than not, difficult to determine. Consider examples such as the following. The clause introduced by *da* (and with the supine *pojatъ* 'to take') in (1) conveys a final or consecutive sense; but this does not necessarily imply that it depended structurally on the preceding clause, it can even be read as inserted direct speech with an optative or hortative meaning.[13] The same applies even after verbs denoting manipulative verbal behaviour as in (2). Optative-hortative meaning clearly emerges in (3)–(4) where *da* introduces an independent clause with the imperative.[14]

(1) i   posla   °csrъ   po   filosofa brata
     and   send[PFV].AOR.3SG   tsar.NOM.SG   for   philosopher_brother.ACC
     jego.   vъ   kozary.   **da**   pojatъ   i   sъ   soboju
     his   in   khazars.ACC   CON   take.SUP   him.ACC   with   REFL.INS
     na   pomoštь.
     on   help.ACC
     'and the tsar sent for his brother, the philosopher. to the khazars. **in order to take him with him as support.**'(VM 4; MMFH II, 142)

(2) star'ci.   naustišę   narody.   **da**
     seniors.NOM   incite[PFV].AOR.3PL   people.ACC.PL   CON
     isprosętъ   varaavǫ.
     request[PFV].PRS.3PL   PN.ACC
     'The venerable men. incited the folks. **that** they (may) ask for Barrabas.' (Mt 27:20)

---

[12] This contrast can be seen in ex. (6).
[13] This ambiguity was still noted for *da*-clauses in 14th century Serbian (Grković-Major 2004: 197). Cf. also Mladenov (1929: 308) for OCS.
[14] These examples are adduced from Večerka (1993: 80–81, 1996: 30, 2002: 395). Although *da*+imperative was quite rare in the earlier canon of texts, this collocation can be observed without doubt in younger OCS texts and in Old East Slavonic chronicles (e.g., *reče imъ Olьga. da glagolite* 'Olga said to them. may you(PL) speak'); cf. Večerka (1993: 81). Moreover, this construction can be encountered in Croatian Glagolitic documents, for instance, in certificates and other official documents ("ist im kroat.-glagol. Schrifttum, etwa auch in der Urkundensprache, nicht selten belegt"; Večerka 1996: 77). Cf. also Grković-Major (2004: 190) on Old Serbian, where *da*+imperative, in turn, is claimed to rarely have occurred.

(3) viždǫ   že   tę [...]   i   dobroličьna,   **da**
    see[IPFV].PRS.1SG PRT 2SG.ACC and educated.ACC.SG.M CON
    ubo   poslušai   mene   druže.
    PRT   listen[PFV].IMP.SG 1SG.GEN friend.VOC
    'I see you [...] and educated, **so (you should)** listen to me, friend.'
    Germ. '[...] nun, Hör mir zu!' (Su 100. 12–14)

(4) ᵒgi.   **da**   ispravi   ny   i   očisti.
    Lord.VOC PRT   improve[PFV].IMP.SG 1PL.ACC and clean[PFV].IMP.SG
    ne našichъ dělъ radi. nъ oběta tvoego radi.
    'Lord, **may** you improve and clean us. not for the sake of our matters. but for the sake of your promise.'
    Germ. 'Herr, nun!, bessere und reinige uns [...].' (K 3v 8–11)

In general, *da*-clauses with finite verbs have been considered as equivalents of infinitival complements and brought into connection with the loss of the infinitive in Balkan Slavonic. Whereas this connection is beyond doubt,[15] and whereas it seems now to be accepted that Greek was the "instigator" of infinitive loss in the Balkans (Joseph 1983), it is by no means sure as to what extent Greek influence on every bit caused an increase of *da*-clauses (at the expense of infinitival complements) in OCS and subsequent varieties of South Slavonic. Večerka (2002: 338–343) argued that Greek infinitival conjuncts were reasonably often translated by *da*-clauses in OCS and that the alleged predominance of different-subject constructions with *da*-clauses (against same-subject constructions with the infinitive) turns out to be exaggerated. In other words, no clear distribution regarding subject vs. object control constructions or same vs. different subject linkage in final clauses could be confirmed.[16] Within Old Serbian, Grković-Major (2004: 193) found a tendency toward distinguishing *da*+V_{fin} (→ different subjects) vs. *da*+INF (→ same subject) in the earliest documents, but this observation was restricted to clauses after *xotěti* 'want'. After all, the reasons for

---

15 More adequately we should say that infinitive clauses were successively ousted by *da*-structures that had already existed beforehand (Asenova 2002: 143). For comprehensive treatments cf. Mirčev (1937) and Minčeva (1985).

16 Greek infinitival complements with object control were readily ("problemlos") translated with the Slavonic infinitive or supine, but OCS avoided adjunctival infinitive constructions (e.g., the *dativus cum infinitivo*) and *nomina actionis*. When these occurred in the Greek texts, we often find them replaced with *da*-clauses in the OCS translations; this was even the rule for purpose clauses (Večerka 1997: 377). Another factor enhancing the functional range of *da*-clauses might have been the loss of participles (Genadieva-Mustafčieva 1970: 18).

an increase of *da*-clauses in different types of clause linkage must have partially been endogenic to South Slavonic. Večerka (2002: 338) claimed that the use of *da*-clauses in same-subject final clauses was "legitimate" but typical only for the South Slavonic area of late Proto-Slavonic ("nur dem südslavischen Areal des Späturslavischen eigen"). At any rate, the infinitive still belonged to the favoured categories of the verb for different types of nexus and juncture (Asenova 2002: 143, relying on Minčeva 1979: 28), while it is also known that *da*-V$_{fin}$ and infinitival complements occurred variably in different places even within identical texts (Mladenov 1929: 300).

Furthermore, '*da* + PRS.IND'-clauses were the most frequent alternative to infinitival complements after (impersonal) CTPs with a modal or irreal meaning (Večerka 1996: 107; 2002, 411–412). Compare:

(5) nevъzmožьno estъ **da** ne pridǫtъ
 impossible.N be.PRS.3SG COMP NEG come[PFV].PRS.3PL
 sъblazni.
 temptation.NOM.PL
 'It is impossible (unimaginable) **that** temptations won't arise.'
 (Lk 17:1)

(6) °gljǫ bo vamъ. ěko ešte psano
 se podobaetъ **da** sъkonьčaetъ sę o m'ně.
 REFL be_likely COMP end[PFV].PRS.3SG REFL about 1SG.LOC
 'For I am telling you. as it is written it might happen **that** it will end on me.'
 (Lk 22:37)

(7) i lěpo že ubo **da** byste carъstvovali.
 and good.N PRT PRT COMP SUBJ.2PL reign[IPFV].L-PTCP.PL
 'and it would be good **if** you (really) reigned.'
 (1 Cor 4:8)

Da was relatively infrequent in quotes (Večerka 2002: 422–423). In complement structures, its use can usually be subsumed under *oratio obliqua*, notwithstanding notorious problems in determining the borderline between direct and indirect speech (see 4.2), which, however, is only a symptom of the more general problems in determining the syntactic status (i–iii) of *da* pointed out above. Note further that, in OCS, we do not find *da*+V$_{fin}$ as a replacement of *da*+INF after modal verbs (or incipient modal auxiliaries). Thus, we encounter structures like *mogǫ*.PRS.1SG *krъstiti*.INF *sę*.REFL 'I can make myself baptized' but not something like **mogǫ*.PRS.1SG *da krъštǫ*.PRS.1SG *sę*.REFL lit. 'I can that they baptize me / I can that I make myself baptized' (Večerka 2002: 440).

3.3 South Slavonic: From subordinator to part of the verbal paradigm

The employment of *da* in auxiliary complexes with modals or phasal verbs appeared later. At any rate, it constitutes a rather late stage of *da*'s spread in the South Slavonic morphosyntax.[17] The crucial processes to comment on can be found in the analyses presented by Grickat (1975) and, first of all, by Grković-Major (2004) of Old Serbian.[18] The Štokavian (Croatian-Serbian) dialect continuum has the advantage that, until today, it shows reflexes of practically all historical stages of development in a synchronic nutshell, whereas in Macedonian and Bulgarian, the earliest stages cannot be "seen" any more since the infinitive has vanished. Moreover, the functional range of *da* in Balkan Slavonic has expanded less widely (or more slowly) than *da* has in the Northwestern part of South Slavonic along a cline of different complement-taking predicates (CTPs, see Tab. 1 below) toward those complements which are semantically less integrated. In fact, in the latter, *da* has conquered almost the entire range of CTPs, simultaneously leaving variation for different CTPs with infinitival complements (e.g., with subject control verbs), which I will however not dwell upon here. These two general observations are remarkable insofar as areal diffusion over the South Slavonic continuum has been claimed to have proceeded generally from Southeast to Northwest (Sedláček 1970). If this observation is correct, one may be inclined to conclude that the territory which was affected by this diffusion later turns out to be "faster" and more consequential in expanding the inner-Slavonic innovation (irrespective of whether and how contact with non-Slavonic varieties might have played a role). As we will see in 4.2, a more or less analogous conclusion can be drawn for 'as if'-complementizers and items associated with them.

Grković-Major accepts the viewpoint that *da* derived from a demonstrative (see 3.1). In Old Serbian (12th–15th centuries), we encounter it as a paratactic or adjunctive connective, usually with an optative, hortative or "expectative" (after 'hope' and similar verbs) function. See an example from 13th century writings ("Stare srpske povelje i pisma"), quoted from Grković-Major (2004: 198):

(8) *Da vi ni ste rekli da se stanemo.*
    PTC 2PL.NOM 1PL.DAT be.2PL say[PFV].PST.PL CON(?) REFL meet.PRS.1PL
    'Well, you told us. Let's meet!'

---

17 I have been unable to find any remark in the work of specialists that would allow us to pinpoint when *da* after modal auxiliaries became established.
18 For a summary cf. Wiemer and Hansen (2012: 80–83).

The second part (*da se stanemo* 'Let's meet!') could still be interpreted as direct speech, loosely attached to the preceding verb form *ste rekli* 'you(PL) said'. The hortative potential of *da* was compatible with one of the possible readings of the speech act verb, namely: that it was used as a directive (and not in order to introduce a report about an accomplished fact). Initially, this semantic compatibility was established on mere discourse grounds, without tighter syntax.

The subsequent development can only be interpreted as a process by which such a loose bond was strengthened as the syntactic relation between both parts was reanalysed. Certainly, this process was favoured by the implicature arising from the compatibility of a possible non-factive reading of the speech act verb and the inherent non-factive semantics of *da*. The reanalysis is schematized in Fig. 1 with the corresponding clause pair in modern Serbian (which in principle still allows for both syntactic interpretations):

(8) a. [*Ta vi ste nam rekli*]_{CLAUSE1} | [*da se sastanemo*]_{CLAUSE2}.
   (juxtaposed clauses)

   b. > [*Ta vi ste nam rekli* [*da se sastanemo*]].
   (matrix clause + complement clause)
   'Well, you told us to meet / that we should meet.'

Figure. 1: Reanalysis: juxtaposition > complementation.

Already at the beginning of the 15th century we come across examples like the following, in which *da* introduced a clausal argument of a perception verb indicating inference or even hearsay (from Grković-Major 2004: 198):

(9) | *a* | *s'di* | **ču-l-i** | | *smo* | *da* | *su* | *něki* |
|---|---|---|---|---|---|---|---|
| and | here | hear[IPFV].L-PTCP.PL | | 1PL | COMP | AUX.3PL | some.NOM |
| *naši* | | *torgovci* | *tamo* | *uběn-i.* | (1402) | | |
| our.NOM | | trader.NOM.PL | there | killed.PL | | | |

'And here **we heard that** some of our traders had been killed there.'

In such cases, the clausal argument of *čuti* 'hear' did not code the content of immediate perception (it thus did not contain just a state of affairs, SoA), but a proposition, i.e. an "object" that could be assessed in terms of the speaker's certainty ('some of our traders were killed there').[19] We do not know how regular

---

19 This interpretation was probably supported by the contrast of *s'di* 'here' vs. *tamo* 'there'. I am obliged to Barbara Sonnenhauser for drawing my attention to this detail.

such changes from immediate perception (SoA-complements) to propositional complements were at that time. Grković-Major (2004) notes that the process by which *da*-complements with finite verbs became established in Serbian lasted for several centuries. Thus, instances like (9) might have been the heralds of a continuous change, but for a long period might have also remained casual. Definitely, more research is necessary (also for other South Slavonic varieties) in order to establish the manner and speed of transitions from SoA- to propositional complements with *da*-finite clauses.

In parallel, *da* became more customary in adverbial subordination (Grković-Major 2004: 199). This process probably started with final adjunct clauses[20] before it spread to an increasing number of other clause types with *da* eventually becoming the most ubiquitous connective in South Slavonic. After reanalysis took place, further steps followed with the newly born complementizer (but not the conjunction). Already during the 14th century complement-clauses with *da* started encroaching into same-subject constructions (J. Grković-Major, p.c.). This process has not yet come to an end in our days. It is visible in the contemporary stage of Croatian-Serbian where the complement of 'want' requires a verb in present tense and only same-subject interpretation is possible. Compare (10) for older Serbian: the translation on the left of the arrow corresponds to older Serbian and the translation on the right to the modern stage:

(10) *xotehu$_i$... da skažu$_{i/k(?)}$*
 want.IMPF.3PL COMP say[PFV].PRS.3PL
 'they$_i$ wanted that they$_{i \vee k}$ say' > 'they$_i$ wanted that they$_{i/*k}$ say'
 (= 'they wanted to say')

After manipulative and desiderative verbs (see 10), *da* also entered into tight correlation with modal and tense auxiliaries as well as with phasal verbs. These steps yielded patterns of complex predicates (in monoclausal units). Such a pattern might be considered in a structuralist view as an expansion of *da* into patterns of analytical morphology. Alternatively, we may assess the participation of *da* in the formation of complex predicates as the result of expansion whereby *da* appeared in complementation patterns that rank high in terms of semantic

---

20 Grković-Major (2004: 196–197) remarked that, even in final clauses, *da* appeared rather late, i.e. not before the 13th century. Instead, *jako* had been used, and *da* only became more frequent during the 15th century; afterwards it eventually ousted *jako* (which, independently of this, seems to have been replaced by *kako*; see 4.2). These findings somewhat contradict the well-attested use of *da* as the final conjunction in OCS and subsequent stages in early Bulgarian (see 3.2). Here, too, we need a better understanding of the more fine-grained chronology of parallel changes with different clause connectives and in different subareas of South Slavonic.

integration. Semantic Integration Hierarchies (SIHs) have been proposed since Givón (1980); a recent elaborate version was presented by Cristofaro (2003: 122), reproduced here as Tab. 1:

Table 1: Complement-taking predicates and semantic integration.

Semantic Integration Hierarchy	
semantic integration:	no semantic integration:
phasals > modals > manipulatives1 ('make') > manipulatives2 ('order'), desideratives, perception	knowledge,[21] propositional attitude, utterance

From this angle, the diachronic path of expansion of *da*-clauses can be captured as an increase in syntactic tightness. In this process, biclausal patterns (as in 8 and 9) should be assumed to have been the first ones to appear (out of juxtaposition) before expansion into monoclausal patterns (i.e. sentences consisting only of one predicative core) started. In all these complementation patterns, *da* has become obligatory in the southeastern part of the South Slavonic continuum (= Balkan Slavonic) while variation with infinitival clauses increases to the northwest. By contrast, *da* can get deprived of its non-factive semantics in the northwestern part, as it is used as an epistemically neutral complementizer ('that') in Serbian, Croatian and Slovene, whereas this happens only rarely in Balkan Slavonic (see 3.4).

This, however, is not the end of the "story of *da*". In different parts of South Slavonic, we observe an even more far-reaching development, namely: the rise of epistemic particles via univerbation.[22] A prominent case in point is Mac. *mora da* 'probably, certainly'. The history of this tight collocation can be understood properly if we jointly account for three factors (cf. Wiemer 2014 for details). First, *mora* 'must' has gradually been losing verbal features, in particular agreement marking; this happened to the extent that *mora (da)* now combines with a lexical verb into a verbal complex in which the agreement features are carried by that

---

[21] This includes inferential and reportive uses of perception CTPs (e.g., *I see that he has left.*, *I hear that you passed the exam.*).
[22] Epistemic particles should probably be evaluated distinctly from the formation of complex conjunctions of which *da* forms a part (e.g., Balkan Slavonic *dali* 'if', *za da* 'in order to') and which have often been discussed in the literature on South Slavonic and Balkan linguistics (cf. Mišeska Tomić 2006, and others).

lexical verb. Second, *mora* has to be "linked" to a lexical verb by a clitic connective, and it combines with no clitic other than *da*. This process additionally enhanced the tightness of this collocation, although it applies not only to *mora* as a verb inflected for tense and agreement-categories (11a), but also as a morphologically complex modal marker (11b and 12):

(11) a. *Moram   da   dojdam   /   Moraš   da*
       must.PRS.1SG   CON   come[PFV].PRS.1SG   must.PRS.2SG   CON
       dojdaš.
       come[PFV].PRS.2SG
    b. *Mora   da   dojdam   /   dojdaš.*
       MUST   CON   come[PFV].PRS.1SG   come[PFV].PRS.2G
       'I / you must come.'

(12) *Mora   da   odea   porano   na   rabota.*
     MUST   CON   leave[IPFV].IMPF.3PL   early   to   work
     'They had to leave early for work. / Probably, they had to leave …'
     → epistemic (can be iterative)

Third, loss of agreement features is much more pronounced if the necessity modal *mora (da)* is interpreted epistemically (with a possible inferential extension). See (12) and (13); examples (11–13) by courtesy of E. Petroska:

(13) *Mora   da   doağaat.   Gi   sluša-m.*
     MUST   CON   come[IPFV].PRS.3PL   they:ACC   hear[IPFV].PRS.1SG
     'They must be coming. I can hear them.'
     (i) '(it) must be (that) they are coming.'
     (ii) 'certainly / necessarily / obviously, they are coming.'

The collocation *mora da* is on the verge of becoming an epistemic particle. A similar conclusion has been drawn by Kovačević (2009) concerning the Serbian cognate expression; we can observe an analogous process in Croatian. SCr. *bit će da / biće da* seems to be developing into an epistemic univerbation as well (Wiemer and Vrdoljak 2011: 114).[23]

---

[23] Compare these cases with Pol. *może* and Russ. (coll.) *možet* (as POSS equivalent to these NEC particles); cf. Hansen (2010). They differ, though, in that no "ex-complementizer" remains attached to them. Remarkably, this is also the case for Mac. *može*, which can occur without *da* (e.g., *Može znae* 'Maybe s/he knows', *Može doznal* 'Maybe he found out'; U. Gajdova, p.c.); cf. Wiemer (2014: 146). There is possibly some deeper reason for which NEC and POSS modals differ in morphosyntax and lexicalization patterns.

3.4 Looking more broadly: *Da* spreading into opposite directions

The increase in morphosyntactic tightness of *da*, up to univerbation with modals to form epistemic particles, is one part of *da*'s "career" in South Slavonic. The other half has recently been pinpointed by Sonnenhauser (2015). Based essentially on Grković-Major (2004), her main conclusion concerning the evolution of *da* as a complementizer amounts to saying that, in South Slavonic, *da* started from a high level of semantic integration (in OCS) and has been "working through" the SIH toward lesser semantic integration (according to Tab. 1). In the Southeastern subarea (= Balkan Slavonic), this move has stopped short with complements of perception verbs, whereas in the Northwestern part (most of the Serbo-Croatian dialect continuum and Slovene) it has gone further so that *da* can also function as an epistemically neutral complementizer (often called 'factive'). This general move is certainly correct, however, three additional facts should be remembered: first, the difference between epistemically neutral (or factive, 'that') and marked (or non-factive) use does not, as such, relate to the SIH. Once a complementizer is used with propositional complements, an epistemic modification of that proposition does not, by itself, change the degree of semantic integration with the CTP (matrix clause) because this modification operates with the same propositional content as would be contained in an epistemically neutral complement; in fact, any epistemic modification presupposes propositional content. Second, even in Bulgarian, *da* occurs rather freely (instead of *če*) after at least some negated verbs of knowledge or cognitive attitude (e.g., *Ne pomnja **da** sъm mu daval pari* 'I don't remember **that** I have given him money', *Ne mislja **da** e glupav* 'I don't think **that** he is stupid'; cited from Genadieva-Mustafčieva 1970: 22). This holds true for Macedonian as well, although the specific verbs and the frequency with *da* (vs. *deka* or *oti*) may differ.[24] And, third, *da* has also expanded into the opposite direction of the SIH since it now shows up in the domain of modals and phasal verbs, i.e. complement types that are semantically more integrated than the original types ('manipulatives2' and 'desideratives', see Tab. 1). This expansion points to higher degrees

---

[24] For instance, Mac. ?? *Ne mislam da e glupav* 'I don't think that he is stupid' sounds awkward while *Ne veruvam da e tolku glupav* 'I don't believe that he is that stupid' sounds much better. Clearly, an explanation of these rather subtle differences depending on types of CTPs would contribute to a better understanding of how complementation patterns change. This is another issue requiring more in-depth research.

of semantic integration and belongs to the first part of the "story of *da*" sketched in 3.1.3, while the former kind of (incipient?) expansion tends toward the pole of lowest semantic integration.[25]

Apart from these issues, the convergent development of epistemic modifiers (particles) in South Slavonic is noticeable especially because Bulg. *trjabva (da)* 'must' is derived from a noun (Proto-Slavonic **trěba*) meaning 'necessity, need' and only acquired verbal properties (tense and agreement marking plus the suffix {va} used to derive imperfective stems) at a later stage; this acquisition of verbal properties has nothing to do with the decline of the infinitive. On the contrary, *morati > mora (da)* 'must' has lost its originally verbal properties, and the same seems to be occurring with Croatian/Serbian *bit će (da)* 'probably, certainly': it has been turning into a petrified 3SG-form of the future of *biti* 'be' which coalesces with *da* (the latter, obviously, still being optional if the whole complex is used like a particle). This process is an indirect consequence of the retreat of the infinitive. In other words, the development of particles as markers of epistemic necessity in South Slavonic proceeded from lexical items with initially different part-of-speech characteristics. It is only indirectly connected to the retreat and loss of the infinitive, and possibly only to the extent that petrified verbal forms began to tightly collocate with *da* so that new lexical items have been arising. Note further that this development has become possible only because *da*, initially being a marker of clauses with directive or manipulative functions, developed into opposite directions on the SIH: it had to combine with modals (high degree of integration) and had to expand into the domain of propositional clausal complements (low degree of integration) since epistemic modification (judgments of certainty) presupposes propositional content. Otherwise one would have to assume that *mora da* etc. had become epistemic particles prior to their occurrence with propositional arguments (as in (12)–(13)). Such an assumption does not seem very plausible, though, since it raises more questions than it explains.

The significance of convergence in the rise of epistemic modifiers, however, becomes less spectacular if we compare the South Slavonic (and Balkan) continuum with an area of contact, both among Slavonic and between Slavonic and

---

[25] This usage is reminiscent of Russ. *čtoby* and Pol. *żeby, aby* used as marked complementizers (in contrast to *čto* and *że*) optionally after CTPs of the same semantic classes (cf. Hansen, Letuchiy, and Błaszczyk 2016: 179–186). Again, however, this marked choice is based on a dimension other than the SIH since it operates on subjective certainty concerning propositional complements. All complements on the right side of the SIH are propositional whereas none of the complements on the left side are.

non-Slavonic varieties, at another periphery of the Slavonic-speaking world. Nau (2012) showed that, in varieties spoken in the area of intimate Baltic-Slavonic contacts, epistemic particles of both necessity and possibility can be identified as a convergent feature if one describes them by eight joint system-building principles. I do not see how such a consistent system of principles can be deduced for equivalent units in the Balkans since they are too scattered.

4 North Slavonic 'as if'-complementation

The Slavonic source expressions of comparison markers are CS. *kako and *jako. The former was originally an interrogative marker (cognate with Lat. *qualis*), the latter probably derived from IE. *j*-stem (relative or anaphoric) pronouns. An exclamative origin (with the Latin cognate *ecco*) has also been considered, but is less plausible (cf. ĖSSJa 1981: 171; ESJaS 1995: 268; Večerka 2002: 178). Although in Proto- and Common Slavonic both expressions were probably customary over the whole Slavonic territory, their functions later got mixed up. Eventually, *kako* became generalized in South and East Slavonic,[26] while in West Slavonic, to the contrary, *jako* took over the usage domains of *kako*. In other words: *jako* and *kako* enchroached into each other's domains and, thus, ousted each other in complementary subregions of Slavonic.

The units we will be dealing with now are etymological continuations of *jako* in North Slavonic whose development is judged from a time when *kako* presumably had become obsolete and *jako* took over its functions in West Slavonic. Remarks on *kako* will be inserted only in passing and no systematic comparison with *jako* is intended.

4.1 *Jako(že)* in OCS

The functional range of *jako* was extremely broad (or rather: vague). It occurred as a general connective (particle, adverb, conjunction and an emergent complementizer) and often in connection with other particles leaning on *jako* as enclitics (cf. Večerka 2002: 28 et passim for some remarks on that account). Among these,

---

[26] In South Slavonic, *kako* co-occurred with *da* for a considerable time (for Old Serbian cf. Grković-Major 2004, for Macedonian Bužarovska 2006 and Gjurkova 2008: 118, for Middle Bulgarian up to the 20th century Sonnenhauser 2015).

že, by and *da* seem to have figured prominently, and in some cases such combinations (*jako*+enclitic) became lexicalized via univerbation, with *jakoby* being just one of these items (see 4.3.2). According to Večerka (1996: 124; 2002: 265–266, 268, 273–278), *jako* was also used in OCS as a general marker of approximation (often with merged *-že* and following *i: jako(že) i*). It seems that this marker was capable of modifying units even on a propositional level ('as if X did S') and it was employed to link secondary predicates to the main predicate (Večerka 1993: 233; 2002: 268–269, 276–278). Otherwise, its scope differed greatly: *jako* could not only modify argument-NPs or numerals (e.g., Lk 1:56: *prěbystъ že mariě sъ nejǫ ěko i tri °mscę* 'Mary spent **about** three months with her'), but also introduced whole clauses with propositional content. *Jako* was the most usual complementizer of declarative clauses (Večerka 2002: 393). Večerka (2002: 266) remarked that *jako(že) i* increased over time and testified to the frequent usage in the spoken language of that time. He also claimed, however, that this usage was influenced by Byzantine Greek models (ὡς καί, καθὸς καί) as might have been the case for *jako da* as a final conjunction modelled on Greek ὡς ἵνα (Večerka 1997: 364). As difficult as such claims are to substantiate,[27] if sustainable, they would supply a nice example of how internal resources and external models can support and amplify each other.

Večerka (1996: 124) also adduced cases in which a clause described a situation that was judged by the author (= metaspeaker) as unreal (14), or the clause introduced by *jako* specifies the content of another person's utterance (15). For clarification I will provide the parallel quotations from the Old Czech Bible (*Biblie Královská*) and from Luther's translation into early New High German as they were supplied by Večerka; note that the German equivalents contain the subjunctive:

(14) i   bystъ.   ěko   i   mrъtvъ
    and   be.AOR.3SG   COMP   PRT   dead.NOM.SG.M
    'and he was **like** dead / **as if** he were dead'
    (Mk 9:26)
    OCz.   *I učiněn jest člověk ten **jako** mrtvý.*
    Luther, NHG   *Und er ward, **als** wäre er todt.*

---

27 Bláhová (2008: 57–58) reported that *jakože* was very infrequent in translation equivalents of Greek infinitival clauses.

(15) tъ   oklevetanъ   bystъ   kъ   nemu.
    3SG.NOM.M   slandered.NOM.SG.M   be.AOR.3SG   to   him.DAT
    ěko   rastačaj-ę   iměnьě   ego.
    COMP(?)   waste[IPFV].PPRSACT:NOM.SG.M   wealth.ACC.N his
    'He was defamed (because people said) to him. **that / as though** he was wasting his wealth.'
    (Lk 16:1)
    OCz.   ten obžalován jest před nim, **jako** by mrhal statek jeho.[28]
    Luther, NHG der ward vor ihm berüchtigt, **als** hätte er ihm seine Gütter umgebracht.

It is remarkable that *jako* here already occurred with propositional clauses that were marked as syntactically embedded (see the participial predicate *rastačaję* 'wasting' in ex. 15). This circumstance can be considered as a clear indication of *jako* already being able to function as a complementizer at that time.[29] Note that proving this with a (morphologically) finite predicate in the clause introduced by *jako* (as in the Old Czech translation) is much more troublesome (on Old Polish see 4.3.2).

As a complementizer, *jako* appeared after certain predicatives with nominal morphology like *(j)avě / vědomo (jestъ)*, *jako* '(it is) evident / known **that** [lit. *how*]', or *vědomo bo jestъ jako samъ stvori °mtrъ* 'for it is known **that** he himself created the mother' (Bes 25, 162aβ 17 sq).[30] No doubt is conveyed here, although the fact that the metaspeaker has based his assertion on (seemingly) accepted knowledge does not make it improbable that he distanced himself from conveyed knowledge, wanting to remain epistemically "agnostic". The question remains open, however, as to whether *jako* served as a signal of epistemic distance (in the latter sense) in such cases or fulfilled the function of a neutral complementizer (void of any meaning connotations). After all, Večerka (2002: 393) identified *jako* as the most usual complementizer of embedded declarative clauses ("in den deklarativen Inhaltssätzen das weitaus gebräuchlichste *jako*").[31] One wonders whether this statement implies that *jako* stripped off

---

[28] Note that, in this translation, Old Czech *jako* occurred with the enclitic *by* still used as a real subjunctive marker. In OCS, *jako(že)* + subjunctive (*by, bi*) was encountered only as an exception (Večerka 2002: 278).

[29] Such instances have to be distinguished from cases in which *jako* introduced propositional clauses but served as a conjunction (adverbial subordinator). Compare, for example: *načǫšǫ °glati iněmi ǫzyky. jako °dchъ daaše imъ prověštavati* 'They started speaking in other languages. **as if / since** (?) the spirit let them preach' (Ap 2, 4; Ochr.; cited after Večerka 2002: 268).

[30] Quoted from Večerka (1996: 117), see there for further comments.

[31] Compare also Večerka (2002: 416) on reported speech complements and (2002: 420) on *jako* introducing direct speech (cf. also Gjurkova 2008: 115–117).

connotations which might have connected it to earlier usage types; regardless, its epistemically neutral character did, of course, not exclude compatibility with epistemically modalized complements. The fact that *jako* must have been able to introduce reported speech and other complement clauses without any epistemic distance can be inferred from examples like the following; after predicates denoting declarative speech acts or perceptual events in the first person present indicative, or after *věděti* 'know' (cited from Večerka 2002: 394–395):

(16) sъvěděteľъstvuemъ.   **ěko**   °ось   posla
     testify[IPFV].PRS.1PL COMP father.NOM send[PFV].AOR.3SG
     °sna   svoego.
     son.ACC   POSS.ACC.SG.M
     'we testify that the Father sent His Son.'
     (Jn 4:14)

(17) °gi   viždǫ   **ěko**   prorokъ
     Lord.VOC see[IPFV].PRS.1SG COMP prophet.NOM
     esi   ty.
     be.PRS.2SG you(SG).NOM
     'Lord, I see **that** you are the prophet.'
     (Jn 4:19)

(18) vědętъ   bo [...]   **jakože** vъ   gradě   ni
     know[IPFV].PRS.3PL because COMP   in   town.LOC NEG
     smoky   bǫdetъ.   ni   dǫbъ   nikakъže.
     fig_tree.NOM.PL be.FUT.3SG NEG oak.NOM.SG no_way
     'Because they know **that** in the town there won't be any fig or oak (tree).'
     (Su 301, 9–12)

Note further that, in OCS, *jako(že)* not only occurred clause-initially, so that it could be interpreted as a conjunction or complementizer, but also was used as a particle. Večerka (2002: 275) adduces an example in which *jakože* occurs within direct speech:

(19) rekošę   že   voini.   my   **jakože**
     say[PFV].AOR.3PL PRT soldier.NOM.PL 1PL.NOM as_though
     izmrъli   běchomъ   sъnomъ.   onъ   že
     exhausted.NOM.PL be.IMPF.1PL sleep.INS he.NOM PRT
     bъdě.
     keep_vigil.PRS.3SG
     'The soldiers said: (while) we were exhausted (and lying) **as though** in a sleep, he kept (lit. keeps) vigilant.'
     (Su 79. 15–17)

This brings us to the much debated issue of connectives in direct and indirect speech, a borderline which admittedly happens to be difficult to draw. First of all, *jako(že)* not only occurs **within** direct speech (as in ex. 19), but also in clauses introducing direct speech (Večerka 2002: 281). In many cases, it cannot be established with certainty whether *jako* belongs to the matrix clause and, as it were, cataphorically refers to the clause to follow, or rather introduces that clause as a complementizer. See an example cited from Daiber (2009: 367):[32]

(20) *Mužь   někto [...]   pověda*
     man.NOM.SG   some.NOM.SG   tell[IPFV].AOR.3SG
     *glagol-ę   **jako**   něcyi   °o   strany*
     say[IPFV].PPRSACT:NOM.SG.M   COMP (?)   some.NOM.PL   from   side.GEN
     sikileiski   korablemъ   iděaxu   vъ   rimъ.
     Sicilian.GEN   ship.INS   go[IPFV].IMPF.3PL   in   Rome.ACC
     'A certain man told a story and said **that** some people from Sicily went on ship to Rome.'
     (GdG 170a 17–22)

The problem in determining clause boundaries (and their possible reanalysis) is reminiscent of the history of 'that'-complementizers in Germanic languages (cf. Diessel 1999: 123–125 for a summary). If this parallel is adequate, we would have confirmation of polygenetic sources of clausal complementation rooted in syntactic reanalysis, for which the role of contact might have played a minor or no role.

Many scholars have pondered whether the appearance of *jako* as a marker (complementizer?) of direct or indirect speech was due to Greek influence (via the Bible translation), and it has been further doubted whether *jako* can be judged as "organic" to early Slavonic (cf., for instance, Collins 1996: 34). Daiber (2009: 366–367) was certainly right in taking a critical stance toward such assumptions about the "imported" nature of *jako*. In the end, however, neither position can be proved or disproved. Moreover, we have to account for the impact of typically oral features of speech which can be transferred into written patterns of speech reports (among other types of clause linkage) at any time in any sufficiently diversified speech community.[33] From this angle, if *jako* was of exclamative origin,

---

[32] This syntactic ambiguity showed up systematically (Daiber 2009).
[33] Gjurkova (2008: 117) seems to have just this in mind when she connects *jako*'s purported exclamative origin with a "mixing of direct and indirect speech", regardless in which of the involved languages. Greek-Slavonic bilingualism might have had an impact on spoken habits, but one can only speculate about the direction of influence (from written to oral communication or vice versa).

this "oral trait" would have further favoured its inclusion in emergent patterns of clausal complementation in young stages of written traditions; additionally, after such clause linking devices are entrenched, older patterns based in spoken language habits can exist further, which would result in layering.

It has been accepted that *jako* continued to exist in East Slavonic as a complementizer for reported speech up to more or less the 17th century when it was replaced by *čto* (cf. Bulaxovskij 1958: 416, whose findings have been reiterated by other scholars). However, the fate of *jako* appears to have split from the development of *jakoby* considerably earlier than that, and the problem of distinguishing direct (quoted) from indirect (reported) speech[34] does not appear that markedly for *jakoby*, in part perhaps because quotations obviously played a minor role in its evolution in both Russian and Polish.

Before we continue with the development of *jakoby* in North Slavonic (4.3), let me comment on its closest parallel in South Slavonic.

4.2 *Kako* in South Slavonic

The history of *kako* cannot be depicted here for the entire South Slavonic area. I will, therefore, restrict myself mainly to Macedonian and compare it with the remaining territory only in passing. The major difference between Macedonian and, for instance, Croatian-Serbian apparently lies in the fact that *kako* has evolved into a complementizer in Macedonian while, in Croatian-Serbian, it has been attested in adverbial subordination, i.e. as a conjunction for final clauses (B. Hansen, p.c.). This holds true for Old Serbian as well where a final *kako* often implied a consecutive nuance (J. Grković-Major, p.c., after Pavlović 2009: 292–294).

As concerns the oldest attested stages of South Slavonic, *kako*, in contrast to *jako*, was closely associated with verbs of perception. Consequently, it occurred in other types of complement clauses, predominantly those which denoted events unfolding simultaneously with a perceptual event (cf. Večerka 2002: 396, 404; Gjurkova 2008: 112 for examples). This would imply that *kako*-complements coded SoAs. Apart from that, *kako* was used for secondary predicates ("prädikative Supplemente"), i.e. in a function close to relative clauses (Večerka 2002: 414, with examples).

---

[34] Cf. Daiber (2009) for a more elaborate discussion of methodological pitfalls in that domain and retracing Bulaxovskij's aforementioned finding in later works (2009: 364–366).

In younger stages of South Slavonic, particularly in Macedonian, *kako da* has gone through a path of semantic evolution schematized by Bužarovska (2006) in the following way

[1] hypothetical similarity > appearance > epistemic/inferential.

Evidently, South Slavonic *kako da* constitutes the combination of a general comparison marker (*kako*) with a general marker of suspended assertiveness (*da*, as analysed in 3.1). Bužarovska (2006: §3) regarded *kako da* as a successor of *jako da*, which, in turn, might have been a calque (structural borrowing) from Greek (see 4.1). This functional development is very close to West Slavonic *jakoby* and its Russian cognate (see 4.3), which, again, is an exact equivalent of *kako da* in terms of its "ingredients" with *jako* coding the comparison relation and *by* the suspension of assertiveness. Both items can be captured as the results of univerbation (which seems to be still in flux in Macedonian, Czech and Slovak; see below), depicted in [2] (see 4.3.2). However, from Bužarovska's analysis one can infer that Mac. *kako da* functions as a complementizer only after perceptual or appearance verbs ('behave', 'seem'; see 21); otherwise it is sort of a "comparison connector", i.e. an 'as if'-conjunction, (22), or a particle, (23):

(21) *Toj   se   odnesuva   kako da   znae*
     he.NOM   REFL   behave[IPFV].PRS.3SG as_if   know[IPFV].PRS.3SG
     sè.
     everything
     'He behaves **as if** he knows everything.'

(22) *Popot   go   razgleduvaše   kako da   e*
     priest.DEF_NOM he.ACC look[IPFV].IMPF.3SG   as_if   be.PRS.3SG
     živa igračka.
     live toy
     'The priest looked at him **as if** he were a live toy.'

(23) *Ti   kako   nešto   da   misliš.*
     you(SG).NOM as   something   CON   think[IPFV].PRS.2SG
     'You look **like** you are thinking about something.'

Note that *kako da* can be disrupted both as a particle, see (23), and as a subordinator. At first sight, this fact indicates that *kako da* has not yet become a new holistic unit. However, this morphotactic behaviour is rather caused by strict rules pertaining to proclitics, of which *da* is one; it is debatable to what extent discontinuative use can be considered *per se* as an indicator of incomplete univerbation.[35]

---

[35] For an argument concerning analogous behaviour of Mac. *mora da* cf. Wiemer (2014: 155–156).

Irrespective of this, *kako da* has not developed further into a complementizer of CTPs situated on the right ('semantically non-integrated') side of Tab. 1.

Similar remarks hold true for the Croatian-Serbian cognate unit *kao da*, which can be used as a particle (also clause-initially) or subordinator with the meaning 'as if'; as such, it is restricted to verbs referring either to behaviour or to perception (I. Vrdoljak, p.c.).[36] Whether *kao da* can be disrupted (as can Mac. *kako da*) in any usage type, and whether there are other subtle differences in comparison to its Macedonian cognate, has yet to be established in further research. In general, the systematic investigation of the functional range, contemporary behaviour and diachronic rise of 'as if'-units in South Slavonic constitutes another huge desideratum. For the time being, we can state that Mac. *kako da* and Croat. *kao da* very closely correspond to Czech and Slovak 'as if'-units, although they are composed of different etyma in both their syntactic behaviour and their functional range (see 4.3).

4.3 *Jako + by > jakoby* in North Slavonic

In order to gain an impression of how variation in cognate 'as if'-units in the most recent stages of North Slavonic languages mirrors their diachronic development, let me start this subsection with a West Slavonic survey in reversed chronological order (4.3.1). This will be followed by a summary of facts known about *jakoby*'s evolution in Polish (4.3.2) and Russian (4.3.3).

4.3.1 The latest stages in West Slavonic

Jędrzejowski and Schenner (2013) argue that in modern Polish the complementizer *jakoby* is no longer interpreted as a hypothetical comparative conjunction *as if*, but rather as a hearsay complementizer (= *that + allegedly*). In particular, the authors show that Pol. *jakoby* cannot be used to embed clauses under perceptual CTPs or a SEEM-verb anymore; see their constructed example:

(24) **Firmie   wydaje   się   jakoby ...*
     company.DAT   seem[IPFV].PRS.3SG   REFL   as_if
     intended: 'It seems to the company **as if** ...'

---

[36] Compare, for instance, *On se ponaša kao da ništa ne zna* 'He behaves **as if** he didn't know anything' (complementizer), *Plakao je kao da je dete* 'He cried **as if** he were a child' (conjunction; example by courtesy of B. Hansen), *Kao da sam čuo nešto o tome* '**It seems**, I've heard something about that' (clause-initial particle).

This restriction must, however, be rather recent since *jakoby* still occurred after perception and DREAM-verbs until the end of the 19th century. At least such examples from the belles-lêttres like the following one from Orzeszkowa's novel "Nad Niemnem" (1888) can still be found:

(25) *Przeszłej nocy* **śniło** *mu się,* **jakoby**
  last night.GEN dream[IPFV].PST.3SG.N him.DAT REFL as_if
  gruszki z drzewa rwał.
  'Last night **he dreamt as though** he plucked pears from a tree.'

Today such usage sounds old-fashioned, and informants would not use *jakoby* after the aforementioned types of CTPs anymore. We can, however, still observe this earlier stage in active use in Czech, (26a), and Slovak, (27a), where, in turn, the reportive function, predominant in modern Polish,[37] proves to be barred, (26b), (27b):

Czech

(26) a. *Zdálo se,* **jako by** *byl opilý*
  seem[IPFV].PST.3SG.N REFL
  'It seemed **as though** he were drunk.'
  b. **Firma popřela,* **jako by** *byly nahlášeny*
  company.NOM deny[PFV].PST.3SG.F
  jakékoliv vadné karty
  intended: 'The company denied **that** there were reports about any faulty cards.'

Slovak

(27) a. *Zdá sa* **ako by** *svadby stávali*
  seem[PFV].PRS.3SG REFL
  vždy väčšími a vydarenejšími
  'It seems **as if** weddings became bigger and more eccentric.'
  b. **Firma popriela* **akoby** *boli oznánenia*
  company.NOM deny[PFV].PST.3SG.F
  chybných kariet
  intended: 'The company denied **that** there were reports about any faulty cards.'

---

[37] It would, however, be an exaggeration to claim that Pol. *jakoby* has become entirely restricted to reportive meanings and that, in particular, no inferential function exists anymore (cf. Wiemer 2015: 220–223).

These examples are quoted according to Jędrzejowski and Schenner (2013). The patterns touched upon by them are confirmed by other sources. Actually, as a complementizer, Slovak *akoby* occurs with verbs of appearance ('seem', 'look like'), but does not introduce complements of verbs denoting epistemic attitudes or speech acts:[38]

(28) *Vyzerá   to,   **ako   by**   to*
     look[IPFV].PRS.3SG DEM.SG.N how   SUBJ   this.ACC.N
     urobila   naschvál.
     make[PFV].PST.3SG.F   intentionally
     'It seems **as though** she did it intentionally.'

(29) *Vidí   sa   mi,   **ako   by**   v   tom*
     see[IPFV].PRS.3SG REFL   1SG.DAT how   SUBJ   in   this.LOC
     mali   prsty   Sovieti.
     have:PST.PL   fingers.ACC   Soviets.NOM
     'It seems to me **as though** it was the Soviets who had their fingers in this.'

In fact, *ako by* is still thought of as "composed" from the comparative *ako* plus the subjunctive marker *by*. This is reflected in orthography (disjoint writing) and applies to *ako by* as a HOW-complementizer, too:

(30) *Neviem,   **ako   by**   som   sa*
     NEG-know[IPFV].PRS.1SG   how   SUBJ   AUX.PRS.1SG   REFL
     čo najľahšie   dostal   na stanicu.
     most_easily   get[PFV].PST.3SG.M
     'I don't know **how** I **might** get myself most easily to the railway station.'

Otherwise *akoby* occurs as a conjunction with an approximative meaning ('as if, as though'):

(31) *Cítil **som** v srdci,*
     ktoré   mocne   bilo,   akoby
     RELPRON:NOM.SG.N   heavily strike:IPFV.PST.3SG.N   as_if
     chcelo   vyletieť   mi z pŕs ...
     want:PST.3SG.N   fly_out[PFV].INF
     'I felt in my heart, which beat heavily **as if** it wanted to fly out of my breast ...'
     (Ctibor Štítnický)

---

[38] If not indicated otherwise, the Slovak examples are taken from the Slovak National Corpus (by courtesy of M. Ivanová).

In this function, *akoby* is written together, as it is if used as a particle with the same approximative meaning 'as though':[39]

(32) No   Matej   **akoby**   ťa   odmietol
     but   PN.NOM   as_though   2SG.ACC   refuse[PFV].PST.3SG.M
     brať   na vedomie.
     take[IPFV].INF   in consciousness
     'But Matej **as though** refused to take you into account.'
     (M. Dzvoník)

This stage is reflected also for Czech. Dictionaries of the 19th and 20th centuries only register the comparison use for contexts in which Cz. *jakoby* can be regarded as a subordinator or a particle. The following examples from entries on *jako* and *jakoby* in Kott (1878: 596–597) illustrate this:

(33) Mlčí,   **jakoby**   mu   ústa
     keep_quiet[IPFV].PRS.3SG   as_if   him.DAT   mouth.PL.ACC
     zašil.
     sew_up[PFV].PST.3SG.M
     lit. 'He is keeping quiet **as if** you sewed up his mouth.'

(34) **Jakoby**   kámen   do   vody   uvrhl.
     as_though   stone.ACC.SG.M to   water.GEN   throw[PFV].PST.3SG.M
     '(It is) **as though** someone had thrown a stone into water.'

(35) Jest   mladý   ještě   muž   a   **jakoby**
     be.PRS.3SG   young.NOM.SG.M   yet   man.NOM.SG   and   as_if
     zrozen   k   úřadu   svému.
     born.NOM.SG.M   to   appointment.DAT.SG.M   REFLPOSS.DAT.SG.M
     'He is yet a young man and, **as it were**, born for what his appointment requires from him.'

Similarly, as for the contemporary stage, PSJČ (1935–37/I: 1161) and SSJČ (1960/I: 758) only adduce *jako(by)* in such contexts. MČ (1987/III: 514, 520–521) refers to *jako* and *jakoby* as complementizers after perception verbs, often with an implication of pretence (e.g., *I cítí,* **jako by** *ji někdo vzal za ruku* 'And she feels **as if** somebody took her at her hand').[40]

---

[39] Cf. Pauliny, Ružička, and Štolc (1968: 322), Horecký (1994) and the entries on *akoby* in http://slovniky.juls.savba.sk/.
[40] Characteristically, *jakoby* is claimed to require the subjunctive ('kondicionál') regardless of whether it is written jointly or disjointedly with *by*.

In summary, Czech *jakoby* and Slovak *akoby/ako by* have remained in a stage which pretty much resembles *jakoby* in 14th–16th century Polish (Wiemer 2015). Unfortunately, as far as I have been able to learn, no research has been conducted on the diachronic development of Cz. *jakoby* / Slov. *akoby*, so our knowledge about these languages is even worse than for the Polish cognate, to which we now turn.

4.3.2 Development in Polish

The later development of Pol. *jakoby* has recently been accounted for by Jędrzejowski and Schenner (2013). Wiemer (2008: 363–368) articulated some considerations concerning the more recent development of Pol. *jakoby* and its Russian cognate *jàkoby*, and Wiemer (2015) gave a first account of the earliest periods of *jakoby*'s development based on the respective entries in SłStar and SłXVI (end of 14th–end of 16th century). From these pieces of research, an idea can be formed about how *jako+by* > *jakoby* has been evolving in functional terms. It could even be possible to make conjectures regarding correlations between *jakoby*'s functional development and its syntactic distribution in the major part of West Slavonic and in Russian. In what follows here and in 4.3.3, I provide a summary of these few existing studies, to which the reader is referred for further details.

Jakoby resulted from the agglutination of the initially subjunctive marker *by* to the general comparison unit *jako* 'how, like'. *By* had survived as the 3SG-remnant of the aorist of *byti* > *być* 'be':

[2] *jako* + *by* (= 'be'.SUBJ < 3SG.AOR) > *jakoby* → univerbation
(= new lexical unit)

The aorist had become extinct in times prior to the first written documents appearing in Polish (end of 14th century).[41] The question of whether *by* began to isolate from its aorist-paradigm, and thus to petrify, already in OCS need not concern us here since the process schematized in [2] implied that *by* was already considerably isolated from its former paradigm. However, the etymological provenance of both *jako* and *by* remained transparent through almost

---

41 It appears that the agglutination process behind this change was not ultimately finished by that oldest period. We may infer this from the fact that, in quite a few examples and in particular the SłXVI devoted to a later period, other enclitics interfere between *jako* and *by*, above all -*że*/-*ż* (yielding *jako-ż-by* etc.).

the entire period represented in SłStar and SłXVI inasmuch as the combination of 'how'(*jako*)+'non-factive'(*by*), written also disjointedly, is visible saliently through most of the examples.

From the end of the 14th to the end of the 16th century, *jakoby* was used as a general indicator of comparison with virtually any sort of entity whose reality was judged as illusory, doubtful or even false;[42] virtually any sort of syntactic unit could occur in its syntactic scope (indicated by square brackets). The marking of manner of action clearly predominated, as shown in the next example:

(36) *Myly   Iesus   potem   schedl [...]   kv   szvyątemv*
     dear   Jesus.NOM   then   go[IPFV].PST.3SG.M   to   holy
     *dnyv   nye   yavnye,   alye   **yakoby***
     day.DAT   NEG   publicly   but   as_if
     [potayejmnye]   (compare Latin *sed quasi in occulto*).
     secretly
     'Then dear Jesus went [...] toward the holy day not in an obvious manner, but **as though** [secretly].'
     (SłStar; Rozm 431)

Although in many instances *jakoby* could be interpreted with semantic scope comprising a proposition, this wide semantic scope more often than not remained implicit; compare (37):

(37) *Kazaly   zvyązacz   mylego Iesusa   povrozmy ...,*
     order[PFV].PST.3PL   bind[PFV].INF   dear Jesus.ACC   rope.INS.PL
     ***yakoby**   [zlodzyeya].*
     as_if   thief.ACC
     'They ordered to bind dear Jesus with ties, **as if** he were [a thief].'
     (SłStar; Rozm 744)

Note that such contexts could serve as "bridges" from comparison marking to a more pronounced propositional marking because the phrase comprised by *jakoby* could be read as reflecting the metaspeaker's emotional, and thus subjective, distance to the content which was contrasted to the proposition outside of *jakoby*'s scope. Whether or not such contexts were really interpreted in this way cannot be established firsthand. Further research, however, might be able to find a method that would provide a reliable answer to this question. Remarkably, however, no clear signs of an incipient epistemic function arose when *jakoby* served as an

---

[42] In both SłStar and SłXVI, *jakoby* often occurred as the translational equivalent of Lat. *quasi*, *velut* or *tanquam*. See ex. (36).

adverbial subordinator (conjunction), even if the clause that it headed contained a proposition. As a rule, these were final clauses; compare:

(38) Ony   mvsa   szye   troszkacz   o   tho,
     they.NOM   must.PRS.3PL   REFL   care[IPFV].INF for   that
     aby   taky ortel   wydaly,   **yakoby**
     COMP_IRR   such_order.ACC   issue[PFV].PST.3PL   in_order_to
     szwey   przysządze   dosycz   vczynyly.
     REFLPOSS.DAT.SG.F   VOW.DAT.SG.F enough   make[PFV].PST.3PL
     lit. 'They have to take care that they issue such an order, **in order to** comply with their vow.'
     (StStar; OrtKał 185)

Final clauses might have been ambiguous with manner clauses, and they are tightly associated with complements of desiderative CTPs and CTPs with complements embedding directive speech acts ('in order to'). In all these functions, complements with finite modal auxiliaries figured quite prominently; compare an example with a manner reading:

(39) Nye   vyem,   y<a>kobychmy   y   mogly
     NEG   know[IPFV].PRS.1SG   COMP.SUBJ.1PL   him.ACC   can.PST.3PL
     zataycz.
     hide[PFV].INF
     'I don't know **how** we could hide him.'
     (StStar; Rozm 588)

The quite frequent occurrence of modal auxiliaries as finite heads of clausal complements makes one inclined to assume that they created another door-opener for *jakoby*-complements to become propositional clauses. Until the end of the 16th century, the majority of *jakoby*-clauses attested by the dictionaries were not about facts; instead, virtually all of them are about the **manner** of performing an action. Evidently, during that period, *jakoby* still functioned not as a 'that/if'-complementizer, but as a 'how'-complementizer.

A remarkable difference between *jakoby* in the 15th–16th century and in contemporary usage lies in its enormous increase as an adnominal complementizer. This usage was still infrequent throughout the 16th century:

(40) Gdy   **nowiná,**   **iákoby**   zeiść
     when   news.NOM.SG.F   as_if   pass_away[PFV].INF
     miał   z   świátá,   przyſzłá.
     have:PST.3SG.M   from   world.GEN   arrive[PFV].PST.3SG.F
     'When the **news as if** he had passed away arrived.'
     (StXVI; CiekPotr 1 (4))

As Tab. 2 illustrates, the overall frequency of complements to nominal attachment sites in the 16th century was 2.9% (compared to 21.3% as a complementizer with verbal attachment sites), while a pilot study conducted on contemporary data from the NKJP yielded 19.4% (with nominal attachment sites) compared to 12% (with verbal attachment sites). If only complementizer-tokens are taken into consideration, we see that the proportions between nominal and verbal attachment sites of *jakoby* as a complementizer have almost inverted, i.e. *jakoby* has become significantly more frequent as an adnominal complementizer (chi-square test, df = 1, p << .001).

Table 2: Relation of adverbal vs. adnominal complementation for Pol. *jakoby*.

	16th century		20th–21st centuries	
adverbal	1,206 (21.3%)	87.9%	59 (12%)	38.3%
adnominal	166 (2.9%)	12.1%	95 (19.4%)	61.7%
sum	1,372 (24.2%)	100% for all complementizers	154 (31%)	100% for all complementizers
jointly against all *jakoby*-tokens	5,671 (100%)		490 (100%)	

Moreover, in the 16th century, complementizer use only slightly outweighed conjunction use (24.2% compared to 19.3% for all 5,671 tokens). By the 20th century, however, the use as an adverbial subordinator vanished altogether (for details cf. Wiemer 2015: 282–290). Evidential uses were still unattested by the end of the 16th century, and reportive use must have arisen considerably later. On the basis of Jędrzejowski and Schenner (2013), it could be possible to infer that an increase in the use as an evidential complementizer (after suitable CTPs) did not occur before the 19th century, but then must have happened rapidly. Moreover, the door to the reportive and inferential domain seems to have been through nominal attachment sites, possibly independently of particle use. The latter has been persisting since Old Polish, but it is difficult to tell established meaning apart from contextually triggered epistemic or even evidential implicatures. It is also difficult to determine when *jakoby* as a particle really marked inferences or hearsay instead of serving as a hedge expression, which can equally be derived from its original comparison function. Finally, as already mentioned, *jakoby* must have only quite recently started losing its original comparative function (which has largely been taken over by *jakby*).

4.3.3 *Jakoby* in Russian

How the cognate unit *jàkoby* (stressed on the first syllable with vowel reduction on the following one) found its way into Russian must still be clarified. It could have been borrowed (rather late) from Polish, and such provenance can be argued for because of the high coverage of identical evidential functions and because we can plausibly detect a common pathway (see below) in the development of Pol. *jakoby* and Russ. *jàkoby* over the past 200 years. Alternatively, *jàkoby* might be a Church Slavonicism of an older age in view of the fact that, as a comparison marker, *jako* (or *ako*) appeared as a Slavonicism from the time of the oldest East Slavonic documents throughout the history of Russian until recent times. In particular, it was used as a sign to mark off quoted speech (Molotkov 1962: 179–189), which closely resembled the so-called '*jako* recitativum' in OCS (Daiber 2009). We also have to take into account the fact that *jakoby* does not exist in contemporary Ukrainian (at least as far as the western variants are concerned; Lj. Popović, p.c.); however, *jako* (without *by*) is used instead of *kako*. These facts might demonstrate that the spread of *jakoby* was also a matter of diastratic (not only diatopic) diversification. In addition, we cannot exclude the possibility that for *jàkoby*, as it has developed since the 18th century, both historical sources (Polish and South Slavonic) "merged" to yield the unit we know from 19th–21st century Russian. For, among other things, both East Slavonic *jako+by* and Pol. *jakoby* (more precisely: either of the components *jako* and *by*) are derived from the same Common Slavonic source and subsequently have shown a very similar functional (syntactic and semantic) development. This similarity, which may have evolved in parallel in different parts of the Slavonic-speaking world, could have supported convergent factors jointly establishing *jàkoby* in Russian by (or during) the 18th century. However, which of these factors (or their joint impact) was decisive can only, at best, be clarified after thorough philological work.

Despite this, the univerbation process, as schematized in [2], seems to have only occurred by the 17th century, and – as with Pol. *jakoby* in the 14th–16th centuries – *jako+by* written disjointedly can still be encountered in many instances even in the 18th century. By that time, the unit *jako+by* occurred as a syntactically versatile marker of unreal or approximate comparison with syntactic scope over units of virtually any format, similar to the function of Pol. *jakoby* (see 4.3.2). The use of *jàkoby* as a final and manner conjunction obviously preceded its exploitation as a complementizer, and we encounter the same diagnostic problems with regard to delimiting its particle functions as we do for Pol. *jakoby*.

Since the late 17th century, *jako+by* appeared after verbs denoting speech acts or cognitive attitudes, thereby emerging as an inferential or reportive complementizer, as in (41):

(41) ne   mni (...),   **jako by**   nam
     NEG   think[IPFV].IMP.SG   COMP.SUBJ   1PL.DAT
     otverščisja   istinnaja vera Xristova.
     open[PFV].AOR.3SG-REFL
     'Don't think **as though** Christ's true faith has revealed itself before us.'
     (Širokova 1966: 144, cited after Neumann 2013: 13)

In the late 18th century, *jakoby* occurred with more or less equal frequency as a comparison and a reportive marker (either as complementizer or as particle). A noticeable difference in comparison to Pol. *jakoby* is that instances in which a clausal complement introduced by *jàkoby* contains a modal auxiliary appear to have been very infrequent at all times.

A significant change in the semantic motivation of *jakoby* manifested itself during the 18th century. Like its Polish "cousin", as long as the functional load of the "subjunctive particle" *by* in Russ. *jàkoby* remained transparent, this unit required a finite verb in its clause to take the past tense form (*l*-participle). However, by the middle of the 18th century, *jàkoby* as a complementizer allowed for clauses with predicates other than in the past tense (*l*-form); compare ex. (41) and an example cited from Neumann (2013: 35):

(42) [...] moi nedobroxoty [...] predstavili na menja Pravitel'stvu,
     jakoby   ja [...]   **rešu**   vse   dela
     as_if   1SG.NOM   decide[PFV].PRS/FUT.1SG   all.ACC   matters.ACC
     protivno gosudarstvennym uzakonenijam [...].
     '[...] my enemies presented the Government with facts (testimonies, documents?) **that I will decide** on all matters against the laws of the state.'
     (Krylov: "Počta duxov")

This testifies to a partial loss of etymological motivation: the component *by* no longer required the finite verb to appear with the *l*-suffix (= past tense marker). Instead, relative time reference could be indicated by a **free** choice of tense markers. Simultaneously, the initial comparative function started getting lost as well.[43] Both facts show that Russ. *jàkoby* differs markedly from its Polish cognate.

---

[43] *Jàkoby* with NPs in the original comparative function is now exceptional and judged as archaic, no less than its Polish cognate. For instance, *Čerez minutu, izmennym golosom,* **jakoby** *barina:* "..." 'A minute later, with an altered voice, **as if** of a landowner: ...'. Instead, *budto* 'as if' or *kak by* 'as though' would be expected in modern usage.

It does not seem implausible to assume that both processes have evolved in parallel with other changes not observed for Pol. *jakoby*. By the mid-19th century, the use of Russ. *jàkoby* as a complementizer dropped drastically, and there were hardly any more instances of it as a conjunction. From among 98 examples analysed for the period 1840–1870 (from the Russian National Corpus), Neumann (2013: 47–50) registered only 13 cases as a complementizer and three as a conjunction. The remaining cases (84%) showed *jakoby* as a particle. From the semantic point of view, this change was paralleled by a dramatic decrease of the comparison function (12 cases) compared to an enormous increase of the reportive function (64 cases); inferential meaning was registered only 16 times. Both trends continued in the subsequent periods. It thus appears that the tendency toward particle use correlated with a growing restriction in favour of the reportive meaning; the change in syntactic distribution went hand in hand with a narrowing of semantic functions.

By 1920, *jakoby* became extremely rare as a subordinator (Neumann 2013: 83) and has now been ousted from this use, being employed only as a particle (Wiemer 2008: 363–368). As such, it conveys an epistemic "overtone" which is at once stronger than with Pol. *jakoby* and differs from the latter also in that it is a stable (conventionalized) component, i.e. cannot be cancelled by the context (Plungjan 2008: 305; Wiemer and Socka 2017: 88–89). Certainly this meaning component was inherent to *jakoby*-units for all their attested history in Russian (as well as in Polish) and can be considered as "inherited" from the original meaning of irreal comparison. Whether, however, it could always be regarded as a stable component (and when it conventionalized) in Russ. *jàkoby*, is an issue open for in-depth research.

To summarise, regardless of whether modern Russ. *jàkoby* really goes back to a Polish loan, or at least was influenced by Pol. *jakoby* since the 18th century, it has outdistanced its Polish cognate in that it changed more rapidly both in syntactic and semantic terms. It has been restricted (again) to particle use after it, as it were, had run through a circle of subordinator functions, and it has not only dissociated entirely from its initial comparison meaning, but has also even been restricted to reportive use; inferential use has become obsolete.

4.4 *Jakoby*: Knitting the threads together

Evidently, contemporary Czech and Slovak reflect an archaic stage whereas Polish and Russian demonstrate a much more advanced stage in which *jakoby* has undoubtedly become an evidential marker (with epistemic overtones that are cancellable for Polish) and lost its former function as a comparison marker.

Fig. 2 is intended to provide a schematic survey of the functional (semantic) and structural (syntactic) development of the cognate units in North Slavonic. It should be "read" in the following way: the historical development goes from left to right; the small arrows (>) indicate succession. FUNCTIONS relate to the purported path in terms of semantics; SYNTACTIC STATUS captures the distribution in terms of minor word classes (so-called function words). The rounded boxes housing 'complementizer' and 'particle' are meant to show how long their status has been stretching from their appearance until the present day. In fact, particle use is primary and can reasonably be assumed to have never ceased to exist, while complementizer use started with appropriate predicates able to take clausal complements. Arguably, complementizer use was preceded by the use of *jakoby* as a conjunction in diverse types of adverbial subordination, but primarily in hypothetical comparison clauses, in final clauses, and in directive clauses. It died out later (we don't know when), but complementizer use has persisted in Polish until now, whereas it has become obsolete in Russian and *jàkoby* now occurs only as a particle and has almost entirely lost its function as a comparison marker. Regardless of this, the inferential function seems to have existed for both Pol. *jakoby* and its Russian cognate only as a complementizer under suitable predicates (namely, denoting cognitive attitudes); the same applies (rather trivially) to its use after perceptual predicates able to take clausal complements. Thus, in general, the movement toward reportive use seems to correlate with a tendency toward particle use, which, however, has not led to ousting Pol. *jakoby*

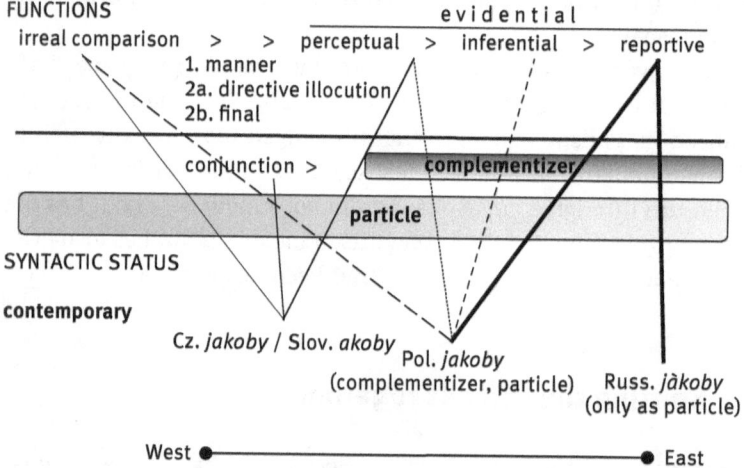

Figure 2: Outline of the development of *jakoby* in North Slavonic.

as a complementizer. The dotted, thin solid and thicker solid lines roughly indicate increasing degrees of association.

In a sense, thus, Russ. *jàkoby* proves to be more innovative than Pol. *jakoby*, irrespective of what the correct explanation for its appearance and maintenance in Russian might turn out to be. Polish, in turn, is much more innovative than its south(west)ern neighbours within West Slavonic: Czech and Slovak appear to have preserved a state of *jakoby / akoby* which is reminiscent of the earliest attestations in Polish. We are tempted to conclude that the Slovak and Czech units have never changed, but should be careful to do so since, at the very least, we lack a reliable analysis of material from earlier periods. Regardless, the contemporary picture nicely illustrates how an inner-Slavonic areal cline (from (south) west to (north)east) correlates with stages of diachronic development. The big caveat which we have to have in mind is that regardless of when *jàkoby* entered into Russian, or its predecessors (and what helped entrench it in the speech community), it might have been an "import" alien to folk speech. This import, again, was restricted to inner-Slavonic contacts, non-Slavonic models that might have been replicated by either of the Slavonic languages discussed here need not be asked for. But note also that, in East Slavonic, *jàkoby* does not occur anywhere other than in the Russian standard language; this unit is practically unknown in Ukrainian (although jako is *used*). This shows that we have to account for the diastratic dimension as well.

Continuing with areal considerations, we might wonder whether the inner-North Slavonic cline sketched above can be inscribed into any larger cline. As I am unable to give a comprehensive answer to this question at present, let me add a few remarks which make one inclined to give an affirmative answer to this question, at least as far as the connection with languages west from West Slavonic, i.e. Germanic, is concerned. For example, Engl. *as if, as though* and *like* have been developing into complementizers after verbs of appearance and perception. See three examples from López-Couso and Méndez-Naya (2012: 174, 182–183):

(43) *It seemed **as though** she were always auditioning.*
(Brown F09)

(44) *The landlord, a plump and harassed man named Barry, looked **as if** he had spent too much time enjoying his own product.*
(FLOB A33)

(45) *I told her that I'd had to take these tablets and that's why I felt **like** I wasn't thinking properly.*
(DCPSE: DI-A13)

Among other things, López-Couso and Méndez-Naya (2012), who looked at different corpora of several varieties of contemporary and historical English, emphasized that "all the predicates selecting *as if*, *as though*, and *like* complements in our data belong to the group of Propositional Attitude Predicates" (2012: 183). This is tantamount to saying that the complement contains a proposition (and not just a SoA). In so saying, it should be noted that the attitude reading becomes possible only because the complement codes not so much the description of a perceptual event, but rather an inference made by the speaker of the utterance. This inference does not proceed further to any other domain related to evidentiality; in particular, the aforementioned English 'as if'-units – as far as one can conclude to date – are not used after CTPs denoting speech acts; nor do they occur as adnominal complementizers (cf. also López-Couso and Méndez-Naya 2015 and p.c.). Similar remarks can be made with respect to Germ. *als ob* 'as if'. Thus, from the side of the Germanic neighbours to Slavonic (from the west), the evolution of 'as if'-units into complementation has proceeded to a considerably lesser extent than it has in Polish and Russian; and the two Germanic languages show pretty much the same picture as West Slavonic (except Polish) and South Slavonic do, although for the latter language groups much more research is necessary (see the remarks on Macedonian and Croatian-Serbian in 4.2).

Furthermore, to my knowledge, in English and German 'as if'-units are rather unknown as particles (with the exception of Engl. *like*). This might be interpreted as an indication that the history of 'as if'-units in Germanic and Slavonic differed radically as far as the onset of such a development is concerned: as shown above, the initiators of the development with Slavonic *jakoby*-units are most probably particles, and whenever they became established in clausal subordination they must have started from there. If, thus, for the evolution of 'as if'-units we notice an areal cluster comprising English, German, Czech and Slovak, from which Polish has "split off", this small zone of Germanic-West Slavonic convergence probably rests on developmental stages at which these units started being used as adverbial subordinators and complementizers after perceptual, 'behave' and 'pretence' verbs, but not more than that (considering movement on the SIH toward lesser integration).

Looking now in the opposite geographic direction, namely towards the Baltic area, we notice that 'as if '-units of different etymological provenance have long been on their way to becoming complementizers. Only some of these units, however, also occur after verbs other than of appearance or perception, namely after CTPs denoting propositional attitudes or speech acts. All of them are of different etymological origin. Latv. *it kā* 'as if', Lith. *esą* 'as though, as if; allegedly', and *lyg* 'like' and questionable *neva* belong to this group.⁴⁴ Only Lith. *lyg* etymologically derives from a comparison meaning (compare the adjective *lyg-us* 'even; equal' and the verb *lyg-ti* 'be equal, of equal power/quality').

In summary, Polish and Russian, together with Baltic, as it were, in between, turn out to be languages with (emergent or established) complementizers that arguably specialize in some evidential domain, in particular the reportive one. In Russian, the relevant 'as if'-unit (*jàkoby*) has become obsolete as a complementizer and largely been supplanted by *budto*-units. All relevant evidential complementizers in Polish, Russian and Baltic are heterosemic with particles; they differ among each other regarding the extent to which epistemic overtones can be suppressed. This, however, is certainly a general feature requiring more accurate modelling on the pragmatics-semantics interface (Wiemer and Socka 2017). Therefore, we feel justified in posing the question of whether Polish and the territory to the northeast might not be considered as a tiny, but distinctive spread zone of evidential complementizers; for we do not find any parallel in South Slavonic or the area southwest from Polish (protracting into remaining West Slavonic and Germanic) where 'as if'-units (or functionally equivalent units) have developed into complementizers to some extent, but not in the evidential domain; even inferential functions have only evolved to a limited extent (as with Engl. *as if, as though, like*).

In terms of triangulation, this interim result means that genealogical considerations cannot explain why this small area comprises languages of two groups (Slavonic and Baltic), but not the closest "relatives" of Polish and Russian, respectively. These relatives, however, show less advanced (and earlier) stages of the same evolution; these stages can, in turn, be evinced in languages of another group, namely Germanic (English, German). The natural conclusion to be drawn here is that we might be dealing with an inner-(North)Slavonic diffusion triggered by some specific types of contact, which still have to be established, all the more as this contact gains a diastratic dimension (as concerns Russ. *jàkoby*). Finally, the fact that English 'as if'-units demonstrate a similar development into complementizers of complements with propositional status leads one to believe that this kind of functional (syntactic and semantic) development is polygenetic, i.e. occurs spontaneously in languages that are comparatively unrelated

---

44 Compare with the likewise questionable Pol. *niby* (Wiemer 2006: 45–48). For details and references concerning the mentioned units cf. Wiemer (2010: 291–294) and Holvoet (2016), who gives a comprehensive account of complementation in Baltic and discusses many borderline cases of complementizers, to which all the units which I have mentioned here belong.

in areal and/or genealogical terms. The big caveat to hold in mind here is that 'as if'-units, as such, have been investigated very poorly on a European-wide (let alone a world-wide) scale, so that it is time to conduct case studies guided by methodologically impeccable principles in order to achieve an empirically reliable picture.

5 Preliminary conclusions and postulates

Let me now summarize the most essential findings concerning areal spread and chronology.

As elaborated on in 3.4, South Slavonic *da* appears to have experienced an expansion through the SIH into two opposite directions. On the one hand, it moved into tighter types of clause combination ending up with auxiliary and phasal verb complexes; on the other hand, it became established with propositional complements after cognitive CTPs with an epistemic restriction (less than full certainty). As concerns the latter direction, the functional evolution of *da* somehow resembles later stages of expansion along the SIH of *jakoby* in North Slavonic (see 4.2). Admittedly, the usage of the latter after negated epistemic attitude CTPs (or epistemic CTPs with a lexically inherent meaning of doubt) has meanwhile been ousted by Russ. *čtoby* entirely and by Pol. *żeby*, *aby* to a large extent. This replacement, however, belongs to a later period. In view of these parallels in the initial stages, it would be intriguing to learn whether the later stages, i.e. the expansion of complementizers from the domain of volitive-desiderative complements into the domain of propositional complements (with an effect of epistemic or evaluative distance) in South Slavonic (with *da*) proceeded along the same lines as *jakoby* and other 'as if'-units in North Slavonic did. There is no reason to assume that South and North Slavonic influenced each other to any extent, so that South Slavonic *da* and North Slavonic 'as if'-units must have developed in parallel, but independently from each other. In North Slavonic, this development has been obliterated by the fact that *jakoby*'s functions in clausal complementation have largely (Polish) or entirely (Russian) been replaced by other units, whereas for South Slavonic *da* the functional range and significance in morphosyntax has tremendously increased. This expansion has affected the "tighter" (monoclausal) end of the SIH to a larger extent than its "looser" end (biclausal, with propositional complements).

Curiously (and incidentally), inner-Slavonic clines in South and North Slavonic run into opposite geographic directions insofar as we account for functions of *da* and *jakoby*. Whereas *jakoby* in North Slavonic shows a cline from southwest (Czech) as the most conservative region to northeast (Russian) as the most innovative one (see 4.2), South Slavonic *da* shows a cline from Balkan Slavonic in the southeast, which in functional terms seems to be more conservative, toward the northwest (Slovene), where more "innovative" loss of original features of *da* can be observed since the former restriction to non-factive complements is dropped.

The investigation presented here is just a pilot study; it is fragmentary and requires detailed research into many specific questions and "holes" in geographic, diastratic and diachronic terms. If, on this preliminary basis, one wants to subsume findings and formulate guidelines for further research, the following should be said: the common heritage of functional lexemes (clitic or free morphemes) in both North and South Slavonic obviously supplied a favourable ground for similar developments in both functional and structural terms but with a complementary geographic distribution (*da*-based constructions and units in the South, *jako*-based units and constructions in the North). At later stages – roughly, after these units had expanded into clausal complementation, in particular with propositional complements – their lines of evolution began to differ: although both *da*- and *jako*-based units partook in the rise of modal particles (thus, in lexicalization via univerbation and petrification), only *da* has either become part of "analytic morphology" (in Balkan Slavonic) or has continuously been acquiring properties of a neutral, or "all-purpose", complementizer (in Serbian-Croatian). Contrastingly, *jako*-based units have either been supplanted as complementizers of propositional clauses (with a firm residuum in Polish) or have remained in a stage not surpassing the stage of PRETENCE- and SEEM-verbs (in the rest of West Slavonic).

I have hardly scraped the surface of the issue of contact with non-Slavonic varieties. Regarding *da*, though, it has often been stated that its pervasive "career" in South Slavonic has to be judged within the context of general features common to languages associated to the so-called Balkan League (cf. Sedláček 1970; Mišeska Tomić 2006, among many others). The basis for this claim seems to be self-evident for specialists in Balkan languages – to an extent that one wonders whether those investigating "Balkanisms" might not have forgotten about complementation patterns as an outstanding areal feature arisen and entrenched by mutual contact influence. Despite this, the concrete diachronic steps and their relation to functional explanations, such as those based on the SIH, still wait for an empirically thorough and systematic investigation. Turning to North Slavonic, the question remains as to whether any non-Slavonic influence can be attested in that area in the domain of clausal complementation, in particular for 'as if'-units, in a similar way as this has been assumed with respect to South Slavonic *da*. The picture I have been able to uncover suggests that the area with a highly advanced development of 'as if'-units is, firstly, very restricted geographically and, secondly, probably developed (and pertains to exist) on a diastractically smaller basis than *da* in South Slavonic did since, even in Polish and Russian, *jakoby* is predominantly known to educated speakers. Regardless, *jakoby* is a property of standard speech (in a very restricted number of specific contexts) and not of dialects. Irrespective of this proviso, the case studies conducted in the main body of this article should have demonstrated that it is not only (and often not so much) contact with non-Slavonic varieties, but also inner-Slavonic contact that contributes to areal diffusion. This holds true particularly if, during some earlier period, Slavonic dialects (and other varieties) had dissimilated from each other before, at a later stage, some element or structure protrudes from one subarea and varieties into other varieties of the same or contiguous areas. As for the cases considered here, *jakoby* seems to show this even more prominently than *da*.

Last but not least, a remark is due concerning the relation between spoken language and habits introduced by writing traditions, which I mentioned in passing in 4.1. This relation, which to some extent intersects with diastratic differentiation, has also been considered with respect to South Slavonic *da*. Večerka (1997: 364) wrote: "The Byzantine spoken language situation may have accelerated the spread of OCS conjunction constructions with *da*, modelled on popular Greek constructions with ἵνα, esp. in main imperative clauses (as a translation equivalent of the Standard Greek imperative or subjunctive) and in expressing hypothetical modality." Since attempts to reconstruct oral Slavonic speech prior and simultaneously to the appearance of OCS – and of understanding how Slavonic-speaking populations construed reports on other people's speech acts or other kinds of clause linkage even after the introduction of this first written form of Slavonic – are rather senseless, there seems to be only one thing that we can do in order to diminish speculation. One can try to specify the probability with which clausal complementation (in particular as a means of reported or quoted speech) emerges in different places and at different times, i.e. one can try to develop more reliable tools to produce probability judgments concerning the polygenesis of the chosen phenomenon assuming fundamental principles of cognition and communication. Such principles are inherently assumed in discussions on typical (or even universal) features of vernaculars (vis-à-vis more standardized and/or written varieties), as are assumptions related to the Uniformitarian Hypothesis claiming that spontaneous speech of all people at all times has been guided by the same cognitive and communicative needs (Labov 1972: 275). An understanding of the polygenesis of clause linkage (in particular of the appearance of complementation indicated by complementizers) would enhance the chance of gaining a better assessment of how probable it is that patterns of clause linkage arise spontaneously. The correctness of a hypothesis (internal development vs. external influence) can never be assured entirely, and probability scenarios that are derived from an empirically verified picture about the occurrence of clause linkage (in particular, complementation) patterns in the world's languages and, more specifically, in the closer surrounds of the language under investigation for the particular time period at hand must suffice. After all, on the basis of a solid probabilistic model, it would be inadequate to claim that "spontaneous" development and influence via contact are mutually exclusive. Rather, some "conspiracy" between both should realistically be assumed[45] as has also been postulated by Kuteva and Heine (2012). After all, since replacements – or shifts in preferred usage patterns – do not occur overnight, and since they rest on the expansion of previously existing minor patterns, the proportions of co-occurring marking devices (including lack of marking) must be quantified. Therefore, no meaningful assertion about triangulation (or any other procedure by which different factors are weighed against each other) can be sufficient without quantification using reliable stochastic methods.

Acknowledgments

I am obliged to Martina Ivanová (Slovak), Veronika Kampf, Petar Kehajov (Bulgarian), Eleni Bužarovska, Liljana Mitkovska (Macedonian), Ivana Vrdoljak (Croatian), Ljudmila Popović (Ukrainian) for their help as informed native speakers, to Piotr Sobotka for etymological information, and an anonymous reviewer for pointing out some minor mistakes. I also want to thank Barbara Sonnenhauser and María José López-Couso for their cooperative sharing of recent papers and exchange of thoughts on particular issues dealt with in this paper. I want to also thank all three volume editors for their helpful remarks made on the first version of this article. Of course, the usual disclaimers apply.

---

45 Independently of all these considerations, the possibility always exists that the increase (and areal diffusion) of a pattern in the replica language departs from the usage (functional range) of its purported model and may even "supersede" the latter. Thus, Daiber (2009: 381) remarked that the inner-Slavonic development of *jako recitativum* led (at least in some medieval texts) to mark direct speech with no claim as to verbatim quotation ("direkte Rede ohne Anspruch auf wörtliche Zitation"), and he mentioned that this development cannot be explained by a Greek model (assumed by many). However, this, in turn, does not give us any substantial hint as to whether *jako* was introduced into Slavonic (OCS) only due to Greek influence or not. A similar remark would be appropriate for the development of *jakoby* in Russian, which – regardless of whether its immediate source is a Polish or an older South Slavonic one – has evidently developed faster than its Polish cognate (see 4.3.3).

List of abbreviations

1, 2, 3	first, second, third person
ACC	accusative
AOR	aorist
AUX	tense auxiliary
COMP	complementizer
CON	connective (without specification of level of juncture)
DAT	dative
DEM	demonstrative
DEF_NOM	definite article (nominative)
F	feminine
FUT	future
GEN	genitive
IMPF	imperfect
INF	infinitive
INS	instrumental
IPFV	imperfective
LOC	locative
L-PTCP	l-participle
M	masculine
MUST	indeclinable 'must'
N	neuter
NEG	negation
NOM	nominative
PFV	perfective
PN	proper name
PPRSACT	participle present active
PRS	present
PST	past
PRT	particle
REFL	reflexive marker
REFLPOSS	reflexive possessive pronoun (inflected)
RELPRON	relative pronoun
SUBJ	subjunctive
SUP	supine
VOC	vocative

References

Asenova, Petja. 2002. *Balkansko ezikoznanie. Osnovni problem na balkanskija ezikov săjuz* [Balkan linguistics. Basic problems of the Balkan Sprachbund]. Veliko Tărnovo: Faber.

Bláhová, Emilie. 2008. K překladu řeckých infinitivních konstrukcí v staroslověnském apoštolu [On the translation of infinitival constructions in the Old Church Slavonic Apostle]. In Ilona Janyšková & Helena Karlíková (eds.), *Varia Slavica. Sborník příspěvků k 80. narozeninám Radoslava Večerky.* [Varia Slavica. Festschrift on the occasion of the 80th birthday of Radoslav Večerka], 53–64. Praha: Nakladatelství Lidové noviny.

Bulaxovskij, Leonid A. 1958. *Istoričeskij kommentarij k russkomu literaturnomu jazyku* [Historical comment on the Russian standard language], 5th edn. Kiev: Radjans'ka škola.

Bužarovska, Eleni. 2006. Pathways of semantic change: From similarity marker to sensory evidential. *Slavia meridionalis. Studia linguistica et balcanistica* 6. 185–311.

Collins, Daniel. E. 1996. The pragmatics of indirect speech in Old Church Slavonic and other early Slavic writings. *Studies in Slavic and General Linguistics* 23. 21–86.

Cristofaro, Sonia. 2003. *Subordination*. Oxford: Oxford University Press.

Croft, William. 2003. *Typology and universals*, 2nd edn. Cambridge: Cambridge University Press.

Daiber, Thomas. 2009. Direkte Rede im Russisch-Kirchenslavischen (Zum pragmatischen Wert des *jako recitativum*). In Juliane Besters-Dilger & Achim Rabus (eds.), *Text – Sprache – Grammatik. Slavisches Schrifttum der Vormoderne. Festschrift für Eckhard Weiher*, 363–386. München & Berlin: Sagner.

Diessel, Holger. 1999. *Demonstratives: Form, function, and grammaticalization*. Amsterdam & Philadelphia: Benjamins.

ESJaS: Havlová, Eva (ed.). 1995. *Etymologický slovník jazyka staroslověnského*, t. 5 [Etymological dictionary of Old Church Slavonic, vol. 5]. Praha: Academia.

ĖSSJa: Trubačev, Oleg N. (ed.). 1981. *Ėtimologičeskij slovar' slavjanskix jazykov, praslavjanskij leksičeskij fond*, vyp. 8 [Etymological dictionary of Slavonic languages, Proto-Slavonic lexical inventory, vol. 8]. Moskva: Nauka.

Genadieva-Mustafčieva, Zara. 1970. *Podčinitelnijat săjuz da v săvremennija bălgarski ezik* [The subordinate conjunction *da* in contemporary Bulgarian]. Sofija: Izdatelstvo na Bălgarskata akademija na naukite.

Givón, Talmy. 1980. The binding hierarchy and the typology of complements. *Studies in Language* 4. 333–377.

Gołąb, Zbigniew. 1984. South Slavic *da* + indicative in conditional clauses and its general linguistic implications. In Kot K. Shangriladze & Erica W. Townsend (eds.), *Papers for the V. Congress of Southeast European Studies (Belgrade, Sept. 1984)*, 170–198. Columbus, Ohio: Slavica Publishers.

Grickat, Irena. 1975. *Studije iz istorije srpskohrvatskog jezika* [Studies from the history of the Serbo-Croatian language]. Beograd: Narodna biblioteka Srbije.

Grković-Major [Grković-Mejdžor], Jasmina. 2004. Razvoj hipotaktičkog *da* u starosrpskom jeziku [Development of the hypotactic *da* in Old Serbian]. *Zbornik Matice srpske za filologiju i lingvistiku* 47 (1–2). 185–203.

Gjurkova, Aleksandra. 2008. *Sintaksa na složenata rečenica vo makedonskite crkovnoslovenski rakopisi* [Syntax of the compound sentence in Macedonian Church Slavonic manuscripts]. Skopje: Institut za makedonski jazik "Krste Misirkov".

Hansen, Björn. 2010. Constructional aspects of the rise of epistemic sentence adverbs in Russian. In Björn Hansen & Jasmina Grković-Major (eds.), *Diachronic Slavonic syntax. Gradual changes in focus* (Wiener Slawistischer Almanach – Sonderband 74), 75–87. München, Berlin & Wien: Otto Sagner.

Hansen, Björn, Alexander Letuchiy & Izabela Błaszczyk. 2016. Complementizers in Slavonic (Russian, Polish, and Bulgarian). In Petar Kehayov & Kasper Boye (eds.), *Complementizer semantics in European languages*, 175–223. Amsterdam & Philadelphia: Benjamins.

Haspelmath, Martin. 2006. Against markedness (and what to replace it with). *Journal of Linguistics* 42 (1). 25–70.

Heine, Bernd & Tania Kuteva. 2000. *World lexicon of grammaticalization*. Cambridge: Cambridge University Press.

Heine, Bernd & Tania Kuteva. 2005. *Language contact and grammatical change*. Cambridge: Cambridge University Press.

Holvoet, Axel. 2016. Semantic functions of complementizers in Baltic. In Petar Kehayov & Kasper Boye (eds.), *Complementizer semantics in European languages*, 225–264. Amsterdam & Philadelphia: Benjamins.

Horecký, Ján. 1994. O spojení *ako by* a spojke *akoby* [On the connector *ako by* and the conjunction *akoby*]. *Kultúra slova* 28 (6). 354–355.

Ježek, Elisabetta & Paolo Ramat. 2009. On parts-of-speech transcategorization. *Folia Linguistica* 43 (2). 391–416.

Jędrzejowski, Łukasz & Mathias Schenner. 2013. From an inferential C to a reportative C: The case of evidential *jakoby* clauses in Polish. Handout of talk delivered at the 21st International Conference on Historical Linguistics. Workshop New Insights into the Syntax and Semantics of Complementation, University of Oslo, 5–9 August.

Joseph, Brian D. 1983. *The synchrony and diachrony of the Balkan infinitive: A study in areal, general, and historical linguistics*. Cambridge: Cambridge University Press.

Joseph, Brian D. 2013. Demystifying drift: A variationist account. In Martine Robbeets & Hubert Cuyckens (eds.), *Shared grammaticalization. With special focus on the Transeurasian languages*, 43–65. Amsterdam & Philadelphia: Benjamins.

Koptjevskaja-Tamm, Maria & Bernhard Wälchli. 2001. The Circum-Baltic languages: An areal-typological approach. In Östen Dahl & Maria Koptjevskaja-Tamm (eds.), *The Circum-Baltic languages. Typology and contact. Vol. 2: Grammar and typology*, 615–761. Amsterdam & Philadelphia: Benjamins.

Kott, František Št. 1878. *Česko-německý slovník zvláště grammaticko-fraseologický, díl první: A-M* [Czech-German dictionary, particularly grammatical-phraseological, part one: A–M]. Praha: J. Kolář.

Kovačević, Miloš. 2009. Je li glagolski oblik *mora* uvijek glagol? [Is the verbal form *mora* always a verb?]. *Radovi Filozofskog Fakulteta* (Istočno Sarajevo) 10 (1). 35–47.

Kuteva, Tania & Bernd Heine. 2012. An integrative model of grammaticalization. In Björn Wiemer, Bernhard Wälchli & Björn Hansen (eds.), *Grammatical replication and borrowability in language contact*, 159–190. Berlin & Boston: De Gruyter Mouton.

Labov, William. 1972. *Sociolinguistic patterns*. Philadelphia: University of Pennsylvania Press.

Lehmann, Christian. 2002. New reflections on grammaticalization and lexicalization. In Ilse Wischer & Gabriele Diewald (eds.), *New reflections on grammaticalization*, 1–18. Amsterdam & Philadelphia: John Benjamins.

Lichtenberk, František. 1991. Semantic change and heterosemy in grammaticalization. *Language* 67. 475–509.

López-Couso, María & Belén Méndez-Naya. 2012. On the use of *as if*, *as though*, and *like* in present-day English complementation structures. *Journal of English Linguistics* 40 (2). 172–195.

López-Couso, María & Belén Méndez-Naya. 2015. Secondary grammaticalization in clause combining: From adverbial subordination to complementation in English. *Language Sciences* 47. 188–198.

Mendoza, Imke. 1996. *Zur Koordination im Russischen: i, a, da als pragmatische Konnektoren*. München: Sagner.

Minčeva, Angelina. 1979. Typologische Bedeutung der Balkanismen in den altbulgarischen Denkmälern. Linguistique *Balkanique* XXII. 19–34.

Minčeva, Angelina. 1985. Za xaraktera na konkurencijata meždu infinitiv i *da*-izrečenija v starobălgarskite pametnici [On the character of the competition between infinitive and *da*-clauses in the Old Church Slavonic monuments]. In Johannes Reinhart (ed.), *Litterae Slavicae Mediaevi. Francisco Venceslao Mareš Sexagenario Oblatae*, 211–221. München: Verlag Otto Sagner.

Mirčev, Kiril. 1937. Kăm istorijata na infinitivnata forma v bălgarskija ezik [On the history of the infinitive form in Bulgarian]. *Godišnik na Sofijskija universitet. Istoriko-filologičeski fakultet* XXXIII (12). 3–34.

Mišeska Tomić, Olga. 2006. *Balkan Sprachbund morpho-syntactic features*. Dordrecht: Springer.

Mladenov, Stefan. 1929. *Geschichte der bulgarischen Sprache*. Berlin & Leipzig: De Gruyter & Co.

Molotkov, Aleksandr I. 1962. Osobye sintaksičeskie konstrukcii dlja peredači čužoj reči v drevnerusskom jazyke [Special syntactic constructions for conveying reported speech in Old Russian]. *Issledovanija po grammatike russkogo jazyka* III [Investigations on Russian grammar III] (= *Učenye zapiski Leningradskogo gosudarstvennogo universiteta* 302, 61 (3)). 162–192. Leningrad: Izdatel'stvo Leningradskogo gosudarstvennogo universiteta.

Nau, Nicole. 2012. Modality in an areal context: The case of a Latgalian dialect. In Björn Wiemer, Bernhard Wälchli & Björn Hansen (eds.), *Grammatical replication and borrowability in language contact*, 465–508. Berlin & Boston: De Gruyter Mouton.

Neumann, Jasmin. 2013. *Funktionale Veränderungen bei jakoby und budto im Russischen der letzten 250 Jahre (eine korpusbasierte Studie)*. Mainz: Johannes Gutenberg-Universität Mainz MA thesis.

Olson, Wendy K. 2004. Triangulation in social research: Qualitative and quantitative methods can really be mixed. *Developments in Sociology* 20. 103–121.

Pauliny, Eugen, Jozef Ružička & Jozef Štolc. 1968. *Slovenská gramatika* [Slovak grammar], 5th edn. Bratislava: Slovenské pedagogické nakladateľstvo.

Pavlović, Slobodan. 2009. *Starosrpska zavisna rečenica od XII do XV veka* [The Old Serbian dependent clause from the 12th to the 15th century]. Sremski Karlovci & Novi Sad: Izdavačka Knjižarnica Zorana Stojanovića.

Plungjan, Vladimir A. 2008. O pokazateljax čužoj reči i nedostovernosti v russkom jazyke: *mol, jakoby* i drugie [On markers of reported speech and unreliability in Russian]. In Björn Wiemer & Vladimir A. Plungjan (eds.), *Lexikalische Evidenzialitäts-Marker in slavischen Sprachen*, 285–311 (Wiener Slawistischer Almanach – Sonderband 72.). München & Wien: Otto Sagner.

PSJČ: *Příruční slovník jazyka českého, díl I: A–J* [Concise Czech dictionary, part I: A–J]. 1935–37. Praha: Státní nakladatelství.

Robbeets, Martine & Hubert Cuyckens. 2013. Towards a typology of shared grammaticalization. In Martine Robbeets & Hubert Cuyckens (eds.), *Shared grammaticalization. With special focus on the Transeurasian languages*, 1–20. Amsterdam & Philadelphia: Benjamins.

Sedláček, Jan. 1970. Srpskohrvatske potvrde o razvitku rečenica sa *da* u južnim slovenskim jezicima [Serbo-Croatian evidence of the development of *da*-clauses in South Slavonic languages]. *Zbornik za filologiju i lingvistiku* XIII (2). 59–69.

SłStar: Urbańczyk, Stanisław (ed.). 1960–1962. *Słownik staropolski*, vol. III [Old Polish dictionary, vol. III]. Warszawa & Kraków: Wydawnictwo PAN.

SłXVI: Mayenowa, Maria Renata (ed.). 1975. *Słownik polszczyzny XVI wieku*, vol. IX [Dictionary of the 16th century Polish, vol. IX]. Wrocław, Warszawa, Kraków & Gdańsk: Ossolineum, Wydawnictwo Polskiej Akademii Nauk.

Sonnenhauser, Barbara. 2015. Functionalising syntactic variance: declarative complementation with *kako* and *če* in 17th to 19th century Balkan Slavic. *Wiener Slavistisches Jahrbuch. Neue Folge* 3. 41–72.

SSJČ: Havránek, Bohuslav (ed.). 1960. *Slovník spisovného jazyka českého, I: A–M* [Dictionary of literary Czech, I: A–M]. Praha: Nakladatelství Československé akademie věd.

Stolz, Christel & Thomas Stolz. 2001. Mesoamerica as a linguistic area. In Martin Haspelmath, Ekkehard König, Wulf Oesterreicher & Wolfgang Raible (eds.), *Language typology and universals: An international handbook*, vol. 2, 1542–1553. Berlin & New York: De Gruyter.

Širokova, Natal'ja A. 1966. *Iz istorii sojuznyx konstrukcij vyražajuščix otnošenija sravnenija* [From the history of comparative conjunction constructions]. Kazan': Izd-vo Kazanskogo Universiteta.

Večerka, Radoslav. 1993. *Altkirchenslavische (altbulgarische) Syntax II. Die innere Satzstruktur*. Freiburg i. Br.: Weiher.

Večerka, Radoslav. 1996. *Altkirchenslavische (altbulgarische) Syntax III. Die Satztypen: Der einfache Satz*. Freiburg. i. Br.: Weiher.

Večerka, Radoslav. 1997. The influence of Greek on Old Church Slavonic. *Byzantinoslavica* LVIII (2). 363–386.

Večerka, Radoslav. 2002. *Altkirchenslavische (altbulgarische) Syntax IV. Die Satztypen: Der zusammengesetzte Satz*. Freiburg. i. Br.: Weiher.

Wälchli, Bernard. 2012. Grammaticalization clines in space: Zooming in on synchronic traces of diffusion processes. In Björn Wiemer, Bernhard Wälchli & Björn Hansen (eds.), *Grammatical replication and borrowability in language contact*, 233–272. Berlin & Boston: De Gruyter Mouton.

Wiemer, Björn. 2004. Population linguistics on a micro-scale. Lessons to be learnt from Baltic and Slavic dialects in contact. In Bernd Kortmann (ed.), *Dialectology meets typology. Dialect grammar from a cross-linguistic perspective*, 497–526. Berlin, New York: Mouton de Gruyter.

Wiemer, Björn. 2006. Particles, parentheticals, conjunctions and prepositions as evidentiality markers in contemporary Polish (A first exploratory study). *Studies in Polish Linguistics* 3. 5–67.

Wiemer, Björn. 2007. Sud'by balto-slavjanskix gipotez i segodnjašnjaja kontaktnaja lingvistika [The fate of the Balto-Slavonic hypotheses and contact linguistics today]. In Vjač. Vs. Ivanov & Petr M. Arkad'ev (eds.), *Areal'noe i genetičeskoe v strukture slavjanskix jazykov (Materialy kruglogo stola)* [Areality and genealogy in the structure of Slavonic languages (Materials from a Round table)], 17–30. Moskva: Probel.

Wiemer, Björn. 2008. *Pokazateli s citativnoj i inferentivnoj funkcijami v russkom i pol'skom jazykax – kommunikativnye mexanizmy semantičeskogo sdviga* [Markers with reportive and inferential functions in Russian and Polish – communicative mechanisms of a semantic change]. In Björn Wiemer & Vladimir A. Plungjan (eds.), *Lexikalische*

Evidenzialitätsmarker im Slavischen, 337–378. (Wiener Slawistischer Almanach – Sonderband 72.) München.

Wiemer, Björn. 2010. Lithuanian *esą* – a heterosemic reportive marker in its contemporary stage. *Baltic Linguistics* 1. 245–308.

Wiemer, Björn. 2014. *Mora da* as a marker of modal meanings in Macedonian: On correlations between categorial restrictions and morphosyntactic behaviour. In Elisabeth Leiss & Werner Abraham (eds.), *Modes of Modality. Modality, typology, and universal grammar*, 127–166. Amsterdam & Philadelphia: Benjamins.

Wiemer, Björn. 2015. An outline of the development of Pol. *jakoby* in 14th–16th century documents (based on dictionaries). In Björn Wiemer (ed.), *Studies on evidentiality marking in West and South Slavic*, 217–302. München: Sagner.

Wiemer, Björn (2017). Main clause infinitival predicates and their equivalents in Slavic – Their impact on factivity and the issue of insubordination. In Łukasz Jędrzejowski & Ulrike Demske (eds.), *Infinitives at the syntax-semantics interface: A diachronic perspective*, 265–338. Berlin & Boston: De Gruyter.

Wiemer, Björn & Björn Hansen. 2012. Assessing the range of contact-induced grammaticalization in Slavonic. In Björn Wiemer, Bernhard Wälchli & Björn Hansen (eds.), *Grammatical replication and borrowability in language contact*, 67–155. Berlin & New York: Mouton de Gruyter.

Wiemer, Björn, Il'ja Seržant & Aksana Erker. 2014. Convergence in the Baltic-Slavic contact zone (Triangulation approach). In Juliane Besters-Dilger, Cynthia Dermarkar, Stefan Pfänder & Achim Rabus (eds.), *Congruence in contact-induced language change. Language families, typological resemblance, and perceived similarity*, 15–42. Berlin & New York: Mouton de Gruyter.

Wiemer, Björn & Anna Socka. 2017. How much does pragmatics help to contrast the meaning of hearsay adverbs? (Part 2). *Studies in Polish Linguistics* 12 (2). 75–95.

Wiemer, Björn & Ivana Vrdoljak. 2011. Evidenzielle Partikeln vs. Satzadverbien im Serbisch-Kroatischen und Slovenischen (Teil I. Ein Forschungsbericht). *Die Welt der Slaven* LVI (1). 100–130.

Jasmina Grković-Major
The development of perception verb complements in the Serbian language[1]

Abstract: This paper investigates the evolution of perception verb complements in Serbian. In order to present the late Proto-Slavonic situation, we first give a survey of complementation strategies in Old Church Slavonic: accusative with participle, inherited from Proto-Indo-European, and *jako-*, *kako-* and *kъde*-clauses. Accusative with participle was lost in Old Serbian before the first written records. It was transformed into accusative with gerund, which was later replaced with a clause. The process of creating clausal complements was at work for centuries. After a period of competition between *jer(e)-* and *da-*clauses, the system seen in the contemporary language was established: *da-*clauses for knowledge acquired and *kako-*, *gde-*clauses for object of perception. We argue that the changes in complementation strategies are the result of an interplay between internal and contact-induced factors. The main internal driving force was the typological drift toward a transitive, configurational system, causing the loss of participial complements. This induced the gradual creation of clausal complements by restructuring parataxis into hypotaxis. Going through this phase of instability, the system was susceptible to foreign influences, which directed further development, as shown by the expansion of *da-*clauses into the indicative domain under Romance influence.

1 Introduction

Cross-linguistically, perception verb complements can encode two types of meaning: a) the direct, immediate perception of a situation, and b) knowledge acquired about a situation. They are labelled differently: event vs. fact, object of perception vs. knowledge acquired, immediate perception vs. mental perception, state of affairs vs. propositional content, ungrounded vs. grounded

---

[1] This research was conducted within the project *The History of the Serbian Language* (№ 178001) financed by the Ministry of Education, Science, and Technological Development of the Republic of Serbia.

https://doi.org/10.1515/9783110531435-012

processes, etc.[2] In this paper we will use the terms object of perception and knowledge acquired.

It has been observed that cross-linguistically there is tendency for knowledge acquired to be morphosyntactically more complex, revealing the iconic relation between language and cognitive complexity (Croft 2003: 203–204; Boye 2010). Thus the difference between knowledge acquired and object of perception is often encoded as finite vs. nonfinite clauses such as participles or infinitives. Noonan (2007: 101) argues that "the stronger the semantic bond between the events described by the matrix and complement predicates, the greater the degree of syntactic integration there will be between the two clauses". But there are other strategies as well, like the use of different complementizers (Horie 2001: 984), distinguishing meanings related to the information source, i.e. the category of evidentiality (Aikhenvald 2004: 120–122). This is the case with Slavonic languages today (Běličová and Sedláček 1990: 71). The difference between the two types of perception verb complements in Slavonic was pointed out already by Bauer (1960: 116), who defined the opposition between Czech *jak-* and *že-*clauses as the one between presenting the perceived situation as an ongoing process vs. presenting it as a whole, a fact, with no reference to its internal dynamics.

The goal of this paper is to investigate the development of perception verb complements in the history of Serbian. Keeping in mind that syntactic change is a gradual process, we will start with a brief presentation of the situation in Old Church Slavonic (OCS). The reason we start with OCS is that, although submitted to Greek influence to a certain degree, it is a valuable source for reconstructing late Proto-Slavonic (PS) syntactic patterns,[3] which were inherited by early Slavonic vernaculars, among them Old Serbian. Then, we will give an overview of complementation strategies and their development in the history of Serbian. Finally, we will analyse the causes and mechanisms of the changes.

---

[2] For a survey see e.g. Horie (2001); Boye (2010).
[3] Although OCS syntax was influenced by Greek, this impact was chiefly on the frequency of certain constructions (Bauer 1972: 71–72), the choice between different Slavonic syntactic strategies (Grković-Major 2013: 61) and hypotactic structures, not being developed in late PS (see Bauer 1972: 213). Recent investigations which include Indo-European and comparative Slavonic perspective, show that OCS shares many archaic syntactic structures with early Slavonic vernaculars (e.g. Grković-Major 2013: 98–115). Many cases where there is one to one correspondence between Greek and OCS syntactic structures can be attributed to their common Indo-European syntactic origins.

2 Perception verb complements in OCS

The investigation is based on the *Codex Marianus* (CM), which is close to the original translation of the Gospels (EM: 4), representing the Thessaloniki phase of OCS.[4] CM exhibits two types of clausal complementation with perception verbs: nominal (accusative with participle) and verbal (introduced with *jako, kako* and *kъde*).

2.1 Accusative with participle

The accusative with participle is an inherited Proto-Indo-European (PIE) construction, a special form of the double accusative (Desnickaja 1984: 81–124; Ambrazas 1990: 145–149). It belongs to the repertoire of nominal forms (participles, verbal nouns, nominal compounds) used to express semantic subordination, a type of which was contextually induced. In OCS it preserved its semipredicative character (Večerka 1996: 195).

With the present active participle, denoting a situation taking place at the same time with the matrix verb, it encodes an object of perception:

(1) *viděsimona i anъdrěję bratra togo*
see-3SG.AOR Simon-ACC and Andrew-ACC brother-ACC.SG that-GEN
simona vъmetajǫšta mrěžę vъ more
Simon-GEN cast-PRS.ACT.PTC.ACC.DU.M nets-ACC in sea-ACC
'He saw Simon and Andrew, Simon's brother, casting nets into the sea.' (Mk 1:16)

(2) *slyšašę že farisěi narodъ rъpъštǫštь*
listen-3PL.AOR PRT pharisees crowd-ACC.M say-PRS.ACT.PTCP.ACC.SG.M
o nemь se
about he-LOC this-ACC
'The Pharisees heard the crowd saying this about him.' (Jn 7:32)

With the past active participle, denoting a situation preceding the matrix verb and having resultative semantics, it encodes knowledge acquired:

(3) *slyšašę i sъtvorъšь znamenie*
listen-3PL.AOR he-ACC do-PST.ACT.PTCP.ACC.SG.M miracle-ACC
'They heard that he had done a miracle.' (Jn 12:18)

---

4 Later translations exhibit innovations, among them the beginning of the adverbialization of participles, e.g. *Codex Suprasliensis* (Miklosich 1868–1874: 828).

(4) viděvъšiimъ   ego   vъstavъša   iz
    see-PST.ACT.PTCP.DAT.PL he-ACC   rise-PST.ACT.PTCP.ACC.SG.M   from
    mrъtvyihъ   ne   jęsę   věry
    dead-GEN.PL NEG   take-3PL.AOR faith-GEN
    'They did not believe those who had seen him risen from the dead.' (Mk 16:14)

The present (5) and past passive participles (6), having resultative semantics,[5] encode knowledge acquired. They are semantically equivalent to the double accusative with adjective (Večerka 1996: 197):

(5) vidě   tъštǫ   ego   ležęštǫ
    see-3SG.AOR mother-in-law-ACC.F   he-GEN   lye-PRS.ACT.PTCP.ACC.SG.F
    ognemъ   žegomǫ
    fire-INS   burn-PRS.PASS.PTCP.ACC.SG.F
    'He saw his mother-in-law lying in bed being burned by fever.'
    (Mt 8:14)

(6) vidě   tu   °čka   ne   oblъčena
    see-3.SG.AOR there   man-ACC.M   NEG   dress-PST.PASS.PTCP.ACC.SG.M
    vъ   oděanie   bračьnoe
    in   garment-ACC   wedding-ADJ
    'He saw a man there not dressed in a wedding garment.' (Mt 22:11)

Although in most cases the Slavonic accusative with participle translates the same Greek construction, it also renders the Greek accusative with infinitive (Miklosich 1868–1874: 824–825; Večerka 1996: 196). This proves that it was an indigenous PS syntactic strategy, productive at the time of the first OCS translations. As seen in (1)–(6), it indicates both types of perception.[6]

2.2 *Jako*-complement

Jako is originally a manner adverb derived from the demonstrative *jakъ (< *j-akъ, ESJS, 5: 268), meaning 'in this way'. According to Vaillant (1974: 329), its formant

---

[5] Cross-linguistically passive participles, according to Haspelmath (1994: 159), should be understood as resultatives; they are adjectives expressing state.
[6] We also see this in Baltic languages (Ambrazas 1990: 143), genetically close to Slavonic, even to this day (Arkadiev 2012: 294).

-ko- is a grammaticalized instrumental of the PIE interrogative **kʷo-*. It is used to translate Greek *hóti*, etymologically also a combination of the demonstrative and the interrogative pronoun (< *hóstis*, Chantraine 1968–80, III: 834).

Jako was highly polyfunctional (SS: 793–795), not yet grammaticalized. This is clearly seen in *jako recitativum*: *onъ že reče emu ěko bratrъ tvoi pride* 'and he said to him (*in this way*): your brother came' Lk 15:27, which reveals the original asyndetic structure, preceding the formation of compound sentence. Used to translate Greek *hóti*, it "acquired" the status of a complementizer in the literary language. *Jako*-complements give information about knowledge acquired:

(7) egda   že   uslyša   ěko   bolitъ
    when   PRT   hear-3SG.AOR   COMP   be.sick-3SG.PRS
    'When he had heard that he was sick.' (Jn 11:6)

The agent of the perceived situation could be put in focus as a direct object, followed by the *jako*-complement (cf. Pichkhadze 2012: 54):

(8) viděvъše   marijǫ   ěko   jędro   vъsta
    see-PST.ACT.PTCP.NOM.PL   Mary-ACC   COMP   hastily   rise.up-3SG.AOR
    'Having seen Mary, that she rose up hastily.' (Jn 11:31)

2.3 *Kako*-complement

Kako (< PIE **kʷo-*) belongs to the same set of adverbs as *jako* (ESJS 5: 299), meaning 'in which way, how'. It was polyfunctional (SS: 280), with perception verbs used for Greek *põ:s* of the same, interrogative origin (Chantraine 1968–1980, III: 922).

The *kako*-clause emerged from a juxtaposed interrogative sentence. According to Bauer (1960: 128–129) it was an exclamative, emotionally coloured utterance, as a reaction to a direct perception of a situation. It is used for an object of perception, still retaining its original semantics:

(9) viděaše   kako   narodъ   metetъ   mědь   vъ
    watch-3SG.IMPF   COMP/how   people   cast-3SG.PRS   money-ACC   in
    gazofilakijǫ
    treasury-ACC
    'He watched how people cast money into the treasury.' (Mk 12:41)

2.4 Kъde-complement

Kъde is a spatial interrogative adverb (< *kъ-de/kъ-dě 'where', ESJS, 7: 391). It was polyfunctional (SS: 300), used with perception verbs to render Greek poũ, of the same origin (< PIE *kʷo-, Chantraine 1968–80, III: 922).

The kъde-complement emerged from a juxtaposed interrogative sentence (Bauer 1960: 2015), and denoted an object of perception:

(10) zьrěašete   kъde   i   polagaahǫ
     watch-3DU.IMPF   where   he-ACC   lay-3PL.IMPF
     'They watched where he was being laid.' (Mk 15:47)

3 Perception verb complements in the history of Serbian

Our corpus consists of documents from the first written records in the 12th century onward. Since Old Serbian language situation is generally characterized by diglossia, Old Serbian and Serbian Church Slavonic being in complementary distribution (cf. Pavlović, this volume), we included only vernacular texts, not influenced by Church Slavonic. The corpus encompasses different genres: various types of charters and letters (more than 1000), legal codes and documents, novels, stories, chronicles etc. (see *Sources*). In order to capture diatopic variation and the spread of innovations we included texts from different dialectal areas. Besides verbs of visual and auditory perception, verbs meaning 'to find' are also included in this category (Grickat 1975: 177; Běličová and Sedláček 1990: 72).

3.1 Accusative with participle / gerund

The loss of agreeing participles (Daničić 1874: 346–385) caused the disappearance of the accusative with active participles in the earliest records.[7] Examples from

---

[7] Several examples in Old Serbian documents are found in the charters structured by principles of diglossia, under Church Slavonic influence (e.g. ACh: 466; Zb: 321). The same is seen in Old Russian: it is not found in the vernacular charters, except for the citations from the gospels (Borkovskij 1968: 128).

folk poetry show that it was first replaced with the accusative with a non-agreeing form (present gerund) construction:[8]

(11) kada   mi   te   začuju   moje   ime
     when   I-DAT   you-ACC   hear-3PL.PRS my   name-ACC
     klikujući
     shout-PRS.GER
     'When they hear you shouting my name.' (B: 19.60)

In the charters and letters from the 12th to the 15th century, we find only passivized participial complements, with both the present (12a) and the past participle/gerund (12b), mostly with verbs meaning 'find'. This shows that long after accusative + participle was removed from the object position, its passive counterpart, with patient of perception verbs in the subject position, existed:

(12) a. ako   li   se   obrěte   zlatarь   u   gradu
        if   PRT   REFL   find-3SG.PRS   goldsmith   in   city-LOC
        kove   dinare   taino
        forge-PRS.GER   dinars-ACC   in secrecy
        'If a goldsmith is found in the city forging money in secrecy.' (DZ: 202)
     b. tko   se   obrěte   ubyvь   otьca   ili
        who   REFL   find-3SG.PRS   kill-PST.GER   father-ACC   or
        materь
        mother-ACC
        'Who is found to have killed [their] father or mother.' (DZ: 184)

From the 15th to the 19th century accusative with gerund is documented exclusively in language contact situations: (13) is from a mining legal code composed under German influence,[9] and (14) from a text translated from Latin:

(13) ako   bi   ga   do poslě   iznašli   gvarci
     if   be-3PL.AUX   he-ACC   later   find-PTCP.PRF   workers
     krijući   dělově
     hide-PRS.GER   parts-ACC
     'If the workers would later find him hiding parts.' (ZR: 42)

---

8 This was a general Slavonic tendency, cf. Old Czech *když kokota slyšel pějíce* (Trávníček 1956: 135), Old Croatian (Čakavian) *i slišah glas govoreči mi* (Mihaljević 2011: 192), Old Russian *viděli molodcevъ sěduci, da ne viděli molodcevъ poěduči* (Potebnja 1958: 313). This complement type still exists in Russian dialects (Kuz'mina and Nemčenko 1971: 231, 268).

9 The code might have even been composed by Saxon miners (ZR: 27). It should be noted that Old Saxon, as well as Old High German permits an accusative with a predicative participle after verbs of perception, including *finden* 'find' (Zeitlin 1908: 36).

(14) vidje   ženu   po   objedu   plačući
     see-3SG.AOR   woman-ACC   after   meal   cry-PRS.GER
     'He saw a woman crying after the meal.' (AZ: 83)

The accusative with the present passive participle was lost before the first records. The past passive participle was preserved as an adjectival modifier. The gradual nature of the change is seen in the fact that it kept its original double accusative word order for centuries:

(15) očima   vidiesmo   štetu   učinjenu
     eyes-INSTR   see-1PL.AOR   damage-ACC.F   do-PST.PASS.PTCP.ACC.F
     'We saw the damage done with our own eyes.' (P: 35)

Such constructions existed at least until the 19th century (see RJA, XX: 817). But in the past century they have been subjected to syntactic restriction, so that in standard Serbian today the object has to be an agent or experiencer (Petrović and Subotić 2002: 54). If not, the word order changed:[10]

(16) videli   smo   učinjenu   štetu
     see-PTCP.PRF   be-1PL.AUX   do-PASS.ADJ.ACC.F   damage-ACC.F
     'We saw the damage which was done.'

3.2 *Jer(e)*- and *da*-complements

Jer(e) is a demonstrative (< **je-že*, ESJS, 5: 287), found in the syntactic positions of OCS *jako* from the earliest records.[11] In paratactic text structure, dominant in Old Serbian documents for several centuries, it functioned as a deictic, while

---

10 Cf. the same process in the history of Russian: *viděše stada vъzjata* > *uvidali vzjatye stada* (Potebnja 1958: 300). In the history of Slavonic languages agreeing modifiers changed word order from postposition to pre-position to the modified noun (Pavlović 2013: 92–93), thus the word order change of the verbal adjective shows the change in its syntactic status.
11 It appears already in OCS texts translated in Bulgaria (all examples of the complementizer *ježe* given in SS: 802 are from *Codex Suprasliensis*). In Old Czech we have (*j*)*eže*, *že* (Bauer 1960: 142), in Old Russian *ože/aže* (Borkovskij and Kuznecov 2006: 482) etc. It can be assumed that PS had several emerging possibilities for knowledge acquired, among them *jako*- and *ježe*-sentences. The translators of OCS texts chose *jako* as a semantic equivalent of the Greek complementizer (see above).

different semantic relations between two sentences were contextually induced.[12] The complement clause emerged from juxtaposition:[13]

(17) *vidě kraljevstvo mi jere* || *ulazi popъ*
     see-3SG.AOR Majesty I-DAT this come.in-3SG.PRS priest
     'My Majesty saw this: the priest is coming in.' (Zb: 148)

Without prosodic information it is not possible to determine when exactly the reanalysis of the constituent structure began. The only clear evidence are examples with enclitics and we will focus the following analysis on such cases. Predicate phrase enclitics take the Wackernagel's, post-initial position in the majority of cases in early Old Serbian records (see Pavlović, this volume). Thus, if *jere* was in the clause initial position when used as *relativum generale* it was the orthotonic host for such enclitics:

(18) *dobitъkъ* || *jere smo rekli dati*
     profit which be-1PL.AUX say-PTCP.PRF give
     'The profit which we said we would give.' (SPP 14.30)

The original asyndetic pattern with perception verbs is revealed in (19), where the enclitic *je* is at the end of the second sentence, while *jerъ* was the object constituent of the first one:

(19) *čujemo jerъ* || °*gdnъ stefanъ knezъ došalъ*
     hear-1PL.PRS this lord Stefan prince come-PTCP.PRF
     je
     be-3SG.AUX
     'We hear this: lord prince Stefan came.' (SPP 195.3)

The first examples of the new pattern with an enclitic after *jer(e)*, testifying to the boundary shift, are from the early 14th century:

(20) *ako se iznađe* || *jer su znajuće*
     if REFL find out-3SG.PRS COMP be-3PL.AUX knowing
     krivo opravili
     wrongly acquit-PTC.PRF
     'If it is found out that knowing they wrongly acquitted.' (DZ: 139)

---

[12] Two main semantic interpretations were: 'complement' and 'cause' (see Pavlović 2009: 74–80, 242–243).
[13] The simple juxtaposition of sentences was an ordinary syntactic strategy in Old Serbian, e.g.: *a viděa* || *onь gradь sokolь malo je vrědanь bez župe* 326.54–55 'and he saw: the city of Sokol is not worth much without the *župa*'.

Examples with clitics are rare in the corpus. We found only 6 in the 14th century: 2 asyndetic and 4 complement structures. In the 15th century the ratio of asyndetic and complement structures was 10% (2) : 90% (20), revealing that the change of the juxtaposition of independent sentences to subordination was coming to an end.

We also find structures with correlatives, as an intermediary stage from parataxis to hypotaxis:[14]

(21) viděsta   to   jere   prěvari   prějamušь
     see-3DU.AOR   COR(that)   COMP   deceive-3SG.AOR   Prejamuš
     kralja
     king-ACC
     'They saw this: that Prijamuš deceived the king.' (RT: 38)

As seen from (17)–(20) the *jer(e)*-pattern had the same function as the OCS *jako*-complement, to denote knowledge acquired.

The first examples with the complementizer *da*[15] replacing *jer(e)* are from the end of the 14th century. The instability of the *jer(e)*-clause in that period was fertile ground for the spread of the *da*-complementizer:

(22) čujemo   da   ste   u   rashoměri   i   u
     hear-1PL.PRS   COMP   COP   in   discord-LOC   and   in
     nemiru
     turbulence-LOC
     'We hear that you (two) are in discord and turbulence.' (SPP 803.5)

The competition between *da* and *jer(e)* also led to the repetition of the two complementizers in the same sentence:

(23) čujemo   po   ljudehь   **jerь**   vьse   što   je   bilo
     hear-1PL.PRS   by   people   COMP   all   which   COP   be-PTCP.PRF
     uzeto   **da**   je   vьse   kь   njemu
     take-PASS.ADJ   COMP   be-3SG.AUX   all   to   he-DAT
     poneseno
     carry-PASS.ADJ
     'We hear from people that all that was taken was carried to him.'
     (SPP 332.12–13)

---

14 Such correlative constructions are witnessed to in Old Russian as well (Preobraženskaja 1991: 142).
15 On the origin and grammaticalization of *da* in Old Serbian see Grković-Major (2007: 204–230).

Da-complements spread in the western Štokavian dialects in the 15th century and the ratio of the two competing strategies was: *da* 61% : *jer(e)* 39%. In the documents from the eastern area we find exclusively *jer(e)* up to the end of the century. The first examples with *da*-complements are from the late 15th century:

(24) viděše   da   se   gragjane potrebiše   izъ   grad(a)
     see-3PL.AOR COMP   REFL citizens run-3PL.AOR from   city-GEN
     protivu   voiscě
     against   army-DAT
     'They saw that the citizens ran from the city against the army.' (RT: 72)

In the 16th century *da*-complements prevailed in the west. In LMR the *da*-clause is documented in 99% of cases and the *jer(e)*-one in 1%. The process was slower in the east: documents in P from the end of the 16th and the beginning of 17th century still show the competition of the two models. In the 17th century *da* prevailed in this area too, as seen from AZ: *da* 98% : *jer(e)* 2%. As *da* was spreading, *jer(e)* was being restricted to adverbial (cause) clauses. However, in some dialects the process was even slower. In the 19th century there are still rare *jer(e)*-complements, even with correlatives, testifying to a gradual spread of syntactic change, both in terms of the internal change and its areal diffusion:

(25) to   kad   viđe   Namik Alil paša   jere   Turci
     that-COR   when   see-3SG.AOR   Namik Alil pasha COMP   Turks
     pleći   okrenuše
     backs-ACC   turn-3PL.AOR
     'And when Namik Alil-pasha saw that the Turks turned their backs.' (OS)

As seen from (20)–(22), *da*-clauses denote knowledge acquired like the *jer(e)* ones. In standard Serbian today the function of the *da*-complement is the same. It cannot encode a situation seen as a process, thus it is not used for immediate perception with verbs marked with intentionality (+), such as *posmatrati* 'observe', *slušati* 'listen', *gledati* 'watch' (**posmatramo da pada kiša* 'we observe that the rain falls', **slušamo da pada kiša* 'we listen that the rain falls'). This is in accordance with Noonan's findings (2007: 144) that cross-linguistically only non-intentional ("non-deliberate") forms express knowledge acquired. If verbs marked with intentionality (+) are combined with the *da*-clause, their meaning shifts:

(26) oni   udaljeniji   gledaju   da   budu
     those   distant-CMP.PL   watch-3PL.PRS COMP   be-3PL.PRS
     neutralni
     neutral-PL
     'The ones which are more far away try to be neutral.' (CG)

3.3 *Kako*-complement

In the texts from the 12ᵗʰ to the 15ᵗʰ century *kako* was highly polyfunctional (Pavlović 2008). The earliest example with a perception verb shows the origin of the *kako*-complement from the juxtaposition of an interrogative sentence:

(27) da   vidi   kralevstvo mi   kako   mi   svrьšiti
     OPT.PRT   see-3SG.PRS   Majesty   I-DAT how   I-DAT do-INF
     hokešь   size   posьlь
     want-2SG.PRS this   job-ACC
     'Let my Majesty see: how will you do this job for me.' (SPP 37.7–8)

Correlative constructions were a step toward creating hypotactic structures:

(28) viděˇ   to   jagupa go(s)pa kako se   troja
     see-3SG.AOR   that-COR   Jagupa lady   COMP REFL Troy
     sko(n)čavaje(t)
     end-3SG.PRS
     'Lady Jagupa saw that: how Troy was coming to an end.' (RT: 72)

The *kako*-clause encodes an object of perception if: a) two predicates denote situations which are taking place at the same time, while the dependent one is ongoing (cf. Cristofaro 2003: 111), and b) if the complement clause refers to something that can be an object of immediate perception (27). Such clauses do not present simply the perceived situation, but the manner in which it takes place.[16] If one of the two requirements is not met, it encodes knowledge acquired:

(29) vide   kako   naasь   °gdnь   kralь   ostoja i
     see-PRS.GER   COMP   we-ACC   lord   king   Ostoja and
     °gda   bosanьska   ljube
     lords   Bosnia-POSS.ADJ   love-3PL.PRS
     'Seeing that lord king Ostoja and the Bosnian lords love us.' (SPP 463.18–20)

(30) čuli   smo   kako   si   putovalь   i
     hear-PTCP.PRF   be-AUX.1PL   COMP   be-2SG.AUX   travel-PTCP.PRF   and
     opetь   se   domom   zdravo   i   počteno   vratilь
     again   REFL   homes-DAT   healthy and   honorably   return-PTCP.PRF
     'We heard that you travelled and returned home healthy and honourably.' (SPP 262.3–4)

---

[16] This was a general Slavonic tendency. *Kako*-clause was grammaticalized in this function in South and East Slavonic. In Old Czech *kako*-complements were quite numerous, but were later replaced with the *jak*-ones (Bauer 1960: 130).

In comparison with the *da*-clause, the *kako*-complement has a nuance of manner semantics. If we compare (31a) and (31b) we see that this is expressed in the complement predicate, the one in (31a) denoting an action, and the one in (31b) a state. Both sentences are written in the same year and by the same scribe:

(31) a. čuli   smo   kako   našěmь   trьgovcemь
        hear-PTCP.PRF be-1PL.AUX COMP   our-DAT   merchants-DAT
        jest   dana   zabava
        COP   give-PASS.ADJ obstruction
        'We heard that(how) our merchants were obstructed.'
        (SPP 190.3–4)

   b. eto   smo   čuli   da   je   našěmь
      PRT   be-1PL.AUX   hear-PTCP.PRF COMP   be-3SG.PRS   our-DAT
      trьgovcemь   zabava
      merchants-DAT obstruction
      'So we heard that there is obstruction to our merchants.'
      (SPP 268.9)

Still at the end of the 19th century, *kako*-clauses with perception verbs were labelled interrogative (RJA: II, 108; XX, 826). Grammars of standard Serbian in the 20th century note that these complements carry a nuance of the "way an action is performed" (Stevanović 1969: 796; Kovačević 1998: 176). In RSANU (9: 95) *kako* with perception verbs is defined as a "declarative-manner" complementizer. Ružić (2006: 171) writes that in standard Serbian today it is used with perception verbs when a dynamic aspect of an ongoing situation is emphasized.

3.4 *Gde*-complement

In the documents from 12th to the 15th century *gde*-complement introduced primarily spatial clauses (Pavlović 2009: 143–146), spreading in the 14th century to the temporal ones by metaphorical extension:

(32) g/d/e   komu   daje   dubrov'čaninь   svoi   dobitьkь...
     when   who-DAT   give-3SG.PRS   citizen.of.Dubrovnik   his   money-ACC
     da   se   klьne   latininь
     OPT.PRT   REFL   swear-3SG.PRS   Roman
     'When a citizen of Dubrovnik gives his property to someone...let the Roman pledge oath.' (SPP 66.71–75)

From the 15th century on it introduced other types of adverbial clauses (RJA, III: 122–124), as well as perception verb complements:

(33) viděhъ   u   sně   gdi   izidě   is
     see-1SG.AOR in   dream-LOC   COMP   come.out-3SG.AOR   from
     troje   medvedъ
     Troy-GEN   bear
     'I saw in a dream that a bear came out of Troy.' (RT: 61)

It is noticeable that in (33) the *gde*-complement has a spatial adverbial (*is troje*), and this is a regular strategy in folk tales:

(34) vidi   gde   ljudi   s   oružjem   ulaze
     see-3SG.PRS COMP   people   with   weapons-INST   go.in-3PL.PRS
     u   crkvu
     in   church-ACC
     'He sees the people with weapons going into the church.' (SNP: 211)

This kind of correlative construction (*gde...u crkvu*) points to the origin of *gde*-complements from juxtaposed sentences.

The *gde*-complement refers to an object of perception. In RJA (III: 123–124) it is pointed out that this is the main difference between *da*- and *gde*-clauses: *čujem da ljudi govore* 'I hear that people are talking' : *čujem gdje ljudi govore* 'I hear people talking'. According to Kovačević (1998: 176), the *gde*-complement still retains a nuance of spatial meaning in standard Serbian.

3.5 Accusative object + *da-* / *gde-* / *kako*-complements

These are syntactic variants of the three complementation models given above, used to put the agent of the perceived situation in focus: the accusative object is followed by *da-* (35), *gde-* (36) or *kako*-complements (37):

(35) kad   ih   vidje   da   su   došli
     when   they-ACC   see-3SG.AOR   COMP   be-AUX.3.PL   come-PTCP.PRF
     'When he saw that they came.' (SM: 74)

(36) vide   unutra   sveću   gde   gori
     see-3SG.AOR   inside   candle-ACC   COMP   burn-3SG.PRS
     'He saw inside a candle burning.' (SNP: 211)

(37) mi   ga   ugledasmo   kako   preskoči   preko   grede
     we   he-ACC   see-1PL.AOR   COMP   jump.over-3SG.AOR over   beam-GEN
     'We saw him jump over the beam.' (LL)

Such constructions are documented late, with the first examples from the 16th century (cf. RJA, XX: 817), only after the *da-*, *gde-* and *kako*-clauses were highly grammaticalized. That is why *jer(e)*-complement is not present in this position, since by that time it was almost completely replaced by the *da*-clause. This speaks in favour of Potebnja's hypothesis (1958: 317) that the complement clause replaced the participle, in the case of Serbian – the gerund. In standard Serbian today *kako* is regular in this position, with *da* and *gde* found sporadically (Ružić 2006: 178).[17]

3.6 Accusative with infinitive

Thanks to the *irrealis* semantics of the PS infinitive, dative(-locative) by origin, it could not be used as a perception verb complement in Slavonic (Grković-Major 2013: 78).[18] The construction is not found in the vernacular texts from the 12th to the 15th century, except for several examples of its passive counterpart, as a result of language contact (38) (cf. (12)):

(38) tko   se   nagje   ot gragjanь   vino   prodavati
     who   REFL   find-3SG.PRS   of citizens-GEN   wine-ACC sell-INF
     na   pazaru
     at   market-LOC
     'A citizen who is found selling wine at the market.' (ZR: 53)

From the beginning of the 16th century, it is documented in the language of the writers from Dubrovnik and coastal Montenegro (39), as a calque of the Romance pattern, directly or through Croatian Čakavian. As Zima (1887: 309) pointed out, this complement was a contact-induced feature of older Čakavian (cf. Mihaljević 2011: 195). In the literary works of writers from Vojvodina (40), it emerged under German influence:

(39) gledajući   oni   narod   klanjati   se   idolom
     watch-PRS.GER   that   people   bow-INF   REFL   idols-DAT
     'Watching the people bowing to idols.' (AZ: 164)

---

17 Our insight into the contemporary Serbian situation is limited to standard language. Unfortunately, we do not have studies on perception verb complements in Serbian dialects today, which would reveal the possible areal distribution of *kako-* and *gde-*clauses.
18 Medieval Slavonic vernaculars used other strategies with perception verbs, see e.g. Pichkhadze 2012 for Old Russian. Accusative with infinitive could emerge as a secondary phenomenon, under foreign influence. For example, instead of *vidím tě ležet* in Czech today, Old Czech had accusative with participle: *vizu tě ležiec* (Trávníček 1956: 167). For the origin and status of the accusative with infinitive with other verb classes, especially cognitive and communicative, having double accusative constructions as their internal motivation, see Kurešević (this volume).

(40) čujem   dvojicu   razgovarati   se
    hear-1SG.PRS   two.men-ACC   talk-INF   REFL
    'I hear two men talking.' (Jerković 1972: 273–274)

4 Discussion and conclusions

The data presented testify to the restructuring of PS perception verb complements (as testified to by OCS) in the history of Serbian, from the PS nominal (accusative with participle) to the verbal complement clause. It was caused, as we believe, by the typological drift of PIE and its daughter languages.

As Meillet (1908: 320–342) already pointed out, PIE was a system with autonomous sentence elements, with no argument structure, where apposition and agreement were the basic principles of syntactic structuring. Subordination was expressed with various nominal forms (participles, verbal nouns, nominal compounds) and syntax was paratactic (Lehmann 1980: 117–124). This was a manifestation of the early PIE typological profile: it was a non-nominative language type, lacking transitivity, presumably active-stative (Gamkrelidze and Ivanov 1984: 267–368).[19]

The development of PIE and its daughter languages testifies to the typological drift toward the nominative language type with transitivity as its main feature, leading to syntactic restructuring and the creation of configurational systems.[20] This is strongly supported by investigations in the domain of Slavonic historical syntax (Grković-Major 2007: 77–97; 2010; 2013: 8–193; Pavlović 2013: 9–136).

With the finite verb (predicate) becoming the centripetal core of the sentence and the adverbial protoaccusative ('in reference with *x*') being grammaticalized into its object argument, the accusative with participle, as an autonomous nominal construction with predicative force, was gradually transformed. In late PS it was still a semipredicative nominal complement, encoding both the object of perception and knowledge acquired. By the time of the first Serbian written records, the active participial complement, marked with agentivity (+) was lost, not being in accordance with the nominative language type, where agentivity is the distinctive feature of the grammatical subject. This was a gradual process,

---

[19] We find convincing the hypothesis that PIE was, in terms of Georgij Klimov's typology, active-stative at some earlier stage (Gamkrelidze and Ivanov 1984: 267–368), or that it might have been a linguistic type of its parent language (Pre-Indo-European, Lehmann 2002). Studies of different IE languages (see Grković-Major 2013: 83) speak in favour this hypothesis.
[20] On configurationality see Luraghi (2010).

in which the participle was first replaced by the non-agreeing form (gerund), as in other old Slavonic languages. It was removed early on from the object position, existing for a period only in passive constructions (subject position) before it completely disappeared. The tendency to remove the second predicative form in the sentence also caused the transformation of the past passive participial complement into an adjectival modifier.

The withdrawal of nominal complement clauses was concomitant with the rise of hypotaxis from parataxis. Serbian grammaticalized independent *kako-* and *gde-* sentences to denote object of perception, which was a further development of late PS tendencies and was seen in other Slavonic languages as well. The grammaticalization of the two adverbials in this function is clear from the cognitive point of view, since perceiving 'how' (*kako*) and 'where' (*gde*) a situation takes place implies immediate perception.

The PS *jako*-pattern for knowledge acquired was lost in prehistorical times since, due to the disappearance of the opposition between **j-* and **k-* pronoun types, the opposition between *jako* and *kako* was lost. *Jako* was replaced with *jer(e)*, as in other early Slavonic vernaculars. However, *jer(e)* was polyfunctional, used to introduce adverbial clauses as well. In the 15th century, the *da*-complement, a west South Slavonic innovation, started replacing the *jer(e)*-one, with *jer(e)* being specialized for adverbial (cause) clauses. The change was gradually diffusing in the Serbian dialects over the following centuries. Analogous processes are seen in other Slavonic languages at the same time.[21] While early Slavonic vernaculars had the same basic patterns: **j*-pronoun type for knowledge acquired (Old Serbian *jer(e)*) and **k*-type for the object of perception (Old Serbian *kako*, *gde*), in the 14th–15th centuries the Slavonic continuum disintegrated in this respect.

Generally speaking, all Slavonic languages followed the same path: from the system where, thanks to the autonomy of sentence elements, both types of perception were encoded by nominal complements to systems in which they are encoded with verbal complements. In other words, they moved from asyndetic, nominal, to hypotactic, verbal structures, which was a general IE scenario (Bednarczuk 1971: 160).

As Serbian was going through the process of creating hypotaxis, it was met with foreign language influences in the Balkans. A major role was played by Romance idioms, on the levels of: a) vernaculars, since the Romance speaking

---

21 Bulgarian *če* developed in the 14th–15th centuries (Grickat 1975: 154), in Czech *ež, ježe, ješte, jenž* went out of use by the 15th century texts, giving way to *že* (Bauer 1960: 138), in Old Russian *čto*-clauses spread at the expense of the *ože*-ones in the 15th century (Borkovskij and Kuznecov 2006: 483).

population was situated deep in the Balkans, being gradually assimilated by the Slavs; b) written language, due to the usage of Romance textual forms.

The main contact-induced change in the domain of complementation was the expansion of the subjunctive *da* into the indicative domain. It was the replication[22] of the situation in Romance, where the distinction between subjunctive *ut-* and indicative *quod*-clauses was lost in favour of *quod* (Sedláček 1970; Grickat 1975: 172). Romance influence is proven by the fact that the indicative *da* spread at the fastest rate in the documents written in Dubrovnik, where intense Romance-Slavonic contacts were at work for centuries.[23] As hypotaxis was being structured, the Romance pattern was used to solve the problem of the polyfunctional *jer(e)*-clauses.

In conclusion: the main driving force causing the demise of the accusative with participle and the grammaticalization of verbal complement clauses with perception verbs in Serbian was the typological drift toward a transitive, configurational language type. But the final result emerged from the interplay of language-internal and contact-induced processes since, due to its typological change, the system was going through a phase of instability, which made it susceptible to foreign influences.

Sources

ACh: Petit, Louis R. P. & B. Korablev. 1915. *Actes de Chilandar*. Petrogradъ.
AZ: Zmajević, Andrija. 1996. *Ljetopis crkovni* [The ecclesiastical annals]. 1–2. Cetinje: Obod.
B: Bogišić, Valtazar. 1878. Narodne pjesme, iz starijih, najviše primorskih zapisa [Folk songs, from the older, mostly coastal records]. *Glasnik Srpskog učenog društva* 10. 1–430.
CG: Karadžić, Vuk. *Crna Gora i Crnogorci* [Montenegro and the Montenegrins]. <http://www.rastko.rs/knjizevnost/vuk/vkaradzic-crnagora.html#_Toc44869810> (accessed June 2013).
CM: Jagić, Vatroslav (ed.). 1960 [1883]. *Quattuor Evangeliorum versionis palaeoslovenicae Codex Marianus glagoliticus*. Graz: Akademische Druck- u. Verlagsanstalt.
DZ: Begović, Mehmed (ed.). 1975. *Zakonik cara Stefana Dušana. 1: Struški i Atonski prepis* [The legal code of the emperor Stefan Dušan. 1: The Stuga and Mount Athos manuscripts]. Beograd: Srpska akademija nauka i umetnosti.
LL: Lazarević, Laza. *Pripovetke* [Stories]. http://www.rastko.rs/knjizevnost/umetnicka/proza/llazarevic-pripovetke_c.html#_Toc526845037 (accessed August 2013).

---

22 On contact-induced grammaticalization see Wiemer and Hansen (2012).
23 Dubrovnik was a Roman city in which Slavonic population was the majority from the 13th century onward. In the 14th century the aristocracy was being Slavonicized, and from the 15th century onward the Republic has been dominantly Slavonic (Ćorović 2004: 390)

LMR: Rešetar, Milan. 1926. Libro od mnozijeh razloga. Dubrovački ćirilski zbornik od 1520 [Libro od mnozijeh razloga. The 1512 Cyrillic *miscellanea* from Dubrovnik]. *Zbornik za istoriju, jezik i književnost srpskog naroda* XV. 1–221.
OS: Njegoš, Petar Petrović. *Ogledalo srpsko* [Serbian mirror]. http://www.rastko.rs/rastko-cg/umjetnost/ppnjegos-ogledalo1_c.html (accessed August 2013).
P: Božić, Ivan, Branko Pavićević & Ilija Sindik. 1959. *Paštrovske isprave XVI–XVIII vijeka* [The Paštrovići documents from the 16th to the 18th centuries]. Cetinje: Državni arhiv Narodne Republike Crne Gore.
RT: Ringheim, Allan. 1951. *Eine altserbische Trojasage*. Prague & Upsal: Imprimerie de l'état à Prague.
SM: Ljubiša, Šćepan Mitrov. 1889. *Pripovijesti crnogorske i primorske* [Montenegrin and coastal stories]. U Dubrovniku: Nakladom knjižare Dragutina Pretnera.
SNP: Karadžić, Vuk. 1985. *Srpske narodne pripovijetke* [Serbian folk tales]. Beograd: Prosveta & Nolit.
SPP: Stojanović, Ljubomir. 1929, 1934. *Stare srpske povelje i pisma I/1–2* [Old Serbian charters and letters]. Beograd: Srpska akademija nauka i umetnosti.
Zb: Mošin, Vladimir, Sima Ćirković & Dušan Sindik. 2011. *Zbornik srednjovekovnih ćiriličkih povelja i pisama Srbije, Bosne i Dubrovnika 1: 1186–1321* [The collection of medieval Cyrillic charters and letters from Serbia, Bosnia and Dubrovnik 1: 1186–1321]. Beograd: Istorijski institut.
ZR: Radojičić, Nikola. 1962. *Zakon o rudnicima despota Stefana Lazarevića* [The Mining code of Despot Stefan Lazarević]. Beograd: Naučno delo.

References

Aikhenvald, Alexandra Y. 2004. *Evidentiality*. Oxford: Oxford University Press.
Ambrazas, Vytautas. 1990. *Sravnitel'nyj sintaksis pričastij baltijskix jazykov* [Comparative syntax of Baltic participles]. Vil'njus: Mokslas.
Arkadiev, Peter M. 2012. Participial complementation in Lithuanian. In Volker Gast & Holger Diessel (eds.), *Clause linkage in cross-linguistic perspective. Data-driven approaches to cross-clausal syntax*, 285–334. Berlin & Boston: Walter de Gruyter.
Bauer, Jaroslav. 1960. *Vývoj českého souvětí* [Development of the Czech compound sentence]. Praha: Nakladatelství Československé akademie věd.
Bauer, Jaroslav. 1972. *Syntactica slavica. Vybrané práce ze slovanské skladby* [Slavonic syntax. Selected works on Slavonic syntax]. Brno: Universita J. E. Purkyně.
Bednarczuk, Leszek. 1971. *Indo-European parataxis*. Kraków: Wydawnictwo Naukowe Wyższej szkoły Pedagogicznej.
Běličová, Helena & Jan Sedláček. 1990. *Slovanské souvětí* [The Slavonic compound sentence]. Praha: Československá akademie věd.
Borkovskij, Viktor I. 1968. *Sravnitel'no-istoričeskij sintaksis vostočnoslavjanskix jazykov. Členy predloženija* [Comparative-historical syntax of East Slavonic languages. Sentence constituents]. Moskva: Nauka.
Borkovskij, Viktor I. & Petr S. Kuznecov. 2006. *Istoričeskaja grammatika russkogo jazyka* [Historical grammar of the Russian language]. Moskva: Akademija nauk SSSR.

Boye, Kasper. 2010. Reference and clausal perception-verb complements. *Linguistics* 48 (2). 391–430.
Chantraine, Pierre. 1968–1980. *Dictionnaire étymologique de la langue grecque. Histoire des mots. I–IV*. Paris: Éditions Klincksieck.
Cristofaro, Sonia. 2003. *Subordination*. Oxford: Oxford University Press.
Croft, William. 2003. *Typology and universals*. Cambridge: Cambridge University Press.
Ćorović, Vladimir. 2004 [1989]. *Istorija Srba* [The history of the Serbs]. Bor: Publik-Praktikum.
Daničić, Đuro. 1874. *Istorija oblika srpskoga ili hrvatskoga jezika do svršetka XVII vijeka* [The history of forms of the Serbian or Croatian language until the end of the 17th century]. Beograd: Državna štamparija.
Desnickaja, Agnija V. 1984. *Sravnitel'noe jazykoznanie i istorija jazykov* [Comparative linguistics and the history of languages]. Leningrad: Nauka.
EM: *Evangelie ot Matfeja v slavjanskoj tradicii* [The gospel according to Matthew in the Slavonic tradition]. 2005. Sankt-Peterburg: Sankt-Peterburgskij gosudarstvenyj universitet, Filologičeskij fakul'tet, Sinodal'naja biblioteka Moskovskogo Patriarxata & Rosijskoe biblejskoe obščestvo.
ESJS: Havlová, Eva (ed.). 1989–. *Etymologický slovník jazyka staroslověnského. 1–*. [Etymological dictionary of Old Church Slavonic. 1–.]. Praha: Academia.
Gamkrelidze, Tamaz V. & Vjačeslav Vs. Ivanov. 1984. *Indoevropejskij jazyk i indoevropejcy. Rekonstrukcija i istorikotipologičeskij analiz prajazyka i protokul'tury I*. [Indo-European and the Indo-Europeans. A reconstruction and historical typological analysis of a proto-language and a proto-culture I]. Tbilisi: Izdatel'stvo Tbilisskogo universiteta.
Grickat, Irena. 1975. *Studije iz istorije srpskohrvatskog jezika* [Studies from the history of the Serbo-Croatian language]. Beograd: Narodna biblioteka Srbije.
Grković-Major [Grković-Medžžor], Jasmina. 2007. *Spisi iz istorijske lingvistike* [Studies in historical linguistics]. Sremski Karlovci & Novi Sad: Izdavačka knjižarnica Zorana Stojanovića.
Grković-Major, Jasmina. 2010. The role of syntactic transitivity in the development of Slavonic syntactic structures. In Björn Hansen & Jasmina Grković-Major (eds.), *Diachronic Slavonic syntax. Gradual changes in focus* (Wiener Slawistischer Almanach – Sonderband 74), 63–74. München, Berlin & Wien: Otto Sagner.
Grković-Major [Grković-Medžžor], Jasmina. 2013. *Istorijska lingvistika: Kognitivnotipološke studije* [Historical linguistics: Cognitive-typological studies]. Sremski Karlovci & Novi Sad: Izdavačka knjižarnica Zorana Stojanovića.
Haspelmath, Martin. 1994. Passive participles across languages. In Barbara A. Fox & Paul J. Hopper (eds.), *Voice: Form and function*, 151–177. Amsterdam & Philadelphia: John Benjamins.
Horie, Kaoru. 2001. Complement clauses. In Martin Haspelmath, Ekkehard König, Wulf Oesterreicher & Wolfgang Raible (eds.), *Language typology and language universals I–II*, 979–993. Berlin & New York: Walter de Gruyter.
Jerković, Jovan. 1972. *Jezik Jakova Ignjatovića* [The language of Jakov Ignjatović]. Novi Sad: Matica srpska.
Kovačević, Miloš. 1998. *Sintaksa složene rečenice u srpskom jeziku* [The syntax of the compound sentence in the Serbian language]. Beograd: Raška škola.
Kurešević, Marina (this volume). The status and origin of the *accusativus cum infinitivo* construction in Old Church Slavonic.
Kuz'mina, Irina B. & Elena V. Nemčenko. 1971. *Sintaksis pričastnyx form v russkix govorax* [The syntax of participle forms in Russian vernaculars]. Moskva: Nauka.

Lehmann, Winfred P. 1980. The reconstruction of non-simple sentences in Proto-Indo-European. In Paolo Ramat (ed.), *Linguistic reconstruction and Indo-European Syntax. Proceedings of the Colloquium of the Indogermanische Gesellschaft, University of Pavia, 6–7 September 1979*, 113–144. Amsterdam: John Benjamins.

Lehmann, Winfred P. 2002. *Pre-Indo-European*. Washington D.C.: Institute for the Study of Man.

Luraghi, Silvia. 2010. The rise (and possible downfall) of configurationality. In Silvia Luraghi & Vit Bubenik (eds.), *Continuum companion to historical linguistics*, 212–229. London & New York: Continuum International Publishing Group.

Meillet, Antoine. 1908. *Introduction à l'étude comparative des langues indo-européennes*. Deuxième édition corrigée et augmentée. Paris: Hachette.

Mihaljević, Milan. 2011. Dopune percepcijskih glagola u hrvatskome crkvenoslavenskome jeziku [Perception verb complements in Croatian Church Slavonic]. *Suvremena lingvistika* 37. 187–200.

Miklosich, Franz. 1868–1874. *Vergleichende Syntax der slavischen Sprachen*. Wien: Wilhelm Braumüller.

Noonan, Michael. 2007. Complementation. In Timothy Shopen (ed.), *Language typology and syntactic description. Volume 2: Complex constructions*, 2nd edn., 52–150. Cambridge: Cambridge University Press.

Pavlović, Slobodan. 2008. Sintaksičko-semantički potencijal starosrpskog veznika *kako* [Syntactic-semantic potential of the Old Serbian conjunction *kako*]. *Zbornik Matice srpske za filologiju i lingvistiku* LI (1–2). 17–30.

Pavlović, Slobodan. 2009. *Starosrpska zavisna rečenica od XII do XV veka* [The Old Serbian dependent clause from the 12th to the 15th century]. Sremski Karlovci & Novi Sad: Izdavačka knjižarnica Zorana Stojanovića.

Pavlović, Slobodan. 2013. *Uzroci i mehanizmi sintaksičkih promena u srpskom jeziku* [Causes and mechanisms of syntactic changes in the Serbian language]. Sremski Karlovci & Novi Sad: Izdavačka knjižarnica Zorana Stojanovića.

Pavlović, Slobodan (this volume). Mechanisms of word order change in 12th and 13th century Serbian.

Petrović, Vladislava & Ljiljana Subotić. 2002. Atribucija objekta uz glagole percepcije (dijahrono-sinhroni plan) [Object attribution with perception verbs (diachronic-synchronic aspects)]. *Naučni sastanak slavista u Vukove dane* 30 (1). 53–59.

Pichkhadze, Anna A. 2012. Subject of subordinate clause as object with verbs of perception, thought, and communication in Old Russian. *Slověne* 1 (1). 52–60.

Potebnja, Aleksandr A. 1958. *Iz zapisok po russkoj grammatike. Tom I–II* [From the notes on Russian grammar. Volume I–II]. Moskva: Akademija nauk SSSR.

Preobraženskaja, Marija N. 1991. *Služebnye sredstva v istorii sintaksičeskogo stroja russkogo jazyka XI–XVII vv.: složnopodčinennoe predloženie* [Syntactic words in the history of the syntactic structure of the Russian language from the 11th to 17th century: complex sentence]. Moskva: Institut russkogo jazyka AN SSSR.

RJA: *Rječnik hrvatskoga ili srpskoga jezika. I–XXIV* [Dictionary of the Croatian or Serbian language. I–XXIV]. 1880–1976. Zagreb: Jugoslavenska akademija znanosti i umjetnosti.

RSANU: *Rečnik srpskohrvatskog književnog i narodnog jezika. 1–* [Dictionary of the standard and vernacular Serbo-Croatian language. 1–]. 1959–. Beograd: Srpska akademija nauka i umetnosti & Institut za srpski jezik.

Ružić, Vladislava. 2006. *Dopunske rečenice u savremenom srpskom jeziku* [Complement clauses in the contemporary Serbian language]. Novi Sad: Matica srpska.

Sedláček, Jan. 1970. Srpskohrvatske potvrde o razvitku rečenica sa *da* u južnim slovenskim jezicima [Serbo-Croatian evidence of the development of *da*-clauses in South Slavonic languages]. *Zbornik za filologiju i lingvistiku* XIII (2). 59–69.

SS: Cejtlin, Ral'a M., Radoslav Večerka & Emilie Blagova (eds.). 1994. *Staroslavjanskij slovar' (po rukopisjam X–XI vekov)* [Old Church Slavonic dictionary (based on the manuscripts from the 10th to the 11th centuries)]. Moskva: Russkij jazyk.

Stevanović, Mihailo. 1969. *Savremeni srpskohrvatski jezik II. Sintaksa* [Contemporary Serbo-Croatian language II. Syntax]. Beograd: Naučna knjiga.

Trávníček, František. 1956. *Historická mluvnice česká III. Skladba* [Historical grammar of Czech III. Syntax]. Praha: Státní pedagogické nakladatelství.

Vaillant, André. 1974. *Grammaire comparée des langues slaves. Tome IV. La formation des noms.* Paris: Éditions Klincksieck.

Večerka, Radoslav. 1996. *Altkirchenslavische (altbulgarische) Syntax III. Die Satztypen: Der einfache Satz.* Freiburg. i. Br.: Weiher.

Wiemer, Björn & Björn Hansen. 2012. Assessing the range of contact-induced grammaticalization in Slavonic. In Björn Wiemer, Bernhard Wälchli & Björn Hansen (eds.), *Grammatical replication and borrowability in language contact*, 67–155. Berlin & Boston: De Gruyter Mouton.

Zeitlin, Jacob. 1908. *The accusative with infinitive and some kindred constructions in English.* New York: The Columbia University Press.

Zima, Luka. 1887. Ńekoje, većinom sintaktične razlike između čakavštine, kajkavštine i štokavštine [Some, mostly syntactic differences between Čakavian, Kajkavian, and Štokavian]. *Djela JAZU* VII. 1–343.

Andrii Danylenko
A tale of two pathways:
On the development of relative clause chaining in East Slavonic

Abstract: This paper elaborates on the developmental scenario of relative clauses in East Slavonic. Premised on a system of areal, diachronic, and socio-typological criteria, the author offers a cross-dialectal typology of relative clause types and their overt linkage markers both inflected U *jakyj*, B *jaki*, R *kakoj*; U *kotryj*, B *katory*, R *kotoryj* 'which' and uninflected U *ščo*, B *što*, R *čto* 'what'; U *de*, B *dze*, R *gde* 'where'. I argue that, instead of a unilateral developmental trend from the free juxtaposition of clauses to hypotaxis to subordination, one should distinguish between two developmental clines (micro-pathways), one leading from parataxis to paratactic subordination and the second conducive to hypotactic subordination in East Slavonic. In the view of parallel relativization strategies in other Indo-European languages, in particular German dialects, I maintain that the formation of paratactic and hypotactic subordination is dependent on a historically prevalent type of discourse within a language community. Such a type is preconditioned by a particular number of societal factors, including the amount of language contact (based on adult second-language learning). The latter is likely to bring about reduction in syntagmatic redundancy leading to a 'simpler' syntactic organization, in particular the development of paratactic subordination.

1 Introduction

The present study attempts to reconstruct a developmental scenario of relative clauses in East Slavonic. In order to further elaborate on a seemingly well-researched phenomenon, we intend to establish a cross-dialectal typology of relative clause formation in various East Slavonic dialects that have customarily remained beyond the research focus of language historians and typologists (cf. Danylenko 2014). Such a cross-dialectal typology will enable us to challenge some of the premises of the theory of grammaticalization across clauses, including the genesis of relative clause subordination and the use of resumption.

For this topic, one can profit from Givón's (2009a, 2009b) theory about the rise of syntactic complexity, in particular of clause subordination and recursive language structures as part of large-scale grammaticalization (Heine 2009). Based on strong cumulative evidence, Givón (2009a: 10) argued that the developmental cline in the genesis of syntactic complexity, in diachrony, ontogeny, and no doubt in evolution, is primarily compositional (synthesis), following the general trend:
a. single words > simple clause
b. simple clause > clause chains (parataxis)
c. clause chains > complex/embedded clause (syntax)

The last stage (c) is well documented in diachrony, and especially in Indo-European languages characterized by rich inflecting morphology, as is its direction – from parataxis to syntax (Heine and Kuteva 2007: 210–261). That is, composition (synthesis) rather than expansion (analysis) is the prevalent trend.

In their monograph on the genesis of grammar, Heine and Kuteva (2007: 210–261), following Givón's explanation of grammatical evolution, argued that clause subordination is the product of grammaticalization of non-subordinate sentence structures. They also suggested a binary typology for the paths through which subordinate clauses arise: either via expansion, that is, the reinterpretation of a nominal as a clausal (propositional) participant, or via the integration of two independent sentences within one sentence. One can mention in this respect Hopper and Traugott's (2003: 176–178) cline of clause chaining leading from parataxis via hypotaxis as a combination of the features [+dependent] and [-embedded] to subordination as a combination of the features [+dependent] and [+embedded]:

parataxis	>	hypotaxis	>	subordination
–dependent		+dependent		+dependent
–embedded		–embedded		+embedded

Arguably, the aforementioned three-way distinction is premised on the idea of a unidirectional cline from relatively free juxtaposition to syntactic and morphological bondness within the framework of grammaticalization broadly construed (Heine and Kuteva 2007: 214).

In this paper, we turn to the development of relative clause structures, with particular attention to some of the clause linkage markers used either with or without resumption, that may contribute to increased dependency in the second part of the cline of hypotaxis > subordination. We are ready to challenge the framework of unidirectionality and linearity, accepted with rare exceptions, in literature on the rise of syntactic complexity. As a rare dissenting voice, Deutscher (2009; cf. Dahl 2009) argued that the two channels, expansion and integration, as outlined by Heine and Kuteva, run the risk of explaining the 'rise' of subordination by presupposing what they aspire to explain. The accounts of expansion take as their starting point nominalized structures that to all intents and purposes are already subordinate, and many examples of 'integration' also merely describe the rearrangement of already subordinate structures (Deutscher 2009: 200). Having compared the evidence adduced for the integration process in the demonstrative-derived relative clause from Akkadian and Germanic, Deutscher (2009: 212) hypothesized that the demonstrative pronouns seemed to have started as heads of already existing relative clauses. In this case, the ultimate origin of relative clauses in Germanic may also be expansion, and therefore nominalization.

Another dissenting opinion was expressed by Dahl (2009) who, instead of having three distinct stages of grammatical evolution with a linear increase of tightness, postulated different kinds of integrative processes which tend to be interconnected with each other in complex ways. Thus, instead of three stages – Parataxis (two separate intonation contours) > Syntax (one single intonation contour) > Lexis (co-lexicalization into a single word) – that characterize the diachronic rise of complex syntactic structures such as complex verb phrases and relative clauses, and presumably of various other grammatical phenomena, Dahl (2009: 240) postulated the following processes that tend to take place simultaneously and partly presuppose themselves:

a. paratactic constructions > syntactic constructions
b. syntactic constructions > inflectionally marked words
c. syntactic constructions > morphologically complex words

With respect to the relative clause interlacing in East Slavonic and, by extension, in other Indo-European (inflecting) languages constituting Standard Average European (cf. Fiorentino 2007; Cristofaro and Ramat 2007), we venture to claim that the evolution from parataxis to syntax (encompassing hypotaxis and subordination, in terms of Hopper and Traugott) should be viewed as a non-linear trend, thus allowing for parallel pathways of linking relative clauses into tighter amalgamations. We will show that the growth of inflectional morphology and syntax and the development of tighter, relative clause linkage demonstrate a rather strong negative correlation in East Slavonic. In other words, the rise of relative clause formations in East Slavonic does not necessarily follow the cline of clause chaining leading from parataxis via hypotaxis to, ultimately, subordination as posited in Hopper and Traugott (2003: 175–211).

There is, in fact, dialect evidence for speaking, at least, of two separate (parallel) pathways of relative clause chaining in East Slavonic, rather than two (or more) successive stages in one linear development. Thus, instead of a unilateral developmental trend from fairly simple (free) juxtaposition of clauses to hypotaxis to subordination, we posit two developmental clines, one leading from parataxis to 'paratactic subordination' (P-Subordination) (Danylenko 2014: 198–199; cf. Potebnja 1899: 322), and a second leading from parataxis to hypotaxis and ultimately to 'hypotactic subordination' (H-Subordination) (see *Scheme* 1). The latter type of subordination is characterized by complete dependency, in which a margin (subordinate clause) is wholly included, with the help of an inflected relative marker, within a constituent of the nucleus (matrix clause) (Hopper and Traugott 2003: 177). 'Paratactic subordination' is premised, however, on the partial integration of a subordinate clause due to the use, in particular, of an uninflected relative marker (or their combinations) either without or with resumption (see Sections 2.2 and 3).

In order to substantiate the aforementioned development of relative clauses in East Slavonic, a system of the areal, diachronic, and socio-typological criteria is applied in this study. In Sections 2–2.3 and 4, we make use of the areal criterion with an eye to outlining a distribution of the existing relative clause types and their overt linkage markers within the context of wider areal-typological implications. A simultaneous discussion of changing patterns in the distribution of such types and markers since the time of their emergence in the 'pre-national' varieties of East Slavonic capitalizes on the diachronic component of our methodology. In Section 3, we offer a socio-typological interpretation of relativization patterns in East Slavonic. All this allows us to explicate the existence, in diachrony and evolution, of the aforementioned two pathways of relative clause chaining in East Slavonic and other Indo-European languages (Kurzová 1981).

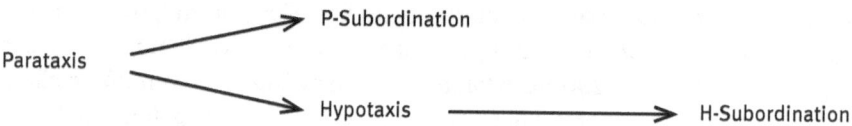

Scheme 1: Two pathways of relative clause combining in East Slavonic.

2 Distribution of the relative clause formations in East Slavonic

Among the relative elements observed in East Slavonic, we identify four basic markers of both P- and H-subordination. Tentatively, we make a primary twofold distinction between inflected and uninflected relative markers, constituting a minimum of four basic types as presented in Tab. 1. Best known from English and some North (Low) Saxon dialects of Schleswig in German, zero relatives are not observed in standard varieties of East Slavonic (cf. Fleischer 2004: 226), though they are still attested in its non-standard varieties (Danylenko 2014: 198–199).

Tab. 1: Inventory of basic relative markers in modern East Slavonic[1]

Inflected markers	(1) U *jakyj*, B *jaki*, R *kakoj*
	(2) U *kotryj*, B *katory*, R *kotoryj* 'which'
Uninflected markers	(1) U *ščo*, B *što*, R *čto* 'what'
	(2) U *de*, B *dze*, R *gde* 'where'

The aforementioned typology can be expanded through adding some uninflected relative markers of the type *že*, *žy*, and *žo* attested in the archaic southwestern Ukrainian dialects (see Section 2.1; Danylenko 2014: 191). What is more important, however, is that the four basic types tend to be further divided into several subtypes found in both standard and non-standard varieties of East Slavonic.[2] For instance, some of the inflected relative markers can occur in conjunction with uninflected relative markers and vice versa. In addition, the uninflected relative markers can be used together with resumptive elements depending on the

---

[1] The following abbreviations are used here: ACC, accusative; AH, Accessibility Hierarchy; B, Belarusian; Bl, Bulgarian; coll, colloquial; CES, Common East Slavonic; CS, Common Slavonic; DAT, dative; dial., dialectal; DEM, demonstrative; F, feminine; Fr, French; folk., folkloric; FUT, future; GEN, genitive; I, Italian; IMP, imperative; INF, Infinitive; INS, instrumental; IREL, inflected relative marker; Kursk, Kursk dialects; Lemk., Lemkian dialects; LOC, locative; M, masculine; MB, Middle Belarusian; MU, Middle Ukrainian; N, neuter; NEB, Northeast Belarusian; NOM, nominative; NP, noun phrase; P, Polish; P, particle; PPP, past passive participle; Podil., Podillja dialects; PRS, present tense; PST, preterit tense; R, Russian; RES, resumptive element; Rm, Rumanian; S, Spanish; SEU, Southeast Ukrainian; SG, singular; Slv, Slovene; SR, South Russian; *Steppe*, steppe dialects; SU, standard Ukrainian; SWB, Southwest Belarusian; SWU, Southwest Ukrainian; PL, plural; R, Russian; Rm, Rumanian; U, Ukrainian; Transc., Transcarpathian dialects; UCM, uninflected clause marker; UREL, uninflected relative marker.

[2] The notion of 'non-standard' includes diatopically, diastratically or diaphasically marked varieties. This allows pigeonholing as 'non-standard' all constructions that in reference works are identified as 'colloquial', 'regional', 'dialectal', 'informal', that is sociolinguistically marked (Murelli 2011: 33). Due to space constraint, results of hybridization of Ukrainian (*suržyk*) and Belarusian (*trasjanka*) as the matrix and Russian as the embedded language (or vice versa) are not taken into consideration (cf. Hentschel et al. 2014). Both *suržyk* and *trasjanka* as sub-standard varieties with predictable (structural) regularities and pejorative connotations are relatively late formations to have a structural impact on relativization strategies in Ukrainian and Belarusian (Danylenko 2016).

position of a relativized noun in the Accessibility Hierarchy (AH) (Keenan and Comrie 1977, 1979) or even in combination with each other as attested not only in East Slavonic but also in other Indo-European non-standard varieties (cf. Murelli 2011: 87–112).

In Sections 2.1–2.3, the cross-dialectal emergence and spread of the relative clause patterns is discussed in tandem with an overview of the changes in dialect distribution of competing variants in the Ukrainian-, Belarusian-, and Russian-speaking territories correspondingly.

2.1 Ukrainian

The relative pronouns *jakyj* and *kotryj* 'which' are the basic type for relative clause formation in Standard Ukrainian (Bilodid 1972: 336). The uninflected marker *ščo*, accompanied by a resumptive pronoun for most of the nominal case roles, save for the subject in the AH, is commonly viewed as a 'secondary' relative clause type (Vyxovanec' 1993: 335–336).

(1) SU
    On toj čolovik,   ščo   z   nym   ja
    he that-NOM.SG.M man-SG.N UREL   with   whom-RES   I
    rozmovljav   u centri   mista
    talk-PST.SG.M   in center-LOC.SG.M town-GEN.SG.N
    'That is the man with whom I was talking in the town centre'
    (Pugh and Press 1999: 179)

It should be borne in mind, however, that the relative marker *kotryj* tends to be employed where the emphasis is on identifying a particular entity; as a regular linkage marker, the relativizer *kotryj* is also attested in a Ukrainian heavily influenced by Russian (Pugh and Press 1999: 296) or, in the case of the western Ukrainian standard, by Polish (Danylenko 2003: 186).

Not surprisingly, in the entire literary output of the major Ukrainian poet Taras Ševčenko (1814–1861), whose language reflects the aforementioned distribution, one comes across only three cases of the relative marker *kotryj*. At the same time, the uninflected marker *ščo* was numerically predominant in all his writings and *jakyj* was still observed in its qualitative meaning 'what sort of' or in the distributive meaning; in the latter case, the relative clause was found in the prenominal position (Danylenko 2003: 190). This nineteenth-century distribution was discussed by Potebnja (1899: 337, 342) who argued that 'pure relativization' in Ukrainian was achieved through the use of the relative 'particle' *ščo* or the relative pronoun *jakyj* but not by the marker *kotryj* influenced allegedly either by standard Russian or Polish.

In fact, the relative markers *kotryj* and *jakyj* demonstrate a rather limited scope of usage. For instance, the inflected marker *kotryj* is largely employed in Southwest Ukrainian, in particular in Transcarpathian dialects, and sporadically in some other Ukrainian dialects (Bevzenko 1980: 172–173). Attested cross-dialectally (cf. AUM 3, part 4: 186), the marker *kotryj* retains a distributive meaning typical of the pre-posed relative clause (Mel'nyčuk 1962: 116).

(2) SWU (Lemk.)
Kotryj   *vyhrat,*   *to*   *tot*
IREL-NOM.SG.M win-FUT.SG.M   then   that-NOM.SG.M
toho   *z'jist*
that-GEN.SG.M   eat-FUT.SG.M
'That one who wins, he will eat the other one'
(Verxratskij 1902: 170)

In general, from the early 19th c. onward the relative marker *kotryj* has been gradually disappearing in Ukrainian dialects at the expense of *jakyj* which replaced parallel *k*-forms like *kakъ* (*kakyj*, *kakovъ*) 'what kind of; which' retained in most Russian dialects (Korš 1877: 28). Although rarely attested in the Poltava region, the relative marker *kotryj* is still attested in postposed relative clauses in some other Steppe dialects (Bevzenko 1980: 173).

(3) SEU (Steppe)
Ljublju   *dytynu,*   *kotra*   *sluxajit'sja*
love-PRS.1SG   child-ACC.SG.F   IREL-NOM.SG.F   obey-PRS.3SG
'I like a child who behaves himself'
(Žylko 1966: 125)

Showing residually weaker relative clause linkage, one comes across sporadic occurrences of the double encoding of the relativized head noun, that is, once by means of the relative marker *kotryj* and once by the resumption (repetition) of the head noun outside the matrix clause, in particular, for the subject position in the AH.

(4) SEU (*Steppe*)
Byry   *toj*   *kavun,*
take-IMP.2SG   that-ACC.SG.M   watermelon-ACC.SG.M
kotryj   *kavun*   *vit*
IREL-NOM.SG.M   watermelon-NOM.SG.M   from
koryn'cja   *soxne*
root-GEN.SG.M   dry-PRS.3SG
'Take a watermelon which dries from its root cap'
(Žylko 1966:125)

The status of the Ukrainian inflected marker *jakyj* is reminiscent of *kotryj*. Cross-dialectally, *jakyj* may occur in a relative clause preceding the matrix one. However, in the postposed position of the relative clause the marker *jakyj* is observed only in a limited number of dialects. In southern Podillja, this marker is not attested at all. If used in a postposed relative clause, the pronoun *jakyj* parallels the meaning of *kotryj*, thus revealing its distributive semantics. From the 19th c. onward the relative pronoun *jakyj* has been gradually spreading across the Ukrainian-speaking territories, most likely under the influence of its counterpart employed in nascent standard Ukrainian (Mel'nyčuk 1962: 115; Danylenko 2015).

If viewed in diachrony, the use of the uninflected marker *ščo* has been most consistent in dialects and spoken varieties of the language. Fulfilling various clause functions, it gradually became most representative as a relative marker already in the Middle period, both in the vernacular standard called Ruthenian (*prostaja mova*) and the local (Meletian, after Meletij Smotryc'kyj) recension of Church Slavonic (Korš 1877: 28–29; Mel'nyčuk 1962: 112; Danylenko 2006: 109–110). As an example of *što* accompanied by a resumptive pronoun consider (5), excerpted from the Peresopnycja Gospel (1556–1561):

(5) MU
    i   *poperevrъtae(t)*   *vsě rěči,*   *što*   *je(st)*
    and   turn-FUT.3SG   all things-NOM.PL.F   UREL   be-PRS.3SG
    v   *ni(x)*
    in   they-LOC
    'And she will turn all the things which are in them'
    (PG 1556–1561: 286)

With parallels in almost all Slavonic languages (Gallis 1958; Gołąb and Friedman 1972: 37, 41–43; Danylenko 2003: 194–197; Křížkova 1970), and even beyond (cf. Murelli 2011: 324–331), the relative clause type involving the uninflected marker *ščo* is fully integrated in modern Ukrainian dialects (AUM 3, part 4: 186). Yet this type is particularly abundant in Southeast and North Ukrainian (Bevzenko 1980: 172). Due to a rather weak interlacing of the matrix clause with the relative one with the uninflected marker *ščo*, Potebnja (1899: 322–323) defined this relationship as 'paratactic subordination'. Indeed, the uninflected marker neither encodes the syntactic role of the relativized item nor provides coreference with the head noun in the matrix clause. Historically, both functions tend to be fulfilled by a resumptive personal pronoun for almost all the positions in the AH, sporadically even for that of subject. It is noteworthy that the latter is relativized today less frequently as in the 19th c. Moreover, the use of *ščo* without any resumption was most common in all the Ukrainian dialects in the 19th c. or even earlier (Smerečyns'kyj 1931: 201–207).

Rarely and mostly in the transitional dialects, the weak relative clause linkage may be compensated by combining the uninflected marker *ščo* with an inflected relative pronoun of the type R *kakoj* and *kotoryj* 'which.'

(6) SWU
tomu	vpade	bil'še,	ščo	kotryj	ukrav
that-DAT.SG.M	get-FUT.3SG	more	UREL	IREL-NOM.SG.M	steal-PST.SG.M

'That one who stole will get more'
(Smerečyns'kyj 1932: 202)

As late as the Middle period, the aforementioned combination was attested in postnominal relative clauses, where *ščo* was used as an identifier and *kotryj* in its distributive meaning.

(7) MU
a	što	kotory(i)	ko(p)cy[...]	byli
and	UREL	IREL-PL.NOM	hump-NOM.PL.F	be-PST.PL

po(p)sovany,	tye	napravi(ti)
spoil-PPP.NOM.PL	those-ACC	fix-INF

'As far as those humps which were deranged are concerned, one should fix them' (16th c., Zadorožnyj and Matvijenko 1995: 84)

Since the 19th c. all the Ukrainian dialects have been demonstrating a tendency toward the postnominal position of the dependent and non-embedded relative clauses (Hendery 2012: 21). A few examples illustrate this vividly:

(8) SWU (Lemk.)
O	vdovi,	ščo	mala	paserbycju
about	widow-LOC.SG.F	UREL	have-PST.SG.F	stepdaughter-ACC.SG.F

'About a widow who had a stepdaughter'
(Verxratskij 1902: 170)

(9) SWU (Podil.)
Bo	to	buv	takyj	pip,
because	that-DEM	be-PST.SG.M	such-NOM.SG.M	priest-NOM.SG.M

ščo	vin	duže	napyvavsja
UREL	he-RES	very	to.get.drunk-PST.SG.M

'For that was such a priest who used to get drunk'
(Levčenko 1928: 130)

(10) SWU (Transc.)
To   tot   dido,   ščo   ho
that-DEM   that-NOM.SG.M   codger-NOM.SG.M   UREL   he-RES.ACC
nahorodyly
award-PST.PL
'This is that codger whom they awarded'
(Žylko 1966: 125)

The use of postposed dependent but not embedded relative clauses is especially representative in Southwest Ukrainian which employs a widearray of uninflected markers (AUM2, map 256). In addition to *ščo*, one finds there, for instance, *ož* (*oš*) as a continuation of CES *o-že* (Mel'nyčuk 1962: 82, 113) but not the bookish (primarily, Church Slavonic) *i-že*, *ja-že* from *yo- (cf. Rabus 2010); deserving of attention are *že, žy, žo, žu* derived from CS *že* (> Slv *ki*, cf. Gołąb and Friedman 1972: 41) rather than from P *že* (Meillet 1924: 427; cf. Murelli 2011: 125).

(11) SWU (Transc.)
Tot   legin',   ož   vydiv   nas
that-NOM.SG.M   guy-NOM.SG.M   UREL   see-PST.SG.M   us
'That fellow who saw us'
(Bevzenko 1980: 173)

The uninflected forms *že, žy, žo, žu* and *ož* seem to be the earliest to become grammaticalized as relative markers in these dialects. As a rule, they do not take any resumption, thereby encoding largely either the nominative or accusative position in the AH. Thus, co-reference with the head noun in the matrix clause is not marked in this type of postposed relative clauses.

Of interest is the locative-specialized relative element *de* 'where' (< *hde* < *gde* < *kъde*) which is used cross-dialectally and is reminiscent of similar relativization formations in other Indo-European languages, belonging in particular to the Balkan Sprachbund cf. Bl *deto* (< *kădeto*) and Rm *de* 'where' (< *unde*) (Murelli 2011: 189–193). The *wh*-adverbial marker can be compared to the uninflected relative marker *ščo* in that it does not encode the syntactic role of the head noun in the matrix clause. The marker *de* can also be rarely accompanied by a resumptive pronoun as illustrated in example (13). With no resumption, the co-reference with the relativized item in gender and number agreement is conspicuously absent. The two clauses are still paratactically interlaced, although under a single intonation contour provided by a mere presence of the marker *de*, as shown in example (12). The difference between (12) and (13) lies in a degree of the residual paratactic subordination which is minimally stronger in the case of resumption. Analogically, one finds paratactic subordination in example (8); this syntactic relationship appears tighter, however, in Sentences (9) and (10) where resumption is employed with the uninflected marker *ščo*.

(12) SWU
    Ce   ta   konjaka,   de   Matvij
    this-DEM that-NOM.SG.F mare-NOM.SG.F UREL Matvij
    jizdyt'
    ride-PRS.3SG
    'This is a mare which Matvij rides'
    (Bevzenko 1980: 173)

(13) SEU
    Ta   baba   pomerla,   de   vony
    that-NOM.SG.F old.lady-NOM.SG.F die-PST.SG.F UREL they-RES.NOM
    z   neji   nasmixalys'
    at   her-GEN   sneer-PST.PL
    'That old lady, at whom they had sneered, died'
    (Žylko 1966: 126)

Tentatively, the introduction of the *wh*-adverbial *de* in relative clause chaining might have been provoked by language contacts as observed in the Balkan Sprachbund or some transitional Ukrainian-Russian dialects (Akimova 1964: 142) (see Section 2.3). Consequently, one finds it difficult to concur with Gołąb and Friedman (1972: 45) viewing the function of Bl *deto* as a general 'hypotactic conjunction' meaning 'where' as a calque from the Greek (see Section 2.2).

2.2 Belarusian

Standard Belarusian employs mostly the inflected relative pronouns *jaki* and *katory* 'which,' although the latter one appears to be stylistically marked (Biryla and Šuba 1986: 292). Unlike Ukrainian, the uninflected relative marker *što* is viewed as colloquial and folklore-restricted (Atraxovič 1966: 608).

The current distribution is a result of changes that have been taking place over the last five centuries. Thus, in the 16th–17[th]cc. the relative clauses with *katory* were prevalent in Ruthenian (*prostaja mova*), as a precursor of both Belarusian and Ukrainian. In neighbouring (Middle) Polish the exclusive use of *który* at the expense of 'colloquial' *co* 'what' could be explained by Latin – and, to some extent, Czech – influence (Urbańczyk 1939: 52). Historically, *jaki* tended to oust *katory* as found today in Belarusian dialects and standard Belarusian. Somewhat surprisingly, *katory* is attested, although sporadically, in all major Belarusian dialects (Akimova 1964: 141), although *što* became their principle relative marker as in Ukrainian (Astrėjka 2009: 196, 392, 396). So, the overall changes in the distribution of the aforementioned competing markers in Ruthenian (I) and, subsequently, in Belarusian (IIa) and Ukrainian (IIb) are documented in *Scheme* 2; the major difference between Belarusian and Ukrainian lies in an optional status of the contact-induced *kotryj* in the latter language.

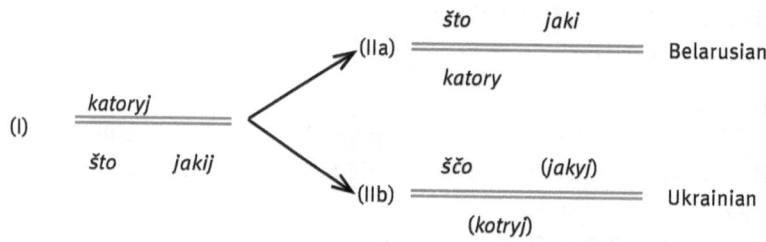

Scheme 2: Changes in the relativization patterns from Ruthenian (I) to Belarusian (IIa) and Ukrainian (IIb).

In Belarusian dialects, the use of *katory* and *jaki* has a clear-cut territorial distribution. The pronoun *jaki* is mostly attested in northeastern, central, and Palessian (U Polissian) dialects, spreading even as far as the adjacent Russian (Pskov) dialects (Akimova 1964: 141). At the same time, the pronoun *katory* is widespread in Southwest Belarusian, thus cutting the Belarusian territories in half (Blinava and Mjacel'skaja 1969: 121). The use of *jaki* in Southwest Belarusian does not exceed 10 percent of the relative clauses recorded in this dialectal area (Baxan'koŭ 1960: 120). What is remarkable is that the two relative pronouns tend to compete primarily in the transitional Belarusian-Russian dialects:

(14) B dial.
To   byŭ   Lën'ka,   katory / jakej   sa   Smalensku
that-DEM   be-PST.SG.M Lën'ka   IREL   from Smalensk-GEN
'That was Lën'ka who was from Smalensk'
(Proxorova 1991: 82)

As evidenced from *Scheme* 2, the uninflected relative marker *što* has followed the same developmental cline as the Ukrainian counterpart *ščo*, including its common use in relativization without resumption (Karskij 2006 [1911]: 464–465). However, the Belarusian marker *što* appears to be more exemplary from the point of view of its relative clause linkage leading, ultimately, to the strengthening of

paratactic subordination. In fact, the marker *što* is found in three types of postposed relative clauses:
I. Uninflected *što* + no resumption. This relative clause pattern is widespread in both Southwest and Northeast Belarusian (Baxan'koŭ 1960: 122).
II. Uninflected *što* + resumption. This relative clause pattern is also used cross-dialectally (Akimova 1964: 141–142) with resumption possible in all the positions of the AH; this means that this distribution is determined by specific socio-typological variables rather than by the geographical factor. As an example of the oblique case-role, consider:

(15) B dial.
Toj   stary   dom,   što
that-NOM.SG.M old-NOM.SG.M house-NOM.SG.M UREL
ja   u   jaho   zašla
I   in it-RES.ACC.SG.M enter-PST.SG.M
'That old house, into which I stepped'
(Baxan'koŭ 1960: 125)

III. Inflected *što* + no resumption. This relative clause pattern is found, in particular, in Southwest Belarusian. The pronoun *što* takes mostly the form of the instrumental case as found in example (16a), although some other oblique case-roles are also possible, for instance with the preposition *na* 'on' as exemplified in (16b). This relative clause type is traced back to the common East Slavonic period (Borkovskij 1958: 124–125); examples of the inflected *što* without resumption are attested in Ruthenian (Middle Belarusian and Middle Ukrainian) as well as in Middle Russian (Baxan'koŭ 1960: 125).

(16) a. SWB
daj   pilu,   čym   rezac'
give-IMP.2SG saw-ACC.SG.F IREL-INS   cut-INF
'Give me a saw with [the help of] which one can cut'
(Baxan'koŭ 1960: 124)

b. SWB
zapražy   kanja,   na   čom
harness-IMP.2SG horse-ACC.SG.M   on   IREL-LOC
jexac'
ride-INF
'Harness the horse which we will ride'
(Baxan'koŭ 1960: 124)

c. MB

A	*koni*	*namъ*	*u*	*vas*	*u Rize*
and	horses-ACC	we-DAT	at	you-GEN	in Riga

kupiti,	*na*	*čemъ*	*u verxъ*	*jexati*
buy-INF	on	REL-INS	upward	ride-INF

'And we need to buy horses from you, in Riga, by which we will go upward' (1407; Borkovskij 1958: 125)

Examples (15), (16a) and (16b) with the complimentary distribution of the inflection of *što* and resumption demonstrate tighter amalgamation of the relative clause which remains, nevertheless, relatively independent within the framework of paratactic subordination. Even occurring as an inflected form, the marker *što* is not capable of modifying an NP in the matrix clause. In Indo-European and its historical dialects, this interrogative-based marker can refer to/focus on the whole nucleus only (Danylenko 2001: 255).

Finally, one should mention the *wh*-adverbial *dze* used as an uninflected relative marker in some Belarusian dialects or spoken Belarusian as exemplified in (17).

(17) B coll.

Ja –	*taja*	*Ljuba,*	*što*	*byla*	*ў*
I [am]	that-NOM.SG.F	Ljuba	UREL	be-PST.SG.F	at

mlynara,	*dze*	*vy*	*mlyn*	*pravili*
miller-GEN.SG.M	UREL	you-PL	mill-ACC.SG.M	renovate-PST.PL

'I am that Ljuba who was at the miller's whose mill you were renovating' (Atraxovič 1966: 610)

We do not have reliable statistics. However, like in some Ukrainian and insular Russian dialects, Balkan Slavonic, and some Polish dialects (cf. Murelli 2011: 220–225), the Belarusian relative marker *dze* appears to be used more often than not in the situation of language contact as, for instance, in the transitional Belarusian-Russian dialects spoken in the Smolensk region. Remarkably, one finds in these transitional dialects the whole set of major relative markers (*katory*, *jaki* and *što*) used intermittently. Interestingly, *što* tends to be used without resumption in these dialects, even for the direct object position.

(18) NEB

Xaču	*s"jest'*	*supu,*	*što*	*ty*
want-PRS.1SG	eat-INF	soup-GEN.SG.M	UREL	you

variš
cook-PRS.2SG

'I want to eat some soup that you are cooking' (Proxorova 1991: 82)

The latter fact speaks for further strengthening of paratactic subordination as a result of language contact in the transitional Russian-Belarusian zone which, according to Proxorova (1991: 3–31, 82), is characterized by a number of 'Balto-Slavonic innovations', especially in relativization.

2.3 Russian

In the 16th–17thcc., the Russian lay texts demonstrated various relative clause types based on the inflected markers *kotoryj*, *kto* and the uninflected element *čto* occurring in both pre- and postnominal constructions. As early as the 18th–19th cc., a substantial reduction of such types occurred in all genres and registers (Troickij 1968: 251; Borkovskij and Kuznecov 1965: 523). All this eventually led to the present-day opposition between a small number of constructions with *kotoryj* in standard Russian and a full variety of constructions encountered in its non-standard varieties. Standard Russian reached the most advanced level of grammaticalization of the relative pronoun *kotoryj* at the expense of *kakoj / jakoj* and the marker *čto* (Mel'nyčuk 1962: 212–218). Used without any resumption, the latter encodes the head noun in the subject or direct object position only and is treated as colloquial and vernacular-oriented (Švedova et al. 1980: 524; Minlos 2012: 80).

In northern and western central Russian dialects, one encounters the relative pronoun *kotoryj*, used also in the prenominal relative clause (Meščerskij 1972: 255). In South Russian, one finds the relative pronoun *kakoj* (or *jakoj*) as a main relative marker which commonly reveals the distributive meaning (Kuznecov 1973: 199). The uninflected relative marker *čto* is attested cross-dialectally, especially in South Russian, although its frequency is smaller than in Belarusian and especially Ukrainian (Akimova 1964: 142).

Two other types of relative markers are of special interest. The first one is illustrated by the *wh*-adverbial *gde* 'where' in example (19) and the second is represented by the uninflected relative marker *čto* 'what' in combination with other relative markers as shown in Sentences (20) and (21). Thus, the uninflected relative marker *gde* is found in some insular Russian dialects spoken in modern Latvia. Ruke-Dravinja (1964) viewed the introduction of this relative markeras internally motivated. We believe, however, that the formation of this relative clause should be linked with language contact as is the case in some Ukrainian dialects, see examples (12) and (13). Suffice it here to mention a similar *wh*-adverbial use of *kur* 'where' in Latgalian, a regional language spoken in East Latvia, which has long been in contact with some Russian Old Believer frontier dialects (cf. Nau 2011: 97).

(19) R dial.

vot	u menja	lampъčka,		gde	garit
here	at I-GEN	lamp-NOM.SG.F		UREL	light-PRS.3SG

letъm
in.the.summer
'Here is a lamp that lights in the summer'
(Ruke-Dravinja 1964: 115)

Another relative clause type is the uninflected dial. *štu* 'what' (< *čto*) used in combination with either the adverbial *jde* 'where' (<*gde*) or the inflected relative marker *kakoj* 'which'. Cited by Akimova (1964: 142) from a work on the syntax of the Kursk dialects, and most recently by Murelli (2011: 101–102), these examples were filed as southern Russian:

(20) SR (Kursk)

Da	pašli	my pa	tej ta	darogi,
PRT	go-PST.PL	we along	that-DAT.SG.F	road-DAT.SG.F
štu	jde	tada	mjašok	patirjali
UREL	UREL	then	sack-ACC.SG.M	loose-PST.PL

'And we went along the same road where we had lost the sack'

(21) SR (Kursk)

Dyk	edit'	ža	on von	na	toj-ta
PRT	ride-PRS.SG.M	PRT	he DEM on		that-LOC.SG.F
lošadi,		štu	u kakoj	dva	ž'rjabënka
horse-LOC.SG.F		UREL	at IREL-GEN.SG.F	two	foal-GEN.SG.M

ž'rjabilis'
to.be.born-PST.PL
'There he goes on that horse that gave birth to two foals'

Remarkably, Akimova (1964: 142) noticed correctly that examples (20) and (21) have much in common with a similar, in particular adverbial-based relativization in some Belarusian and Ukrainian dialects. This connection becomes even more obvious if one takes into consideration the area where these examples come from. As we suggested elsewhere (Danylenko 2014: 196), examples (20) and (21) might have been recorded in a transitional Ukrainian-Russian dialectal zone, with a Ukrainian Sloboda or eastern Polissian dialect in interaction with a southern Russian (Kursk or Belgorod) dialect. For our discussion, the data from the Kursk dialect is of utmost importance. The point is that in this transitional dialectal zone the speakers use almost exclusively the uninflected relative marker *što* / *štu*; the relative pronoun *kotoryj* is not found in this contact zone, while *kakoj* / *jakoj*, which is typical of South Russian, is attested in the Kursk dialect only sporadically (Baxan'koŭ 1960: 127).

As we have shown for Belarusian, the use of the adverbial relative marker *jde* in combination with the uninflected marker *štu* in the Kursk dialect is not a unique case in (the history of) East Slavonic and its dialects (Korš 1877: 29). In fact, as a principle relative marker, the uninflected U *ščo* / B *što* / R *štu* tends to combine with any other relative clause linker in Belarusian and Ukrainian. Yet such a combination of relative markers does not change the degree of relative clause amalgamation which allowed Potebnja (1899: 322) to label them as 'paratactic subordination'.

3 Discussion

The foregoing survey of relativization in East Slavonic has been conducted on a comparatively minor historical scale; we left aside Common Slavonic and early medieval East Slavonic relative clause types. We also disregarded some relative markers like *iže* found in the Old Church Slavonic and early Middle East Slavonic written languages (Mel'nyčuk 1962). We largely remained in the domain of postnominal relative clause subordination and its two basic inflected and two basic uninflected markers. Some other, primarily uninflected markers typical of Southwest Ukrainian are not discussed either in the remainder since they do not shed any additional light on the development of relative clauses in East Slavonic.

Yet the major diachronic changes outlined above are sufficient for making several observations of the diachronic and typological nature, especially in regards to our hypothesis about the two pathways of relative clause chaining in East Slavonic. As evidenced in scholarly literature (e.g., Mel'nyčuk 1962; Akimova 1964) the number of non-standard relative clause types in Russian dialects seems to equal those in Belarusian and Ukrainian. The difference between Russian, on the one hand, and Belarusian and Ukrainian, on the other, lies in the systemic adaptation of the aforementioned relative clause types. Of the four overt relative markers noted, the Russian dialects tend to use today mostly the inflected relative markers *kotoryj* and *kakoj* 'which' rather than uninflected elements for the interlacing of relative clauses (Danylenko 2014: 200–201); the uninflected markers *čto* 'what' and, especially, *gde* 'where' occur rarely and more often than not in the dialects which have been in contact with other languages or dialects, irrespective of their genealogical closeness. One can mention here the insular and some Russian Old Believer frontier dialects in the northeast of Latgalia in Latvia and the Russian transitional Kursk-Orel dialects in contact with the Ukrainian Sloboda dialect.

The Belarusian dialects too differ from the Ukrainian ones. The inflected relative markers seem to be more widespread in Belarusian than in Ukrainian where the markers *kotryj* and, historically, *jakyj* 'which' have been largely influenced by the adjacent Polish and Russian dialects and the corresponding literary traditions. As early as the 16th–17th cc. these markers represented non-native, artificial trends as cultivated in the written language (cf. Rabus 2010: 158–166). It is not surprising that, for instance, U *kotryj* and respectively B *katorŷ* 'which' have largely retained their distributive meaning cross-dialectally in both Ukrainian and Belarusian-speaking territories.

Diachronically and typologically, the uninflected marker *ščo* 'what' appears to be most representative for the Ukrainian-and Belarusian-speaking territories. As one of the oldest vernacular-oriented relativization strategies in East Slavonic (Mel'nyčuk 1962: 102), *ščo* still functions as a general overt linker for two clauses in juxtaposition. In such cases, the semantic relationship between the two clauses is by inference only; cf. the causative adverbial function as inferred in example (22):

(22) U folk.
Ne	puskaje	maty,	ščo	ja	moloda
not	let-PRS.3SG	mother	UCL	I	young-NOM.SG.F

'My mother doesn't let me go out because I am young'
(Korš 1877: 27)

As follows from the above, the level of incorporation of the margin clause in (22) is low; although overtly linked to the matrix clause, the margin one remains in the realm of parataxis and can be called, following Potebnja, a paratactic subordinate (relative) clause.

Conceivably, the nature of paratactic subordination does not change when the overt uninflected clause marker relates to an NP in the matrix clause, thus initiating relative clause linkage, as exemplified in (23):

(23) U folk.
A	de ž	taja	krynyčen'ka,	ščo
And	where	that-NOM.SG.F	well-NOM.SG.F	UREL
holub		kupavsja?		
pigeon-NOM.SG.M		bathe-PST.SG.M		

'And where is the well in which the pigeon bathed?'
(Korš 1877: 28)

The developmental cline of paratactic subordination as reconstructed for the relative clause chaining in East Slavonic involves two possible resolutions, or 'micro-pathways,' both attested in diachrony and contemporary dialects (see Section 2.2; Korš 1877: 15).

The first micro-pathway is premised on the use of the uninflected marker U *ščo* / B *što* / R *čto* 'what' in combination with a resumptive pronoun, as shown in Sentences (15), (24), and (25); the locative-specialized relative marker U *de* / B *dze* / R *gde* is also part of this micro-pathway as exemplified in Sentences (12), (13), (17), and (19).

(24) MU
Počerpalo: každaja   rečь,   ščo
Scooper   [is] every   thing-NOM.SG.F   UREL
čerpajutъ   neju
scoop-PRS.PL it-INS.SG.F
'Scooper can be anything with the help of which one scoops'
(1627; Berynda: 91)

(25) SR (Rjazan')
a   žena   nesët   emu   mladenca,
and   wife-NOM.SG.F   carry-PRS.3SG   he-DAT   baby-ACC.SG.M
čto   nego   rodila
UREL   he-ACC give.birth-PST.SG.F
'And his wife is carrying a baby whom she gave a birth'[3]
(Borkovskij 1981: 206)

The evolution of paratactic subordination along the second micro-pathway omits any resumption and presupposes, instead, the use of inflecting forms of the relative marker U *ščo* / B *što* / R *čto*, in particular in the instrumental and prepositional locative cases. Less advanced and rarely attested in the contemporary dialects, this micro-pathway was, nevertheless, rather productive in the Old and Middle periods of the history of East Slavonic (Borkovskij 1958: 124–125). It was ultimately replaced by the uninflected relative marker in combination with resumptive pronouns.

What we have shown here is thus that the aforementioned micro-pathways represent a distinctive developmental cline (pathway) of so-called paratactic subordination. Demonstrating a linear increase of syntactic amalgamation, this cline nevertheless is not conducive to the formation of 'complete' (hypotactic)

---

[3] We glossed *nego* as the direct object. However, this form is hard to interpret – the form *nego* may also stand for the agentive genitive *ot nego* '(impregnated) by him' or, as Minlos (2012: 78) suggested, the PP *dlja nego* 'for him'; it might also be a prothetic genitive form *nego ~ jego*.

subordination characterized by a complete dependency of the embedded relative clause. Linked with the help of such inflected relative markers as U *jakyj* / B *jaki* / R *kakoj* and U *kotryj* / B *katorŷ* / R *kotoryj* 'which', the developmental cline of hypotactic subordination also shows an increase of syntactic tightness. However, the latter tightness should be treated as a result of a separate diachronic and evolutional trend leading to a new stage in the genesis of syntactic complexity. In other words, the aforementioned pathways of relative clause chaining in East Slavonic represent separate (parallel) trends on integrative processes which tend to interlace with each other, though never losing their distinctive developmental tracks. All this clearly entitles us to argue that, instead of a unilateral developmental trend from free juxtaposition of clauses to hypotaxis to subordination, one should distinguish between two developmental clines, one leading from parataxis to paratactic subordination and the second leading to hypotactic subordination. In the view of the two historical resolutions (micro-pathways) to the development of paratactic subordination (P-Subordination) as opposed to hypotactic subordination (H-Subordination), we propose a modified representation of relative clause chaining for P-Subordination in East Slavonic in *Scheme 3*.

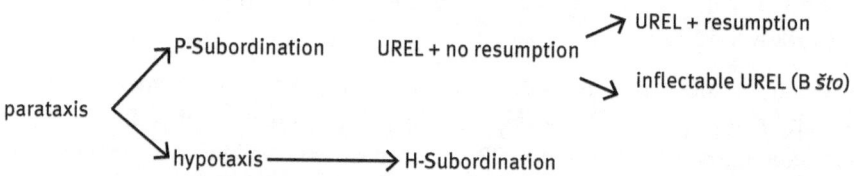

Scheme 3: A modified representation of clause combining for P-Subordination in East Slavonic.

What is left to determine here is what preconditions the developmental clines leading to the formation of paratactic and hypotactic subordination. As we hypothesized elsewhere (Danylenko 2014) in terms of social typology, the formation of paratactic and hypotactic subordination is dependent on a historically prevalent type of communication (discourse) within a language community. The prevalent type of communication is determined ultimately by a particular constellation of societal (extralinguistic) factors like the amount of adult language contact, type of social stability, size of a speech community, type of social networks, and amounts of communally shared information (Trudgill 2011: 13–14, 62, 146; 2013). Such a constellation preconditions the formation of a particular 'internal determinant' defined as a principal feature optimizing the whole system of a particular language (Danylenko 2006: 215–217). As a result, whether a language accrues complexity, in particular in the formation of hypotactic subordination in relativization, or simplifies, while strengthening the paratactic type of subordination, depends on a particular internal determinant of the language system. Since language contact (based on adult second-language learning) leads to an increase in simplification, the inflecting system tends to acquire more analytic features, which is likely to bring about regularization of irregularizations, an increase of morphological transparency, a reduction in syntagmatic redundancy conducive to a 'simpler' syntactic organization, including the development of paratactic subordination (cf. Trudgill 2011: 62).

As evidenced in its history (Danylenko 2001, 2006: 195–217), East Slavonic has been influenced by varying extralinguistic factors. This is why its dialects tend to demonstrate two developmental clines in relativization. The major, synthetic tendency has been leading to the strengthening of hypotactic subordination, while the second, analytic one to the strengthening of paratactic subordination in East Slavonic. As we have shown, the Belarusian and largely Ukrainian dialects have gone along the pathway conducive to the formation of paratactic subordination, while the bulk of Russian dialects have been developing hypotactic subordination with the complete dependency of embedded relative clause.

4 Areal-typological outlook

The existence of the two pathways of relativization is not limited to East Slavonic. They can be postulated for any inflecting Indo-European language which demonstrates either the analytic or synthetic tendency as outlined above. Since most Slavonic languages have retained the primary synthetic features and acquired some secondary analytic features (Danylenko 2013: 153–156), one can find some Slavonic dialects whose relative clause chaining is based either on the inflected relative clause linkage (e.g., Russian), or the uninflected relative clause linkage as found in Balkan Slavonic and most of the Ukrainian and Belarusian dialects (cf. Gołąb and Friedman 1972). In fact, this correlation can be applied to the rest of the Indo-European languages, conceived of in terms of Standard Average European. For instance, from the point of view of relativization patterns, Fiorentino (2007) divided Europe into two parts. On the one hand, Continental West Germanic languages (Dutch, German) still use an inflected Indo-European relative pronoun, while Romance languages, Greek, and English, on the other, adopted a mixed system with an invariant marker, cf. Fr and S *que*, I *che*.

The aforementioned generalization seems to be realistic. One can mention here those German dialects, e.g., Oberrotweil, Balse, East Pomeranian and others, which use the uninflected *wo* 'where' without resumption (Fleischer 2004: 224–227); the latter relativization strategy, as we have mentioned, is observed in the transitional Ukrainian, Belarusian, and Russian dialects found in contact with other languages. Of interest also is another German parallel, i.e., the use of uninflected *was* 'what' in combination with a resumptive pronoun, one of the most wide-spread innovations in the northwest (in the North Saxon dialect of Husby in Schleswig) and, predominantly, in the east, namely, in East Pomeranian, the Upper Saxon dialect of northwestern Bohemia, North Bavaria, and the Lubica linguistic island within the Slovak language area. Fleischer (2004: 235) hypothesized that, under the Slavonic influence, the eastern occurrences of this relative clause type might have been contact-induced.

Fleischer's contact hypothesis would be a partial explanation only. The point is that it has been very tempting in historical linguistics, for reasons that are far from obvious, to cast around for contact explanations of grammatical change. However, as Givón (1991: 301) noted, its scope is rigidly circumscribed. In the spirit of Givón's doubts, our inclination has always been to defer to the following methodological principle: explain by contact only changes that are counter-normative, i.e., go against the more common diachronic drift. The material discussed in this study allows us to claim that paratactic subordination tends to develop 'naturally', i.e., not as a replication, within an inflecting language system with analytic properties evolved due to contacts with speakers of other languages or conditions of spoken discourse (Kurzová 1981: 80; Givón 1991: 303). All this seems to corroborate our hypothesis about two separate pathways of relative clause chaining in East Slavonic and, by extension, other Indo-European languages that meet the requirements of either analytic or synthetic changes in their morphosyntax. But how these changes are correlated with the societal variables of linguistic patterning is a topic for future research on the diachronic syntax of Slavonic.

References

Akimova, Galina N. 1964. Tendencii v razvitii ornositel'nogo podčinenija v sovremennyx vostočnoslavjanskix jazykax [Tendencies in the development of relative clause subordination in the contemporary East Slavonic languages]. *Izvestija Akademii nauk SSSR. Serija literatury i jazyka* 23 (2). 138–144.

Atraxovič, Kandrat K. (ed.). 1966. *Hramatyka belaruskaj movy*, T. 2: *Sintaksis* [Belarusian grammar. Vol. 2: Syntax]. Minsk: Akadèmija navuk BSSR.

Astrèjka, V. D. 2009. *Xrèstamatyja pa belaruskaj dyjalektalohii. Cèntral'naja zona* [A reader for the Belarusian dialectology. The central zone]. Minsk: Belaruskaja navuka.
AUM: Matvijas, Ivan H. et al. (eds.). 1988. *Atlas ukrajins'koji movy*. T. 2: *Volyn', Naddnistrjanščyna i sumižni zemli*; 2001, T. 3: *Slobožanščyna, Doneččyna, Nyžnja Naddniprjanščyna, Pryčornomor''ja i sumižni zemli* [Atlas of the Ukrainian language. Vol. 2, Vol. 3]. Kyiv: Naukova dumka.
Baxan'koŭ, Arcëm Ja. 1960. Skladanazaležnyja skazy z dadanymi aznačal'nymi ŭ paŭdnëvazaxodnix belaruskix havorkax [Compound sentences with relative clauses in the southwestern Belarusian dialects]. *Vesci Akadèmii navuk Belaruskaj SSR. Seryja hramadskix navuk* 4. 116–128.
Berynda: Nimčuk, Vasyl' V. (ed.). 1961. *Leksykon slovenoros'kyj Pamvy Beryndy* [A Slavonic-Ruthenian Lexicon by Pamva Berynda]. Kyiv: Akademija nauk URSR.
Bevzenko, Stepan P. 1980. *Ukrajins'ka dialektolohija* [Ukrainian dialectology]. Kyiv: Vyšča škola.
Bilodid, Ivan K. (ed.). 1972. *Sučasna ukrajins'ka literaturna mova. Syntaksys* [Contemporary Ukrainian literary language. Syntax]. Kyiv: Naukova dumka.
Biryla, Mikalaj V. & Pavjal P. Šuba. 1986. *Belaruskaja hramatyka 2: Sintaksis* [Belarusian grammar 2: Syntax]. Minsk: Navuka i tèxnika.
Blinava, Èvelina D. & Evdokija S. Mjacel'skaja. 1969. *Belaruskaja dyjalektalohija* [Belarusian dialectology]. Minsk: Vyšejšaja škola.
Borkovskij, Viktor I. 1958. *Sintaksis drevnerusskix gramot: složnoe predloženie* [Syntax of the Old Russian charters: The compound sentence]. Moskva: Akademija nauk SSSR.
Borkovskij, Viktor I. 1981. *Sintaksis skazok. Russko-belarusskie paralleli* [Syntax of tales: Russian-Belorusian parallels]. Moskva: Nauka.
Borkovskij, Viktor I. & Pëtr S. Kuznecov. 1965. *Istoričeskaja grammatika russkogo jazyka* [A historical grammar of the Russian language]. Moskva: Nauka.
Cristofaro, Sonia & Anna Giacalone Ramat. 2007. Relativization strategies in the languages of Europe. In Paolo Ramat & Elisa Roma (eds.), *Europe and Mediterranean as linguistic areas: Convergence from a historical and typological perspective*, 63–93. Amsterdam & Philadelphia: John Benjamins.
Dahl, Östen. 2009. Two pathways of grammatical evolution. In Talmy Givón & Masayoshi Shibatani (eds.), *Syntactic complexity. Diachrony, acquisition, neuro-cognition, evolution*, 239–248. Amsterdam & Philadelphia: John Benjamins.
Danylenko, Andrii. 2001. Russian *čto za*, Ukrainian *ščo za*, Polish *co za* 'was für ein'. A case of contact-induced or parallel change? *Diachronica* 28 (2). 241–265.
Danylenko, Andrii. 2003. *Predykaty, vidminky i diatezy v ukrajins'kij movi: istoryčnyj i typolohičnyj aspekty* [Predicates, cases and diatheses in Ukrainian: Historical and typological aspects]. Kharkiv: Oko.
Danylenko, Andrii. 2006. *Slavica et Islamica: Ukrainian in context*. Munich: Otto Sagner.
Danylenko, Andrii. 2013. Ukrainian in the language map of Central Europe: questions of areal-typological profiling. *Journal of Language Contact* 6 (1). 134–159.
Danylenko, Andrii. 2014. On the relativization strategies in East Slavic. In Motoki Nomachi, Andrii Danylenko & Predrag Piper (eds.), *Grammaticalization and lexicalization in the Slavic languages*, 183–204. Munich: Otto Sagner.
Danylenko, Andrii. 2015. How many varieties of standard Ukrainian does one need? *Die Welt der Slaven* 60 (2). 223–247.

Danylenko, Andrii. 2016. *Iazychie* and *Surzhyk*: Mixing languages and identities in the Ukrainian borderlands. In Tomasz Kamusella, Motoki Nomachi & Catherine Gibson (eds.). *The Palgrave handbook of Slavic languages, identities and borders*, 81–100. New York: Palgrave Macmillan.

Deutscher, Guy. 2009. Nominalization and the origin of subordination. In Talmy Givón & Masayoshi Shibatani (eds.), *Syntactic complexity. Diachrony, acquisition, neuro-cognition, evolution*, 199–214. Amsterdam & Philadelphia: John Benjamins.

Fiorentino, Giuseppe. 2007. European relative clauses and the uniqueness of the relative pronoun type. *Rivista di Linguistica* 19 (2). 263–291.

Fleischer, Jürg. 2004. A typology of relative clauses in German dialects. In Bernd Kortmann (ed.), *Dialectology meets typology*, 211–243. Berlin & New York: Mouton de Gruyter.

Gallis, Arne. 1958. Flektiertes Relativum und Relativum generale, insbesondere im Serbokroatischen. *Scando-Slavica* 4. 137–148.

Givón, Talmy. 1991. The evolution of dependent clause morpho-syntax in Biblical Hebrew. In Elizabeth Closs Traugott & Bernd Heine (eds.), *Approaches to grammaticalization*, 257–310. Amsterdam & Philadelphia: John Benjamins.

Givón, Talmy. 2009a. *The genesis of syntactic complexity*. Amsterdam & Philadelphia: John Benjamins.

Givón, Talmy. 2009b. Multiple routes to clause union. In Talmy Givón & Masayoshi Shibatani (eds.), *Syntactic complexity. Diachrony, acquisition, neuro-cognition, evolution*, 81–118. Amsterdam & Philadelphia: John Benjamins.

Gołąb, Zbigniew & Victor A. Friedman. 1972. The relative clause in Slavic. In Paul M. Peranteau, Judith N. Levi & Gloria C. Phares (eds.), *The Chicago which hunt. Papers from the Relative Clause Festival, April 13, 1972*, 30–46. Chicago: Chicago Linguistic Society.

Heine, Bernd. 2009. From nominal to clausal morphosyntax. Complexity via expansion. In Talmy Givón & Masayoshi Shibatani (eds.), *Syntactic complexity. Diachrony, acquisition, neuro-cognition, evolution*, 23–51. Amsterdam & Philadelphia: John Benjamins.

Heine, Bernd & Tania Kuteva. 2007. *The genesis of grammar. A reconstruction*. Oxford: Oxford University Press.

Hendery, Rachel. 2012. *Relative clauses in time and space. A case study in the methods of diachronic typology*. Amsterdam & Philadelphia: John Benjamins.

Hopper, Paul J. & Elizabeth Closs Traugott. 2003. *Grammaticalization*, 2nd edn. Cambridge: Cambridge University Press.

Karskij, Evimij F. 2006 [1911]. *Belorusy 2: Jazyk belorusskogo naroda 2* [Belarusians 2: Language of the Belarusian people]. Minsk: Belaruskaja Ėncyklapedyja.

Keenan, Edward L. & Bernard Comrie. 1977. Noun phrase accessibility and Universal Grammar. *Linguistic Inquiry* 8 (1). 63–99.

Keenan, Edward L. & Bernard Comrie. 1979. Data on the noun phrase Accessibility Hierarchy. *Language* 55 (2). 333–351.

Korš, Fëdor. 1877. *Sposoby otnositel'nogo podčinenija. Glava iz sravnitel'nogo sintaksisa* [Means of relative clause subordination. A chapter from comparative syntax]. Moskva: Katkov.

Křížkova, Helena. 1970. Relativní věty v současných slovanských jazycích [Relative clauses in contemporary Slavonic languages]. *Slavia* 39. 10–40.

Kurzová, Helena. 1981. *Der Relativsatz in den indoeuropäischen Sprachen*. Hamburg: Buske.

Kuznecov, Pëtr S. (ed.). 1973. *Russkaja dialektologija* [Russian dialectology]. Moskva: Prosveščenie.

Lehmann, Christian. 1984. *Der Relativsatz. Typologie seiner Strukturen. Theorie seiner Funktionen, Kompendium seiner Grammatik*. Tübingen: Gunter Narr.

Levčenko, Mykola Z. (ed.). 1928. *Kazky j opovidannja z Podillja v zapysax 1850–1860 rr., fasc.1–2* [Tales and stories from Podillja in the records from the 1850s–1860s]. Kyiv: Vseukrajins'ka akademija nauk.

Meillet, Antoine.1924. *Le slave commun*. Paris: Édouard Champion.

Mel'nyčuk, Oleksandr S.1962. Istoryčnyj rozvytok systemy vidnosnyx sliv v ukrajins'kij movi [Historical development of the system of relative words in Ukrainian]. *Slov'janske movoznavstvo* 4. 80–121.

Meščerskij, Nikita A. (ed.). 1972. *Russkaja dialektologija* [Russian dialectology]. Moskva: Vysšaja škola.

Minlos, Filipp R. 2012. Slavic relative *čto/co*: Between pronouns and conjunctions. *Slověne* 1. 74–91.

Murelli, Adriano. 2011. *Relative constructions in European non-standard varieties*. Berlin & Boston: De Gruyter Mouton.

Nau, Nicole. 2011. *A Short Grammar of Latgalian*. Languages of the World (Materials 482). Munich: Lincom Europa.

PG 1556–1561: Čepiha, Inna P. (eds.). 2001. *Peresopnyc'ke Jevanhelije 1556–1561* [The Peresopnycja Gospel of 1556–1561]. Kyiv: Nacional'na akademija nauk Ukraini.

Potebnja, Aleksandr A. 1899. *Iz zapisok po russkoj grammatike* 3 [From the notes on Russian grammar 3]. Kharkiv: Zil'berberg.

Proxorova, Svetlana M. 1991. *Sintaksis perexodnoj russko-belorusskoj zony: areal'no-tipologičeskoe issledovanie* [Syntax of the transitional Russian-Belorusian area: An areal-typological study]. Minsk: Universitetskoe izdatel'stvo.

Pugh, Stefan & Ian Press. 1999. *Ukrainian. A comprehensive grammar*. London & New York: Routledge.

Rabus, Achim. 2010. Die Relativisatoren im Ruthenischen. In Björn Hansen & Jasmina Grković-Major (eds.), *Diachronic Slavonic syntax. Gradual changes in focus* (Wiener Slawistischer Almanach – Sonderband 74), 155–168. München, Berlin & Wien: Otto Sagner.

Ruke-Dravinja [Ruke-Dravina], Velta.1964. Dial. *gde* [=*kotorj*]. In Igor Vahros & Martti Kahla (eds.), *Lingua Viget. Commentationes slavicae in honorem V. Kiparsky*, 115–119. Helsinki: Suomalaisen Kirjallisuuden Kirjapaino Oy.

Smerečyns'kyj, Serhij. 1932. *Narysy z ukrajins'koji syntaksy* [Studies on Ukrainian syntax]. Xarkiv: Radjans'ka škola.

Švedova, Natalija J. (ed.). 1980. *Russkaja grammatika. Tom 2: Sintaksis* [Russian grammar. Vol 2: Syntax]. Moskva: Nauka.

Troickij, Veniamin I. 1968. *Otnositel'noe podčinenie v jazyke russkoj pis'mennosti XVI–XVII vekov* [The relative clause subordination in the Russian literary language of the 16th–17th centuries]. Kazan: Izdatel'stvo Kazanskogo universiteta.

Trudgill, Peter. 2011. *Sociolinguistic typology. Social determinants of linguistic complexity*. Oxford: Oxford University Press.

Trudgill, Peter. 2013. Contact and sociolinguistic typology. In Raymond Hickey (ed.), *The handbook of language contact*, 299–319. Chichester, West Sussex, Malden, Mass.: Wiley-Blackwell.

Urbańczyk, Stanisław. 1939. *Zdania rozpoczynane wyrazem co w języku polskim* [Sentences introduced with the word *co* in Polish]. Kraków: Nakład Polskiej akademii umiejętności.

Verxratskij, Ivan. 1902. *Pro hovor halyckyx lemkiv* [On the dialect of the Galician Lemkos]. Lviv: Naukove Tovarystvo imeny Ševčenka.
Vyxovanec', Ivan R. 1993. *Hramatyka ukrajins'koji movy* [Ukrainian Grammar]. Kyiv: Lybid'.
Zadorožnyj, Vasyl' B. & Antonina M. Matvijenko (eds.). 1995. *Volyns'ki hramoty XVI st.* [Charters from the Volhyn' of the 16th century]. Kyiv: Instytut ukrajins'koji movy NAN Ukrajiny.
Žylko, Fedot T. 1966. *Narysy z dialektolohii ukrajins'koji movy* [Studies on the dialectology of the Ukrainian language]. Kyiv: Radjans'ka škola.

Barbara Sonnenhauser
Relativisation strategies in Slovene: Diachrony between language use and language description

Abstract: The Slovene relativisation markers *ki* and *kateri*, which contribute to the very individual nature of Contemporary Standard Slovene among the Slavonic languages, constitute a prime example for the complex processes underlying diachronic syntactic change. Their formal and functional development as evinced in historical data and analysed in linguistic descriptions shows a multitude of factors that interact not only on the linguistic, but also on the descriptive level. The specific situation in contemporary Slovene thus results from a development that has taken place at the interface of language and linguistics, being affected by both language use and language description.

1 The 'oziralna dvoica' *ki* and *kateri*

Brozović (1988: 187) emphasizes that the "complex and extraordinarily interesting nature of Contemporary Standard Slovene" can only be understood against the background of "its material base, the way it evolved, its special paths of development and [...] the specific circumstances in which it was elaborated" (1988: 185). Among the examples illustrating the specific nature of Slovene and the concomitant need for a multifactorial analysis are its relativisation strategies. This pertains in particular to indeclinable *ki* and adjectival *kateri*, which are both used for restrictive and non-restrictive relative clauses.[1] This *oziralna dvojica* 'relativisation pair' – as Toporišič (2000: 341) calls it – is puzzling in terms of synchronic usage patterns and diachronic development.

The contemporary usage patterns are briefly illustrated in (1) and (2). Both may be used for the relativisation of subjects, cf. (1a) and (1b):

---

[1] In free and correlative relative clauses, *wh*-pronouns + *r* (*kdor*, *kakor*, etc.) are used; see Chidambaram (2007) for a short overview.

(1) a. *Zid,* **ki** *je delil svetove*
 wall which aux.3SG divide.PST.3SG worlds
 'The wall, which divided the worlds'
 (FidaPLUS)[2]
 b. *Ne bomo žalovali kakordrugi,*
 NEG will.1PL mourn.PST.PTCP like others,
 kateri *nimajo upanja.*
 which not.have.3PL hope.GEN.SG
 'We will not mourn like the others that do not have any hope.'
 (FidaPLUS)

As regards the relativisation of non-subjects, *ki* requires a resumptive pronoun, as *jih* 'them' in (2a). For prepositional cases, only *kateri* is possible (see Topolińska 2003 for exceptions), cf. (2b):

(2) a. *Podatki$_i$,* **ki jih$_i$** *je sporočil*
 information which them AUX.3SG tell.PST.3SG
 'The information$_i$, which [them$_i$] he told'
 (FidaPLUS)
 b. *Zagledal je hišo,* **v katero**
 notice.PST.M.SG AUX.3SG house.ACC into which
 so vstopali ljudje
 AUX.3PL enter.PST.PL people
 'He noticed the house, **which** people stepped **into**.'
 (FidaPLUS)

For the relativization of direct and indirect objects both can be used. Elaborating the parameters underlying the choice between *ki* and *kateri* in these contexts is beyond the scope of the present paper (see, e.g., Topolińska 2003; Sonnenhauser 2013 for suggestions). The focus here will be on the diachronic development underlying the current state of affairs. As will be shown, different factors – usage based and description based – have to be taken into account: (i) language internal development, i.e. paths of development that can be motivated by general Slavonic processes, (ii) external, i.e. contact-related influences,

---

[2] The FidaPLUS corpus is a morphosyntactically tagged reference corpus for Slovene covering literary and non-literary written texts from 1979 to 2006. A detailed description of the corpus can be found in Krek and Kilgarriff (2006); see also http://www.fidaplus.net/Info/Info_index_eng.html (last accessed February 4, 2016). The FidaPLUS corpus has been included in the Gigafida corpus, which also includes texts from 2006 onwards (see http://www.gigafida.net/ for access to the corpus and information concerning its makeup).

and (iii) metalinguistic factors influencing language description and grammar writing.

2 Diachrony I: Usage

To begin with, an overview of the usage of *ki* and *kateri* in older stages of Slovene will be given. Needless to say, 'usage' refers to the occurrence of both relativisation markers in written documents, which does not necessarily reflect oral language usage. However, since the usage in these documents is not yet subject to prescriptive norms, it can be taken as a good starting point for reasonable assumptions – at least concerning the scribe of the respective document. Differences encountered may thus be taken as evidence of regional variance and of potential contact influence.

One of the problems in dealing with the usage patterns of *ki* and *kateri* in older stages of Slovene is the poor data basis. There are only a few sources for the 10th to 16th century. During the reformation in the 16th century the number increases, but again decreases for the 17th to 18th century. The situation again changes with the beginning of the 19th century, when efforts to standardize Slovene set in.

2.1 The Freising manuscripts (10th/11th century)

The first written documents including what might – with all due caution – be called Slovene vernacular elements, are the Freising manuscripts (FM), dating to the late 10th/early 11th century. Here, forms of *iže* can be found, cf. *iſe* in (3a), which can also be inflected and be used for non-subject (or rather non-nominative) relativisation, as indicated by *emuſe* in (3b):

(3) a. *Naſ gozbod zueticruz   iſegeſt   bali   teleznaſſih* [...]
       our lord   holy.Christ   who.is   physician   bodies.ours
       'Our Lord, the holy Christ, *who* is the physician of our bodies'
       (Manuscript II.89–90; Toporišič 1981: 399)
    b. *ili eſe   mizetomu   chotelo   emuſe   mibi*
       or because   me.that   wanted.N.SG   which   me.would
       ne   doztalo   choteti [...]
       NEG   suited.N.SG   want.INF
       'or because I wanted something [*which*] I ought not to have wanted'
       (Manuscript I.16–17; Toporišič 1981: 396)

Another relativising element encountered in the FM is *choi*, cf. (4) where it is accompanied by the resumptive pronoun *ih* 'them.ACC.PL':

(4) *Eſeroti* **Choi** *ſe*   **Ih**   *nepazem* [...]
    or.oaths which PRT   them   NEG.we.keep
    'or oaths *which* we do not keep [*them*]'
    (Manuscript II.23–24, Toporišič 1981: 398)

As an interrogative-based relativising element, *choi* is to be distinguished from anaphora-based *iže* (Dogramadžieva 1989: 65, 66; see also Sections 3.1, 4), which Dogramadžieva (1989: 67) counts among those elements that have been kept from Proto-Slavonic without major changes. While both *iže* and *choi* are accompanied by the particle *ſe* (*že* in contemporary orthography[3]), they differ in agreement marking, which is morphologically expressed for *iže*, cf. (3b), and with a resumptive pronoun for *choi*, see (4).

2.2 Early Slovene manuscripts (14th–16th century)

The few manuscripts dating to the 14th–16th century exhibit different instances of what look like variants of later *ki*, such as *kyr*, *kher* or *kir*:[4]

(5) a. *Yaſt*   *veruyo*   *wu boga othſcho* [...]   *yno*   *wu iheſuſſa criſtuſſa* [...]
       I   I.believe in god father   and   in Jesus Christ
       kyr   *ye poczett*   *od ſwetiga ducha* [...]
       who[5]   is conceived   from Holy Ghost
       'I believe in God the Father and in Jesus Christ, *who* is conceived of the Holy Ghost'
       (*Rateški rokopis*, 1362–1390;[6] Mikhailov 1998: 99, 3.I–IV)

---

3 The FM were written in Latin alphabet, which had not yet been adapted to the needs of Slovene at that time (the elaboration of the Slovene alphabet towards its contemporary form took until the mid-19th century).
4 In his edition and linguistic analysis of these manuscripts, Mikhailov (1998: 386) lists the emergence of the relativising element *ki* among those questions which come to mind when analysing these documents.
5 Mikhailov (1998: 101) analyses *kyr* as *ker* 'because': "*kyr* müßte die Kausalkonjunktion mod. slow. *ker* 'weil' und nicht irgendwelches Relativpronomen (vgl. *ki*) sein" [*kyr* must be the causal conjunction mod. Slov. *ker* 'because' and not some relative pronoun (cf. *ki*)]. The same holds for *kher* in (5b), cf. Mikhailov (1998: 207). The Slovene edition of these prayers has *ki* in both cases (Mikhailov 1998: 100, 206).
6 For the dating of the manuscripts see Mikhailov (1998: 16–18).

b. *Otzha nafch* **kher** *fy vnebeffich*
   father our   who you.are in.heaven
   'Our Father *who* (you) are in heaven'
   (Starogorski rokopis, 1492–1498: Mikhailov 1998: 206, 1.I)
c. *ja odpušo vsejm tejm* **kir** [...]
   I I.forgive all those   who
   'I forgive all those *who* [...]'
   (Stiški rokopis, 1428–1440; Mikhailov 1998: 145, 5.LVII–LVIII)

The *Černejski rokopis* has *chi*,[7] cf. (6a), which may also be inflected, as in (6b). Mikhailov (1998: 244) analyses *fchich* as genitive plural to *ki*:

(6) a. *treti del   jednoga mafa vmefti*   **chife**   *clize vpechol*
       third part of.one estate at.place which.REFL calls 'vpekol'
       'the third part of an estate at a place *which* is called 'v Pekol''
       (Černejski rokopis, 1497–; Mikhailov 1998: 250–251, 9(50))
   b. *jeft   oftauil* [...]   *marach zeternaift* **fchich**
       AUX.3SG bequeathed.M.SG   Marks fourteen   with.which
       marach jeft cuplegno   dua ftara   pfefnize [...]
       Marks AUX.3SG bought.N.SG   two measures of.grain
       'He has bequeathed fourteen Marks, *with which* Marks two heaped measures of grain have been bought.'
       (Černejski rokopis, 1497–; Mikhailov 1998: 243, 4(45))

Only a few forms can be found in the Early Slovene manuscripts that seem related to *kateri*: the Starogorski rokopis has *kheter*, (7a) (vs. the Rateški rokopis, cf. (5a)) the Kranjski rokopos has *khatero*, (7b), and *sa khatere*, (7c):[8]

---

7 Possibly, this spelling is to be attributed to the influence of Italian orthography, if not to Italian itself, which has *chi* as relative pronoun. Given that the manuscript originates from Friaul (Mikhailov 1998: 79), this assumption seems not unwarranted.

8 Further relativisation markers, besides those related to *ki* and *kateri*, found in the documents dating to this period are *kemer* and *kigar*, see (i) and (ii).

(i) *Ya fe dalfan dam vffeymi greychy zkemer ta czlovik more greyffity* [...] (*Stiški rokopis*, 1428–1440; Mikhailov 1998: 129, 4.XII–XIII)
    'I admit being guilty through all the sins *with which* man can transgress'
(ii) *fam ze volnw wdall ty ablafti tyga /chudic zakygar* [...] *fam fe odpoueydall* [...] (*Stiški rokopis*, 1428–1440; Mikhailov 1998: 139, 5.VIII–IX)
    'I rendered myself voluntarily to the realm of the Evil *which* I have abjured'

Miklosich (1876: 149) derives *kemer* from *kyimiže*, i.e. *kyj*, which he assumes to underlie also the 'Croat Slovene' *ki, ka, ko* (ibid.).

(7) a. *Yest veryo   na boga [...]   ynuy   na Jheſuſſa chriſtuſſa*
     I I.believe   in god   and   in Jesus Christ
     *[...], **kheter**   ye podtzhett   od ſwetiga ducha [...]*
     who   is conceived   from Holy Ghost
     'I believe in God and in Jesus Christ, who is conceived by the Holy Ghost'
     (Starogorski rakopis, 1492–1498; Mikhailov 1998: 211, 3.I–V)
  b. *Jeſt   Vaſʒ opomenim,   da   Vy wote pouedalli.   per thi*
     I   you I.admonish   that   you will report   with this
     *teleſʒni Rotwi   **khatero**   Ste Vy [...]   perſeglj.*
     bodily oath   which   aux.3PL you.PL   took.PST.PL
     'I admonish you to report with this bodily oath *which* you took.'
     (Kranjski rokopis, 1140–; 1998: 185, V)
  c. *vtih rečeh.   **sa khatere**   Vy wodete   Vpraſchanj*
     in.these things   about which   you.PL will.2PL   asked
     'concerning these things *about which* you will be asked'
     (Kranjski rokopis, 1140–; 1998: 185, V)

Since the Kranjski rokopis is available only as transcript from 1871 (Mikhailov 1998: 181), these data have to be treated with caution, albeit it seems unlikely that the editor of the transcript would have interfered with syntax that essentially.

2.3 Protestant texts (16th century)

With the onset of the Reformation and its aim to propagate Protestantism among as many people as possible, the amount of texts increases from the mid-16th century onwards. In these texts, *kateri* is well attested in a relativising function and appears regularly, alongside *ki(r)*.

In (8a), *kateri* may be interpreted both as a free-choice pronoun (which indicates its interrogative origin) and a relative pronoun, while in (8b) it unambiguously functions as a relative pronoun.

(8) a. *Vsaketeri,   **kir**   mene spozna   pred tejmiludmi,   tiga*
     everyone   who   me recognizes   in.front.of these people,   that.one
     *istiga   jest hočo   tudi spoznati [...];   **kateri** pak   mene*
     the.same   I I.want   also to.recognize   who but   me
     pred ludmi   zataji [...],   tiga istiga   jest hočo   zatajiti [...]
     in.front.of people   disowns   that.one the.same   I I.want   to.disown
     'Everyone *who* recognizes me in front of those people, I also want to recognize; but *he who* disowns me, that one I will also disown.'
     (Primož Trubar, *Ena regišter ... ena kratka postila*, 1558; Freidhof 1981: 19f)

b. *ta ortografija   drži,   **katero***
   that orthography   keep.IMP   which
   našiga jezika idioma   inu natura   potrebuje [...]
   of.our language idiom   and nature   requires
   'keep that orthography *which* the characteristics and nature of our language require'
   (Sebastian Krelj, *Postila slovenska*, 1567; Freidhof 1981: 63f)

In the course of the Counter Reformation, letter print came to a halt in central Slovenia. However, reformist books kept being printed in the periphery, notably in the Slovene-speaking regions under Hungarian Rule such as Prekmurje (see Jesenšek 2008 for a comparison of Trubar's and Küzmič's language in their catechisms). In these texts, *ki* and *kateri* appear, with *šteri* as an alternative form to *kateri*, cf. (9):

(9) *Jožef pa   i Maria   Mati Jezušova*
   Jožef PRT   and Maria   mother of.Jesus
   *sta se čüdivala   nad onim,   **štera***
   AUX.2DU REFL wonder.PST.2DU   about these.things,   which
   so povejdana   od njega.
   are told   from him
   'But Joseph and Maria, the mother of Jesus, wondered about that *which* was told by him.'
   (Mikoš Küzmič, *Sveti Evangjeliomi*; Novak 1936, 39)

Since the present paper is concerned with the development towards the contemporary standard language, which is based on central Slovene dialects, the Prekmurian data (and other data from peripheral dialects of Slovene) will not be focused upon in more detail.

2.4 Contemporary Slovene

From the late 19th century onwards both *ki* and *kateri* have been in general use in written sources, with *ki* dominating in mere numbers[9] (see the texts on http://www.intratext.com/8/slv/). It remains to be investigated as to whether there is a functional difference associated with the choice of form in contexts, where – from a syntactic point of view – both are equally possible (see Section 1). Several

---

[9] This is based on evidence by inspection not on a thorough counting of tokens. As clear as this surface impression is, it cannot – of course – claim to be based on a representative sample.

factors have been suggested to play a role in this respect, such as register or type of relative clause (e.g. Gołąb and Friedman 1972). However, none of them seems to exhibit a statistically significant correlation with the choice of *ki* or *kateri*. A slight tendency can be observed for complex head NPs and relative clause attachment, in that *kateri* is preferred for NP_2-attachment, *ki* for NP_1-attachment (see Sonnenhauser 2013). Complex head NPs being rarer in the spoken than in the written mode, the preference for *ki* in oral communication may possibly emerge as a side effect of this syntax-based distribution.

2.5 Summing up

While various forms of putative predecessors of *ki* can be found already in the earliest documents, *kateri* appears in regular usage as a relativisation marker only from the 16th century onwards. The data prior to the 16th century being so rare and being restricted in terms of lexicon and topics (as pointed out also by Mikhailov 1998: 13f), this evidence has to be interpreted very carefully. These restrictions notwithstanding, the early Slovene manuscripts are of great value in that they indicate the complexity of the data and the multitude of analyses that might be applicable. This latter type of variety will be shown in the following section.

3 Diachrony II: Descriptions

The poor data basis is not only problematic for the identification of possible usage patterns, it also impedes the investigation of the formal and functional development of *ki* and *kateri*. This has brought forth various different analyses.

3.1 *Ki*

The origin and development of *ki* are fairly opaque and, as a consequence, explained in manifold ways (see also Sonnenhauser 2013: 156–159 for an overview). This pertains to two main questions: 1) whether *kir*, which is found until the 19th century, and contemporary *ki* are identical or derive from different sources, and 2) in which way *ki* and/or *kir* relate to *kateri*.

One line of analysis regards the emergence of *ki* as an instance of the general Indo-European replacement of **jo*-based pronouns by **kwo*-based ones (e.g. Kurzová 1981: 44). This fits the observation that OCS and the Freising manuscripts still have *iže*, while in later manuscripts only *ki(r)* is found. According to another kind of analysis (see Cazinkić 2001: 56 and Snoj 1997: 228 for an overview of proposals), *ki* emerges from **yo* via *kir* < *ki-že* < *iže*. While final *r* can be accounted for in terms of rhotacism, i.e. the development of *ž* into *r* (a common development in Slovene), this proposal faces difficulties in accounting for the initial *k-*. This is then motivated in terms of analogy to other interrogative and relative pronouns.

Another assumption derives *ki* from **kъjь* 'who, which', via *kyjь*, *kaja*, *koje* (e.g. Topolińska 2003; Gołąb and Friedman 1972; Křížková 1970). One early attestation that could support this assumption is *choi* in the Freising documents (II, 23–24, cf. (4) above), which Dogramadžieva (1989: 65, 66) analyses as relativizing adverb with an interrogative root. Gallis (1956) draws a parallel to Kajkavian *ki*, *ka*, *ko* which he analyses as 'contracted forms' of *koji*, *koja*, *koje*, etc. While this could be supported by *ſchich* in the FM (see (6b) above), the development of *ki* into an indeclinable element remains to be accounted for.

Miklosich (1876) assumes *ki* and *kir* to be of different origins. He relates *kir* to **kъde-že* 'where' (via *kir* < *kjer* < *kder* < *kъde že*), and inflected forms of *ki* to 'Croat Slovene' (i.e. Kajkavian) *ki*, *ka*, *ko*. For the latter he cites one example from Krelj's *Postila Slovenska* (1567): *v kim mestu* 'at which place' (1876: 149). This is interesting insofar as Krelj, unlike Trubar, aimed at a literary language that was closer to Croatian (see Kopitar 1808: 28; Seitz 1997: 98–101). Miklosich (1876: 149) further differentiates inflected and uninflected *ki*, arguing that the latter is a 'recent' (relative to his time) development and not found in older documents:

> *Das heutzutage gebräuchliche* ki, *das mit dem demonstrativen* i *verbunden und als relativum gebraucht wird [...] findet sich in den älteren denkmälern nicht: statt dessen gebrauchten trub.* [Trubar, BS] *und seine zeitgenossen das mit* kъde že *zusammzustellende* kir *aus* kjer, kder (1876: 149; italics in the original, BS)
> [Contemporary *ki*, which is combined with demonstrative *i* and used as a relativising element is not found in the older documents: instead, Trubar and his contemporaries used *kir* which is to be grouped together with *kъde že*, deriving from *kjer*, *kder*]

In addition, Miklosich (1876) proposes a separate approach for 'contemporary' (i.e. 19th century) *kir*, which he distinguishes from *ki*. This is suggested by his analysis of *choi* in example (4) as deriving from *kyže*, which corresponds to „*heutzutage* kir" 'nowadays *kir*' (1876: 149; italics in the original, BS). This obviously amounts to assuming two different kinds of *ki* and two different kinds of *kir* – a highly complex situation. However, given the variety of the data (cf. Section 2), this seems not categorically unlikely.

A relation between *ki* and 'where' is proposed also by Nuorluoto (2010), albeit a more indirect one than assumed by Miklosich. Nuorluoto does not regard *ki* as an immediate successor of *kъdeže*, but assumes *ki* to have lost its inflection – which is still present in some Čakavian dialects – due to German influence: German *wo* 'where', which also functions as a relativisor (see also Danylenko this volume), has triggered the reanalysis of *ki(r)* as *kje* 'where' (Nuorluoto 2010: 42; see also Kopitar 1808).[10]

The complex situation concerning *ki* is also reflected in dictionaries. The *Dictionarium Latino-Carniolicum* (1608–1710; cf. Latinski) lists three entries for *kir*: one as a pronoun, one as locative adverb and one as conjunction (the latter giving Latin *ubi* as translation). Pleteršnik (2010 [1894]) has three entries that seem related to contemporary *ki*, cf. (10): one relating *ki* as a relative pronoun to *ker* and *kir*, one regarding it as part of a paradigm *ki, ka, ko* deriving from *kyj*, and a third one relating *ki* to *ker*, which in turn is assumed to relate to *kъdeže*, cf. (10):

(10) a. *kì*, pron. rel. indecl. [...] — prim. ['cf.'] *ker, kir*.
  b. *kí, ka, ko*, pron. = *kateri* [...] — prim. stsl. ['cf. old Slavonic'] *kyj*.
  c. *kèr*, I. conj. [...] zato, *ker* [...] II. pron. rel. = *kir, ki*, Krelj; —
  „ker entspricht wohl einem altslov. kъdeže" ['ker corresponds to Old Slavonic kъdeže'], Mik[losich]. [...]

The entries in Pleteršnik suggest that three different lexemes might have been conflated in contemporary *ki*: ki_1 and ki_2 differ in tone, with ki_1 having a short falling (*kì*), ki_2 a long raising (*kí*) accent. Since tone is not equally prominent in all Slovene dialects, it may very well be the case that for some speakers, a difference between ki_1 and ki_2 was not noticeable, which in turn provided the basis for reanalysing them as identical – the more so, as their function is virtually identical. Reanalysis might also have been involved in the development of *ker* from *kъdeže*, accompanied by phonetic erosion (*ki* < *kir* < *ker*) and rhotacism (*r* < *že*).

The assumption of different origins for *ki* and *kir* and the distinction between contemporary uninflected *ki* and inflected *ki* is also reflected in the entry for *ki* in Snoj's (1997) etymological dictionary, which proposes (1997: 228) that "[v] današnje *ki* sta verjetno sovpadli dve prvotno razližni besed" 'in contemporary *ki*, most likely, two originally different words have coincided', namely *kir* < **jь že* and **kъjь* (*že*).

---

[10] The fact that many influential Slovene writers grew up in a German speaking environment may also have played a role.

3.2 *Kateri*

While the etymology of *ki* is fairly obscure, the origins of *kateri* are more obvious. It derives from a **kwo*-based pronominal element amended with **-(t)ero-*, an Indo-European comparative suffix expressing relative contrasts such as the choice between a pair of entities (Meier-Brügger 2002: 225). This is also pointed out by Kopitar (1808: 297–298):

> K a t e r i selbst ist, mittels der auch bey den Zahlwörtern und sonst z.B. m n o g i t e r i (mancherley), vorkommenden Ableitungssilbe e r i (t e r i) von k d o (oder der Wurzel ki (k')?) abgeleitet. [spacing in the original, BS]
> [*Kateri* is derived from *kdo* (or the root *ki* (k')?) by means of the derivation syllable *eri* (*teri*), which appears also with numerals and also, for instance, *mnogoteri* (*some*).]

It remains to be investigated in more detail whether the semantics 'which of two' (see also Gołąb and Friedman 1972) may account for the subtle functional differences between contemporary *ki* and *kateri* (as suggested in Sonnenhauser 2013).

One of the puzzles concerning *kateri* is the fact that on the one hand it "continues Common Slavonic *kъterъ-jъ*, with a secondary *a* inserted by analogy with pronouns such as *kako* and *kakšen*" (Topolińska 2003: 310), while on the other, it is rarely attested in a relativising function until the mid-16th century, i.e. until the Protestant texts (the situation is similar for West Slavonic). In its relativising function it has cognates in other present day Slavonic standard languages – except for South Slavonic. Kajkavian, however, seems to be closer to Slovene: Gallis (1956: 115) notes the appearance of "a new pronoun, namely *koteri* (*kteri*)" in the Kajkavian literature of 1500–1800, whereby 'new' obviously refers to its function only. Miklosich (1876: 150), too, points out that Croatian (i.e. Kajkavian) has *kteri* and *koteri*, besides *ki*, *ka*, *ko* (see also Vasilev 1973: 534 on this Slovene-Kajkavian parallel).

Moreover, forms of *kateri* can be found in the peripheral Slovene dialects, such as Prekmurian. The Prekmurian dictionary (cf. Prekmursko) mentions *šteri* as relative pronoun, equivalent to *ki* and *kateri*, and as an indefinite, free choice pronoun. Pleteršnik lists *šteri* (cf. Section 2.3) as well and annotates it as being attested at the river Ščavnica in lower Styria.

Obviously, thus, forms of *kateri* were extant in older stages of South Slavonic, at least in interrogative and indefinite function, but seem to have become out of use in the course of time. In Slovene, however, judging from the written documents available for that time, they have (re-)appeared in the 16th century, exhibiting now (also) a relativising function.

3.3 Summing up

As concerns the diachronic development of *ki* and *kateri*, we are faced not only with a diversity of forms, but also a diversity of descriptions. This leads to a rather complex picture. As regards *ki*, it remains unclear whether the forms discussed are indeed 'different', in the sense of having followed different diachronic paths, or whether they are 'made different' by the way they are described. For *kateri*, the question remains as to why it cannot be found in older documents and why/how it (re-)appeared in a relativising function in the 16th century.

4 Interplay of factors

The different analyses presented in Section 3 do not yield a clear picture concerning the origin and diachronic development of *ki* and the (re-)appearance of *kateri*. This fits the very essence of language, as Joseph (2013: 687–688) emphasizes:

> Given the inherent complexity of language, of the creatures who use language, and of the social networks in which that use takes place, it should come as no surprise that it is rare to find single-factor answers to why aspects of language are as they are or to find single sources for synchronic phenomena in a language.

For the development towards the contemporary system of relativisation in Slovene, several factors must have been at work: (i) language internal development (derivation of *ki* from **kyj*, **iže* or *kъde že*; emergence of relativizing function for interrogative-based *kateri*), (ii) language contact by language users (reanalysis of *ki* as 'where') and grammarians ((re-)introduction and propagation of *kateri*), and (iii) factors influencing language description.

4.1 Internal development: Language change

The different explanations for the emergence of *ki* depicted in Section 3 can all be given inner Slavonic support, if older stages of closely related languages, mainly West Slavonic, are considered as well. Changes concerning **jo*-based pronouns – be it replacement or formal development – can be observed in Sorbian (which has *kiž* and *kenž*, as pointed out already by Škrabec 1994 [1886]) and Czech (which has *jenž*, e.g. Kurzová 1981). Whether this supports the assumption of fronting *k-* to *iže* or the assumption of *ki* deriving from **kyj* remains an open question. In any case, a parallel development in Slovene and West Slavonic can be observed, with the exact stages being subject to language specific processes (such as rhotacism, which is not found in Sorbian and Czech but is typical of Slovene).

The assumption that *ki* has resulted from a contraction of *koj* can draw on a parallel in terms of Kajkavian *ki, ka, ko*. Supportive evidence might be provided by *choi* found in the FM as well as *chi* and inflected forms thereof in the Early Slovene documents. Finally, the relation between *kъde že / wo* 'where' and *ki(r)* too can be justified on language-internal grounds, see, for instance, Bulgarian *deto < kъde-to* (already found in the early damaskini).

In order to judge the respective plausibility of these different analyses, more data would be needed. But even then it might well be the case that no clear-cut answer can be found. Conceivably, there is not one single source for *ki* and the (re-)introduction of *kateri*. Instead, different sources and different interacting developments are plausible which may, in addition, have been subject to processes of reanalysis.

4.2 External stimuli: Language contact

Given the pronounced multilingualism in the Slovene territories (see Ahačič 2014 for a description of the situation in the 16th century), contact influences are highly probable to have played a role in the development of the relativisation system.

Most of the Early Slovene and Protestant texts are composed by non-native speakers of Slovene or by bilingual individuals. The Early Slovene manuscripts are not only characterized by a mixture of dialects (Mikhailov 1998: 76), they are in part also composed by clergymen of Czech origin (e.g. the Stiški rokopis, Mikhailov 1998: 68–70) or written in a bilingual environment (e.g. the Starogorski rokopos, which has been written in the Slovene-Italian regions at the river Natisone, Mikhailov 1998: 76). Mikhailov (1998: 14) regards these circumstances as a crucial obstacle for obtaining a comprehensive picture of the situation and the development of the Slovene language at that time. From a different point of view, however, these data allow insights into language contact. Not yet striving for an over-individual, dialect-levelling norm, the Early Slovene manuscripts provide evidence for possible contact influences. The reanalysis of *ki* as 'where' may very well have been due to contact with German (which has *wo* 'where' as relativisation marker) – both as regards the language users and those describing the language. Also, Italian *chi* might have played a role in the formation of *ki*.

The 16th century marks a turning point in the history of Slovene, since first attempts of forming a literary language and establishing a norm date to this period. Ahačič (2014: 33) speaks of a "watershed in the sociolinguistic development" of Slovene. The first books were printed in Slovene in order to propagate Protestantism to as many recipients as possible. To fit the new needs, the language had to be adapted. This adaption was driven by the need to convey high contents in a language as close to the spoken varieties as possible. Since no cross-dialectally valid norms had been developed for Slovene, and since it had not yet been elaborated to fit the needs for such abstract contents, the language in these documents may display dialectal features that are not present in all Slovene dialects, and exhibit features that are taken from or influenced by patterns available in other languages. The latter might be an explanation for the increasing usage of *kateri* as a relativisation marker. Possibly, *kateri* was (re-)introduced or calqued as a 'high-level' relativisation marker, by analogy with German *welcher*.[11] If so, this influence has to be one concerning the usage and distribution (interrogative as relative) of a native element. Matras and Sakel (2007: 829–830) describe this mechanism as pattern replication:

> [T]he formal substance or matter is not imported but is taken from the inherited stock of forms of the recipient or replica language [...] it is the patterns of distribution, of grammatical and semantic meaning, and of formal-syntactic arrangement at various levels (discourse, clause, phrase, or word) that are modelled on an external source.

The fact that in addition to internal development, language contact on different levels seems to have contributed the (re-)analysis of *ki* and the (re-)introduction of *kateri* fits Joseph's (2013: 682) assumption that "[i]n some instances [...] contact with speakers of other languages can be one of the multiplicity of sources". He goes on to point out that words may enter from outside even if there is a native word, which then yields a synchronic situation in which "there are multiple forms with a single – or at least related – meaning" (ibid.); again this situation can also be observed for Slovene.

Language contact is possible not only on the level of the languages themselves. It may as well be effective on the descriptive level, in terms of influences on the descriptors and their analyses. Contact-induced reanalysis is thus plausible both with speakers when using the language, and with speakers describing the language and propagating prescriptive rules.

---

[11] For Polish *który*, Gallis (1956: 11) assumes Latin influence. In a more general perspective, this type of relativization marker deserves closer diachronic and comparative analysis among the Slavonic languages, in terms of functional (interrogative, relative), syntactic (introducing relative clauses preceding or following the matrix clause, relative clauses with 'internal nuclei'; e.g. Mendoza 2010; Mendoza and Sonnenhauser 2015) and formal, i.e. morphological (see Majer 2015) respects.

4.3 Metalinguistic factors: Language description

In addition to internal development and contact-induced changes, metalinguistic factors, too, have contributed to the shaping of the contemporary system of relativizing strategies in Slovene. This encompasses the choice of the data basis underlying linguistic analysis and grammatical description, the tradition into which the individual grammarians place their analyses, and prescriptive rules derived from these analyses. The latter can exhibit considerable influence on language use and may thereby become reinforced over time.

The writers and pre-codifiers of the 16th century most probably did not have any knowledge of the earlier sources. The FM and the Early Slovene manuscripts came to be known only in the course of the 19th century. Kopitar (1808: XXIX), as well, was not yet aware of the Early Slovene manuscripts, as is indicated by his statement "Es ist nicht wahrscheinlich, dass die krainische Sprache vor der Reformation je wäre geschrieben worden." [It is unlikely that the Carniolian language had been written before the Reformation.]. Even though he edited the FM in 1822 and 1836, respectively, he could not have taken them into account already in his 1808 grammar. Miklosich (1876) knew both the FM and some of the Early Slovene manuscripts (he edited the Stiški rokopis in 1858 and the Škofeloški rokopis in 1868; see Mikhailov 1998: 75), and cites examples from both.

One case in point illustrating the role of the poor data basis is the analysis of *ki(r)* as an abbreviation to *kateri* (see Section 3). Metelko (1825: 204), for instance, wonders whether *kir* is just another, older, variant of *ki* or whether it is an abbreviation from *kateri* and hence to be distinguished from *ki*. Regarding it as an abbreviation, Pohlin (1783), Kopitar (1808), amongst others, assume *ki(r)* to be preferred by ordinary people. Accordingly, *ki* and *kateri* are assigned to different registers and styles: *ki* to a lower, *kateri* to a higher level. This analysis and interpretation is probably related to the lacking access to the early documents, which exhibit forms that resemble later *ki*, but not of *kateri*. This should have ruled out the assumption of *ki* being an abbreviated form of *kateri*. Be that as it may, these underlying assumptions on formal development and functional differentiation continue to be repeated in traditional grammars and textbooks (Bajec, Kolarič, and Rupel 1964; Breznik 1934).

Their data basis being that sparse, Kopitar, Miklosich and their predecessors – such as Pohlin (1783) – had to rely in their etymological analyses and functional assumptions on reconstruction and intuition. Since these intuitions in turn are influenced by their respective dialectal backgrounds and language environments, language contact is most likely to have had a bearing on the metalinguistic level as well. Presumably, this influence is visible in Kopitar's (1808) description of *ki* as resulting from the reanalysis of *ki(r)* as *kje* 'where'. This he infers from the observation that Slovene speakers use a German (dialectal) relativising construction with *wo* 'where' when speaking German:

> Die städtischen Krainer halten dieses ihr ki für die Particula loci: ki, kje wo? Denn wenn sie Deutsch sprechen, übersetzen sie diesen Slavismus so: Der Mann, wo (er) bey mir war [...] (Kopitar 1808: 294)
> [The urban people from Carniola take their *ki* for the locative particle: *ki, kje, wo* ['where']? Since when they speak German, they translate this Slavism as follows: The man wo [i.e. who] was with me]

Moreover, 16th century Slovene, i.e. the language serving as point of reference for the standardisation efforts in the 19th century, was to a considerable degree influenced by the language background of the respective authors, which was predominantly German. In addition to that, the Slovene texts were translations, mainly from German, but also Italian or Croatian (see Seitz 1997 for more details). The input data for the codifiers of the early 19th century thus not only provided imperfect evidence for a diachronic description, but was also the result of language interference. Accordingly, the frequent usage of *kateri* in these texts may thus be related to the development of literary Slovene as shaped to a great deal by only a handful of writers (Trubar and his contemporaries) with their very specific linguistic and theoretical backgrounds.

Moreover, in the standardisation process, which relied on central Slovene as the basis for the literary language, the data available in other dialects and alternative literary developments, such as Prekmurian, were not taken into consideration. Neither were alternative proposals for the make-up of the literary language, such as bringing the Slovene standard closer to Croatian, as was proposed in the 16th century by Sebastjan Krelj (see Seitz 1998 for more details on this discussion). By these decisions, neighbouring developments and similarities to closely related South and West Slavonic languages had been disregarded, which again contributed to the very 'individual' character of Slovene.

Obviously, the picture that emerges for Slovene described in textbooks and grammars is to a considerable extent shaped by the tradition of earlier analyses. These earlier analyses, in turn, are influenced by different metalinguistic factors: the data available as a source for description as well as the linguistic background of the linguists and codifiers involved.

5 Conclusion

As has been shown in this paper, the relativisation strategies encountered in contemporary Standard Slovene result not only from language-related factors, such as internal development and external contact, but also from factors relating to data selection, description and interpretation.

Relativisation by means of *ki* and/or *kateri* thereby provides a prime example of 'multiple sources and variation' playing a role in language change (Joseph 2013: 685) and of the multiplicity of factors involved in the emergence of linguistic structures. One of these factors is language internal development which may interact to different degrees with contact related input. This interaction may lead to conflicting hypotheses in language description:

> The important thing to realize about such disagreements is that although scholars often act as if only one etymological hypothesis can be correct, in principle more than one could be right, with different constructs in an earlier stage converging or external sources influencing the direction of development of a particular internal etymon. (Joseph 2013: 681)

Moreover, contact influence and multilingualism may contribute to – again possibly conflicting – speaker-internal processes of reanalysis, as Joseph (2013: 618) points out:

> [S]peakers are not necessarily aware of multiple etymologies, though different speakers might make different connections in their 'synchronic etymologizing', i.e. in the connections that they make among forms as they set about constructing their own mental grammars.

Since grammarians and linguists are first of all speakers themselves, they are hardly devoid of a specific linguistic background, i.e. their own etymologizing and reanalysing. Therefore, different hypotheses in etymological analyses "may well reflect the reality of varied – and multiple – pressures that speakers feel on their usage" (Joseph 2013: 682).

How exactly the various factors pointed out here – internal, external and metalinguistic – have interacted in the development of the contemporary system of relativisation in Slovene requires further investigation and in-depth analyses. Questions such as to whether the emergence of *kateri* in relativising function is to be analysed as an indication of an isogloss encompassing Slovene and West Slavonic, as the introduction of a new function for an existing form triggered by inner Slavonic language contact (Slovene, Polish, Czech) or by functional calquing (German) – on the level of language usage or on the descriptive level (grammar writing[12]) – or whether it is not new at all but simply not attested in the rare documents available, needs to be investigated in a broader perspective.

---

[12] As to influences on the descriptive level see Ahačič (2014) for the 16th century, and Pavkovič (2011) for the 17th and 18th centuries.

However, it might as well not be possible to reveal that interaction in detail, the more so, as no speaker judgments are available. But even if they were, speakers might not be aware of the variance of forms – and one would still be left with a multiplicity of explanations.

References

Ahačič, Kozma. 2014. *The history of linguistic thought and language use in 16th century Slovenia*. Frankfurt/Main: Peter Lang.

Bajec, Anton, Rudolf Kolarič & Mirko Rupel. 1964. *Slovenska slovnica. Druga popravljena izdaja izdaja* [Slovenian grammar. Second upgraded edition]. Ljubljana: Državna založba Slovenije.

Breznik, Anton. 1934. *Slovenska slovnica za srednje šole. Četrta, pomnožena izdaja* [Slovenian grammar for high schools. Forth, extended edition]. Celje: Družba sv. Mohorja.

Brozović, Dalibor. 1988. Contemporary standard Slovene: A complex linguistic phenomenon. *Slovene Studies* 10 (2). 175–190.

Cazinkić, Robert. 2001. Kategorizacija in razvrstitev oziralnikov *ki* in *kateri* [Categorization and classification of the relative pronouns *ki* and *kateri*]. *Slavistična revija* 49 (1–2). 55–73.

Chidambaram, Vrinda. 2007. Relative and pseudo-relative clauses in Slovene. *Slovenski jezik* 6. 287–301.

Danylenko, Andrii (this volume). A tale of two pathways: On the development of relative clause chaining in East Slavonic.

Dogramadžieva, Ekaterina. 1989. Săjuznite sredstva văv Frajzingskite pametnici [Means of conjunction in the Freising Manuscripts]. In Jože Toporišič (ed.), *Obodobje srednjega veka v slovenskem jeziku, književnosti in kulturi. Mednarodni simpozij v Ljubljani od 29. Junija do 1. Julija 1988* [The period of Middle Ages in the Slovenian language, literature and culture. International symposium in Ljubljana from June 29 to July 1, 1988], 63–68. Ljubljana: Univerza Edvarda Kardelja v Ljubljani.

FidaPLUS: *Korpus slovenskega jezika* [Corpus of the Slovenian language]. (http://www.fidaplus.net/).

Freidhof, Gerd (ed.). 1981. *Slowenische Texte aus der Reformationszeit*. München: Sagner.

Gallis, Arne. 1956. *The syntax of relative clauses in Serbo-Croatian. Viewed on a historical basis*. Oslo: Aschehoug.

Gołąb Zbigniew & Victor A. Friedman. 1972. The relative clause in Slavic. In Paul M. Peranteau, Judith M. Levi & Gloria C. Phares (eds.), *The Chicago which hunt. Papers from the Relative Clause Festival, April 13, 1972*, 30–46. Chicago: Chicago Linguistic Society.

Jesenšek, Marko. 2008. Trubarjeva in Küzmičeva različica slovenskega knjižnega jezika [Trubar's and Küzmič's versions of literary Slovene]. *Slavistična revija* 56 (4). 199–209.

Joseph, Brian. 2013. Multiple sources and multiple causes multiply explored. *Studies in Language* 37 (3). 675–691.

Kopitar, Jernej. 1808. *Grammatik der Slavischen Sprache in Krain, Kärnten und Steyermark*. Laibach: Wilhelm Heinrich Horn.

Krek, Simon & Adam Kilgarriff. 2006. Slovene word sketches. *Proceedings of the 5th Slovenian / First International Languages Technology Conference*, Slovenia, October 2006. http://www.kilgarriff.co.uk/Publications/2006-KrekKilg-Ljub-SloveneWS.pdf (accessed 4 February 2016).

Křížková, Helena. 1970. Relativní věty v současných slovanských jazycích [Relative clauses in the contemporary Slavonic languages]. *Slavia* 39. 10–40.
Kurzová, Helena. 1981. *Der Relativsatz in den indoeuropäischen Sprachen*. Hamburg: Buske.
Latinski: *Slovensko-latinski slovar po: Matija Kastelec – Gregor Vorenc, Dictionarium Latino-Carniolicum (1608–1710)* [Slovenian-Latin dictionary according to: Matija Kastelec – Gregor Vorenc, Dictionarium Latino-Carniolicum (1608–1710)]. www.fran.si (accessed 6 June 2015).
Matras, Yaron & Jeanette Sakel. 2007. Investigating the mechanisms of pattern replication in language convergence. *Studies in Language* 31 (4). 829–865.
Meier-Brügger, Michael. 2002. *Indogermanische Sprachwissenschaft*. Berlin & New York: de Gruyter.
Majer, Marek. 2015. Russian *kotóryj*, Czech *který*, Slovene *katęri*: Vowel variation in the reflexes of Proto-Slavic *koterъ(jь) 'which (of the two)'. *Scando-Slavica* 61 (2). 154–179.
Mendoza, Imke. 2010. Relativsätze mit *który to*. *Wiener Slawistischer Almanach* 65. 105–118.
Mendoza, Imke & Barbara Sonnenhauser. 2015. Restricting grammatical variation. The case of Slavic relative constructions. Paper presented at the 10th Annual Meeting of the Slavic Linguistics Society, Heidelberg, 4–6 September, 2015. https://www.academia.edu/15538283/Restricting_grammatical_variation_The_case_of_Slavic_relative_constructions (accessed 4 February 2016).
Metelko, Franz S. 1825. *Lehrgebäude der Slowenischen Sprache im Königreiche Illyrien und in den benachbarten Provinzen. Nach dem Lehrgebäude der böhm. Sprache des Hrn. Abbé Dobrowsky*. Laibach: Leopold Eger.
Mikhailov, Nikolai. 1998. *Frühslowenische Sprachdenkmäler. Die handschriftliche Periode in der slowenischen Sprache (XIV. Jh. bis 1550)*. Amsterdam: Rodopi.
Miklosich, Franz. 1876. *Vergleichende Grammatik der slavischen Sprachen. Dritter Band: Wortbildungslehre*. Wien: Wilhelm Braumüller.
Novak, Vilko. 1936. *Izbor prekmurske književnosti* [A collection of Prekmurian literature]. Celje: Družba sv. Mohorja.
Nuorluoto, Juhani. 2010. Central Slovak and Kajkavian structural convergences: A tentative survey. *Slovo* 50. 37–45.
Pavkovič, Aleksander. 2011. *Tschechisch und Slovenisch im Vergleich ihrer schrift- und standardsprachlichen Entwicklung*. München: Sagner.
Pleteršnik. 2010 [1894]. *Pleteršnikov Slovensko-nemški slovar. Spletna izdaja* Pleteršnik's Slovenian-German dictionary. Internet edition]. Ljubljana 2010. http://bos.zrc-sazu.si/pletersnik.html. [Pleteršnik, M. 1894–1895. *Slovensko-nemški slovar*. Ljubljana].
Pohlin, Marko. 1783. *Kraynska grammatika* [Grammar of the Carniolan dialect]. Laybach: Lorenz Bernbacher.
Prekmursko: Novak, Vilko. 2006. *Slovar stare knjižne prekmurščine* [Dictionary of the old literary Prekmurje dialect]. Ljubljana: Založba ZRC, ZRC SAZU. www.fran.si. (accessed 6 June 2015).
Seitz, Elisabeth. 1997. "Wäre doch Truber ein Kroat gewesen!". Slovenische Variationen über das Thema einer gesamtsüdslavischen Schriftsprache von der Reformation bis zum Neoillyrismus. *Slovene Linguistic Studies* 1. 91–124.
Seitz, Elisabeth. 1998. *Primus Truber – Schöpfer der slovenischen Schriftsprache? Versuch einer Antwort unter besonderer Berücksichtigung seines Satzbaus*. München: Sagner.
Škrabec, Stanislav. 1994 [1886]. Slovniški pomenki. 'kir' in 'kéri' in pa še kaj [Notes on grammar.'kir' in 'kéri' and others]. In Jože Toporišič (ed.), *P. Stanislav Škrabec. Jezikoslovna dela 1* [Linguistic works 1], 236–288. Nova Gorica: Frančiškanski samostan Kostanjevica v Novi Gorici.

Snoj, Marko. 1997. *Slovenski etimološki slovar* [Slovenian etymological dictionary]. Ljubljana: Mladinska knjiga.
Sonnenhauser, Barbara. 2013. Relative clauses in Slovene: Diachronic puzzles, synchronic patterns. *Wiener Slavistisches Jahrbuch. Neue Folge* (1). 150–187.
Topolińska, Zuzanna. 2003. Means for grammatical accommodation of finite clauses: Slovenian between South and West Slavic. *Sprachtypologie und Universalienforschung* 56 (3). 306–322.
Toporišič, Jože. 1981. *Slovenska zvrstna besedila* [Slovenian text types]. Ljubljana: Univerza Edvarda Kardelja.
Toporišič, Jože. 2000. *Slovenska slovnica. Četrta, prenovljena in razširjena izdaja* [Slovenian grammar. Fourth, renewed and expanded edition]. Maribor: Obzorja.
Vasilev, Christo. 1973. Slovenisch und Westslavisch. In Johannes Holthusen, Erwin Koschmieder, Reinhold Olesch & Erwin Wedel (eds.), *Slavistische Studien zum VII. Internationalen Slavistenkongress in Warschau 1973*, 526–541. München: Trofenik.

Index

accusative with participle 339, 341, 342, 344, 353, 354, 356
accusativus cum infinitivo 7, 261, 262, 264
adverbial 209
adverbial participle 210, 215, 217, 218, 220, 231, 232, 233, 234, 236, 247, 248, 249, 250, 251, 254
agreement 6, 33, 34, 95, 96, 98, 99, 100, 101, 102, 107, 111, 114, 115, 118, 119, 129, 130, 145, 152, 153, 154, 155, 165, 171, 188, 198, 201, 302, 303, 305, 354, 370, 390

bookish neologism 7, 261, 262, 263, 279
Bosnian 65, 127, 145, 150, 212, 247

cases and prepositions 81, 83, 84, 86, 89
clitics 37, 65, 149, 150, 151, 152, 155, 189, 205, 290, 348
Codex Marianus 30, 31, 261, 268, 341
complement clause 7, 34, 133, 146, 219, 223, 224, 232, 235, 236, 243, 277, 300, 301, 309, 311, 347, 350, 353, 354, 355, 356
configurational system 7, 339, 354
contact induced change 3, 5, 133, 285, 290, 356, 401
coreference 210, 217, 218, 248, 249, 250, 254, 368
Croatian 6, 7, 64, 65, 73, 84, 97, 98, 110, 125, 126, 127, 128, 129, 131, 134, 135, 136, 137, 138, 139, 140, 142, 144, 146, 147, 148, 149, 150, 154, 155, 209, 210, 212, 214, 216, 217, 220, 221, 222, 230, 231, 232, 233, 234, 235, 236, 237, 245, 247, 249, 251, 254, 255, 296, 299, 301, 302, 303, 304, 311, 313, 326, 331, 353, 395, 397, 402

double accusative 262, 266, 267, 268, 271, 272, 273, 274, 275, 277, 278, 341, 342, 346, 353
drift toward analyticity 84, 85, 86, 88, 90

East Slavonic 8, 285, 286, 292, 293, 295, 296, 306, 311, 321, 325, 350, 361, 363, 364, 365, 366, 373, 377, 378, 379, 380, 381, 382
enclitics 7, 187, 188, 189, 190, 191, 192, 197, 202, 204, 205, 306, 317, 347

German 6, 7, 8, 82, 98, 125, 126, 127, 128, 131, 132, 137, 138, 140, 141, 142, 143, 144, 145, 146, 147, 148, 149, 151, 152, 153, 154, 155, 161, 178, 179, 180, 204, 209, 211, 212, 236, 237, 247, 248, 288, 307, 326, 345, 353, 361, 365, 381, 382, 396, 399, 400, 402, 403
Germanic 326
grammaticalization 1, 2, 6, 70, 83, 98, 130, 131, 132, 133, 144, 155, 161, 164, 169, 171, 177, 178, 179, 180, 285, 286, 291, 292, 348, 355, 356, 361, 362, 375
grammatical replication 179, 263

heritage languages 6, 126, 127, 128, 136, 140, 150
hypotactic subordination 8, 361, 364, 380, 381
hypotaxis 339, 348, 355, 356, 361, 362, 363, 364, 380

infinitive 7, 37, 96, 131, 133, 134, 143, 146, 180, 210, 247, 254, 263, 264, 265, 266, 269, 272, 273, 274, 275, 277, 279, 295, 297, 298, 299, 305, 340, 342, 353
*jo 394, 398

juxtaposition 300, 302, 347, 348, 350, 361, 362, 364, 378, 380

*kwo 394, 397

language contact 2, 5, 6, 8, 63, 84, 89, 125, 127, 130, 131, 132, 133, 154, 155, 161, 179, 209, 211, 223, 234, 236, 237, 247, 254, 261, 263, 277, 279, 288, 289, 345, 361, 371, 374, 375, 380, 381, 398, 399, 400, 401, 403

language death 68, 81, 88, 89
Latin 4, 6, 81, 82, 85, 87, 161, 179, 180, 236, 254, 263, 275, 279, 306, 318, 345, 371, 390, 396, 400

matrix clause 117, 217, 218, 224, 231, 233, 235, 242, 243, 249, 250, 277, 300, 304, 310, 364, 367, 368, 370, 374, 378, 400
metalinguistic 8
Molise Slavonic 6, 63, 64, 89, 130, 132, 133

non-configurational syntax 203, 204
non-standard 130
non-standard varieties 82, 365, 366, 375
(NP) enclitics 189

Old Church Slavonic 5, 6, 7, 13, 14, 29, 96, 101, 200, 220, 235, 243, 261, 293, 339, 340, 377
Old Russian 271
Old Serbian 7, 187, 188, 189, 190, 196, 197, 200, 202, 204, 236, 261, 262, 270, 272, 277, 278, 296, 297, 299, 306, 311, 339, 340, 344, 346, 347, 355

paratactic subordination 8, 361, 364, 368, 370, 373, 374, 375, 377, 378, 379, 380, 381, 382
parataxis 361, 362, 363, 364, 378, 380
pattern replication 1, 6, 125, 126, 127, 129, 137, 141, 247, 248, 400
perception verbs 271, 272, 275, 279, 304, 316, 341, 343, 344, 345, 347, 351, 353, 356
Polish 6, 7, 128, 132, 161, 162, 164, 165, 168, 171, 176, 177, 178, 179, 180, 182, 210, 216, 217, 231, 247, 254, 286, 288, 295, 308, 311, 313, 314, 317, 320, 321, 322, 323, 324, 325, 326, 327, 328, 329, 330, 331, 365, 366, 371, 374, 378, 400, 403
polysemy copying 6, 130, 132, 133, 142, 144, 146, 149, 155
prescription 3

reanalysis 2, 286, 294, 300, 301, 310, 347, 396, 398, 399, 400, 401, 403

relative clause 8, 311, 361, 362, 363, 364, 366, 367, 368, 369, 370, 371, 372, 373, 374, 375, 376, 377, 378, 380, 381, 382, 387, 394, 400
relative marker 364, 365, 366, 367, 368, 370, 371, 372, 374, 375, 376, 377, 379, 380
relativisation marker 8, 387, 389, 391, 394, 399, 400
replica grammaticalization 179
replication 179, 212, 236, 237, 247, 263, 356, 382, 400
resultative construction 6, 161, 162, 163, 164, 170, 174, 175, 176, 178
resumption 361, 362, 364, 367, 369, 370, 371, 372, 373, 374, 375, 379, 380, 382

Serbian 4, 5, 6, 7, 25, 73, 89, 98, 125, 126, 127, 128, 130, 131, 134, 136, 137, 138, 139, 140, 142, 144, 146, 149, 150, 154, 155, 187, 188, 189, 192, 195, 197, 198, 199, 200, 202, 203, 204, 205, 212, 245, 247, 277, 296, 299, 300, 301, 302, 303, 311, 313, 326, 329, 339, 340, 344, 346, 349, 351, 352, 353, 354, 355, 356
Serbian Alexander Romance 261, 273
Serbian Church Slavonic 188, 261, 272, 273, 344
Slovene 8, 302, 304, 329, 365, 387, 388, 389, 390, 391, 393, 394, 395, 396, 397, 398, 399, 400, 401, 402, 403
social typology 380
standardisation 2, 402
structural borrowing 129, 179, 312
syntactic calque 144, 262, 263, 276, 279
syntactic complexity 32, 362, 380
syntactic Graecism 261, 262

transitivity 188, 196, 202, 203, 276, 277, 279, 354
translation 2, 5, 13, 14, 16, 17, 18, 19, 21, 22, 23, 24, 25, 29, 30, 31, 50, 57, 82, 89, 145, 146, 147, 148, 165, 182, 214, 216, 217, 221, 222, 223, 230, 236, 237, 238, 240, 241, 247, 251, 252, 253, 262, 268, 269, 297, 301, 307, 308, 310, 330, 341, 342, 396, 402
translational 144, 318

valence 6, 137, 138, 139, 140, 141, 142, 144, 146, 155, 219
valency 44, 59, 87, 88, 138, 219, 234
verba dicendi 7, 209, 222, 223, 224, 233, 234, 235, 238, 239, 242, 244, 247, 251, 253, 254, 255

word order 5, 6, 7, 29, 30, 31, 34, 35, 37, 38, 39, 40, 41, 42, 59, 149, 150, 151, 167, 168, 176, 177, 178, 180, 187, 188, 203, 204, 346

www.ingramcontent.com/pod-product-compliance
Lightning Source LLC
Chambersburg PA
CBHW051242300426
44114CB00011B/853